The Dynamics of Nonviolent Action

part three of:

Extending Horizons Books

A study prepared
under the auspices of
Harvard University's Center
for International Affairs

The Politics of Nonviolent Action

Gene Sharp

With the editorial assistance of Marina Finkelstein

Porter Sargent Publishers, 11 Beacon St., Boston, Ma. 02108

Each of these specific "nonviolent weapons" is illustrated with actual cases.

The Dynamics of Nonviolent Action examines the complex operation of this technique against a violent, repressive opponent.

Groundwork which may precede the struggle is explored, as well as basic requirements for effectives. Then the focus turns to the initial impact of the nonviolent challenge.

Repression is probable. Determined, yet nonviolent, continued resistance is needed to fight it. The opponent's repression may rebound by "political *jiu-jitsu*", weakening his power by loss of support and increased resistance.

Three main mechanisms by which nonviolent action may produce victory are examined: conversion (the rarest), accomodation, and nonviolent coercion. Massive noncooperation may paralyze and disintegrate even an oppressive system.

All these elements of the dynamics of nonviolent struggle are illustrated with examples.

The resisting group itself is also changed: it gains in self-respect, confidence and power.

Empowerment of the struggle group, the accompanying strengthening of the non-State institutions, ability to defeat repressive elites, and the extension among the populace of a nonviolent struggle capacity, contribute to long-term social changes by redistributing power.

Biographical Sketch of Gene Sharp

1949:   Bachelor of Arts with High Distinction in Social Sciences, Ohio State University

1951:   Master of Arts in Sociology, Ohio State University

1951-55:   Studied history of nonviolent action and Gandhi independently in New York City

1953:   Imprisoned as a conscientious objector (served nine months, ten days of a two year sentence); supported in his position by Dr. Albert Einstein

1954:   Personal secretary to A. J. Muste, America's leading pacifist

1955-58:   Assistant Editor of the weekly *Peace News,* London

1957:   Writer and Lecturer for two months at the Institute for Philosophy and the History of Ideas of the University of Oslo, Norway

1958-60:   Research Fellow, Institute for Social Research, Oslo, Norway

1960:   Consultant, Positive Action Conference on Peace and Security in Africa, held in Accra

1961-64:   Doctoral studies at St. Catherine's College, Oxford, England

1964:   Organizer and participant, international Civilian Defense Study Conference, St. Hilda's College, Oxford

1964-65:   Assistant Lecturer, Institute of Philosophy and the History of Ideas, University of Oslo

1965-72:   Research Fellow, Center for International Affairs, Harvard University

1967-69:   Visiting Lecturer and Assistant Professor, Department of Politics, University of Massachusetts at Boston

1968:   Doctor of Philosophy, Oxford University
Faculty of Social Studies (in political theory)

1969-70:   Lecturer, Department of Government, Boston University, Mass.; Lecturer, Lesley College, Cambridge, Mass.; Lecturer, Experimental College, Tufts University, Medford, Mass.

1970:   Participant, International Gandhi Seminar, Gandhi Peace Foundation, New Delhi, India

1970-71:   Visiting Lecturer, Brandeis University, Waltham, Mass.

1971-72:   Lecturer, Department of Social Relations, Harvard University
Associate Professor of Sociology and Political Science, Southeastern Massachusetts University

1972:   Participant, Conference on Non-military Forms of Struggle, Uppsala, Sweden; also, World Council of Churches' Cardiff Consultation on Violence, Nonviolence and the Struggle for Social Justice, Wales

1972-73:   Lecturer, Department of Psychology and Social Relations, Harvard University
Chairman, Department of Sociology, and Professor of Sociology and Political Science, Southeastern Massachusetts University

1973-74:   Professor of Sociology and Political Science, Southeastern Massachusetts University

BY THE SAME AUTHOR

Gandhi Wields the Weapon of Moral Power (India)
"The Political Equivalent of War"—Civilian Defense
Civilian Defense: An Introduction (co-editor, India)
Exploring Nonviolent Alternatives
Buki naki minshu no teikō (Japan)
An Abecedary of Nonviolent Action and Civilian Defense (forthcoming)

CONTENTS

Chapter Four

THE METHODS OF SOCIAL NONCOOPERATION

Chapter Five

THE METHODS OF ECONOMIC NONCOOPERATION: (1) ECONOMIC BOYCOTTS

Chapter Six

THE METHODS OF ECONOMIC NONCOOPERATION: (2) THE STRIKE

Chapter Seven

THE METHODS OF POLITICAL NONCOOPERATION

Chapter Eight

THE METHODS OF NONVIOLENT INTERVENTION

PART THREE: THE DYNAMICS OF NONVIOLENT ACTION

Chapter Nine

LAYING THE GROUNDWORK FOR NONVIOLENT ACTION

Chapter Ten

CHALLENGE BRINGS REPRESSION

Chapter Eleven

SOLIDARITY AND DISCIPLINE TO FIGHT REPRESSION

Chapter Twelve

POLITICAL JIU-JITSU

Chapter Thirteen

THREE WAYS SUCCESS MAY BE ACHIEVED

CONTENTS *xvii*

Chapter Fourteen

THE REDISTRIBUTION OF POWER

PART THREE:
The Dynamics of Nonviolent Action

INTRODUCTION
TO PART THREE

An understanding of how nonviolent action "works," of its dynamics in struggle, and of its mechanics of change is of extreme importance. Without that insight our extensive catalogue of its methods will lack the vitality which is characteristic of social change and political conflict, and the view of power upon which this technique rests will remain an exercise for specialists in political philosophy. But with awareness of the dynamics of nonviolent action, we can understand the operation of this technique in society and politics, and evaluate intelligently its potential utility in various types of conflict situations.

The dynamics of nonviolent action is a relatively uninvestigated phenomenon. There have been important pioneers in the field—especially Richard Gregg,[1] E.T. Hiller,[2] and Leo Kuper,[3] and a few others who will be cited later. Certain activists in the application of the technique have also made significant observations on the subject, especially M.K. Gandi.[4]

In these final six chapters we shall draw on the insights of these theorists and activists. But primarily we shall draw on the events in several significant cases of nonviolent action to construct, largely by an inductive approach, an analysis of how this technique works. This analysis contains many hypotheses awaiting further critical examination and testing, including the use of a wider selection of case material.

Throughout the exploration of this topic, it is essential to remember that the operation of nonviolent action in struggle is always a dynamic process. It involves continuous change in the various influences and forces which operate in that process and are constantly influencing each other. No discussion in static terms of how nonviolent action works can be valid. Also, the process is very complicated; for reasons which will become clear, it is more complicated than conventional military warfare or even guerrilla warfare.

NOTES

1. Gregg, **The Power of Nonviolence.**
2. Hiller, **The Strike.**
3. Kuper, **Passive Resistance in South Africa.**
4. See, for example, M. K. Gandhi, **Non-Violence in Peace and War** (two vols.; Ahmedabad, India: Navajivan Publishing House, 1948 and 1949), and **Non-Violent Resistance;** Ind. ed.: **Satyagraha.**

9

Laying the Groundwork for Nonviolent Action

INTRODUCTION

Nonviolent action is a means of wielding social and political power, even though it does not involve its practitioners in the use of violence. If nonviolent action is capable of wielding power, it must be able with its power to act upon the power wielded by the opponent. This it does by means which differ radically from those involved in political violence, i.e., violence for political purposes. Nonviolent action can be viewed as acting against the opponent's power in two ways, either *indirectly* against it, or more *directly* than violence against it. We shall now see how this is the case.

CONFRONTING THE OPPONENT'S POWER

The opponent is frequently a government; where it is not, the opponent often has the support of the State machinery. In either case, the nonviolent group may find arrayed against it the government's troops, police, prisons and the like. In nonviolent action there is no attempt to combat these by using the same types of instruments, as would be the case if both sides were using violence. Instead, in strategic terms, the nonviolent group counters this expression of the opponent's power *indirectly,* in various ways. These weaken the opponent's relative power position rather than strengthen it by, for example, alienating existing support and undermining the opponent's ability (and at times weakening his will) to continue the policy and the repression. The opponent is usually well equipped to apply military and other violent means of combat and repression, as well as to fight violent and military means of struggle. Instead of meeting him directly on that level, where he is strong, nonviolent actionists rely on a totally different technique of struggle, or "weapons systems," which is designed to operate to *their* advantage. The whole conflict then takes on a very special assymetrical character; the combatants are fighting but they are using very different types of weapons. Given an extensive, determined, and skillful application of nonviolent action, the opponent is likely to find that nonviolent actionists' insistence on fighting with their choice of "weapons system" will cause him very special problems which will tend to frustrate the effective utilization of his own forces.

A close consideration of the strategic problems of military conflict shows that frontal resistance or attack may not necessarily be the wisest course of action—precisely because this is where the enemy has concentrated his strength. Napoleon wrote, for example:

It is an approved maxim in war, never to do what the enemy wishes you to do, for this reason alone, that he desires it. A field of battle, therefore, which he has previously studied and reconnoitered, should be avoided, and double care should be taken where he has had time to fortify and entrench. One consequence deductible from this principle is, never to attack a position in front which you can gain by turning.[1]

This approach to strategy has been developed by the late Sir Basil Liddell Hart, who argued:

. . . throughout the ages, effective results in war have rarely been attained unless the approach has had such indirectness as to ensure the opponent's unreadiness to meet it. The indirectness has usually been physical, and always psychological. In strategy the longest way round is often the shortest way home. . . .

To move along the line of natural expectation consolidates the opponent's balance and thus increases his resisting power. . . . In most campaigns the dislocation of the enemy's psychological and physical balance has been the vital prelude to a successful attempt at his over-throw. [2]

This indirect approach to conventional military strategy has been carried to a more extreme development in modern guerrilla warfare.

Nonviolent struggle carries indirect strategy still further, to the point where the military opponent is confronted not only with differing strategies but with a contrasting technique of struggle and a nonmilitary "weapons system." Nonviolent action involves opposing the opponent's power, including his police and military capacity, not with the weapons chosen by him, but by quite different means. (The possibility of both sides instead using nonviolent action is discussed briefly in Chapter Eleven.) The result of using nonviolent weapons against violent action may be a significant increase in the actionists' total combat effectiveness. In this special type of assymetrical conflict, the opponent's violent action is always confronted indirectly, i.e., not by the same type of action in direct confrontation but by nonviolent resistance and intervention. This can be viewed as an extreme development of indirect strategy as discussed above. Repression by the opponent is used against his own power position in a kind of political *jiu-jitsu,* and the very sources of his power (analyzed in Chapter One) thus reduced or removed, with the result that his political and military position is seriously weakened or destroyed. The opponent's balance is thereby dislocated, his resistance power undermined, and in extreme cases his ability to continue the struggle eliminated.

There is also a sense in which nonviolent action impinges upon an opponent's power *more directly* than would violence. In varying degrees, depending upon a number of factors, nonviolent action is capable of striking at the availability of the sources of political power of the ruler: authority, human resources, skills and knowledge, intangible factors, material resources, and even sanctions themselves. The ruler's power, as discussed earlier, is dependent upon these sources. Through various processes which take place in a large-scale nonviolent struggle, the supply of those sources may be threatened, curtailed, or cut off. The degree to which the sources of power are restricted in individual cases varies considerably, of course. This potential of the nonviolent technique is illustrated most clearly perhaps in strikes and mutinies. For example, nonviolent actionists may try to destroy the opponent's army as an effective force of repression by inducing deliberate inefficiency and open mutiny among the soldiers, without whom there can be no army. In contrast, military actionists would usually fight that army intact and attempt to defeat it by destroying its weapons and killing its soldiers. Such attacks on them would usually reinforce, not disrupt or destroy, their obedience patterns.

Therefore, in the sense that nonviolent action cuts off the *sources* of the opponent's power, rather than simply combatting the final power product of those sources, nonviolent action is a more direct attack on an opponent's power than is violence.

RISKS AND VARIATIONS IN NONVIOLENT ACTION

As a substitute for violence in political conflicts, nonviolent action also involves risks. The first risk is possible defeat. This technique is not foolproof. The simple choice of nonviolent action does not guarantee success, especially on a short-term basis. This should not be surprising, since this technique too involves the matching of forces and must be ably and skillfully used if it is to produce success. No technique of struggle can guarantee success every time; after all, in cases in which both sides use violence, one of them usually loses.

Nonviolent action is not a safe means of struggle; there is no such thing. People are liable to be hurt and to suffer in various ways, including economic loss, physical injury, imprisonment, and even death; this is the second risk. There are, of course, risks in passivity—especially in letting an oppressive regime go unchallenged—and in any type of alternative violent action which might be taken. It is claimed, however, that the injuries, deaths, suffering and destruction are significantly less—even on the resisters' side alone—when one side relies on nonviolent action than when both sides use violence.[3]

A third risk is that political violence may break out during the use of nonviolent action. Gandhi recognized this risk and took measures to prevent the outbreak of violence, and to isolate and eliminate such violence if it occurred. This risk did not in his opinion mean that the nonviolent campaign should not be launched. His view was that the outbreak of political violence (with its consequent detrimental effects on all concerned) was far more likely if he did nothing in a tense conflict situation than if was if people were offered a nonviolent substitute course of action. Gandhi wrote in 1920:

. . . the risk of supineness in the face of a grave issue is infinitely greater than the danger of violence ensuing from organizing non-co-operation. To do nothing is to invite violence for a certainty.

. . . the only way to avoid violence is to enable them to give such expression to their feelings as to compel redress. I have found nothing save non-cooperation.[4]

He felt that with greater experience and with the accumulation of visible successes in nonviolent struggle, the chances that people would turn to violence in such a situation would be considerably reduced.

No two cases of nonviolent action are alike, and they may indeed differ radically from each other, as the illustrations in Chapter Two and the examples of various methods in Part Two illustrate. There are other important variations which need to kept in mind. The campaign may have been deliberately planned and prepared for, or it may have broken out spontaneously or "semi-spontaneously." There may be a clear leadership group, or not. The movement may start spontaneously and without leadership and end up organized and with leaders; or the process may be exactly the opposite. There may be general preparations which arouse the will to resist and give general ideas of how to do so, but the specific movement may start accidentally. Or the preparations may be for a very limited action, with people not knowing what to do in other situations. The range of methods applied may differ widely, as may the numbers of actionists involved and the intensity of the penalties they are willing to undergo. A given movement may avow "love" for the opponent or hatred as intense (at certain stages at least) as in many military conflicts. Nonviolent actionists may aim to convert or to coerce their opponent. The types of issues at stake and their relative importance to the contending groups may differ widely. Similarly, the composition and characteristics of the respective groups will differ from case to case, as will their resources, allies, strengths and weaknesses. The degree of severity of repression, too, will differ. Whether the police are partisan or neutral between the contending groups will be important. The extent and depth of understanding of the technique of nonviolent action among its practitioners will differ considerably, as will the degree and adequacy of the strategy and tactics used. Other important variables will add considerably to the difficulty of describing the various processes and mechanisms involved in the working of nonviolent action in conflicts.

Certain assumptions will therefore be made here in order to reduce somewhat the difficulties in the way of analysis. It is assumed, for example, that the methods used include those of noncooperation (not simply nonviolent protest and persuasion), and some methods of nonviolent intervention. The participation of fairly large numbers of people is assumed, which means that most of them are not believers in a creed enjoining nonviolence but are acting under a nonviolent discipline for the conflict's duration. It is also assumed that the struggle takes place where there are at least some civil liberties, although these may be reduced as the campaign continues. The use of nonviolent action against totalitarian systems requires separate discussion.

CASTING OFF FEAR

One of the prerequisites of nonviolent struggle is that the participants must cast off fear of acting independently and fear of the sufferings which may follow. A high degree of courage is required of nonviolent actionists. The accusation of cowardice, which has often been unjustly made against people who for conscientious reasons refuse to take part in war, cannot even be levelled against nonviolent actionists—except perhaps by those totally ignorant on the subject.

Indeed, Gandhi was most emphatic in his condemnation of cowardice, arguing that "cowardice and *ahimsa* [nonviolence] do not go together any more than water and fire." [5] The coward seeks to avoid the conflict and flees from danger, the nonviolent actionist faces the conflict and risks the dangers involved in pursuing it honorably. "Cowardice is impotence worse than violence," concluded Gandhi. [6] "Nonviolence cannot be taught to a person who fears to die and has no power of resistance . . ." [7] "There is hope for a violent man to be some day nonviolent, but there is none for a coward," [8] "Fear," argues Gregg, "develops out of an assumption of relative weakness." [9] The coward, being fearful, cannot use nonviolent action effectively. The nonviolent actionist must have confidence in the right and strength of his cause, in his principles, and in his technique of action.

The emphasis which Gandhi and other nonviolent actionists have placed on casting off fear has political roots and consequences. Despotism, they have insisted, could not exist if it did not have fear as its foundation. "The Government takes advantage of our fear of jails," argued Gandhi. [10] In the earlier theoretical analysis of the roots of political power, in Chapter One, it was emphasized that sanctions *themselves* do not produce obedience; but the *fear* of sanctions does. If there is great fear among the subjects, even minor sanctions may produce great conformity, while severe sanctions in face of a high degree of fearlessness may not secure the regime. This difference is crucial for the operation of nonviolent means of struggle in face of violent repression.

Nonviolent actionists have not been alone in pointing to the paralyzing political effect of fear and in arguing that liberation can only come after fear has been cast off. The nineteenth century Russian revolutionary Alexander Herzen, for example, devoted the first page of the first issue of his *Free Russian Press* (published in London in 1853) to this objective. [11]

If fear, then, plays an important role in maintaining oppressive regimes, the liberation of the subjects by their own efforts requires a change in them toward fearlessness and self-confidence. This view is also shared by advocates of violent revolution. Bakunin, for example, linked "mental liberation" with "socio-economic liberation."[12] The Russian Jacobin Petr Tkachev, from whom Lenin learned so much, argued for the need of fearlessness if revolution were to be possible: "When the people see that terrible power that they dreaded and before which they were accustomed to tremble and to denigrate themselves, is disorganized, split and befouled, when they see that they need not fear anybody or anything, then the accumulated bitterness will break out with irrestible force."[13] There were others.[14] Michael Prawdin writes that in Russia in early 1917 "the people had lost their fear of punishment and the bogey of the state had lost its power to terrify."[15]

Gandhi repeatedly emphasized the importance of this inner psychological change from fear and submission to fearlessness and self-respect as a necessary prerequisite of real political freedom. In this context, his emphasis on the primacy of "inner conditions" over "external conditions" gains new significance. Speaking of India's millions, Gandhi wrote: "We have to dispel fear from their hearts. On the day they shed all fear, India's fetters shall fall and she will be free."[16] This is not to say that fear must initially be *fully* cast off, and that only then can nonviolent action follow. Fear may be cast off by degrees, and certain groups in the population may become less afraid than other groups. Also, participation in nonviolent action often seems to lead to a loss of fear.

Casting off fear is closely tied to gaining confidence that one possesses power and can act in effective ways to change a situation.[17] This was apparently the case in Montgomery, Alabama, during the bus boycott. Martin Luther King, Jr. reported that when repression began, "a once fear-ridden people had been transformed. Those who had previously trembled before the law were now proud to be arrested for the cause of freedom."[18] It is clear that a great deal of the strength of the Norwegian teachers in their resistance to the Quisling regime lay in their open defiance and refusal to bow to fear.[19]

The qualities of bravery and courage are not, of course, limited to nonviolent action. They are present in other situations and certainly where people struggle heroically by violent means, as Gandhi often acknowledged[20] He argued, however, that "the use of nonviolence requires greater bravery than that of violence"[21] and that nonviolent struggle constitutes a weapon "of the stoutest hearts."[22] According to the theories of nonviolent action, violence is removed, not by yielding to it, but by remaining firm in its face. Courage in this technique is not simply a moral virtue; it is a practical requirement of the technique.

Assuming that the actionists maintain courage, the specific type of action possible will be determined by the *degree* to which the participants have become fearless. As E.D. Nixon said at the beginning of the Montgomery bus boycott: ". . . if we are afraid we might just as well fold up right now."[23] If the groups which have been dominated by the opponent are afraid, there can be no nonviolent action, no challenge to the opponent, and no willingness to risk his sanctions. If the nonviolent actionists become fearful in the midst of the struggle, then the movement collapses.

Fear interferes with or destroys the operation of most of the processes of change upon which nonviolent action depends, whether these be conversion of the opponent by convincing him of a new, more favorable, image of the grievance group, or be paralysis of the system by the massiveness of noncooperation despite repression. Fear may also contribute to the continuation of brutalities rather than their diminuation and cessation; *the shortest way to end brutalities is to demonstrate that they do not help to achieve the opponent's objectives.* Courage is required if the nonviolent struggle is to continue and to lead to the increasing strength of the nonviolent group and an undermining of the opponent's power.

Gandhi argued that bravery expressed nonviolently is more powerful than bravery expressed in violence.[24] The emphasis on fearlessness in Gandhian thought, and in various cases of nonviolent struggle, is well advised, for it is a casting off of one's fear—or at least the deliberate reduction and control of one's fear—which makes possible the challenge, the persistance in face of repression, and the capacity to bring into operation the sources of strength and change which can finally lead to victory. This courage makes possible nonviolent discipline in face of severe repression and provocation; and this nonviolent discipline is in turn necessary for the operation of the technique. The nonviolence in nonviolent action rests upon courage.

SOCIAL SOURCES OF POWER CHANGES

The total combat strength and military power of belligerents in conventional military wars are not determined solely by the leaders of the contending governents or even by the soldiers in the front lines. Actions of other sections of the populations, and at times the assistance of other countries in providing various types of necessary support, are also important. Because of this aid, combat strength in military war is variable and depends on the extent and type of support for and participation in the war effort. Similar variations occur in the combat strength of two contending groups when one of them relies on nonviolent action, but with important differences.

The variations in the respective power of the contending groups in this type of conflict situation are likely to be more extreme, to take place more quickly, and to have more diverse consequences. In addition, the nonviolent group may, by its actions and behavior, control the increase or decrease in the relative strength of the opponent group, and this to a much greater degree than occurs in purely military conflicts.

On both sides the leadership groups are dependent on a variety of types of support from large numbers of people and groups, many of which provide specialized types of assistance and serve other essential social roles. The conflict is therefore not one between two clear-cut groups of fixed composition and strength. *Instead, the power of both groups varies.* The process by which their relative and absolute power is altered is complicated, but it can be simply illustrated. The strength of the nonviolent group will be strongly influenced by the people who are actually carrying out the action: the men and women who refuse to work in a strike, the volunteers who disobey laws in a civil disobedience campaign, the people who refuse taxes, who parade in the streets, and who leave boycotted goods on the shelves. If they participate fully, and persist despite the punishments meted out to them, the nonviolent movement is likely to be strong. If significant numbers of the nonviolent actionists decide, however, not to continue to take part, then the nonviolent movement will be weakened.

The opponent group's leadership—say, the government—is similarly dependent on the participation of many people on its side, such as administrators, civil servants, soldiers, policemen, members of the prison system, and the like. All of these may of course not be directly involved in the struggle at any given point. They are, however, the agents (the term is used in a morally neutral sense) on whom the opponent relies in carrying out his policies and countermeasures. If they support the opponent and carry out his policies and instructions fully and efficiently, they will help to maintain or increase his relative power position. But this is not necessarily the case. There are examples of persons in such positions who become lax in carrying out their duties—for example, by not passing important information up the hierarchy, by not relaying orders clearly to their subordinates, by not carrying out their own responsibilities efficiently, or by refusing outright to obey. Should this happen on a widespread basis, the opponent's relative power position is likely to be significantly weakened. There are indications that such laxness in carrying out measures for the regime and against the opposition is likely to occur more frequently, extensively and seriously when the opposition is using nonviolent means of struggle than when it is applying some type of political violence.

The degree to which the participants on *each* side give their wholehearted assistance in behalf of their group's objective varies, therefore. This instability and variability of general participation on *both* sides is an important characteristic of conflicts in which one side uses nonviolent action. The course of the struggle is significantly determined by the supporters of each side. It is they who wage the actual struggle. Without their participation and active assistance neither the leadership of the nonviolent group nor that of the opponent group could increase or even maintain its power. This is a first source of the constant variation in the strengths of each side. There are two others.

Rarely, if ever, does either the nonviolent or the opponent group include the whole "population," or group of people, whom they purport to represent or serve. In a given nonviolent campaign the active participants are usually a relatively small percentage of the whole population in whose interests the nonviolent group claims to be acting. On occasion, of course, participation may be extraordinarily high. The small percentage of actual combatants is not peculiar to nonviolent action. Generally it is even more so in violent struggles, whether international wars or violent revolutions. The attitudes and activities of that wider population associated with the nonviolent struggle are, however, highly important: its approval or disapproval of the nonviolent campaign may influence the morale and hence the behavior of the active participants. If sympathetic, the wider group may provide funds, facilities and supplies, take less dangerous symbolic actions of support, or provide new volunteers for the more militant action; on occasion the whole group may move toward noncooperation with and defiance of the opponent. Conversely, their disapproval of the struggle and withholding of assistance may seriously weaken or undermine the nonviolent actionists. The degree of sympathy and support from the larger group is likely to be influenced by many factors, especially by the issues at stake, the behavior of the opponent group, and the behavior of the nonviolent actionists.

A similar dependence exists for the opponent, for the attitudes and actions of his usual or potential backers are also likely to influence his relative strength. It is on this general population that he is likely ultimately to depend for his financial and material resources, and (in many cases) the operation of the economic system. So, too, he will have to rely on that population for new recruits for the army, police, civil service and the like, and for the general approval of his policies. That approval—or disapproval—may significantly influence the morale and behavior of the officials, police and soldiers who implement the policies and carry out the repression. In some situations a change in attitude in the general population could lead to changes in government policy, and even to a change in government. Here, too, the degree of sympathy and support for the regime, its policies and its measures against the nonviolent actionists is likely to be influenced by the issues at stake and by the behavior of the opponent group and of the nonviolent group. As will become clear, there are important indications that the nonviolent group may be able directly and indirectly both to increase internal opposition to the opponent regime and also to encourage among that regime's general population sympathy and support for the nonviolent group; all this to a far greater degree than would be possible if the nonviolent group had used violence.

In summary, the degree to which the respective "populations" give or withhold their encouragement and assistance to the active protagonists is a very important factor in determining the relative strengths of the two protagonists and the outcome of the conflict. This is a second source of the constant variation in the relative strengths of the respective groups. There remains one more.

Usually this type of conflict occurs within a wider "universe." It may be national or international or both. The importance of national and world opinion to the outcome of the struggle varies considerably and can be highly exaggerated. Such opinion may at times, however, influence the morale of the respective groups, and hence the outcome of the conflict. Or, such opinion may at times take on more concrete expression: public statements by national leaders or pronouncements by international organizations, political intervention by national leaders, economic and other types of support for the nonviolent actionists, economic boycotts and embargoes against the opponent, diplomatic representations, severance of diplomatic relations, and various other forms, depending on the particular situation. These are often ineffective, but on occasion they may tip the scales to bring victory. As will be discussed briefly in Chapter Eleven, this factor was important in the 1963 Buddhist struggle in Vietnam and influential even in unsuccessful struggles.

Because of the variability of the strengths of the protagonists and the dependence of the leadership groups on various other groups, the objectives of the two groups, and their means of action, their wider strategies, tactics, specific methods, and behavior are all likely to have effects far beyond the particular time and place in which they occur. These effects will rebound to strengthen or weaken one group or the other. The ever-present potential for extreme variability in the power of the contending groups, and the widespread and complex character of the reverberations and influences of actions and their effects, are highly important in understanding how this technique of struggle works and why certain types of behavior may have consequences which would not otherwise be expected.

LEADERSHIP IN NONVIOLENT STRUGGLE

Socially significant nonviolent action does not just happen. In every case—whether such action occurs spontaneously, "semi-spontaneously," or is deliberately planned—considerable groundwork has prepared the way for the use of this particular technique of struggle. This groundwork may have been laid quite unconsciously as the result of a variety of influences. Frustration at the blocking of conventional channels of change, or at their uselessness in certain situations, may have finally led people to think of unorthodox ways of acting. The situation itself may have become unbearable or threatening, thus requiring radical action. Other types of action—such as violence—may have been defeated or may appear hopeless. An example of nonviolent action in some other place or time may suddenly be seen as relevant to the immediate situation. People may have grasped hope that something can be done to improve their lot and that they can do it. They may have lost their fear. New insights into accepted beliefs may have gained. The pleas or example of an apparently ignored minority may finally have produced results. New leadership may have arisen. There may have been other factors, but before socially significant nonviolent action can take place, *something* must have prepared the situation for it.

Unfortunately, we know very little of the conditions under which spontaneous cases occur and to what degree the groundwork for these can be consciously cultivated even though the actual resort to nonviolent action remains unplanned. Detailed comparative studies of cases of spontaneous nonviolent action might shed light on this and prove to be extremely important, especially for political situations which make it difficult to organize nonviolent action on a large scale. Such studies might also shed light on whether, and if so how, particular problems—such as strategy, discipline and tenacity—involved in spontaneous nonviolent action could be satisfactorily solved. For the sake of simplification, in these chapters we are assuming deliberate planning. We can therefore assume that some recognizable leadership for the movement exists.

The leadership group will usually initiate as well as plan and give continuing direction, at least in the early stages, to the nonviolent action, although in some cases it may be called to or assume its position after the action has begun. Leadership in such situations serves a very important role, especially where knowledge and understanding of the principles and practice of nonviolent action are not widespread and deep among the general population. Machiavelli pointed to the tendency of threats of disobedience to collapse if there is no effective leadership to assist in implementing them. [25] Recent struggles give evidence to support Machiavelli's view. For example, Eugen Stamm has argued that the decisive shortcomings of the 1953 East German Rising were "lack of organizational preparations; lack of central leadership; the incapacity of local strike leaders to keep in touch with one another."[26]

It would be rash, however, to say that without central leadership nonviolent struggle can never be successful. Much depends on the extent and depth of understanding of the nature and requirements of this technique of struggle. There is evidence that, in the late stages of a campaign, a nonviolent resistance movement can continue even after all the central leadership has been imprisoned or otherwise removed. If so, there is no intrinsic reason why a movement which started without central leadership could not be effective, given wide popular understanding of this type of action. It is not necessarily true that the stronger the leadership the better. For example, it has been argued that during the British General Strike of 1926 the General Council of the Trades Union Congress (influenced especially by Ernest Bevin) attempted too much centralized control.[27]

In most cases at the present stage of the development of the technique, however, some type of central leadership will be present and will be important for a variety of tasks. These would include working out strategy and tactics for action, negotiating with the opponent, encouraging willingness to resist, promoting discipline, choosing the best moment for action, and recommending continuing tactics and counterresponses as the struggle continues. Gandhi was, for example, convinced of the importance of strong leadership for a major movement using nonviolent action. He did not mean only the top leadership but also a larger band of well-trained volunteers "who thoroughly understood the strict conditions of Satyagraha. They could explain these to the people, and by sleepless vigilance keep them on the right path."[28] Referring to the participation of many thousands in the 1930-31 campaign, Gandhi said: "Their belief in nonviolence was unintelligent.... But their belief in their leaders was genuine."[29]

The main tasks of leadership in conflicts have been listed by Miller: to serve as spokesmen for those who are less articulate, to offer solutions to the problems they face, and to organize the implementation of those solutions.[30] Also, in the course of a struggle there will arise a host of problems and situations in which decisions based on knowledge and experience are to be preferred to decisions based on little understanding, or to no decisions at all because there is no one to take them.

The origins and structure of leadership in nonviolent struggles have differed widely. Where an existing organization resolves upon a course of nonviolent action, that body can itself provide a considerable degree of the leadership and organizational framework for the ensuing conflict. The Trades Union Congress and other trades union bodies served such roles in the British General Strike of 1926, for example (especially the General Council's Strike Organization Committee)[31] and the Indian National Congress, with Gandhi in a strong role, composed most of the leadership in the Indian struggles. The leadership has also taken the form of a self-selected group which operates an underground giving instructions for open nonviolent resistance by the general population, as in Finland in 1901.[32] A leadership committee may be elected by popular vote; a sixty-member committee to carry out the economic boycott against Great Britain was so elected at the City Hall in New York City on November 22, 1774.[33] In nonviolent action in support of the government, against invaders or *coups d'etat,* the top leadership may be the legal government and its ministers, as happened in the *Ruhrkampf* of 1923.[34]

In other cases, a self-selected leadership group may be formed shortly before or immediately after conflict has broken out into the open. At other times the people directly involved in the action may elect a leadership committee: frequently several such committees may federate to form a wider leadership committee. For example, in Halle, East Germany, where strikers were able to fall back on a long trade union tradition, local strike committees joined together on June 17, 1953, to form an Initiative Committee, which called a mass meeting and conducted negotiations for the successful occupation of a radio station and newspaper office.[35] During the student sit-in movement in 1960, in Raleigh, North Carolina, students from two colleges joined to set up leadership committees, composed of persons who had emerged "by natural selection." Elsewhere student presidents stepped into leadership in the new situation. In Raleigh, students formed a central Intelligence Committee (executive committee) with four specialized subcommittees to deal with particular tasks.[36] In Atlanta, Georgia, the 1960 sit-ins were led by a policy-making board of about fifteen members from six colleges, the Committee on Appeal for Human Rights; there was a general staff, a top officer called *"le Commandante,"* a "Deputy Chief of Operations," a field commander, deputy commander, and area commanders.[37] New leaders were also "thrown up out of the situation" in the bus boycott by the Africans of Alexandra Township near Johannesburg in 1957.[38] On May 20, 1917, mutinous French troops at the XXXIInd Corps replacement depot elected three delegates to present the officers with an ultimatum, and others a few days later elected "deputies" on the style of the Russian Soldiers' Councils.[39]

Top leadership in nonviolent action movements has so far taken one of three forms: group or committee leadership, an individual (especially Gandhi) acting much like a general in an army with all others carrying out orders, or a combination of the two. There are advantages and objections to all.

The individual leadership system makes it possible for the most experienced person with deepest insight into the technique, the social and political situation, the condition of the expected volunteers and general population, and other factors to work out the plans and strategy as a comprehensive whole. This is important, for the particular actions and stages of the movement can only be most significant if they are seen in relation to the wider movement to which they contribute. Gandhi argued that if the movement in crisis situations were to avoid temptations to resort to violence, or to take actions which might lead to violence, the leadership of the movement must be in the hands of those who believed in nonviolence as a moral principle. Also, in the preparation for a struggle there is often time for only limited detailed discussions and arguments in committee. Depending of course on the composition of the specific committee, such bodies can help; but they can also involve "interminable" discussions and arguments on trivial or irrelevant points. Sometimes such meetings can fairly be described as sessions in which mutual ignorance is pooled. There would be times in which to have the direction of a large-scale struggle in such hands could prove disastrous.

On the other hand, if no individual obviously stands well above the group in the qualities needed for this leadership position, it could be dangerous to give power of overall direction to one not prepared for it. Consequently, the alternative procedure—usually followed in the West—is for the leadership and planning to be in the hands of a special committee. The members may bring to it various backgrounds, skills, knowledge and insights, which ideally will combine to give the committee as a whole the qualities, skills and information to fulfill its tasks. The presence on the committee of members who lack the ability to listen to others, who talk incessantly, argue over irrelevancies, are unstable, arrogant, or simply difficult persons must be avoided. If so, and suitable persons who are capable of working smoothly together and of recognizing useful insights and suggestions from other members are included, then the group leadership will possess advantages over individual leadership and may usefully contribute to the further training of top leadership personnel. It is arguable which could operate best in crisis situations.

Even in the case of individual leadership, however, the situation is not as authoritarian as it appears at first sight, for the leader would be selected by the group concerned with the grievance and given authority to prepare plans for the action. For example, Gandhi was authorized by the

Indian National Congress—the nationalist party—to plan the civil disobedience campaign in 1930. But the leader's continued authority would always be subject to the continuance of the group's voluntary recognition of it. There is likely to be—often there must be—a pyramid of leadership with two or three or more ranks. But despite this hierarchical leadership structure, the leader cannot force his will upon those unwilling to accept it. The group could decline to accept the leader's plans. Any individual could decline to volunteer for the struggle, and at any time he could withdraw from the group if he could no longer conscientiously support the movement and its actions. As long as the volunteer remains a volunteer, however, he should carry out instructions. As Gandhi put it, he "may not remain a unit in his regiment and have the option of doing or not doing things he is asked to do." [40] In Western practice, people usually do not volunteer for a long-term nonviolent campaign, but for a specific demonstration or action, usually because long-term campaigns are rarely planned. Hence there is very little or no chance of their being ordered into a specific action of which they may disapprove, thus having to withdraw from the movement. But if a campaign or a more limited action has been carefully planned it is extremely important that all participants be willing to abide by the plans if the action is to be coherent and disciplined.

The nonviolent leadership has only nonviolent sanctions at its disposal for the enforcement of its decisions and instructions. These sanctions will be discussed in more detail later, but their relationship to the character of nonviolent leadership requires attention here. One sanction is the disapproval by other members of the nonviolent group. Sometimes social boycotts have been used. The leader himself has sanctions which only he can impose. For example, Gandhi first fasted and then called off the 1919 campaign against the Rowlatt Act because some demonstrators had resorted to violence. [41] When striking mill workers being led by Gandhi in Ahmedabad in 1918 began to go back on their pledges of behavior for the course of the strike, Gandhi's fast restored morale and adherence to their earlier promises. [42] However effective such extreme sanctions may sometimes be, they are clearly of a different character than the extreme sanctions at the disposal of leaders in a violent struggle—imprisonment or execution. This difference in enforcement sanctions is only one of the factors which separate the operation of military leadership from even the most authoritarian forms of leadership in a nonviolent movement. In addition, nonviolent leaders have frequently emphasized that they did not wish people to follow them blindly, but to follow only if convinced of the policy and proposed actions. [43]

One of the most important justifications for strong leadership in nonviolent struggles has been that only a few people had sufficient understanding of this technique to make wise decisions as to how to take action. It is very possible that widespread self-education and spread of knowledge about nonviolent action may facilitate the development of a more diffused system of leadership and increased self-reliance.

Whatever form it takes, the quality of the leadership for nonviolent action is very important in developing the movement along sound lines, gathering support, maintaining confidence, keeping up morale, and guiding it directly or with prepared plans through difficulties to a successful conclusion. The personal qualities of the leader or the leadership group and the perceived wisdom of their plans for action determine whether their guidance is accepted voluntarily by the participants in the struggle. If not, those "leaders" will be rejected and become unsuccessful claimants to leadership positions. Gregg lists as necessary qualities of nonviolent leaders a high degree of love, faith, courage, honesty and humility.[44] There are other qualities, however, which are highly important. Leaders for this type of struggle are likely to be most capable if they possess an active mind, have thorough expertise in the technique they are applying, are able to develop wise strategy, plans and actions, and understand the opponent's case, his psychology, resources, and the changing views and attitudes of his supporters. The nonviolent leader will need to understand the potentialities, limitations and nature of the volunteers, sympathizers and the population. His past record will also be important, especially his experience, service and integrity. He must be willing to accept sacrifice and to set an example for the movement.

In some cases the leadership will be more diffused and harder to locate—especially where the movement has been spontaneous rather than planned, and also in advanced stages of planned movements when the original leadership has been entirely removed. Leadership may then be provided by larger numbers of individuals and small groups who offer leads for action which are accepted and followed by others. The quality of this type of leadership is important too, for it must not lead in the wrong direction if the campaign is to be a success.

PREPARING FOR NONVIOLENT STRUGGLE

Whether a campaign is to be massive, including many millions of participants, or small, with only a handful of volunteers or even a single person, careful planning and preparations are essential. Gandhi's careful attention to detail in laying plans for *satyagraha* and in solving organizational problems has been acknowledged as one of the reasons for his effectiveness. This has not always been the case in nonviolent struggles, of course. Lindberg pointed out in 1937 that military campaigns have almost always been carried out by disciplined men acting under trained leaders, while nonviolent campaigns have never taken place under such favorable conditions. "They have always been characterized by inadequate preparations." However, since the time of Gandhi's major experiments with this technique in India, there has been increasing emphasis on the need for preparations if the technique is to be effective. As Lindberg wrote: "Every form of nonviolent campaign of a merely spontaneous character is threatened either by death in indifference in the course of a short time, or is threatened by a much too rapid growth and blooming in a transition to violence." [45] Investigation may show ways to combine general preparations for nonviolent struggle with spontaneity as to the exact moment and form of action; this might be especially useful in political situations where open advance preparations and organization are impossible. However, Gandhi and others who have given considerable thought to the problem would come very close to full agreement with Lindberg.

The exact order in which various types of preparation or actions are carried out, or ought to be carried out, for greatest effectiveness will vary with the particular situation. The order of the topics discussed here ought not therefore to be identified with an unchangeable pattern.

A. Investigation

Where the use of nonviolent action is contemplated, the movement will be strengthened by an advance investigation of alleged grievances. Few things can weaken such a movement as much as the revelation that the actionists did not really know the facts nor have accurate information on the situation they were complaining about. Where full and accurate information is not readily available, some type of investigation will have to be undertaken. That investigation should be as accurate and as fair as possible; this will help in the wide acceptance of its results. The investigation should not be limited only to the facts as seen by the group with the grievances, but should include the facts as seen by the opponent group and by third parties. Following the investigation, a statement of desired changes should be formulated. The greater the accuracy and fairness in the statement of grievances and of facts, and the greater the restraint shown in concentrating on only the clearest and most important demands, it has been said, the stronger the appearance of the nonviolent group's case and the weaker that of the opponent. Furthermore, basic issues should not be confused with secondary ones.

Sometimes in rigid political systems the facts may come to light not by an investigation—which might be impossible—but by simply "leaking out." For example, in Nazi Germany news of the gassing of mentally ill persons which began in September 1939 leaked out even though it was top secret; this led to significant protest from Roman Catholic church leaders until the euthanasia program was stopped in August 1941.[46]

After the information has been gathered by investigation or other means, the widest possible publicity is to be given to the facts of the case, the grievances, and the aims of the nonviolent group. This publicity is not part of the investigation, which is normally done quietly, but belongs in the phase of "generating cause-consciousness" which is discussed below. This publicity may itself bring pressure for a change. Even if it does not, the dissemination of the results of investigation will contribute to a stronger position for the nonviolent group during the ensuing struggle.

B. Negotiations

At this stage of the conflict negotiations with the opponent are usually undertaken or intensified, through personal meetings and letters, often unpublicized. Initiation of nonviolent action, especially in its more radical forms, is a serious undertaking. Efforts to solve the problem before taking direct action are desirable. In addition an effort at negotiations—whether or not immediately successful—may also *contribute* to a satisfactory resolution of the conflict. Negotiations in this context are therefore not seen as a full substitute for nonviolent action, but as a step which might make it unnecessary in some cases and more effective in others.

Where the issues at stake are serious, especially where they affect the relative power positions of the groups, it should not be surprising if a solution satisfactory to the nonviolent group is not reached by negotiation. The effort may, however, serve other purposes. Negotiation is one channel for maintaining contact between the two groups, helping the opponent understand the grievances, and communicating to him why nonviolent action is going to be taken. In negotiations the nonviolent group can also explain the type of struggle which will be used. Very important in some cases, negotiations may also help the opponent and the negotiators to achieve a relationship between human beings as such. This may counterbalance or prevent the mutual distortions of each other's images which often occur in conflict and which may reduce the chances of a settlement.[47] It is also important that the nonviolent group should make, and be seen to make, every effort at a settlement before launching direct action. This greatly increases its moral position, in its own eyes and in those of the opponent group and of third parties. It will also aid the perception that the more extreme action has been forced upon the nonviolent group and is therefore more justified.[48] When the nonviolent group begins direct action, that perception may influence various reactions and thus the relative support the two contending groups receive.

In negotiations, the representatives of the nonviolent group will make clear their minimum demands, as distinguished from secondary issues on which compromise may be possible, or which may even not be pressed. Where basic moral or political principles are involved they will not be subject to compromise, however. Once the demands are set, it is generally recommended that they be kept unchanged during the struggle, and not raised or lowered with variations in the nonviolent group's chances of victory. Usually, such changes in demands are likely to reduce sympathy and support for the nonviolent group, and lower its credibility.[49]

Preparation for nonviolent action is likely to increase the chances of successful negotiations, for the mere possibility of such struggle may on occasion encourage the opponent to make concessions.[50] This relationship is important at this stage of the conflict. The practitioner of this technique is much more realistic about the role of power than is his more naïve friend who favors negotiations as a *substitute* for open struggle. Negotiations do not take place in a vacuum, and they are rarely resolved solely on the objective merits of the respective arguments and evidence. Behind every case of negotiations is the stated or silent—but mutually understood—role of the relative power positions of the negotiators; that is, what each can do if no agreement is reached. Gandhi said, for example: "I do not believe in making appeals when there is no force behind them, whether moral or material."[51] The nonviolent actionists' capacity and willingness for further action distinguishes his approach from that of those who vaguely prefer peace and think that talking is a substitute for war. The nonviolent army, Gandhi said, "should be so well prepared as to make war unnecessary."[52] Theodor Ebert has called "a credible determination to fight a prerequisite for negotiations."[53] Ebert has pointed out that on some occasions Indian leaders demanded not only concrete promises in negotiations, but some "advance deeds as proof that the promises would later be kept," such as the release of political prisoners.[54]

All cases may not follow this pattern, of course. In actual events, negotiations may occur simultaneously with other actions, such as a strike or a civil disobedience campaign. Or the opponent may refuse to negotiate, demanding, for example, that the nonviolent group give up all plans for direct action, or, if such action has begun, declaring that he will not negotiate until it is called off. The nonviolent actionist will refuse to be intimidated or sidetracked by such tactics. However, Gandhi and others have emphasized that as long as the opponent does not impose unreasonable preconditions for negotiations, the nonviolent group should be willing and even eager to negotiate at any stage of the conflict, in the hope of finding an acceptable settlement which will make continued direct action unnecessary.

C. Sharpening the focus for attack

Nonviolent action is a technique of struggle in which the participants are able to advance their cause in proportion to the degree that the opponent's desire and ability to maintain the objectionable policy are weakened, and that the nonviolent group is able to generate the will and power to give it the internal strength to effect the change. The skillful choice of the point of attack is important in this connection. In intellectual arguments one often concentrates on the weakest links in the opponent's case. In war, instead of attacking with equal force on the whole front simultaneously, one usually concentrates forces on what are believed to be the enemy's weakest points in the belief that a breakthrough there will lead to a weakening or collapse of other sections of the front. So in a nonviolent struggle the nonviolent leadership will show wisdom in concentrating action on the weakest points in the opponent's case, policy, or system. This will contribute to the maximum weakening of his relative position and the maximum strengthening of that of the nonviolent group.

In nonviolent action it is necessary to have a pivot point on which to place the lever which is to remove the evil. The selection of this pivot or issue is very important for the whole consequent campaign. One does not, in Gandhi's view, launch a nonviolent campaign for such general objectives as "peace," "independence," "freedom," or "brotherhood." "The issue must be definite and capable of being clearly understood and within the power of the opponent to yield." [55] In applying this technique of struggle under less than perfect conditions, success may depend, Miller writes, on "phasing strategy in such a way as to score a series of minor gains or to secure a single major victory in the most accessible sector, rather than trying for a cluster of major objectives at the same time." [56] Whether the specific objective(s) chosen is (are) highly limited or very ambitious will hinge in part on the nonviolent group's assessment of its relative strength and capacity for action.

In a study of the defeated campaign in Albany, Georgia, in 1962, Professor Howard Zinn wrote:

There has been a failure to create and handle skillfully a set of differentiated tactics for different situations. The problem of desegregating Albany facilities involves various parties: some situations call for action by the city commission; some for decision by the Federal Courts; some for agreement with private businessmen. Moreover, there are advantages to singling out a particular goal and concentrating on it. This is an approach not only tactically sound for Negro protest but also creates a climate favorable to a negotiated solution. The community is presented with a specific concrete demand rather than a quilt of grievances and demands which smothers the always limited ability of societies to think rationally about their faults.[57]

Martin Luther King, Jr., reached a similar conclusion in the same case:

> . . . we decided that one of the principal mistakes we had made there was to scatter our efforts too widely. We had been so involved in attacking segregation in general that we had failed to direct our protest effectively to any one major facet. We concluded that in hard-core communities a more effective battle could be waged if it was concentrated against one aspect of the evil and intricate system of segregation.[58]

Without question there were other serious causes of the Albany defeat, but those do not invalidate these observations.

Instead, then, of a campaign for some very general objective, Ebert writes: "In working out the staged plan, it is essential for the success of the campaign to find the correct point of attack or one flash-point among many in social relationships which symbolizes all the other conflicts."[59] In the Vykom campaign, sketched in Chapter Two, the issue was the right of people to use a road that led to their homes. In the 1930–31 independence movement the specific issue which initiated the campaign was that of the Salt Laws, which touched the lives of most of the people in India; other wider political aims were condensed into eleven demands.[60]

This is not a matter of being moderate in one's aims, but of concentrating one's strength in ways which will make victory more likely. The planners choose the point of attack, the specific aspect of the general problem which symbolizes the "evil" which is least defensible by the opponent and which is capable of arousing the greatest strength against it. Success in such limited campaigns will in turn increase the self-confidence of the actionists[61] and their ability to move effectively toward the fuller achievement of their larger objectives as they gain experience in the use of effective means of action to realize their aims.

The choice of the point of attack requires considerable understanding and a keen perception of the total situation. Amiya Chakravarty has described very well Gandhi's ability to combine short-run and long-run plans in the selection of a focal point for action. It sometimes happens, Chakravarty writes, that "in following one obvious remedial line we have hit upon a symptom which symbolizes, demonstrates and challenges a root situation." A series of attacks on these points makes it possible to move "from one total situation to another." The issue should be kept clear and clean, he continues, pointing out that, for example, segregation in opium parlors would be an erroneous choice as a point for attack on racial segregation, while the right to pray in unsegregated churches "would be an issue of overwhelming convergence." Repression against nonviolent actionists concentrating on such a point of attack could but strengthen their cause. "Again and again, Gandhiji showed an instinct, a spiritual instinct, for the right issue, for the converging issues which supported each other at a point." [62]

This approach to political action has strong support from a quite different source, namely, Lenin, who wrote: "The whole art of politics lies in finding and gripping as strong as we can the link that is least likely to be torn out of our hands, the one that is most important at the given moment, the one that guarantees the possessor of a link the possession of the whole chain." [63]

D. Generating "cause-consciousness" [64]

During the stage of investigation, publicity will usually, but not always, have been avoided. After the information has been gathered, however, and the minimum demands determined, it is necessary to publicize the facts, the issues and the arguments advanced by the nonviolent group. "The investigation into the causes of the conflict, the documentation of actual grievances and the resulting demands of the oppressed must be widely disseminated in a form which is comprehensible to the public and to the oppressor," writes Ebert. [65] The need for such a period of motivational preparation has been long recognized as important to a well-supported and sustained nonviolent movement. For example, in 1769, in correspondence with George Washington about the details and implementation of a nonimportation plan, his neighbor James Mason argued that it would be necessary to publish "something preparatory to it in our gazettes, to warn the people of the impending danger and to induce them the more readily and cheerfully to concur in the proper measures to avert it." [66]

This phase may begin prior to negotiations with the opponent, or it may occur simultaneously with negotiations, or follow them when they have failed. It may proceed by stages, moving from the effort to inform the public in general of the grievances, to encouraging people to feel that nonviolent action is needed to correct them, and finally to enlisting paricipants for the coming struggle. A very important part of this activity is aimed at arousing the feeling that something can and ought to be done, and at increasing confidence that this can and should be done along non-violent lines.

A variety of means may be used for these purposes. Pamphlets, leaflets, books, articles and papers dealing with the issues and the implications of the dispute may be issued. Public meetings, speeches, debates, discussions on radio, television and before existing organizations may be held. Sometimes the cinema, theater, catchy songs, slogans and symbols may be used, as well as house-to-house canvassing, petitions and personal contacts. The degree to which specific means are used openly depends somewhat on the regime and political situation in the country. A properly conducted journal can be of immense help in such a campaign, as most leaders of political dissent, including Gandhi, have recognized.

The emphasis in this effort to arouse ''cause-consciousness'' must be placed on quality rather than on speed or quantity, and strict efforts must be made to avoid exaggerations, distortions and falsehoods. Neither should feelings of hatred or intolerance be aroused. Oppenheimer and Lakey write that, without compromising, it is important ''to try to limit the amount of antagonism from potential allies.'' This involves both ''cutting down on actions which can be misinterpreted to be hostile and negative'' and also improving the interpretation of all activities. ''Remember,'' they add, ''that many people are only looking for an excuse *not* to support the movement.''[67]

The duration of this stage of the movement will vary with the situation and previous work.[68] Sometimes, some of the publicity efforts started when the grievance group had not yet considered taking nonviolent action will be continued. Sometimes, also, widespread individual discontent will coalesce into general awareness of collective dissent. For example, before the East German Rising of June 16-17, 1953, workers had become increasingly vocal about their dissatisfaction with working conditions and with an increase in the work norms, which reduced wages but not the amount of work. They had managed to discuss their grievances, and the Rising itself was preceded by some sixty local strikes during the first half of June.[69]

Arousing "cause-consciousness" may be divided into several phases. Special efforts will be necessary to develop understanding of the issues. When the decision is finally made to launch nonviolent action and specific plans are announced, further efforts will be needed to inform the population and possible participants of the nature of the contemplated action, the requirements for its success, the importance of engaging or not engaging in particular acts, and similar points.

A variety of efforts may then be made to justify and legitimatize resort to direct action. Persons about to launch nonviolent action may regard themselves as acting in defense of the constitution and the law, while the opponent's actions are regarded as having no legal basis.[70] Alternatively, the action may be taken in an attempt to restore a system or constitution which was illegally and violently overthrown by the opponent. Justification may also be made in terms of democratic popular will against minority or foreign oppression, or in terms of the basic rights of man or of religious principles. Frequently, too, reliance on the technique of nonviolent action will be regarded as adding legitimacy and justification to the cause, especially when various means of violent action are regarded as inappropriate or wrong for social and political as well as moral reasons.

The nonviolent leaders may also at this stage warn of the hardship and suffering which will be incurred during the struggle. They may seek to arouse confidence that those penalties will be worth incurring, because this type of action is more likely than any other to procure victory. Sometimes such leaders and participants believe that the combination of a just cause and the use of this technique of action will in the long run ensure victory. Frederic Solomon and Jacob R. Fishman argued that the confidence of civil rights workers in inevitable desegregation—coming from a just cause and use of nonviolent action—was psychologically useful because "it heightens [their] own strength and resolve" and also "undermines that of the opposition."[71] Various types of symbolic action (among them methods described in Chapter Three) may be used at this stage to dramatize the issues, strike the imagination of the general populace, and arouse the will to take direct action.

E. Quantity and quality in nonviolent action

In planning and conducting nonviolent action very careful consideration must constantly be given to the relationship between the numbers participating in the conflict and the quality of their participation. This appears to be a more complex relationship than is recognized by those who argue that *only quantity* or *only quality* is important. The way in which this relationship is resolved and expressed has a very significant effect upon the whole course of the movement and its consequences. Clearly both are important, but they are not always equally important. Within certain limits the relationship between numbers and quality may vary considerably, changing with the situation, the stage of the movement, and the methods which are to be used. Certainly in a technique of action which in large degree depends for its effectiveness on the withdrawal of consent, cooperation and obedience, the numbers of participants are significant to its relative impact. But to concentrate on numbers alone may prove unwise because the effectiveness and consequences of nonviolent action are not in simple proportion to the numbers involved. If large numbers are involved, the strength thus demonstrated must be genuine if the movement is not to collapse in crises and if it is to persist and grow. The genuineness of this strength is in turn related to such factors as the degree of fearlessness, discipline, willingness to persist despite sanctions, and wisdom shown in the choice of strategy, tactics and methods of action. These are all closely associated with the quality of the movement.

In a sense nonviolent action is by its very nature qualitatively different from other means of struggle. It requires, for example, fearlessness and determination, an ability to maintain nonretaliation, sometimes forgiveness, and always nonviolence in face of the opponent's sometimes brutal repression. At the same time it requires courageous persistence in the intended course of action, and selfless commitment to the cause of the grievance group.

The degree of quality required in a given movement may vary with conditions, especially those conditions which may make it difficult to use this technique, and also with the type of opponent being confronted. In a labor strike, for example, under normal conditions in Western countries today, as long as the men stay away from work, their chances of success are high. They usually have some form of financial assistance to help them through the strike. The chances of severe repression by police or the military are now slight. Strikebreakers are rarer than before. Provocation to violence is usually no longer extensive. Objectives are usually quite limited and do not threaten the opponent seriously. The duration of the strike is not likely to be long. Under such conditions, the actionists can "get away" with a lower overall quality in the movement than would be desirable or necessary if contrasting conditions existed. This certainly does not mean that increased quality in behavior of participants under such conditions would not be desirable and even highly beneficial, but that it is no longer so necessary.

However, when the chances of success are not large, when repression may be severe, when the opponent provokes violence, when the objectives seriously threaten the opponent's ego or position, and the struggle may be a long one, then high quality in the movement becomes essential. The problem is how to achieve it. Sometimes people may out of desperation, newly gained confidence, courage, or intuition rise to the demands of the situation. On other occasions they may be willing to follow wise guidance from leaders who understand what is needed. Sometimes the development of quality behavior in large numbers of participants may follow a series of smaller demonstrations of brave and disciplined nonviolent action.

There is a tradition within nonviolent action, especially in the labor movement and among advocates of the general strike in achieving social revolution, which emphasizes the importance of numbers. So, too, there is another tradition (clearly expressed by Gandhi) which emphasizes the role of quality and the disproportionate effect which a small number of actionists may have. Gregg has argued that a minute force can lead to a large change and that frequently a weak stimulus may even be superior to a stronger one.[72] He speaks of the "primary influential power of disciplined individual persons."[73] Bondurant relates Gandhi's concepts of the power of the individual to his concern for individual freedom within society and to Western concepts of the dignity of the individual.[74] Fewer numbers of volunteers with fuller understanding of the nonviolent approach are likely, she explains, to prove more reliable in crises. Lakey suggests that quality may be more important, even at the cost of numbers, when the nonviolent group aims at persuading or converting the opponent. He writes:

> This may be explained by recourse to our view that communication of images is an important part of any conflict. The image which is presented by the nonviolent actor is more important than the number of persons comprising the image. In Goffman's terms, the person for whom nonviolence is a matter of faith is more likely to give a "consistent performance"—thereby presenting a clear-cut image of suffering and courageous humanity. The fewer "slips" there are into angry retorts or frantic retreats, the more likely it is that the opponent and public will perceive in the campaigner an important common quality and respond to it with a lessening of violence.[75]

It may be useful briefly to survey Gandhi's views on the dependence of both success and numbers in nonviolent action on quality, since his conclusions differ considerably from the popular expectation. Numbers, Gandhi insisted, were not necessary in a just cause.[76] In a nonviolent struggle fewer *satyagrahis* would be needed than would regular soldiers in a violent conflict.[77] Nonviolent action of high quality and small numbers could have a powerful impact, he insisted.[78] "I attach the highest importance to quality irrespective almost of quantity . . ."[79] "Even a handful of true satyagrahis well organized and disciplined through selfless service of the masses, can win independence for India."[80] "I am convinced that there is safety in fewness so long as we have not evolved cohesion, exactness and intelligent cooperation and responsiveness."[81] Even a single perfect *satyagrahi,* Gandhi believed, could "defy the whole might of an unjust empire . . . and lay the foundation for that empire's fall or regeneration."[82] Unfortunately, Gandhi admitted, such perfection was not possible, but this did not alter the general principle of the overwhelming importance of quality in a nonviolent movement.

It is clear that Gandhi saw this quality as influencing the opponent and making him more likely to accept the demands of the nonviolent group, as paving the way for larger numbers when, inspired by the example, more people learned to cast off fear and to rely on disciplined nonviolent action to remedy the grievance.[83] Quality would be contagious and multiply; the number of nonviolent actionists enrolled under Gandhi's leadership in South Africa, for example, rose from sixteen to sixty thousand.[84] In contrast, undisciplined numbers would fade away. Furthermore, the growth in numbers was important for another reason. Even if it were possible for a single individual or a very few nonviolent actionists by their own actions to achieve the desired change, it would be wiser, Gandhi felt, for them to use their abilities to educate the masses of the people in the means by which they themselves could right their wrongs. The maintenance of quality was important in this. "Mass instruction on any other terms is an impossibility."[85]

In other words, the maintenance of high quality in nonviolent action is necessary at all stages; if this is done when the numbers are small, it will make possible a very considerable increase in the numbers of nonviolent actionists capable of the strength necessary for effectivenenss. Large numbers not able to maintain the nonviolent discipline, the fearlessness, and other necessary standards of behavior could only weaken the movement,[86] but large numbers capable of maintaining the necessary standards and discipline become "irresistable."[87]

In summary, because of the nature of the technique of nonviolent action itself, attention to the maintenance of the quality of the movement, including such factors as fearlessness and maintaining the nonviolent discipline, is always required. Large numbers may frequently be necessary to effect particular changes. However, such numbers can be obtained as reliable participants only by maintaining and not lowering the standards of the movement.

F. Organizing the movement

Some type of organization is usually helpful or necessary if the action campaign is to implement decisions and carry out specific tasks. Important jobs cannot be simply left to chance; they require efficient organization to ensure that they are done. Among the tasks of such an organization are those which relate to the public, the volunteers, the leadership and the movement as a whole. These tasks will include publicizing the facts and grievances, promoting sympathy for the nonviolent group and its aims, informing the public of the intentions of the nonviolent group and its plans for action, and mobilizing financial and other resources for the movement. Another group of tasks relating to volunteers includes recruiting participants for the campaign, preparing volunteers and potential participants for action, and training these volunteers for specific and immediate tasks. Also, when new sympathizers and supporters appear, it will be necessary to show them how to help the movement in specific ways and to incorporate them into groups of other active participants. Leadership and organization are related; the organization may provide in advance for several successive stages of leadership to replace immediately arrested leaders, and may determine the procedure for further selection of leadership as long as conditions permit its operation as a clear group. The organization may also provide the leadership with accurate information about the condition of the movement and various factors influencing it. Other tasks which the organization may tackle include steps to keep up the movement's morale, to maintain discipline, and to prepare participants to act without leaders in times of severe repression.

The degree to which such organization has been formal has in past campaigns varied considerably. The numbers involved, their understanding of the technique of action, whether they are used to working together, and the situation in which they are operating—all have an influence in this regard. Sometimes an organization may be set up on the spot, as by striking workers who have no trade union. Sometimes an existing organization may be turned to the new task of nonviolent action; there are sometimes advantages to that, especially as the body may already be a legitimate group with a definite place in the society. Sometimes local or regional or even central government may become the resistance organization, especially if such government is responsive to popular will. Local and regional government may be involved when the opponent is the central government; together with the central government, local and regional governments may be involved in facing an internal usurper carrying out a *coup,* or a foreign invader. On other occasions a new action organization for the specific purpose may be set up before nonviolent action is launched. Both tried and respected persons and leaders of other groups and new and hitherto inexperienced and unknown persons may help to build and operate the organization.

An organization for nonviolent struggle should not be unwieldy, it must not be corrupted, it should be able to put its full weight into the struggle without pursuing any basically inconsistent further objective, and it should be able to operate under a voluntary formal or informal discipline.[88] An effective system of communication between the various branches and levels of the direct action organization will usually be required. If the opponent's police measures and control of communications and transportation make such communication difficult or impossible, then the planners will need to determine in advance the points and issues on which opposition will be launched and how this will be done. Then, despite lack of contact between resistance groups, they may still be able to act, even as part of a joint action for the same objectives.[89]

Regardless of the precise form which organization takes in a particular conflict situation—and that subject itself merits detailed study[90]—the importance of organization for effective nonviolent action remains of high priority. As Gandhi wrote in 1920:

> But the greatest thing in this campaign of non-cooperation is to evolve order, discipline, cooperation among the people, coordination among the workers. Effective non-cooperation depends upon complete organization.[91]

Ebert has supported this view:

> The fact that the state of organization and advance preparation has been so decisive in past nonviolent campaigns suggests that nonviolent resistance can develop into an alternative to violent resistance only in so far as it assumes visible organizational shape and is adequately prepared.[92]

Sometimes part of the preparatory organizational work will include obtaining pledges to participate in the campaign. Such pledges will often include clauses committing the signer to abide by the movement's nonviolent discipline as a contribution to success. Pledges are not a recent innovation. Pledges, oaths and agreements to carry out resistance plans, especially for nonviolent economic resistance, were widely used during the struggle of the American colonists.[93] In 1775, for example, radicals in Virginia sought the signature of every inhabitant in the colony to the Continental Association resistance plan adopted by the First Continental Congress.[94] The Congress had in that document pledged continued adherence to the plan until repeal of the offending laws of Parliament had been achieved.[95]

Mass meetings have often been used to contact possible volunteers and to stimulate their willingness to join the coming struggle. If formal pledges are used in the campaign, signatures may then be sought. In other cases there have been no formal pledges, with reliance being placed instead on adherence to the general principles of the movement, high morale and group pressures to ensure continued participation and discipline. Where volunteers have continuing confidence in the efficacy of nonviolent action, considerable understanding of and experience in the use of this technique, and also a good grasp of the planned course of action, then the need for formal pledges may not be so severe. However, in light of existing experience, strong commitment of the volunteers to participation and adherence to the campaign's plans and standards remain crucial. Effective means for promoting these are therefore important at this and other stages of the struggle. In preparing the volunteers and the general population for the struggle, extreme attention must be given to three closely related qualities of this technique: fearlessness, nonviolence, and their corollary, openness or nonsecrecy.

OPENNESS AND SECRECY IN NONVIOLENT STRUGGLE

Secrecy, deception and underground conspiracy pose very difficult problems for a movement using nonviolent action. No matter from what ideological or philosophical position one starts there is often no easy solution to them.

Believers in nonviolence as a moral principle have often asserted that an associated principle—that of truthfulness—should also be accepted by persons using nonviolent means; they have therefore concluded that nonviolent action movements must never use secrecy. When based simply on assertions of moral principles, these arguments have generally had little influence on persons not sharing them. The relative success of these believers in influencing nonviolent action movements to operate openly and to reject secrecy is probably rooted less in the impact of their arguments than in the evidence provided by various campaigns and action projects that openness worked.

Nevertheless, some persons taking part in nonviolent struggle have at times tried to get the action organization to use secrecy and conspiratorial behavior. This has happened not only where the movement was under political dictatorship, where such an approach might seem reasonable, but even under relatively liberal political conditions, as in Britain. Within the anti-nuclear weapons Committee of 100 in its heyday, there were, for example, members who were acting, or pressing the Committee to act, by secret and conspiratorial means. They argued that it was naïve and "emotional" to attempt to apply such moral principles as openness and truthfulness to the hard reality of political struggle. The choice of tactics and the decision whether to be open or secretive must not, they maintained, be unreasonably restricted by emotion, religion or prejudices; practical answers to practical problems had to be worked out solely in light of the demands of the situation. However, if one asks what the consequences of secrecy and deception for the movement and the society are, or their effects on the dynamics of nonviolent action, or what the practical alternative means to openness in building and conducting an effective movement are, the weaknesses of the intellectual case for underground conspiratorial means become apparent.

In this section we shall look at the relationship between openness or secrecy and the dynamics of nonviolent action. We are not here concerned with moral imperatives to openness and truthfulness, but with the psychological, social and political effects of such behavior. The basic conclusion of this discussion will be contrary to what might commonly be assumed: the dynamics of this technique require that, in most situations at least, nonviolent action movements operate openly if they are to achieve their maximum strength and advantage in the struggle.

Openness in nonviolent action means that the organization backing the action act openly: that the names and activities of their leaders be revealed to the public and the opponent, that written protests be signed by the person or groups making them, that actions of protest, resistance and intervention be taken openly without attempt at deceit or hiding the behavior. Usually it has also even meant that the opponent and often the police be directly notified in advance, usually in writing, of the date, place, time, often the names of participants, and of the type of action to be taken. Gandhi was well known for this type of behavior, typified by his letter of March 2, 1930, to Lord Irwin, the Viceroy. In that letter Gandhi said that if his appeal for major political changes were not granted by March 11, he would, with his co-workers, begin his plan to disobey the provisions of the Salt Laws. On March 12, the names, ages, and identification of those who were to march with him to the sea to make salt were published in his paper, *Young India;* the plans included provision for immediate mass civil disobedience, should he be arrested at any point before he broke the law.[96] Similar plans for action in case openness led to early arrests were followed on other occasions. Similar openness has been used by American nonviolent civil rights groups. For a long period it was followed in South Africa by the African National Congress—for example, during the 1952 Defiance Campaign.[97] This openness in nonviolent action is not, however, something new introduced by Gandhi. Openness in defiance was a prominent feature of the Russian Revolution of 1905. Father Gapon himself told the Russian government of the plans for the march to the Winter Palace with a petition on January 9, 1905 (which became "Bloody Sunday");[98] liberals during the spring of 1905 were, in contrast to previous times, "operating virtually in the open";[99] instead of repeating the former practice of indoor and secret May Day celebrations in 1905, the socialists let it be widely known that they would conduct open demonstrations accompanied by political strikes (despite police arrests "the plans were carried out, with somewhat irregular success, in scores of places throughout the country").[100]

The problems of openness and secrecy under extreme dictatorships, especially totalitarian regimes, require special consideration. In this analysis we assume that the movement is not operating under such extreme difficulties. Improved understanding of the conditions and consequences of secrecy and openness in these milder situations may assist later examination of the problem under totalitarian conditions. However, it is not these extreme situations with which opposition groups are usually faced, even under milder dictatorships and colonialism and where civil liberties are in decline. Further, the answer to the problem of secrecy and openness in nonviolent action against totalitarian regimes does not necessarily determine the answer in the far greater number of situations more frequently faced.

However, the fact that open protest and resistance have taken place even under extreme totalitarian situations, when the actionists were improvising without special knowledge and understanding of this technique, shows that the case against the open operation of nonviolent action against totalitarian systems is not as firm and closed as many might believe. Indeed, the courage involved in such open action may strike especially hard at totalitarian systems, which are characterized by the instillation of fear and submissiveness in the subjects. Open defiance was a major characteristic of the East German Rising, for example, [101] and in the successful resistance in Berlin in 1943 to the deportation of Jews—especially those in mixed marriages—to the extermination camps, as described briefly in Chapter Two. In his study *The Final Solution,* Reitlinger cites Goebbels's entries in his diaries in March 1943 referring to these events, including the crowd demonstration against the evacuation of a home for aged Jews which resulted in the suspension of the whole action: "We can save it up for a week or two." Even Hitler's personal complaints to Goebbels at the continued presence in Berlin of Jewish intellectuals produced no results. Goebbels wrote: "After a terrific commotion in artistic circles, particularly among actors, a number of Jews married to Aryans had to be released." [102] Reitlinger concludes that this attempt to deport the partners of mixed marriages and their children, "like the euthanasia programme for the insane and incurable, was one of Hitler's defeats." [103] In the history of Nazism these were minor defeats, but these instances illustrate the simple point that openness in successful resistance was possible under even the conditions in the Third Reich.

Discussions in favor of secrecy in nonviolent action often seem to assume that it is not difficult to keep the opponent or the government from finding out what is to be kept secret. In many situations this is a very naïve assumption, both for small and large movements. While it may be possible to keep certain matters secret for some time, it is likely that sooner or later the police will learn not only the most important general intentions, but often the detailed plans as well. Modern electronic devices of various types may be used in addition to the older methods of opening the mail, telephone tapping, volunteer informers, planting of agents, spying and the like. If there are no secrets and planned action is not dependent on secrecy, such measures are not likely to impede the movement seriously. But when the implementation of plans for action depends on maintenance of secrecy, then such police methods may pose serious threats. Even under the Russian tsarist regime—which was scarcely as efficient as modern governments—police agents and spies penetrated the revolutionists' organizations continually, frequently rising to top positions of trust.[104] The British government apparently tried to have informers and agents in strike organizations during the General Strike of 1926.[105] In Nazi Germany opposition groups had immense difficulty in keeping resistance plans secret; informers and agents frequently penetrated underground groups and even operated inside concentration camps and prisoner-of-war camps.[106]

However, the most powerful single objection to secrecy in a nonviolent action movement is that secrecy is not only rooted in fear but that it contributes to fear. Fear is often a block to action even when people are stirred to indignation. As has been discussed earlier in this chapter, willingness to use nonviolent action depends in large degree upon the casting off of fear.

To produce change, nonviolent action operates on much more fundamental psychological, social and political levels than other techniques of action, especially more so than the several types of political violence with which conspiratorial behavior is usually associated. These more fundamental levels of operation in nonviolent action, which may produce shifts of loyalties and invisibly undermine the power of a hostile regime, often operate more quickly than dramatic acts which might only be possible by secrecy. But the more basic changes will be far more important. Therefore, it is highly dangerous to threaten the operation of those sometimes less obvious but much stronger forces by a secret effort to produce a quick temporary victory on some subordinate point. If the nonviolent actionists are to maximize their strength, they must act in harmony with the dynamics of this technique and its requirements. Especially important in these requirements are the maintenance of fearlessness and nonviolent discipline.

If—because of an inadequate understanding of their own technique and its dynamics, or because of the temptations of shortsighted expediency, or because of undisciplined behavior—the nonviolent actionists introduce into their struggle qualities and means appropriate to a violent struggle, they reverse important processes necessary for their success. At the same time they strengthen the opponent. The introduction of secrecy into a nonviolent action movement operates strongly against the maintenance of fearlessness and nonviolent discipline. Thus openness—that is, being truthful in statements and frank with the opponent and the public concerning intentions and plans—appears to be a corollary of the requirements of fearlessness and nonviolent discipline.

The openness of the movement and even its effrontery in daring to state its intentions publicly will have a significant impact on the non-violent group itself, on the opponent, and on third parties. Conversely, resorting to secrecy, deception and underground conspiracy is likely to have a detrimental impact on all three groups.

Secrecy in a nonviolent action movement is likely to involve the leaders' going into hiding and seeking to avoid arrest. Whatever the leaders' motivation may be when this happens, the impression may spread that they are in fact seeking to avoid prison or other suffering. The lack of daring leadership by example is likely to have a disastrous effect on the willingness of others in lesser positions in the movement to do anything which might lead to danger or risks that the leaders are not taking. When such leaders are caught, sometimes the opponent may feel able to impose larger penalties on them under conditions which bring the leaders and movement less sympathy and support than if the punishments were imposed after open defiance. Leaders in hiding may even under some conditions become a liability to the movement. In contrast, imprisoned nonviolent leaders who have challenged the regime openly are more likely to be seen as heroes and martyrs, disturbing the complacent and inspiring the resisters.

When there are serious attempts to maintain secrecy in a nonviolent resistance movement, an atmosphere of fear spreads—fear that plans will be discovered, fear that hidden leaders will be captured, fear that the secret organization will be broken, fear that key members and masses of supporters will be imprisoned. As this happens among actual and potential supporters, the spirit of resistance is dampened. Instead of open nonviolent action demonstrating that repression is powerless, fear that secrets and plans will be revealed and that personnel will be captured permeates the movement; this leads to a kind of degeneration, demoralization and weakening which inevitably tends to undermine the movement.

Gandhi charged that resort to secrecy during the Indian 1932-33 struggle had been a prime cause for that movement's collapse. He said: ". . . the secrecy that has attended the movement is fatal to its success . . ." "There can be no doubt that fear has seized the common mass. The ordinances have cowed them down and I am inclined to think that the secret methods are largely responsible for this demoralisation."[107]

Certain theorists and practitioners of nonviolent struggle thus blame fear and other factors associated with secrecy for producing a series of undesirable influences which weaken the movement. It is significant that

Nehru—who, it is emphasized, did not share Gandhi's philosophical or religious beliefs nor his ethical commitment to nonviolence—had a similar view of the effects of secrecy during the campaigns of 1930-31 and 1932-33:

> Our experience of 1930 and 1932 showed that it was easily possible for us to organise a secret network of information all over India. Without much effort, and in spite of some opposition, good results were produced. But many of us had the feeling that secrecy did not fit in with the spirit of civil disobedience, and produced a damping effect on the mass consciousness. As a small part of a big open mass-movement it was useful, but there was always the danger, especially when the movement was declining, of a few more or less ineffective secret activities taking the place of the mass movement.[108]

Secrecy is most likely to be used by a movement to maintain itself when it feels too weak to operate openly. However, the secrecy may in fact lead to fewer participants rather than more,[109] not only because of the above factors, but also because, in many situations at least, the movement which is "security conscious" will have to reduce the number of people who plan and carry out policy. Under some conditions, numbers may also be reduced by the alienation of persons who were becoming sympathetic to the movement when it operated openly, but who distrust a secret political organization; this is especially likely to be the case where the nonviolent action is being applied in a society with a liberal democratic form of government.

The use of police spies, agents and informers is likely to seem more justified against a movement organized and operating on the basis of secrecy than against one which is not. Openness will not necessarily eliminate such agents. However, whether people see the use of police spies as justified or not justified, and whether or not sympathy is given to the police or to the nonviolent actionists, may influence the outcome of the conflict. It has also been suggested that secrecy concerning plans for nonviolent action may increase the chances of more brutal reaction from the opponent's forces than might have been the case had they known what to expect and had time to consider their counteraction carefully.

Secrecy may also threaten the very capacity of the movement to remain nonviolent—and this is crucial to the success of such a movement. This threat is most clearly illustrated by the problem of how to deal with an informer or police agent in possession of information which—it is believed—the opponent must not learn if the movement is to succeed. Various nonviolent types of persuasion and pressure might be used, plans could be changed, and the agent ostracized in the future once his identity is known (see Chapter Eight), but there is no nonviolent means of guaranteeing that the agent will not pass the information to the police or others. Past revolutionary and resistance movements using both secrecy and violence have not hesitated to murder the agent (or suspected agent, for it has sometimes proved later that the suspicions were unfounded). But resort to violence in a nonviolent action movement would reverse the operation of the mechanisms of change upon which that movement depends. The attempt to apply violence only on a very selective and restricted basis is likely to alter the conflict situation radically. It is likely to contribute to a major switch from the nonviolent technique to a violent one. In turn, that switch would enhance the opponent's relative power position, since he is better equipped to wage violent struggle.

In summary, a nonviolent movement which attempts to maintain a policy of secrecy concerning its planning, actions and organization faces problems and obstacles which are likely to prove insurmountable and which will, at best, severely threaten its requirements for casting off fear and the maintenance of nonviolent discipline. It is for such reasons that in their handbook for American civil rights demonstrators Oppenheimer and Lakey wrote:

> It is possible to confuse and delay the obtaining of "secret" information by your opponents in various ways. However, if your opponents are determined, this is pointless. It results in *inefficiency* because you have to cover up much that you do from your own members, *authoritarianism* because you cannot tell your members what is going on, and *mistrust*. In any case, your opponents, if they are determined, will plant "informers" and/or modern electronic devices in such a way that your activities will be an open book. You may as well open the book and be fully honest about your plans to begin with. You should try to plan tactics . . . which do not depend on secrecy for their value.[110]

Openness concerning intentions, plans, organizations and the like will also, it is argued, produce certain positive results which will help to strengthen the nonviolent group. This certainly does not imply that the movement will not face difficult problems, but openness contributes to the growth of *genuine* strength in the movement, as distinct from showy passing feats. In nonviolent action it is the buildup of genuine strength which is required; unreal appearances of strength are never lasting, and the movement may in fact be weakened if they are sought at the expense of undermining prerequisites of nonviolent power.

There are several specific ways, it has been argued, in which openness assists the nonviolent movement. Gregg, for example, feels that a policy of openness may promote wider knowledge of the existence, aims and activities of the resistance movement, and make the opponent's attempts at censorship and suppression of news more difficult.[111] It is true that open opposition is likely to become more difficult as the society becomes less democratic. But on the other hand, it also appears that the more monolithic a society, the greater the likely impact of any dissent. News of such opposition is likely to spread widely even when it is treated with silence in the official news media.

The contrast between the contending groups when one side relies upon nonviolent action is sharpened when that group also maintains a policy of truthful statements and openness concerning its intentions and plans. The contrast between the behavior of the conflicting groups is important in influencing the sympathies of third parties. Such sympathies are of course not decisive, but at times they may be important, especially when they take the form of concrete action against the opponent or in support of the nonviolent actionists. Sympathy and support may come as well from members of the broader grievance group who have not yet joined the struggle, and even from within the opponent's group itself. Therefore behavior which contributes to changes of perception and attitudes is very important. Here the visible contrast between the two groups plays a key role.

One side resorts to violence, brutality and repression; the other persists with courage in its action, accepts the suffering as the price of change, pledges itself anew to only nonviolent means, and refuses to retaliate. One group resorts to spies, deception, tricks and secrecy, while the other announces its intentions, plans, personnel and objectives publicly. One group demonstrates fear and uncertainty as to the present and future, while the other remains calm, determined, confident and fearless. In the process, the nonviolent group actively affects the power relationships between the groups. As the movement continues and the nonviolent actionists maintain their qualities and behavior, the perception that this movement differs qualitatively from the opponent group and from conventional political groups will gradually spread. This will, in turn, tend strongly to increase support for the nonviolent group from all sources and to weaken that for the opponent. The distinguishing qualities between the nonviolent group and the opponent will not appear so sharp if deception is used by both sides. Suspicions concerning the movement's real intentions, objectives and plans will spread, and sympathy for the actionists from third parties will be less likely.

Because nonviolent action is based upon that view of power which claims that all governments, hierarchical systems, oppression and injustice are ultimately dependent upon the submission, cooperation and assistance of the multitude of the citizens, subordinates and victims, it follows that the key to change by this technique lies in psychological and attitudinal changes among the subordinates. Feelings of apathy, impotence, fear and submissiveness will need to be shattered and replaced by their opposites. Gandhi implied that openness in defiance was necessary to break the habit of submissiveness and that a great deal of the effect of nonviolent action lay in the indifference of its users to measures for self-protection and in their willingness to take severe risks.[112] In the struggle to attain freedom, it was necessary to behave like free men: "A free man would not engage in a secret movement."[113] Openness, Gandhi argued, contributed to the morale of the rank and file of the movement, and enhanced their dignity and respect in their own eyes and in those of the opponent and third parties. A demonstration of confidence and daring is also often needed to inspire in others confidence and willingness to take risks. Gandhi insisted on this on several occasions:

No secret organization, however big, could do any good. . . . We have to organize for action a vast people that have been crushed under the heel of unspeakable tyranny for centuries. They cannot be organized by any other than open truthful means.[114]

No underhand or underground movement can ever become a mass movement or stir millions to mass action.[115]

Only open challenge and open activity is for all to follow. Real *Swaraj* [self-rule] *must* be felt by all—man, woman and child. To labour for that consummation is true revolution. . . . The millions of India would not have been awakened but for the open, unarmed struggle. Every deviation from the straight path has meant a temporary arrest of the evolutionary revolution.[116]

Once again Nehru's experience in open action showed him the psycologically liberating effects of struggle without secrecy, and also how this affected the British agents:

> Above all, we had a sense of freedom and a pride in that freedom. The old feeling of oppression and frustration was completely gone. There was no more whispering, no round-about legal phraseology to avoid getting into trouble with the authorities. We said what we felt and shouted it out from the house-tops. What did we care for the consequences? Prison? We looked forward to it; that would help our cause still further. The innumerable spies and secret-service men who used to surround us and follow us about became rather pitiable individuals as there was nothing secret for them to discover. All our cards were always on the table. [117]

Honesty, openness and lack of secrecy may also have certain effects on the opponent group, at least under certain conditions. These will be especially important where the nonviolent group aims at changes in attitudes in the opponent, most clearly where conversion is attempted. This has been emphasized by Ebert:

> So long as the oppressor fears the resistance fighters, i.e., so long as he is not convinced of their nonviolent attitude, he will be inclined to strengthen his own position. Only an open resistance organization can convince the oppressor that its professed belief and the demands which arise from it correspond to the true aims of the campaign. [118]

This does not mean that the opponent will immediately interpret the nonviolent group's motives, aims, intentions and plans correctly; only that this is more likely under conditions of openness than under conditions of attempted secrecy. Direct contact with the opponent group may be repeatedly sought as a means of avoiding or correcting distortions in perception which could seriously affect the course of the conflict. Advance notice to authorities of demonstrations, for example, may not only help to reduce brutalities by surprised police uncertain of what may happen, but may be interpreted as "clean fighting" and chivalry. These perceptions may contribute to increased respect for the nonviolent actionists among members of the opponent group. [119]

Usually there will be a time lag in changes in the opponent's perception of the nonviolent group, but constant repetition of behavior inconsistent with the opponent's view of members of that group may eventually lead to a correction of his perception. As Irving Janis and Daniel

Katz point out, openness may affect the opponent's view of the action-ists, e.g., his view of their moral status:

> Revealing material that is ordinarily kept secret may influence the ri-vals' attitude concerning the *moral status* of the acting group (e.g., they may become suspicious that something more important is being kept secret, or they may become much more respectful of the sincerity of the group). [120]

Openness may cause a distortion in perception of their strength in either direction:

> Revealing tactical plans that will handicap the acting group may influ-ence the rivals' attitudes concerning the *strength* of the acting group (e.g., admission of one's plans may be perceived as signs of weakness and ineptness in conducting the struggle or as signs of an exception-ally powerful movement that is capable of being successful without re-sorting to secrecy). [121]

Similarly, Janis and Katz write, telling the opponent in advance of the intended plans for nonviolent action "may have the effect of increasing or decreasing the magnitude of frustration and the intensity of the aggressive impulses aroused when the deprivations subsequently materialized." [122] This refers to the opponent's *initial* response to the action. Specialists in this technique have not claimed that openness always reduces hostility in the initial stages of a conflict, but that it tends to do so over a period of time.

There may also be even more important long-term consequences for the society as a whole of an atmosphere of secrecy, distrust and fear, or conversely of open expression of views and intentions, but these have as yet received little attention.

BASIC ELEMENTS IN NONVIOLENT STRATEGY

The strategy and tactics of war have been carefully developed and studied, and major attempts have been made to develop underlying theory. Maxims, rules and systems for conducting war have been formulated in response to "urgent want." [123] In the field of nonviolent action there has been to date no comparable development. Gandhi made the most im-portant conscious efforts to develop strategy and tactics in this technique of struggle. He was, however, neither an analyst nor a theorist; hence, despite his contribution in practice and his passing observations, the analysis and formulation of strategy and tactics have been left to others. Only comparatively recently has attention been turned to the examination of the problems and possibilities of strategy and tactics in nonviolent struggle against would-be internal dictators or invaders. [124] Attention is needed both to the broad field of strategy and tactics and to the specific problems which are likely to arise in facing particular opponents and in achieving particular objectives.

Strategy and tactics are of course present in various forms and degrees in many aspects of social life. They are, however, especially important in military action and nonviolent action, which are both techniques by which social and political conflicts are conducted when they have developed to the point of open struggle and a pitting of strength. There appear to be some points at which insights from military strategy may be carried over into nonviolent strategy; and there are also points at which military insights must *not* be carried over, because the nature and dynamics of the two techniques of struggle differ radically. This section is therefore not purely descriptive or analytical of existing observations on strategy in nonviolent action; it also involves the incorporation of principles of military strategy where these seem valid for the nonviolent technique, and where the military sources are clearer and more explicit than observations from nonviolent actionists.

Here are some brief definitions of basic strategic terms: grand strategy is the broadest conception which serves to coordinate and direct all the resources of the struggle group toward the attainment of the objectives of the conflict. Strategy, a more narrow term, is the broad plan of action for the overall struggle, including the development of an advantageous situation, the decision of when to fight, and the broad plan for utilizing various specific actions in the general conflict. Tactics refers to plans for more limited conflicts within the selected strategic plan. Fuller definitions of these terms are provided in the author's *An Abecedary of Nonviolent Action and Civilian Defense.*

A. The importance of strategy and tactics

Strategy is just as important in nonviolent action as it is in military action. While military strategic concepts and principles cannot automatically be carried over into the field of nonviolent action, the basic importance of strategy and tactics is in no way diminished. Attention is therefore needed to the general principles of strategy and tactics appropriate to this technique (both those peculiar to it and those which may be carried over from military strategy and other types of conflict). These aspects need to be considered, of course, within the context of the unique dynamics and mechanisms of nonviolent struggle.

People from a military background may find it strange to discover certain exponents of nonviolent means stressing the importance of strategy and tactics. And people from a background in religious or philosophical nonviolence may also be surprised to find strategy and tactics stressed instead of moral principles and conscience. Therefore, some brief discussion is needed of the function of strategy and tactics in nonviolent action.

In order to influence the outcome of a struggle, it is important to choose the course of action wisely and carry it out carefully and intelligently. It is quite inadequate simply to say that one will be moral and do what is right, for there may be several courses of action which are all morally "right"; what is "right" may involve maintaining or creating maximum opposition to "evil," and if so the problem is how to do this; in order to meet one's moral responsibility and maximize the effects of one's action, those actions must be carefully chosen and carried out at the right time. Specialists in the study and conduct of war have long since learned that the best results were not achieved simply by an uncontrolled outburst of violence and sacrifice. As Liddell Hart has said: ". . . the conduct of war must be controlled by reason if its object is to be fulfilled. . . . The better your strategy, the easier you will gain the upper hand, and the less it will cost you." [125] As in war, strategy and tactics are used in nonviolent action so that the courage, sacrifice, numbers, and so on of the nonviolent actionists may make the greatest possible impact.

The course of the struggle may take any of a wide variety of forms. depending on the strategies, tactics and methods chosen to meet the particular needs of the situation. The specific acts of protest, noncooperation and intervention in the course of a nonviolent campaign will be most effective if they fit together as parts of a comprehensive whole, so that each specific action contributes in a maximum way to the development and successful conclusion of the struggle. The optimal combination of specific actions is therefore best achieved where leaders with an adequate grasp of the situation and the technique are able to chart the course of the campaigns. "Only the general who conducts a campaign can know the objective of each particular move," wrote Gandhi. [126] Gandhi chose the issues, places, times and methods of action with extreme care, so that his movement was placed in the strongest position possible *vis-à-vis* the British, and so that the actions themselves conveyed the greatest understanding to his fellow Indians and aroused the maximum sympathy and support from everyone. Just as strategy is important in labor strikes,[127] so it is important in more highly developed types of nonviolent struggle—even more so when it is directed against extreme dictatorships.

There is ample historical evidence of the importance of strategy and tactics.[128] Sometimes this evidence is of a negative type, showing effects of the absence of strategy or of failure to make important decisions on strategic and tactical questions. Sometimes difficult problems which arose in the course of given conflicts could have been avoided or more satisfactorily resolved had there been greater understanding of the role and principles of nonviolent strategy. On other occasions, nonviolent campaigns have been continued after the point when achievement of almost all the objectives and demands was possible—far more than is usually the case in military conflicts; subsequent events then led to the defeat of the movement. Or in other cases the nonviolent movement *regarded* itself as defeated even though by normal standards it was victorious; as a result, that nonviolent action was eventually replaced by military action which was *believed* to be more effective. The American colonists' struggles against the British government can without difficulty be interpreted in this way. Considerable light would be shed on the problems and general principles of nonviolent strategy if careful strategic and tactical analyses were undertaken of a series of nonviolent struggles. It is also important to have acceptance by the grievance group of the strategy for the struggle; in the case of Finland in 1901, disagreement on *how* to deal with the opponent seems to have severely accentuated existing internal conflicts.[129]

B. Some key elements in nonviolent strategy and tactics

Despite the relative absence of strategic analyses of past nonviolent struggles and the lack of systematic studies of basic principles of nonviolent strategy, it is possible to list certain fairly clear general principles which have taken concrete form in particular struggles. Clausewitz wrote that in the case of war it was easier to make a theory of tactics than of strategy.[130] Both theories are very difficult in nonviolent action, and the list of principles offered here is necessarily incomplete and provisional.

1. The indirect approach to the opponent's power   The technique of nonviolent action can be regarded as an extreme development of "the indirect approach" to military strategy as formulated by Liddell Hart, and discussed earlier in this chapter.

Liddell Hart argued that direct strategy consolidates the opponent's strength, while an indirect approach is militarily more sound; generally effective results have followed when the plan of action has had "such indirectness as to ensure the opponent's unreadiness to meet it." Therefore, instead of a direct attack on the opponent's positions of strength, Liddell Hart emphasized the importance of psychological factors; the purpose of strategy then becomes "to diminish the possibility of resistance . . ." "Dislocation" of the enemy is crucial, he insisted, in achieving the conditions for victory, and the dislocation must be followed by "exploitation" of the opportunity created by the position of insecurity. It thus becomes important "to nullify opposition by paralysing the power to oppose" and to make "the enemy do something wrong." [131] These general principles are all applicable to the use of nonviolent action against an opponent using military means, so that the opponent's means of action are always confronted indirectly and his power of repression made to rebound against him in a kind of political *jiu-jitsu*. Finally, the very sources of his power are reduced or removed without having been confronted directly by the same means of action.

2. Psychological elements   Some of the psychological elements in military war have equivalents in "war without violence." But the carryover is not automatic. For example, surprise has been regarded as an essential element in certain types of military strategy. In nonviolent action, however, such objectives as throwing the enemy off guard, benefiting from his incapacity to meet the attack, and so on, which surprise has been intended to produce, are likely to a significant degree to be achieved simply by insistence on using a technique different from that of the opponent in the struggle. At times, however, the element of surprise in nonviolent action may operate to the detriment of the nonviolent actionists, by increasing the possibility of jumpiness among troops which may in turn mean more severe repression and less chance of disaffection among them.

Morale among the actionists will be important in nonviolent conflict just as it is in military conflict. It will be crucial for the population as a whole to understand well that the opponent's military might does not give him either control or victory. Confidence in nonviolent action would be fundamental, along with the qualities of "a warlike people" as described by Clausewitz: "bravery, aptitude, powers of endurance and enthusiaasm." [132]

3. Geographical and physical elements   Neither possession of nor gaining of control over particular places is regarded even in military war as important for its own sake but as "intermediate links," as "means of gaining greater superiority" so as finally to achieve victory.[133] While not to be *totally* ignored in nonviolent action, these elements assume a considerably lesser role, because the technique of struggle is dependent primarily upon the will and actions of human beings rather than on possession of geographical positions. It is possible, for example, for a territory to be physically occupied by troops without the regime which commands them having effective control over the population of the territory. Particular places, buildings and so on may on occasion become important in nonviolent action, especially where they have high symbolic value; in such cases, the methods of nonviolent obstruction, nonviolent raids and nonviolent invasion are likely to be applied. Even then, however, the physical possession of particular points is of secondary importance to the fulfillment of the conditions which make possible the operation of the mechanisms of change in nonviolent action. There are other geographical and physical elements; on occasion the terrain, time of day and weather may be important, and there may be "camps" for volunteers and hospitals to care for the wounded.

A careful nonviolent strategist is likely to be attentive to the choice of the place at which given acts of opposition are to be undertaken. Gandhi usually paid considerable attention to this point, as was illustrated by his plans for civil disobedience of the Salt Laws in 1930. As the place where he would make salt and spark the national struggle, Gandhi chose the little-known Dandi beach on the Gulf of Cambay, not significant in itself, but a point which allowed Gandhi and his followers to walk for twenty-six days—the now-famous Salt March—during which time he could arouse public interest and focus attention on his plans for civil disobedience.[138] Also during his investigation of the plight of the peasants in Champaran, Bihar, in 1917, when Gandhi expected arrest he went to Bettiah, preferring to be arrested among the most poverty-stricken peasants of the district.[135]

4. Timing   The timing of the implementation of tactics can be extremely important in nonviolent action. This timing may be of several types. For example, it is necessary to be able to judge when people are ready to take direct action, and also when a call for action would meet only a weak response or be ignored.[136] Timing needs to be considered in light of the whole situation; Nehru paid tribute to Gandhi's ability to do this when he wrote: ". . . he knows his India well and reacts to her lightest tremors, and gauges a situation accurately and almost instinctively, and has a knack of acting at the psychological moment."[137]

It has been argued that the Irish "No-Rent Manifesto" would have been more successful if issued in February 1881—as the extreme wing of the Land League wanted—instead of six months later, after the leaders had been jailed and reforms were dampening the will to resist. [138]

Sometimes the launching of nonviolent action may be timed to coincide with some significant day or occasion. The choice of April 6, 1930, as the start of the Indian civil disobedience campaign, for example, coincided with the beginning of National Week, which was observed in homage to the victims of the Amritsar Massacre of 1919. [139] Timing may also be important in another sense. The hour and minute at which given nonviolent actionists are to be at certain places and the synchronization of actions of various groups may be crucial; this has been the case in certain student actions in the U.S. South. [140]

In still a different sense, timing may refer to the choice of the stage at which to resist an opponent who is attempting to impose or extend his control over a society. On occasion, the opponent's demands and action may require prompt reaction and resistance if his efforts to establish or extend control are to be thwarted. In the case of an invasion, for example, this may be particularly true at three points. The first occurs after the formal seizure of power and the occupation of the country. The second is at the stage when the invader seeks the collaboration and assistance of important groups, such as police, civil service and trade unions. The last is at the point where he attempts to destroy the independent social institutions, bring all organizations and institutions under his control, and atomize the population. When each of these attacks occurs, it will be important that resistance be undertaken without delay and that people do not "wait and see" or just drift. Only prompt action can be effective. In other conflict situations, the timing of action at various stages of the struggle may also be important.

5. Numbers and strength   While numbers may be extremely important both in nonviolent action and in military action, [141] they are certainly not the only important factor and do not guarantee victory. It is fallacious to attempt "to analyze and theorize about strategy in terms of mathematics" and to assume that victory is determined simply by "a superior concentration of force at a selected place." [142] In nonviolent action—especially when nonviolent coercion is being attempted, as in a general strike or a mutiny—numbers may at times be decisive. But numbers must not be considered alone; large numbers may even be a disadvantage, either for tactical reasons or because discipline and reliability have been sacrificed to obtain them, as discussed earlier in this chapter. Particular tactics and methods may in the given circumstances have their own requirements concerning the numbers of actionists. Large numbers unable to maintain nonviolent discipline and to continue action in face of repression may weaken the movement, but with the necessary standards and discipline they may become "irresistible." [143]

6. The issue and concentration of strength   If there are to be wise strategy and tactics for conducting nonviolent action most effectively, then a careful selection of the points on which to fight is crucial, as discussed above. In conventional military campaigns, such points may in large degree be determined by consideration of topography, supplies and the like. But in nonviolent campaigns they are almost exclusively determined by political, psychological, social and economic factors.

There is no substitute for genuine strength in nonviolent action. If this is lacking, then the attempt to fight for an objective which is too vast to be achieved may be unwise. To be effective, nonviolent action needs to be concentrated at crucial points which are selected after consideration of one's own strength, the objectives and position of the opponent (including his weaknesses), and the importance of the issue itself. Napoleon's maxim that it is impossible to be too strong at the decisive point applies here as well. [144] In selecting that point consideration must also be given to the probable consequences if that particular battle is either lost or won. This is very closely related to the first of the axioms of military strategy and tactics outlined by Liddell Hart:

> *Adjust your end to your means.* In determining your object, clear sight and cool calculation should prevail. It is folly "to bite off more than you can chew," and the beginning of military wisdom is a sense of what is possible. So learn to face facts while still preserving faith: there will be ample need for faith—the faith that can achieve the apparently impossible—when action begins. Confidence is like the current in a battery: avoid exhausting it in vain effort—and remember that your own continued confidence will be of no avail if the cells of your battery, the men upon whom you depend, have been run down. [145]

There may be particular circumstances, such as the attempt to atomize the population, which may require that action be taken despite weaknesses; but even then consideration of one's real strength is required, and in formulating strategy and tactics an attempt should be made to see if the existing strength can be used to best advantage and the weaknesses either bypassed or urgently corrected.

"The principles of war, not merely one principle, can be condensed into a single word—'concentration.' But for truth this needs to be amplified as the 'concentration of strength against weakness.'" [146] This principle of military action applies also in nonviolent action and was stressed by Gandhi. Concentration in nonviolent struggles will primarily be on certain political, social or economic points which symbolize wider general conditions. This is related to another of Liddell Hart's axioms: "*Keep your object always in mind,* while adapting your plan to circumstances. Realize that there are more ways than one of gaining an object, but take heed that every objective should bear on the object." [147] Nonviolent actionists will seek to attack the specific aspect which symbolizes the "evil" they are fighting, which is least defensible by the opponent and which is capable of arousing the greatest strength among the nonviolent actionists and the wider population. Success on such a limited point will increase their self-confidence and ability to move forward effectively toward the fuller realization of their objectives. Having chosen the point for concentrated attack, they must not allow themselves to become sidetracked to a lesser course of action or a dead-end issue. [148]

7. The initiative   In nonviolent action it is highly important—even in defensive phases of the struggle—for the actionists to obtain and retain the initiative. "An able general always gives battle in his own time on the ground of his choice. He always retains the initiative in these respects and never allows it to pass into the hands of the enemy," wrote Gandhi. [149] One of the important distinctions indicated by Nehru between the 1930 campaign—which could be described at least as a "draw"—and the 1932 campaign, which was a clear defeat for the Indians, was that in 1930 the "initiative definitely remained with the Congress and the people" whereas "the initiative early in 1932 was definitively with the Government, and Congress was always on the defensive." [150] The nonviolent leadership group needs to be able to control the situation and to demonstrate that it has that control. [151] Nirmal Kumar Bose writes that a leader of a nonviolent campaign ". . . should not allow the adversary to dictate or force any step upon him . . . [nor] allow himself to be buffeted about by every temporary event." [152] Wherever possible, then, the nonviolent group, not the opponent, will choose the time, issue and course of action and seek to maintain the initiative despite the opponent's repression. In cases where the conflict has been precipitated by the opponent, as in a *coup d'etat* or invasion or when new repressive measures are imposed, the nonviolent actionists will endeavor to restore the initiative to themselves as quickly as possible.

C. The choice of weapons

In order to achieve optimal results, the choice of nonviolent weapons to initiate and conduct the campaign will need to be made carefully and wisely. It will be necessary to determine which of the specific methods of nonviolent action described in Part Two (and possibly other methods) are most appropriate to this particular conflict. This decision will need to be taken in the light of a variety of factors. These include the issues at stake, the nature of the contending groups, the type of culture and society of each, and the social and political context of the conflict. Other factors are the mechanisms of change intended by the nonviolent group (as to convert or to coerce), the experience of the nonviolent group, and their ability in applying nonviolent action. Finally, there are also the type of repression and other countermeasures expected, the ability of the nonviolent group to withstand them, and the intensities of commitment to the struggle within the nonviolent group. There are of course others.

The number of methods used in any single conflict will vary from only one to dozens. The choice of the specific methods to be used in a given campaign will be based on several factors. One of these is a judgment as to whether or not the basic characteristics of the method contain qualities desired for that particular conflict. For example, generally speaking, the methods of the class of nonviolent protest and persuasion (Chapter Three) are largely symbolic in their effect and produce an awareness of the existence of dissent. Their impact is proportionately greater under authoritarian regimes where opposition and nonconformity are discouraged and rare. Depending on the numbers involved, the methods of noncooperation (Chapters Four, Five, Six and Seven) are likely to cause difficulties in maintaining the normal operation and efficiency of the system. In extreme situations, these methods may threaten its existence. The methods of nonviolent intervention (Chapter Eight) possess qualities of both groups, but in addition usually constitute a more direct challenge to the regime. This class of methods makes possible a greater impact with smaller numbers, providing that fearlessness and discipline are maintained.

Moving from the class of nonviolent protest and persuasion to that of noncooperation and thence to nonviolent intervention generally involves a progressive increase in the degree of sacrifice required of the nonviolent actionists, in the risk of disturbing the public peace and order, and in effectiveness. The methods of noncooperation can be interpreted as withdrawal of cooperation from an evil system, and hence as having connotations of a defensive moral action. The use of this class of methods, as compared to nonviolent intervention, may also contribute to producing a *relatively* less explosive and dangerous social situation, in that they simply withdraw existing cooperation or withhold new forms of cooperation with the opponent.[153] The penalties and sufferings imposed directly or indirectly upon noncooperators, although severe at times, may be relatively less than those involved in nonviolent intervention. Also, the risk of such repression in any particular case may be less. It may also be easier to get people to refrain from doing something which has been ordered, i.e., to noncooperate, than to get them to do something daring which is prohibited.

For effective noncooperation, larger numbers of participants are usually required than for either symbolic protest or intervention, and the action usually continues over longer periods of time. Often a long duration is necessary for the noncooperation to achieve its impact. In 1930 Gandhi said that whereas the cooperation of three hundred million people would be necessary for a foreign-cloth boycott campaign to be successful, for the civil disobedience campaign an army of ten thousand defiant men and women would suffice.[154] Many of the methods of nonviolent intervention can only be practiced for limited periods of time. A continuous effect therefore is achieved only by constant repetition of the action. These methods therefore require more skilled, reliable and determined practitioners than methods of noncooperation. Because of this, the quicker methods of nonviolent intervention usually require considerable preparations in order to be successfully applied. Also, those methods are often best combined with other forms of nonviolent action. The movement using intervention methods, too, must be more highly disciplined and better led. "The quickest remedies are always fraught with the greatest danger and require the utmost skill in handling them."[155]

Another important factor in the selection of the specific methods to be used in the campaign is whether the actionists intend to produce change by the mechanism of conversion, accommodation, or nonviolent coercion. Within that context, the specific inducements for change by the opponent which the nonviolent group is attempting to produce may be important; these may include, for example, economic losses, weakening of political position, guilt feelings, new perceptions, and the like. Where conversion of the opponent is sought, such methods as the general strike, mutiny and parallel government are obviously not appropriate. But where nonviolent coercion is intended these may be precisely the methods needed, whereas forms which rely for their impact on psychological and emotional effects on the leaders of the opponent group may be a waste of time and effort. The problem is complicated, however, and frequently methods which apply differing pressures and use different mechanisms may be combined effectively within the same campaign. Fast rules are not possible.

In most cases more than one method will be used; then the order in which the methods are applied, the ways in which they are combined, and how they influence the application of other methods and contribute to the struggle as a whole become highly important. The methods to be used in a given situation must be considered not only for their specific and immediate impact on the conflict situation and the opponent. Also important is their contribution to the progressive development of the movement, to changes in attitudes and power relationships, to alterations in the support for each side, and to the later application and effects of more radical nonviolent methods.

Sometimes the combination of methods is relatively simple, especially in a local or limited type of action. Economic boycotts have been used, for example, in support of sit-ins against racial discrimination, and picketing is commonly used in support of strikes. When a general strike is used to support the mutiny of government troops, however, the situation begins to become more complicated, with larger numbers of methods likely to become involved quickly.

For large-scale planned campaigns against determined opponents the question of how to combine the use of several methods is not easy to answer; it must be considered in the context both of the overall strategy of the struggle and its more localized and restricted phases. In a long struggle phasing is highly important, and the choice and sequence of methods may be the most important single factor in that phasing. Waskow speaks, for example, of the " 'escalation' of disorder without violence." [156] The importance of this phased development of a nonviolent campaign has been stressed by specialists in Gandhi's type of nonviolent action, such as Bose [157] and Bondurant. As one of nine "fundamental rules" of *satyagraha* Bondurant lists:

> *Progressive advancement of the movement* through steps and stages determined to be appropriate within the given situation. Decision as to when to proceed to a further phase of the satyagraha must be carefully weighed in the light of the ever-changing circumstance, but a static condition must be avoided. [158]

It may, therefore, be determined that certain methods must precede others, in order that it may be possible later to use more radical forms.

Gandhi frequently used the response of the volunteers and public to some specific action as a means of testing whether or not some further, more radical, form of action were possible, in such terms as degree of commitment, willingness to act, ability to withstand the opponent's sanctions, degree of discipline, and ability to remain both fearless and nonviolent. In his testimony before the Hunter Committee in 1920, for example, Gandhi said:

> *Hartal* was designed to strike the imagination of the people and the government. . . I had no means of understanding the mind of India except by some such striking movement. *Hartal* was a proper indication to me how far I would be able to carry civil disobedience. [159]

He also used the consumer's boycott to test readiness for civil disobedience. Gandhi wrote in 1921: "It is my firm conviction that if we bring about a successful boycott of foreign cloth, we shall have produced an atmosphere that would enable us to inaugurate civil disobedience on a scale that no Government can resist." [160]

In May 1920 Gandhi had reported in *Young India* that the organizers of the coming noncooperation movement had decided that it should take place in four stages: 1) relinquishment of honorary posts and titles, 2) progressive voluntary withdrawal from government employment, 3) withdrawal of members of the police and the military from government service ("a distant goal"), and 4) suspension of payment of taxes ("still more remote"). [161] The first stage involved the minimum danger and sacrifice, [162] while the last two involved the greatest risks. [163]

The 1930-31 movement was planned with a different strategy. It began with methods of nonviolent protest, such as the Salt March itself and mass meetings, and mild forms of political noncooperation, such as limited withdrawals from the provincial legislatures—all involving small numbers of people. The mass movement itself began directly with civil disobedience of a law regarded as immoral, and then developed to include both milder forms of noncooperation and more radical forms of noncooperation and nonviolent intervention. [164]

D. Selecting the strategy and tactics

The general strategy, types of tactics, and choice of methods planned by the leaders in advance will usually determine the general direction and conduct of the campaign throughout its course. Their selection is therefore highly important. As in war, a large number of factors must be considered in the selection of strategy and tactics. However, the quite different dynamics and mechanisms of nonviolent struggle appear to make the interrelationships of these factors more intimate and complex than in military struggle.

Fundamental to this task is careful consideration of the opponent's primary and secondary objectives, and the various objectives of the nonviolent group. It will be highly important to evaluate accurately the opponent's and one's own strengths and weaknesses, and to take these into account in the formulation of strategy and tactics. Failure to do so may lead either to overly ambitious plans which fail because they are not based on a realistic assessment of possibilities, or to excessively timid plans which may fail precisely because they attempt too little. Evaluation of the strengths and nature of the opponent group may assist the nonviolent leadership in formulating a course of action most likely to produce or aggravate weaknesses and internal conflicts within it. Correct assessment of the weaknesses of the nonviolent group itself may be used in the selection of strategy and tactics which are intended to bypass them, and which may possibly also contribute to strengthening them. Estimates as to the length of the forthcoming struggle will be needed and will be important for outlining the course of action. But provision must also be made for an error of judgment in such estimates and for contingency tactics if the struggle turns out to be long instead of brief.

Careful consideration of other factors in the general situation will be necessary to determine whether conditions are suitable for the launching of nonviolent action, and, if so, what the general and specific conditions of the situation mean for the planning of the campaign. Sibley has emphasized that

> . . . the effective use of nonviolent resistance depends not only on adequate training and commitment, but also on the "objective" situation: external conditions must be ripe for effective campaigns, and if they are not, it is the part both of wisdom and of morality not to resort to nonviolent resistance. [165]

Gandhi insisted that in formulating and carrying out the strategy and tactics of the struggle the leaders need to be responsive to the demonstrated qualities of their movement and to the developing situation:

> In a satyagraha campaign the mode of fight and the choice of tactics, e.g. whether to advance or retreat, offer civil resistance or organize nonviolent strength through constructive work and purely selfless humanitarian service, are determined according to the exigencies of the situation. [166]

Strategy and tactics are of course interdependent. Precise tactics can only be formulated in the context of the overall strategy, and an intimate understanding of the whole situation and the specific methods of action which are open. Skillful selection and implementation of tactics will not make up for a bad overall strategy, and a good strategy remains impotent unless carried to fulfillment with sound tactics: ". . . only great tactical results can lead to great strategical ones . . ." [167]

Liddell Hart has suggested that the particular course of action should have more than one objective.

> *Take a line of operation which offers alternate objectives.* For you will thus put your opponent on the horns of a dilemma, which goes far to assure the chance of gaining one objective at least—whichever he guards least—and may enable you to gain one after the other.
>
> Alternative objectives allow you to keep the opportunity of gaining *an* objective; whereas a single objective, unless the enemy is helplessly inferior, means the certainty that you will not gain it—once the enemy is no longer uncertain as to your aim. There is no more common mistake than to confuse a single line of operation, which is usually wise, with a single objective, which is usually futile. [168]

To a large degree this frequently happens in nonviolent action anyhow without particular planning, since the nonviolent group aims at achieving both particular objectives and more general changes in attitudes and power relationships within each group and between the contending groups. These more general changes are likely to be taking place during the whole course of the conflict, and may be achieved to a considerable degree even in instances where the particular political goal is not won. However, attention is also needed to the possibility of applying Liddell Hart's strategic principle to concrete limited goals, so long as this does not violate the principle of concentration discussed previously.

The progressive development of the movement, partially characterized by the staged introduction of new methods of action (as discussed in the previous section), will also benefit from careful strategic planning. Such development will help to ensure that the alteration of methods and new courses of action will contribute to the maximum utilization of the actionists' forces, facilitate an improvement in their morale, and increase the chances of vistory. Without clear strategic insight, changes from one type of action to another may take place without good purpose or effect, and the discouraging results which may follow can lead first to increased uncertainty as to what to do, then to demoralization, and finally to disintegration of the nonviolent movement.

Strategic phasing of nonviolent campaigns is not new of course. However, greater understanding of the nature of the technique and of principles of strategy now make possible a fuller development and more effective utilization of such phasing than has been possible before. Three earlier examples of phasing are offered here. The provincial convention of Virginia, meeting in early August 1774, outlined a phased campaign of economic noncooperation to achieve its objectives. The convention set dates at which new phases of their campaign were to go into effect, subject to alterations agreed to by Virginia delegates in the Continental Congress. Starting at once, no tea was to be imported or used. If Boston were compelled to reimburse the East India Company for losses (as of tea in the Boston Tea Party), the boycott would be extended to all articles sold by the company until the money was returned. On November 1, an absolute boycott was to be imposed on all goods (except medicines) imported directly or indirectly from Britain, including all slaves from wherever they were brought. If colonial grievances were not corrected by August 10, 1775 (a year later), then an absolute program of nonexportation of all articles to Britain was to be imposed. The year interval before nonexportation took effect allowed for payment of debts to British merchants, and for Virginia tobacco growers to shift to crops which could be used at home.[169] This phased campaign drafted by Virginians foreshadowed the program adopted by the First Continental Congress.

A phased campaign of peasant action was issued in Russia by the Second Congress of the Peasants Union, meeting in Moscow in November 1905, during the revolution of that year. The Congress called for the use of methods of peaceful pressure (such as the peasants' collective refusal to buy or rent land from the landlords) to achieve the free transfer of land to the peasants. If these methods did not produce results, then the Union would call for a general agrarian strike to coincide with a general strike in the cities. If the tsarist government harassed the Union, it would call on the peasants to refuse to pay taxes or to serve in the armed forces.[170]

The Pan-Africanists in South Africa had planned their campaign of defiance of the Pass Laws in the spring of 1960 as simply the first stage of a three-front long-range struggle: 1) *political,* with the international aim of isolating South Africa (including United Nations condemnation and expulsion from the British Commonwealth) and the domestic aim of ending collaboration and submission by the African people upon which the government depended; 2) *labor,* the withdrawal of cheap African labor would bring an economic collapse, and therefore stay-at-home strikes were designed to induce industrialists to demand changes in government policies; and 3) *psychological,* the Africans "would discover the power they have even without weapons and they would never be the same again." Despite clear thought and certain planning for a phased campaign, however, the organization had not anticipated that the government would seize the initiative by declaring a state of emergency. [171]

While specific tactics for the later stages of the struggle cannot be formulated in advance, it is possible to explore a variety of general approaches for later consideration. Tactics for use in the early (and possibly intermediate) stages may, however, be successfully selected in advance if one has accurately anticipated the situation and form of attack.

A variety of approaches may be used in tactics, involving different fronts, groups, time periods, methods and other factors. For example, the brunt of the responsibility for carrying out the action may, after certain periods of time or certain political events, be shifted from one group to another, or different roles may be assigned to particular groups. The most dangerous tasks (involving, for example, the use of the most daring methods, such as those of nonviolent intervention) could be assigned to groups with especially high discipline, experience, skill, or training, while other important but less dangerous tasks could be undertaken by groups more typical of the general population. At times particular responsibilities would fall upon certain occupational or geographical groups because of the policies and actions of the opponent. Where the initiative lay with the nonviolent actionists, they could deliberately choose to undertake simultaneous actions on more than one front if their strength and the general situation were such as to make this wise. At times tactics could involve geographical fronts as well as political fronts, as in the use of nonviolent raids or obstruction; far more often, however, there would be no semblance of a geographical front and the resistance would be more diffuse and general, as in the case of a stay-at-home. The selection of tactics will be influenced significantly by the immediate and long-term political aims of the nonviolent actionists, and by the mechanisms through which change is sought. Various types of tactics will produce different problems for the usurper and have different effects on the nonviolent population.

Variation in tactics may be important in order to add variety and interest (and often newsworthiness) to the campaign. Such changes may serve other purposes, such as to involve new sections of the population, to augment psychological, political and economic pressures on the opponent, expand or contract the front and to test the discipline, morale and capacity of the nonviolent actionists. Tactical changes may be designed to achieve a variety of effects on the opponent, leadership, bystanders, or police and troops charged with repression. For example, Ebert points to the deliberate use in some cases of small groups of demonstrators (instead of large ones) and time gaps between demonstrations (instead of continuous ones), as means of reducing brutality in the repression by making it easier for the opponent's police and troops to see the actionists as individual human beings, and by allowing them time for reflection and reconsideration between particular demonstrations. [172]

The unrolling of the strategy and implementation of tactics in specific acts takes place in a context of a sensitivity and responsiveness to the developing conflict situation. Very careful and precise plans may have been prepared for commencing the attack. Following the beginning of the struggle, however, room must be allowed for flexibility in the further development, modification and application of the strategy and tactics. [173] Liddell Hart has emphasized the importance of flexibility in the formulation and implementation of the anticipated course of action:

> *Ensure that both plan and disposition are flexible—adaptable to circumstances.* Your plan should foresee and provide for a next step in case of success or failure, or partial success—which is the most common case in war. Your dispositions (or formation) should be such as to allow this exploitation or adaption in the shortest possible time. [174]

The capacity to respond to unforeseen (or unforeseeable) events must be acutely developed. Especially important is the response, morale and behavior of the nonviolent actionists and potential supporters. If they have proved too unprepared and weak to carry out the plans, the plans must be altered, either by taking "some dramatic step which will strike the imagination of the people, and restore confidence in the possibility of full resistance through nonviolence," or by calling a temporary retreat in order to prepare for a future stronger effort. [175] There is no substitute for, or shortcut to, strength in a movement of nonviolent action. If the necessary strength and ability to persist in face of penalties and suffering do not exist, that fact must be recognized and given an intelligent response. "A wise general does not wait till he is actually routed; he withdraws in time in an orderly manner from a position which he knows he would not be able to hold." [176] The leadership will, just as in a military conflict, need to recognize frankly the weaknesses in their volunteers and potential supporters and find ways of correcting these. [177]

The means for doing this will vary with the conditions of the given situation.

On the other hand, the struggle may reveal significant weaknesses in the opponent which may call for prompt alteration of the tactics and speeding up the tempo of the struggle. At times, too, the struggle may reveal the nonviolent actionists and the general population to be stronger than had been expected, and then it may be possible to make a more rapid advance on a sound basis than originally conceived.

THE ULTIMATUM

If negotiations with the opponent are not showing signs of producing satisfactory results, the strategy and early tactics must be settled, and various types of organizational preparations completed. In some types of nonviolent struggle—primarily Gandhian or neo-Gandhian—the next stage will be the issuance of an ultimatum to the opponent. In other traditions of nonviolent struggle there may be no ultimatum, because the idea is unknown, because the planners hope to take the opponent by surprise, because the conflict has already broken out spontaneously, or for some other reason. Where the ultimatum is used, however, it is very similar to ultimatums which in the old days used to be issued by governments before they declared war on their opponent: the demands are stated, and an offer is made to cancel plans for attack if the opponent grants those demands (or a major part of them) by a given day and hour. [178]

Like negotiations, the ultimatum is intended to influence both the opponent and the general public. Negotiations are aimed not only at influencing the opponent to grant the demands of the nonviolent group through greater appreciation of their justice and for other reasons, including that granting them may be the better part of political wisdom. Negotiations—especially long, sincere negotiations which have really sought a solution short of open struggle—may also help to put the adversary in the wrong in the eyes of all concerned and to bring sympathy to the nonviolent group for attempting diligently and patiently to find a peaceful settlement. Similarly, the ultimatum may be intended to encourage the opponent to agree to the demands, by telling him in clear terms the consequences of a failure to achieve a mutually agreed change in the matters at stake. At the same time, however, the ultimatum is also a means of showing everyone who may be interested that, while maintaining firmness and dignity, the nonviolent group is giving the opponent one last chance to settle the conflict peacefully. This may endow the nonviolent group with an aura of defensiveness—which may be psychologically advantageous in several ways—even while they are preparing for militant nonviolent action. An ultimatum may also be important in building up morale and willingness to act in the grievance group.

In its ultimatum the leaders of the nonviolent group list their grievances and demands without exaggeration. A time limit is set for the granting of these minimum demands. This ultimatum may be likened to a conditional declaration of war. The nonviolent group may in the ultimatum include assurances to the opponent intended to correct misunderstandings and remove fears he may have about the group and their objectives, and it may remind him that only nonviolent means are intended. Without compromising basic issues and principles, the ultimatum may be worded in such a way as to leave the opponent a way of saving face. The nonviolent group hopes that the opponent will grant the demands and that the threatened action will thus be avoided. If not, the time will have arrived for nonviolent action.

On occasion an ultimatum may take the form of a general public declaration—intended for the opponent and others—of what will happen if the demands are not met by a given date. This may be a part of a plan of escalation of resistance. This type of ultimatum was included in the plan for American colonial resistance, the Continental Association, adopted by the First Continental Congress. The nonimportation phase had already begun in late 1774, but the nonexportation phase was to be launched a year after the meeting of the Continental Congress—if victory had not by then been achieved:

> The earnest desire we have, not to injure our fellow-subjects in Great-Britain, Ireland, or the West-Indies, induces us to suspend a non-exportation until the tenth day of September, 1775; at which time, if the said acts and parts of acts of the British parliament herein after mentioned are not repealed, we will not, directly or indirectly, export any merchandise or commodity whatsoever to Great-Britain, Ireland, or the West-Indies, except rice to Europe. [179]

Ultimatums have also been issued in the course of unplanned nonviolent resistance, as during the French army mutiny in 1917 when defiant soldiers intended for the 162nd Regiment demonstrated on May 20 at the XXXIInd Corps replacement depot demanding more pay, more leave, and better food, and in the evening elected three delegates to present their ultimatum. [180]

The 1952 Defiance Campaign in South Africa was preceded by an ultimatum to the government from the African National Congress, which stated:

At the recent annual conference of the African National Congress held in Bloemfontein from 15th to 17th December, 1951, the whole policy of the Government was reviewed, and, after serious and careful consideration of the matter, conference unanimously resolved to call upon your Government, as we hereby do, to repeal the aforementioned Acts, by NOT LATER THAN THE 29TH DAY OF FEBRUARY 1952, failing which the African National Congress will hold protest demonstrations and meetings on the 6th day of April 1952, as a prelude to the implementation of the plan for the defiance of unjust laws. [181]

The classic ultimatum in the tradition of Gandhian nonviolent struggle remains Gandhi's letter to the British Viceroy, Lord Irwin, written on March 2, 1930. He began the long letter by addressing the representative of the King-Emperor simply as "Dear Friend." Gandhi then went straight to the point: "Before embarking on civil disobedience and taking the risk I have dreaded to take all these years, I would fain approach you and find a way out." No harm was intended to any Englishman, Gandhi continued, although he held British rule to be a curse. As no significant steps toward independence had been taken, there was now no option, he wrote, but to carry out the 1928 Indian National Congress decision to declare independence if the British had not acted in that direction by the end of 1929. Gandhi then stated why, as he saw it, the British had not acted: "It seems as clear as daylight that responsible British statesmen do not contemplate any alteration in British policy that might adversely affect Britain's commerce with India or require an impartial and close scrutiny of Britain's transactions with India." Unless something were done, Gandhi predicted, the already severe exploitation would continue and India would "be bled at an ever increasing speed."

This Gandhi could not tolerate: ". . . if India is to live as a nation, if the slow death by starvation of her people is to stop, some remedy must be found for immediate relief." He then rejected the proposed Round Table Conference as a remedy. "It is not a matter of carrying conviction by argument. The matter resolves itself into one of matching forces. Conviction or no conviction, Great Britain would defend her Indian commerce and interests by all the forces at her command. India must consequently evolve force enough to free herself from that embrace of death." Indians advocating political violence were gaining support, Gandhi pointed out, while British-organized violence was inflicted on India. The answer to both, he asserted, was nonviolent struggle.

Gandhi then turned to his plan of action: "It is my purpose to set in motion that force as well against the organized violent force of the British rule as the unorganized violent force of the growing party of violence. To sit still would be to give rein to both the forces . . ." The civil disobedience and noncooperation which were contemplated were intended to convert the British, he continued. The civil disobedience plan would include attacking a number of specific injustices which he had outlined in the letter. When these were removed, he continued, "the way to friendly negotiation will be open. If the British commerce with India is purified of greed, you will have no difficulty in recognizing our independence." Gandhi then invited the Viceroy "to pave the way for an immediate removal of those evils, and thus open the way for a real conference between equals."

Gandhi, however, did not expect the British Empire to give way so easily, and he turned to the plan of resistance: "But if you cannot see your way to deal with these evils and my letter makes no appeal to your heart, on the 11th day of this month, I shall proceed with such co-workers of the Ashram as I can take, to disregard the provisions of the Salt Laws." If the Viceroy were to arrest him first, Gandhi expressed the hope there would "be tens of thousands ready, in a disciplined manner, to take up the work after me, and, in the act of disobeying the Salt Act to lay themselves open to the penalties of a law that should never have disfigured the Statute Book." Gandhi offered to discuss the issues if the Viceroy found substance in the letter. "This letter is not in any way intended as a threat but as a simple and sacred duty peremptory on a civil resister." [182] He signed the letter, "I remain, your sincere friend, M.K. Gandhi," and sent a young British Quaker to deliver it to Lord Irwin.

The nonviolent actionists are not naïve enough to expect that such an ultimatum will often lead to capitulation by the opponent. There may be various reasons for this. He may not, for example, see nonviolent action as a credible threat of which he need take notice. Even more often, however, the opponent is likely to see such a communication as an unjustified challenge to his authority, an affront to his dignity, and a usurpation of status, highly improper behavior for people of a subordinate position. The opponent may therefore become angry, he may break off any negotiations in progress, he may totally ignore the communication, or he may say it should have been directed to some subordinate official. Or he may, as did Lord Irwin, have his secretary send a terse four-line acknowledgment of the letter.

In such a case, the time has come for action. The nonviolent actionists will then speak of courage, daring and sacrifice, and call on the people opposed to the opponent's policies to combat them in open struggle, as did Mr. Ahmed Kathrada at the beginning of the 1952 civil disobedience campaign in South Africa:

> The time has come for action. For too long have we been talking to the white man. For three hundred years they have oppressed us . . . And, friends, after three hundred years I say that the time has come when we will talk to the white man in the only language he understands: the language of struggle. [183]

NOTES

1. Napoleon, **The Officer's Manual** or **Napoleon's Maxims of War** (New York: James G. Gregory, 1861) Maxim XVI, pp. 58-59.
2. B. H. Liddell Hart, **Strategy: The Indirect Approach** (New York: Frederick A. Praeger, 1954. Br. ed.: London: Faber and Faber, 1954), p. 25.
3. See Lindberg, *"Konklusionen: Teorien om Ikke-vold,"* p. 209 in Lindberg, Jacobsen and Ehrlich, **Kamp Uden Vaaben**; Oppenheimer and Lakey, **A Manual for Direct Action,** pp. 116-117; and Frederic Solomon and Jacob R. Fishman, "The Psychosocial Meaning of Nonviolence in Student Civil Rights Activities," *Psychiatry*, May 1964, pp. 91-99.
4. Gandhi, **Non-violent Resistance**, pp. 116-117; Ind. ed.: **Satyagraha**, pp. 116-117. See also pp. 362-363; Sharp, **Gandhi Wields the Weapon of Moral Power,** pp. 83 and 87; and Nirmal Kumar Bose, **Studies in Gandhism** (Second Edition); Calcutta: Indian Associated Publishing Co., 1947, p. 171.
5. Gopinath Dhawan, **The Political Philosophy of Mahatma Gandhi,** Ahmedabad, India: Navajivan, 1962, (Third Revised Edition), p. 72.
6. *Ibid.*
7. *Ibid.,* p. 73.
8. *Ibid.,* pp. 72-73. See also Gandhi, **Non-violence in Peace and War,** vol. II, pp. 5-6.

9. Gregg, The Power of Nonviolence, p. 50.
10. Gandhi, Non-violent Resistance, p. 172; Ind. ed.: Satyagraha, p. 172.
11. Venturi, Roots of Revolution, p. 92.
12. *Ibid.,* p. 432.
13. Prawdin, The Unmentionable Nechaev, p. 174.
14. There were several 19th century cases of such psychological and attitude changes among the peasants, some of them deliberately cultivated. See for example, Venturi, Roots of Revolution, pp. 64, 214, 576.
15. Prawdin, The Unmentionable Nechaev, pp. 171-172.
16. Gandhi, Non-violence in Peace and War, vol. II, p. 38.
17. See *Ibid.,* vol. I, p. 12.
18. King, Stride Toward Freedom; U.S. ed., p. 119; Br. ed., p. 140.
19. See Sharp, Tyranny Could Not Quell Them.
20. See Sharp, "Gandhi's Defence Policy," in Mahadevan, Roberts and Sharp, eds., Civilian Defence: An Introduction, pp. 15-52.
21. Gandhi, Non-violence in Peace and War, vol. I, pp. 131-132. See also pp. 76 and 151, and vol. II, pp. 38, 133, 233, and 247; Gandhi, Non-violent Resistance, p. 51; Ind. ed.: Satyagraha, p. 51; and Krishna Kripalani, ed., All Men Are Brothers: Life and Thoughts of Mahatma Gandhi as told in his Own Words (Paris: Unesco, 1958), p. 101; Ind. ed.: (Ahmedabad: Navajivan, 1960), p. 135.
22. Gandhi, Non-violence in Peace and War, vol. I, p. 109.
23. Quoted in King, Stride Toward Freedom, U.S. ed., pp. 46-47; Br. ed., p. 55.
24. See, e.g., Gandhi, Non-violence in Peace and War, vol. II, pp. 220-221.
25. See Machiavelli, The Discourses of Niccolo Machiavelli, vol. I, pp. 339-340.
26. Eugen Stamm and Helmut Kastner, Juni 53: Der Volksaufstand vom 17 Juni 1953 in Ost-Berlin und der Sowjetischen Besatzungszone (Bonn: *Bundesministerium für gesamtdeutsche Fragen,* 1961) p. 43. Quoted in Ebert, "Nonviolent Resistance Against Communist Regimes?" pp. 193-194. On the lack of leadership in that Rising, see Ebert's account, *ibid.,* pp. 177-179 and Brant, The East German Rising, pp. 73 and 113.
27. Symons, The General Strike, p. 137.
28. M. K. Gandhi, An Autobiography or the Story of My Experiments With Truth, (Ahmedabad, India: Navajivan, 1956) pp. 470-471.
29. Quoted in Miller, Nonviolence, p. 139.
30. *Ibid.,* p. 136.
31. Symons, The General Strike, p. 63.
32. Jutikkala, A History of Finland, p. 233.
33. Gipson, The British Empire Before the American Revolution, vol. XII, The Triumphant Empire, Britain Sails into the Storm, 1770-1776, p. 179.
34. Halperin, Germany Tried Democracy, pp. 251-259.
35. Ebert, "Nonviolent Resistance Against Communist Regimes?" p. 182.
36. Miller, Nonviolence, p. 307.
37. C. Eric Lincoln, "The Strategy of a Sit-in" p. 296, in Sibley, ed., The Quiet Battle.
38. Luthuli, Let My People Go, p. 179.
39. Watt, Dare Call it Treason, p. 185.

40. M. K. Gandhi, **Young India,** vol. II; quoted by Dhawan, **The Political Philosophy of Mahatma Gandhi,** p. 122.

41. See D. G. Tendulker, **Mahatma: Life of Mohandas Karamchand Gandhi** (Delhi: Government of India, Publications Division, 1960), vol. I, p. 255 and 261.

42. *Ibid.,* pp. 219-221.

43. See for example, Gandhi, **Non-violent Resistance,** pp. 30 and 301; Ind. ed.: Satyagraha, pp. 30 and 301; and Dhawan, **The Political Philosophy** . . . , p. 120.

44. Gregg, **The Power of Nonviolence,** p. 49.

45. Lindberg, *"Konklusionen: Theorien om Ikke-vold,"* in Lindberg, Jacobsen and Ehrlich, **Kamp Uden Vaaben,** p. 208.

46. Guenter Lewy, **The Catholic Church and Nazi Germany** (New York and Toronto: McGraw-Hill, 1964, and London: Weidenfeld and Nicholson, 1964), pp. 263-267.

47. See Gregg, **The Power of Nonviolence,** pp. 56, 76 and 123, and Miller, **Nonviolence,** pp. 145-147.

48. See Bose, **Studies in Gandhism,** pp. 142-143.

49. *Ibid.,* pp. 138-139.

50. See M. K. Gandhi, **Satyagraha in South Africa** (Ahmedabad, India: Navajivan, 1950), p. xii.

51. Gandhi, **Non-violence in Peace and War,** vol. I, p. 52.

52. Quoted in Dhawan, **The Political Philosophy** . . . , p. 216.

53. Theodor Ebert, "Theory and Practice of Nonviolent Resistance: A Model of a Campaign," manuscript, p. 138. Unpublished English translation (by Hilda Morris) of a doctoral thesis in political science presented at the University of Erlangen, Germany, 1965. Published as **Gewaltfrier Aufstand: Alternative zum Bürgerkrieg** (Freiburg: Verlag Rombach, 1968), and paperback abridgement (Frankfurt am Main and Hamburg: Fischerbücheri, GmbH, 1970).

54. *Ibid.,* p. 142.

55. Gandhi, quoted in Bose, **Studies in Gandhism,** p. 134. See also Gandhi, **Non-violent Resistance,** pp. 30 and 174; Ind. ed.; **Satyagraha,** pp. 30 and 174.

56. Miller, **Nonviolence,** pp. 168-169.

57. Howard Zinn, **Albany** (Atlanta: Southern Regional Council, 1962), p. 19, quoted in *ibid.,* p. 328. Miller also cites on this Wyatt Tee Walker, "Achievement in Albany," in **New South** (Atlanta), June, 1963.

58. Martin Luther King, Jr., **Why We Can't Wait** (New York: The New American Library, Signet Books, 1964), p. 54.

59. Ebert, "Theory and Practice of Nonviolent Resistance," MS. p. 171.

60. See Sharp, **Gandhi Wields** . . . , pp. 56-57 and 59-60.

61. Gandhi, **Satyagraha in South Africa** (rev. sec. ed.; trans. from the Gujarati by Valji Govindji Desai; Ahmedabad, India: Navajivan, 1950), p. 46.

62. Amiya Chakravarty, **A Saint at Work: A View of Gandhi's Work and Message** (William Penn Lecture 1950; Philadelphia: Young Friends Movement of the Philadelphia Yearly Meetings, 1950), pp. 29-31.

63. V.I. Lenin, "What is to be Done? Burning Questions of Our Movement," in V.I. Lenin, **Selected Works in Three Volumes** (New York: International Publishers, and Moscow: Progress Publishers, 1967), vol. I, pp. 232-233. Also in Lenin, **Selected Works in Two Volumes** (Moscow: Foreign Languages Publishing House, 1950) vol. I, p. 379.

64. The term is used by Shridharani, War Without Violence, U.S. ed., p. 7; Br. ed., p. 30.
65. Ebert, "Theory and Practice of Nonviolent Resistance," MS. p. 128.
66. Schlesinger, The Colonial Merchants and the American Revolution, p. 136. "Preliminary agitation" took place that autumn in Providence, Rhode Island. See ibid., p. 153.
67. Oppenheimer and Lakey, A Manual for Direct Action, p. 50.
68. For other descriptions of this stage, see Shridharani, War Without Violence, U.S. ed., pp. 7-9; Br. ed., pp. 30-32 and Bose, Studies in Gandhism, pp. 139-142.
69. Ebert, "Nonviolent Resistance Against Communist Regimes?," pp. 176-177.
70. See, for example, Jutikkala, A History of Finland, p. 233, and Gipson, The Coming of the American Revolution, pp. 98, 182, 199 and 211.
71. Soloman and Fishman, "The Psychosocial Meaning of Nonviolence in Student Civil Rights Activities," Psychiatry, vol. XXVII, no. 2 (May 1964), p. 98.
72. Gregg, The Power of Nonviolence, pp. 114-120.
73. Ibid., p. 147.
74. Bondurant, Conquest of Violence, pp. 29-30.
75. George Lakey, "The Sociological Mechanisms of Nonviolent Action," (M.A. thesis in sociology, University of Pennsylvania, 1962), p. 53; also published in Peace Research Reviews (Oakville, Ontario: Canadian Peace Research Institute), vol. II, no. 6 (Dec. 1968), p. 34.
76. Gandhi, Non-violent Resistance, p. 33; Ind. ed.: Satyagraha, p. 33.
77. Ibid., p. 362.
78. See ibid., pp. 91 and 294.
79. Gandhi, quoted in Dhawan, The Political Philosophy . . . , p. 225.
80. Ibid., p. 225.
81. Ibid., p. 225.
82. Gandhi, Young India, vol. I, p. 262.
83. Gandhi, Non-violent Resistance, p. 295; Ind. ed.: Satyagraha, p. 295.
84. Dhawan, The Political Philosophy . . . , p. 225.
85. Bose, Studies in Gandhism, p. 129.
86. Gandhi, Non-violent Resistance, p. 288; Ind. ed.: Satyagraha, p. 288, and Dhawan, The Political Philosophy . . . , pp. 224-225.
87. Dhawan, The Political Philosophy . . . , p. 225.
88. See Gandhi, Non-violent Resistance, p. 296; Ind. ed.: Satyagraha, p. 296.
89. For a discussion of difficult problems of organization in "civilian defence" – i.e., prepared nonviolent action for purposes of national defence – see Ebert, "Organization in Civilian Defence," in Roberts, ed., Civilian Resistance As a National Defense, Br. title: The Strategy of Civilian Defence, pp. 255-273.
90. For suggestions on methods of organization for U.S. civil rights groups, see Oppenheimer and Lakey, A Manual for Direct Action, esp. pp. 42-55.
91. Quoted by Ebert in "Organization in Civilian Defence," in Roberts, ed., op. cit., p. 256.
92. Ibid., p. 257.
93. See Schlesinger, The Colonial Merchants . . . , p. 360, 370, 501 and 521, and Gipson, The British Empire Before the American Revolution, vol. XI, The Triumphant Empire: The Rumbling of the Coming Storm 1766-1770, pp. 143,

145, 181-182 and 187-188; and vol. XII, pp. 152-153 and 208.

94. Schlesinger, **The Colonial Merchants** . . . , p. 513.
95. *Ibid.*, p. 612.
96. See Sharp, **Gandhi Wields** . . ., pp. 61-72.
97. Luthuli, **Let My People Go**, pp. 117 and 160.
98. Harcave, **First Blood**, p. 84.
99. *Ibid.*, p. 142.
100. *Ibid.*, p. 150.
101. See Brant, **The East German Rising**, pp. 62, 66, 87-88, 91-95, 98-99, 104, 108, 111-112, 124, 136, and 140-141, and Ebert, "Nonviolent Resistance Against Communist Regimes?," MS. pp. 176-183.
102. Reitlinger, **The Final Solution**, p. 161.
103. *Ibid.*, p. 179.
104. See, for example, Prawdin, **The Unmentionable Nechaev**, pp. 153-155, 157, 159 and 160-61, and Charques, **The Twilight of Imperial Russia**, pp. 70, 83, 176, 186 and 201-202. For an instance of how a worker informant gave the police information which enabled them to crush a whole organization, see Venturi, **Roots of Revolution,** p. 533. These are simply examples which could be multiplied from other cases also.
105. Symons, **The General Strike**, p. 145.
106. See Wheeler-Bennett, **The Nemesis of Power**, pp. 550, 565, 593 and 628, and Delarue, **The Gestapo**, pp. 127, 193-194, 210, 227, 239, 272, 297, 304-305 and 316.
107. Bose, **Studies in Gandhism**, pp. 144-145.
108. Jawaharlal Nehru, **An Autobiography** (New edition; London: The Bodley Head, 1953), p. 337.
109. Bose, **Studies in Gandhism** and Gandhi, **Non-violence in Peace and War**, vol. II, p. 3.
110. Oppenheim and Lakey, **A Manual for Direct Action**, p. 48.
111. Gregg, **The Power of Nonviolence**, p. 80.
112. See Gandhi, **Non-violence in Peace and War**, vol. II, pp. 2-3.
113. Gandhi, quoted in Bose, **Studies in Gandhism**, p. 146.
114. Gandhi, **Non-violent Resistance**, pp. 379-380; Ind. ed.: **Satyagraha**, pp. 379-380.
115. Quoted in Dhawan, **The Political Philosophy** . . . , p. 223.
116. Gandhi, **Non-violence in Peace and War**, vol. II, pp. 50-51.
117. Nehru, **An Autobiography**, p. 69.
118. Ebert, "Theory and Practice of Nonviolent Resistance," MS. p. 116.
119. Gregg, **The Power of Nonviolence**, p. 80.
120. Irving L. Janis and Daniel Katz, "The Reduction of Intergroup Hostility: Research Problems and Hypotheses," **Journal of Conflict Resolution,** vol. III, no. 1 (March 1959), p. 87.
121. *Ibid.*
122. *Ibid.*
123. Clausewitz, **On War**, vol. I, p. 96.
124. This has been especially stimulated by examinations of how prepared nonviolent struggle might be used in national defence—i.e., "civilian defence". See, for example Sir Stephen King-Hall, **Defence in the Nuclear Age** pp.

196-205; (Nyack, N.Y.: Fellowship, 1959; Br. ed.: London: Gollancz, 1958), and Adam Roberts, "Civilian Defence Strategy," in Roberts, editor, **Civilian Resistance as a National Defense,** Br. ed.: **The Strategy of Civilian Defence,** pp. 215-254.

This chapter, however, is restricted to examination of basic principles of strategy and tactics in nonviolent action generally, and will not therefore examine how these principles might be applied in specific conflicts or for particular purposes.

125. Liddell Hart, **Strategy,** p. 369.

126. Gandhi, **Satyagraha in South Africa,** p. xi.

127. Hiller, **The Strike,** p. 126.

128. On strategic and tactical problems in the struggles of the American colonists, see Morgan and Morgan, **The Stamp Act Crisis,** pp. 174 and 240; Gipson, **The British Empire . . . ,** vol. XI, pp. 265-271; and Schlesinger, **The Colonial Merchants . . . ,** pp. 213-215, 218-220, 226-234, and 400-401.

On the lack of strategy in the East German Rising, see Brant, **The East German Rising,** pp. 73, 103 and 188-189.

On the lack of strategic planning for the *Ruhrkamf,* see Ehrlich (Raloff), *"Ruhrkampen,"* p. 184, in Lindberg, Jacobsen and Ehrlich, **Kamp Uden Vaaben.** Lack of advance strategic planning for certain aspects of the 1926 British General Strike is mentioned by Symons, in **The General Strike,** p. 51. On strategic and tactical questions in the spontaneous 1905 Revolution, see Schwarz, **The Russian Revolution of 1905,** pp. 99-112, and (on conflicting views on whether strikes should lead to a violent rising) pp. 132-143, and Harcave, **First Blood,** pp. 165-167, 175, 199-206, 209-210, and 215; p. 199 raises the question of when the optimum results might have been achieved by ending that particular struggle. On the tactical problem of what the *Duma* should have done when dissolved in February 1917, see Katkov, **Russia 1917,** pp. 293-294. On strategic and tactical planning of a sit-in campaign in Atlanta, see C. Eric Lincoln, "The Strategy of a Sit-in," in Sibley **The Quiet Battle,** pp. 296-297. On when to call off an African bus boycott in South Africa, see Luthuli, **Let My People Go,** p. 178.

129. See Jutikkala, **A History of Finland,** pp. 233-235.

130. Clausewitz, **On War,** vol. I, p. 107.

131. See Liddell Hart, **Strategy,** pp. 340-41, 25, 337, 349, 359 and 350.

132. Clausewitz, **On War,** vol. I, p. 183.

133. *Ibid.,* p. 173.

134. Sharp, **Gandhi Wields . . .** pp. 70-90.

135. *Ibid.,* pp. 14-15.

136. Miller, **Nonviolence,** p. 150.

137. Nehru, **An Autobiography,** p. 253.

138. Sheehy-Skeffington, **Michael Davitt,** pp. 120-121. On debate in 1775 on the timing of the American Colonists' nonimportation and nonexportation movement, see Schlesinger, **The Colonial Merchants . . .** pp. 414-421.

139. Sharp, **Gandhi Wields . . .** p. 84.

140. See Miller, **Nonviolence,** p. 308; and Lincoln, "The Strategy of a Sit-in," p. 297.

141. Clausewitz, **On War,** vol. I, p. 192.

142. Liddell Hart, **Strategy,** p. 342. See also Clausewitz, **On War,** vol. I, p. 97.

143. M. K. Gandhi, **Non-violent Resistance,** p. 288; Ind. ed.: **Satyagraha,** p. 288; and Dhawan, **The Political Philosophy . . . ,** pp. 224-5.

144. Clausewitz, **On War,** vol. I, p. 214.
145. Liddell Hart, **Strategy,** p. 348.
146. *Ibid.,* p. 347.
147. *Ibid.,* p. 348.
148. *Ibid.*
149. Bose, **Selections from Gandhi,** p. 202.
150. Nehru, **An Autobiography,** pp. 215 and 327-328.
151. Miller, **Nonviolence,** pp. 146 and 150.
152. Bose, **Studies in Gandhism,** p. 152.
153. Gandhi, **Non-violent Resistance,** p. 156; Ind. ed.: **Satyagraha,** p. 156.
154. Sharp, **Gandhi Wields** . . . , p. 72.
155. Gandhi, **Nonviolent Resistance,** p. 173; Ind. ed.: **Satyagraha,** p. 173.
156. Waskow, **From Race Riot to Sit-in,** p. 246.
157. Bose, **Studies in Gandhism,** p. 176.
158. Bondurant, **Conquest of Violence,** p. 38.
159. Gandhi, **Non-violent Resistance,** p. 25; Ind. ed.: **Satyagraha,** p. 25.
160, *Ibid.,* p. 173.
161. *Ibid.,* pp. 115-116.
162. *Ibid.,* p. 127.
163. *Ibid.,* p. 151.
164. Sharp, **Gandhi Wields** . . . , pp. 51-206.
165. Sibley, ed., **The Quiet Battle,** p. 371.
166. Bose, **Selections from Gandhi,** p. 202.
167. Clausewitz, **On War,** vol. I, p. 241.
168. Liddell Hart, **Strategy,** p. 348.
169. Schlesinger, **The Colonial Merchants** . . . , pp. 369-370.
170. Harcave, **First Blood,** pp. 219-220.
171. Interview with Pan-Africanist representative Peter Molotsi in Accra, 26 April 1960; reported in Gene Sharp, "No Co-existence with Oppression," *Peace News,* 13 May 1960.
172. Ebert, "Theory and Practice of Nonviolent Resistance," MS pp. 313-314.
173. See Liddell Hart, **Strategy,** pp. 343-344 and Clausewitz, **On War,** vol. I, p. 166.
174. Liddell Hart, **Strategy,** p. 349.
175. Bose, **Studies in Gandhism,** p. 153.
176. Gandhi, quoted in Bose, **Selections from Gandhi,** p. 202.
177. See Bondurant, **Conquest of Violence,** pp. 38-39 and Bose, **Studies in Gandhism,** p. 176.
178. On the nature and role of the ultimatum in satyagraha, see Shridharani, **War Without Violence,** U.S. ed., pp. 11 and 133-134, and Br. ed., pp. 33-34, 98 and 128, and Bondurant, **Conquest of Violence,** pp. 40 and 85.
179. Schlesinger, **The Colonial Merchants** . . . , p. 609.
180. Watt, **Dare Call It Treason,** p. 185.
181. Kuper, **Passive Resistance in South Africa,** p. 234; Appendix B, pp. 233-247, contains the full text of this exchange of letters with the government.
182. The full text is quoted in Sharp, **Gandhi Wields** . . . , pp. 61-66.
183. Kuper, **Passive Resistance in South Africa,** p. 114.

10

Challenge
Brings Repression

INTRODUCTION

The time comes when passivity, acquiescence and patience give way to open nonviolent struggle. This time for action may have been determined by various factors discussed in the previous chapter: tactical and strategic considerations, the opponent's actions, the absence of solutions through milder measures, and the state of mind of the grievance group.

This time for action is also the time for self-reliance and internal strengthening of the struggle group. During an Irish rent strike campaign in 1879 and 1880 Charles Stewart Parnell repeatedly called on the peasants to "rely on yourselves," not on any one else, to right their grievances:

> It is no use relying on the Government . . . You must only rely upon your own determination . . . . help yourselves by standing together . . . strengthen those amongst yourselves who are weak . . . ,

band yourselves together, organize yourselves . . . and you must win . . .

When you have made this question ripe for settlement, then and not till then will it be settled. [1]

Self-reliance and organization (or, occasionally, spontaneous united action) contribute to change by increasing the strength of the groups near the bottom of hierarchically organized social, economic and political systems. The dominant groups in such systems are usually well organized and capable of united action for their objectives. Subordinates in such systems are frequently not so. They may be large in numbers, and the dominant groups may be in fact dependent upon them. Yet the subordinates may often be incapable of effective joint action because they lack confidence in themselves, because they remain a mass of separated individuals and disunited groups,[2] and because they do not know how to act. Nonviolent action may change this situation. The grievance group may take joint action by a technique which mobilizes power among the subordinates and enables them to exert control over their present and future lives. Of course, to win, the actionists must do more; they must persist despite repression and must bring into operation the forces which can bring success.

A HALT TO SUBMISSION

Nonviolent action means that submission and passivity are cast off. Nonviolence, said Gandhi, "means the pitting of one's whole soul against the will of the tyrant." [3] Nehru's view was similar.[4] This determination to struggle will be expressed in the use of the psychological, social, economic and political forces at the disposal of the actionists. These forces operate in concrete ways utilizing the methods of action which have been described in detail in Chapters Three to Eight. This period is the time of the matching of forces. If advance planning has preceded action, now will be the time to disseminate precise instructions on what action should take place, when, and which persons and groups are to act. If advance pledges to act have been made, this is the time to put them into practice.

The initial forms of action in a nonviolent struggle may differ widely. Methods of nonviolent protest—marches, parades, display of flags and the like—often begin a campaign, or in other cases some type of psychological nonviolent intervention—such as fasts—may be used. Other struggles begin directly with noncooperation—civil disobedience or a large-scale strike, for example. Initial dramatic actions symbolic of the issues at stake, conducted in a disciplined manner, may strike the imaginations of all concerned, shatter inertia, awaken awareness, increase the morale of the grievance group, and set the tone for the struggle which has begun.[5]

Particular conflicts will differ widely in the pace with which the strategy is unrolled and the full strength of the movement is mobilized and applied. Sometimes a slow and deliberate development is most effective, while at other times it may be stunningly rapid. Since nonviolent campaigns differ widely, there are no universal steps or stages for them all. Therefore, in this and the next chapters the focus will be on the general processes, forces and mechanisms of change operating in this type of conflict. Their specific implementation will differ from case to case.

With the launching of nonviolent action, basic, often latent, conflicts between the respective groups are brought to the surface and activated. Through ensuing "creative conflict and tension"[6] it becomes possible to produce change to resolve the underlying conflict.

Unlike many religious pacifists, most exponents of nonviolent action would agree with Frederick Douglass:

> Those who profess to favor freedom and yet deprecate agitation, are men who want crops without plowing up the ground. They want rain without thunder and lightning. They want the ocean without the awful roar of its many waters. The struggle may be a moral one; or it may be a physical one; or it may be both moral and physical. But it must be a struggle. Power concedes nothing without demand. It never did and it never will.[7]

Indeed, nonviolent actionists insist that in sharp conflicts, only effective nonviolent struggle can lead to a satisfactory solution which avoids both passive submission and political violence.

In some cases members of the grievance group may become enthusiastic at the prospect of nonviolent hostilities. As tension increases, morale rises and large numbers of formerly passive people become determined to take part in the coming struggle. "Such enthusiasm in the face of future suffering may be due to the fact that a community which has been oppressed and humbled, looks forward to the opportunity of proving their full and equal worth in combat," writes Ebert.[8]

The changes which nonviolent struggle brings to the struggle group will be explored more fully in Chapter Fourteen, but a brief mention of them is required here. Some will be psychological—a shattering of attitudes of conformity, hopelessness, inertia, impotence and passivity. Others will be more directly political—learning how to act together to achieve objectives, the long-term results of which will obviously be most significant where success is achieved. Participation in nonviolent action may give people increased self-respect, confidence and an awareness of their own power. Thus, writes Hiller, "Recognition of laborers as formidable opponents undoubtedly helps to improve the status of every workingman. The strike, although it brings no material gain, is felt to bring a triumph if it brings this sense of importance." [9] The experience in India was similar. Jawaharlal Nehru wrote that Gandhi's example and leadership changed the millions in India from a demoralized mass of people without hope or capacity for resistance, into people with self-respect and capacity for self-reliant struggle against oppression. [10]

The withdrawal of consent, cooperation and submission will challenge the system. How seriously, will vary with the quality and forms of action, the numbers of the actionists, and their persistence in face of repression. The social and political milieu is also important. This includes: how much nonconformity the system can tolerate, how much support for, or hostility to, the regime there is, what the chances are of the resistance spreading, and how much the opponent's sources of power are threatened by the action. The final outcome of the challenge will be determined by some kind of balance between the seriousness of the challenge and the degree to which the social and political milieu favors each side. The opponent's own efforts are clearly important, but, *in themselves,* they are not decisive. Take repression, for example. To be effective, repression must produce submission. But at times it does not. Repression may even be counterproductive, and forces started by the nonviolent actionists and outside of the opponent's control may even reduce or destroy his *ability* to act. An end to the submission of the grievance group initiates changes which may bring fundamental alterations in the relations of the contending groups.

INITIAL POLARIZATION FOLLOWED BY SHIFTING POWER

The launching of nonviolent action will almost always sharpen the conflict, cause the conflicting groups to become more sharply deliniated, and stimulate previously uncommitted people to take sides. This polarization seems to be a quality of all forms of open conflict. [11] At the beginning of nonviolent struggle, Lakey observes, "those initially inclined toward the opponent tend to move closer to his position and support it, while those initially inclined toward the campaigner may move in the campaigner's direction." [12] The point at which this occurs varies. Oppenheimer and Lakey point out that the previous period of indifference is likely to be replaced by one of "active antagonism, the time when tide often runs highest against the movement." [13]

This polarization of support for the opponent is well illustrated by reactions in the 1952 Defiance Campaign in South Africa. Before the campaign, the Europeans were usually indifferent to the many prosecutions of Africans and other nonwhites for breaking the Pass Laws and certain other regulatory laws. However, when the *Apartheid* laws and regulations were deliberately and publicly disobeyed by the nonwhites who used jail-going as a protest, the Europeans' indifference was shattered, and they reacted "with active emotions of hate or sympathy." A related political shift occurred also; the opposition United Party, committed to white domination in a milder form than the ruling Nationalist Party, "moved toward the assimilation of its non-European policy with that of the Government, and United Party supporters moved into the ranks of the Nationalist Party." [14] In this case the struggle ended without a major reversal of this trend although, as discussed in Chapter Twelve, under certain circumstances which include continuation of the struggle, this polarization in favor of the opponent is likely to be a passing phenomenon. In the South African case it was not, since the campaign collapsed just as disunity of the opponent group had started to appear.

During this initial polarization, which may be short or long, it is especially important for the nonviolent actionists to be most careful in their behavior. "Actions which confirm the prejudices of the opponent will be seized upon and magnified; those which counter the prejudices will have more impact than ordinarily." At this stage, the grievance group will be worse off than before the campaign started since repression has been added to the initial grievances. If the struggle halts at this stage the grievance group will remain worse off than before. But a continuation of the struggle in a disciplined manner is likely to lead to a new stage, characterized by the disunity of the opponent. [15] In this new stage the opponent is likely to lose even support he had before the struggle while support for the nonviolent actionists may grow.

Seifert supports this view of the instability of the initial polarization, drawing largely upon the cases of minority nonviolent action for social reform. Because the first public reaction to the nonviolent challenge may well be negative, the actionists should attempt to keep to a minimum defection of this pre-campaign support for the desired changes. But, Seifert argues, there seems to be nothing the actionists can do to prevent a temporary strengthening of the opponent group. In addition, the supporters of change may become divided between nonviolent militants and more conventional moderates. After this initial stage, Seifert continues, the first shifts in favor of correcting the grievances "are likely to come at an agonizingly slow rate." A "tipping point" will come, however, after which the shifts in opinion, support and power will proceed at a rapid rate, and, for many, even become "the thing to do."

In the long run, therefore, successful nonviolent campaigns produce a strengthened solidarity among the nonviolent militants, a growth of wider support for correction of the grievance and a fragmentation and disintegration of support for the opponent. Seifert acknowledges, of course, that the factors making for this shift may not always be present; at times other factors, such as economic interests, may dictate a very rapid adjustment by the opponent to the new situation produced by the nonviolent challenge. [16]

This instability of the initial polarization, the tendency of a section of intermediary opinion to shift toward the nonviolent group, of the opponent's camp to split, and of support for the actionists' objectives to grow, are not inevitable. They appear to develop only so long as the group remains nonviolent. For reasons discussed in Chapter Eleven, if violence is used by or on behalf of the actionists the tendency toward both a relative and an absolute increase of their strength and support seems to reverse.

As intermediary opinion shifts toward the nonviolent actionists the new support may be expressed not by nonviolent action but by more conventional attacks on the grievances. This has occurred in several cases. Nonviolent sit-ins in the U.S. South, for example, are reported to have stimulated other less militant antisegregation action, such as voter registration, integration of schools and integration of all-white professional organizations. [17] There is other scattered evidence of this tendency. For example, the 1930-31 civil disobedience campaign in India prodded the Liberals (who had opposed it) to take stronger action by constitutional means, and to act as intermediaries in negotiations between the Indian National Congress and the British *Raj.* [18] The Defiance Campaign of 1952 in South Africa contributed significantly to the formation of the Liberal Party and the Congress of Democrats—both antiapartheid political groups. In that same campaign, the African National Congress experienced a jump from seven thousand to one hundred thousand in paid-up members. The objectives of the campaign also received support from various church groups not previously involved. [19]

Support for the nonviolent actionists and increased participation in the campaign itself are also likely to grow as the initial polarization is reversed. When these various changes take place, the extreme polarization which first occurred between the nonviolent group and the opponent is revealed as unstable. There tends to develop what Harvey Seifert has called the "progressive detachment of groups arranged in a spectrum of potential support." [20] The course of the struggle may be viewed as the attempt of the nonviolent actionists continually to increase their strength (numerical and otherwise), not only among their usual supporters and third parties but even in the camp of the opponent, and by various processes to reduce the strength of the opponent group.

During the campaign the respective strengths of the two contending groups are therefore subject to constant change, both absolutely and relatively. Such change takes place to a much greater degree and more quickly than it does in struggles in which both sides use violence.

The nonviolent actionists' behavior may therefore influence the strength or weakness of both their own group and also of the opponent. In addition the conduct of the nonviolent group will influence whether third parties turn to the support of either of the groups. The extreme and constant variability of the strength of both contending groups is highly important to the nonviolent actionists in choosing and applying strategy, tactics and methods. This highly dynamic and changeable situation means that particular acts within a nonviolent strategy may have extremely wide and significant repercussions on the power of each side, even more so than comparable acts in war. Each particular action, even a limited one, therefore needs to be selected and evaluated in terms of its wider influences on the overall struggle.

If possible, the specific acts should not only demonstrate the present strength of the actionists, but also help to increase their absolute power and to diminish that of the opponent. This may happen even when the immediate political objective has *not* been achieved. Naturally, short-term successes which also contribute to a favorable alteration of relative strengths are to be preferred if possible, but short-term successes at the *cost* of an unfavorable alteration of relative strengths are most questionable. It is possible to *appear* to lose all the battles except the last and yet clearly to win that last one because of the changes in relative strengths that have occurred during the previous battles.

Improvements in the relative strength of the nonviolent actionists after the initial polarization will be highly important in determining the course of events in the intermediate and later stages of the campaign. An increase in genuine strength of the nonviolent group at each stage will make it easier for the group to meet unforeseen circumstances, will maximize its relative strength in the next stage of the struggle, and will increase the possibility of full success.

THE OPPONENT'S INITIAL PROBLEM

The opponent's initial problem arises from the fact that the nonviolent action disrupts the status quo and requires of him some type of response. The type and extent of the disruption will differ. The opponent's tolerance will vary. And his reactions, both psychologically and in countermeasures, may range widely and may change as the struggle continues.

In mild cases, initiation of nonviolent action may disturb the existing situation only slightly. In extreme cases, however, it may shatter the status quo. The opponent will no longer be able to count on the submission of the members of the grievance group. He will no longer be able to assume they will do nothing fundamental to alter their plight; they are actively protesting, noncooperating and perhaps intervening to block implementation of his policies or to produce changes of their own. The opponent will have to respond to the new challenge. Generally he will try to end the opposition. To do so, the opponent will need to take a series of decisions about his own countermeasures. He will need to make similar decisions when the challenge is instead made by violent means, but, as later discussion will show, nonviolent means may be especially conducive to creating difficulties in making those decisions. Nonviolent action also tends to produce and aggravate conflicts within the opponent's camp about appropriate countermeasures.[21]

It is to the advantage of the nonviolent actionists to prevent and correct misperceptions of their intentions and activities. At the initial stage such misperceptions may cause the opponent group to make first responses which may be harmful to all concerned. If the misperceptions continue into later stages, they are likely to disturb—though not destroy—the normal operation of the mechanisms of change of nonviolent action, especially the processes associated with the conversion mechanism. Problems of accurate perception of nonviolent intentions existed even before Gandhi's campaigns. Nehru, who knew the English well, has written: "The average Englishman did not believe the *bona fides* of nonviolence; he thought that all this was camouflage, a cloak to cover some vast secret design which would burst out in a violent upheaval one day."[22] Past cases of violence during and following a nonviolent struggle therefore produce detrimental influences which the nonviolent group will need to counter, both at the initiation of the campaign and throughout its course. Frequently it will also be necessary to counter a general disbelief in the possibility of effective but strictly nonviolent struggle.

Sometimes—but not always—when confronted with nonviolent action the opponent and his officials become confused, especially when they have been taken by surprise by the events or when they are unfamiliar with this type of behavior. This confusion is not, of course, necessarily beneficial to the actionists and their cause. French army officers were, for example, confused and uncertain about what to do when faced with mass mutiny in 1917. [23] East German officials, police and Party leaders, especially on the local level, were confused and uncertain when confronted with strikes and demonstrations in June 1953. [24] Heinz Brandt—then secretary for agitation and propaganda in the Berlin organization of the Socialist Unity Party—has described the Party propagandists as "completely bewildered" as they witnessed the first "genuine working class movement" of their lives which, contrary to all they had been taught, was acting against the "workers' party." [25] Furthermore, a similar response came from higher officials: "Party and state officials were taken by surprise and increasingly paralyzed. A monstrous event was occurring before their very eyes: workers were rising against the 'worker-peasant' state. The world collapsed round their ears." [26] Workers rebelling against the Communist State often sang "The Internationale." [27] These events suggest that confusion may be especially likely when the nonviolent action takes the forms which shatter the perception of the world contained in official doctrines and ideology.

Confusion in the ranks of the opponent may have other sources as well. It may arise from excessive optimism and false confidence that others see his actions and policies as entirely good. When attempting to overthrow the Weimar Republic, Dr. Kapp "staked all on a great popular welcome, and when confronted with blank hostility, he showed himself bewildered, weak and helpless." [28] Nehru records British confusion and uncertainty as they faced the 1921 noncooperation movement:

> As our morale grew, that of the Government went down. They did not understand what was happening: it seemed that the old world they knew in India was toppling down. There was a new aggressive spirit abroad and self-reliance and fearlessness, and the great prop of British rule in India—prestige—was visibly wilting. Repression in a small way only strengthened the movement, and the Government hesitated for long before it would take action against the big leaders. It did not know what the consequences might be. Was the Indian Army reliable? Would the police carry out orders? As Lord Reading, the Viceroy, said in December 1921, they were "puzzled and perplexed." [29]

Sometimes in the past, one source of the opponent's confusion has been surprise at the explicitly nonviolent character of the action movement. Such surprise may or may not have helped the nonviolent group. However, with increasing use of the nonviolent technique, the surprise element has declined; it will finally disappear. Governments are also rapidly accumulating experience in dealing with this type of challenge.[30] Although these developments may reduce the brutality of repression, they will not necessarily reduce the effectiveness of the technique. The struggle potential of nonviolent action is not dependent upon surprise or novelty.

At times, instead, the opponent may be ignorant of its nature and workings. Ignorance of the power of nonviolent struggle may cause the opponent to be overconfident and hence to react extremely mildly to the nonviolent challenge. This reaction may also derive from misperceptions of the intentions of the grievance group, or in overconfidence rooted in belief in the regime's omnipotence, or in long absence of effective challenge. Tsarist officials clearly miscalculated the gravity of the spreading illegal strike movement in St. Petersburg in the first few days of January 1905, a short while before the march on the Winter Palace on Bloody Sunday.[31] Even in later months, despite events and warnings from advisers, tsarist officials again underestimated the seriousness of the trouble spots throughout the Empire. In both instances they did so because of overconfidence in the regime's ability to deal with trouble should it erupt.[32]

In other situations, the opponent may clearly recognize the danger to his system or policies which the nonviolent action poses. Any given nonviolent action will not, however, be equally threatening to all regimes. There are variations in tolerance, i.e., in the degree to which the opponent can safely ignore the challenge or take only mild action against it. Several factors will be involved: the issues at stake, the numbers involved, the methods of nonviolent action used, and the expected future course of the movement. The degree to which the opponent can tolerate dissent may also be influenced by the degree to which the society is democratic or nondemocratic. Gandhi argued for example: "A civil resister never uses arms and hence he is harmless to a State that is at all willing to listen to the voice of public opinion. He is dangerous for an autocratic State, for he brings about its fall by engaging public opinion upon the matter for which he resists the State."[33] Many systems will not, and some cannot, tolerate defiance without taking repressive counteractions.

This is not to say that all hostile responses to nonviolent challenges arise solely from an intellectual recognition of the objective dangers which they pose to the opponent's policies or system. Frequently, an opponent may react to nonviolent challenge emotionally, seeing it largely as an affront, an indignity, as offensive behavior, and as a repudiation of his authority and position. He may regard these aspects of the challenge as more important than the actual issues at stake. The opponent may then try to obtain either verbal acknowledgement of his authority and position, or a cancellation of the nonviolent campaign, or both, before he will consent to negotiations or reconsider the disputed policies. Even written protests and petitions, and correspondence concerning grievances between responsible bodies—which are far short of actual disobedience—may provoke this indignant reaction. Such mild acts by American colonists and their legislatures, for example, aroused highly emotional reactions in Britain, from the King and from members of both Houses of Parliament; until the colonials had acknowledged the supremacy of British laws and their responsibility to help support the government of the Empire, there was no disposition to consider objectively their grievances or petitions.[34]

Sometimes this reaction of indignation may accompany recognition that the nonviolent challenge is genuinely serious. The British government's reaction to the 1926 general strike, for example, was partially emotional, the strike being seen as an affront, as offensive, and as a repudiation of authority; but it was also rational, the strike being seen as a serious threat which had to be defeated in order to halt such challenges once and for all. In the days before the strike, the government broke off negotiations and demanded "an immediate and unconditional withdrawal of the instructions for a General Strike."[35] As the time for action came, even government supporters who had earlier favored conciliation hardened their position, and concluded that, once begun, the struggle had to be fought to an end.[36] At almost the last minute, Labour M.P. Arthur Henderson (who opposed the strike) attempted a final appeal for a settlement to Sir Winston Churchill (leader of Cabinet "hard-liners"). When Henderson arrived, however, Churchill asked: "Have you come to say that the strike notices are withdrawn? . . . No? Then there is no reason to continue this discussion."[37]

In many instances, the opponent may be less concerned with challenges to his dignity or authority and more with the immediate issues at stake. He may recognize that his interest will be better served by concentrating primarily or exclusively on the issues in dispute. This does not necessarily mean that he will take the nonviolent challenge without concern, especially if withdrawal of the subordinates' usual cooperation and support brings realization to a somewhat startled opponent that his power is in fact based upon the support which is now denied. For example, Watt reports that during the 1917 mutiny, French Army "officers suddenly found that they were not in control of their men . . ."[38] The Russian 1905 Revolution, concludes Katkov, brought to the tsarist government a "newly-discovered need for popular support . . ."[39] In his report to the Tsar on January 17, 1905, just over a week after Bloody Sunday, the Minister of Agriculture, Alexis Ermolov, reminded him that the strength of the throne was dependent on the support of the people.[40] Despite these insights the Russian government persisted in underestimating the power of various strike waves until they produced undeniable economic paralysis.

As already noted, the strong reactions to the British general strike of 1926 were in part rooted in a perception of the power of nonviolent economic struggle, which Conservatives saw as a challenge to the existence of the British constitutional system. An editorial written for the *Daily Mail* reflected this view. The general strike was not "an industrial dispute," it declared, but "a revolutionary movement" which, by inflicting suffering upon the general community, was intended "to put forcible constraint upon the Government." The general strike, the draft editorial continued, could "only succeed by destroying the Government and subverting the rights and liberties of the people." Therefore no civilized government could tolerate it, and "it must be dealt with by every resource at the disposal of the community."[41] With such a perception, the British government prepared to meet the crisis by withdrawing warships from the Atlantic fleet for use at home, dispersing soldiers and naval contingents to various parts of the country, and canceling all army and navy leaves.[42]

The Nazis also saw mass noncooperation in the form of the general strike as a dangerous weapon if used against them. For example on March 1, 1933, after the burning of the *Reichstag* (the German parliament building) on February 27, the Nazis issued a decree which provided punishments both for "provocation to armed conflict against the State" and for "provocation to a general strike." Delarue in his study, *The Gestapo,* writes, "What the Nazis feared the most was a general strike, which could be the sole effective weapon of the divided Left."[43]

Recognition of the power of nonviolent action will sometimes lead the opponent to make concessions in the hope of ending the challenge. The opponent may grant major demands claimed by the nonviolent actionists if they appear just to others and if he expects that otherwise the movement will grow and become increasingly difficult to control. He may see serious concessions to be in the long run the easiest way out. Or, he may hesitate to take such action because of fear that other groups with less justified claims might resort to similar means. While conceding demands, the opponent may seek to save face, as by suddenly discovering that a long-standing commission or board had just submitted its recommendations which included changes demanded by the nonviolent group: "If only they had been patient and trusted us . . ."

At other times, the opponent will make major concessions only after a considerable period of struggle, that is, after he has recognized the real power of the movement. For example, the tsarist regime in 1905, especially during the Great October Strike, had "to become acquainted with the new force and form of the opposition and to meet unexpected problems." In the first days of the October strike, "the government seemed paralyzed; and in many ways it was." Very reluctantly, not knowing what else to do, the Tsar issued the imperial October Manifesto, in which he renounced his role as unrivaled autocrat, granted civil liberties and extension of the vote in principle to all, established that *Duma* (parliamentary) consent was required for all laws, and guaranteed effective popular supervision of appointed officials.[44] These concessions were, however, too mild to halt the revolution, for many people now aimed at bigger objectives.

Instead of major concessions, the opponent may offer comparatively minor ones. For example, after it was announced that the 1930-31 campaign in India would begin with civil disobedience of the Salt Act, the government referred the salt tax question to the Tariff Board; the aim was to lower the price of taxed salt to that of untaxed salt if the salt tax were abolished. Gandhi, however, affirmed that he would not be satisfied with this concession, and besides there were yet other forts to be stormed.[45] In a very different conflict, in early August 1953 during the peak of the strike in the Vorkuta prison camps, the State Prosecutor arrived with a retinue of generals from Moscow offering minor concessions: two letters could be mailed a month instead of a year, one family visit a year, removal of identification numbers from clothes, and removal of iron bars from windows. These were rejected in an open letter from the prisoners. Their reply was ignored and General Deravyanko traveled from camp to camp within the Vorkuta group promising better food, higher pay, shorter shifts, with "some effect on weaker and less politically active elements."[46] Often in ordinary labor strikes the employer offers certain limited improvements as a counter to trade union demands. The East German regime responded to the developing strikes and the Rising on June 16, 1953—which had been to a significant degree sparked by an increase in the amount of work required in the factories—by minor concessions. Very quickly government loud-speaker vans announced that the Politburo would "reconsider" the increased work norms, and later the same day the Polit-buro did in fact rescind them. [47]

Relatively minor concession, however, frequently will not satisfy a determined movement. The Diem regime in South Vietnam on several oc-casions responded unsuccessfully to the Buddhist campaign of 1963 with minor concessions and gestures of conciliation. These included removal of certain local government officials, apologies for the actions of some sub-ordinate officials, renewal of talks with the Buddhists, release of some Buddhist prisoners, removal of barbed wire around pagodas. [48] Minor concessions are related to what has become called "tokenism" in the Afro-American freedom movement, i.e., minor changes intended simply to end protest and pressure, as Martin Luther King, Jr., described it. [49]

But concessions, large or small, may not weaken the resistance, but strengthen it. The concessions may give confidence to the actionists, as occurred in the East German Rising. Striking and demonstrating workers were elated by their first gains, and cancellation of the increased work norms brought confusion to Party members who had been defending them. [50]

Many opponents have difficulties in granting major concessions, or in acceding to all the actionists' objectives as long as they still have a choice. These difficulties may be rooted in beliefs, prestige, or in power considerations. Occasionally an opponent—however autocratic—may gen-uinely believe that concessions, compromise, or surrender are out of the question if he is to be "true" to his mission or duty. Such a belief was very important in the qualms of conscience which Tsar Nicholas II experi-enced before deciding to abdicate in March 1917. [51] The opponent's sin-cere belief that he is right and that his policies and repression are correct and necessary may be highly important factors in particular conflicts. Un-der certain conditions, international prestige may also discourage certain opponents from making major concessions. [52] In other cases concessions may be difficult because of the opponent's desire to appease some of his supporters who strongly oppose the nonviolent group.

Even more serious can be the opponent's fear that once he surren-ders on some specific issues, he may have to surrender everything. This was a frequent reaction to the predominantly nonviolent economic and political resistance campaign of the American colonists prior to April 1775. For example, in England there was a strong feeling against the im-pending repeal of the disrupted Townshend duties on the grounds that, says Gipson, "the government could not give way without bringing about a disruption of the Empire.' [53] In 1774 when repeal of the remaining tax on tea was being debated, Solicitor General Widderburn told Edmund Burke: ". . . if you give up this tax, it is not here you must stop, you will be required to give up much more, nay, to give up all." [54]

Rather than repression, the opponent may use psychological influences to induce the nonviolent actionists to be submissive again and to withdraw from the struggle. Usually the opponent may try to convince them that not only can the movement not succeed, but that it has already begun to lose strength. These tactics are commonly used in strikes, in the form of inspired reports that more and more of the strikers are returning to their jobs. In one major American steel strike, for example: "Full page advertisements begged the men to go back to work, while flaming headlines told us 'men go back to mills,' 'steel strike waning!' and 'mills operating stronger'; 'more men back at work'; and so forth." [55] At one point a false report of a settlement was issued in an attempt to bring the Montgomery bus boycott to an end. [56] In the Bardoli revenue refusal campaign in 1928 there were repeated attempts to induce key people to pay the land revenue which was being withheld in the hope that this would weaken the will of others. [57]

False rumors may also be spread about the movement, its intentions, and its leadership. [58] Attempts may be made to split off groups supporting the movement or to turn leaders against each other. [59] Or a more direct counterattack may be mounted, with the opponent making a major effort to justify existing policies and to show that there is no justification for the demands of the nonviolent group. This effort is intended to reduce the support that the nonviolent group can mobilize and retain.

It is common for nonviolent resistance to be met with repression when the opponent is unwilling or unable to grant the actionists' demands. Repression is an acknowledgement of the seriousness of the challenge. Sometimes the severity of repression will be in proportion to the seriousness of the nonviolent challenge, but this is by no means a standard pattern. In cases of civil disobedience, for example, in certain political situations, the fact that a law chosen for open disobedience is unimportant will not necessarily reduce the intensity of the opponent's reaction. [60] Gandhi acknowledged that when people practiced civil disobedience ". . . it was impossible for the Government to leave them free." [61] True, the opponent's need to bring an end to defiance may in certain situations be largely symbolic. But in other situations of widespread nonviolent action which is likely to become increasingly effective, the pressures on the opponent to halt it by some means or other will be overwhelming. Such strong pressures will especially occur where the system cannot stand major dissent.

For example, Luthuli pointed out that one reason for the South African Government's attempt to break the 1957 bus boycott by Africans living in Alexandra township, near Johannesburg, was that it needed "to break all demonstrations of African unity . . ." [62] (The boycott nevertheless succeeded.) "The first problem of an autocratic ruler is . . . how to maintain firm control of his subjects . . . ," Hsiao writes. [63] In any conflict situation, involving an autocratic regime or not, if the nonviolent opposition is widespread or especially daring, the opponent really cannot ignore it without appearing to be helpless in the face of defiance and thereby running the risk of its spread. He must then take some kind of counteraction. Sometimes he will respond with police action even to public declarations of opposition and of intent to carry out resistance at some future time. [64] Sometimes the opponent's need to act against the nonviolent challenge will to a significant degree be rooted in his reactions of fear and uncertainty in face of challenges to his dominance, authority, status and wealth. [65] Economic noncooperation (especially by tax refusal and rejection of the government's paper money) may so threaten the financial stability of the regime that it constitutes "a challenge that could not be ignored" —which was the case in Russia in December 1905. [66] Repeated American colonial campaigns of economic and political noncooperation finally confronted the British Parliament with ". . . the alternative of adopting coercive measures, or of forever relinquishing our claim of sovereignty or dominion over the colonies," —as Lord Mansfield declared in February 1775, two months before the violence at Lexington and Concord. [67] The morning after the general protest strike against Nazi maltreatment of Jews began in Amsterdam on February 25, 1941, the German occupation officials realized that it constituted a major challenge. Originally planned for only one day, the strike had been extended, had spread to towns outside Amsterdam, and large crowds were continuing to demostrate within the city. "These constituted a serious threat to the occupying power, which could not tolerate a display of popular strength in defiance of its orders." Consequently Nazi officials ". . . felt that ruthless and quick action was needed, including the establishment of a state of seige during which harsher punishments would be meted out by summary courts." [68]

As these examples illustrate, an opponent who is unwilling to grant the demands of the nonviolent actionists, and who knows no other type of response to such a challenge, is likely to resort to sanctions. These sanctions will vary. In a strike, they may simply involve cutting off wages, or a lock-out. In other situations, however, when the opponent is the State, or has its support, the sanctions are likely to involve the use of the police, the prison system and the armed forces. This response is repression.

Whether the opponent uses repression or some other means, as long as the actionists persist in struggle while maintaining nonviolent discipline, the opponent will experience difficulties in dealing with that struggle. These difficulties are associated with the dynamics and mechanisms of the technique and their tendency to maximize the influence and power of the nonviolent group while undermining those of the opponent.

REPRESSION

Nonviolent actionists who know what they are doing will not be surprised at the repression inflicted by the opponent. "If we choose to adopt revolutionary direct action methods, however nonviolent they might be, we must expect every resistance," wrote Nehru.[69] The Buddhists struggling against the Diem regime in South Vietnam also expected repression.[70] Repression is especially likely when the nonviolent action takes forms and expressions which present a serious challenge to the opponent. As most political systems use some type of violent sanctions against dissidents, through police, prisons and the military forces, these are likely also to be used against the nonviolent challengers. In acute social and political conflicts the actionists must often pay a price in the struggle to achieve their objectives. Freedom is not free.

Once the opponent has decided to use repression, the questions are: what means of repression will he use, will they help him to achieve his objectives, and what will be the response of the nonviolent group and others to the repression. We turn first to the means of repression. Some of the sanctions which the opponent may use will be official while some may be unofficially encouraged. Sometimes there will be threats; other times the sanctions will be simply carried out. Some sanctions involve open police or military action (i.e., repression), others more indirect means of control and manipulation, and some even nonviolent sanctions. Many of the means of repression are also used in quite different conflict situations.

The sanctions the nonviolent actionist can expect will take many forms and involve different degrees of pressure. They may be discussed under eight general headings:

A. Control of communication and information

These methods will include: censorship of all means of public information and communication; suppression of particular newspapers, books, leaflets, radio and television broadcasts, etc.; dissemination of false news reports; severance of private communication between members and sections of the nonviolent group, as by intercepting mail and telegrams; and tapping telephone conversations and the like.

B. Psychological pressures

Although many other methods also have psychological influence, certain methods are intended to be primarily psychological. These include verbal abuse as name-calling, swearing, slander and rumors; ostracism; efforts to obtain defections and changes in plans by bribing key people, directly or indirectly, as with job offers; vague threats of various types of severe action if certain things are, or are not, done; threats of specific brutal actions; making "examples" of a few by severe punishment; retaliation against families and friends of resisters or other innocent people; and finally, severe mental pressures.

C. Confiscation

These methods include confiscation of property, funds, literature, records, correspondence, offices and equipment.

D. Economic sanctions

These range widely, from those imposed by courts and officials to popular economic boycotts. They include direct or indirect efforts to deprive nonviolent actionists of their livelihood, especially by dismissal from jobs and blacklisting; restrictions on trade, commerce, materials, supplies and the like; cutting off utilities, as water, gas and fuel; cutting off food supplies; consumer and other economic boycotts; individual fines and collective fines.

E. Bans and prohibitions

These are government orders which prohibit certain types of acts and activities. They include orders declaring organizations illegal; the banning of public meetings or assemblies; interfering with travel of nonviolent actionists; curfews; and court injunctions against certain behavior associated with the struggle.

F. Arrests and imprisonment

These are the sanctions which are commonly used to punish disobedience of the State's laws and regulations. They include: arrests for serious and minor charges related to the nonviolent action; arrests and legal harrassing on unrelated or imagined charges, as traffic violations; arrests of negotiators, delegations and leaders; and prison sentences of varying lengths.

G. Exceptional restrictions

These methods involve unusual or more severe forms of detention and restrictions on normal public liberties. They include: new laws or regulations to deal with the defiance; suspension of *habeas corpus* and other rights; declaration of martial law and states of emergency; mobilization of special forces, as "special constables" or "deputy sheriffs," and use of army reserves, territorial army, national or state guards, or other military units normally assigned to other duties; forced labor, as in prison camps and road gangs; prosecutions on charges more serious than for the simple act of resistance, as for conspiracy, and incitement; conscription of nonviolent actionists into armed forces, where they will be subject to court martial for indiscipline; mass expulsion of the resisting population; exile or other removal of leaders; detention without trial; and concentration camps.

H. Direct physical violence

These methods include official beatings and whippings; rough physical treatment, including manhandling, pushing, unofficial beatings including encouragement or permission for third parties (as hoodlums) to attack the nonviolent group physically; use of dogs, horses and vehicles against demonstrators; use of water from fire hoses, such instruments as electric cattle prodders and the like; bombings and other destruction of homes, offices and other buildings; individual assassinations; torture; shooting, discriminate or indiscriminate, of demonstrators or general population; executions, open or secret, individual, group, or mass; and bombings by airplanes.

Almost all of these have already been used in some cases of nonviolent action, and any of them—and others—could be used in extreme cases in the future. The amount and type of repression used by the opponent will vary with his perception of the conflict situation, the issues involved, his understanding of the nature of nonviolent action, and the anticipated results of the repression both in restoring "order" and in alienating needed cooperation, support, etc., of others. In small local cases of nonviolent action, the number of means of repression may be few, while in large movements a considerable number may be involved. In some situations the opponent may operate on the basis of an overall strategy against the nonviolent movement, while in other cases specific means of repression may be selected or improvised to deal with particular nonviolent acts only.

Seifert has pointed out that the severity of repression frequently tends to increase significantly as the campaign continues and as earlier forms of repression prove ineffective. For example, when the first Quakers came to Massachusetts Bay Colony in defiance of Puritan legal prohibitions, they were immediately imprisoned and deported. Later they were whipped in addition. Then ear-cropping was instituted, and finally the Quakers were banished under threat of execution. Between 1659 and 1661 four Quakers were hanged, including a woman. Over two and a half centuries later, when woman suffragists first picketed the White House while Woodrow Wilson was President, they were not interfered with officially for nearly six months, but after several stages of escalation of repression, prison sentences of six and seven months were given out. [71]

The introduction of special laws, edicts and ordinances to deal with various forms of nonviolent action is nothing new. Confronted with the noncooperation of the bakers of the city of Ephesus in the second century A.D., the Roman Proconsul of Asia issued an edict: "I therefore order the Bakers' Union not to hold meetings as a faction nor to be leaders in recklessness, but strictly to obey the regulations made for the general welfare and to supply the city unfailingly with the labor essential for breadmaking." He threatened violators with arrest and a "fitting penalty." [72] Very strong Roman laws against strikes were issued about the middle of the fifth century, A.D. [73]

In modern times, strikes for the purpose of achieving wage increases and improved conditions were illegal for decades in many countries, and in many cases antistrike laws were only repealed after considerable struggle. Laws against economic boycotts are still on the books of many American states.

There is also a record of laws against various types of nonviolent action used to achieve political objectives. In a direct attempt to deal with economic resistance by the American colonists, Lord North sponsored bills which became law in March and April 1775, which provided that until the nonimportation campaign ended and peaceful conditions of business were restored, certain of the provinces would not be permitted to trade with any part of the world except the British Isles and the British West Indies, and after a short time with minor exceptions, those provinces would be prohibited from sending out fishing fleets also. One type of disruption of trade was to be matched by another type, to be backed by the means at the disposal of the British government.[74] One measure which Austria used to counter Hungarian economic nonviolent resistance around 1860 was to issue an ordinance declaring "exclusive trading" illegal.[75]

When the French and Belgian occupiers of the Ruhr were confronted with German government-sponsored nonviolent resistance, they issued innumerable regulations. "Soon there was nothing which was not forbidden or punishable under some regulation issued by General Degoutte or one of his subordinates," writes Grimm, who enumerates a multitude of aspects of life to which they applied. He concludes: ". . . finally [there was] a law for the suppression of passive resistance, which put an end to free speech and threatened with five years' imprisonment anyone evincing doubts about the justice and validity of the orders and directions issued by the occupation authorities. General Degoutte's decrees reached the remarkable number of 174."[76]

Two special laws were enacted in response to the South African 1952 civil disobedience movement. One of these, the Public Safety Act, No. 3 of 1953, provided the machinery for the introduction of wide emergency powers, the reorganization of the police and a change in their functions. This Act specified the conditions under which police violence might be used, and enabled the police to act before, rather than after, the event.[77] The other, the Criminal Law Amendment Act, No. 8, of 1953, is probably one of the first legislative acts created especially to deal with civil disobedience (as distinct from other forms of nonviolent action). This Act provides:

> Whenever any person is convicted of an offence which is proved to have been committed by way of protest or in support of any campaign for the repeal or modification of any law or the variation or limitation of the application or administration of any law, the court convicting him may, notwithstanding anything to the contrary in any other law contained, sentence him to (a) a fine not exceeding three hundred pounds; or (b) inprisonment for a period not exceeding three years; or (c) a whipping not exceeding ten strokes; or (d) both such fine and such imprisonment; or (e) both such fine and such whipping; or (f) both such imprisonment and such a whipping.[78]

Kuper reports that even more drastic penalties are imposed by the Act on persons convicted of promoting or assisting offenses by way of protest against any law.[79] In actual practice it was not necessary to use the new powers bestowed on the government by the new laws. The mere assumption of these powers had an effect.

Another Act already on the books, the Supression of Communism Act, could also be used against nonviolent action since charges of promoting "Communism" amazingly included "unlawful acts or omissions, actual or threatened, aimed at bringing about any [sic!] political, industrial, social or economic change." There were, of course, other South African laws against nonviolent action, such as the Native Labour (Settlement of Disputes) Act, which made strikes by Africans illegal.[80] One of the new laws decreed shortly after the end of World War II and the beginning of the occupation of the Eastern Zone of Germany by Soviet troops was one against "incitement to War, Murder and Non-cooperation."[81] The point is simply that special laws against various forms of nonviolent action are nothing new, but have occurred under diverse historical and political conditions.

Various other countermeasures may be used by the opponent along with repression. These differ widely, depending on the situation and forms of nonviolent action being fought. Countermeasures taken by the British government during the 1926 General Strike included a government newspaper, advance stockpiling of food, coal and fuel and the organization of alternative supplies and transportation. An unofficial Organization for the Maintenance of Supplies, said to include about one hundred thousand ready volunteers, was set up well in advance and its control was handed over to the government just before the outbreak of the strike.[82] The French during the Ruhr struggle also used various counter means to control the resistance as well as strictly violent repression. For example, they disbanded the police force of Essen and banished its members.[83] In other cases the opponent regime has responded by changes in its own structures and command system. This was illustrated during the February Revolution of 1917 by the Tsar's appointment of General Ivanov as Commander-in-Chief of the Petrograd garrison with full powers even over government ministers.[84] Very different countermeasures were used in South Vietnam in 1963 when the Diem regime in combatting Buddhist resistance attempted to show "popular support" for the government; rival pro-government Buddhist organizations were set up and "elections" were held which produced 99.8 percent of the votes for prominent government personalities.[85]

Some people (including certain pacifists) have seen the opponent's violent repression as created by the nonviolent group through its radical action; hence these people have often preferred milder means short of direct action. This reaction is, however, based upon both an inadequate understanding of the operation of the nonviolent technique and upon a very superficial view of political violence and the social system in which it is prominent. The absence of open violence by the ruler does not mean that violence is absent. Nor, if violence is the opponent's reaction to nonviolent action, does it mean that the nonviolent group created the violence. Rather, there is an intimate relationship between the kind of social system and the degree of violence the power holders in that system are prepared to use if it is challenged.

Political violence is not expressed only in beating, shooting or imprisoning people, but also in the readiness, threat and preparations to inflict such violence if the situation "requires" it. Political violence is also present in hierarchical political systems where status, wealth, effective decision-making and control are concentrated in an elite willing and able to use political violence to implement its will and to maintain dominance. In such a system, as long as the subordinates submit passively, there will be no need to implement the reserve capacity for violent repression and thus to show clearly the system's character and ultimate sanction. Nevertheless, the continuing domination by the elite through threats of violent sanctions for insubordination is from this perspective a case of constant political violence. Opponents of such systems describe them as "oppression," "exploitation," or "tyranny." In less extreme systems such as Western democracies, violence also remains the accepted sanction for dealing with law-breakers, insurrections, subversion, or external aggression.[86] The degree to which any particular political and social system depends for its existence upon covert or overt violence varies considerably. Where the degree of this dependence is small, where the citizens effectively influence and determine the government's policies, where there is confidence in ultimate sanctions other than violence for dealing with crises, there one can expect proportionately less violence in response to internal nonviolent action. Probably the chances of nonviolent action within the system will also be less. The converse would also follow.

When a system largely characterized by political violence is actively, albeit nonviolently, challenged, one can expect that the basic nature of that system will be more clearly revealed in the crisis than during less difficult times. The violence upon which the system depends is thus brought to the surface and revealed in unmistakable terms for all to see: it then becomes more possible to remove it.

In support of this view, Kuper argues that the 1952 response of hostility and violence from the South African whites to the civil disobedience had its roots in the nature of the oppressive system, which was revealed by nonviolent action: "The explanation of this violence lies in the nature of the domination itself." The original "naked force of conquest" had been translated into the sanctity of law. When the subordinate group challenged *any* law, even a trivial one, this was seen as "rebellion," and increased "force" was applied to suppress the rebellion. Kuper points out that civil disobedience brought the violence behind the law and the domination into actual operation. "Satyagraha strips this sanctity from the laws, and compels the application of sanctions, thus converting domination again to naked force." The nonviolent challenge had not created, but only revealed the violence. "Force is implicit in white domination: the resistance campaign made it explicit." [87] Kuper's observations on this point are consistent with Gandhi's conclusions. In Gandhi's view this process of making the violence inherent in the system explicit could be an important step in the destruction or radical alteration of the system. It could alienate support for the regime among its usual supporters and agents, promote greater solidarity and resistance within the subordinate group, arouse the opinion of third parties against the oppressor, and demonstrate that not even violent repression can compel the resisters to submit.

April Carter, an English direct actionist and political scientist, also supports this interpretation of violent repression against nonviolent actionists. She writes that civil disobedience is sometimes intended ". . . to force the opponent into overt use of the means of violence at his command," which reveals to the people and to the world at large the degree "to which the regime is oppressive and prepared to use violence to maintain itself." In that light, ". . . the true character of the South African Government was revealed at Sharpeville, the true character of segregation in the Deep South when the Freedom Riders were mobbed." The social violence inherent in *Apartheid* and segregation was made clear by those events, an important step toward changing the status quo. [88]

If one is not familiar with the workings of nonviolent action, the enumeration of the many possible means of repression and realization of the severe character of many of these, may prove rather staggering. It may then be difficult to see how one could hope for effectiveness from this technique. For example, during the Algerian War, Algerian nationalist leaders were asked why they had chosen to rely on political terrorism and guerrilla tactics instead of on massive nonviolent noncooperation. They replied that they had indeed tried strikes and boycotts which had been carried our relatively effectively. The French had not, however, responded nonviolently but with the use of military might and Algerian people had been injured. Therefore, they said, the Algerians, too, had turned to political violence. But, we may ask, if the nonviolent action had been so ineffective and harmless to the established system, why was the repression so harsh? Why should the French authorities (or anyone else) bother to repress actions which are supposedly so impotent?

The fact is, of course, that while it is true that the severity of the repression may be out of proportion to the seriousness of a threat, the repeated application of repression which has occurred against nonviolent action in Algeria, South Africa, Nazi Germany, India, the Soviet Union, East Germany, the Deep South, England, occupied Norway and many other places, is very strong evidence that nonviolent action does frequently pose a serious threat to the established order. This repression is a confirmation of and a tribute to the power of nonviolent action. Refusal to submit to this repression while maintaining nonviolent discipline is crucial if the desired shift in policies and power relationships is to be achieved.

The opponent's repression may succeed in defeating the nonviolent actionists and in restoring passive submission, as has happened in various cases. Whether this happens will in large degree be determined by the nonviolent actionists' response; if they become frightened and weaken in their resolve, then, just as in military combat, the front lines will fall back and the whole front will be threatened.

However, repression will not necessarily cause a collapse of nonviolent action. As was pointed out in Chapter One, if sanctions are to be effective, they must operate on the minds of the subjects, and produce fear and willingness to obey. However, these necessary intervening processes may not occur because of the nonviolent actionists' lack of fear, or because of their deliberate control of fear, or because of their commitment to some overriding loyalty or objective; when fear does not control the mind the repression may not succeed. Exponents of nonviolent action have stressed the limits of repression in obtaining submission and obedience. In 1917, Gandhi for example said that tyrannical rulers could not effectively use violent force against a nonviolent actionist who continued to refuse his consent and submission: ". . . without his concurrence they cannot make him do their will." [89] Since the ruler's sanctions are not effective in restoring submission and obedience unless the will of the nonviolent actionist is changed, the repression is not necessarily effective. It remains possible for the nonviolent actionists to achieve their objectives. "Nothing is more irritating and, in the final analysis, harmful to a government," wrote Nehru, "than to have to deal with people who will not bend to its will whatever the consequences."[90]

The opponent faces an additional problem in making repression effective: the means of repression are more appropriate to deal with violent opposition than with nonviolent action. Since, however, nonviolent action operates quite differently from violent action, repression used against the nonviolent group may fail to produce the desired results, and may even weaken the opponent, as we shall see. In contrast, when a movement of violent terrorism, or a military revolt is met with violent repression the two conflicting groups are applying essentially the same means of struggle. Violent repression then has a certain logic and a greater chance of effectiveness and is more likely to be justified in the eyes of the general population and third parties. This is not true when one side instead struggles nonviolently. This is not to say that violent resistance poses no threat to a regime, or that violent rebellion is always easily squashed, but it is to say that nonviolent struggle can be more difficult to deal with and that violent repression against it is less likely to be effective than against violent resistance.

One of the ways in which nonviolent action functions is to exhaust the opponents' means of repression and demonstrate their impotence. In this, the actionists' attitude of fearlessness is crucial. Without fear of sanctions, the sanctions lose their power to produce submission. The actionists may therefore—instead of fearing the repression—openly defy laws, seek imprisonment and may even ask the opponent to do his worst. The result may be to make repression impotent.

The peculiar problems of repression against a nonviolent movement were felt by the British in India during the 1930-31 struggle:

> . . . during the year there were violent disturbances and acts of terrorism in many parts of the country, but these the forces of law and order in India as elsewhere, were trained to counter. What perplexed them was the mobilization of inertia, the large crowds silently awaiting punishment, the well organized processions refusing to yield in face of attack.[91]

When people deliberately court arrest by practicing civil disobedience, imprisonment ceases to be a deterrent to their defiance. Indeed, imprisoned nonviolent resisters are sometimes more of a difficulty for the opponent than if they had been left safely in their homes. Other specific means of repression and other specific methods of action by the nonviolent group present their own difficulties for the opponent. Continued defiance by nonviolent noncooperation and intervention by hundreds, thousands, hundreds of thousands, and even millions of people despite the opponent's repression can create a political nightmare for an autocratic ruler. Not only is his repression then ineffective; it may even multiply the problems created by the nonviolent challenge.

PERSISTENCE

Faced with repression, nonviolent actionists have only one acceptable response: to overcome they must persist in their action and refuse to submit or retreat. As Gandhi put it, "In the code of the satyagrahi, there is no such thing as surrender to brute force." [92] Without willingness to face repression as the price of struggle, the nonviolent action movement cannot hope to succeed. Kuper argues, for example, that unwillingness to accept the vastly increased sanctions for violation of the laws in question was an important reason for the collapse of the 1952 Defiance Campaign. [93]

The opponent applying the repression is likely to be a believer in the effectiveness of political violence and to assume that repression, if severe enough, will produce submission. Therefore, as we have noted, once repression has begun, the opponent is likely to increase it when it is not immediately effective. [94] An unconsidered reaction by persons seeking to minimize suffering might then be to halt the nonviolent challenge and submit, or to seek a "compromise," or in effect a sell-out. This is a very shortsighted reaction, however. Such behavior confirms the opponent in his belief in the efficacy of repression, and encourages him to become increasingly brutal by showing him that sufficient cruelty will bring the nonviolent action to an end. Hence, stopping the movement in order to reduce repression while the actionists are still capable of continuing the struggle is likely in the long run to contribute to an increase in the extent and severity of repression against nonviolent action. Furthermore, a collapse of the movement at this stage will make it impossible to bring into operation the mechanisms of change upon which nonviolent action depends for success. It is necessary and possible at this point to break the usual repression-fear-submission pattern, that is, of repression producing fear, fear bringing submission, and submission causing a continuation of the objectionable policies or the intolerable regime.

Fearlessness, or deliberate control of fear, discussed in Chapter Nine is especially important at this stage of the struggle. Standing firm at this point will make it possible to refute stereotypes of the subordinate group. One of these may be that they are cowards: for example, " . . . that 'Negroes, like animals, will be scared away by a show of force.'" [95] Firmness will make it possible for mass noncooperation to produce its coercive effects. Under certain circumstances persistence may also contribute to sympathy and respect for the defiant nonviolent actionists. [96]

Submission to violence is contrary to the nature of the nonviolent technique. Nonviolently resisting volunteers must be able to stand against apparently overwhelming physical force. Throughout history there have been many instances of an individual or a small number of men standing firmly for their convictions, struggling to achieve a wider social end, or fighting to defend their people or principles against "impossible" odds. Defiance without retaliation may enable the nonviolent actionists to remove the policy or regime to which they object and to make the repression impotent. "Strength does not come from physical capacity. It comes from an indomitable will," [97] wrote Gandhi. "No power on earth can make a person do a thing against his will. Satyagraha is a direct result of the recognition of this great law . . ." [98]

There are various examples of nonviolent actionists standing firm in face of repression. At Vorkuta, for example, when the Russian authorities on July 20, 1953, arrested the Pit No. 1 Strike Committee (recognized as the central leadership) even before the prisoners could initiate their strike, the prisoners' response was to elect a new committee. The strike was thus merely postponed for twelve hours. Later, when the Strike Committee went to meet officials for negotiations but never returned, the strikers nevertheless continued. [99] When, during the Montgomery boycott, white officials resorted to mass arrests and private persons resorted to bombings, the result was a demonstration of increased determination and fearlessness by the Afro-Americans. [100] "The members of the opposition . . . ," wrote Martin Luther King, "thought they were dealing with a group who could be cajoled or forced to do whatever the white man wanted them to do. They were not aware that they were dealing with Negroes who had been freed from fear. And so every move they made proved to be a mistake." [101] When the Ku Klux Klan rode through the Negro section, hoping to repeat its usual tactic of striking terror into the Negroes who would then lock their doors and darken their houses, they met with a surprise. The Negroes kept the lights on, the doors open, remained casual, as though watching a circus parade, some even waved to the cars. Nonplussed, the Klan disappeared into the night. [102]

The Quakers who kept coming with their religious message to Puritan Massachusetts Bay Colony were undeterred by deportations, whippings, imprisonments and even death penalties, as Seifert reports:

In spite of increasing severity, the same persons came back again and again "to look the bloody laws in the face." Although about sixty

PART THREE: DYNAMICS

years of age, Elizabeth Hooton came to Boston at least six times, being expelled each time, and was four times whipped through several towns out of the jurisdiction. Even the death penalty proved to be no deterrent. While William Leddra was being tried for his life, Wenlock Christison, who had already been banished upon pain of death, walked calmly into the courtroom. Then while Christison was on trial, Edward Wharton, who had also been ordered to leave the colony or forfeit his life, wrote from his home in Salem that he was still there. Such a succession of applications for execution identified a people who were not to be turned aside by any terrors their persecutors might devise. [103]

There are many other examples of defiance in face of repression. In November 1905 the Central Bureau of the Union of Railroad Workers in tsarist Russia defiantly called for anti-government strikes in retaliation for the court-martial sentencing to death of a railroad engineer named Sokolov and others for their participation in a recent strike at Kushka Station on the Central Asian Railroad. [104] Reitlinger gives a large measure of credit for the saving of over 75 per cent of the Jews in France from the Nazi extermination plan to the refusal of Frenchmen to submit and comply in face of Gestapo terror and other intimidation: "the final solution . . . failed in France because of the sense of decency in the common man, who, having suffered the utmost depths of self-humiliation, learnt to conquer fear." [105] Although Russian tanks had been roaming the streets of Halle, East Germany, and the People's Police had been firing warning shots into the air, an estimated sixty thousand to eighty thousand people attended a mass antigovernment meeting in the market place on June 17, 1953. [106]

Examples of this refusal to submit to repression, and this assertion of fearlessness, could be multiplied. It is especially important that the leaders of the nonviolent struggle be, and be seen to be, courageous and unbowed in face of repression and threats of future punishments. Albert Luthuli's compliance with various restrictions imposed by the South African government, which removed him from active political work without placing him in prison, is therefore an example which ought *not* to be followed, and is a response to repression which may encourage submission by others and help to discredit nonviolent struggle as a militant and effective technique. [107]

Courageous persistence must, of course, continue to be expressed through disciplined nonviolent behavior if the movement is not to be seriously weakened. This leaves room for, and indeed often requires, flexible and imaginative responses suitable to the particular situation. In various cases the nonviolent actionists may make certain tactical moves to avoid unnecessary provocation of more severe repression. Miller writes, for example:

> We must be careful not to corner our opponent . . . Firmness should never become dogmatic rigidity. Although nonviolence places a premium upon the capacity of the nonviolent cadre to endure suffering, each team of cadres should have sufficient tactical flexibility to be able to choose whether to extricate the individual members from a catastrophic situation or, if this alternative is foreclosed, to endure martyrdom with a composure that may cause their attackers to repent afterward. [108]

Sometimes nonviolent actionists may alter their behavior at the moment when repression is likely to begin or has just begun. For example, in 1959, when ordered to disperse by police who prepared to make a baton charge, African women demonstrators at Ixopo, South Africa, went down on their knees and began to pray. In that instance at least the baton charge was not made and the "police hung around helplessly." [109]

Sometimes certain methods of action will by their nature be more difficult to deal with by repression and less likely to put resisters to the test of withstanding severe brutalities. Some strike leaders from the East German Rising concluded that strikers who had stayed at home or had conducted a stay-in strike at their jobs were more difficult for the regime to cope with than demonstrators in the streets who could usually be easily dispersed by tanks. Ebert calls this "the avoidance of mass confrontations, which is not the same thing as renouncing resistance." [110] Nonviolent actionists or others may appeal to the opponent's troops and police urging them to restrict their repression in some way. Such appeals were planned in Berlin in June 1953, but both a prepared broadcast in Russian to members of the Soviet occupation forces by the acting mayor of West Berlin, Ernst Reuter, and appeals by Russian émigrés at the border with East Berlin to Russian soldiers not to use violence against demonstrating workers, were blocked by Western officials in Berlin. [111] Flexibility and alternative responses to repression while continuing the struggle may at times depend upon the recognition that in a given conflict situation victory will not come quickly and the campaign may be protracted. [112]

Any possible variations in tactics in response to repression must not, however, alter the basic nonviolent counteraction to repression: persistence, determination, nonviolent discipline and an end to fearful cringing before the opponent's threats and punishments. With this response, change is possible, for "the grip of fear" is broken, [113] and "an immediate and relentless and peaceful struggle" is under way. Those words are from the call for resistance issued by Maxim Gorky and nine others shortly before their arrest the day after Bloody Sunday, 1905.[114]

THE NECESSITY OF SUFFERING

Facing repression with persistence and courage means that the nonviolent actionists must be prepared to endure the opponent's sanctions without flinching. The nonviolent actionists must be prepared to suffer in order to advance their cause. Some people may interpret this suffering in a metaphysical or spiritual sense, but this view is not necessary for the technique; it is sufficient if the volunteers see something of the contribution which withstanding repression makes to achieving their objectives. Nonviolent action has long been regarded as a "two-edged Sword"—a phrase used in 1770 by Governor Wright of Georgia to describe the colonists' nonimportation program.[115] While the analogy is accurate, it is not complete, for it may imply that direct actionists are likely to suffer only when they use the nonviolent technique, instead of violence, or when they do nothing. This is of course not true.

Political violence, too, especially in the forms of civil wars, terrorist movements. guerrilla war, violent revolution and international wars, involves the risk of suffering and usually high casualties. Accounts of certain nonviolent campaigns are sometimes gory with detailed descriptions of beatings and other brutal treatment of nonretaliating actionists, while histories of wars often cite casualties only in impersonal statistics. Such bloody events in nonviolent struggles are, of course, usually comparatively mild in both seriousness and extent compared with comparable scenes in major cases of political violence, accounts of which rarely describe in detail the human suffering which accompany them. Descriptions of brutalities incurred in nonviolent struggles are simply honest accounts of unpleasant events which for fairness should be balanced with equally detailed reports of suffering in violent conflicts. It is inappropriate for supporters of those violent means to object (as they sometimes do) to nonviolent action on the ground that somebody might get hurt. When only some form of direct action is judged to be an acceptable response to the situation, then suffering is an inherent consequence of that decision. The intelligent response is not to ask simply what means will most effectively release frustration and hatred. The likely consequences of violent action or of nonviolent action are also important.[116]

The fact that suffering is likely or inevitable with both violent and nonviolent action does not mean that there are no important differences.

Other questions remain, such as will there be more or less suffering with one technique or the other, and will the sacrifices incurred by use of each type of action really advance the long term objectives of the grievance group. There have been no careful comparative studies of casualties in violent and nonviolent struggles, but there are reasons for suggesting that both total casualties and suffering on both sides, and also those of only the nonviolent actionists and grievance group, are significantly less than when both sides use violence.

When both belligerents use violent methods, a pattern frequently occurs in which the violence of each side is met with counterviolence in a continuing cycle. Even without significant escalation in the severity and extent of its application, this process produces a continuing accumulation of violence, and of casualties and suffering until one side accedes. When, however, one side is fighting with a different, nonviolent, weapons system, the constant circle of violence is broken. Suffering will still occur, and at times it will be severe, but the substitution of nonviolent persistence for violent retaliation tends to reduce the severity of repression and to contribute in the long run to a reduction in political violence.

This break in the political violence cycle, produced by the willingness of the nonviolent group to accept nonretaliatory suffering as the price of achieving its goals, seems in that immediate struggle to reduce the casualties on both sides. Gregg, for example, argued in these terms:

> In the Indian struggle for independence, though I know of no accurate statistics, hundreds of thousands of Indians went to jail, probably not more than five hundred received permanent physical injuries, and probably not over eight thousand were killed immediately or died later from wounds. No British, I believe, were killed or wounded. Considering the importance and size of the conflict and the many years it lasted, these numbers are much smaller than they would have been if the Indians had used violence toward the British. [117]

There were, however, a few Indian policemen in British service killed in the conflict. But the total casualties were still very small, as compared with the 1857 Indian violent struggle against the British—the idea that Indians are somehow by nature nonviolent is just not true—or compared with the number of Algerian dead in the Algerian revolution against the French, estimated variously, but by some as high as nearly a million out of a population only ten times that size.

It also appears that the introduction of violence into a nonviolent struggle will increase the casualties. Bondurant writes: "A comparison of campaigns of civil disobedience which remained nonviolent with others in which satyagraha deteriorated into violence, indicates significantly greater incidence of injury and death in the latter cases." [118] In the series of strikes in Soviet prison camps, especially in 1953 and 1954, there appears to be a significant correlation between the degree of brutality used in repression and the casualties inflicted on the prisoners on the one hand, and the degree to which the prisoners remained nonviolent or resorted to serious violence against the prison camp officials, police and troops. [119] Nazi repression and retaliation for the two day strike in Amsterdam and nearby towns in protest against persecution of Jews were severe: several people were wounded in the streets; seven were killed on the second day; Himmler authorized brutalities and the arrest and deportation of one thousand strikers; over one hundred Communists and others suspected of instigating the strike were arrested; fines were imposed on Amsterdam and other municipalities; the mayors of Amsterdam and nearby Haarlem and Zaandam were dismissed and other Dutch officials were also accused of not making sufficient efforts to suppress the strike. [120] There seems no question however that a comparable two day violent Dutch uprising in the same area and by the same number of people would in light of Nazi actions elsewhere against violent resistance (Warsaw, for instance) have produced many times that number of dead, wounded and imprisoned.

In addition to human suffering, a variety of economic losses have also occurred during nonviolent resistance campaigns, as, for example, in the American colonists' struggles, and in the *Ruhrkampf*. Writing about the effects of the nonimportation movement in Boston in 1770, Samuel Adams said: "The Merchants in general have punctually abode by their Agreement, to their very great private loss." [121] Later, when the British closed the port of Boston in retaliation for the city's various and continued acts of defiance and noncooperation, it was not only the merchants who suffered economically. Hundreds of workmen were thrown out of jobs, and it proved necessary to find ways to feed the poor without giving in to the British. [122] However, the most severe example of economic suffering and dislocation accompanying nonviolent resistance is probably the *Ruhrkampf*. Much of the economic disruption of the German economy as a whole can be blamed, however, on the German government's decision to finance the resistance by unsupported paper money. [123] Within the Ruhr, shortages of milk in the cities endangered the health of children and of ill adults so severely that the death rate for children increased, and only evacuation of about a half million children to unoccupied Germany reduced their danger. Furthermore, in the occupied Ruhr district and the Rhineland, the number of unemployed reached two million out of a total population of about nine million. [124] An immense inflation took place throughout Germany with disastrous economic results.[125] But even in such a case, one does not have to be very imaginative to see that a military war for repossession of the territory (had Germany been then capable of it) could well have been still more disastrous economically, not only for the Ruhr which would have become a battleground but for all Germany because of the required financial expenditure, the likely destruction of the Ruhr's productive capacity, and the extreme loss of lives.

Not all suffering is the same, nor does it have the same effects. The suffering involved in nonviolent action has more in common with the suffering of certain violent resisters than with the suffering of helpless terrorized and submissive people. Accordingly, the results of suffering of courageous resisters are likely to differ radically from that of the submissive. Gandhi himself pointed to some instances of violence as being almost comparable to those of courageous nonviolence. These cases of violence involved great courage in defying overwhelming forces with very little or no hope of victory, and with the certainty of major suffering. A woman defending herself from rape, a single man (even with a sword) defending himself against a horde of fully armed bandits and killers, or the Poles who ". . . knew that they would be crushed to atoms, and yet they resisted the German hordes." All three cases, he said, had in common ". . . the refusal to bend before overwhelming might in the full knowledge that it means certain death."[126] Suffering endured in such courageous violence had more in common with suffering in nonviolent action than the latter had with that of the terrified, passive victim of brutalities. However, this is not, of course, to say that the social and political results would be the same with equally courageous violent and nonviolent resistance.

In common with participants in violent revolution and war, the nonviolent actionists must be willing in extreme crises to risk their lives.[127] Gandhi repeatedly emphasized that rather than submitting to the violence of the opponent, the nonviolent actionist must be willing to make severe sacrifices including, if need be, his own life.[128] Those planning nonviolent action will need to consider the degree of suffering the volunteers are willing to endure, as this may determine which methods of action can be used and how firmly the volunteers will be able to defy the opponent's repression. If the degree of expected tolerable suffering is low, then the volunteers may require further preparation, or they will have to limit themselves to milder forms unlikely to require serious sacrifice.[129]

People may remain nonviolent, not for moral or ideological reasons, but because they realize this behavior is necessary for the practical operation of the technique. "Without suffering," wrote Gandhi, "it is not possible to attain freedom."[130] It was from this perspective that Motilal

Nehru, father of the late Prime Minister, declared on the eve of his own imprisonment in 1930:

> We have not yet paid one hundredth part of the price of freedom and must go forward with unflinching step defying the enemy and all the cruel refinements of torture that he is capable of inventing. Do not worry for those who have been taken. See to it that every man, woman and child left behind gives a good account of himself or herself to the nation. [131]

This persistence through repression and willingness to suffer will have a number of effects. Two are: 1) the numerical or quantitative (sometimes almost mechanical) effect of many defiant subjects refusing to obey despite repression on the opponent's ability to control the situation and to maintain his policies, and 2) the psychological or qualitative (or moral) effect of the sacrifices on the opponent, his supporters, third parties and others. Both of these are complicated processes; frequently their operation depends on intervening processes, and in overcoming problems in accurate perception. We shall return to these effects and processes in the final chapters.

In many conflicts the repression and other counter action will be relatively mild or moderate. The intensity and extent of suffering among the actionists and the grievance group will therefore be within the range which can be withstood without extreme difficulty. However, in some cases there will be brutalities.

FACING BRUTALITIES

Brutalities may arise from three main general sources.

First, the regime may be one in which brutality is commonplace. Terror may be used against all opponents, real or imaginary, in an effort to make the regime omnipotent. Such regimes are usually described as tyrannical or, in extreme forms, totalitarian.

Second, a nontyrannical regime may, when effectively and fundamentally challenged, react with brutal repression. This may follow from a decision that only drastic action can crush the resisters (especially if milder measures have failed) or from exasperation at the actionists' defiant behavior or refusal to submit in face of less severe repression.

Finally, without orders from the regime, local officers, or individuals, in the army, police, or even the general public, may on their own initiative perpetrate brutalities on the nonviolent actionists. These brutalities may result from sadistic personalities, from frustration produced by the defiance, or from inner conflicts aroused by the situation and the qualities of the nonviolent actionists.

The first two sources may be described as official brutality and the third as unofficial brutality.

A. Official and unofficial brutalities

There must be no illusions. In some cases nonviolent people have not only been beaten and cruelly treated but killed, not only accidentally or as isolated punishment, but in deliberate massacres. Refraining from violence is not a guarantee of safety, although contrary to popular opinion it is arguable that nonviolent behavior has better "survival value" than violence. There are disturbing cases of major killings. The 1919 British massacre of at least 379 Indians (and wounding of 1,137) meeting peaceably in Jalianwala Bagh, Amritsar, is one such case. [132]

There have been some massacres of pacifists, although not always when engaged in nonviolent action. In the context of Ohio frontier wars and raids in 1782, two hundred white frontiersmen with full deliberation slaughtered a group of pacifist native American Indians, converts to the Moravian Church which held to nonresistant pacifism. These were wrongly believed to have killed a woman and her five children in a raid on a settler's farm. Twenty-nine men, twenty-seven women and thirty-four children (including at least twelve babies) were slaughtered two by two; almost all were then scalped by the whites. [133] Luthuli reports that in South Africa in 1924 "a hundred Hottentots were butchered for refusing to pay an incomprehensible tax on dogs." [134] It should be pointed out that the massacre of the Moravian Indians took place in the context of warfare, and involved mistaken identity. The victims were not engaged in nonviolent action as defined in this study although they were nonviolent. The case is included here simply to acknowledge that such events have occurred against peaceful people.

But the Indians in Amritsar were holding a peaceful protest meeting and the Hottentots were refusing to pay a tax—both methods of nonviolent action. The shootings on Bloody Sunday are another example. Massacres of nonviolent actionists can take place. Such killings also occur, probably much more frequently, when people resist violently, and even people who passively submit to their oppressors may die as victims of their policies and brutalities. There is no guarantee of safety as long as the underlying conditions contributing to brutality continue. If there is no immediate way to guarantee protection from brutalities, it is at least wise to be aware that they may occur against nonviolent actionists and to determine how to respond to them in accordance with the technique's requirements for effectiveness.

The more tyrannical the regime and system generally, the more probable will be extreme brutalities against the nonviolent actionists. Among all regimes and systems which to any considerable degree depend on violence, the common response when they are challenged, even though by nonviolent means, will be violence against the dissenters. As Bose put it, "the violence of the rulers, which was formerly implicit or camouflaged, now becomes explicit." [135] The degree of severity of repression and of brutalities will vary considerably. Frequently, the response may be quite out of proportion to the seriousness of the challenge. As Hiller pointed out: ". . . the stronger party (especially when it is irresponsible) tends to respond violently to a mild act of resistance or of assertion by the weaker, and especially by a despised party." [136]

Early in the conflict the opponent may have interpreted the actionists' nonviolence as cowardice or stupidity, only to discover it was neither. Continued nonviolent defiance may have proven to be difficult to crush and it may have come to threaten the opponent's continued dominance and control. When the opponent's will is thwarted, violent retaliation is a very likely response. [137] Brutalities may then be deliberate, as we have seen. Seifert has pointed to this type of motivation for brutalities: "This buildup in brutality may be the result of normal and rather rational goal-directed behavior." To the opponent, the established social order, institutions and policies may be good, and he may see the defeat of the resisters as the only way to protect them. "Since, so far as he knows, the only way to accomplish this defeat is to increase severity, he . . . becomes more repressive. This seems to him to be the best possible expedient among the choices available . . ." He is, "given his presuppositions . . . acting in a rational, defensible manner." [138] "Insofar as nonviolence is interpreted as a sign of weakness, it 'makes sense' to increase hostile pressure in the expectation that this will cause collapse of the resisters' cause." [139]

The degree of brutality inflicted as official policy will vary. It may be influenced by the degree to which the opponent understands what is happening, including his comprehension of the dynamics of nonviolent action, and the process of political *jiu-jitsu,* which will be discussed in Chapter Twelve. Confusion, uncertainty and fear will increase the likelihood of official brutalities.

Unauthorized and unofficial brutalities may also be committed on nonviolent actionists. Sometimes highly disproportionate repression may be quite accidental, especially when police or troops are threatened or attacked by undisciplined persons or groups, as was apparently the origin of the famous Boston Massacre of 1770. [140] Brutalities may be committed deliberately, although unofficially, for a variety of motives. A paternalistic ruler who has been rejected by his subjects may commit brutalities.

> Within a paternalistic, imperialist framework he may have expressed considerable kindness to a subject race so long as its members stayed "in their place." He may even have thought he was requiring participation in God's own true religion, an essential to the eternal salvation of the resister. [141]

Such an opponent, shocked at having his supposed "good" acts denounced as "evil" by the subordinates, and his egoism revealed and rejected, may resort to extreme acts. "When anyone strips away our cherished self-images and exposes what we really are, he invites punishment." [142] This is closely associated with the wider phenomenon of status-usurpation by the nonviolent actionists.

The agents of repression, and the dominant group in general, may see the nonviolent actionists of the subordinate group as behaving in ways they have no "right" to behave. That is, they are no longer acting like subordinates, but have behaved like equals, no longer cowed and submissive, but erect and insistent. One Deep South store manager faced with a sit-in declared, "Who do these niggers think they are?" [143] Speaking of self-suffering produced by nonwhite civil disobedience in South Africa, Kuper argues that one reason it may alienate sympathy of the whites is that "there is a quality of impudence about it, of status-usurpation, when looked at from the point of view of the dominant group." [144] This, too, may be conducive to brutalities.

The individual policemen or soldiers and the lower rank officers may be in a very difficult position, which may press them toward extreme actions. Not only are they used to having people obey them in such situations, but they are themselves required to obey and carry out orders from their superiors. If they fail to do so, they may be subjected to reprimands, sanctions and withholding of promotions. They may have been given orders to prevent certain actions by the nonviolent group, or to disperse and halt the action if it has already begun. With the nonviolent group remaining fearless, refusing to obey their orders and standing firm, the police, or troops, may find their ability to cope with the situation by the usual permitted means of action blocked. Fearing the consequences of a failure to carry out their orders, the men and lower officers may in desperation or frustration resort to extraordinary means in an effort to complete the tasks commanded by their superiors.

When, despite normal sanctions and repression, the actionists remain fearless, continue their defiance while remaining nonviolent and refusing to be provoked into retaliation, the opponent's police, troops and the like are likely to become frustrated and irritated. Such behavior, in which people neither fear nor obey them, drastically reduces the ability of such agents to control the situation and to carry out their duties. In addition, as we have noted, they are likely to feel insecure when due deference is not given to their position. Irritation and inadequacy may lead to brutality. Seifert also describes this factor:

> When measures taken against resisters have proved ineffectual, and when an opponent faces a personal loss of status or threat to his personality, he may lay on all the harder. Feeling powerless and being unable to tolerate such a feeling of impotence, he resorts to force to give himself the illusion of strength. [145]

This seems to have happened in India in 1930-31. [146]

In his autobiography, Nehru describes an earlier occasion in 1928 when he and other nonviolent demonstrators were beaten seriously by both foot police and a large number of cavalry or mounted police. Some Indians were permanently injured but, though badly beaten and wounded, Nehru recovered fully. He wrote:

> But the memory that endures with me far more than that of the beating itself, is that of many of the faces of those policemen, and especially of the officers, who were attacking us. Most of the real beating and battering was done by European sergeants, the Indian rank and file were milder in their methods. And those faces, full of hate and blood-lust, almost mad, with no trace of sympathy or touch of humanity! [147]

On occasion it will be private individuals who commit brutalities. Such attacks sometimes occurred during lunch counter sit-ins in the United States South in 1960. One such instance was against high school anti-segregation sit-inners in Portsmouth, Virginia. The student sit-inners had not expected such violence and lacked both specific instructions and training to meet it. Hence, they finally reacted with violent retaliation. It started on February 15, 1960, when a group of young white hoodlums arrived on the scene to provoke violence and attack the sit-inners and other Negro youths. A participant, Edward Rodman, writes:

> Outside [of the store] the [white] boy stood in the middle of the street, daring any Negro to cross a certain line. He then pulled a car

chain and claw hammer from his pocket and started swinging the chain in the air.

He stepped up his taunting with the encouragement of others. When we did not respond, he became so infuriated that he struck a Negro boy in the face with the chain. The boy kept walking. Then in utter frustration the white boy picked up a street sign and threw it on a Negro girl. [148]

In other cases, brutalities may at times take place as a consequence of an inner moral or psychological conflict within the individual committing them, a conflict produced at least in part by the behavior of the nonviolent actionists. [149] Disturbed, consciously or unconsciously, by the challenge of the nonviolent group, their claims and behavior, and by the acts against them he is expected to perform, the individual agent may seek to dismiss this inner conflict or to assert his loyalty to the opponent by extra vigor in repression. Sometimes it is the situation which Seifert describes: ". . . he knows that the resisters are right, but he cannot bear the knowledge. Therefore he represses it and strikes those who irritate his conscience." [150] On other occasions, he may still think the opponent right, but may find himself inflicting punishment which he knows is reprehensible, especially against nonviolent persons:

But he has too much emotional capital invested in his policy to admit he has been wrong . . . When the opponent doubts the defensibility of terror, he may intensify it as a way of convincing himself that he was right all along. He may beat the more to try to avoid a feeling of guilt for those already beaten. [151]

In addition, some of the extreme aggression against the nonviolent group may be the result of their providing, apparently, a safe group on which to vent aggressions against other, known or unknown, persons or conditions. [152] Unless and until the nonviolent behavior of the actionists is perceived as bravery and strength, some persons may see it as weakness and therefore express irrational hostility because of their own inadequacies, as Seifert points out:

Some persons are basically cowardly, but put on an outer show of bravado. When they see action which they interpret as weakness or cowardice, they strike out at it as though despising it wholeheartedly. Not being able to strike at the weakness in themselves, they hit the harder at the resister. For such persons the sight of suffering endured may become provocative. Nonviolent resistance brings out the bully in those inclined to be bullies. [153]

A contrasting situation exists when the demonstrators do not firmly adhere to their nonviolent discipline, or when the police, troops, etc., on the spot do not understand that the group is going to remain nonviolent and is not attacking them violently. The police and others may then be inspired by fear in what they believe to be a highly insecure and threatening situation, especially if the group is large. This fear may lead them to inflict brutalities on the nonviolent group and to be generally hostile. [154] Such acts of violence may occur even in defiance of general orders from superior officers. Lord Hardinge, the British Ambassador to St. Petersburg, claimed, for example, that (contrary to a widely held belief) on Bloody Sunday 1905 it was Prince Vassiltchikoff, commander of the Guards Division, who was on the spot (not the Grand Duke Vladimir), who gave the order to fire on the peaceful demonstrators. Hardinge added that Prince Vassiltchikoff also disobeyed an order from the Grand Duke to stop firing, "saying he could not be responsible for the safety of his troops or of the town unless they used their arms." [155] Lord Hardinge's testimonial may or may not be true, but this is the type of situation in which police and troops immediately in charge of maintaining order or of inflicting repression may fear the worst and act accordingly.

There will be a strong tendency to brutalities when the agencies of repression include a considerable number of persons with strong sadistic tendencies. Katz and Janis have pointed "toward a fit between unusual institutional roles and basic personality patterns." "When an institution permits violence as part of its function, people will be attracted to this role who derive satisfactions from the nature of the work. Thus there is a self-selection process for brutal roles." Even when the person is not especially brutal on entering such institutions, there will be a strong tendency for him to change or leave; in either case those people with strong sadistic or hostile drives will tend to continue and dominate the organization. [156] While this tendency is not universal it may be sufficiently common to help to explain brutalities committed by police, and other official bodies when they do occur. Seifert has also discussed the tendency for individuals to be harsher in their behavior when they are acting as members of a group, with its backing and on the basis of institutional decisions, than they would be as single individuals. Private inhibitions are thus reduced, and "the barrier of institutional decision can insulate a person from emotional involvement." [157]

In some situations, there will also be a considerable possibility that brutalities may be perpetrated on nonviolent actionists by members of the general population and by special civilian groups and organizations, as well as mobs. This has happened frequently in the Deep South.[158] Such private brutalities may be entirely independent of the police, or with their conveniently remaining elsewhere during the attacks, or watching the attacks as passive bystanders. At other times, nonofficial brutalities may be perpetrated despite active attempts by the police to prevent them.

B. Remaining firm

Therefore, the informed actionist is not, in crisis situations, surprised by the occurrence of brutalities against the nonviolent group. As already noted, they may even be expected. Their occurrence in situations where many people would least expect them—as in India under British rule[159] or in the United States—should leave little doubt that they may certainly be expected in a system comparable to Nazi Germany or Stalinist Russia. The response of the nonviolent actionists—if the movement is to continue and not be crushed—must be essentially the same as to normal repression. Either to halt the action or to resort to violence would have serious consequences and would certainly rebound to the opponent's favor. To be effective, the actionists must persist through the brutalities and suffering and maintain their fearlessness, nonviolence and firmness.

This will doubtless mean considerable suffering until it becomes clear that the brutalities are not effective in cowing the actionists, that instead they may be weakening the opponent's position, or until there is a change of policy or attitude toward the nonviolent group and their demands. This process, it must be clear, will often take some time and it may be necessary to have repeated demonstrations to the opponent and his agents that brutalities will not crush the movement.[160] The price the nonviolent actionists may thus have to pay may be at times severe, but it is, in terms of the dynamics of nonviolent action, a price which sometimes must be paid if fundamental changes are to be made. This has military parallels, although there are significant differences.

The leadership in a nonviolent struggle will not, on the basis of any criteria, be wise to demand that the actionists undergo suffering, or court brutalities, beyond their abilities to bear them. Certainly a new course of action which is liable to intensify repression and brutalities must be considered most carefully, and if an unwise course of action has been started it should not be continued out of dogmaticism or stubbornness.

Wise leadership will take great care to avoid unnecessary brutalization of the opponent. It is also desirable to seek to remove motives or influences which might produce brutalities when this can be done without weakening the movement, or giving in to cruelties intended to induce submission. However, there should be no retreat when maintenance of a firm stand, or even still more daring action, is required.

There are occasions when, in Gandhi's view, the nonviolent actionists ought to intensify resistance in face of severe repression and be willing to court additional suffering. This would demonstrate, he maintained, first that the repressive might of the opponent was incapable of crushing the resistance. This would also set in motion a number of forces which would lead to a relative weakening of the opponent, to a strengthening of the nonviolent group and to increased support for the latter from third parties. This is involved in the political *jiu-jitsu* process which is examined in Chapter Twelve. Such provocative nonviolent action may also sometimes be deemed necessary for the internal strengthening of the nonviolent group. A demonstration by a smaller group of some daring form of fearless dramatic action which, if known in advance, may bring upon them "the most intense form of repression possible," [161] may contribute to improving morale and combating a growth of fear of repression.

The reasons for daring to take provocative nonviolent action and for risking cruel retaliation from the opponent are primarily concerned with the effects of such action on the nonviolent group, on the opponent, or sometimes on third parties, or a combination of these. In any case, the nonviolent group may deliberately seek to reveal to all the extreme brutality of which the opponent and his agents are capable. This type of provocative nonviolent action, it should be made clear, is especially Gandhian. Explicit advocacy of such a course, and theoretical justification for it, do not occur widely in other traditions of nonviolent action, although there are examples in actual practice.

Early in the Indian 1930-31 campaign scattered acts of brutality occurred against the nonviolent volunteers. Gandhi then decided that if this was going to happen anyhow, it would be best to challenge the regime in such a way that such brutality could be revealed publicly in unmistakable terms in order to alienate further support from the government. Gandhi wrote to the Viceroy:

> . . . I feel that it would be cowardly on my part not to invite you to disclose to the full the leonine paws of authority, so that the people who are suffering tortures and destruction of their property may not

feel that I, who had perhaps been the chief party inspiring them to action that has brought to right light the Government in its true colours, had left any stone unturned to work out the Satyagraha programme as fully as it was possible under given circumstances. [162]

He therefore planned a nonviolent raid to seize the government salt depot at Dharasana, an act which because of its daring and challenge would inevitably bring either Government acquiescence or—far more likely—severe repression and brutalities.

This example should make it clear, if there be still any doubt, that it is an error to equate being nonviolent with keeping the opponent "good-natured." The nonviolent strategist regards both the provocation of extreme repression in rare cases and the more usual willingness to withstand repression against more conventional nonviolent action, as interim stages, temporary phases, of a larger and more complicated process of change, a process which is necessary to alter an intolerable situation.

No opponent is likely to appreciate a serious challenge to his power or policies, even if the challenge is peaceful. The nonviolent actionist recognizes that the desired change may only come as the consequence of a difficult and temporarily disruptive struggle. Gandhi wrote:

> Our aim is not merely to arouse the best in [our opponent] but to do so whilst we are prosecuting our cause. If we cease to pursue our course, we do not evoke the best in him but we pander to the evil in him. The best must not be confounded with good temper. When we are dealing with any evil, we may have to ruffle the evil-doer. We have to run the risk, if we are to bring the best out of him. I have likened nonviolence to a septic and violence to antiseptic treatment. Both are intended to ward off the evil, and therefore cause a kind of disturbance which is often inevitable. The first never harms the evil-doer. [163]

April Carter has drawn an analogy between the tensions and conflict involved in a civil disobedience struggle, and those the patient goes through under psychoanalysis, it being necessary in both cases to bring the conflict into the open and to experience it in order to remove it and allow a more healthy condition to be achieved. [164]

As the Gandhian nonviolent actionist understands the process, as long as the opponent is not simply becoming brutalized, and as long as the actionists are able to withstand the repression, there need be no alarm when the opponent temporarily becomes angry and inflicts repression, even brutalities. The situation must, however, be handled wisely and if the above qualifying conditions no longer exist a change in tactics and methods may be urgently required. Barring that, the nonviolent actionists persist while remaining brave and nonviolent. If this can be achieved, there are good grounds for believing that the brutalities will be a temporary phase, though not necessarily a brief one. Seifert points out that while it is not always the case, ". . . it is entirely possible for the worst persecution to come shortly before capitulation by their opponents." [165]

The precise factors which may lead to a reduction or cessation of brutalities will vary widely with the particular situation. These factors will be closely associated with 1) the operation of one or more of the mechanisms of change discussed in later chapters, and especially 2) the ways in which repression may rebound against the opponent's position as will be discussed in Chapter Twelve. For example, members of the opponent group may learn that the nonviolent actionists are in fact both brave and strong. With nonviolent discipline, the opponent group may realize it need not fear a violent attack on itself, and hence its hostility may be reduced. [166] Gandhi argued that when the opponent's violence was met with nonviolence, the result would be finally be a weakening of the opponent's desire or ability to continue his violence; in this way nonviolence would "blunt the edge of the tyrant's sword." [167] An important factor in this process would be the opponent's realization that, rather than strengthening his position, his own repression and brutalities were reacting against him and weakening him, while increasing the relative strength of the nonviolent group.

The change will, however, come only if the nonviolent actionists and the wider grievance group are able to maintain and increase their solidarity. It is to this task and the means for doing so that the discussion now turns.

NOTES

1. From Parnell's speeches at Tipperary, on 21 September 1879, and at Ennis, on 19 September 1880, quoted in O'Hegarty, **A History of Ireland Under the Union, 1880-1922,** pp. 490-491.

2. For examples of this, see Franco Venturi, **Roots of Revolution,** pp. 490, 573 and 651, and Gipson, **The British Empire Before the American Revolution,** vol. XII, **The Triumphant Empire, Britain Sails into the Storm, 1770-1776,** p. 239.

3. Gandhi, **Non-violent Resistance,** p. 134; Ind. ed.: **Satyagraha,** p. 134.

4. Nehru, **An Autobiography,** p. 551.

5. Seifert, **Conquest by Suffering,** p. 64.

6. Farmer, **Freedom — When?,** p. 73. See also Kuper, **Passive Resistance in South Africa,** p. 74.

7. Quoted by Farmer, *loc cit.*

8. Ebert, "Theory and Practice of Nonviolent Resistance," MS p. 168.

9. Hiller, **The Strike,** pp. 22 and 88.

10. Jawaharlal Nehru, **India and the World: Essays by Jawaharlal Nehru** (London: Geo. Allen & Unwin, Ltd., 1936), p. 173. See also Diwakar, **Satyagraha,** p. 28.

11. Hiller, **The Strike,** p. 30.

12. Lakey, "The Sociological Mechanisms of Nonviolent Action" (thesis), p. 110; also in **Peace Research Reviews,** vol. II, no. 6 (Dec. 1968), p. 73.

13. Oppenheimer and Lakey, **A Manual for Direct Action,** p. 23.

14. Kuper, **Passive Resistance in South Africa,** pp. 22 and 180. See also pp. 154-159 and 178-180.

15. Oppenheimer and Lakey, **A Manual for Direct Action,** p. 23. See also Miller, **Nonviolence,** p. 311, and Luthuli, **Let My People Go,** p. 181.

16. Seifert, **Conquest by Suffering,** pp. 61-62. See also p. 46.

17. Lakey, "The Sociological Mechanisms of Nonviolent Action" (thesis), p. 110, and **Peace Research Reviews,** vol. II, no. 6 (Dec. 1968), pp. 73-74, cites: Paul Ernest Wehr, "The Sit-Down Protests: A Study of a Passive Resistance Movement in North Carolina" (unpublished M.A. thesis, University of North Carolina, 1960), and Martin Oppenheimer, "The Sit-In Movement: A Study in Contemporary Negro Protest" (unpublished Ph.D. dissertation, University of Pennsylvania, 1962), pp. 111 and 134.

18. See Sharp, **Gandhi Wields the Weapon of Moral Power,** p. 124. On their role in negotiations, see pp. 170, 178, 202-203, and 205-207.

19. See Kuper, **Passive Resistance in South Africa,** pp. 209, 146, and 146-149.

20. Harvey J. D. Seifert, "The Use by American Quakers of Nonviolent Resistance as a Method of Social Change" (unpublished Ph.D. dissertation, Boston University, 1940), p. 145.

21. On conflicts within the East German regime and in Moscow about the handling of the Rising, or as a consequence of it, see Ebert "Nonviolent Resistance

Against Communist Regimes?" pp. 186-187 and Brant, **The East German Rising,** pp. 167-175.

22. Nehru, **An Autobiography,** p. 70.

23. Watt, **Dare Call it Treason,** p. 182.

24. See Brant, **The East German Rising,** pp. 155-157 and Ebert, "Nonviolent Resistance Against Communist Regimes?" pp. 184-188.

25. Ebert, "Nonviolent Resistance Against Communist Regimes?" p. 184.

26. *Ibid.,* p. 187.

27. *Ibid.*

28. Wheeler-Bennett, **The Nemesis of Power,** p. 78.

29. Nehru, **An Autobiography,** p. 70.

30. Kuper, **Passive Resistance in South Africa,** p. 87. On Gandhi's views of the ways in which the government is unprepared for nonviolent action, essentially because it does not expect it, see Gandhi, **Satyagraha in South Africa,** p. 214.

31. Harcave, **First Blood,** pp. 76-77.

32. *Ibid.,* p. 169.

33. Gandhi, **Non-violent Resistance,** p. 174; Ind. ed.: **Satyagraha,** p. 174.

34. Gipson, **The British Empire Before the American Revolution,** vol. XI, **The Triumphant Empire: The Rumbling of the Coming Storm,** 1766-1770, pp. 151-152, and vol. XII, pp. 309-311.

35. Symons, **The General Strike,** pp. 47-48.

36. *Ibid.,* p. 52.

37. *Ibid.,* p. 53.

38. Watt, **Dare Call It Treason,** p. 186.

39. Katkov, **Russia 1917,** p. xxv.

40. Harcave, **First Blood,** p. 125.

41. Symons, **The General Strike,** p. 49.

42. *Ibid.,* pp. 52-53.

43. Delarue, **The Gestapo,** p. 8.

44. Harcave, **First Blood,** p. 189. On other instances of recognition by officials of the need to prevent spread of strikes, see also pp. 97, 174, and 196.

45. Sharp, **Gandhi Wields . . . ,** p. 81.

46. Gerland, "The Great Labor Camp Strike at Vorkuta," *Militant,* 7 March 1955.

47. Ebert, "Nonviolent Resistance Against Communist Regimes?" pp. 179 and 185. After the rising more significant concessions were made. See Brant, **The East German Rising,** pp. 163-164, and 166.

48. *Newsweek,* 17 June 1963, and *New York Times,* 19 July and 9 October 1963, cited in Roberts, "The Buddhist Revolt", MS pp. 13, 17 and 37.

49. King, **Why We Can't Wait,** pp. 30-32.

50. Ebert, "Nonviolent Resistance Against Communist Regimes?" p. 185. On elation and determination to continue the struggle in Russia after the "October Manifesto" see Harcave, **First Blood,** pp. 199-203.

51. Katkov, **Russia 1917,** pp. 322-323 and 332.

52. Jutikkala, **A History of Finland,** p. 229.

53. Gipson, **The Coming of the Revolution, 1763-1775,** p. 193.

54. Gipson, **The British Empire . . . ,** vol. XII, p. 130. For similar statements, see

also pp. 295 and 310-311, and Schlesinger, **The Colonial Merchants and the American Revolution**, pp. 537-538.

55. William Z. Foster, **The Great Steel Strike and Its Lessons** (New York: B. W. Huebsch, 1920), p. 116. I am grateful to George Lakey for this reference. See also Symons, **The General Strike**, pp. 158, 182-186 and 196.

56. King, **Stride Toward Freedom**, U.S. ed., pp. 100-102; Br. ed., pp. 118-120.

57. See Mahadev Desai, **The Story of Bardoli**, pp. 71-72, 88-89, 90, 94-95.

58. See King, **Stride Toward Freedom**, U.S. ed., 98-99; Br. ed., p. 116.

59. *Ibid.*

60. Kuper, **Passive Resistance in South Africa**, p. 86.

61. Gandhi, **Non-violent Resistance**, p. 208; Ind. ed.: **Satyagraha**, p. 208.

62. Luthuli, **Let My People Go**, p. 175.

63. Hsiao, **Rural China**, p. 3.

64. Luthuli, **Let My People Go**, p. 159. This refers to reaction to the issuing of the Freedom Charter in 1955.

65. Seifert, **Conquest by Suffering**, p. 49.

66. Harcave, **First Blood**, p. 232.

67. Gipson, **The British Empire** . . . , vol. XII, p. 287. On a similar warning by General Gage in 1767, see *ibid.*, vol. XI, p. 57.

68. Warmbrunn, **The Dutch Under German Occupation 1940-1945**, p. 110.

69. Nehru, **An Autobiography**, pp. 328-329.

70. Malcolm W. Browne (of Associated Press), *Japan Times,* 31 August 1963, quoted by Roberts, "The Buddhist Revolt," MS p. 45.

71. Seifert, **Conquest by Suffering**, pp. 39-40.

72. Buckler, "Labour Disputes in the Province of Asia Minor," p. 31. On other repression against strikes and tax refusal, see Rostovtzeff, **The Social and Economic History of the Roman Empire**, vol. I, p. 449.

73. Ramsay MacMullan, "A Note on Roman Strikes," *Classical Journal*, vol. LVIII (1962-1963), pp. 269-271.

74. Schlesinger, **The Colonial Merchants** . . . , pp. 538-539.

75. Griffith, **The Resurrection of Hungary**, p. 34.

76. Friedrich Grimm, **Vom Ruhrkrieg zur Rheinlandräumung** (Hamburg: *Hanseatische Verlagsanstalt,* 1930), p. 105. Quoted in translation by Sternstein, "The *Ruhrkampf* of 1923," pp. 121-122.

77. Kuper, **Passive Resistance in South Africa**, p. 63.

78. *Ibid.*, p. 62.

79. *Ibid.*

80. Luthuli, **Let My People Go**, p. 149.

81. Brant, **The East German Rising**, p. 20.

82. See Symons, **The General Strike**, pp. 20-22, 26-27, 94 and 154-155.

83. Halperin, **Germany Tried Democracy**, p. 250.

84. Katkov, **Russia 1917**, pp. 307-308.

85. *New York Times*, 30 September 1963, quoted in Roberts, "The Buddhist Revolt," *MS pp. 15 and 34.*

86. Bondurant, **Conquest of Violence**, p. 218.

87. Kuper, **Passive Resistance in South Africa**, pp. 86, 79 and 206.

88. April Carter, **Direct Action** (pamphlet; London: *Peace News,* 1962), p. 22.

89. Dhawan, **The Political Philosophy of Mahatma Gandhi**, p. 142.
90. Nehru, **Toward Freedom**, p. 249.
91. Gopal, **The Viceroyalty of Lord Irwin**, p. 64.
92. Gandhi, **Non-violent Resistance**, p. 81; Ind., ed.: **Satyagraha**, p. 81.
93. Kuper, **Passive Resistance in South Africa**, p. 86.
94. See Seifert, **Conquest by Suffering**, p. 39.
95. Oppenheimer and Lakey, **A Manual for Direct Action**, p. 23.
96. Fredric Solomon and Jacob R. Fishman, "The Psychosocial Meaning of Nonviolence in Student Civil Rights Activities," **Psychiatry**, vol. XVII, no. 2 (May 1964), p. 96.
97. Gandhi, **All Men Are Brothers** (Ahmedabad, India: Navajivan, 1960), p. 138.
98. Gandhi, **Non-violent Resistance**, p. 347; Ind. ed.: **Satyagraha**, p. 347.
99. Brigitte Gerland, "The Great Labor Camp Strike at Vorkuta," *Militant* (New York), 7 March 1955, p. 3
100. King, **Stride Toward Freedom**, pp. 106-122; Br. ed.: pp. 126-144.
101. *Ibid.*, U.S. ed.: p. 122; Br. ed.: p. 144.
102. *Ibid.*, U.S. ed.: p. 132-133; Br. ed.: p. 156. On other examples from the Afro-American movement, see Farmer, **Freedom—When?**, p. 10, and Solomon and Fishman, "The Psychosocial Meaning of Nonviolence in Student Civil Rights Activities," pp. 95-97.
103. Seifert, **Conquest by Suffering**, p. 41.
104. Harcave, **First Blood**, p. 231.
105. Reitlinger, **The Final Solution**, p. 328.
106. Ebert, "Nonviolent Resistance Against Communist Regimes?" p. 182.
107. Luthuli, **Let My People Go**, pp. 11, 78, 145-147, 150-153, 155-157, 161, 170, 209, 214-217, 226, and 229, and Appendix C, and also Sharp, "Problems of Violent and Nonviolent Struggle," *Peace News*, 28 June 1963.
108. Miller, **Nonviolence**, p. 162.
109. Luthuli, **Let My People Go**, p. 196.
110. Ebert, "Nonviolent Resistance Against Communist Regimes?" p. 193.
111. *Ibid.*, p. 192.
112. Ebert, "Theory and Practice of Nonviolent Resistance," MS pp. 438-439.
113. Brant, **The East German Rising**, p. 164.
114. Harcave, **First Blood**, p. 116.
115. Gipson, **The British Empire . . .** , p. 186 On economic hardships on the colonists of that campaign in 1770, see p. 273.
116. Niels Lindberg as early as 1937 attempted, and appealed for, a comparative evaluation on practical grounds of the advantages, disadvantages and consequences of nonviolent action, military resistance, terrorist resistance and guerilla war. See Lindberg, *"Konklusionen: Theorien om Ikke-vold,"* in Lindberg, Jacobsen and Ehrlich, **Kamp Uden Vaaben**, pp. 203-213.
117. Gregg, **The Power of Nonviolence**, p. 100.
118. Bondurant, **Conquest of Violence**, p. 229.
119. See *Monthly Information Bulletin* of the International Commission Against Concentration Camp Practices (August-November 1955), pp. 19-35, and 66-68.
120. Warmbrunn, **The Dutch . . .** , p. 110.
121. Schlesinger, **The Colonial Merchants . . .** , p. 183.

122. *Ibid.*, p. 315.

123. Ehrlich, *"Ruhrkampen,"* p. 189.

124. *Ibid.*, pp. 188-189.

125. Halperin, **Germany Tried Democracy**, pp. 252-254.

126. Gandhi, **Non-violence in Peace and War**, vol. I, p. 338. See also, pp. 43, 226, 278, 323, and 337-339. For other discussions of suffering in nonviolent action, see *ibid.*, vol. II, pp. 63, 145, 166 and 288; Gandhi, **Non-violent Resistance**; Ind. ed.: **Satyagraha**, p. 134, and 172; Gregg, **The Power of Nonviolence**, pp. 53, 78, 84, and 129-130; Bose, **Selections from Gandhi**, p. 183; Case, **Non-violent Coercion**, pp. 397-401; Dhawan, **The Political Philosophy** ... , pp. 139-141; Kuper, **Passive Resistance in South Africa**, pp. 78-93, and Wolff, editor, **The Sociology of Georg Simmel**, pp. 224-249, esp. p. 226.

127. See Bondurant, **Conquest of Violence**, pp. 29 and 198 and Gandhi, **Non-violence in Peace and War**, vol. II, p. 21.

128. See Gandhi, **Non-violence in Peace and War**, vol. II, pp. 36, 59 and 63, and Bose, **Selections from Gandhi**, p. 189.

129. Gandhi, **Non-violent Resistance** p. 67; Ind. ed.: **Satyagraha**, p. 67.

130. *Ibid.*, p. 115.

131. *Young India* (weekly), 10 July 1930 nr. 28.

132. Sharp, **Gandhi Wields** ... , p. 76.

133. Miller, **Nonviolence**, pp. 224-229.

134. Luthuli, **Let My People Go**, p. 92.

135. Bose, **Studies in Gandhism**, p. 161.

136. Hiller, **The Strike**, p. 151.

137. See Lakey, "The Sociological Mechanisms ... " (thesis), p. 84; *Peace Research Reviews*, vol. II, no. 6 (Dec. 1968), pp. 54-55.

138. Seifert, **Conquest by Suffering**, p. 47.

139. *Ibid.*, p. 50. See also p. 49.

140. Schlesinger, **The Colonial Merchants** ... , p. 180 and Gipson, **The British Empire** ... , vol. XI, pp. 276-280.

141. Seifert, **Conquest by Suffering**, p. 47.

142. *Ibid.*, p. 48.

143. Quoted by Lakey, "The Sociological Mechanisms ... " (thesis), p. 83; *Peace Research Reviews*, vol. II, no. 6 (Dec. 1968), pp. 54-55.

144. Kuper, **Passive Resistance in South Africa**, p. 89.

145. Seifert, **Conquest by Suffering**, p. 48.

146. See Gopal, **Viceroyalty of Lord Irwin**, p. 65.

147. Nehru, **An Autobiography**, p. 180.

148. Edward Rodman, "Portsmouth: A Lesson in Nonviolence," pp. 80-81, in Peck, **Freedom Ride**.

149. See Kuper, **Passive Resistance in South Africa**, p. 85.

150. Seifert, **Conquest by Suffering**, p. 48.

151. *Ibid.*, p. 50.

152. *Ibid.*, pp. 48-49.

152. *Ibid.*, pp. 48-49.

153. *Ibid.*, p. 50.

154. Lakey, "The Sociological Mechanisms . . . ," (Thesis) p. 85; *Peace Research Reviews*, vol. II, no. 6 (Dec. 1968), pp. 55-56.

155. Lord Hardinge of Penschurst, **Old Diplomacy: The Reminiscences of Lord Hardinge of Penschurst** (London: James Murray, 1947), p. 114.

156. Janis and Katz, "The Reduction of Intergroup Hostility," p. 99.

157. Seifert, **Conquest by Suffering**, p. 51.

158. Miller, **Nonviolence**, p. 164.

159. See Sharp, **Gandhi Wields . . .** , pp. 101-102; 104-105; 108-111; 115; 139-141; 142-144; 148-149; 162-166.

160. Gregg, **The Power of Nonviolence**, pp. 59, 83, 118, 120 and 126.

161. Bose, **Studies in Gandhism**, p. 153.

162. Sharp, **Gandhi Wields . . .** , p. 117.

163. Quoted in Bose, **Studies in Gandhism**, p. 168.

164. April Carter, **Direct Action** (pamphlet), p. 23.

165. Seifert, **Conquest by Suffering**, p. 63.

166. Gregg, **The Power of Nonviolence**, p. 48, and Janis and Katz, "The Reduction of Intergroup Hostility," **Journal of Conflict Resolution**, vol III, no. 1 (March 1959), p. 95.

167. Dhawan, **The Political Philosophy . . .** , p. 141.

PART THREE: DYNAMICS

11

Solidarity and Discipline to Fight Repression

INTRODUCTION

Faced with repression and suffering, the nonviolent actionists will need to stand together, to maintain their internal solidarity and morale, and to continue the struggle. As the opponent attributes violence to them and tries to provoke them to commit violence—with which he could deal more effectively—the nonviolent actionists will need to persist in reliance on their chosen technique of struggle and to maintain nonviolent discipline. As the conflict deepens, the nonviolent actionists will need to continue to pursue the struggle in order to bring into operation the changes that will alter relationships and achieve their objectives.

THE NEED FOR SOLIDARITY

The need for solidarity has been recognized in many campaigns, both in the initial stages and in the later more difficult phases. During the initial stages, when the effort is to rally as much support as possible, the nonviolent group is likely to identify with the grievance group as a whole and its needs. This will continue, Lakey points out, as long as the group of participants is growing; "little if any emphasis is placed on a boundary between the nonviolent actor and the public."[1] In some cases the whole population group is more or less involved, although not always equally so. In other cases, the nonviolent actionists may be a minority and a highly visible group, in comparison to the general population or even the group whose grievances are being championed.

Sometimes people will hesitate to commit themselves to nonviolent action unless they are convinced that there will be sufficiently solid support to make it effective. In the spring of 1768 New England merchants were, for example, cautious about a nonimportation campaign; they wanted assurances that merchants in the colonies down the coast would also take part. New York merchants made their adoption of the plan later that year dependent on continued support from Boston and the adoption of similar measures in Philadelphia.[2]

Nonviolent actionists will aim for the full participation which was shown at the beginning of the British General Strike of 1926:

> The workers' reaction to the strike call was immediate and overwhelming. There can be no doubt that its completeness surprised the Government, as well as the TUC. From district after district reports came into the TUC headquarters at Eccleston Square, sending the same message in various words: the men were all out, the strike was solid. This is a very rare thing . . . this one, almost unprepared and imperfectly coordinated, might have been expected to show signs of collapse from the start. Instead, the response was in effect complete.[3]

On June 16, 1953, similar solidarity was shown by East Berlin workers. Workers from *Volkseigener Betrieb Industriebau*'s Block 40 section were indignant at the approximately ten percent increase in their work norms, which had been announced by the ministerial council. At first it was decided to send delegates to Ulbricht and Grotewohl to protest the change, but, Ebert reports:

> At an improvised meeting a foreman said that it was time to act. All the workers should go, not just the delegates. One of the workers has described this decisive movement in the history of the uprising: "A colleague came forward. 'Take your choice. If you are with us, step over to the right: if not step over to the left.' The whole gang moved to the right." The uprising began in that instant. The workers re-

solved to protest openly. After that there was no turning back. The fact that they had all taken the same step gave them strength and confidence.[4]

It should not be assumed, however, that such initial unanimity will always be possible, nor that it is always required (however desirable it may be). If near unanimity of participation is not likely, or does not materialize, this fact will have to be considered in the selection, or modification, of the strategy, tactics and specific methods for the campaign. Where the active participants in the nonviolent struggle are only a section of the general population, deliberate efforts may be needed to strengthen their morale. This strengthening may involve developing the nonviolent actionists as a *self-conscious* group distinguished from the rest of the population. Lakey writes that this drawing of boundaries may happen "as soon as campaigners cease to be recruited at a high rate."[5] When maximum possible support has at that stage been rallied, the nonviolent group is likely without conscious influence to develop its internal solidarity as it faces the coming struggle. Deliberate efforts may also be made to develop and maintain group solidarity.

The maintenance of morale in nonviolent struggles is extremely important. There appear to be roughly four ways of doing this (and here we follow Hiller's analysis of morale-building in strikes[6] with some modifications and additions). These are: 1) maintaining rapport, feelings of group participation and group solidarity; 2) generating incentives to carry on the struggle; 3) lessening incentives to give it up; and 4) possessing or using restraints on participants wishing to abandon the struggle.

A. Maintaining rapport

The ability of the participants to face repression will be very significantly increased if they constantly feel that they are part of a much larger movement which gives them, personally, support and strength to carry on. Even when the individual is physically separated from the group, the awareness that others are continuing in solidarity with him will help him to resist temptations to submit. Regular contacts and demonstrations of "togetherness" are therefore important ways of maintaining group morale.[7] This explains the role of regular mass meetings during strikes.[8] During the Montgomery bus boycott, regular mass prayer meetings were held, first twice a week and later once a week.[9]

Other specific actions seemingly intended as resistance against the opponent or as an effort to reach the public may in reality help to maintain internal group solidarity and morale. For example, parades and marches may be used. As Hiller points out in the case of strikes: "Marching before spectators is a declaration 'to the world' that one's lot has been cast with the group in its rivalry with others. Self-display before a public causes one to feel identified with those similarly placed and associated." Picketing has an effect, not only on the public, strikebreakers, etc., but on the strikers themselves. Hiller describes this effect as being "more influential upon the strikers than upon the scab and the employer. The very antagonism which these efforts provide helps to maintain the conflict, boost morale, and lessen desertions." [10]

During the Indian 1930-31 campaign, for example, there were a significant number of parades, picketing, the hoisting or carrying of the Indian national flag, the burning of foreign cloth and mass meetings. The *hartal* was not only a form of protest but also a means of keeping up morale. Singing was frequently used by large crowds in crisis situations. [11] At the beginning of the campaign, Gandhi, writing in *Young India,* stated that during the movement *satyagrahis* should find themselves:

1. In prison or in an analogous state, or
2. Engaged in civil disobedience, or
3. Under orders at the spinning wheel, or at some constructive work advancing *Swaraj* [self-rule]. [12]

Thus in the crises, work on the constructive program (intended to remove social evils, educate the people, and build new, self-reliant, institutions) also helped to keep people involved and active in the overall movement, whether or not engaged in civil disobedience. In 1952 mass meetings were used in South Africa both to build up a spirit of resistance and solidarity and to spread the objectives and plans of the civil disobedience movement. The campaign was preceded by a day of prayer in many African locations throughout the country. [13]

In some situations temporary camps for volunteers may be set up, as in India in 1930. These are particularly necessary in combat situations, as during the nonviolent raid at Dharasana, [14] and serve not only to meet elementary physical needs but also to maintain group spirit.

Sometimes the wearing of certain symbols of unity will help people to identify with the movement and show their support for it. For example, Elizabeth Gurley Flynn tells how this worked in an American labor strike:

The strike was in danger of waning for lack of action. We got every striker to put on a little red ribbon . . . and when they got out of their homes and saw the great body that they were they had renewed energy which carried them along for many weeks in the strike. [15]

Norwegians during the Nazi occupation wore paper clips in their lapels, a sign of "keep together," and students and pupils took to wearing necklaces and bracelets of paper clips. Red caps were worn as a sign of resistance. Pupils wore tiny potatoes on match sticks in their lapels. Every day they became larger, indicating that the anti-Nazi forces were growing. The smallest Norwegian coin, showing "H VII" for King Haakon VII, was brightly polished and worn. Flowers were widely worn on the King's seventieth birthday. Such symbolic actions not only irritated the Nazis—several hundred Norwegians were arrested for them—but also served to boost feelings of solidarity among the Norwegians. [16]

Explaining why a strikers' picnic was held on Sunday (when the strikers could have had a rest and break), Flynn pointed out that the reasons went "deep into the psychology of a strike." She then elaborated on the importance of conscious efforts to maintain solidarity if the strikers were to win. "You have got to keep the people busy all the time, to keep them active, working," she explained. This was the reason why the Industrial Workers of the World had "these great mass meetings, women's meetings, children's meetings . . . [,] mass picketing and mass funerals. And out of all this . . . we are able to create that feeling . . . 'One for all and all for one' . . . we are able to bring them to the point where they will go to jail and refuse fines, and go, hundreds of them, together . . ." [17]

B. Generating incentives

A second way of maintaining morale is to promote determination to carry on the struggle. The participants must believe that they have very good reasons for continuing, that their action is justified, that the objectives when won will be worthwhile, and that the means of action to achieve them have been wisely chosen. "The biggest job in getting any movement off the ground," wrote Martin Luther King, Jr., "is to keep together the people who form it. This task requires more than a common aim: it demands a philosophy that wins and holds the people's allegiance; and it depends upon open channels of communication between the people and their leaders." [18]

The leaders in Montgomery put much effort into explaining nonviolent action and "Christian love" in the mass meetings. Morale is likely to increase if the nature of the technique, the plan of action and tactics, the significance of the repression and the response to it are understood. Sometimes the opponent's repression will by its brutality make waverers more firm on their resolve. If the goals and means of struggle are, or can be, related to deep religious or philosophical convictions *already held* by the participants and the wider population, their resolve and morale are likely to be stronger.

C. Reducing grounds for capitulation

At certain stages in nonviolent campaigns, the participants may become discouraged or fatigued, and specific attention must then be given to counteract these conditions. Wise nonviolent leaders will have anticipated this development and may have tried to reduce its severity by advance measures. It is highly important that at least the original participants continue support and that none desert. The failure to maintain lasting internal solidarity among the inhabitants of the Ruhr led to serious weakening of the movement. "The united front against occupiers, which had been firm and strong at the outset, now began to disintegrate," writes Sternstein about the months of August and September, 1923. [19]

Where fatigue or monotony occur, special entertainment may be marginally useful. There was a considerable effort in this direction during the 1926 British General Strike. The General Council of the Trades Union Congress suggested the organization of sports and entertainment, and local Strike Committees organized concerts, football matches and other sports. In many cases strikers played football matches against teams of local policemen. All over Britain, local Strike Committees organized "Sport and Entertainment" sections. The Cardiff, Wales, Strike Committee advised the local men: "Keep smiling. Refuse to be provoked. Get into your garden. Look after the wife and kiddies. If you have not got a garden, get into the country, the parks and the playgrounds." [20]

Where, because of participation in the struggle, the nonviolent actionists and their families suffer from lack of food, housing, money and the like, or if they may do so in the future, there may be a major effort to supply these needs. This assistance would relieve the nonviolent combatants and their families of immediate worries, and enable them to carry on longer than otherwise possible. Such efforts to equalize the burdens and provide mutual help have been made in various recent campaigns, but the practice is an old one, having been used by American colonists. South Carolinians, for example, devised a scheme for equalizing the burdens which would come with the plan for economic resistance contained in the Continental Association; the possible adverse effects on rice planters were regarded as especially important. [21] When the British closure of the port of Boston brought economic hardship to the city's merchants and unemployment for workingmen, other cities and towns, and indeed other colonies at some distance, provided various forms of mutual help, ranging from free use of storerooms and wharves for Boston merchants in nearby Marblehead to financial assistance for Boston's needy.[22] Modern forms of such assistance have included legal representation, bail funds, financial assistance to families, and (where the campaign was in support of the government) advance guarantees of compensation for financial losses arising from the struggle. For example, the German Minister of Traffic, Gröner, in 1920 promised all staff members, officials and workers in the State railroads that in accordance with the policy of refusing all cooperation with French efforts to run the railroads in the Ruhr, the government would reimburse them for all injury and loss. This compensation policy was also extended to industrialists of the territory for their losses during the struggle, and 715,000,000 marks were later paid in compensation.[23] In other cases, where the resistance organization was a private one with little or no financial reserve, volunteers have sometimes been asked to sign a statement acknowledging that there will be no claim for, or pledge of, financial remuneration for any losses or difficulties arising from the struggle.

The sufferings incurred in the course of nonviolent struggle are sometimes interpreted by nonviolent leaders in ways which make them seem more bearable. Where this effort is successful, further grounds for capitulation will be reduced. Various speakers emphasized such interpretations during the 1952 South African Defiance Campaign:

I know you will be called upon to make many sacrifices and you may have to undergo many sufferings. But what are these sufferings compared with the sufferings of other people in this country to-day . . . . Our people suffer every day, and it is all wasted. What we say is, suffer, but for a cause, and let us rather die for a good cause.

If they put you in gaol, I ask you: is your condition better outside?

They can bring their machine-guns, as they did on the first of May, and shoot us down—innocent men—without provocation. And what will happen to you if you die? I ask you. My friend, let me tell you that when you die they must take that chain off you and you will be free in your death.

. . . their power is great. But are we going to be frightened of that power? . . . The power of man is greater than the power of machine-guns . . . And if justice and truth is on our side, no machine, no police, no power can stop us from marching onwards.[24]

D. Restraints or sanctions

The last, most extreme, and least used, means of maintaining solidarity is the threat or use of nonviolent restraints or sanctions. Such restraints or sanctions may be applied to those who have refused to join the movement, or to members of the nonviolent group who have weakened and withdrawn from the campaign. These nonviolent sanctions differ radically from the sanctions for indiscipline applied in violent conflicts, which are imprisonment or execution.

The nonviolent alternative sanctions may under suitable circumstances be powerful and effective. Sometimes verbal persuasion is sufficient to restore adherence to the movement. When this is not adequate, other methods are available, including vigils, public prayers, picketing, fines, publication of names, suspension of membership, social boycott, economic boycott, fasting and nonviolent interjection. [25]

If such pressures are to be used, considerable care will be needed in their application. Intimidation and threats of physical harm must not be used, or the movement is likely to slide into a struggle with violence applied against one's own people. Rejection of threats is certainly a minimum limitation on sanctions for maintaining solidarity. Frequently nonviolent leaders insist that the attitude toward the persons whose behavior requires these pressures must be a benevolent one. Gandhi insisted, for example, that such means must be applied without vindictiveness or hostility. This is contrary to attitudes frequently accompanying Western labor conflicts when nonstrikers are ostracized or "sent to Coventry." Social boycotts, it should be remembered, do not require bitterness and hatred. In any case, supplies of food and all other necessities must be maintained; if necessary these must be provided to those who are being socially boycotted.

The activists among American colonists during their noncooperation campaigns against British laws, regulations and government probably still furnish the outstanding example of these types of restraints and sanctions. (This is not to deny that threats of physical violence were also on occasion used against recalcitrants.) For example, in 1769 residents of Massachusetts Bay Colony used various nonviolent methods against those not complying with the nonimportation campaign, including distribution of thousands of handbills urging people to shun the shops of merchants not abiding by the agreement, refusal to do business with any vessel which loaded forbidden goods at any British port, and publication in newspapers of the names of violators. [26]

This is, however, simply one illustration of many which might be offered. Various committees were set up throughout the colonies to enforce the provisions of the ongoing campaign, and these achieved considerable effectiveness.[27] In Connecticut the Continental Association was enforced by open, fair trials of persons accused of violations of its provisions.[28] In order to prevent a skyrocketing of prices as a consequence of short supplies during nonimportation, colonials controlled prices by instituting investigations (at times demanding examinations of accounts), publishing names of violators, and imposing economic boycotts on those who sought to profit from the crisis.[29] The most important nonviolent sanctions were the "naming" of people—i.e., publishing their names in newpspapers—imposition of social boycott, and in the case of merchants and traders, the application of secondary economic boycotts against them. In practice it was often difficult to separate the operation of the methods of "naming," social boycott and economic boycott.[30] One ultraradical wrote in late 1774:

The [Continental] Congress, like other Legislative bodies, have annexed penalties to their laws. They do not consist of the gallows, the rack, and the stake . . . but INFAMY, a species of infamy . . . more dreadful to a freeman than the gallows, the rack, or the stake. It is this, he shall be declared in the publick papers to be *an enemy to his country* . . .[31]

In certain situations certain austerities adopted for resistance, including the ban against gambling, were also enforced by such means. The enforcement measures took a variety of additional forms depending on the situation, including dismissal from their jobs of ship captains or masters who had taken on prohibited goods and the refusal of lawyers to provide services for violators of the noncooperation plan.[32]

Enforcement of the nonimportation and other measures by such means was frequently effective. Banned goods were sometimes returned to England without being unloaded, while at other times such imports were unloaded but placed in storage for the duration of the campaign, or sold at auction for the benefit of the resistance movement.[33] Occasionally shopkeepers were "sentenced" to burn boycotted tea in their possession.[34]

The Lieutenant Governor of Massachusetts Bay, Thomas Hutchinson, writing of the period when he acted as Governor before General Gage replaced Governor Bernard, confirmed the effectiveness of the various means of enforcement:

The design, at this time, was to enforce the compliance with the former subscription, and to compel all other persons to abstain from importation. The first step for this purpose was the publication in the newspapers, of the names of such persons as were most notorious for persisting in importing goods contrary to the agreement of the merchants, "that there might be the concurrence of every person upon the continent in rendering their base and dangerous designs abortive." Many persons, at first, appeared determined not to submit to so arbitrary a proceeding, but the subscription was general, with few exceptions only.[35]

Hutchinson also offered several examples of pressures which involved a shift toward physical intimidation to enforce the noncooperation provisions.[36] Without doubt there was at times both a strong tendency for suppression of contrary opinions and violation of freedom of speech, and a development of quasi-military groups,[37] but such developments do not necessarily follow from the nonviolent enforcement of resistance policy: indeed, they need to be prevented.

In an unusual extension of this type of enforcement, colonies which were firmly supporting nonimportation applied secondary economic boycotts not only against towns where the expression of opposition was weak,[38] but even against whole colonies which had been lax in launching or maintaining noncooperation, especially Rhode Island, South Carolina and Georgia.[39]

During the Irish rent refusal campaign, Charles S. Parnell, Member of Parliament and President of the Land League, called for social boycott against Irishmen who did not maintain solidarity with their resisting compatriots. Parnell declared at Ennis on September 19, 1880:

Now what are you to do to a tenant who bids for a farm from which another tenant has been evicted? I think I heard somebody say shoot him. I wish to point out to you a very much better way—a more Christian and charitable way, which will give the lost man an opportunity of repenting. When a man takes a farm from which another has been evicted, you must shun him on the roadside when you meet him—you must shun him in the streets of the town—you must shun him in the shop—you must shun him on the fair-green and in the market place, and even in the place of worship, by leaving him alone, by putting him into a moral Coventry, by isolating him from the rest of his country, as if he were the leper of old—you must show him your detestation of the crime he has committed . . .[40]

Examples of the use of nonviolent interjection, for example, to press nonstrikers to stay away from work have also been offered in Chapter

Eight in the description of that method.[41] On occasion fasts have been used to maintain solidarity. For example, during the Ahmedabad textile workers' strike led by Gandhi in 1918, after four weeks the strikers became dispirited and some began to return to work. Gandhi regarded their weakening as a breaking of their pledge not to do so. Accordingly, he reminded the workers of their pledge and undertook a fast, saying, "unless the strikers rally and continue the strike till a settlement is reached, or till they leave the mills altogether, I will not touch any food." This restored morale and solidarity.[42]

In late 1930, when tax refusal was added to the methods of resistance used by the Indians and the government consequently seized properties of tax resisters, fasts were applied against fellow Indians who sought to profit from the struggle. In Siddapur *taluka* (subdistrict), in Kanara, Karnatak province, thirty-seven women fasted at the doors of persons who had bought the seized properties of tax resisters, and at Mavinagundi such a fast lasted thirty-one days.[43]

It is possible, of course, that in face of repression, despite such means of promoting solidarity, both determination and fearlessness may weaken and the movement may collapse. If, however, the nonviolent actionists remain determined and fearless, are willing to undergo the suffering and maintain their solidarity and high morale, it is highly likely that the movement will continue. This will present severe problems for the opponent. It will mean, among other things, that his effort to crush the movement by his strongest means of action—repression—will have failed. To achieve this, however, the actionists must maintain nonviolent discipline, for there are strong chances that the opponent will falsely attribute violence to them and seek to provoke them into committing it. That is to his advantage.

INHIBITING REPRESSION

The difficulties which the opponent faces in attempting to defeat a nonviolent action movement arise from 1) the fact that the opponent strongly tends to be more limited in the means of repression which he may use against nonviolent action than against violent action, and 2) the nature of his means of repression, which are generally most effective in dealing with *violent* action.

Extremely severe and brutal repression against a group pledged to non-violence and to harm no one is much more difficult to justify to everyone concerned than is such repression against a group engaged in injuring and killing people. Awareness of this in advance, or as a result of experience, will in many cases cause the opponent to make his counteraction less severe than against violent actionists. He learns that disproportionate repression may react against him, not only in terms of opinion but also in weakening his own relative power position. This reaction includes increased support for the nonviolent group, less support for, and greater open opposition to, the opponent's policies, repression and regime generally.

Lakey puts it this way:

> . . . the strategy of the nonviolent actor is to limit the means of repression which can be included in the definition of the situation of the opponent. The nonviolent actor does this by persuading his opponent that some means are inappropriate for use against him. Even if the opponent has traditionally exploited or been violent against the campaigner, the latter seeks to protect an image of himself which will remove the justification for the opponent's violence. [44]

It is true that the British were far more brutal in putting down the Indian nonviolent movement than most people today realize. [45] However, it is also true that they were by no means as ruthless as they *could* have been, and as they in fact *were* in putting down the 1857 uprising in India and the Mau Mau movement in Kenya, or in the bombings of German cities in World War II. At least a major part of the reason for the comparative British restraint in dealing with the Indian nonviolent movement was that the Indians' continuing nonviolence limited the British in the means of repression which are effectively open to them. Focusing on labor strikes, Hiller points to the influence of the presence or absence of a public on the kinds of repression which may be used against strikers. [46]

Explaining the British Government's refusal to arrest Gandhi during his Salt March to the sea to commit civil disobedience in 1930, Gandhi said:

> . . . the only interpretation I can put upon this noninterference is that the British Government, powerful though it is, is sensitive to world opinion which will not tolerate repression of extreme political agitation which civil disobedience undoubtedly is, so long as disobedience remains civil, and, therefore, necessarily nonviolent. [47]

The degree to which a regime will feel able to defy world—or internal —opinion will of course vary, depending on several factors. These include the kind of regime it is, whether it thinks the events can be kept unknown, the degree to which it is threatened by the events, and whether opinion against the regime will be translated into assistance for the non-violent group and into actions against the opponent.

Censorship kept the news of the 1919 massacre of Jalianwala Bagh in Amritsar, India, from reaching the United States for eight months—but it did eventually leak out.[48] In dealing with the defiant nonviolently resisting Norwegian teachers Quisling could obviously have been more ruthless than he was and could have shot some or all of them. However, he was not really free to do so because he knew that if he took harsher measures against the teachers than sending them to concentration camps he might irrevocably increase public hostility to his regime and make forever impossible his hope of gaining the consent and cooperation he needed for establishing the Corporative State in Norway.[49]

The British in India clearly faced some very difficult decisions concerning what means of repression should be used and when they should be applied. Nehru described this situation in late 1921: "The nerves of many a British official began to give way. The strain was great. There was this ever-growing opposition and spirit of defiance which overshadowed official India like a vast monsoon cloud, and yet because of its peaceful methods it offered no handle, no grip, no opportunity for forcible repression."[50] Gopal, who had access to government correspondence and reports, describes some of the problems during the 1930-31 struggle and the differences of opinion within the government about measures of repression.[51] These are simply indicative of the general problem which an opponent faces when confronting nonviolent action. The decisions are difficult for him if he is to consider the effects of his action on his own position, strength and future; the responses offered to this problem may vary considerably.

In other cases, too, there is suggestive evidence that the maintenance of nonviolent discipline in face of repression tends significantly to restrict the repression and to cause especially difficult problems for the opponent. For example, in South Africa, in an effort to crush a strike by Africans which began on March 22, 1960 (the day after the shooting at Sharpeville), police invaded the Nyanga location near Capetown on April 4; for four days they unleashed a reign of terror including extensive whippings of men, use of batons and some shootings and killings. (This was after extensive unprovoked police brutality against Africans elsewhere, which had produced important white protests against the police.) Norman Phillips of the *Toronto Star* reports the inhibiting effects of nonretaliation even in this situation: "For sheer sadism, the closest comparison to what happened at Nyanga was when the Gestapo sealed off the Warsaw ghetto and began to annihilate it. Had Nyanga fought back, it, too, would have been wiped out; but the Africans employed nonaggressive tactics that puzzled the police."[52] The French commander confronted with nonviolent resistance in the Ruhr acknowledged that it was not very easy to crush the movement; he told the German author Friedrich Grimm: "You have no idea of the difficulties I had, nor of the opportunities you had of exploiting them."[53]

Sir Basil Liddell Hart offered further evidence of the special problems of repression against nonviolent actionists from German occupation experience in World War II:

> When interrogating the German generals after the Second World War, I took the opportunity of getting their evidence about the effect of the different kinds of resistance which they had met in the occupied countries.
>
> Their evidence tended to show that the violent forms of resistance had not been very effective and troublesome to them, except in wide spaces or mountainous areas such as Russia and the Balkans, where topography favoured guerrilla action. In the flat and thickly populated countries of western Europe, it rarely became a serious handicap unless and until the Allied armies were able, and close enough, to exert a simultaneous pressure.
>
> Their evidence also showed the effectiveness of nonviolent resistance as practised in Denmark, Holland and Norway—and, to some extent, in France and Belgium. Even clearer, was their inability to cope with it. They were experts in violence, and had been trained to deal with opponents who used that method. But other forms of resistance baffled them—and all the more in proportion as the methods were subtle and concealed. It was a relief to them when resistance became violent and when nonviolent forms were mixed with guerrilla action, thus making it easier to combine drastic repressive action against both at the same time.[54]

THE OPPONENT PREFERS VIOLENCE

Because of the special difficulties of repressing a nonviolent resistance movement, the opponent may seek to ease them by attributing violence to the nonviolent actionists. The British policy in 1930-31 was to publicize widely all the violence that occurred and, it often seemed, to issue deliberately false reports. The official report for the year, *India in 1930 -31,* stated that between April 6 and July 7, 1930, there was a considerable number of "riots and serious disturbances" and "disorders" throughout the country. Fifty-three such happenings were listed—with no attempt to distinguish between violent riots and nonviolent "disorders."[55] During the 1952 Defiance Campaign in South Africa, as we have seen, there was considerable attempt to identify the civil disobedience movement with the Mau Mau movement in Kenya.[56] The opponent may also plant incriminating evidence "proving" violent intentions and unsavory political associations within the nonviolent group. For example, according to Denis Warner in the *Daily Telegraph* (London) the South Vietnamese Diem regime planted weapons, explosives and "Communist propaganda" in the Xa Loi pagoda in Hué, in 1963.[57] This was to help "justify" severe repression, harsh raids, and large-scale arrests.

Frequently fearing nonviolent resistance more than violent resistance, officials have on occasion preferred that the actionists resort to violence. On the other hand, an opponent who genuinely holds humanitarian and moral views may be partially grateful that the actionists use nonviolent means.[58] However, if the opponent is more interested in maintaining policies which are difficult to justify, in preserving his dominance, and in crushing opposition than he is in upholding an ethical outlook, he may try to provoke violence. In the history of the labor movement, for example, there are frequent instances in which employers have found that resort to violence by the strikers was counterproductive for them but an advantage for the employers.[59] In the United States, Oppenheimer and Lakey report as follows: "Again and again in the civil rights struggle police have been itching to shoot into demonstrations but have not fired because they could not find the excuse of 'self-defense' or 'rioting.'"[60]

Toward the end of Gandhi's struggle in South Africa, one of the secretaries to General Smuts said to Gandhi: "I often wish you took to violence like the English strikers, and then we would know at once how to dispose of you."[61] Gopal reports that whereas the British found Gandhi's nonviolent action "bewildering," "nothing would have suited the British better than to have been confronted with a series of weak, armed rebellions . . ."[62] Benjamin Tucker argued: "There is not a tyrant in the civilized world today who would not rather do anything in his power to precipitate a bloody revolution rather than see himself confronted by any large fraction of his subjects determined not to obey."[63]

Even minor breaks in discipline and very limited violence may be the occasion for quite disproportionate response by the agents of repression; this happened both at Sharpeville in 1960 when stones were thrown at the police and in Birmingham, Alabama, in 1963, when initial taunting of the police produced high pressure water hosing against Negro demonstrators, a step which led to the Negroes' hurling stone paving-blocks at police in a struggle which lasted an hour-and-a-half.[64] Even a little violence will give the opponent the excuse for which he may well have waited to use his overwhelming violence and repression. Severe repression may, of course, occur even when nonviolent discipline is maintained; but in that case, the repression is more likely to rebound against the opponent's power, as is discussed in Chapter Twelve.

Where both sides rely on violence, despite their disagreements, "in reality they conduct their fight on the basis of a strong fundamental agreement that violence is a sound mode of procedure."[65] The use of nonviolent means against a violent opponent, however, creates a condition of disequilibrium within the dynamics of the conflict which operates to the benefit of the nonviolent group.

It is clear that Hitler and the Nazi regime generally regarded some type of "provocation" as necessary, or at least highly desirable, when they were about to launch some major international or domestic power grab which might otherwise have met with considerable opposition. If the provocation desired by the Nazis did not happen on its own, then it was "necessary" to fake a provocation. Detailed study of archives and documents might show whether or not the Nazis consciously applied this as a general practice to resistance movements of various types; this extensive research has not been possible. However, the available evidence shows that even in the Nazis' opinion provocation greatly facilitated international aggression, internal usurpation and brutalities against and murder of hated people. This Nazi desire for provocations adds plausibility to the view that violence used by or on behalf of nonviolent actionists is likely to be counterproductive and help the opponent to inflict overwhelming repression and brutalities. Since the Nazi regime would be expected to be most indifferent to a need for such "justification," these cases are especially significant. Several such instances will therefore be surveyed here. In all these the Nazis wanted violence from their opponents. If it did not happen anyhow, the Nazis either falsely attributed violence to the opposition or provoked them to commit it. Then the Nazis utilized such violence for their own political advantage.

In 1933 Hitler clearly saw provocation to be necessary if he were to use his precarious position as Chancellor representing a minority party in a coalition cabinet operating under a democratic constitution, to abolish the Weimar Republic and to establish a one-party Nazi system. Communist violence was seen as necessary for the "legal" destruction of the Communist Party, and the Nazis would accordingly wait.[66] The burning of the *Reichstag,* the parliament building, provided the occasion. Although one might expect such a dramatic act of presumed opposition to the Nazis to weaken them, it in fact strengthened them. Arriving at the burning building, Hitler declared: "This is a sign from God. No one can now prevent us from crushing the Communists with a mailed fist." [67] As far as the role which the fire played in the Nazi rise to power is concerned, it makes little or no difference whether one believes the fire was (as the Nazis said) started by the Communists as part of a plot, or was (as anti-Nazis said) started by the Nazis themselves for the purpose of blaming the Communists, [68] or was (as Fritz Tobias says) started only by Marius van der Lubbe. [69] The fact remains that the fire provided the necessary provocation which enabled the Nazis by several actions to rout the Communists, abolish constitutionally guaranteed liberties, arrest members of the *Reichstag,* and achieve passage of the disastrous Enabling Act—which suspended the constitution and made it possible for Hitler's National Socialist German Workers Party to become undisputed ruler of Germany.

In international adventures, Hitler always sought to shift the blame to someone else and to show that his peace-loving regime had only acted in the interest of order and self-defence after the most extreme provocation and, if possible, attack by his victims. On July 1, 1940, Hitler told the Italian ambassador, Dino Alfieri, "it was always a good tactic to make the enemy responsible in the eyes of public opinion in Germany and abroad for the future course of events. This strengthened one's own morale and weakened that of the enemy." [70] Accordingly, considerable preparations preceded the German occupation of Austria so that the act might appear, not as military aggression, but as an altruistic act intended to save Austria from violence and civil war; these preparations may even have included plans for the murder of the German Ambassador Franz von Papen. [71] The advance planning for the 1939 invasion and take-over of Czechoslovakia included extensive manipulation of the victim's internal situation designed to make it possible for Hitler to pose as the savior of the cruelly persecuted and terrorized German minority. By threats Hitler even gained the submission of the Czechoslovak government in order to maintain the appearance of "legality" for the actual occupation. [72] In the later case of Poland, the Nazis were not content with justification of the invasion on the basis of persecution of the German minority, but on August 31, 1939, even staged a fake border incident in an attempt to show that the Poles had attacked first and seized a German radio station near the border; as "proof" that Polish troops had made the attack, a dozen or so condemned German criminals in Polish uniforms were left dead, with appropriate wounds, at the scene.[73] The next day at dawn the German armies invaded Poland.

Acts of violence against Germans provided favorable opportunities for the Nazis to carry out the brutalities they wanted to commit. The murder of the young Ernst vom Rath, anti-Nazi third secretary at the German Embassy in Paris, in November 1938 by seventeen-year-old Herschel Gryszpan, son of one of the Jews who had been deported across the Silesian border, was met with "the week of broken glass." Well-organized "spontaneous" reprisals took place against Jews throughout Germany in what became the "first ruthless and undisguised suppression of Jews in Germany on a wholesale scale," and various anti-Jewish laws and economic measures were also then introduced.[74] The assassination of Reinhardt Heydrich on May 29, 1942, near the village of Lidice, Czechoslovakia, by agents from England was followed by the execution of 1,690 persons. These included 199 from Lidice (the village itself was razed to the ground), 152 Jewish hostages in Berlin, and 1,339 other persons in Prague and Bruenn.[75] Attacks on German soldiers and acts of sabotage in several occupied countries were met with brutal retaliation.[76] Hitler even regarded some provocation necessary for the planned extermination of Polish intellectuals, nobility, clergy and Jews. The original excuse, a faked rising in the Galician Ukraine, was set aside as the Nazis waited for a more favorable moment. The extermination was then "justified" by the claim that it was necessary to end agitation dangerous to the security of the troops.[77] It was clear that Hitler was quite conscious in his utilization of violent opposition as the occasion for disproportionately brutal retaliation; he said, for example, that partisan warfare launched in occupied areas of the Soviet Union "enables us to eradicate everyone who opposes us."[78]

These various cases show two simple points: 1) that even Hitler and his cohorts were strongly convinced that their own ruthlessness and agression would be much more easily committed and have greater success if it could be portrayed as retaliation for the violence of others, and 2) that the common assumption that violence by the grievance group can only strengthen their position and not weaken it is, in many situations, not true. This does not prove, of course, but it does make more plausible, the view that violence committed by or in support of nonviolent actionists operates to the advantage of the opponent, and is indeed precisely what he may want in order to consolidate his position and to apply ruthless repression.[79]

The opponent may therefore attempt to provoke the nonviolent actionists and grievance group to violence. This may be attempted in several ways. One of the common means is to make the repression so severe that the actionists break the nonviolent discipline spontaneously, or a group of them begins to advocate violent retaliation openly and to gain a following. This is how Gandhi interpreted the government's declaration of martial law and other harsh repressions in Bardoli in 1928 when the whole area was refusing to pay the land revenue: "It is evident that by the latest form of 'frightfulness' the Government is seeking to goad people into some act of violence, be it ever so slight, to justify their enactment of the last act in the tragedy." [80] This had already happened in 1919 during the *satyagraha* campaign against the Rowlatt Act when people in Ahmedabad, Viramgam, and other parts of the Gujarat heard of Gandhi's arrest. Gandhi later testified: "They became furious, shops were closed, crowds gathered and murder, arson, pillage, wirecutting and attempts at derailment followed." [81] Describing a scene in Bihar in 1930, Rajendra Prasad, later President of India, reported: "The police are, it seems, now determined upon provoking violence so that they get an excuse for using their guns." [82] Writing to the Viceroy after the beginning of the 1930-31 campaign, Gandhi once again commented on this tendency: "If you say, as you have said, that the civil disobedience must end in violence, history will pronounce the verdict that the British Government, not bearing because not understanding nonviolence, goaded human nature to violence which it could understand and deal with." [83]

Similar claims were made by African speakers early in the 1952 Defiance Campaign in South Africa:

And the police who are supposed to uphold order but who only start riots, shot down a hundred at Bellhoek, May 1st, 1951! I don't need to remind you that in many African townships the police started the riots. If the Africans will not fight, the police make them fight. [84]

They [the volunteers] must behave well as the police will provoke them. Tomorrow the police will say, *"Ek het 'n kaffer geskiet, hy het met'n klip gegooi."* ("I've shot a kaffir. He threw a stone at me.") But that policeman has never been injured. But what will they say now? *"Hoe gaan ons werk, kerels, die mense baklei nie."* ("What shall we do, chaps? These people don't fight.") You must give them that headache. [85]

Police in Birmingham, Alabama, on May 3, 1963, appeared to be deliberately provoking Negroes to violence, using first torrents of water from fire hoses, then dogs, then "a state police investigator deliberately swerved his car into the crowd." At that point the Negroes threw bricks and bottles at the police. After a settlement had been reached, white extremists unsuccessfully tried to get white leaders to provoke the Negroes to new violence as a pretext for repudiation of the agreement.[86]

The opponent may also employ spies and agents in an effort to defeat the nonviolent movement, including *agents provocateurs*. If the nonviolent action campaign is being operated without secrecy—as is common in nontotalitarian countries—spies and agents will not be much good for gathering secret information, for there will be none. They may, however, be useful in stirring up "jealousies and resentments among the campaigners and spreading morale-disturbing rumors."[87] The opponent may by such means make serious attempts to demoralize the movement internally, to divide it on policies or personal matters, or to bog down its policy-making meetings with endless bickerings or to prevent effective operation of the group's normal decision-making process.

Agents provocateurs may also be used in a deliberate attempt to provoke the group to violence. At an earlier stage of the labor movement, employers used *agents provocateurs* widely to combat the development of trade unions and to defeat particular strikes. One method is to place agents inside the nonviolent group. These agents then agitate for a switch to violence, or, defying group decision and discipline, commit violence themselves. The hope is to incriminate the whole group or to provoke wider violence. Sometimes they may operate outside the nonviolent group as such, and seek in difficult situations to provoke large nonviolent demonstrations into violence, or to commit acts of violence which, though actually separate from the plans of the nonviolent group, can be identified in the public's mind with their resistance.

This danger was emphasized by Gregg:

> Who in this actual world of hard realities does or ever would for an instant fear this so-called weapon of nonviolent resistance?
> The answer is known to every student of history, every detective, secret service man or C.I.D. officer, every really "hard-boiled" ruthless executive of an American industrial corporation which has had a strike of employees, every American trade union leader, every leader of a subject people striving for political freedom. The answer is that every "blood and iron" type of governor fears nonviolent resistance so much that he secretly hires *agents provocateurs* who go among the nonviolent resisters pretending to be of them, and invite them to deeds of violence or actually throw bombs or do deeds of violence themselves. This was the method of the tsarist government of old Russia. Rulers in power immediately make great outcry, stir up public indig-

nation against the "miscreants," call out the police or soldiery, and "repress the uprising" with considerable brutality, meanwhile assuring the world that these are stern but necessary steps taken only in the interests of public safety, law and order. Those striving for freedom or more privileges are indeed often violent in the first instance. But if they are not violent, their opponents or the underlings of their opponents frequently stir up violence in order to take advantage of the public reaction against it. That they feel they need to adopt such tactics shows how much they fear nonviolent resistance.[88]

Kuper also points to the dangers of agents:

In certain circumstances, the rulers may incite the resisters to violence, by use of *agents provocateurs* and of extreme provocation, for two reasons. First, force is more readily mobilized against violence . . . Second, the severe repressive measures, which the ruler may wish to use and is organized to use, require some justification. The violence of the resisters is the best justification for violent counteraction; this explains the tendency of the ruling groups in South Africa to identify the passive resistance campaign with Mau Mau.[89]

Nehru claimed after the violence at Chauri-Chaura in 1922 that "numerous *agents provocateurs,* stool pigeons, and the like . . . [have] crept into our movement and indulged in violence themselves or induced others to do so."[90] In 1936, in his presidential address at the forty-ninth session of the Indian National Congress at Lucknow, Nehru again reported the existence of ". . . a wide network of spies, and [a] . . . tribe of informers and *agents provocateurs* and the like."[91] An examination of the relevant archives would be useful in checking these charges and possibly shedding more light on the subject. In England itself, during the 1926 General Strike, the British Army had agents all over the country who mixed with strikers; whether they would have been used to provoke violence is nor clear, but certainly they were instructed to gather information and report current attitudes of strikers—a much milder role.[92]

In combatting the Finnish nonviolent noncooperation movement for independence from tsarist Russia, the Russian Governor-General of Finland, General Nikolai I. Bobrikov, arranged for *agents provocateurs* (hired by the Ochrana, the Russian secret police) to commit violence themselves against Russians, or to provoke the Finns to adopt violence. The aim was to help justify savage repression.[93] Despite the pleas of innocence of the last head of the police under the Tsar, A.T. Vassilyev,[94] there is impressive evidence that the Ochrana did use *agents provocateurs* against the Russian revolutionary groups,[95] in addition to very effectively infiltrating its agents into these groups in order to gain information.[96]

These means of counteracting a movement of nonviolent action will not necessarily be successful, however. Provocation is, indeed, highly dangerous for the opponent. If it should be publicly revealed (as is always possible) that he had deliberately attempted to provoke violence, this could disastrously affect his normal support and relative power position. Even if his agents do not publicly reveal their activities, there are other ways in which they may be unmasked (see Chapter Eight, on "disclosing identities of secret agents"), and in which their provocations may be blocked or nullified. The nonviolent group will need to give careful attention to this problem, and additional research and analysis on it are needed. The opponent's provocation to violence emphasizes still further the importance of strict adherence to nonviolent discipline. To resort to violence, declared Gandhi, is to "cooperate with the Government in the most active manner."[97] "Restraint under the gravest provocation," he insisted, "is the truest mark of soldiership." Just as even a novice in "the art of war knows that he must avoid the ambushes of his adversary," so nonviolent actionists must see every provocation as "a dangerous ambush into which we must resolutely refuse to walk."[98]

If the actionists can maintain such discipline under very difficult circumstances, they will not only help expose *agents provocateurs* and reveal the opponent, not only as an upholder of order, but as one who prefers resisters who injure and kill to disciplined nonviolent resisters; they may also help to prevent the most ruthless repression and to bring the actionists success. This is because nonviolent struggle, like other techniques for conducting conflicts, has requirements which must be fulfilled if it is to "work." One such requirement is that the nonviolent actionists and their supporters maintain nonviolent behavior.

THE NEED FOR NONVIOLENT BEHAVIOR

The requirement that volunteers maintain their nonviolent behavior is rooted in the dynamics of the technique of nonviolent action and is not an alien emphasis introduced by moralists or pacifists.[99] Without nonviolence, the opponent's repression will not rebound to undermine his power through political *jiu-jitsu* (discussed in Chapter Twelve), and the mechanisms of this technique (discussed in Chapter Thirteen) will not operate. This is not a new perception. In 1861 Francis Deák warned fellow Hungarians not to be betrayed into acts of violence nor to abandon legality (i.e., the old Hungarian constitution) as the basis of their struggle against Austrian rule: "This is the safe ground on which, unarmed ourselves, we can hold our own against armed force." [100] As Gandhi put it, "victory is impossible until we are able to keep our temper under the gravest provocation. Calmness under fire is a soldier's indispensable quality." [101] "Nonviolence is the most vital and integral part of noncooperation. We may fail in everything else and still continue our battle if we remain nonviolent." [102] Nonviolent conduct is "a strategic imperative." [103]

Nonviolent means are often perceived to be more legitimate (or sometimes less illegitimate) than violent means in the same situation, especially if the nonviolent ones seem effective. This reaction may be partly intuitive, partly emotional and partly rational. It is especially likely among third parties, usual passive supporters of the opponent, and members of the grievance group not yet participating in the struggle. These are precisely the groups whose shifts of position and loyalty may, as we shall see in later chapters, help to determine the outcome of the conflict.

Nonviolent behavior is likely to contribute to achieving a variety of positive accomplishments. Four of these are: 1) winning sympathy and support, 2) reducing casualties, 3) inducing mutiny of the opponent's troops and similar disaffection, and 4) attracting maximum participation in the nonviolent struggle. We shall consider each of these briefly here; and some of them will be discussed in more detail in the following chapter.

The sympathy and support which a nonviolent political stance tends to bring to the actionists has often been anticipated by groups using nonviolent means, even at times ones which did not exclude possible later use of violence. This was the case, for example, in the Suffolk Resolves passed by delegates in Suffolk County, Massachusetts Bay, in 1774. These Resolves were later approved by the First Continental Congress. While the Suffolk delegates clearly provided for military preparations in case hostilities broke out, they preferred peaceful forms of struggle which would bring respect and sympathy to the colonials.

... we would heartily recommend to all persons of this community not to engage in any routs, riots, or licentious attacks upon the properties of any person whatsoever, as being subversive of all order and government: but, by a steady, manly, uniform, and persevering opposition, to convince our enemies that in a contest so important—in a cause so solemn, our conduct shall be such as to merit the approbation of the wise, and the admiration of the brave and free of every age and of every country. [104]

The tendency already discussed for the opponent's repression to be relatively limited against nonviolent actionists obviously only operates so long as they remain nonviolent. Even then, the limitations on repression are not complete, and brutalities may occur. The murder of three young civil rights workers in Mississippi in 1964 is evidence of the fact that brutalities must be expected, but does not refute this tendency on nonviolent behavior to limit the repression; in fact, Robert Moses, head of the Mississippi 1964 Summer Project, has stated: "One reason we've survived is that we haven't had guns and everyone knew it." [105]

A nonviolent stance in face of repression may help undermine the morale and loyalty of the opponent's police, troops and other important aides so much that they may mutiny or express their disaffection in other strong ways. One important example of such mutiny and disaffection occurred in Petrograd in the February 1917 Revolution and was largely responsible for the final disintegration of the Tsar's regime. This instance will be described in more detail in the following chapter on political *jiu-jitsu*. There seems little doubt that serious disaffection and mutiny are much more likely in face of heroic nonviolent resistance than in face of violence when the safety and lives of the police, troops and the like are threatened. When mutiny occurs on a large scale, it demonstrates that nonviolent behavior may deal with the opponent's violent repression in a fundamental and effective way.

There is one final reason why adherance to nonviolence strengthens the movement: the use of nonviolent action will allow the maximum degree of active participation in the struggle by the highest proportion of the population. [106] Nonviolent action can be actively applied by men and women, old and young, city dwellers and rural people, factory workers, intellectuals and farmers, educated and uneducated, able-bodied and the physically weak. Virtually no one in the population need be excluded. This makes possible a much higher number of active combatants than in any other technique. The realization of this potential hinges, of course, on people's will to act and on their skill and persistence in doing so, but the technique makes possible the participation of the highest numbers of all possible forms of struggle. This will not only increase the strength of the grievance group, but this large and diverse popular participation is also likely to cause especially severe problems for the opponent. There will be many more people against whom he must act. It will often be more difficult to separate "combatants" from "noncombatants." Application of his usual control measures and repression against the old, women, the young, handicapped people, etc.—the very groups usually excluded from active combat—is especially likely to provoke reactions which weaken his power position and strengthen that of the nonviolent group. (How this happens is discussed in the next chapter.) Maintenance of nonviolent behavior is therefore extremely important in this technique for practical reasons.

HOW VIOLENCE WEAKENS THE MOVEMENT

Political violence "works" in quite different ways from nonviolent action. The introduction of violence into a nonviolent campaign by the nonviolent actionists or the grievance group, or on their behalf, is highly dangerous because the process which in nonviolent action produce strength, and could lead to success, will thereby be reversed. This reversal is likely to lead to reduced strength for the nonviolent actionists, to increased effectiveness of the opponent's measures to retain or regain control, and to the defeat of the nonviolent group. "Two opposite forces can never work concurrently so as to help each other," stated Gandhi.[107] In his study of the strike, Hiller pointed out that violence "reverses the character of the response" to the resistance.[108] It is no accident that, as we have noted, opponents confronted with nonviolent action often attribute violence to the nonviolent group when it is not present, and that, when it occurs, they concentrate on it, and exaggerate its seriousness. One example, out of the many possible, is the reaction to the predominantly nonviolent East German Rising. On June 23, 1953, the official Communist paper *Neues Deutschland* sought to justify violent suppression by recounting alleged violent actions by demonstrators and strikers during the Rising: "On 17 June . . . Fascist hordes roamed the streets, murdering, pillaging, destroying and screaming."[109] Similarly, a few days after the event, the government described speakers who had actually advised disciplined behavior at a city strike meeting of twenty thousand in the Goerlitz town square as "fascist provocateurs, criminals and bandits," and charged that they had incited the crowd to sabotage and violence.[110]

The use of violence by the nonviolent actionists, or on their behalf, has a strong tendency to shift attention to that violence and away from the issues at stake in the conflict and from the nature of the opponent's system, and also away from the (usually much greater), violence of his repressive measures. The tendency for the basic issues to be lost sight of in such cases has been pointed out by Mulford Sibley in the case of labor strikes: "If strikers resort to violence, whether initially or in response to provocation, they simply provide an excuse for the government to use force against them; and once force has been employed, the original issues leading to the strike become confused or are often forgotten." [111]

The events which followed the bombing of policemen at a strike meeting in Haymarket Square, Chicago, on May 4, 1886, illustrate both that resistance violence may shift attention from the issues in the struggle and also become the "justification" for overwhelming repression. The bombing occurred during a large and reasonably effective strike movement in various cities for the eight-hour day. In Chicago the labor organizations which believed in violence headed the strike movement, and proviolence anarchists were very influential. The peaceful open-air strike meeting at Haymarket Square had been called after police had fired into a group of two hundred striking workers who had taunted and attacked nonstrikers at a Chicago plant. At least four workers were killed and many wounded. The bomb which was thrown by an unknown person into a group of policemen killed seven and wounded sixty-six; the police had been about to disperse the small remnants of the large meeting. Although the real identity and motives of the bomber could not be established, the blame was placed on anarchists and labor radicals.

The Haymarket bomb had many results, but the eight-hour day and stronger workers' organizations were not among them. Nor was an advance for anarchism. The dead and wounded workers felled by police firings immediately after the bomb exploded were only the beginning of the workers' casualties. "Stimulation of public hysteria became the main activity of the police," writes Yellen. [112] All strike leaders and twenty-five printers of a labor newspaper were arrested. Newspapers throughout the country demanded "instantaneous execution of all subversive persons . . ." There were many police raids; homes, offices and meeting halls were broken into and searched; evidence was often fabricated. Eight strike leaders were found guilty of the bombing and four were sentenced to hang, even though they had been tried primarily on their anarchist convictions rather than on evidence. The State's Attorney admitted they were "no more guilty than the thousands who followed them," and John Altgeld, later Illinois governor, denounced the trial as grossly unfair. There were more savage police attacks on strikers' gatherings; the workingmen's ranks were split; the "Black International" dwindled to a few intellectuals and anarchism never regained a hold on the American labor movement. For many years all radical theory and practice fell into disfavor with American labor organizations. The issue of the eight-hour day was lost, the strike movement for it collapsed, and even in most cases where the eight-hour day had been already granted, employers took it away. [113]

Some people advocate the use of violence for restricted and special use in a campaign in which overwhelming reliance is to remain on non-violent methods. There is evidence, however, that when significant violence is introduced into a nonviolent action campaign, the result will be its collapse, or the abandonment of nonviolent methods, or at least considerably reduced nonviolent action and its subordination to violence as the dominant technique.

Violence by or on behalf of the nonviolent actionists may lead to the collapse of the nonviolent movement. After the peasants of Bardoli district in India had in 1928 successfully refused to pay land revenue increases, Gandhi said that if they had "committed one single act of violence, they would have lost their cause";[114] ". . . we capitulate miserably if we fail in adhering to nonviolence."[115] This is likely to lead to "disaster."[116]

The outbreak of violence in South Africa in 1952 played a very important role in the collapse of the Defiance Campaign. At the peak of the civil disobedience movement, after it had been in motion for about six months, a series of African riots broke out between October 18 and November 9. Six whites were killed and thirty-three Africans. The white dead included a nun who had been a missionary doctor to the Africans; her body was spoliated.[117] This contributed to the sensationalism and to feelings that repression was "justified." The precise causes of the riots are not clear. The resistance leaders demanded an enquiry, which the government refused. There was no evidence that the resistance movement was responsible, and there were suggestions that *agents provocateurs* may have been involved.[118] In any case, the effects of the riots "were to damp down the spirit of resistance."[119] It is possible, Kuper acknowledges, that the campaign was ready to decline anyhow, but even then the riots played an important role:

> In October the movement was still in full vigor. The number of resisters was the highest sent into action—2,354 . . . Probably as many as 1,000 defied the laws in the latter half of October. In November and December, however, the number of resisters fell to 280. Nor did the introduction of white resisters check the decline.[120]

For "all practical purposes," says Kuper, "the resistance campaign was at an end."[121] Other factors in this may include the impending general elections and the arrest of leaders, but,

> Clearly the riots played a decisive role. Quite apart from their effect on the resisters, the riots provided the opportunity for the Government to take over the initiative and to assume far-reaching powers with some measure of justification.[122]

This violence also assisted the Europeans' attempt to identify the civil disobedience movement, not with Gandhi, but with Mau Mau in Kenya.[123]

The transition between nonviolent struggle and violent struggle in the case of the American colonists illustrates that, on occasion at least, a gradual increase in readiness to use violence and the introduction of unplanned violence (Lexington and Concord) may alter the situation so drastically that even a carefully-planned, comprehensive and phased nonviolent campaign with wide popular backing may be abandoned for violence. This is especially likely when there is little deep appreciation of the practical advantages of nonviolent struggle, and when, despite using nonviolent means, people still regard violence as the most effective means of combat. Arthur Schlesinger, Sr., pointed out the vastly disproportionate effect of unplanned minor skirmishes in Massachusetts Bay on the carefully worked-out and phased program of hitherto effective economic noncooperation, the "Continental Association" adopted by the First Continental Congress. After February 1, 1775, ". . . British mercantile houses and manufactories became idle so far as American business was concerned. They were threatened with dull times and industrial depression at a time when their capital was more largely then usual tied up in American ventures." At this point limited firings took place between American irregulars and British troops. After four-and-a-half months of the noncooperation movement these events "changed the whole face of public affairs and rapidly converted the Association from a mode of peaceful pressure into a war measure." The military action at Lexington and Concord, and that which followed, convinced the radicals that ". . . the Association as a method of redress had suddenly become antiquated and that it must be altered, if not altogether abandoned, to meet the greatly changed conditions. This realization was at once acted upon by local committees and by Congress; and by the middle of 1775 the Continental Association was rapidly losing its original character." The political machinery of the Association turned increasingly to military preparations, so that by September 10, 1775, when the nonexportation phase of the noncooperation was to begin, the character of that measure was changed. "Thus, the bold experiment, inaugurated by the First Congress . . . was brought to a premature close by the call to arms."[124]

The introduction of violence is also likely to counter sharply, and to reverse, both the process of political *jiu-jitsu* and the operation of the very special mechanisms of change and dynamics of the technique of nonviolent action, discussed in later chapters. This tendency develops even when the violence is on the relatively small scale of rioting, injury, accidental loss of life in violent sabotage, or individual assassinations. For example, the whole conversion mechanism, which aims at a change of opinions, feelings and outlook, will be blocked. Violence will enable the opponent who had been unsettled by courageous nonviolence to resume his previous certainty and views, saying "I told you so . . ." [125] Also, the opponent's violence will no longer rebound against him by alienating his usual supporters, or by bringing sympathy and support from third parties. As resistance violence leads to a contraction of support for the nonviolent group in the grievance group, the opponent group and among third parties, the chances of change by nonviolent coercion are also almost entirely eliminated. With factors leading to both nonviolent coercion and conversion virtually eliminated, change by accommodation, which falls between them, also becomes most unlikely. Later we shall see in detail how these mechanisms are disrupted by resistance violence.

Success in nonviolent struggle depends to an extremely high degree upon the persistence of the nonviolent actionists in fighting with *their own methods,* and upon their refusing all temptation, whether caused by emotional hostility to the opponent's brutalities, by temptations of temporary gains, or by *agents provocateurs,* to fight with the opponent's "weapons system." If the nonviolent group switches to violence, it has, in effect, consented to fight on the opponent's own terms and with weapons where most of the advantages lie with him. This hands the initiative to the enemy, when the initiative should be retained by the nonviolent group, as we have already discussed. Luthuli points to this shift of initiative as a consequence of the riots, already described, which happened at the peak of the 1952 Defiance Campaign. Before they occurred, he wrote:

> The Defiance Campaign was far too orderly and successful for the Government's liking, and it was growing . . . . The challenge of nonviolence was more than they could meet. It robbed them of the initiative. On the other hand, violence by Africans would restore this initiative to them—they would then be able to bring out the guns and the other techniques of intimidation and present themselves as restorerors of order.
>
> It cannot be denied that this is exactly what happened, and at the moment most convenient for the Government. The infiltration of *agents provocateurs* in both Port Elizabeth and Kimberly is well attested. They kept well clear of the volunteers and the Congress. They did their work among irresponsible youngsters . . .
>
> It was all the Government needed. The riots and the Defiance Campaign were immediately identified with each other in the white South African imagination. The initiative was with the Government.

It is well known that the Government used its recovered initiative harshly and to the full . . . The activities of rioters provided the pretext for crushing nonviolent demonstrators. [126]

Violence by the actionists will also tend strongly to alienate existing support for the struggle by other members of the grievance group. Thus violence may weaken the unity and reduce the combat strength of the general grievance group. There are many examples of this from the history of the Russian revolutionary movement. [127] Katkov points out these effects on one revolutionary party:

> The Socialist Revolutionary Party did not give up its terrorist activities until the double agent, Azef, who directed them, was unmasked in 1908. Terrorism, however, had sapped the organizational capacity of the party and alienated it from the masses, who never understood the purpose of political terror. [128]

Alienation of support by acts of violence also happened during the various struggles of the American colonists; initially it was mob disorders and intimidations which alienated people—especially merchants—who otherwise supported the objectives of the struggle. [129] The destruction of property belonging to someone else—as the dumping of tea into Boston harbor—also alienated other Americans who were not merchants:

> . . . the Boston Tea Party was best calculated to enkindle the public mind; but, to the surprise of the radicals, there was no bursting forth of the flame that had swept over the country at the time of [the nonviolent campaigns against] the Stamp Act and again during the Townshend Acts, save in Massachusetts where the fuse had been carefully laid . . . The merchant class was generally shocked into remorseful silence . . . and many other people, more liberally inclined, were of their cast of mind. [130]

Even Benjamin Franklin called the tea destruction "an act of violent injustice on our part." [131] When military resistance broke out, even some radicals deserted the colonists' cause. [132] There had been a great degree of unity in implementing the earlier noncooperation campaigns. When violent resistance became dominant, Gipson points out, many Americans chose to be Loyalists and to fight for the King and the association with England—giving the contest "all the characteristics of a civil war in many parts of the country." Furthermore, he continues,

> . . . there were vastly greater numbers of colonials hostile to the revolutionary movement. They stood aghast at the acts of terrorism per-

formed by bands of rioters and vandals . . . To people of such conservative tendencies the patriotic cry of liberty was a mockery, when hand in hand with it went acts of violence designed to deprive them of all liberty because they disagreed on the great issue of the day. [133]

The earlier opposition of moderates to the Continental Association plan of resistance by economic noncooperation [134] had thus been multiplied and intensified by the switch to violence.

There is supporting evidence also from the contemporary Afro-American struggle in the United States that violence alienates support. [135] James Farmer, then National Director of the Congress of Racial Equality, predicted this process in 1965, before the large-scale urban riots; his warning has been largely fulfilled.

Widespread violence by the freedom fighters would sever from the struggle all but a few of our allies. It would also provoke and, to many, justify such repressive measures as would injure the movement. None would profit from such developments except the defenders of segregation and perhaps the more bellicose of the black nationalist groups. [136]

There is wide evidence in support of Farmer's view that violence by the grievance group tends to unleash disproportionately severe repression. Such repression would otherwise probably not have happened even though the opponent might well have liked to use it, and if it had happened in face of nonviolent resistance it would probably not have been effective. There are repeated examples of this. The firings at Lexington and Concord led to British occupation of Boston by troops, who turned it into an armed camp. [137]

Irish reforms, an end to English coercion, and the possibility of Home Rule were all destroyed by the assassinations in Phoenix Park, Dublin, on May 6, 1882, of two government officials. These occurred just when the coercion policy had been ended, the Irish leaders Parnell, Dillon and Davitt had been released from prison, and the strongest men in the government, including Gladstone, were coming around to Irish Home Rule. The assassinations were carried out by "The Invincible Society," a group of about twenty youthful Irish patriots. "The result was almost fatal to the national movement," writes O'Hegarty. [138] A new far more severe Coercion Act, which suspended the ordinary processes of law and civil liberties, was enacted. Conservative opinion hardened, and any step toward Home Rule became out of the question. "This year and next, Ireland was under the iron heel." [139] Morley, biographer of Gladstone, writes: "The reaction produced by the murders in the Park made perseverance in a milder policy impossible in face of English opinion, and parliament eagerly passed the Coercion Act of 1882." [140] "The Invincible Society" succeeded in aiding English imperialism with great effectiveness. "No worse blow could have been struck at Mr. Parnell's policy." [141]

Even the youthful Stalin warned workers against individual assaults on employers or managers—"economic terror"—which were becoming widespread, because they would recoil on organized labor. [142]

Casualties also tended to be much higher among violent resisters than among nonviolent resisters. During the 1905 revolution, for example, much greater numbers of dead occurred in instances of large-scale violence than in overwhelmingly nonviolent demonstrations and general strikes. Thus relatively brief violent rebellions in Lodz left three hundred dead; in Odessa, about two thousand dead; and in Moscow, one thousand dead. Nonviolent strikers and demonstrators were also killed, but not in such proportions, even though their challenge to the government's power was often far greater. [143]

The government-sponsored nonviolent noncooperation struggle against Franco-Belgian occupation of the Ruhr was detrimentally affected by the introduction into the struggle of acts of political violence, including destructive sabotage, attacks on French sentries and blowing up of bridges. The distinguished German historian, Erich Eyck, points to their counterproductive effects:

> Although such acts satisfied the bitter mood of many Germans, politically they were absurd, indeed suicidal. Only the politically immature could persuade themselves that these incidents would force France and Belgium to retreat. Their only consequence could be still worse sufferings for the unfortunate people of the occupied zones: arrests, expulsions, and executions . . . [Carl] Severing, [the Prussian Minister of the Interior], and the whole Prussian government were only doing their clear duty when they tried to stop as best they could this playing with fire. [144]

Similar evidence of the tendency for violent action to provoke strong repression may be found in reactions to the United States 1919 race riots, [145] and from the urban ghetto riots of the late 1960s.

Solomon and Fishman have also pointed to the tendency for violence to remove the limitations on the opponent's repression, while maintenance of nonviolence tends to restrict repression. In fact they describe this nonviolent technique as ". . . a means of directly asserting aggression while still trying to minimize provocation. When a group or individual wants to struggle against strong opposition which is capable of inflicting disastrous retaliation, the nonviolent mode of 'defiance' seems to provide a way of resolving the dilemma." [146] Violence by the subordinates, however, removes the limitations on repression imposed by the dynamics of nonviolent action.

Violence by, or in support of, the nonviolent actionists is also likely to bring an abrupt reversal of sympathy for them among the members of the opponent group, and especially end any internal opposition to the objectionable policies or repression. It was, for example, much easier for Englishmen to oppose colonialism and repression in India during the Gandhian struggles than in Kenya during the Mau Mau campaign. Members of the opponent group who have supported the policies and regime out of idealistic motives are especially likely to be alienated by violence; however, had nonviolent discipline been maintained, those people might have proved to be the least reliable of the opponent's supporters. Since nonviolent action operates to aggravate existing dissent in the opponent group, and to create within it support for the nonviolent group, such violence would be especially unfortunate. Increased solidarity in the opponent group behind the policies and repression will sharply reduce the chances of victory for the nonviolent actionists.

American colonial economic noncooperation had by early 1775 aroused British merchants, traders and investors with American connections into a considerable campaign against the Government and for repeal of the coercive acts of 1774. (Total export trade from England to the participating North American colonies dropped by nearly ninety-seven percent from 1774 to 1775.) The merchants carried on systematic activities to convince the King's ministers and Parliament to yield; these included many petitions and were similar to actions which had on earlier occasions brought changes in government policies for America. The ministry did not yield in response, but before the merchants' indignation against government coercive measures against the colonists could find new expressions, the merchants became reconciled to the situation and their opposition faded. One important factor in this was the improvement in mid-1775 in British business conditions as a result of increased European orders and improved payments of debts by American merchants. However, there was another equally important reason for the collapse of the support for the Americans by British merchants. Schlesinger writes: "undoubtedly the affair at Lexington and Concord in April sharpened the understanding of many of them as to the nature of the issues at stake." [147]

Resistance violence is especially likely to restore loyalty and obedience among any of the opponent's troops or police becoming disaffected by the nonviolent action. Soldiers under fire are likely to remain obedient, not mutiny. It is well known that ordinary soldiers will fight more persistently and effectively if they and their friends are being shot, wounded or killed. Resistance violence will tend to remove the influences producing sympathy for nonviolent actionists and shatter possible inner doubts about the issues of the conflict and the soldier's own duty. In nonviolent struggles in which success and failure hinge on whether the opponent's troops can be induced to mutiny, violence against them may spell defeat.

There is suggestive evidence of this counterproductive role of violence from the Moscow general strike and armed rising of December 1905. In the weeks prior to the Moscow strike there was considerable and widely scattered unrest in the armed forces, involving ". . . an unmistakable change in attitude toward authority. The results were mutinous and disorderly conduct that ranged from minor infractions to quite ominous outbreaks." [148] There had been several mutinies of both sailors and soldiers. These, added to lesser instances of insubordination, "made the navy practically worthless as a trustworthy fighting force . . ." [149] Disaffection in the army was widespread, even in the interior of the Empire. Although outright disobedience by soldiers was not so marked in those areas, ". . . there were good reasons for concern about the instrument upon which the regime would have to place its ultimate dependence, its armed forces." [150] Although the Menshevik and Bolshevik wings of the Social Democratic Party in Moscow were both agreed that "the Tsarist government was deliberately provoking the working class . . . ," both supported the plan for an armed rising; although the Bolsheviks favored an immediate armed rising, they agreed to the Menshevik proposal for "a general political strike which should transform itself into an armed uprising." [151] This was in response to the November 27 call from the St. Petersburg Soviet for a general armed rising, issued immediately before it was crushed. [152]

There was no reason to assume at the time that there was a serious chance of victory for an armed rising in Moscow. The militia of the Social Democratic Party in the city numbered only about one thousand, inadequately organized and armed and with less than twenty handmade bombs and grenades. The head of the militia himself opposed an armed rising, and others expressed doubts that the soldiers would support insurrection. [153] Very important, it has been reported that the tsarist government was deliberately provoking violence in order to be able to crush the revolution. [154] Once the decision had been made, workers, party revolutionaries and even Bolsheviks were all uneasy about the plan. They lacked enthusiasm and even believed in "the inevitability of defeat." [155] "Although damaging to the Government's prestige," Keep writes, a violent rising had "no chance of bringing about its overthrow . . ." [156]

Nevertheless, the Bolsheviks had taken the lead in pushing for an armed rising in Moscow. On the basis of available evidence, the Leninist Social Democrats did not seem to have compared the likely effect of an armed rising to alternative courses of action, on the chances of inducing a major mutiny of the Tsar's troops. The "Right Bolsheviks," however, apparently did. The Bolsheviks under Lenin were instead primarily concerned with gaining control of the situation for their own purposes and directing it as they chose to gain Bolshevik political objectives, regardless of the wishes of others or of effects on the revolution. [157] It is also clear the call of the Moscow Bolsheviks for an armed rising was not an "irresponsible" independent act of the local group, for on November 27 there had been a meeting of the Central Committee of the Social Democratic Party in St. Petersburg, attended by Lenin, at which preparations for an armed rising were discussed. [158]

It is difficult to document the Bolsheviks' motives for an armed rising launched when the loyalty of the troops still hung in the balance, and when the chances of mutiny were high while those of military victory were very small. Prawdin writes that "the real purpose of the Bolsheviks was to bring it home to the workers that they could not do without military organization and arms." [159] This interpretation is consistent with Lenin's comments on the need for violence, which he had written before the Moscow rising, [160] and with his comments on the rising written afterwards. [161]

The general strike phase of the Moscow insurrection began on December 7—four days after the mutiny of a regiment stationed in the city. The Social Democratic Party seems to have been either indifferent to the mutiny or incompetent in responding to it. The party offered no practical advice to the disobedient troops in their barracks—not even to become lost in civilian clothes among the general population. All they did was to advise restraint. The mutiny was then suppressed and several units were withdrawn from Moscow. [162] Then the general strike began, and during this phase, Harcave reports, "Two-thirds of the government troops . . . were judged unreliable; one whole regiment had actually undertaken to join the strikers before the fighting began, and had been prevented only by the interposing of loyal troops." [163] There were a number of instances of troops refusing to fire on demonstrators. [164]

The violent insurrection then developed. This included partisan war-fare tactics, street barricades and sniper fire against the soldiers patrolling the city. In contrast to the earlier disaffection, disobedience and mutiny, the troops now obeyed orders.[165] The violent insurrection was defeated. "The Moscow rising was a failure," writes Seton-Watson," and it was clear that the revolution was over. The army's loyalty was by now ensured." [166] Other historians also point to the end of the Moscow rising as the begin-ning of the end for the revolution; Lenin's conclusion on that single point was identical.[167] Further research is needed, but provisionally the evidence suggests that: 1) the failure of the Moscow rising had a significant influ-ence on the revolution as a whole, contributing to its defeat, 2) the Mos-cow rising was a failure because the troops, despite widespread unrest, did not mutiny, 3) the chance of large-scale mutinies of soldiers in Moscow would have been greater if revolutionary activities had been restricted to nonviolent ones not threatening the lives of the troops, and 4) had nonvio-lent discipline been more widespread and a nonviolent Moscow rising re-placed the violent one, the tsarist system might have been destroyed in December 1905-January 1906. The popular view that violence in a resist-ance or revolutionary movement by definition adds to the power and chances of success of that movement can no longer be accepted.

SABOTAGE AND NONVIOLENT ACTION

Hostile conservative critics of nonviolent action sometimes argue that nonviolent struggle should be rejected because it is closely associated with sabotage or leads to sabotage. In contrast, others interested primarily in maximum effectiveness in struggle and who think themselves to be more realistic argue that sabotage should be used along with nonviolent action. Both views reveal an inadequate understanding of the nonviolent technique.

Sabotage, as used here, refers to acts of demolition and related de-struction directed against machinery, transport, buildings, bridges, installa-tions and the like. Because these are acts against *property,* they are not included in the definition of "violence" in this book. Such acts would, however, become "violence" if they bring injury or death to *persons,* or threaten to do so. Certain other types of action fall somewhere between sabotage and nonviolent action, such as removal of key parts from machin-ery and vehicles, removal or release in nondangerous ways of fuel for ma-chinery and vehicles, removal of records and files for various government departments and offices (as police) and even their destruction by means which could not possibly cause physical injury to any persons. Such methods require separate consideration, and this discussion does not apply to them. Those methods are more likely to be compatible with nonviolent action, but are not always so in all situations. They, too, can be detrimental to effective nonviolent action under certain conditions.

Sabotage has on occasion followed nonviolent action, especially when the latter was not immediately effective, as in South Africa. Sabotage has also occurred during nonviolent resistance when there has been no decision to use only certain means of resistance, as in Norway during the Nazi occupation. Even there, however, much if not most of the sabotage was organized from England for Allied military purposes, not by resistance groups in Norway. Also, sabotage has on occasion been used during a consciously nonviolent struggle by persons and groups ignoring or defying the instructions of the leadership to eschew acts of demolition, as was the case in the *Ruhrkampf*. But sabotage has never, to my knowledge, been deliberately applied by a disciplined movement which has consciously chosen to fight by nonviolent action. Gandhi constantly emphasized that sabotage was contrary to this technique.[168] In terms of the principles, strategy and mechanisms of operation, sabotage is more closely related to violent than to nonviolent action. This is true even though the aim of the sabotage may be only the destruction of material objects without taking lives—such as an empty bridge as distinct from a bridge being crossed by enemy troops.

There are strong reasons why the introduction of sabotage will seriously weaken a nonviolent action movement. These are rooted in the differing dynamics and mechanisms of these two techniques. There are at least nine such reasons:

First, sabotage always runs the risk of unintentional physical injury or death to opponents or to innocent bystanders, as in attempts to destroy bridges, factories, etc. Nonviolent action, on the other hand, requires that its supporters refuse to use physical violence and instead protect the lives of opponents and others. Even limited injuries or deaths will rebound against the nonviolent movement.

Second, effective sabotage in difficult situations requires a willingness to use physical violence against persons who discover the plans and are willing and able either to reveal or to prevent them. These may be informers, guards, soldiers, or ordinary people. Nonviolent action, conversely, requires for success the strict maintenance of nonviolence.

Third, sabotage requires secrecy in the planning and carrying out of missions. As already discussed, secrecy introduces a whole series of disruptive influences. These include ultimate dependence on violence (instead of nonviolence), fear of discovery (in place of fearless open action), and wild suspicions among the opponents about the resisters' intent and plans which may increase brutalities and intransigence (in place of the usually openly announced intentions).

Fourth, sabotage requires only a few persons to carry it out and hence reduces the number of effective resisters, while nonviolent action makes possible a large degree of participation among the whole population.

Fifth, confidence in the adequacy of nonviolent action is a great aid to its successful application. The use of sabotage, however, demonstrates a lack of such confidence which is detrimental to effective use of nonviolent action.

Sixth, nonviolent action is based upon a challenge *in human terms* by human beings to other human beings. Sabotage relies on physical destruction of property, a very different approach likely to detract from the operation of the other, potentially more powerful, influences. [169]

Seventh, sabotage and nonviolent action are rooted in quite different premises about how to undermine the opponent. Nonviolent action produces withdrawal of consent by the subjects, while sabotage acts against the opponent by destroying property.

Eighth, where physical injury or death occurs to persons because of sabotage, whether accidental or deliberate, there is likely to be a relative loss of sympathy and support for the nonviolent group and/or an increase of sympathy and support for the opponent—the opposite of what is likely and necessary in nonviolent action.

Finally, therefore, sabotage is likely to result in highly disproportionate repression against the saboteurs or the general population, or both. [170] Contrary to the effects of repression against persistent nonviolent actionists, repression provoked by sabotage is not likely to weaken the opponent's relative power position.

That sabotage does not combine well with nonviolent action is amply illustrated by the 1923 Ruhr struggle. There is further evidence to support the view of Eyck quoted above that sabotage had detrimental effects. Not only were electricity and telegraph wires cut but also various objectives, such as railway lines, canal locks and barges, railway trestles and military trains carrying occupation troops were bombed. Ten Belgian soldiers were killed and forty wounded by the attack on the Rhine bridge near Duisburg. Other acts of violence included terrorist attacks against occupation soldiers, and suspected spies and traitors within the sabotage groups were sometimes murdered. [171] One reason for these developments was the Germans' lack of a plan for nonviolent resistance and their relative lack of effective leadership and organization.[172] Although sabotage and similar acts did harass the occupation officials, there is little indication that the acts were effective in limiting or reducing the occupiers' control or ability to achieve their objectives. However, sabotage had other effects, including extremely severe repression from the occupying forces who sometimes beat and killed people, including innocent bystanders. Also, the unity of the population of the occupied area—which had been achieved under the nonviolent resistance campaign—was destroyed. Repression included a widespread ban on road traffic which, according to Wentzcke, "heralded the end of passive resistance." Internationally, the moral isolation of France and the high degree of world sympathy which had been produced by the nonviolent resistance were not only erased, but to a significant degree reversed.[173]

For these reasons, the idea that sabotage is compatible with nonviolent action must be rejected, as either a false accusation of uninformed critics, or as a highly dangerous action proposal likely to disrupt the processes which could bring strength and victory.

OTHER WAYS TO SLIP INTO VIOLENCE

One reason why the most perceptive exponents and practitioners of nonviolent action have emphasized so strongly the firm and meticulous maintenance of nonviolent behavior is that without strict and conscious attention, the movement could easily slip into progressively greater reliance on violence without a prior conscious decision to do so. This may happen at a variety of points, a number of which are illustrated by instances in the American colonists' struggles. Their struggles probably provide the richest example of this type of development—from systematic and repeated noncooperation to a long war of independence.

Even while the colonists' struggle prior to April 1775 was overwhelmingly nonviolent, there were quite a few points at which actions were taken which were either themselves violent or which potentially set the stage for violence. Until Lexington and Concord, however, these did not expand sufficiently to alter the predominantly nonviolent character of the resistance. They are nevertheless instructive. During the opposition to the Stamp Act there was considerable use of personal and mob threats, physical intimidation, and destruction of personal and public property designed, for example, to induce newly appointed Stamp Distributors to resign their posts.[174] During the same period, there was a general tendency among.

undisciplined elements of the population to act in disregard of the recommended plans of those who had launched the campaign and had selected the means of action which were to be used. [175] Economic boycotts and nonuse of taxed imports lead to smuggling, and "smuggling proved to be the first channel through which violence was injected into the struggle." [176] Sometimes relatively insignificant behavior burst into violence, because "the high tension which public affairs had reached ripened the public mind for violence." [177] Some radicals, such as Thomas Mason, urged that a policy of disobedience to Parliament's laws be defended if necessary by "resort to armed resistance and secession . . ." [178] Sometimes delaying a decision or postponing action provided the necessary opportunity for advocates of violence to win the day. [179] The destruction of property rapidly escalated in seriousness, as from the dumping of tea in Boston harbor to the later burning of a tea-bearing vessel at Annapolis, Maryland. [180]

The exchanges of fire between British troops and colonial irregulars at Lexington and Concord were, as it happened, the actions which resulted in abandonment of a comprehensive plan of economic noncooperation before it had been fully applied and in its replacement by military means. The campaign of economic noncooperation embodied in the Continental Association had been signed by the members of the First Continental Congress on October 20, 1774. It was broadly divided into two phases, the nonimportation of British goods to begin from December 1, 1774, and the nonexportation of American goods to Britain to begin from September 10, 1775. [181] This remained the colonists' resistance strategy, even though tensions were sometimes high and though various groups were on their own initiative preparing for military conflict. In Massachusetts Bay the Provincial Congress took steps in February 1775 to prepare the militia and the "Minute Men" and to raise taxes to pay for weapons. [182] This was independent action taken outside the context of the Continental Association campaign of resistance adopted for all the colonies. Further preparations for military conflict were shortly taken by the Committee of Safety. When seven hundred British troops under orders to destroy the colonists' military supplies hidden at Concord met seventy-five Minute Men on the Lexington village green on April 19, there was an exchange of fire. This was probably initiated by an American who was not among the Minute Men; the latter fled, leaving dead and wounded on the green. Most of the Concord supplies were removed before the British arrived there, and the Minute Men with large reinforcements forced British troops to retreat under fire toward Boston. The Redcoats were continually fired upon by Americans hidden behind stones and trees, and only the arrival of British reinforcements made possible a fighting withdrawal to Charlestown, across the river from Boston.[183]

For the purposes of this study, the significance of these events is the effect that they had on the entire course of the American struggle. The large-scale preparations for military conflict in Massachusetts Bay were undertaken on the initiative of Massachusetts radicals only, and outside of the resistance measures outlined in the Continental Association. These had not even mentioned military resistance, neither to commend it, threaten it, nor to discourage it, except by implication in the statement that nonimportation, nonconsumption and nonexportation measures "faithfully adhered to, will prove the most speedy, effectual and peaceable measures . . ."[184]

Once military preparations against the British had begun in Massachusetts Bay it was to be expected that, short of immediate evacuation, the British would have to take counteraction. The British action was intended to be a very limited one, to destroy supplies of American arms hidden at Concord, the exact location of which they knew from an informer. However, once each side had taken these steps the chances of avoiding an exchange of fire were few. (If the Concord supplies had all been moved, as most of them were, and hidden elsewhere and the Americans had themselves remained out of sight the British troops would have had to return to Boston without having accomplished their mission but also without military hostilities.) The consequence of general military preparations in *one* colony and the unplanned shift to military struggle on April 19 extended to all the colonies and altered the whole approach to the conduct of the conflict.

It is arguable that the American colonists could have won full independence more quickly, with more support within the colonies and from Englishmen, had they continued to rely upon the nonviolent methods of struggle they had so successfully used to that date. *De facto* British control in the colonies was already extraordinarily weak, owing to the Americans' political noncooperation, economic sanctions and development of alternative political institutions to which they gave loyalty. Governor Dunmore of Virginia wrote to Lord Dartmouth on December 24, 1774, that the Continental Association was being enforced there "with greatest rigour," that the "Laws of Congress" (the Continental Congress) received from Virginians "marks of reverence they never bestowed on their legal Government, or the Laws preceding from it." He added:

I have discovered no instance where the interposition of Government, in the feeble state to which it is reduced, could serve any other purpose than to suffer the disgrace of a disappointment, and thereby afford matter of great exultation to its enemies and increase their influence over the minds of the people.[185]

In South Carolina the British Government was so weak compared to the Continental Association that "ministerial opposition is here obliged to be silent," as the General Committee wrote at the time.[186] The Governor of Massachusetts Bay in early 1774 was already of the opinion that "All legislative, as well as executive power was gone . . ."[187] Governor Gage made a similar report from there in September 1774, and by the end of October he had virtually no power except that of his troops.[188] By October 1774, the legal government in Maryland had virtually abdicated.[189] There are also other indications.[190]

By mid-April the nonimportation and nonconsumption phase of the Continental Association resistance plan had only been in operation about four-and-a-half months, and the more extreme nonexportation phase was not due to come into operation for almost another five months. The introduction of the unplanned but obviously significant violence of the Massachusetts Bay Minute Men in the colonists' struggle created a situation in which imitation of their action seemed natural, and a large-scale extension of military preparations and action seemed to be required—"seemed" is used since there was apparently no careful evaluation of the relative advantages of a major shift to military struggle as compared with an attempt to isolate the Lexington-Concord events and to continue to rely upon the established strategy of political and economic noncooperation along with a further development of parallel governmental institutions. One immediate result was confusion, as Robert R. Livingston put it during the Second Continental Congress, which opened on May 10, 1775: "We are between hawk and buzzard; we puzzle ourselves between the commercial and warlike opposition."[191] The uncertainty did not last long, however. Schlesinger summarized the change which took place:

> The tocsin of war, sounded on the historic April day at Lexington and Concord, wrought a radical change in the nature of the opposition directed by the Americans against the British measures. This did not mean that a struggle for independence had begun, but it did mean that armed rebellion had superseded commercial coercion as the dependence of the radicals in their struggle for larger liberties. Thereafter the Continental Association lost its distinctive character as a method of peaceful coercion; it became subordinated to the military necessities of the times.

The transformation which the Association was undergoing revealed itself in five ways: in the widespread adoption of defense associations; in the determination of the Georgian moderates to adopt the Continental Association as a deterrent to the more violent methods advocated by the radicals there; in the spontaneous action of the extra-legal bodies in the several provinces in taking on disciplinary and military functions; in the adoption, by provinces exposed to the perils of war, of non-exportation regulations prior to the time fixed in the Association; and in the important alterations made in the text of the original Association by the Second Continental Congress. [192]

This Second Congress regarded the Lexington events as a declaration of war, began to act like a government, and took direction of the rebellion. In June, 1775, already, George Washington was appointed Commander-in-Chief of the army of the United Colonies, and regulations were announced for the army and navy. On July 6 a declaration was issued which in effect said that the British use of military force required the colonists to change their means of struggle and to reply with military means also. [193]

THE NECESSITY OF DISCIPLINE

If the nonviolent struggle movement is to persist in face of repression, to remain nonviolent, and to carry through the campaign, discipline among the nonviolent actionists is required. Basically, this discipline consists of adherence to certain minimum standards of behavior. The degree and type of discipline required will vary depending on the situation and the nature of the nonviolent group and of the opponent. The absence of discipline will mean that effective use of this technique will become very difficult or impossible. This emphasis on discipline is not, as some might think, associated only with Gandhian nonviolence. The need for it was emphasized by the Danish exponent of nonviolent action, Nils Lindberg, before World War II on the basis of other considerations, [194] and very un-Gandhian East Germans called for discipline in the course of resistance during the rising of June 1953. [195] Although Gandhi antedates these instances, their emphasis on discipline is derived from other sources.

Discipline may be encouraged by leaders through instructions, appeals, pledges, as well as by discipline leaflets, marshals and other means, as discussed below, and, as we have already seen, various nonviolent sanctions may be applied in support of group decisions and discipline. However, in nonviolent action discipline cannot be imposed or forced upon the participants by the leaders; various means of encouraging discipline will be effective only to the degree that they influence or strengthen the will or conscience of the actionists. Despite important measures to promote and maintain discipline, including nonviolent sanctions, by the nature of the technique discipline in nonviolent action must be essentially the self-discipline of the participants.

Discipline in nonviolent action is, therefore, self-discipline and inner discipline. This is true whether the discipline has been promoted by the active leaders of the movement, or has been continued after all distinguishable leaders have been imprisoned, or has been developed intuitively in a spontaneous movement. But there are a variety of ways used to promote nonviolent discipline and there is room for comparative evaluation and choice among these alternative ways. But there must be some type of discipline. Those who out of ignorance or emotional reaction to discipline would ignore or abolish it in nonviolent action place the entire struggle in a perilous position. If their views predominate, effective nonviolent action becomes impossible. It is not necessary to agree with everything Gandhi said on the subject to appreciate his general assessment:

> Freedom of four hundred million people through purely non-violent effort is not to be gained without learning the virtue of iron discipline —not imposed from without, but sprung naturally from within. Without the requisite discipline, non-violence can only be a veneer. [196]

Continued participation in the struggle and refusal to submit to fear are the most crucial aims of discipline. After this, adherence to nonviolent behavior is the most important single aspect of discipline in this technique. Discipline serves other functions also, including increasing the actionists' ability to withstand severe repression. "A group of people who are acting under discipline are less likely to crack under pressure," argues Bradford Lyttle. Just as discipline helps military troops to continue to confront the enemy despite danger, discipline helps nonviolent actionists: "disciplined demonstrators can better resist charge by the police or attack by counter-demonstrators." Discipline, Lyttle writes, will help nonviolent demonstrators to remain calm and firm, and to react effectively in unexpected situations. [197]

Where discipline is weak or absent, there is danger that a nonviolent demonstration may, in a tense situation, lead to a major riot which would most likely both shift attention from the original grievance and also alienate support. Four days of riots in Negro areas of New York City in July

1964 were triggered in this way. On the evening of July 18, a rally was held by several city chapters of the Congress of Racial Equality (C.O.R.E.) to demand a civilian review board to examine cases of alleged police brutality and the removal of the police commissioner. The rally was held two days after an off-duty policeman had shot to death a youth who had attacked him in Harlem. About a hundred people were led by C.O.R.E. organizers to a Harlem police precinct station where they presented their demands. They then sat down in the street, announcing they would stay until at least some of the demands were met. When police tried to push some of the crowd back, several scuffles took place, but the organizers generally maintained control. They were, however, arrested, dragged into the police station, and, some reported, beaten. Its nonviolent leadership removed, the crowd began throwing bricks and bottles at the police, who charged into the crowd. Later a flaming bottle of gasoline was thrown at a police car, police fired at rioters, looting took place, and such activities continued during the night. In Harlem and the Negro ghetto of Bedford-Stuyvesant in Brooklyn similar violence took place, largely between Negro youths and white police, for the next four nights.[198] Had the experienced C.O.R.E. organizers not been arrested, or had the remaining sit-downers maintained discipline, the rioting would probably not have happened, and attention would have remained focused not on Negro rioting, but on charges of police brutality and demands for a civilian control board.

In addition to maintaining nonviolent behavior in organized planned demonstrations, discipline includes adherence to the plans and instructions for the action. If prospective nonviolent actionists do not have confidence in the judgment of those responsible for planning the nonviolent action, then they ought not to take part. If they do have confidence, then the plans and instructions ought to be carried out precisely.

Where advance planning is possible, it should be in the hands of those persons most qualified for the job on the basis of their knowledge of the technique, understanding of the situation and experience. Other important qualities include ability to express themselves and to get along well with others. Persons who accept the planners' recommendations, and therefore wish to participate in the action or campaign, should then have the humility to follow the recommended strategy and course of action. Almost always action should be limited to the forms prescribed for the particular conflict. Not everyone is equally capable of intelligent planning for group or mass nonviolent action, any more than everyone is equally capable of doing anything else. While knowledge of the dynamics, methods and strategy of this technique remains restricted, there are likely to be fewer capable planners. But when such knowledge increases and spreads, more and more persons will become capable of participating in formulation of wise plans for nonviolent struggle. It is either arrogance or deliberate disruption intended to help the opponent which causes a person to join a nonviolent group and then ignore the prepared plans for the struggle, insisting on doing whatever he or she pleases. To the degree possible, leaders should take participants into their confidence and explain to them the reasons for the choice of the given strategy and plans for action, along with discussion of anticipated difficulties and recommended ways of dealing with them. [199]

Well formulated plans take into consideration the best means for achieving maximum impact, given the numbers, strengths and qualities of the nonviolent actionists, the nature of the opponent, the issues, the conflict situation, and the requirements of this technique. If then some participants take other unplanned types of action, while claiming to be part of the planned action, the effectiveness of the whole operation may in serious instances be jeopardized unless the rest of the nonviolent group is able to isolate or to counterbalance the innovations. Undisciplined activities are likely to give the effect of disunity and dissension. As a result other participants may be placed in a situation for which they are not prepared, represented as supporting actions with which they do not agree, or confronted with unanticipated repression by police or troops responding to the unexpected.

Of course, in a given instance, the unplanned innovations may seem to do little harm, or even be beneficial. However, they intrinsically involve dangers. For example, unplanned types of action, or demonstrating at other places than those selected can greatly facilitate the outbreak of counterproductive violence among the grievance group and the application of effective repression by the opponent. Sometimes indiscipline and internal chaos may be promoted by well intentioned but confused people. At other times, they may be emotionally disturbed. On still other occasions, they may be undercover agents for the police or a hostile political organization. Small or large groups of bystanders—whether friendly or hostile—may also present special discipline problems requiring different types of control measures. [200]

Political groups with strong viewpoints, clear policy, internal discipline and ambitions far beyond the immediate demands of the struggle may also seek to "use" the conflict situation to their own advantage, even though promotion of their political advantage may require weakening of the nonviolent struggle and harming its cause, verbal pronouncements notwithstanding. Sometimes such political groups will promote indiscipline themselves and at other times they may try to capitalize on disruption and confusion introduced by others. Groups which have a strong doctrinal belief in the necessity of political violence, such as the Communists, are especially risky potential collaborators. Even when they do not seek to enter the nonviolent opposition movement their behavior may be disruptive. At the beginning of the general strike against the Kapp *Putsch* in Germany in 1920, the Communists refused to support it and thereby refused to act against the attempted military-monarchist seizure of power because they did not wish to help a capitalist republic. Later they supported the strike, but after the collapse of the *coup* the Communists tried to capitalize on the internal crisis by organizing violent rebellion in the Ruhr and by attempting their own *coup* in Sachsen.[201] Communists and their supporters in South Africa who used and supported nonviolent action at certain stages were prominent among those who later denounced nonviolent methods as having "failed" without offering comparative strategic analyses of the problems, advantages and disadvantages of various types of both nonviolent and violent struggle in the situation. The South African Communists' abandonment of nonviolent means could have been, and indeed was, predicted.[202]

Discipline is especially important when there is special danger that violence may break out and when participants lack experience and deep understanding of nonviolent technique. In addition to the multitude of statements by Gandhi on the importance of the volunteers' carrying out instructions, and obeying the rules and resolutions of their own group,[203] various Western groups have also stressed discipline. Peace action groups have often been especially articulate on this point. The 1962 discipline of New York City peace groups, for example, included this pledge:

> We will adhere to the planned program of action for each demonstration, unless a change of plan is communicated to us by the demonstration's sponsors or by their representatives. We will not initiate any unannounced action, unless it has been explicitly approved by the sponsors.
>
> We recognize that conducting an orderly demonstration depends upon mutual cooperation and respect between participants and those who have organized and are responsible for the demonstration. (If requests are made for action which you feel are unwise, you will have an opportunity to discuss your complaint fully with the responsible persons after the demonstration, if it is not possible at the time.) If a request is made which you cannot accept, please quietly disassociate yourself from the demonstration.[204]

The nonviolent group's standards for behavior of participants may cover not only the direct action stage, but also the period of imprisonment following arrests.[205]

Exponents of discipline in nonviolent action have argued that a disciplined movement (as compared to an undisciplined one) is more likely to win the respect of third parties and of the opponent,[206] achieve a greater recognition of the seriousness of purpose involved, be more inspiring and produce a greater impact.[207] Such discipline, Gregg argued, also contributes to inner growth and inner strengthening of individual participants.[208] It will also help to maintain social order even in the midst of major struggle and sharp political conflict. Though not easy, nonviolent discipline is quite within the capacities of the vast majority of people; Gregg argued that discipline in nonviolent action, once understood, is not necessarily more difficult than the quite different type of discipline which is often achieved among soldiers in war situations.[209]

PROMOTING NONVIOLENT DISCIPLINE

In some cases participants may intuitively, or by common accord, adhere to nonviolent discipline without formal efforts to promote it. Strong support for the objectives and general acceptance of nonviolent action as the means to achieve them may be sufficient to ensure the necessary degree of nonviolent discipline in the particular situation. This may be especially true if the participants are experienced in the use of nonviolent technique, if opposition is not strong, if the factors likely to produce violence are minimal, and if the actionists have a strong religious or moral preference for nonviolent means.

However, since the dangers to the movement of indisciplined action and of an outbreak of violence are so serious, one should not passively stand by and hope for the best even when such favorable conditions are present. A movement *may* come through safely, but every effort needs to be made to avoid those threats to success. Furthermore in the larger number of cases without those favorable conditions, stronger efforts still are needed to maintain nonviolent discipline. Some persons with anti-authoritarian personalities or *some* philosophical anarchists react very negatively to any type of discipline. To allow emotional reactions or inadequately considered philosophical generalizations to block efforts to promote nonviolent discipline is most unwise and irrational. There is nothing "wrong" with nonviolent discipline; it is necessary because it "helps prevent actions or reactions which bring disunity or disorder or which work against the objectives of the action [and] provides a way by which a group of people can do corporately what they wish to do," as Charles C. Walker has pointed out.[210]

Nonviolent discipline also frequently includes willingness to carry out humble and undramatic tasks, as well as the more visible and daring ones from which a greater personal sense of importance, recognition, or honor may result. Nonviolent actionists also need to be willing to try to improve their abilities and skills so as to be able to act with greater effectiveness. Dignified, calm behavior may frequently be a part of nonviolent discipline.[211] All this does not in any way imply submissiveness or cringing before the opponent and his police or troops; behavior will be polite but firm. Nonviolent actionists will treat the opponent and his agents as human beings, but the actionists will not be bullied.[212]

It follows from the need for nonviolent discipline that those persons or groups unwilling or unable to abide by it must be asked not to take part. They will help most by remaining outside the movement or withdrawing from it until they feel able to act in accordance with the required standards of behavior.[213] The maintenance of high standards for participants may initially reduce the numbers of nonviolent actionists. However, in the long run both larger numbers of participants and success in the struggle depend on maintaining the quality of the movement, as has already been pointed out. Reducing nonviolent discipline in order to bring in larger numbers will have serious detrimental effects on the movement. Gandhi argued, for example, that the lowering of the standards for volunteers late in the 1930–31 struggle seriously weakened the movement and led to *goondaism* (rioting or violent disorder) in some places.[214]

Persons not familiar with the past practice of nonviolent action are often highly skeptical that nonviolent discipline can be achieved on a group or mass basis. The assumption that only individuals are capable of disciplined nonviolent action is a denial of the facts. It is widely acknowledged that with group encouragement and support many individuals commit acts of violence which they never would commit, acting alone. Group encouragement and support help achieve a similar, but reverse, change in behavior in the case of nonviolent action. Individuals who are not pacifists, and who if attacked individually would reply with counter-violence, have with group encouragement, support and pressures successfully maintained nonviolent discipline even when physically attacked. This happens when the nonpacifist participant is able to see that nonviolent discipline and nonretaliatory persistence are necessary to advance the group's goals which which he shares.[215] There are cases of such group discipline even when advance instructions and training in nonviolent conflict behavior were minimal or absent.[216]

Nonviolent action almost always occurs in a situation of conflict and tension: it generally heightens such conditions rather than reduces them. Given that fact, it requires some skill to prevent violence and to maintain discipline. But it is possible to do this because not all conflict is violent and because tension and aggression can be released in disciplined nonviolent ways. Sometimes—but not always—in situations where the atmosphere strongly favors violence, or where violence has already broken out, nonviolent leaders have judged it best not to start a nonviolent campaign at that point, or to call off a current campaign, until a more propitious moment. For example, Gandhi suspended the campaign against the Rowlatt Bills in 1919 because of the outbreak of violence.[217] In the summer of 1939 Gandhi rejected suggestions that he organize mass nonviolent struggle, arguing:

> . . . the atmosphere is surcharged with violence . . . nonviolent mass movement is an impossibility unless the atmosphere is radically changed . . . If any mass movement is undertaken at the present moment in the name of nonviolence, it will resolve itself into violence largely unorganized and organized in some cases. It will bring discredit on the Congress, spell disaster for the Congress struggle for independence and bring ruin to many a home.[218]

Ruling out mass nonviolent struggle did not, however, necessarily rule out all nonviolent action, as Gandhi had pointed out two weeks earlier: ". . . some active form of Satyagraha, not necessarily civil disobedience, must be available in order to end an impossible situation . . . There must be either effective nonviolent action or violence and anarchy within a measurable distance of time."[219]

Other methods may be used in advance to prevent the creation of an explosive situation. In 1769 during the nonimportation campaign to achieve repeal of the Townshend duties, the decision of Philadelphia merchants to refuse to allow any English goods not ordered before February 6, 1769 to be landed from the ships had this effect. As the goods were returned to England directly, there was no occasion for acts of violence against anyone for possession, use or attempt to sell the prohibited goods, nor for attempts to destroy the goods. It is uncertain whether this calming result was the intended consequence of banning the landing of boycotted goods, but it happened. Schlesinger concluded that in Philadelphia in 1769-70 ". . . the enforcement of nonimportation was free from all exhibitions of mob violence, largely because goods violative of the agreement were immediately re-shipped to Great Britain." [220] This prevention of provocative situations may contribute to nonviolent discipline.

Whenever two hostile crowds have gathered and may meet, the situation is ripe for violence. For example, in New York City on July 7, 1770, during that same campaign, crowds for and against the nonimportation policy encountered each other in Wall Street, "where stiff blows were exchanged with cane and club and the nonimporters finally dispersed." [221] Where opposing groups are likely to gather, or have already done so, nonviolent strategists seeking to maintain peaceful discipline will need to take counter measures. If the hostile group attacks, the nonviolent actionist will need strong self-discipline in order to prevent both a rout and violence. If the leaders wish to avoid a physical encounter, possible lines of action include movement of the nonviolent group away from the violent demonstrators, dispersal, or a switch to some other type of individual or small group nonviolent action. If the possible physical attack by the mob is to be confronted directly, the nonviolent leadership will need to be sure that the actionists will be capable of maintaining both discipline and nonviolence if the conflict is not to degenerate into flight or riot. Sometimes various novel acts may be applied at such a point, including singing religious or patriotic hymns, kneeling in prayer, and sitting down.

In many situations where conflict and tension are widespread the launching of militant nonviolent action may be regarded as a necessary step to prevent the outbreak of violence. Such action is aimed at providing alternative effective means for conducting the conflict and simultaneously releasing feelings of aggression and hostility which have accumulated within the grievance group. Militant nonviolent action may often be risky, but it may be the only alternative to passive submission on the one hand and allowing the forces of violence to gain the upper hand on the other. A decision to launch militant nonviolent action to prevent violence may be made when there is high tension but as yet no open conflict (either violent or nonviolent), or in a tense situation once the nonviolent struggle has begun.

It has been recognized for a long time that certain nonviolent activities may defuse potential violence. For example, in 1765, after Newport, Rhode Island, had already experienced one riot, another threatened as the tense local situation combined with the approach of November 1, when the hated Stamp Act was to go into effect. The result might have been a politically counterproductive explosion. Then, on that date, ". . . in order to forestall any possible riot, the Sons of Liberty attempted to divert popular feeling into an orderly demonstration, by staging a 'grand Funeral of Freedom',' as described in detail in Chapter Three. Many decades later, on a vastly larger scale, Gandhi sought to provide nonviolent means of struggle which would simultaneously be effective for achieving political ends and also would prevent political violence. While there were growing terrorist groups, Gandhi showed the effectiveness of nonviolent struggle and got the Indian National Congress—the nationalist party—to adopt it for achieving independence. Jawaharlal Nehru, who had been an advocate of violent revolution and who never became a believer in nonviolent doctrine, was among those who accepted the nonviolent technique for practical reasons. [222] Later, while the struggle continued, he wrote:

> Terrorists have flourished in India, off and on, for nearly thirty years . . . terrorism, in spite of occasional recrudescence, has no longer any real appeal for the youth of India. Fifteen years' stress on nonviolence has changed the whole background in India and made the masses much more indifferent to, and even hostile to, the idea of terrorism as a method of political action. Even the classes from which the terrorists are usually drawn, the lower middle classes and intelligentsia, have been powerfully affected by the Congress propaganda against methods of violence. Their active and impatient elements, who think in terms of revolutionary action, also realize fully now that revolution does not come through terrorism, and that terrorism is an outworn and profitless method that comes in the way of real revolutionary action. [223]

James Farmer has strongly supported this analysis: ". . . rather than leading to riots, demonstrations tend to prevent them by providing an alternative outlet for frustration." Farmer then supported his view with evidence from New York City and Chicago. In the summer of 1963, in New York, for example, he maintained, "anger and frustration were just as high as they were to be in the riotous summer of 1964." However, in 1963 there were "hundreds of mass demonstrations" against discrimination in the building trades. Many unemployed youths who would otherwise have prowled the streets aimlessly, joined in the demonstrations. They picketed, climbed cranes, and blocked the bulldozers. Furthermore, these youths remained nonviolent. "They did not have to resort to throwing bottles and bricks, and they didn't." In the summer of 1964, however, there were few demonstrations, and there were riots.

Farmer denied a simple cause-and-effect relationship between organized nonviolent protest and avoidance of riots, ". . . but certainly there is some relationship. We have seen it countless times, in the South as well as the North." During the riots of 1964 Farmer walked the streets of Harlem and reported: "I saw more clearly than I have ever before how young men who feel that nothing is being done about grievances so deep they can barely articulate them, will finally spring to violence." He added: "I firmly believe that if Harlemites had been better trained in legitimate mass demonstrations (demonstrating *is* doing something)—and if the police had not acted so unwisely—the Harlem riots [of July 1964] could have been averted." As a general conclusion, Farmer continued: "One way to avert riots is to satisfy people that they can do something—not promise that things will be done, but satisfy them that *they can do something* without turning to self-defeating violence. One thing they can do is demonstrate." (Italics added). This was exactly what happened in the summer of 1965, and the riots which had been predicted did not occur.

Just as labor movement violence has been replaced by legitimizing strikes and other mass labor demonstrations, so racial violence can be replaced by ". . . legitimizing the techniques of mass action developed by the civil rights groups. It seems to me obvious that without demonstrations we will learn what violence and chaos really are. To inhibit mass demonstrations is madness." Of course, Farmer continued, where the only possible result of a demonstration is immediate mob violence it should not be held, but that certainly does not mean abandonment of "all but the most polite demonstrations of protest." Instead, he concluded, ". . . if demonstrations are in danger of courting violence, the remedy is not to stop demonstrating but to perfect our ability to control the more undisciplined participants and to spread our teaching." Farmer also points to the desirability of countering ill-advised demonstrations by the development and use of tactically sounder ones, rather than leaving people with the choice of doing nothing or participating in an unwise action. [224]

This discussion is not to imply that *any* form of nonviolent action can channel aggression and group hostilities away from violence. That obviously is not true, and careful consideration needs to be given to the selection of the precise ways most suitable for the particular situation. The remainder of this section is a survey of the types of efforts to maintain nonviolent discipline that have been used in the past. High morale is important in achieving and preserving nonviolent discipline. Walker emphasizes that high morale requires that participants believe they are members of a group which cares about them as individuals, which gives them the opportunity for creativity, active participation, overcoming obstacles and working together loyally with others who share their outlook and purposes.[225] Mass meetings may be held periodically—daily, weekly, or at some other interval—for the purpose of building morale, as well as increasing understanding of the nonviolent technique and disseminating information; mass meetings have been used in support of nonviolent action in the South, as during student sit-ins, and during the Montgomery bus boycott.[226]

The hope of achieving victory will often help maintain nonviolent discipline, especially among the less reliable elements, and may also help hold together the existing coalition of diverse groups behind the struggle. This was the case during the early stages of the 1905 revolution in Russia: ". . . as long as the possibility of peaceful political change remained in sight . . . the weakly united front of liberals and socialists continued."[227] When this united front dissolved and workers turned toward the more proviolent socialists it was ". . . not so much because of the socialists' ideology as because of their vigorous tactics—which now seemed to many the only means of influencing events and achieving new victories."[228]

Morale will often be increased, also, by feelings among the actionists that some significant source of strength not available to their opponent is supporting them. In some cases these feelings may arise in part from a sense of the power of the technique of action they are using, or the justice of their cause, or the inevitability of their victory. In some cases, such feeling may be rooted in a belief that they have powerful friends whose influence and capacity may finally help to defeat their opponent. Norwegian participants in nonviolent struggle against Quisling's regime and the Nazi occupation frequently point to the importance to their morale of their belief that the Allies were waging a powerful military struggle against the Nazis; civil rights workers using nonviolent action in the Deep South gained inner strength not only from the rightness of their cause and the moral superiority of their methods, but also from ". . . an intimate sense of identification with public opinion and with the movement of the Federal Government—however slow. He [the civil rights worker] is isolated only from the immediate antagonistic community."[229] During the 1920 Kapp *Putsch,* Dr. Kapp and part of the army had to confront a determined population inspired by awareness that they were defending the Republic at the request of the constitutional government. As a result, "an inspired purposefulness reigned in the camp of Dr. Kapp's enemies."[230]

Where the nonviolent actionists are a distinct minority and also do not have access to these sources of feelings of strength, they will need to take compensating measures to support high morale. Such measures should not be simply gimmicks and should be able to survive crises. In any case, it would be dangerous and overly optimistic simply to count on high morale to achieve and maintain nonviolent discipline. There are other ways to promote this.

One of these is that active participants in the struggle, sympathizers and the general population understand well *why* the campaign needs to be kept strictly nonviolent. Such understanding has not always been achieved to a significant degree; instead, a few inadequate generalizations about nonviolence being "better" or "more moral" have often been regarded as sufficient. Fuller and politically more adequate explanation of the need for nonviolent discipline might be more effective both in avoiding scattered violence during the campaign and a later major switch to violence. The groups most likely to advocate or initiate violence are precisely those likely to be least influenced by vague generalizations and moral exhortations to be nonviolent.

As understanding of the reasons for the importance of nonviolent behavior for the operation of the technique spreads, it will be more and more difficult to provoke violence. Also, the chances are increased that if the opponent attempts to do precisely that, his efforts will be publicly exposed. Under this new discipline, violence against the opponent becomes "as traitorous to the cause as desertion is in the army."

> Once that understanding, attitude and discipline are attained among the group of nonviolent resisters, any *agent provocateur* who comes whispering among them or preaching violence, retaliation or revenge will be immediately known for what he is and repudiated. And the group will soon prove its tactics so clearly to the public that the latter will not be deceived by the act of an *agent provocateur* bomb thrower or inflammatory speaker.[231]

The need for outward discipline is thus likely to be reduced as the volunteers gain confidence in the adequacy of nonviolent action to further their cause.[232]

Good organization, wise leadership, carefully laid and intelligently formulated plans and effective means of communication within the movement will contribute significantly to the achievement and maintenance of nonviolent discipline. Conversely, the absence of these will greatly facilitate both indiscipline and violence. "Karl Ehrlich" (pseud. for Karl Raloff) attributed the development of terrorism during the *Ruhrkampf* to the absence of German plans for nonviolent resistance, and the relative absence of leadership and organization for the struggle.[233]

Organization, leadership, plans and communication involve attention to a considerable variety of particular problems and tasks. Strategy, tactics and methods always need to be carefully chosen, but when the atmosphere is especially conducive to violence special care in their choice and formulation will be needed. In some cases methods which rely on the high-quality action of a few people may be more appropriate than those that rely on large numbers of less disciplined participants. [234] For particularly difficult tasks the person or group to carry them out needs to be carefully selected on the basis of reliability and other qualifications, especially when the task is dangerous, or extremely important, as in starting the struggle, [235] or in shifting its direction at a critical point.

The degree to which regular participants in the action should be selected from among the volunteers, or that selection is possible, will differ from one conflict to another. So, too, will the degree and type of advance training of general participants differ. Detailed discussion of methods for training of both general participants and specialist personnel lies outside the scope of this study. Study groups, workshops, seminars and socio-drama have been used widely in the United States by civil rights groups. [236] Such methods, however, obviously only scratch the surface of the possibilities. Consideration of the purposes, levels and means of training large numbers of people or the whole population is essential.

Organizers, leaders and sometimes ordinary participants have used speeches, messages and on-the-spot pleas in efforts to prevent violence and maintain discipline. Initial calls for action and statements by leaders and spokesmen for the grievance group before or at the beginning of the struggle, often emphasize the nonviolent and disciplined nature of the coming action, with the intent of influencing the course of the movement and the behavior of possible participants. Such statements were made, for example, in South Vietnam at the start of the 1963 Buddhist anti-Diem struggle. The conflict began after shootings into crowds of Buddhists in Hué as they objected to restrictions on their religious freedom. The next day (May 9) a Buddhist leader, Thich Tan Chau, wrote a letter addressed to all monks, nuns, and other Buddhists in Vietnam asking support to ". . . protect our just religion in an orderly, peaceful, nonviolent manner." The following day the manifesto of demands to be the basis of the coming struggle, presented in Hué, declared that Buddhists "will use nonviolent methods of struggle." [237] Verbal pleas for nonviolent disciplined behavior, as many persons may expect, were often made by Gandhi, [238] by King, [239] and by leaders of the 1952 Defiance Campaign in South Africa. [240] Such calls have also been made in situations where they might be less expected. It is not so widely known that the manifesto issued by the Pan Africanist

Congress of South Africa before its 1960 campaign against the Pass Laws called for "absolute nonviolence." After several hours of intimidation of the orderly and disciplined seven thousand demonstrators at Sharpeville on March 21, some Africans broke discipline and began throwing stones at the police. (It was only at that point the police without warning began firing into the crowd with the deadly results that are so well known.) The Pan Africanists continued to seek nonviolent discipline, however, Philip Kgosana was notably successful in achieving this with very large demonstrations; on March 30 he led a disciplined peaceful thirty thousand Africans marching thirty abreast through Capetown. (He was later arrested as he led a deputation, when police broke their promise that the deputation would be received by officials.[241]

There were numerous verbal attempts to maintain nonviolent discipline during the 1953 East German Rising. It was repeatedly emphasized that this was a struggle against the East German Communist regime and that all possible steps should be taken not to provoke the Russians. For example, a speaker at a mass meeting of sixty thousand in Halle ". . . asked the crowd to observe strict discipline warning against panic buying, looting and violence—the Red Army, he told them earnestly, must be given no excuse to intervene."[242] It was a similar story in Goerlitz: "At no time had the demonstrators become involved with the occupation troops. Speaker after speaker had warned against provoking the Red Army into taking action and no one had contradicted them."[243] The leader of the insurgents at East Germany's largest chemical plant (the *Leunawerke* near Leipzig), Friedrich Schorn declared: "Everything is at stake. But violence isn't the answer . . . Let's keep order." When factory guards turned over their weapons, Schorn ordered them locked in a storeroom, instead of being used in the rising. When the plant's workers marched to Merseburg for a mass meeting, Schorn again urged the crowd to remain calm, even as Soviet troops advanced on the square where the meeting was being held. When some demonstrators began shouting and spitting at the Russians, signs of possible serious violence in that situation, Schorn after consultations with others urged the strikers to return to their respective factories but not to begin work. "They formed columns and marched off in perfect discipline."[244]

Sometimes more active intervention has been used to halt acts of violence or acts which might lead to serious violence even though they might in themselves not be very serious. For example, on one occasion after an initial clash between police and strikers outside the House of Ministries, in East Berlin, June 17, 1953, a few of the demonstrators tried to prevent others from throwing stones at the police.[245] Night patrols have also been used. In Newport, Rhode Island, on November 1, 1765, for example, as the Stamp Act went into force "the Sons of Liberty endeavored to maintain popular feeling against the Stamp Act without touching off another riot"; after the substitute nonviolent demonstration (in the form of a mock funeral described above) they also took other measures. "In the evening a number of persons patrolled the streets to prevent the gathering of a mob, and the night passed quietly." [246]

Effective organization and communication in the nonviolent group will contribute significantly to achieving and maintaining nonviolent discipline. Certain measures for organization and communication which appear to be directed solely to relations with the opponent or the press, for example, the selection of a spokesman to issue statements, answer questions and speak for the demonstrators during the confrontation[247] also are likely to promote group discipline.

Highly important in promoting nonviolent discipline will be ". . . clear lines of command and communication, and . . . a clear understanding by the participants of what they are to do in a variety of circumstances." [248] One of the most effective means of promoting nonviolent discipline in large scale nonviolent action demonstrations has been detailed instruction and discipline leaflets. Sometimes the detailed instructions for the particular action are combined with the general instructions about how to behave in crises, and sometimes they have been separate leaflets. Clear, simple explanations of the plans, of the nonviolent discipline, and of the reasons for them, combined with recommendations on how the actionist is expected to behave in various specific situations, may help remove much of the uncertainty and potential to violence. Where violence nevertheless breaks out, these detailed instructions may help prevent the nonviolent actionists from being blamed for the violence. Such instruction and discipline leaflets sometimes include brief explanations of why a particular course of action is recommended or rejected.

"Marshals" for demonstrations have also been used to help keep a given action nonviolent and disciplined. These marshals are usually especially experienced, able to remain calm and confident, and well versed in an understanding of the technique. The marshals receive special briefings on the plans and problems expected. They may be assigned to particular small groups of actionists, so that reliable persons who are able to set an example, offer advice and instructions, and relay detailed plans and lines for action to those near them are spread throughout a large demonstration. In the South African struggles in the early 1900s violence would sometimes have broken out but for the "most vigilant supervision," reports Gandhi.[249] In Britain the Direct Action Committee Against Nuclear War, the Campaign for Nuclear Disarmament, and the Committee of 100 all made extensive use of marshals to keep the demonstrations orderly and peaceful. On the Aldermaston marches, such marshals even assisted in directing traffic, relieving the police of some of their normal duties. These marshals played an extremely important role in promoting nonviolent discipline among large numbers of people who may have been new to both demonstrations and nonviolent action. As an extremely effective means to maintain nonviolent discipline, the use of marshals is likely to be adopted and refined increasingly by practitioners of nonviolent action. Marshals have also been used widely in the United States, especially for massive anti-Vietnam-War demonstrations in Washington, D.C. Agitation against marshals—they have been called "peace pigs"—may have various motives, some for destroying the movement, as may other pressures against nonviolent discipline discussed above. In the absence of extraordinary self-discipline and experience, however, efforts to undermine the moral authority and effectiveness of marshals can only benefit the opponent by increasing the chances of violence.

Organizers of nonviolent action have sometimes sought to promote nonviolent discipline by asking volunteers to promise, or to sign a pledge in advance, to adhere to a certain code of behavior. "Success depends entirely upon disciplined and concerted non-cooperation and the latter is dependent upon strict obedience to instructions, calmness and absolute freedom from violence," declared a statement issued in India by the Noncooperation Committee for public information and guidance in 1920.[250] There have been two types of these written standards—campaign pledges and demonstration pledges. In India far more than elsewhere, volunteers have been asked to pledge themselves to participate in a long-term struggle and to abide by certain standards of behavior while taking part. "Long-term" implies the duration of the campaign, from a few to many months. Formal pledges asked of persons volunteering to take part in a whole campaign have included a clause on nonviolent behavior and on obedience to orders.[251] The Indians have not, however, been the only ones to seek pledges for a whole campaign.

An attempt was made in New York during the boycott of tea in 1773 to obtain signatures to a pledge of nonviolent behavior during the struggle, as Schlesinger reports that "the more conservative merchants" saw a clear drift toward mob control. Four days after a mass meeting of two thousand endorsed a secondary boycott of persons helping introduce boycotted dutied teas, a few persons, including Isaac Low and Jacob Walton, sought signatures to a pledge not to resort to violence in opposing the introduction of the tea. Schlesinger reports that the project quickly made some headway, ". . . but was abandoned on the next day because of the excitement aroused by the receipt of news of the Boston Tea Party. From that moment, as Governor Tryon informed Dartmouth, all hope of a temperate opposition was gone." [252]

Codes of discipline for participants in particular demonstrations have been used both in Britain by the Direct Action Committee against Nuclear War and the Committee of 100,[253] and in the United States by peace groups.[254] Some of the basic points in various American peace and civil rights discipline codes have been listed by both Walker[255] and Miller.[256] For several years the Congress of Racial Equality used a general code of nonviolent discipline, and local groups have sometimes prepared their own codes, as that adopted by college students in Nashville, Tennessee, for use in lunch counter sit-ins.[257]

Often the intent to keep a resistance movement nonviolent has been partially frustrated by the arrest of the very resistance leaders capable of preventing violence. O'Hegarty reports this happened in Ireland following the arrests of Parnell, Dillon and other local and national leaders of the Land League in October 1881:

Deprived of their leaders, deprived of their Organization, the people resisted as individuals, and resisted as families, and as communities. With no central direction or policy, violence and outrage and intimidation, the unarmed or poorly armed people's only defence against tyranny, soon held full sway.[258]

This is one reason why it is insufficient for nonviolent actionists to rely only on the established leaders. In any case, most such movements require a constant influx of new blood into the leadership group. Some times the recognized leadership may be arrested before it has been able to formulate plans. In other cases, at an advanced stage of a campaign all the leaders are likely to be imprisoned or otherwise removed. Whether leaders are arrested early or late, it is vital that the other persons be capable of stepping into leadership positions, and finally that the nonviolent actionists become capable of acting courageously and effectively in the absence of a recognizable leadership group.[259] This was emphasized by Gandhi. He spoke of the stage in a campaign ". . . where no one has to look expectantly at another, where there are no leaders and no followers, or where all are leaders and all are followers . . ."[260] He also said: "Discipline has a place in nonviolent strategy, but much more is required. In a satyagraha army everybody is a soldier and a servant. But at a pinch every satyagrahi soldier has also to be his own general and leader." [261]

While capable of free action the leaders will need to take steps to help people maintain the necessary nonviolent discipline when they must act without leaders. These steps will include both general instructions and specific training in the nature of nonviolent action, in the need for non-violent discipline and in ways of maintaining it. Also important is the careful formulation of the initial stages of the campaign so that the early pattern can set the mood and serve as an example for the later stages.

In other situations, the opposite trend may develop: instead of all leadership being removed, the nonviolent forces may become so strong that characteristics of a parallel government emerge, [262] which help maintain nonviolent discipline. For example, during the Continental Association plan for economic nonviolent resistance, Connecticut colonial patriots in 1775 enforced compliance with the resistance provisions by open trials of persons accused of violating the resistance plans. The problem of enforcement was more difficult in that colony because it possessed no commercial metropolis but only several small river and coast towns. The movement started, Schlesinger reports, at a meeting of the committees of inspection of Hartford County on January 25, 1775. It was agreed that proceedings against a person accused of violating the noncooperation program should be conducted in an "open, candid and deliberate manner." Furthermore, formal summonses would be served upon him, containing the nature of the charge, and an invitation to defend himself before the committee six days or more later. Witnesses and other evidence were to be "openly, fairly and fully heard"; and conviction should be made only "upon the fullest, clearest and most convincing proof." New Haven, Fairfield and Litchfield counties adopted the same mode of procedure. Nor were these mere pious platitudes. Schlesinger reports that "trials of offenders by the committees of inspection bore every evidence of being fair and impartial hearings, although mistakes were occasionally made." [263]

REFUSAL TO HATE

It should be clear at this point that nonviolent action does not require its practitioners to "love" their opponent, nor to try to convert him. Clearly this technique has been applied by people who hated their opponent and desired to coerce him. Such emotions and attitudes can coexist with the use of nonviolent means.

However, it is also true that effectiveness with the nonviolent technique may be increased when the actionists are able to refrain from hatred and hostility. This is true for all three mechanisms of change, which are discussed in detail in Chapter Thirteen. Appeals to "love" the enemy may at times be emotionally or religiously motivated appeals of persons who are politically naïve. But it is often similarly naïve to dismiss pleas to regard members of the opponent group as fellow human beings and to treat them with respect, personal friendliness and even "love." If actionists are incapable of making this distinction between persons and the issues, and are able only to abstain from physical violence, they should be credited with that achievement rather than have their behavior and attitudes discredited because they were less than perfect. However, if in addition they can refrain from hostility, ill will and hatred, and perhaps even demonstrate personal goodwill for members of the opponent group, they may have much greater chances of success.

An absence of hostility and the presence of goodwill will facilitate the operation of the conversion mechanism. Repression against people who are not only nonviolent but also personally friendly while persisting in their firm action will often appear less justifiable than repression of hostile persons. Repression may still be applied, but the impact of the resulting suffering on the opponent group and on third parties is also likely to be greater. Where the conversion mechanism is not fully achieved, the non-hostile attitudes of the actionists may facilitate change by accommodation. An absence of personal ill will while fighting for the issue may increase the degree to which the opponent's repression rebounds to weaken his own political position. [264]

Even when nonviolent coercion is sought there are good reasons for deliberate efforts to minimize ill will, hostility and hatred by the nonviolent actionists toward the opponent group and to promote positive personal relationships. Such efforts may, for example, help undermine the loyalty of the opponent's police and troops, possibly leading to reduced efficiency in the carrying out of orders for repression, or even to open refusal to obey.

Gandhi is prominent among those who have argued that there is no room for hatred, malice or ill will in nonviolent action, and that they should be replaced by the gentleness, civility, compassion and love for the opponent. [265] This attitude has also been expressed in Western cases of nonviolent action as illustrated in discipline leaflets for demonstrations by American and British peace groups. A 1962 discipline leaflet adopted by New York City peace organizations include these sentences:

Our attitude toward persons who may oppose us will be one of understanding and of respect for the right of others to hold and express whatever views they wish.

We will not be violent in our attitude, make hostile remarks, shout or call names. If singing or chanting is indicated, it will be in a manner consistent with the nonviolent spirit of the demonstration. [266]

The discipline leaflet issued in Britain by the Committee for Direct Action Against Nuclear War (the predecessor of the Direct Action Committee Against Nuclear war) contained this request:

Do not use any language or take any action which is likely to provoke violence by others. A dignified bearing and courteous determination will greatly contribute to victory for this cause.
If you are jeered or called names, do not shout back or jeer those who differ from our views. Silence and a friendly smile are the best reply to hostility, as you continue [to act] as before the interruption. [267]

The nonviolent action movement against racial segregation in the Deep South placed very great importance on "love" for the white segregationists. "The nonviolent resister not only refuses to shoot his opponent but he also refuses to hate him," wrote Martin Luther King, Jr. "At the center of nonviolence stands the principle of love." [268] This extreme emphasis turned some people away from nonviolent means. When understood as a *requirement* for nonviolent action (rather than a helpful refinement), the demand for "love" for people who have done cruel things may turn people who are justifiably bitter and unable to love their opponents toward violence as the technique most consistent with bitterness and hatred. This confusion of secondary refinements with primary requirements and alienation of many potential users of the nonviolent technique has sometimes been aggravated by attempts of pacifists and believers in the principles of nonviolence to proselytize within nonviolent action movements, and to blur the distinctions between their beliefs and the nonviolent technique. Such efforts may in the long run impede rather than promote the substitution of nonviolent for violent means. Nevertheless, for the sake of effectiveness and beneficial long-term consequences, it is desirable for nonviolent actionists to minimize hostility and hatred and to maximize their goodwill for members of the opponent group while firmly continuing the struggle.

THE INEFFICACY OF REPRESSION

As we have already indicated, repression against a movement of non-violent action does not always produce the desired results. If the nonviolent actionists remain fearless, keep their nonviolent discipline, are willing to accept the sufferings inflicted for their defiance, and are determined to persist, then the opponent's attempt to force them to submit to his will is likely to be thwarted. He may be able to imprison them, to injure them, or even to execute them, but as long as they hold out, his will remains unfulfilled. Even if only a single person remains defiant, to that degree the opponent is defeated. The political potentialities of this thwarting of the opponent's will begin to assume much clearer forms when large numbers maintain this persistence, along with the other necessary qualities of nonviolent action. Where significant sections of the population continue defiance, the results will extend far beyond individual example and martyrdom, perhaps even to the point where the opponent's will is effectively blocked. That is, he is politically unable to carry out his plans even with the aid of repression.

He may arrest the leaders, but the movement may simply carry on without a recognizable leadership. He may make new acts illegal, only to find that he has opened new opportunities for defiance. He may attempt to repress defiance at certain points, only to find that the nonviolent actionists have gained enough strength to broaden their attack on other fronts so as to challenge his very ability to rule. He may find that mass repression fails to force a resumption of cooperation and obedience, but instead is constantly met by refusal to submit or flee, producing repeated demonstrations of impotence. Yet, not only may his repression prove inadequate to control his defiant subjects; his very agencies of repression may in extreme cases be immobilized by the massive defiance.

A. Arresting leaders is inadequate

It is natural for the opponent to believe that arresting the leadership will cause the movement to collapse. This was the view of Thomas Hutchinson, Lieutenant Governor of Massachusetts Bay Colony, when he attempted to counteract the campaign of nonimportation of British goods and other noncooperation; in 1769 and 1770 he urged passage by Parliament of an act to punish organizers and participants in such a movement. He denounced "the confederacy of merchants"—who were providing leadership—as unlawful and wrote that Parliament's laws would always be nullified in America ". . . if combinations to prevent the operation of them and to sacrifice all who conform to them are tolerated, or if towns are allowed to meet and vote that measures for defeating such acts are legal." [269] Operating on such a view, opponents confronted with nonviolent action have often seen their best immediate course of counteraction to be the arrest of the leaders and making the organization of this form of struggle illegal. In certain circumstances, this type of repression may be effective. This is most likely to happen when the movement does not genuinely have the strength it appeared to have, when the people are not fearless and when they do not understand how to conduct nonviolent action.

But when the movement does have strength, when the people are fearless, when they understand how to carry on, then the arrest of the leaders may prove a very inadequate means of crushing the movement. Repression is most likely to be made impotent when there has been a widespread and intensive program of public education in the use of nonviolent action or when the actionists have had considerable experience with the technique. Sometimes the example of a few and the intuition of others may suffice to continue resistance, but this is rare and dangerous; sound preparation is safer. Advance training and a widely distributed manual on how to use nonviolent action may help in compensating for the loss of the leadership. These aids may help the actionists to continue to struggle even though reserve layers of leadership have also been removed.

Provision of successive layers of leadership to replace those arrested, or otherwise removed by the opponent, seems to have been given the greatest attention during the Gandhian struggles in India. Not only was a secondary leadership prepared to take the place of the first-line leadership when it was arrested but a whole chain of successive layers of leadership was selected in advance, sometimes up to the thirtieth successive group, to take over direction of the movement as the previous groups were arrested. Sometimes there was, instead, a clear procedure for selecting later leaders, especially by having an existing leader appoint his successor. But, in a mass defiance campaign against an opponent intent upon repressing it ruthlessly, such measures are only stop gap measures. It is likely that sooner or later the continued operation of centralized leadership will become impossible.

In a struggle using political violence—violent revolution, civil war, or international war, for example—the leadership is in most situations kept back, out of danger. Indeed, the movement may depend upon the safety of the top leadership. In nonviolent action, by contrast, the leaders are usually the first victims of the opponent's repression. Having laid down the basic strategy, tactics and methods by which the struggle is to proceed, having helped to forge the organization to carry out those plans, and having emphasized the importance of fearlessness, persistance and maintenance of the nonviolent discipline, the leaders must *act* accordingly. They must by their own fearlessness, suffering and bearing set an example for the many who shall follow them. It is partly because the leadership will be so quickly removed from the scene that so much emphasis must be laid on the quality of the movement at the very beginning. Said Gandhi, ". . . clean examples have a curious method of multiplying themselves." [270] He emphasized the consequences of the importance of the quality of the participants in a nonviolent movement: ". . . mass instruction on any other terms is an impossibility." [271] The leaders, wrote Bose, ". . . are out of the picture at the first shot, only to leave their example to work as leaven in raising the masses." [272]

"There should be no demoralization when the leaders are gone, and there should be no surrender in the face of fire." [273] Rather than causing a slackening, the imprisonment or death of these and other participants in the struggle ought to cause an intensification of the fight: [274] ". . . surely the memory of imprisonment should act as a spur to greater and more disciplined action. We must be able to stand on our own legs without support even as we breathe naturally and without artificial aid." [275] This leads to a situation in which "self-reliance is the order of the day." [276]

These prescriptions by Gandhi for a successful major nonviolent action movement against severe repression were to a considerable degree filled during the 1930–31 independence campaign. Almost immediately after the launching of this struggle, the government began arresting and imprisoning prominent members of the nationalist party, the Indian National Congress. When Jawaharlal Nehru was sentenced to six months' simple imprisonment, there was a universal, spontaneous and complete *hartal.* He left a message for the people: "Keep smiling, fight on and get through the job." [277] When Gandhi was arrested and imprisoned without trial, there were *hartals* and demonstrations throughout the country and the remaining Congress leadership resolved to intensify the struggle by extending the areas of noncooperation and civil disobedience. [278] Gradually the various Congress organizations were declared illegal. They continued, nevertheless, to function for a considerable time with varying membership. After the Congress Working Committee had been effectively halted in its activities, ". . . civil disobedience lacked steering; but it had by now secured sufficient momentum to continue on its own." [279]

This broad self-reliance and continued resistance were deliberately promoted. In an article in *Young India* Jairamdas Daulatram wrote:

> The Government wishes to disorganize us. Each town, each village may have, therefore, to become its own battlefield. The strategy of the battle must then come to be determined by local circumstances and change with them day to day. The sooner the workers prepare for this state of things, the earlier shall we reach our goal. They should need little guidance from outside.[280]

This decentralization of the battle-planning must, he added, be accompanied by continued firm adherence to discipline and to nonviolence, and continued obedience to leaders as long as they remain at liberty. After nearly all the Congress organizations had been declared illegal, Vallabhbhai Patel declared that thereafter every home must be a Congress office and every individual a Congress organization.[281]

At Mathura when the leaders were all arrested before the plans for civil disobedience could be put into effect, the response was a spontaneous city-wide *hartal,* and a huge procession paraded through the city; eight thousand carried out civil disobedience in the form of making illegal salt.[282] In Bihar, with nearly all the leaders in prison, many more salt centers were opened illegally.[283] Referring to conditions throughout the country as a whole, Gopal commented: "The policy of arresting only the leaders was obviously ineffective in countering a movement which drew its strength from local organizations."[284]

This growth of decentralization and self-reliance developed to such a point that without fear of contradiction Gandhi was able to point to the difficulties of carrying on negotiations with the British when only members of the Working Committee had been released from prison. He maintained that evidently the authorities did not understand that the people as a whole had become so much affected by the movement that, no matter how prominent the leaders, they could not dictate a course of action if the masses were not in accord.[285] Such a development, if it should take place to a significant degree over a large area, would be most difficult to combat.

It would be an error to conclude that continued popular resistance despite arrests of leaders is only possible in India, or only with Gandhi as the inspiring leader even when in jail. There is scattered evidence from other conflicts that this continued resistance may occur in a considerable variety of situations. Officials have sometimes anticipated that increased resistance would result from the arrest of leaders and have accordingly acted with caution. For example, although the tsarist Minister of the Interior, Peter Svyatopolk-Mirsky, in January 1905 issued orders for the arrest of Father Gapon and nineteen of his lieutenants before the planned march to the Winter Palace in St. Petersburg, the Prefect of the capital, General Ivan Fullon, did not carry out the arrests, fearing that his police force could not handle the greater, potentially violent, tumult which he expected as the result of such arrests.[286] At Vorkuta in 1953, as noted earlier, the original strike committee was arrested even before the strike began, but the plans went ahead. In Montgomery, Alabama, during the 1957 bus boycott, there were mass arrests of the leadership. Rather than striking fear into the Negroes, the result was increased determination and fearlessness.[287]

Diffused leadership may also be required as a result of the very effectiveness of the nonviolent struggle. This is illustrated by the Russian 1905 Revolution. Only one newspaper was still being printed (a reactionary one in Kiev); telegraph communications were either cut or under government control; there was generally no public transportation operating; the postal system was almost paralyzed. All this meant that no strike leadership could be effective beyond the local area; consequently, resistance leadership was diffused, with leaders in each city acting in virtual isolation.[288]

B. Repression measures may become new points of resistance

Where the nonviolent actionists are strong, and other favorable conditions are present, various measures of repression may be utilized as new points at which to practice civil disobedience and political noncooperation. This is quite distinct from increasing the group's *demands,* which is regarded as generally unwise once the movement has begun. The extension of resistance to repression measures themselves also differs from expansion of other points of resistance and defiance.

It may have been planned, for example, that if the movement showed sufficient strength new methods of action would be used, or the same ones would be applied at new points. In other cases unexpected vigor and resiliance of the actionists and grievance group may make such an expansion of points of resistance possible and desirable. It must be emphasized that any extension of the points of resistance should only be launched if the movement has demonstrated unmistakably sufficient support, tenacity and discipline to warrant the extension; it would be a grave strategic error to overextend the fronts beyond the ability of the nonviolent group to hold them and to keep the initiative.

If the movement shows such nonviolent power and is even able effectively to extend the struggle against certain measures of repression themselves, the opponent will find the situation particularly frustrating. The more his countermeasures infringe on widely accepted standards of conduct and political practice, the more suitable they may be for selection as new points for nonviolent challenge. For example, in trying to combat the nonviolent movement, the opponent may restrict freedom of the press, or freedom of speech or assembly. Such counteractions and repression provide the nonviolent group with additional points at which to resist and defy the regime on issues which will have the sympathy and support of many people still outside the movement.

The 1930–31 struggle in India probably provides the best examples of the extension of resistance, both to more ambitious forms as part of a planned strategy, and also to the opponent's repressive measures themselves. For instance, Gandhi decided to escalate the massive individual violations of the Salt Laws (in which individuals or groups committed civil disobedience by boiling down sea water or digging salt) to large-scale nonviolent raids on government salt depots.[289] Following Gandhi's arrest, the Working Committee of the Congress expanded the scope of the campaign considerably, intensifying the salt raids and the boycott of foreign cloth, encouraging no-tax campaigns, expanding breaches of the Salt Act by manufacture, civil disobedience of the Forest Laws, initiating a boycott of British goods, banking and insurance, and urging the newspapers to noncooperate with new government restrictions on them.[290]

Among the government measures to deal with the civil disobedience movement was the Press Ordinance. This required all journals and newspapers to deposit a security with the government. If the publication then printed information or views ruled by the government to be subversive, the deposit was forfeited and publication was to cease. The Congress Working Committee urged the newspapers to regard this as a new point of refusal of cooperation with the government and to cease publication as a printed journal. Gandhi's own press closed, but *Young India* continued to be issued in duplicated form. Walls, sidewalks and paved roads served as blackboards for Congress notices. Handwritten and typed newspapers were copied and recopied and widely circulated. Various papers and news sheets appeared, all to be declared illegal. (However, most newspapers, but not all, complied with the government ordinance, thus not completing the extension of the defiance which was made possible by the measures.)[291] When public distribution of certain literature was made illegal, *satyagrahis* sometimes held public readings of the banned material, in a further act of civil disobedience.[292] Other extensions of resistance took place also. For example, at one point political prisoners in several jails in the Central Province were on hunger strike,[293] and elsewhere peasants unable to bear further repression went on a protest-migration *(hijrat)* to areas outside British control.[294] It is significant that during that campaign the United Provinces Government opposed the proposal that the central government should declare all Congress organizations illegal. The former felt that "such action was not justified by local conditions and might well revive an agitation which was more or less at a standstill [in the province]."[295] Gopal reports also that while the imposition of collective fines on villages and districts, and the introduction of whipping, had in limited localities helped to control the nonviolent movement, "elsewhere ordinances only seemed to serve the purpose of providing fresh opportunities for defiance; and when the ordinances lapsed the tendency to lawlessness was keener than before."[296]

If the nonviolent actionists' response to repression is an effective expansion of the points at which noncooperation and defiance are committed, and a significant increase in the numbers of active participants in the struggle, the opponent is faced with a strong movement whose opposition may become total. He is then in serious trouble. Very likely, he will in desperation intensify repression. Not only may this not work, but it may backfire to undermine his power position still further. Having failed to deal with the power of noncooperation and defiance, he may unwittingly have brought yet another force into operation against him: that of political *jiu-jitsu*.

NOTES

1. Lakey, "The Sociological Mechanisms of Nonviolent Action" (Thesis) p. 68; *Peace Research Reviews,* vol. II, no. 6 (Dec. 1968), p. 47.
2. Schlesinger, **The Colonial Merchants and the American Revolution,** pp. 113-115.
3. Symons, **The General Strike,** p. 62.
4. Ebert, "Nonviolent Resistance Against Communist Regimes?" p. 177.
5. Lakey, *loc. cit.*
6. Hiller, **The Strike,** pp. 83-84.
7. *Ibid.,* p. 82.
8. *Ibid.,* pp. 85-86.
9. King, **Stride Toward Freedom,** U.S. ed., p. 67; Br. ed., p. 79.
10. Hiller, **The Strike,** pp. 87 and 123.
11. See Sharp, **Gandhi Wields the Weapon of Moral Power,** pp. 41-210 *passim.*
12. Quoted in *ibid.,* p. 59.
13. See Kuper, **Passive Resistance in South Africa,** pp. 10-19 and 112-122.
14. See Sharp, **Gandhi Wields . . . ,** pp. 133 and 144-148.
15. Quoted in Hiller, **The Strike,** p. 94.
16. See Sharp, **Tyranny Could Not Quell Them.**
17. Quoted in Hiller, **The Strike,** p. 94.
18. King, **Stride Toward Freedom,** U.S. ed., p. 66; Br. ed., p. 78.
19. Sternstein, "The *Ruhrkampf* of 1923", p. 127. See also Ehrlich, "*Ruhrkampen,*" p. 191.
20. Symons, **The General Strike,** pp. 141-142.
21. Schlesinger, **The Colonial Merchants . . . ,** pp. 465-469.
22. *Ibid.,* pp. 314, 480, 485, 489, 514-515, 520 and 611.
23. Ehrlich, "Ruhrkampen" in Lindberg, Jacobsen and Ehrlich, **Kamp Uden Vaaben,** pp. 186 and 192.
24. Kuper, **Passive Resistance in South Africa,** pp. 112-113, 116, 119 and 121.
25. Lakey, "The Sociological Mechanisms . . ." p. 73.
26. Schlesinger, **The Colonial Merchants . . . ,** pp. 156-164.
27. See Schlesinger, **The Colonial Merchants . . . ,** pp. 186-187, 189, 192-193, 205-206, 208, 387, 427-428, 437-438, 441-443, 447 n.2, 498, 504-505, 611-612, and Gipson, **The British Empire Before the American Revolution,** vol. XII, **The Triumphant Empire: Britain Sails into the Storm, 1770-1776,** pp. 217-254.
28. Schlesinger, **The Colonial Merchants . . . ,** pp. 487-488.
29. See *ibid.,* pp. 516-517, 586-587, and 610-611.
30. See *ibid.,* pp. 82, 111-112, 122, 124, 139, 141-143, 146, 148-151, 153-154, 158, 162-164, 173-175, 177, 181-182, 184, 188-189, 195, 198, 203, 205-206,

208-209, 211, 215-219, 227-228, 367-370, 388, 454 n.1, 477-478, 481, 483, 486, 491, 493, 495, 507-508, 515, and 610-611; Gipson, **The British Empire Before the American Revolution**, vol. XI, **The Triumphant Empire: The Rumbling of the Coming Storm, 1766-1770,** pp. 183, 188, and 265n., and vol. XII, pp. 69, 196, 208, 252, and 254.

31. Schlesinger, **The Colonial Merchants . . . ,** pp. 432-433.

32. *Ibid.,* pp. 519, 524-525, 610 and 504-505.

33. In addition to above references, see *ibid.,* pp. 479ff, 489, 498-499, 520-521, 526, 551, and 611.

34. *Ibid.,* pp. 484 and 507.

35. Thomas Hutchinson, **The History of the Colony and Province of Massachusetts-Bay,** vol. III, p. 185. See also, pp. 191 and 193. Cambridge, Mass.: Harvard University Press, 1936. Some additional material on resistance is contained in Catherine Barton Mayo, ed., **Additions to Thomas Hutchinson's "History of Massachusetts Bay"** (Worcester, Mass.: American Antiquarian Society, 1949). I am grateful to Ron McCarthy for locating this.

36. See *ibid.,* vol. III, pp. 185-187 and 191-194.

37. See Schlesinger, **The Colonial Merchants . . . ,** pp. 81-82, 478, 542, 552-559, and 564.

38. *Ibid.,* pp. 363, 367 and 372.

39. *Ibid.,* pp. 189, 225, 267, 269, 360-362, 472, 483ff, 529, 531f, and 612.

40. O'Hegarty, **A History of Ireland Under the Union, 1880-1922,** p. 491. During this struggle violence became applied to a significant degree against Irishmen who did not support the campaign, or who weakened in their resolve. For some cases of this, see Forster, **The Truth About the Land League, Its Leaders and Its Teachings,** esp. pp. 70-71, and 84-85.

41. See above Chapter Eight, method 171, nonviolent interjection.

42. See Shridharani, **War Without Violence,** U.S. ed., pp. 86-87; Br. ed., pp. 90-93; Diwakar, **Satyagraha,** pp. 112-114; Gandhi, **An Autobiography,** pp. 427-428 and 430-432; and Erikson, **Gandhi's Truth,** pp. 351-362.

43. Sharp, **Gandhi Wields . . . ,** p. 183.

44. Lakey, "The Sociological Mechanisms . . . " (Thesis), p. 34; *Peace Research Reviews,* vol. II, no. 6 (Dec. 1968), p. 22.

45. See Sharp, **Gandhi Wields . . . ,** pp. 89-211.

46. Hiller, **The Strike,** p. 149.

47. Sharp, **Gandhi Wields . . . ,** p. 85.

48. See Gregg, **The Power of Nonviolence,** p. 79.

49. Sharp, **Tyranny Could Not Quell Them,** p. 16.

50. Nehru, **An Autobiography,** p. 70.

51. Gopal, **The Viceroyalty of Lord Irwin,** pp. 55, 58-59, 64-66, 69-70.

52. Norman Phillips, **The Tragedy of Apartheid** (New York: David McKay, 1960), p. 172.

53. Sternstein, "The *Ruhrkampf* of 1923", p. 132.

54. Liddell Hart, "Lessons from Resistance Movements—Guerilla and Nonviolent", p. 205. See also Sir Basil Liddell Hart, **Defence of the West: Some Riddles of War and Peace** (London: Cassell, 1950), pp. 53-57 (Chapter VII "Were we Wise to Foster 'Resistance Movements'?").

55. Government of India, **India in 1930-31, a Statement prepared for Presentation to Parliament etc.** (Calcutta: Government of India, 1932), pp. 69-72.

56. Kuper, **Passive Resistance in South Africa,** pp. 87 and 156.

57. *Daily Telegraph,* 4 September 1963; cited in Roberts, "The Buddhist Revolt," MS p. 25.

58. See, e.g., Sharp, **Gandhi Wields . . . ,** p. 98.

59. See, e.g., Hiller, **The Strike,** p. 164.

60. Oppenheimer and Lakey, **A Manual for Direct Action,** p. 116.

61. Dhawan, **The Political Philosophy of Mahatma Gandhi,** p. 141.

62. Gopal, The Viceroyalty of Lord Irwin, p. 5.

63. Quoted by de Ligt, **The Conquest of Violence,** p. 118.

64. Miller, **Nonviolence,** p. 336.

65. Gregg, **The Power of Nonviolence,** p. 44.

66. See Delarue, **The Gestapo,** pp. 6 and 40 (including a quotation to that effect from Goebbels).

67. *Ibid.,* p. 40.

68. See, e.g., Shirer, **The Rise and Fall of the Third Reich,** pp. 191-196, Delarue, **The Gestapo,** pp. 7-10 and 34-46, and Bullock, **Hitler,** pp. 262-274.

69. Fritz Tobias, **The Reichstag Fire.** New York: G.P. Putnam's Sons, 1964.

70. Quoted in Shirer, **The Rise and Fall . . . ,** p. 756.

71. See *ibid.,* pp. 336, 339, 342, and 345n., and Bullock, **Hitler,** pp. 427-428 and 433.

72. See Shirer, **The Rise and Fall . . . ,** pp. 304, 357, 361-363, 377, 383, 387-388, 406, 427, and 443-444, and Bullock, **Hitler,** 443-466 and 482-485.

73. Delarue, **The Gestapo,** pp. 173-176, Crankshaw, **Gestapo,** pp. 101-102 and 109-111, Shirer, **The Rise and Fall . . . ,** pp. 464, 472, 518-520, 546-547, 554 inc. n., 563, 577, 579 n., 582, 593-595, 602, 604 and 615, and Bullock, **Hitler,** pp. 376 and 546-547.

74. See Reitlinger, **The Final Solution,** pp. 10-15, Shirer, **The Rise and Fall . . . ,** pp. 430-435, Crankshaw, **Gestapo,** p. 160, Delarue, **The Gestapo,** p. 268 inc. n., Neumann, **Behemoth,** pp. 118-120.

75. Reitlinger, **The Final Solution,** p. 100.

76. See, e.g., *ibid.,* pp. 309, 330-331, 348, and 361.

77. See Delarue, **The Gestapo,** pp. 177 and 191-192, and Wheeler-Bennett, **The Nemesis of Power,** p. 461.

78. Shirer, **The Rise and Fall . . . ,** p. 941.

79. Another important example of the effect of revolutionary violence in making the regime stronger, more dictatorial and in uprooting opposition is the attempted assassination of Tsar Alexander II of Imperial Russia in 1866. That year Karakozov, an emotionally unstable member of a revolutionary group decided against the opinion of his fellow revolutionaries to assassinate Alexander II. This followed a period of liberalization and certain reforms approved by the Tsar. Karakozov's attempt to shoot the Tsar failed and he was seized.

   "The shooting made an enormous impression [writes Venturi]. It put an end to the few remaining traces of collaboration between the Emperor and the liberal intelligentsia in the direction of reforms—a collaboration that had made possible the freeing of the serfs and the subsequent changes in local administration and justice. A wave of indignation and fear destroyed any liberal dreams that still survived after the repression of 1862. And the period of what is traditionally called the 'White Terror' now began. Even men like Nekrasov, who had inherited the spirit of the Tsar's earliest years on the throne, bowed down and tried to save what could still be saved. They added their voice to the chorus of protests against 'nihilism' and joined with the intelligentsia in a mass condemnation of the desperate and violent younger generation. Muravev, who in 1863 had crushed the Polish rebellion in blood, was put in effective charge of internal affairs. He organized a system of repression which aimed to root out the forces of revolution by striking the intellectual tendences which had given them birth.

"The reaction went deep, and even spread to the people. Exact information is difficult to come by, but all sources are agreed that the peasants stood by the Emperor, often violently."

The workmen in the factories similarly rallied to the Tsar, he reports.

". . . the attempt on the Tsar's life did show how strong was the alliance between the monarchy and the mass of working classes and peasants. It was a bond which could not be cunningly exploited to incite violence against the nobles, as the revolutionaries had hoped. They must have realized now what an abyss still divided them from the people."

After Karakozov's arrest it was not long before the police were able to trace other members of the revolutionary group.

"The entire Moscow group was at once caught. The arrested were taken to St. Petersburg.

"The atmosphere of reaction and terror in which the enquiries were made inevitably had profound effects on the results. The extent of the arrests, which involved several hundred people, eventually provided the police with a large number of facts."

"The repression which followed Karakozov's attempt to kill the Tsar had one immediate and tangible effect. Between 1866 and 1868 there was not a single group in Russia able to carry out clandestine activities or make known its ideas by giving a more general significance to its internal debates."

Venturi, **Roots of Revolution,** pp. 345-350.

80. Gandhi, **Non-Violent Resistance,** p. 212; Ind. ed.: **Satyagraha,** p. 212.

81. *Ibid.,* p. 9.

82. Sharp, **Gandhi Wields . . . ,** p. 103.

83. *Ibid.,* p. 118.

84. Kuper, **Passive Resistance in South Africa,** p. 239.

85. *Ibid.,* p. 131.

86. Miller, **Nonviolence,** p. 333 and 338.

87. Lakey, "The Sociological Mechanisms . . . ",(Thesis), p. 95; *Peace Research Reviews,* vol. II, no. 6 (Dec. 1968), p. 63.

88. Gregg, **The Power of Nonviolence,** pp. 87-88. The use of *agents provocateurs* against nonviolent campaigns is also briefly mentioned in Oppenheimer and Lakey, **A Manual for Direct Action,** p. 116 and Walker, **Organizing for Non-violent Direct Action,** p. 26.

89. Kuper, **Passive Resistance in South Africa,** p. 87.

90. **Nehru, An Autobiography,** p. 81.

91. Nehru, **Toward Freedom,** p. 394.

92. Symons, **The General Strike,** pp. 112-113.

93. Miller, **Nonviolence,** p. 247.

94. Vassilyev, **The Ochrana,** pp. 63-78.

95. See, e.g., Katkov, **Russia 1917,** pp. xxvi, 288 and 419.

96. See, e.g., *ibid.,* pp. 28, 30-31, 33, 170, 288, 420.

97. Gandhi, quoted in Bose, **Selections from Gandhi,** p. 204.

98. *Ibid.*

99. It is sometimes assumed that this emphasis on keeping the struggle nonviolent is a recent innovation stemming from pacifist or Gandhian influences; this is not true. The degree to which the mass use of nonviolent means has been self-conscious has, of course, varied considerably. The nonviolent character of certain mass struggles has often been intuitive or spontaneous in nature and therefore with limited or no explicit efforts to keep it nonviolent. However, in several cases where the ethical view of nonviolence was minimal or absent there have been efforts to maintain nonviolent behavior. In the American colonists' struggles, for example, the noncooperation measures were often seen as a peaceful substitute for war, even though explicit attempts to prevent violence were comparatively limited. (See Gipson, **The British Empire . . .** , vol. XII, pp. 153 and 252-253.) But such efforts to keep the struggle peaceful were made in Virginia, New York and Massachusetts Bay. In this last colony, Lieutenant-Governor Hutchinson wrote in late 1773 of "the greater part" of the merchants, that "though in general they declare against mobs and violence, yet they as generally wish the teas may not be imported." (Schlesinger, **The Colonial Merchants . . .** , p. 283 n.2. See also pp. 93, 96, 129, 189-190, 283, 293, and 605, and Gipson, **The British Empire . . .** , vol. XII, pp. 201-202, and 246.)

　　The Finnish constitutionalists' struggle launched in 1901 against new Russian measures was based on the view, writes Jutikkala, that "the unarmed nation must carry on the struggle with all the means available, without, however, resorting to violence." (Jutikkala, **A History of Finland,** p. 233.) In the predominantly nonviolent Russian 1905 Revolution there were frequent explicit attempts to keep strikes and demonstrations nonviolent. Although significant spontaneous violence did occur, much of the violence can be traced to deliberate initiatives of students and Marxists—especially Bolsheviks; the political wisdom of those initiatives can be challenged most seriously. (See Harcave, **First Blood,** pp. 73, 90, 92-93, 100, 105-106, 116-117, 144, 171, 187 and 219; Schwarz, **The Russian Revolution of 1905,** pp. xi, 65, 68, 132-134, and 138-143; Keep, **The Rise of Social Democracy in Russia,** pp. 157, 159, 172-174, 187, 220, 222, 225-226, 228, 236, 258, 260, 263, 266, 270, and 289-290, and Lord Hardinge of Penschurst, **Old Diplomacy,** p. 114.

　　When the French and Belgians invaded the Ruhr, the proclamation to the entire German people from the President and government urged avoidance of counterproductive action: ". . . take no action which would harm our just cause. Anyone who . . . commits any rash and unconsidered action which in the end would only serve the enemy's ends would be deeply guilty. The public good depends on each and every person exercising the utmost self-control." (Sternstein, "The *Ruhrkampf* of 1923" p. 112.) In the predominantly nonviolent East German rising of 1953 there were spontaneous attempts to keep it nonviolent. (See Brant, **The East German Rising,** pp. 71, 73, 76, 84, 94, 99, 102-103, 115, 124, 126, and 190-191.) Ebert writes: ". . . in general the more reasonable elements among the workers managed to prevent acts of violence. The demonstrators locked up or destroyed any weapons they found." (Ebert, "Nonviolent Resistance Against Communist Regimes?" pp. 190-191.) These few examples illustrate that nonviolent discipline is not an alien emphasis introduced by moralists, but that other practitioners have perceived it to be a necessary aspect of the technique itself.

100. Griffith, **The Resurrection of Hungary,** p. 32. See also pp. 17 and 57.

101. Gandhi, **Non-violent Resistance,** p. 56; Ind. ed.: **Satyagraha,** p. 56. See also p. 187.

102. Gandhi, in Bose, **Selections from Gandhi,** p. 203.

103. The phrase is Miller's. Miller, **Nonviolence,** p. 155.

104. "Suffolk Resolves" Nr.18, **American Archives,** Fourth Series (Washington, D.C.: M. St. Clarke and Peter Force, 1937), vol. I, p. 778.

105. Oppenheimer and Lakey, **A Manual for Direct Action,** p. 121.

106. Lindberg, *"Konklusionen: Teorien om Ikke-vold"*, p. 209, in Lindberg, Jacobsen and Ehrlich, **Kamp Uden Vaaben.** Lenin also acknowledged this tendency in 1905 although he favored violence. See Lenin, "Lessons of the Moscow Uprising" in Lenin, **Selected Works in Three Volumes,** vol. I, p. 577.

107. *Young India* (weekly), 27 March 1930.

108. Hiller, **The Strike,** pp. 171-172.

109. Ebert, "Nonviolent Resistance Against Communist Regimes?" p. 191.

110. Brant, **The East German Rising,** p. 124.

111. Sibley, **The Quiet Battle,** p. 117.

112. Samuel Yellen, **American Labor Struggles** (New York: Harcourt, Brace & Co., 1936), p. 58.

113. This account is summarized from Yellen, *op. cit.,* pp. 39-71.

114. Gandhi, **Non-violent Resistance,** p. 218; Ind. ed.: **Satyagraha,** p. 218.

115. Gandhi, quoted in Bose, **Selections from Gandhi,** p. 203.

116. Gandhi, **Non-violent Resistance,** p. 288; Ind. ed.: **Satyagraha,** p. 288.

117. See Kuper, **Passive Resistance in South Africa,** p. 133-140.

118. See *ibid.,* pp. 140-143.

119. *Ibid.,* p. 140.

120. *Ibid.,* p. 143. On these riots and their effects, see also Luthuli, **Let My People Go,** pp. 127-128 and 130.

121. *Ibid.,* p. 144.

122. *Ibid.,* p. 145.

123. *Ibid.,* p. 156.

124. Schlesinger, **The Colonial Merchants . . . ,** pp. 475-476. For some specific examples of the abandonment or repeal of provisions of the Continental Association, see also pp. 566-568, 572, 583-585 and 589.

125. See Gregg, **The Power of Nonviolence,** p. 133,

126. Luthuli, **Let My People Go,** pp. 127-128.

127. See Yarmolinsky, **Road to Revolution,** pp. 9, 141-142, 161, 177-178, 227, 291; Seton-Watson, **The Decline of Imperial Russia,** p. 72; Schapiro, **The Communist Party of the Soviet Union,** p. 80 and Venturi, **Roots of Revolution,** pp. xxvi, 469 and 527. On the effects of arson, see Yarmolinsky, *op. cit.,* pp. 113-114, and on the effects of robberies, see Schapiro, *op.cit.,* pp. 97 and 104.

128. Katkov, **Russia 1917,** p. xxvi.

129. See Schlesinger, **The Colonial Merchants . . . ,** pp. 92-93.

130. *Ibid.,* pp. 298-299. See also pp. 300 and 308-309.

131. *Ibid.,* p. 299.

132. *Ibid.,* p. 542.

133. Gipson, **The British Empire . . . ,** vol. XII, p. 369.

134. See Schlesinger, **The Colonial Merchants . . . ,** pp. 435-439.

135. See, e.g., Waskow, **From Race Riot to Sit-In,** p. 261 for an early observation of this.

136. Farmer, **Freedom – When?**, p. 79.

137. Schlesinger, **The Colonial Merchants . . .** , p. 531.

138. O'Hegarty, **A History of Ireland Under the Union, 1880-1922**, p. 515.

139. *Ibid.,* p. 522.

140. John Morley, **The Life of William Ewart Gladstone** (New York & London: Macmillan & Co., 1903), vol. III, p. 70.

141. *Ibid.,* vol. III, p. 68.

142. Deutscher, **Stalin,** p. 102.

143. See Harcave, **First Blood,** esp. pp. 155-157, 177 and 238.

144. Eyck, **A History of the Weimar Republic,** vol. I, p. 237. See also Sternstein, "The *Ruhrkampf* of 1923" pp. 120 and 125. He reports especially the taking of hostages, and the deaths of 141 Germans from beatings, arbitrary executions, and firings from guards and patrols.

145. Waskow, **From Race Riot to Sit-in,** pp. 199-202.

146. Solomon and Fishman, "The Psychosocial Meaning of Nonviolence in Student Civil Rights Activities," *Psychiatry,* vol. XXVII (May, 1964), p. 95.

147. Schlesinger, **The Colonial Merchants . . .** , p. 539. See also pp. 536-540. There remained, however, other important British support for the Americans even after Lexington and Concord. See Gipson, **The British Empire . . .** , vol. XII, pp. 340-351.

148. Harcave, **First Blood,** p. 220.

140. *Ibid.,* p. 222.

150. *Ibid.,* p. 223.

151. Keep, **The Rise of Social Democracy in Russia,** p. 249.

152. *Ibid.,* pp. 239-242.

153. *Ibid.,* p. 248.

154. Henry W. Nevinson, who was at the time in Moscow as a special correspondent for the *Daily Chronicle* (London) reported the disaffection and untrustworthiness—prior to the rising—of the soldiers stationed in Moscow. Nevinson also wrote that on December 6 (19) – the day before the general strike began— ". . . the Government was only longing for disturbances as an excuse for military assassination." He reported that on Dec. 8 (21): "They [the revolutionists] were ill-armed, had only eighty rifles as yet; a good many revolvers certainly, but not enough arms. Besides, if the Government wanted a rising, they obviously ought not to rise. It is a bad strategist who lets the enemy dictate the time for battle."

"But the Government had determined that neither delay nor opportunity should be given. Their one thought was the urgent need of money, the power that commands force is the Government, and the power that commands money can command force; that was their just and simple argument. Their one hope was to stir up an ill-prepared rebellion, to crush it down, and stand triumphant before the nations of Europe, confidently inviting new loans in the name of law and order, so as to pay the interest on the old and 'maintain the value of the rouble.' For this object it was essential that people should be killed in large numbers . . . unless the slaughter came quickly the officials could not count upon their pay. The only alternative was national bankruptcy. . . . At all costs the people must be goaded into violence, or the Government's strategy would have failed." Nevinson, Henry W., **The Dawn in Russia or Scenes in the Russian Revolution** (London and New York: Harper & Bros., 1906), pp. 123 and 136-138.

155. Keep, **The Rise of Social Democracy in Russia,** pp. 250-251.

156. *Ibid.,* p. 243.

157. *Ibid.,* pp. 245-246.

158. Louis Fischer, **The Life of Lenin** (New York: Harper & Row, 1965 and London: Weidenfeld and Nicolson, 1965), p. 57.

159. Prawdin, **The Unmentionable Nechaev,** p. 148. Also on the Bolsheviks' view of the Moscow defeat as "beneficial," see Adam B. Ulam, **The Bolsheviks: The Intellectual and Political History of the Triumph of Communism in Russia** (New York: Macmillan, and London: Collier-Macmillian, 1965), p. 236. And Nevinson, **The Dawn in Russia,** pp. 198-199.

160. In July 1905 Lenin wrote: "The revolutionary army is required for the military struggle and the military leadership of the masses of the people against the remnants of the military forces of the autocracy. The revolutionary army is needed because great historical questions can be solved only by *violence,* and the *organisation of violence* in the modern struggle is a military organisation." Lenin, "The Revolutionary Army and the Revolutionary Government," in V. I. Lenin, **Selected Works,** vol. III, **The Revolution of 1905-07** (Moscow and Leningrad: Co-operative Publishing Society of Foreign Workers in the U.S.S.R., 1934 [?]), p. 313. See also p. 315.

    In August he wrote: "... we must clearly and resolutely point out the necessity for an uprising in the present state of affairs; we must directly call for insurrection (without, of course, fixing the date beforehand), and call for the immediate organisation of a revolutionary army. Only a very bold and wide organisation of such an army can serve as a prologue to the insurrection. Only insurrection can guarantee the victory of the revolution ..." Lenin, "The Boycott of the Bulygin Duma and the Insurrection" p. 327 in *op. cit.,* vol. III.

161. "The broad masses, however, were still too naive, their mood was too passive, too good-natured, too Christian. . . . they lacked . . . a clear understanding that only the most vigorous continuation of the armed struggle, only a victory over all the military and civil authorities, only the overthrow of the government and the seizure of power throughout the country could guarantee the success of the revolution." Lenin, "Lecture on the 1905 Revolution" (January 1917), in Lenin, **Selected Works in Three Volumes,** vol. I, p. 795. (Note: the Moscow 1934(?) edition refers to the seizure of power "over the whole state" instead of "throughout the country." See Lenin, **Selected Works,** vol. III, p. 10.)

    "... we should have explained to the masses that it was impossible to confine things to a peaceful strike and that a fearless and relentless armed fight was necessary. And now we must at last openly and publicly admit that political strikes are inadequate; we must carry on the widest agitation among the masses in favour of an armed uprising and make no attempt to obscure this question ... We would be deceiving both ourselves and the people if we concealed from the masses the necessity of a desperate, bloody war of extermination, as the immediate task of the coming revolutionary action.

    "... Another lesson [of the December 1905 events] concerns the character of the uprising, the methods by which it is conducted, and the conditions which lead to the troops coming over to the side of the people. An extremely biased view on this latter point prevails in the Right wing of our Party. It is alleged that there is no possibility of fighting modern troops; the troops must become revolutionary. Of course, unless the revolution assumes a mass character and affects the troops, there can be no question of serious struggle. That we must work among the troops goes without saying. But we must not imagine that they will come over to our side at one stroke, as a result of persuasion of their own convictions. . . . But we shall prove to be miserable pedants if we forget that at a time of uprising there must also be a physical struggle for the troops."

"And the guerrilla warfare and mass terror that has been taking place throughout Russia practically without a break since December [1905], will undoubtedly help the masses to learn the correct tactics of an uprising." Lenin, "Lessons of the Moscow Uprising," in Lenin, **Selected Works in Three Volumes,** vol. I, pp. 579-582.

162. Keep, **The Rise of Social Democracy in Russia,** pp. 246-247.

163. Harcave, **First Blood,** p. 235. On the four phases of the rising, see Keep, **The Rise . . .** , pp. 251-257.

164. Harcave, **First Blood,** p. 235.

165. Keep, **The Rise . . .** , pp. 253-254.

166. Seton-Watson, **The Decline of Imperial Russia,** pp. 224-225.

167. Harcave, **First Blood,** pp. 238 and 243. Nevinson wrote: "The failure at Moscow fell like a blight upon all Russia, and all hope withered." (Nevinson, **The Dawn in Russia,** p. 198.) Lenin later wrote: "In October 1905, Russia was at the peak of the revolutionary upsurge . . . the period of decline set in after the defeat of December 1905 . . ." "The turning point in the struggle began with the defeat of the December uprising. Step by step the counter-revolution passed to the offensive as the mass struggle weakened." Lenin, "Revolution and Counter-Revolution," from *Proletary*, Nr. 17, 20 October 1907, in **Collected Works,** vol. 13, **June 1907–April 1908** (Moscow: Foreign Languages Publishing House, 1962), pp. 114 and 116.

168. "Sabotage, and all it means, including the destruction of property, is in itself violence," wrote Gandhi. Bose, **Studies in Gandhism,** p. 145.

169. See Gandhi, **Non-violent Resistance,** p. 378; Ind. ed.: **Satyagraha,** p. 378.

170. See *Ibid.,* p. 379.

171. See Halperin, **Germany Tried Democracy,** p. 250, Karl Ehrlich, *"Ruhrkampen,"* in Lindberg, Jacobsen and Ehrlich, **Kamp Uden Vaaben,** p. 187, and Sternstein, "The *Ruhrkampf* of 1923" pp. 123-126.

172. Ehrlich, "Ruhrkampen" p. 187.

173. On these negative influences of sabotage, see Sternstein, "The *Ruhrkampf* of 1923" pp. 124-126. The quotation from Wentzcke is on p. 125 from Paul Wentzcke **Ruhrkampf** (Berlin: Reimar Hobbing, 1930), vol. I, pp. 424-425.

174. See, e.g., Schlesinger, **The Colonial Merchants . . .** , p. 71.

175. *Ibid.,* pp. 91-92 and 105.

176. *Ibid.,* p. 97. See also p. 103.

177. *Ibid.,* pp. 179-180.

178. *Ibid.,* p. 368.

179. *Ibid.,* p. 390.

180. *Ibid.,* pp. 391-392.

181. For the text of the Association, see *ibid.,* pp. 607-613.

182. Gipson, **The British Empire . . .** , vol. XII, p. 316.

183. *Ibid.,* pp. 321-323.

184. Schlesinger, **The Colonial Merchants . . .** , p. 608.

185. *Ibid.,* p. 519.

186. *Ibid.,* p. 529.

187. Gipson, **The British Empire . . .** , vol. XII, p. 145.

188. *Ibid.,* pp. 163-164.

189. *Ibid.,* p. 197.

190. See, e.g., *ibid.,* pp. 320-349.

191. Schlesinger, **The Colonial Merchants . . . ,** p. 563.

192. *Ibid.,* p. 541. See also p. 542. On various alterations in the earlier economic sanctions, see pp. 562, 566-568, 572-573, and 576.

193. *Ibid.,* p. 563.

194. See Lindberg,*"Konklusionen: Teorien on Ikke-vold,"* pp. 207-208 in Lindberg, Jacobsen and Ehrlich, **Kamp Uden Vaaben.**

195. See Ebert, "Nonviolent Resistance Against Communist Regimes?" p. 182.

196. Bose, **Selections from Gandhi,** p. 200.

197. Bradford Lyttle, "The Importance of Discipline in Demonstrations for Peace" (duplicated, 2pp. New York: Committee for Non-Violent Action, 1962).

198. Waskow, **From Race Riot to Sit-in,** pp. 255-257.

199. Lyttle, "The Importance of Discipline in Demonstrations for Peace."

200. Luthuli, **Let My People Go,** p. 120.

201. Ehrlich, *"Rene Sociale Klassekampe. Den Ikke-voldelige Modstand, Der. Kvalte Kapp-Kuppet,"* pp. 200 n. and 202, in Lindberg, Jacobsen and Ehrlich, **Kamp Uden Vaaben.**

202. See Kuper, **Passive Resistance in South Africa,** p. 93 and Sharp, "A South African Contribution to the Study of Nonviolent Action: A Review" p. 400, *Journal of Conflict Resolution,* vol. V, no. 4 (December, 1961).

203. For examples of Gandhi's views, see Bose. **Selections From Gandhi,** p. 189; Bose, **Studies in Gandhism,** p. 151; and Gandhi, **Non-violent Resistance,** pp. 57, 98, 100, 194-195, 302, 355 and 362-363; Ind. ed.: **Satyagraha,** same pp.

204. "Discipline for Public Witness Demonstrations" (leaflet).

205. For Gandhi's views on self-discipline in prison, see Gandhi, **Non-violent Resistance,** pp. 60-65; Ind. ed.: **Satyagraha,** pp. 60-65.

206. Gregg, **The Power of Nonviolence,** pp. 80-81.

207. Lyttle, "The Importance of Discipline in Demonstrations for Peace".

208. See Gregg, **The Power of Nonviolence,** p. 71.

209. *Ibid.,* p. 67.

210. Charles C. Walker, **Organizing for Nonviolent Direct Action** (pamphlet) (Cheney, Pennsylvania: The Author, 1961), p. 16.

211. See *ibid.,* pp. 20 and 22.

212. Oppenheimer and Lakey, **A Manual for Direct Action,** p. 108.

213. Gandhi, **Non-violent Resistance,** p. 333; Ind. ed.: **Satyagraha,** p. 333. The Committee of 100 during the period of its greatest strength repeatedly made the same request for its civil disobedience demonstrations.

214. Gandhi, **Non-violent Resistance,** p. 287; Ind. ed.: **Satyagraha,** p. 287.

215. See Gregg, **The Power of Nonviolence,** p. 118.

216. Luthuli paid strong tribute to the discipline of the inexperienced and largely untrained volunteers for the 1952 Defiance Campaign in South Africa, although this did not apply to the whole nonwhite population. See Luthuli, **Let My People Go,** pp. 118 and 125.

217. Gandhi, **Non-violent Resistance,** p. 25; Ind. ed.: **Satyagraha,** p. 25.

218. *Ibid.,* p. 299.

219. *Ibid.,* p. 297.

220. Schlesinger, **The Colonial Merchants . . .**, pp. 193-194. On other cases of reshipment of goods without information on its effect on mob violence, see also pp. 200-201, 217 and 426.

221. *Ibid.,* p. 226.

222. See his statement in Sharp, **Gandhi Wields . . .**, p. 49.

223. Nehru, **An Autobiography,** p. 175.

224. Farmer, **Freedom — When?** pp. 27, 28, and 32-34. On the effect of nonviolent action reducing the chances of violence, see also Waskow, **From Race Riot to Sit-in,** pp. 262 and 285.

225. Walker, **Organizing for Nonviolent Direct Action,** p. 28.

226. Miller, **Nonviolence,** p. 307 and King, **Stride Towards Freedom,** pp. 58-62 and 78-81.

227. Harcave, **First Blood,** p. 149.

228. *Ibid.,* p. 226.

229. Solomon and Fishman, "The Psychosocial Meaning of Nonviolence in Student Civil Rights Activities," p. 98.

230. Halperin, **Germany Tried Democracy,** p. 179.

231. Gregg, **The Power of Nonviolence,** p. 88.

232. See Gandhi, **Non-violent Resistance,** p. 151; Ind. ed.: **Satyagraha,** p. 151.

233. Ehrlich, "*Ruhrkampen,*" p. 187.

234. See Bose, **Studies in Gandhism,** pp. 143-144 and Gandhi, **Non-violent Resistance,** pp. 139-141 and 151; Ind. ed.: **Satyagraha,** pp. 139-141 and 151.

235. See Walker, **Organizing for Nonviolent Direct Action,** p. 20.

236. Oppenheimer and Lakey, **A Manual for Direct Action,** p. 84 and Miller, **Nonviolence,** pp. 306-308, and Walker, **Organizing for Nonviolent Direct Action,** pp. 9-11.

237. Quoted in Roberts, "Buddhism and Politics in South Vietnam" pp. 243-244.

238. Sharp, **Gandhi Wields . . .**, p. 81.

239. King, **Stride Toward Freedom,** U.S. ed., p. 51; Br. ed., p. 60. For an example of on-the-spot pleas for nonviolence from hostile crowds in Birmingham, Alabama, in 1963, see Miller, **Nonviolence,** pp. 334-336.

240. Kuper, **Passive Resistance in South Africa,** p. 119.

241. Miller, **Nonviolence,** pp. 278-280.

242. Brant, **The East German Rising,** pp. 102-103. See also p. 99.

243. *Ibid.,* p. 126.

244. Joseph Wechsberg, "A Reporter in Germany," pp. 38, 49 and 50 in *The New Yorker,* 29 August 1953, quoted in Miller, **Nonviolence,** pp. 352-353.

245. Brant, **The East German Rising,** p. 71.

246. Morgan and Morgan, **The Stamp Act Crisis,** p. 248.

247. Peck, **Freedom Ride,** p. 76 and Walker, **Organizing for Nonviolent Direct Action,** p. 20.

248. Oppenheimer and Lakey, **A Manual for Direct Action,** p. 87.

249. Gandhi, **Non-violent Resistance,** p. 35; Ind. ed.: **Satyagraha,** p. 35.

250. *Ibid.,* pp. 118-119. This view was repeatedly emphasized by Gandhi in very strong terms; see also, pp. 98 and 302.

251. See, for example, Gandhi, **Nonviolence in Peace and War,** vol. I, p. 154; Dhawan, **The Political Philosophy . . .**, pp. 211-213; Sharp, **Gandhi Wields . . .**, pp. 67-69 and 80-81; Gandhi, **Non-violent Resistance,** pp. 205-206; Ind. ed.:

Satyagraha, pp. 205-206; and Bondurant, **Conquest of Violence,** pp. 77 and 133-134.

252. Schlesinger, **The Colonial Merchants . . . ,** p. 293. In late June 1774 the town meeting of Portsmouth deliberately took various other measures—not involving pledges or codes of discipline—to prevent the outbreak of violence when dutied teas was landed, and at the town's insistence and expense re-exported so that it was not sold or used in Portsmouth. See *ibid.,* p. 303.

253. The Direct Action Committee Against Nuclear War issued a general but detailed discipline leaflet — "Demonstrators —" (1958?) intended both for organized demonstrations and for distribution during spontaneous demonstrations. That Committee also issued detailed briefings for participants on the particular plans and behavioral requirements for a given demonstration, as well as legal aspects and a guide for statements in court for those arrested. For example, for one action the following were issued: "Briefing for Non-Violent Obstruction at North Pickenham Rocket Base on Saturday December 6th" (25 November 1958), "Briefing on legal aspects of demonstration on December 6th" (4 December 1958), and "Explanatory statement to be made in Court" (n.d.). Discipline leaflets were also issued both for the National Committee of 100 and affiliated groups, as the Oxford Committee of 100. The Oxford leaflet differed from the D.A.C.A.N.W. leaflet not only in its brevity, but its recommendation that if violence broke out people should not physically place themselves between the fighters, but "immediately withdraw, leave an empty space, and sit down. Isolate the violence."

254. Twelve New York City peace organizations in 1962 issued a "Discipline for Public Witness Demonstrations" and a very detailed binding discipline code was issued by the Committee for Nonviolent Action for its long peace walk focusing on U.S. relations with Cuba: "Group Discipline — Principles of Conduct — or what have you for the Quebec-Washington-Guantanamo walk for peace — sponsored by CNVA."

255. Walker, **Organizing for Nonviolent Direct Action,** p. 16.

256. Miller, **Nonviolence,** pp. 155-156.

257. Sibley, **The Quite Battle,** pp. 299-300.

258. O'Hegarty, **A History of Ireland Under the Union 1880-1922,** p. 514.

259. This is discussed more fully in the last section of this chapter.

260. Bose, **Selections from Gandhi,** p. 203.

261. *Ibid.,*

262. See above pp. 479-491.

263. Schlesinger, **The Colonial Merchants . . . ,** pp. 488-489.

264. Thus Gandhi argued that the purer the suffering, the quicker would be the result. Gandhi, **Non-violent Resistance,** p. 188; Ind. ed.: **Satyagraha,** p. 188.

265. See, e.g., *Ibid.,* pp. 74, 93, 107, 162, 169, 179, 182, 193, 201-202, 207, 284-285, and 357.

266. "Discipline for Public Witness Demonstrations" (leaflet). New York: various peace organizations, 1962.

267. "Demonstrators — " (leaflet). London: Committee for Direct Action Against Nuclear War, 1958 (?).

268. King, **Stride Toward Freedom,** U.S. ed., p. 83; Br. ed.: pp. 97-98.

269. Schlesinger, **The Colonial Merchants . . . ,** p. 172.

270. Gandhi, **Non-violent Resistance,** p. 139; Ind. ed.: **Satyagraha,** p. 139.

271. Bose, **Studies in Gandhism**, p. 129.
272. *Ibid.*, p. 147.
273. Quoted in Bose, **Selections from Gandhi,** p. 202.
274. *Ibid.*, pp. 202-203.
275. *Ibid.*, p. 202.
276. *Ibid.*, p. 203.
277. Sharp, **Gandhi Wields . . . ,** p. 91.
278. See *ibid.*, pp. 118-127 and Gopal, **The Viceroyalty of Lord Irwin,** p. 71.
279. Gopal, **The Viceroyalty . . . ,** p. 79.
280. Sharp, **Gandhi Wields . . . ,** p. 172. See also p. 177.
281. *Ibid.*, pp. 171-172.
282. *Ibid.*, p. 104.
283. *Ibid.*, p. 100.
284. Gopal, **The Viceroyalty** .. , pp. 77-78.
285. Sharp, **Gandhi Wields . . . ,** pp. 202-203. On this possibility, see also Symons, **The General Strike,** pp. 210-211.
286. Harcave, **First Blood,** p. 84.
287. King, **Stride Toward Freedom,** U.S. ed., pp. 115-122; Br. ed.; pp. 136-144.
288. Harcave, **First Blood,** pp. 186-187.
289. See Gopal, **The Viceroyalty** ... , p. 70, and Sharp, **Gandhi Wields . . . ,** pp. 114ff.
290. See Gopal, **The Viceroyalty** ... , p. 71, and Sharp, **Gandhi Wields . . . ,** pp. 125-127 and 174-176.
291. See Gopal, **The Viceroyalty** ... , p. 77, and Sharp, **Gandhi Wields . . . ,** pp. 113-114, 132 and 183. For Gandhi's views on hand-copied newspapers in 1921, see Bose, **Selections from Gandhi,** pp. 200-201.
292. Sharp, **Gandhi Wields . . . ,** pp. 132 and 161.
293. *Ibid.*, p. 200.
294. *Ibid.*, pp. 198-200.
295. Gopal, **The Viceroyalty** ... , p. 78.
296. *Ibid.*, p. 87.

PART THREE: DYNAMICS

12

Political Jiu-Jitsu

INTRODUCTION

Political *jiu-jitsu*[1] is one of the special processes by which nonviolent action deals with violent repression. By combining nonviolent discipline with solidarity and persistence in struggle, the nonviolent actionists cause the violence of the opponent's repression to be exposed in the worst possible light. This, in turn, may lead to shifts in opinion and then to shifts in power relationships favorable to the nonviolent group. These shifts result from withdrawal of support for the opponent and the grant of support to the nonviolent actionists.

Cruelties and brutalities committed against the clearly nonviolent are likely to disturb many people and to fill some with outrage. Even milder violent repression appears less justified against nonviolent people than when employed against violent resisters. This reaction to repression is especially likely when the opponent's policies themselves are hard to justify. Thus, wider public opinion may turn against the opponent, members of his own group may dissent, and more or less passive members of the general grievance group may shift to firm opposition. The effects of this process do not stop there, however. In addition to shifts of opinion *against* the opponent, positive sympathy in *favor* of the nonviolent actionists and their cause is also likely to develop. Most important, all these shifts in opinion may lead to action. The opponent may find more and more groups, even among his normal supporters, resisting his policies and activities; at the same time, increased active support for the nonviolent actionists and their cause may develop.

Thus, precisely because the actionists have rejected violence while persisting in resistance and defiance, the opponent's violence has certain effects on several social groups which tend to shift loyalties, social forces and power relationships against him and in favor of the nonviolent actionists. *Their nonviolence helps the opponent's repression to throw him off balance politically.*[2] *The nonviolent group is also able to gain far more support and power than if it had met violence with violence.*

Political *jiu-jitsu* does not operate in all nonviolent struggles. Most of the many specific methods of action listed in earlier chapters are independent of this particular process. If opponents become more sophisticated in dealing with nonviolent action, so that they drastically reduce, or even eliminate, violent repression and thereby political *jiu-jitsu,* the nonviolent actionists will still be able to win. They will still be able to utilize the many psychological, social, economic and political forces and pressures which the multitude of specific methods brings into play.

Political *jiu-jutsu* operates among three broad groups: 1) uncommitted third parties, whether on the local scene or the world level, 2) the opponent's usual supporters, and 3) the general grievance group. Now we shall explore the ways in which the views and actions of each of these three groups tend to shift away from the opponent and in favor of the nonviolent actionists. We shall begin with third parties whose potential influence is normally the smallest, then consider the opponent's usual supporters who are obviously very important, and conclude with the grievance group, whose role may be crucial.

WINNING OVER UNCOMMITTED THIRD PARTIES

Repression against nonviolent people may attract wide attention to the struggle and strong sympathy for the suffering nonviolent group among persons not involved in the struggle in any way. As the American sociologist Edward Alsworth Ross put it,

The spectacle of men suffering for a principle and *not hitting back* is a moving one. It obliges the power holders to condescend to explain, to justify themselves. The weak get a change of venue from the will of the stronger to the court of public opinion, perhaps world opinion.[3]

A. International indignation

Indeed, some of the main cases used in this study support this conclusion. For example, Bloody Sunday (1905) in St. Petersburg produced, reports Harcave, "immediate and bitter international revulsion" expressed in anti-tsarist demonstrations in England, Germany, Austria-Hungary, Sweden, France, Spain, Italy, Belgium, United States, Argentina and Uruguay.[4] Two days after the massacre, Kokovtsev, the Minister of Finance, reported to the Tsar that not only had the killings impaired morale at home, but that Russian financial credit abroad had been affected.[5] In other words, repression of nonviolent actionists had drawn even foreign "third parties" into the struggle against the regime (even if the creditors' motives were selfish).

Similar results have taken place in such contrasting cases as Germany and India. In 1923 government-sponsored nonviolent resistance in the Ruhr against the Franco-Belgian occupation produced wide sympathy for Germany, brought new discredit to the Treaty of Versailles, and alienated British opinion from the invaders at a time when France needed British support for the international security it wanted.[6] And in the thirties, British repression against nonviolent Indian volunteers helped move world opinion significantly toward the Indians.[7]

International indignation was also aroused by repression against nonviolent actionists in both South Africa and South Vietnam. Sometimes the actionists, aware of this process, have deliberately sought to arouse this international support, as they did in South Africa.[8] For example, the 1952 Defiance Campaign attracted world attention to *Apartheid* in South Africa and the plight of nonwhites there. Press reports hostile to the regime became common. Several Asian governments and African political groups expressed sympathy for the resisters. After India raised the matter in the United Nations General Assembly, a U.N. commission investigated the effects of *Apartheid* legislation.[9] This widespread disapproval of its policies, Kuper writes, posed two problems for the South African government: how to win over world opinion, and how to explain world condemnation to its own European population.[10] The government was more successful in the latter than in the former, but continued major efforts to win international acceptance indicate its importance to that regime.

Eight years later, in 1960, during another nonviolent campaign in that country, the killing of demonstrators at Sharpeville (where Africans had only thrown stones, and that without inflicting serious injuries) produced widespread condemnation and economic sanctions against the South African government. The extreme disproportion between the repression and the demonstrators' behavior shocked world opinion. The shootings had made clear, said Luthuli, "the implacable, wanton brutality of their regime." [11] Throughout far away Norway, for example, flags were flown at half-mast in mourning. The Legums report that the European population in South Africa was in 1960 "staggered by the unanimity of the world's reaction to Sharpeville." By December 1963, hostility at the United Nations had increased to the point that "South Africa stood alone in the face of the world's unanimous condemnation of its policies." The South African Europeans again "reacted with dazed incomprehension or truculent self-justification." [12]

Another quite different case, the 1963 Buddhist struggle against the South Vietnamese regime of President Ngo Dinh Diem, also illustrates that, by being nonviolent, the repressed group is likely to gain significant sympathy from third parties. By 1963 President Diem had for nine years had the support of the United States. Hedrick Smith reported in his article on Diem's overthrow in *The New York Times* series on *The Pentagon Papers* revelations that "until the eruption of Buddhist demonstrations against the Diem regime in May 1963, much of the American public was oblivious to the 'political decay' in Vietnam described in the Pentagon account . . ." [13]

But on May 8 government troops fired into a crowd of Buddhists in Hué who were displaying religious flags in defiance of a government decree. Armored vehicles crushed some of the demonstrators. Nine were killed and fourteen injured. [14] The Buddhist campaign followed, using nonviolent struggle and also suicide by fire, in which monks burned themselves with gasoline. During those weeks the United States government pressed the Diem regime to meet Buddhist demands. On June 12 the deputy U.S. Ambassador, William Truehart, warned Diem that unless the Buddhist crisis was solved the United States would be forced to dissociate itself from him. Finally, on August 15 Diem declared his policy always to have been conciliation with the Buddhists.

Only six days later, however, the South Vietnamese Special Forces, financed by the United States Central Intelligence Agency and commanded by Diem's very powerful brother, Ngo Dinh Nhu, conducted cruel and destructive midnight raids on Buddhist pagodas: 1,400 people, mostly monks, were arrested, many were beaten, and thirty Buddhists were killed. [15] On

August 29, United States Ambassador Henry Cabot Lodge cabled Secretary of State Rusk, in part: ". . . there is no possibility . . . that Diem or any member of the family can govern the country in a way to gain the support of the people who count, i.e., the educated class in and out of government service, civil and military—not to mention the American people. In the last few months (and especially days) they have in fact positively alienated these people to an incalculable degree." [16]

In addition to internal reactions, the pagoda raids brought deep world resentment against the Diem regime, including criticism from the Vatican, [17] plus open United States government criticism and hints that a change of government might not be unacceptable to Washington. [18] The United States government applied pressure to get the arrested Buddhists freed and their grievances corrected. The author of the Pentagon's account of this period wrote of the consequences of the pagoda raids as follows: "In their brutality and their blunt repudiation of Diem's solemn word to [retiring Ambassador] Nolting, they were a direct, impudent slap in the face for the U.S. For better or worse, the August 21 pagoda raids decided the issue for us." [19] Four days after the raids, on August 24, the initial State Department approval of a possible change in government was sent to Ambassador Lodge, signed by Acting Secretary George W. Ball. [20] Between late August and early October decisions were taken to cut various types of economic aid to the regime. [21] From August 24 on, with slight shifts from time to time, United States officials encouraged and, from behind the scenes, assisted an already initiated generals' *coup*. This took place on November 1, after the Buddhist campaign had undermined the moral authority of and support for the regime; Diem and his family were deposed and Diem himself was killed. [22]

South Vietnamese police were obviously aware during the Buddhist campaign that unfavorable news stories and especially photographs were dangerous to the regime. Although a complete news blackout to the outside world was not politically possible, the police took sporadic action against foreign reporters. On July 7 nine Western reporters and cameramen covering a Buddhist demonstration in Saigon were attacked by police. [23] Just before the crucial raids on Buddhist pagodas, many normal channels of communication with the outside world were cut off. [24] Also, on October 5 three American reporters were beaten by plainclothes police after resisting attempts to seize their cameras which had been used to photograph a political suicide by fire. [25]

Nonviolent action by the Buddhists has been credited with extreme importance, both in bringing this sympathy to the Buddhists and in arousing support within South Vietnam for a change in government. Denis Warner has written: "The physical weakness of the Buddhists was their moral strength. If they had had guns, the Ngo Dinhs could have crushed them and neither Vietnam nor the rest of the world would have cared; defenceless they proved beyond defeat." [26]

B. Factors determining the impact of third party opinion

The third parties whose opinions may shift may be local people, or from the wider region or nation, or as the above indicated, from the world as a whole. In any case, although these shifts of opinion are desirable and usually advantageous to the nonviolent group, they alone serve a limited role at best. There should be no naïve assumption that "public opinion" alone will triumph. Disapproval by third parties and condemnation by world opinion may be very important to some opponents. Both may, in certain cases at least, contribute to uncertainty about the type of counteraction and repression being used, and even about overall policies and objectives. [27] Hostile opinion may cause the opponent to try to justify his policies and measures, or to deprecate those of the nonviolent group. But world opinion on the side of the nonviolent group will *by itself* rarely produce a change in the opponent's policies. Frequently a determined opponent can ignore hostile opinion until and unless it is accompanied by, or leads to, shifts in power relationships, or threatens to do so.

Three groups of factors will determine whether or not the opponent is affected by changes in the opinion of third parties: 1) factors related to the nature of the opponent and of the conflict situation; 2) factors related to action based on the changed opinions; and 3) factors related to the effects of opinion changes on the nonviolent actionists themselves. We shall now consider these.

First, opponents are not alike. Some of them are far more sensitive to public opinion than others. A loss of prestige and the imposition of world censure may be an intolerable price for some opponents to pay, while others will be quite willing to do so if they see no other way to their objectives. There is probably a general correlation between the degree of democracy or autocracy in the opponent's regime or system on the one hand and the degree of responsiveness or unresponsiveness to wider opinion on the other. But this is clearly not an inviolate rule, and reverse combinations sometimes occur. At times even the Nazi regime seemed highly sensitive to public opinion. The nature of the regime, its ideology, its attitude to opposition in general, the role of repression, the social system and related factors may all be important in this context. In addition, some issues may be regarded by the opponent as sufficiently important to be worth the cost of alienated opinion.

Furthermore, not all third parties will be of equal importance to the opponent. Esteem and condemnation are clearly of greater significance in some cases than in others. If the opponent is in fact dependent on certain third parties, he is much more likely to be sensitive to shifts in their opinion than he would be otherwise.

Second, changes in third-party opinions are much more likely to be effective if the opinions are transformed into actions affecting the opponent's relative power position, either opposing the opponent's regime and its policies or supporting the nonviolent group and its policies. Both *who* takes the actions and *what* actions are taken are important. All action is not equal.

The proportion of successes among past cases of international nonviolent action, especially by third parties, is extremely small.[28] There are reasons for this. In the past most third-party and international nonviolent supporting actions have been either largely symbolic in character, or, when more substantial (economic sanctions), have not been applied on the systematic and sustained basis required for effectiveness.

International action by third parties has also sometimes been regarded as a *substitute* for effective struggle by the grievance group itself—as in the case of South Africa—when in fact there is a limit to what third-party nonviolent actions alone can do. The capacity of such actions is—and perhaps should be—limited. Reliance on others is not a source of salvation for people who feel themselves oppressed but who are at the moment unable or unwilling to take effective action themselves. It is in the nature of the nonviolent technique that the main brunt of the struggle must be borne not by third parties but by the grievance group immediately affected by the opponent's policies. For third-party opinion and actions to be most effective within the context of political *jiu-jitsu,* they must, regardless of their strength, play the auxiliary role of backing up the main struggle being conducted by the nonviolent actionists from the grievance group itself. Any other view may be dangerous, for overconfidence in the potential of aid from others may distract resistance efforts from their own most important tasks. In fact, third-party support is more likely to be forthcoming when nonviolent struggle by the grievance group is being waged effectively.

Foreign financial support for nonviolent actionists is one form which third-party assistance has taken. Gandhi argued, however, that nonviolent actionists should be financially (and in other ways) self-reliant, and that in some situations foreign funds could be misperceived or misrepresented and hence be counterproductive. Instead, complete financial self-reliance, even when more limited, could be a better policy, he felt. That view does not, of course, exclude other types of third-party supporting action, such as protests, public declarations and demonstrations, diplomatic representations and sanctions, and economic sanctions.

The final way in which shifts in third-party opinion clearly aid the nonviolent actionists is by boosting their morale and encouraging them to persist until they win. Conversely, strong third-party opinion supporting the nonviolent actionists and opposing the opponent's policies and repression may help to undermine the morale of the opponent group as a whole or perhaps primarily that of certain sections of that group.

C. The future of third party support

One reason for the limited use and effectiveness of third party and international supporting actions lies in their primitive state. Conscious attempts to maximize effectiveness of this aspect of the nonviolent technique have been extremely limited, especially when it comes to supporting action for a domestic nonviolent resistance movement.

Perhaps in the future other forms of third party action may be designed to help the grievance group and the nonviolent actionists to increase their nonviolent combat strength. These forms might, for example, include supply of literature and handbooks about nonviolent struggle, of printing facilities or services, radio broadcasting facilities and equipment, and bases and centers for study and training in this type of struggle. Additional possible forms may provide for communication among resisters, especially when under severe repression, and with the outside world. Third parties could also relay messages between the actionists and the opponent when regular communications were severed, and could at times bring them into direct touch.

Over the past fifteen years or so pacifists have discussed the possibility of third party action in the form of international nonviolent intervention on a politically significant scale. This proposal has usually taken the form of illegal nonviolent crossings of national borders in solidarity with an internal resistance group, especially in relation to (the former) Northern Rhodesia, South West Africa and South Africa, but such an invasion has not occurred. Such forms of international nonviolent action may be applied in the future, but they are likely to have very limited effectiveness.

The conscious development of third party and international support for a domestic nonviolent resistance movement raises, of course, a series of difficult problems which lie outside the scope of this study. Some of these are questions of political wisdom, others are practical questions of application and effectiveness. Such support may in the future have far-reaching implications and potentialities, but it can, and should be, primarily in assistance of an internal resistance movement.

AROUSING DISSENT AND OPPOSITION IN THE OPPONENT'S OWN CAMP

Violent repression of nonviolent actionists is far more likely to result in uneasiness and criticism within the opponent's camp than is violent repression of violent actionists. This is so for two general reasons. First, severe repression against nonviolent people is more likely to be seen as unreasonable, distasteful, inhuman or dangerous for the society. Such repression may also be seen by members of the opponent group as too high a price to pay for continued denial of the demands of the nonviolent group. Second, when the actionists are nonviolent instead of violent it is much easier for members of the opponent group to express their possible misgivings, to advise caution, or to recommend changes in the counteractions or in the policy which is at issue. Even without a change of opinion about the issues at stake, a perception within the opponent group that severe repression or brutalities are inappropriate against nonviolent people may detach support from the opponent and arouse active dissent. Seifert suggests that the most likely group to be alienated by violent countermeasures is the vast body of persons who are normally indifferent or apathetic about major issues. When repression becomes "nasty or annoying, they withdraw their support." [29] The violence of repression does not, of course, operate completely in isolation. The issues at stake—what are they, and how important?—and the wider public and international reactions to the conflict may also be significant in this process.

A. Questioning both repression and the cause

Opposition in Britain to British policies in India and to repressive measures against the Gandhian nonviolent struggles is often cited as a reason why nonviolent action could work in that special situation. However, criticisms in Britain, and even within its Parliament, of British policy in India were only in part a result of the nature of British society and institutions, though these were obviously important. These criticisms were also a consequence of the Indians' choice of nonviolent means, which made it easier for people at home to view British rule in India in an unfavorable light.

The Indians were well aware of this aspect of political *jiu-jitsu* and consequently sought to maintain their nonviolent discipline in order to create maximum dissent from British policy in Britain itself. V.J. Patel once made this perception explicit to the American journalist Negley Farson, who had questioned him concerning the program of action for the 1930 campaign. Patel, who had just resigned as Speaker of the Indian Legislative Assembly to show support of the noncooperation movement, said:

> I am going to make you beat me so outrageously that after a while you will begin to feel ashamed of yourself, and while you are doing it, I am going to put up such an outcry that the whole street will know about it. Even your own family will be horrified at you. And after you have stood this scandal long enough, you will come to me and say, "Look here, this sort of business cannot go on any longer. Now, why cannot we two get together and settle something?" [30]

In contrast, the violence of the Mau Mau movement during the Emergency in British-ruled Kenya was far less conducive to criticism and dissent within Britain, either concerning the anti-Mau Mau repression or British colonial policies in Kenya.

In this asymmetrical conflict situation—violent repression versus nonviolent struggle—some members of the opponent group may begin to question not only the *means* of repression, but their cause itself. This is a new stage, for they may then become willing to consider the claims of the nonviolent group. Conversion, or partial steps in that direction, then become possible. In certain conflicts such positive support within the opponent group may contribute to still stronger internal dissent and opposition. Not only is the repression seen as inappropriate or cruel, but even the cause for which it is used is rejected as unjust. Thus both the negative rejection of extreme repression and brutalities, and the positive espousal of some or all of the nonviolent actionists' cause, may lead to withdrawal of support for the opponent's policies and measures. The positive espousal of the actionists' cause may also lead to concrete assistance for it even within the opponent's own camp where he normally counts on solidarity in times of crisis. Seifert points out that nonviolent action is especially conducive to playing upon existing diversities within the opponent group, including age, sex, class, political allegiance, economic interest, ideology, personality type and many others. In fact, he writes:

> In the swing toward more sympathetic regard for the resisters and their rights, it is possible to speak of a spectrum of potential support . . . This continuum ranges from those individuals and groups most

predisposed to alter their position, through various intermediary group-
ings, to those most rigid and tenacious in their condemnation of the
resisters.[31]

This aspect of political *jiu-jitsu* may, in summary, contribute to several types of dissent and supporting reactions among members of the opponent group. These include: 1) feelings that the repression and possible
brutalities are excessive and that concessions are preferable to their continuation; 2) an altered view of the nature of the opponent's regime and
leadership, possibly resulting in a new or greatly intensified conviction that
important changes in its policies, personnel, or even the system itself are
required; 3) active sympathy for the nonviolent group and their cause; 4)
various resulting types of unease, dissidence and even defection and disobedience among members of the opponent group, including officials and
agents of repression; and 5) various types of positive assistance for the
cause of the grievance group and aid to the nonviolent actionists. One,
two, or more of these may occur in the same situation, and at times members of the opponent group may begin with the first of these reactions and
then move on to more extreme ones. Illustrations of these aspects of political *jiu-jitsu* are diverse. First we shall focus on certain cases of attitude
change, and then cite some cases where attitude change was followed by
action.

B. Repression produces defections: three cases

Occasionally an opponent has recognized in advance that, if used,
severe repression would cost him support in his own group and even arouse
active opposition. Because of this recognition, he had limited his repression.
The British government, in late 1765 for example, faced a very difficult
problem in dealing with the American colonists' defiance of the Stamp
Act and their use of the weapons of economic boycott, civil disobedience,
and refusal to pay debts, for these methods stimulated important opposition to the Stamp Act and support for the colonists in England itself. Giving in to the colonists could set a dangerous precedent, but on the other
hand, "... were it to attempt to enforce the Stamp Act by the sword
... it risked uprisings in support of the colonials in many of the leading
trading towns of England."[32]

More often, however, the realization that repression of nonviolent resisters could arouse significant opposition among the opponent's usual supporters has come only after the event. This was true in Russia in January
1905. Superficially, Bloody Sunday was a full victory for the tsarist regime:

it had been demonstrated that protest processions would not be allowed, petitions to the Tsar would not be received, and that tsarist troops could control the streets, ruthlessly routing dissident crowds. But the real result was very different and Bloody Sunday in fact inflicted a defeat on the regime from which it was never to recover.

Not only were the poor who had long believed in the Tsar and his concern for their welfare alienated from him—a point discussed later in this chapter—but the brutality of the repression aroused strong protest among several groups whose support the system required. Liberals who still did not favor revolution obtained 459 signatures for a letter to "Officers of the Russian Army," which declared Russia's need for bread, enlightenment, liberty and a constitution, and asked the officers: should their place be with the Tsar or ". . . with all of honourable and selfless Russia? As men of honour, you will not use arms against the unarmed, you will not take money from the people for its blood, which you have already spilled." The letter asked them to turn their arms against "the enemies of the people." [33] Not only did factory workers go on strike; there developed "what may be called a strike among the educated class, . . . generally peaceful but openly defiant." Lawyers refused to appear in the courts and formally protested against the "pitiless hand of the government." Medical, legal, pedagogical and agricultural societies denounced the regime, calling for a constituent assembly. Because of their participation in the repression of Bloody Sunday, guards officers were refused admittance to the Merchants Club. The Manufacturers Association voted to give financial help to the victims' families, to demand political reforms, and to take no action against workers on strike. A declaration that the events had created the need for a change in government was issued by sixteen members of the august Academy of Sciences, and signed first by 326 distinguished professors and lecturers and then by 1,200 of the country's most noted scholars. [34]

It is not widely recognized that French military action and brutal measures of repression against the nonviolent resistance in the Ruhr alienated Frenchmen at home and played a role in the 1924 electoral defeat of the government which had launched the invasion and been responsible for the repression. In the 1924 elections a coalition of the Left was victorious, and consequently in May Poincaré resigned. Halperin writes that this political upset was partly due to "a nation-wide revulsion against the methods he [Poincaré] had employed in dealing with the whole complex of Franco-German relations . . ." Many Frenchmen, Halperin reports, had begun to realize that both the occupation and "the policy of coercion" against the resistance had been mistakes. Not only had "France . . . failed to attain her objective" but "the invasion cost her more than she was able to get out of it." [35] Not only did Frenchmen at home change their attitudes toward the occupation and repression; so did many French occupation soldiers and civilian occupation aides. The German historian of this struggle, Friedrich Grimm, reports:

> The occupation had repercussions which no one had expected. Thousands of Frenchmen who went to the Ruhr as soldiers and civilians became *"advocats des boches,"* intercessors on behalf of the Germans. For the first time they saw the Germans as they really are . . .There were even many high-ranking officers who had soon to be replaced as unsuitable because of their friendly attitude towards the Germans . . .[36]

C. Four more cases of defections

Even the Nazis had on occasion to consider whether or not they might lose more support by acting against a defiant opponent than by giving in. After the failure of a number of written protests by Catholic and Protestant church leaders against the "top secret" program of systematic extermination of the incurably ill, Bishop Galen, speaking in the St. Lamberti Church in Münster on August 3, 1941, described in detail how the ill were being killed and their families deceived; Galen stamped the actions as criminal, and demanded that the killers be charged with murder. Copies of the Bishop's sermon were circulated throughout the country and among troops at the front. He became so popular that the government—at the height of its military victories—decided in its own interest not to punish him. Martin Bormann (Head of the Nazi Party Chancery) thought Bishop Galen should be executed, but propaganda chief Goebbels feared that if that happened, the population of Münster and perhaps of all Westphalia would be lost to the war effort. Even though Hitler was furious, he feared to make Bishop Galen a martyr; indeed a short while later a *Führerbefehl* was issued stopping the systematic extermination of the incurably ill. By then about seventy thousand had been gassed; only scattered killings occurred later. [37]

Brutalities against nonviolent Africans have aroused sympathies among the dominant Europeans—even in South Africa. Such sympathies developed, for example, during the successful 1957 bus boycott conducted by Africans living in Alexandra location near Johannesburg. Despite official threats, many European automobile drivers gave rides to the walking African boycotters. On the route the Africans had been systematically intimidated and persecuted by the police.[38] Also, after Sharpeville, unprovoked attacks —including whippings—by police against Africans in the Capetown area during an African strike, led to so many European bystanders phoning to report the attacks to Capetown newspapers that the switchboards were jammed; the President of the Cape Chamber of Industries, C.F. Regnier, personally pleaded with the Chief of Police, Col. I.P.S. Terblanche, to stop the assaults.[39]

In the United States also, nonviolent persistence against repression and brutalities in civil rights struggles led to considerable white support and participation in the actions and in other ways; later, when nonviolent means were less prominent and violence increased, this white support was drastically reduced.[40] When official repression and unofficial brutalities against disciplined and courageous nonviolent actionists became especially severe, Southern white communities and even the prosegregationist leadership sometimes split, and significant sections among them counseled moderation, concessions to the Negroes, and a halt to brutalities. Sometimes these defections began to operate behind the scenes before they became public.[41] There are several examples, including some from Montgomery, Atlanta and Birmingham.

After a federal court ordered an end to racial segregation on the buses of Montgomery, Alabama, at the end of the 1956-57 bus boycott, white extremists bombed two homes and four churches. Martin Luther King, Jr., reported that the next morning there were three major defections from the hard-line segregationists' camp. The editor of the *Montgomery Advertiser,* Gus Hall, in a strong editorial entitled "Is it safe to live in Montgomery?" argued that although he supported segregation, the bombings had shifted the issue, and he could not stomach these excesses. Several white clergymen issued a statement, repeated throughout the day by the distinguished Presbyterian minister Reverend Merle Patterson, denouncing the bombings as un-Christian and uncivilized. The businessmen's organization, the Men of Montgomery, also publically opposed the bombings. King wrote: "For the first time since the protest began, these influential whites were on public record on the side of law and order."[42] A few more bombings were attempted, but they were quickly halted. The bombings had lost important support for the extreme segregationists and, reports King, "it was clear that the vast majority of Montgomery's whites preferred peace and law to the excesses performed in the name of segregation."[43]

Later, in 1961, when anti-segregationist "freedom riders" were brutally beaten by white extremists in Atlanta, Georgia, with the police refusing to intervene, many Southern whites were again repelled. The Atlanta *Constitution* editorially criticized the police for not preventing the brutalities against the "freedom riders":

> If the police, representing the people, refuse to intervene when a man—any man—is being beaten to the pavement of an American city, then it is not a noble land at all. It is a jungle. But this is a noble land. And it is time for the decent people in it to muzzle the jackals. [44]

In May 1963 when police brutalities were committed against demonstrating Negro women and children during the civil rights struggle in Birmingham, Alabama, one of the effects was a withdrawal of the white business community from its firm support for segregation. Also, in contrast to earlier situations, most Birmingham whites no longer actively supported or participated in the repressive actions; instead "the majority were maintaining a strictly hands-off policy." [45] After returning from a tour of the Far East, the President of the Birmingham Chamber of Commerce, Sidney Smyer, said that his city had lost much prestige as a result of the violence there against freedom riders. [46]

A similar defection from the opponent's camp occurred in South Vietnam in 1963 in the campaign in which Buddhists charged they were discriminated against by the government, which favored the Roman Catholic minority. Although South Vietnamese Catholics might have been expected to support the Diem regime against the 1963 Buddhist campaign, many Catholics felt they could not support the repressive measures being used. The Roman Catholic Archbishop of Saigon, Nguyen Van Binh, circulated a pastoral letter in August appealing for religious tolerance, stating that some "confuse the political authority that governs Vietnam with the spiritual power that rules the Church in Vietnam." [47] Brutal repression during that struggle led to major defections from the Diem regime, both at the lower levels, and high in the regime; for example, the Foreign Minister and the Ambassador to the United States both resigned. [48] Actual defections of officials as a result of the operation of this aspect of political *jiujitsu* have also occurred in other cases.

D. The troops mutiny

Defections sometimes extend to police and troops who are charged with inflicting repression, as happened in the Vietnamese struggle. After the repression of Buddhist demonstrators in early June 1963, the *New York Herald Tribune* reported "growing unrest among army units in central Vietnam, whose ranks are mostly filled by Buddhists." [49] In August unrest was widely reported even among the wives of secret policemen, with the result that there was often plenty of warning of coming repression.[50] Army unrest extended even to the generals, producing, as we noted, a military *coup* when the government's moral authority had been undermined by the Buddhist campaign, a *coup* backed, but not instigated, by the United States.

Unease and disaffection among the opponent's agents of repression may be expressed by deliberate inefficiency in carrying out their duties. This inefficiency is especially likely if they are unwilling or unable to risk the penalties for open disobedience. In other cases, the police or troops may actually mutiny and defy orders to inflict repression. Both these types of behavior are discussed in Chapter Seven. Out of revulsion against severe repression against nonviolent actionists, regular troops, police and officers may deliberately but covertly restrict their assistance in it, or they may openly defy orders to carry out repression. Both types of behavior may, if sufficiently widespread or if they occur in crisis situations, severely reduce the repressive power of the regime.

The main example which will be offered here of the impact of troop mutiny in face of nonviolent action on the outcome of the struggle is from the February 1917 Russian revolution. This case is sufficiently important to merit detailed attention, especially since many people assume in ignorance that violence was necessary to destroy the tsarist regime.

Even Trotsky, who was no exponent of nonviolence, acknowledged after 1905 that victory or defeat in that revolution had hinged on whether the troops could be made sympathetic to the revolutionaries. He added that the greatest power did not lie in weapons, though they were useful:

> Not the capacity of the masses to kill others but their great readiness to die themselves . . . assures in the last instance the success of a popular uprising . . . the soul of the soldier . . . must experience . . . a profound commotion . . . Even barricades . . . are of significance in reality above all as a moral force . . .[51]

The failure of the 1905 Revolution can be largely traced to the failure to win the soldiers over to massive disobedience on a large scale.

In contrast, large scale mutinies occurred in February 1917 and these were highly significant in the disintegration of the Tsar's power. One of the reasons for these mutinies was the "profound commotion" produced within and among the soldiers by the predominantly nonviolent behavior of the revolutionary people. It is true that for a time there was considerable restraint in the use of violence on *both* sides, and also that violence was used in Petrograd by *both* sides on a scattered basis. However, up to February 25 the government forces had orders not to use firearms on the demonstrating crowds except in self-defense. This made it possible for the demonstrators to talk with the troops. "The soldiers soon caught the mood of the crowd. To them they seemed to be peaceful demonstrators, against whom it would be an outrage to use arms." [52]

Even the Bolsheviks at this point tried to prevent violence by the revolutionaries—though Leninist doctrine stressed the importance of violence. The Bolsheviks in Petrograd now behaved very differently than they had in 1905. In February 1917 they saw prevention of violence against the troops as necessary to induce them to mutiny, after which, the Bolsheviks believed, the former soldiers would make effective military means available for the revolution; the Bolsheviks sought nonviolence only for tactical purposes. This does not, however, destroy the significance of these events. Katkov writes:

> . . . even the Bolshevik leaders seem to have done everything in their power to prevent shooting in the streets. [Alexandr] Shlyapnikov [one of three members of the Russian Bureau of the Central Committee of the Party] is most definite on this point. When workers urged him to arm the demonstrators with revolvers, he refused. Not, he says, that it would have been difficult to get hold of arms. But that was not the point:
>
> "I feared [says Shlyapnikov] that a rash use of arms thus supplied could only harm the cause. An excited comrade who used a revolver against a soldier would only provoke some military unit and provide an excuse for the authorities to incite the troops against the workers. I therefore firmly refused to give arms to anybody who asked for them, and insisted again and again that the soldiers must be brought into the uprising, for in this way arms would be provided for all workers. This was a more difficult decision to carry out than getting a couple of dozen revolvers, but it was a consistent programme of action." [53]

The Tsar had telegraphed an order on February 25 to Khabalov, commander of the Petrograd Military District, to "put an end as from tomorrow to all disturbances in the streets of the capital." Accordingly, the troops fired into demonstrating crowds in Znamensky and Kazansky Squares on the next day. There were many dead and wounded. Katkov reports the impact of the events on the soldiers who had obeyed orders:

> What cannot be too strongly emphasized is the effect of the shooting on the troops themselves . . . When at last they were ordered to open

fire on the same predominantly unarmed crowds they had previously fraternized with, they were appalled, and there is no reason to doubt General Martynov's estimate of the situation: "The overwhelming majority of the soldiers were disgusted with the role assigned to them in quelling the riots and fired only under compulsion." This applied in particular to the training unit of the Volynsky Regiment, consisting of two companies with two machine-guns, which had to disperse the demonstrations of Znamensky Square . . . leaving forty dead and as many wounded lying on the pavement.[54]

The result of this and other shootings was that "order had been restored." That was not, however, the end of the story.

The next day there was a brief mutiny of some members of the Pavlovsky Guards Regiment, two of whose companies had taken part in the shootings. Some went into the streets and called for an end to the bloodshed.[55] Much more significant, however, was the effect of the shootings on the soldiers of the Volynsky Regiment, who had fired on demonstrators in Znamensky Square.

After the officers had left the barracks, the men gathered to discuss the day's events. They could not understand why they had had to shoot . . . Nothing indicates that it was revolutionary conviction that led to the troops' momentous decision to refuse to fire on the demonstrating crowds. They were, far more probably, prompted by a natural revulsion against what they had been doing under the command of a most unpopular officer. Yet they must have known the risks they incurred in adopting a mutinous attitude.[56]

On Monday, the 27th, the day after the shootings, these same troops informed their officer of their refusal to go out into the streets. After he left them he was shot by an unknown assassin. The disobedient troops left their barracks, went into the streets, proclaimed their support for the people's rising, and tried to persuade other regiments to follow their example. Other units did indeed also mutiny, and troop reinforcements had a way of "dissolving" on the way to their destinations, merging with the anonymous crowd. It was not long before the Tsar's regime no longer had an effective military force at its command in the capital.[57] This evidence suggests that had the demonstrators at Znamensky Square fired on the soldiers of the Volynsky Regiment, and had other demonstrators also done so elsewhere, the Tsar's troops would have been more likely to remain loyal, and without their mutiny the Tsar's regime would probably not have disintegrated. The Tsar's capacity for violent repression was detroyed when the troops mutinied after shooting peaceful demonstrators. Exponents of nonviolent action see this process as important in revolutionary situations.

In a very different case, it is significant that the Garhwali mutiny in India in late 1930 occurred immediately after severe repression in Peshawar, where at least 30 and perhaps as many as 125 demonstrators had been killed.[58] "The 2/18th Royal Garhwal Rifles were ordered to Peshawar, but two platoons refused to proceed, on the ground that their duty was to fight enemies from abroad and not to shoot 'unarmed brethren'," writes Gopal.[59] The severe repression against peaceful demonstrators thus produced a situation of great potential gravity for the regime, although insufficient to destroy it.

Some cases of disaffection or open mutiny also occurred during the 1953 East German Rising. For example, as stronger action was taken against the rising, the Russians sent Polish tanks across the border at Goerlitz to disperse demonstrators. Thousands of the demonstrators greeted the tanks. An eyewitness to the encounter, Don Doane, an Associated Press correspondent, wrote:

> The senior Polish officer stepped out of his tank, faced the Germans —and saluted. "I don't fire on German workers," he said. The Germans returned his salute.
>
> When the Russians saw the Poles were not going to resist the Germans, they ordered the Polish troops back across the border and sent in Russian tanks.[60]

East German police and troops and even Russian troops sometimes proved unreliable when ordered to put down the predominantly nonviolent rising. Cases of disobedience of orders occurred both among East German police and Russian officers. The Russians frequently brought in fresh troops who had not previously been in East Germany and would presumably have less inhibitions against carrying out repressive measures against the population.[61]

E. Splits in the opponent regime

Not only may troops defect; splits over the conflict may develop between officials of the regime itself. This should be expected, for internal conflicts sometimes occur in a regime engaged in conflict, even when it is against a *violent* enemy. For example, significant conflicts over policy for the occupied sections of the Soviet Union occurred within the Nazi system—a regime in which most people would not expect to find internal disputes.[62] However, internal conflicts in the opponent group are much more likely when the other party to the conflict is *nonviolent.* This is because the actionists pose no *violent* threat (which usually unifies the opponent's camp), and also because counteracting a nonviolent campaign is especially difficult, conducive to different opinions on what to do, and later to recriminations over the failure of those counteractions. Some of the conflicts within the opponent group may thus be created by the problems of dealing with a nonviolent struggle group, while others may be rooted in earlier problems or rivalries within the regime which have been aggravated by the conflict.

Studies focusing on the relationships between splits within the opponent regime and the use of nonviolent struggle in actual historical cases remain to be undertaken. A comparative study might be undertaken of the opponent's internal conflicts on policy and repression in several cases, for example, the British in dealing with the Indian campaigns, the French in dealing with the Ruhr resistance, and the Norwegian fascists and German Nazis in dealing with the Norwegian resistance. Internal conflicts may be most expected when the campaign lasts some weeks or months, which gives time for conflicts arising over how to deal with the challenge to develop, or for control measures to fail and invite recriminations, or for old rivalries to take on new forms in the context of the struggle. However, the fact that splits among officials occurred almost immediately in the unexpected and very brief civilian insurrection of the East German Rising of June 16–17, 1953, suggests that splits within the opponent's regime may be extremely important in some cases of nonviolent struggle.

In the East German case some of the confusion and splits among officials and Party leaders focused on the problem of the appropriate counteraction, and both East German leaders and the Russians themselves thought that severe repression might cost them more than it would help in crushing the rebellion. The Socialist Unity Party's Central Committee later admitted that some Party organizations, organs, officials and members had given in "to panic and confusion," and that in "many cases" Party members had lost nerve and capitulated or even themselves taken part in meetings and demonstrations against the regime. Also, at the time, the Minister for State Security, Wilhelm Zaisser, and the Editor-in-Chief of the official paper *Neues Deutschland,* Rudolf Herrnstadt, formed a faction in the Politburo and the Central Committee with the intent of overthrowing Ulbricht.[63] Their reasons may not have been directly related to the rising itself, but the timing may be significant. From the beginning some Party officials favored violent repression, but others counseled against it. On June 16 the Russians first prohibited repressive police action against workers marching down the Stalinallee, believing it would be "provocative." Despite pressure from the chief of the East Berlin police, the Berlin district secretary of the Party refused to urge the Russians to permit strong repression, as he did not want to be regarded as a "worker slaughterer."[64] The nature of the East German and Russian regimes, and the rapidity with which internal conflicts appeared, suggest that investigation of the possible relationships between nonviolent struggle and splits in the opponent's camp may be highly important.

F. Provocation and appeals

Nonviolent actionists aware that brutal repression may produce unease, dissent and opposition within the opponent group have on occasion provoked the opponent to violence deliberately. For example, after British woman suffragists were maltreated by bystanders and police and then arrested, some suffragists concluded that their cause had gained more than it had lost by the events, and therefore they in the future deliberately provoked violent police reprisals in order to split the opponents of woman suffrage over the repression, embarrass the leaders of the political parties and get them to act on the demand for suffrage.[65] This type of provocation, however, has limited utility and contains its own dangers. Conversely, fearing the political *jiu-jitsu* effect of severe repression and not wanting opposition "at home," the opponent may try to prevent the facts from being discovered at all and to block the dissemination of existing information. This interpretation was placed on British attempts in 1930–31 to block investigations into severe repression against Indian nonviolent actionists, as by arresting two unofficial committees before their enquiries into police excesses in Rampur, Gujarat, could begin.[66] Censorship may also be applied on a wide scale.

Nonviolent actionists may also encourage splits in the opponent group by quite different means, by direct appeals and efforts to persuade members of that group of the justice of the cause of the grievance group and to solicit their support for it. These efforts may take a variety of forms, including personal conversations, small and large meetings, distribution of literature, and many other means. Luthuli in South Africa, for example, took advantage of a number of opportunities to address all-white meetings and racially mixed gatherings in order to explain the conditions under which Africans were living and to plead their cause.[67] In 1920 the legal German government used leaflets called "The Collapse of the Military

Dictatorship" to spread President Ebert's stirring appeal to defeat the Kapp *Putsch*. Strikers handed the leaflets to troops, and a government plane dropped them over the capital, including over the soldiers barracks.[68]

As the examples in this section show, nonviolent action may accentuate and arouse internal dissent and opposition within the opponent's own group both without deliberate efforts by the nonviolent group to do so, and when the actionists consciously seek to produce such splits—and deliberate efforts are likely to help. The capacity of the nonviolent technique to create and aggravate internal problems for the opponent group puts nonviolent action in a special class among techniques of struggle. Violent techniques, in contrast, usually seem to presume that the opponent group is a fixed entity to be fought and defeated, not a group which could be split and within which major active support could be won. In this respect guerrilla warfare is closer to nonviolent action than other violent techniques, though still at a considerable distance. In conventional warfare, although splits in the opponent group are welcomed when they occur, the usual assumption is that they will not and that the group as a whole must be defeated; in addition, conventional warfare generally contributes to increased unity within the opponent group which rallies together against the dangers of enemy attack.

INCREASING SUPPORT AND PARTICIPATION FROM THE GRIEVANCE GROUP

There is a third way in which political *jiu-jitsu* causes the opponent's severe repression and brutalities to recoil against his power position. The repression may increase the resistance from the grievance group itself, instead of intimidating them into acquiescence. This process will be first illustrated with an example from the Russian revolutionary movement, and then the general process will be discussed with further examples.

A. The victory in Palace Square

Nineteenth century Russian revolutionaries had long been vexed with a severe problem: how to destroy the naïve faith in the Tsar held by the mass of the peasants and workers, how to make them see that the Tsar was not a benevolent well-intentioned father but the head of an oppressive social and political system, how to make them see the system in all its naked violence. Bakunin, for example, had written: "Above all we must destroy within the hearts of the people the remains of that unfortunate faith in the Tsar which for centuries has condemned them to terrible serfdom."[69] Violence by revolutionaries had failed to do this. In 1866, when Karakozov attempted to assassinate Tsar Alexander II, the result was a rallying of sympathy and support from the poor for the Tsar, while the revolutionaries lost both drastically. Venturi reports that ". . . all sources are agreed that the peasants stood by the Emperor, often violently." ". . . the attempt on the Tsar's life did show how strong was the alliance between the monarchy and the mass of working classes and peasants."[70] As long as the workers and peasants believed in the benevolence of the Tsar and consequently supported him, popular mass revolution in Russia would remain a utopian dream of isolated sectarians.

The killing and wounding of hundreds of peaceful marchers who were under instructions to remain nonviolent, which made January 9, 1905 famous as Bloody Sunday, destroyed that alliance of the poor with the Tsar. The sharp contrast between the brutal political violence of the regime and the nonviolence of the marching petitioners shattered the naïve belief of the peasants and workers in the benevolence of the Tsar. Only when that belief was shattered did a popular revolution by the masses of people become possible. The British Ambassador at St. Petersburg, Lord Hardinge of Penhurst, wrote that because of Bloody Sunday ". . . a gulf was created between the Emperor and his people and the story was spread that when his subjects came to present their grievances to the 'Little Father' they were mowed down by his troops."[71] Several historians have also pointed to this change and its significance. Schapiro: ". . . from this day on, . . . faith in the Emperor's love and care for his people was shattered."[72] Charques: ". . . it did perhaps more than anything else during the whole reign to undermine the allegiance of the common people to the throne . . ."[73] Harcave: "After January 9, the liberation movement could count on far greater support and more favorable conditions for expansion and action than ever before." "The socialists . . . had been given just what they had sought for years: an aroused working class."[74] Keep: "It dissipated what remained of peasant ways of thinking and opened their minds to revolutionary propaganda."[75] "Another event like Bloody Sunday might be sufficient to topple the government . . ."[76]

On January 17, six days after the shootings, Minister of Agriculture Alexis Ermolov in his regular report to the Tsar called the shootings a disaster for the government, warned that the army might disobey orders to shoot and that even if it remained loyal it might be inadequate to defeat a rising in the countryside. Ermolov reminded the Tsar that he depended on the people's support, which needed to be regained and maintained.[77]

In addition to turning the middle class, intellectuals, businessmen and nobility against the regime—as discussed earlier—Bloody Sunday began one of the great popular mass revolutions in history. The workers resorted to strike action—in the remainder of January alone more workers were on strike than the whole decade from 1894 to 1904.[78] For the first time in Russia's history the peasants began to act as an organized political force in opposition to the government.[79] The easy "victory" of the Tsar's troops in Palace Square reverberated throughout the Empire, shattered illusions, and recoiled in anger, determination and revolution. The "victory" in clearing the square had created the most important precondition for a mass revolutionary movement.

B. Strength needed to withstand repression

Of course severe repression does not always produce mass revolution or even increased resistance. As has been emphasized throughout this Part of the book, this technique has requirements which must be fulfilled if it is to be successful. The most important of these are the requirements associated with the nonviolent group itself. One of these is that people must not be intimidated by repression. Whether severe repression results in decreased or increased resistance depends to a considerable degree on how much suffering the actionists and the general grievance group are willing and able to endure as the price of change. If their conviction in the rightness of their cause is not strong, if their courage falters, or if the suffering is greater than their capacity to bear it, then whether or not more persons become alienated from the opponent, the numbers of actionists will not increase by additions from the general grievance group, and may even diminish. Under such conditions, growing severity of repression may lower morale in the grievance group and among the nonviolent actionists and reduce resistance. The weak may be weeded out.[80] This is one of the important reasons why numbers alone are not decisive in nonviolent action, and why there is no substitute in this technique for genuine strength. Submission to violence spells defeat.

But violent repression need not spell submission. Contrary to popular opinion, as we have already seen in Chapter Ten, how much suffering people can withstand is *not* determined only by the relative severity of the repression. The strength, resilience and will of the nonviolent group are also very important. In fact, severities and brutalities under certain conditions *increase* resistance and weaken the opponent. Machiavelli argued that when a ruler is opposed by the public as a whole and attempts to make himself secure by brutality, "the greater his cruelty, the weaker does his regime become." [81]

C. Repression may legitimize resistance

When violence is committed against people who are, and are seen to be, nonviolent, it is difficult for the opponent to claim "self-defense" for his use of extreme repression, or to argue that the severe repression was for the good of the society as a whole. Instead, the opponent is likely to appear to many people as a villain, and many will believe that the worst accusations against the opponent are being confirmed, and that they are witnessing "deepening injustice." [82]

When such extreme repression occurs, the chances of the nonviolent group agreeing to a compromise settlement far short of their avowed aims may be sharply reduced. Severe Puritan repression against Quakers in Massachusetts Bay Colony, for example, "made the Quakers all the more certain that the Puritans were anti-Christ." [83] British measures against Indians practicing civil disobedience made many Indians believe the worst possible interpretations of British motives and of the nature of the *Raj.*

When severe repression is directed against nonviolent actionists who persist in the struggle with obvious courage and at great cost, the actionists' persistence makes it difficult for the opponent to claim he has acted to "defend" or "liberate" the people concerned. Instead, it will be seen that the opponent could not win obedience and support on the basis of the merits of the regime and its policies and has therefore in desperation sought to induce submission by severe measures. He is seen as *unable* to rule without extreme repression. Concerning repression in India, J.C. Kumarappa made this point when he wrote in 1930 that "the Government . . . . is . . . demonstrating beyond a doubt its total incapacity to govern by civilized methods." [84] People whose lives have been affected by the grievances, who have nevertheless seen the opponent as benevolent and well-intentioned, may now shift. For them the opponent's positive image may be destroyed and they may become convinced that he deserves not obedience and cooperation but defiance and resistance.

One result of this increased alienation is that the *existing* group of nonviolent actionists may become more—not less—determined to continue their intended course and even to expand their efforts to bring about change. To be imprisoned for disobedience, for example, is interpreted not as a shame but as an honor. This shift took place both in India among nationalist resisters,[85] and in the United States among woman suffragists and civil rights workers.[86] "The result is both legitimization and intensification of revolt."[87] The effects of alienation from the opponent extend still further, however.

D. The numbers of resisters may grow

If determination and willingness to pay the price of resistance become great enough among members of the general grievance group, this increase in alienation from the opponent may mean that more members of that group become active participants in the struggle. The numbers of nonviolent actionists defying the opponent may then increase. This is in line with Gregg's view that in nonviolent action the suffering and even death of the volunteers in face of the opponent's repression are likely to produce new volunteers to take the place of the fallen.[88]

The opponent's problems in dealing with this development will be multiplied because this nonviolent technique can, far more than violence, involve as active participants *all* sections of the population—not only able-bodied young men, but women, the young, and the old.[89] In India in 1930 for example, at Mahuva in Kathiawad, Gujarat, four thousand women and children went on a fast in sympathy with the picketers of shops selling foreign cloth. The dealers in foreign cloth then stopped sales.[90] Also in that campaign, thousands of women took an active part in picketing, parades and in civil disobedience against the Salt Act and other types of noncooperation. This participation of women, usual in Indian society, was difficult for the police to deal with.[91] During the Korean struggle in 1919-22 against Japanese rule, not only women but school children took part in the nonviolent protest campaign. It was reported that police attacked them with drawn swords, beat them, and as a punishment publicly stripped girls taking part in the protest. As a result Koreans were still further alienated from the regime.[92]

Increased resistance has sometimes resulted also when brutal repression has been applied against violent resistance or against mixed violent and nonviolent resistance. There are cases in which the violence of the repression was highly disproportionate to the lesser violence of the resistance. The Nazis encountered this general phenomenon on a number of occasions. In occupied areas of the Soviet Union, they were ruthless in repression, seized people for slave labor in Germany, exterminated many prisoners of war, and did many other such things. The result was not, however, passive submission to Nazi rule, but flaming resentment and resistance. Dr. Otto Bräutigam, deputy leader of the Political Department of Rosenberg's Ministry for the Occupied Eastern Territories, in a confidential report to his superiors, wrote that German policy and practice in the occupied Soviet Union had "brought about the enormous resistance of the Eastern peoples." [93] Shooting of innocent hostages was widely used in Nazi-occupied Europe to terrorize the population into submission and to halt various acts of opposition, usually sabotage or acts of violence. The results were often the opposite of those intended, however. The policy of shooting hostages led to protests to Keitel from both the Commander of the *Wehrmacht* (German Army) in the Netherlands and from the military Governor of Belgium, General Falkenhausen. The latter wrote to Field Marshall Keitel in September 1942, as follows:

> The result is undoubtedly very unsatisfactory. The effect is not so much deterrent as destructive of the feeling of the population for right and security; the gulf between the people influenced by Communism and the remainder of the population is being bridged; all circles are becoming filled with a feeling of hatred towards the occupying forces, and effective inciting material is given to enemy propaganda. Thereby military danger and general political reaction of an entirely unwanted nature . . .[94]

In Denmark, the Nazis were unable to destroy a single Danish resistance organization of any importance throughout the occupation, although they were able to arrest, deport and execute members of those organizations. The Danish occupation historian de J. Hæstrup writes: "It seems that suppression only gave birth to more vigorous resistance. The view might be different in other countries where conditions were more cruel, but the Danish conclusion must be that suppression is a two-edged sword." [95]

Although, as the above cases indicate, a *jiu-jitsu* effect increasing, not reducing, resistance *may* operate in cases of mixed violent and nonviolent resistance, or of repression highly disproportionate to the resistance violence, the *jiu-jitsu* effect is both more frequent and more intensive in cases of exclusively nonviolent action. This is so contrary to the popular assumption that power accrues to the violent, that several cases will now be described or cited in which repression against nonviolent action produced not passive submission but increased alienation and resistance.

In addition to the events of 1905, described earlier in this section, there are many other Russian examples of repression leading to increased alienation of the population and to intensified resistance. Thus, for example, the tsarist regime used the army to intervene in 269 industrial disputes between 1895 and 1899. Keep writes:

> . . . some officers seem to have taken it for granted that bloodshed was an unfortunate but necessary means of intimidating "rebellious elements" into submission. Naturally, where shooting took place, this served to embitter the atmosphere still further. Often it provoked action by workers in other enterprises, which it was the main aim of the military to prevent.[96]

When police used whips to quell student disturbances at St. Petersburg University in 1899, the result was a student strike all over Russia.[97]

The old statement that the blood of the martyrs is the seed of the Church is thus not at all a sectarian religious saying for the comfort of the believers. It is a profound statement about a likely consequence of brutal repression against nonviolent people who stand firm in their convictions—a statement with wide political implications far beyond the treatment of unwanted religious groups. In his tirade against the German philosopher Eugen Dühring, Frederick Engels, no less, argued that Dühring's anti-religious extremism would in fact help religion to survive: ". . . he incites his gendarmes of the future against religion, and thereby helps it to martyrdom and a prolonged lease on life."[98] In the 1920s the Communist Party of the Soviet Union, having ignored Engels' warning, found it difficult to ignore the demonstrated validity of his opinion. "The party," writes Schapiro, "could persecute priests and preach atheism, but the communists were soon to discover that religion thrives on persecution."[99]

The sixteenth century Inquisition begun by Charles V in the Netherlands, if not increasing public defiance, at least added to the numbers of heretics. Pieter Geyl writes:

> . . . after the first deaths by fire—the victims were two Antwerp Augustinian monks, burnt at Brussels in 1523—the number of the martyrs kept steadily growing . . . . And yet this horror . . . achieved no more than that the opinions which it was intended to kill were driven underground. Men who could have given a lead kept quiet or left the country, but the spectacle of the martyrs' sufferings and courage made many thousands of simple souls take the new heresy into their hearts. In the parlour and the market place, in the workshop and in the meetings of the Rhetoricians, passionate discussions went on about the problems of faith. Souls that were inaccessible to the learning of the humanists now thirsted after the new doctrine.[100]

In the American colonies, too, the English soon found that their attempts to force the colonials to obey and to halt political and economic noncooperation by military means or by threats of new punishment usually only heightened the spirit of defiance. The unplanned Boston Massacre heightened the spirit of opposition and increased the practice of resistance not only in Massachusetts Bay but throughout the American colonies—even though the British troops had been provoked. In Boston the deaths of those shot by the troops were deliberately used to arouse more general opposition to the British rule.[101] The commanding officers finally acceded to the demand of the Boston town authorities, supported unanimously by the Council of Massachusetts Bay, that British troops be withdrawn from the city; they were transferred to Castle William in the harbor,[102] a result which the colonials could not easily have achieved by military means. Other colonies also reacted very strongly to the news[103] and the Massacre gave considerable impetus to the economic boycott movement.[104]

Although relatively mild by contemporary standards of State repression, the coercive acts enacted by Parliament in the spring of 1774 evoked widespread opposition and a significant increase in resistance, which they had been intended to quell. The new acts were designed to alter the Massachusetts constitution and destroy the independence of the town meetings in order to halt unrest and to punish the refusal of compensation to the East India Company for the losses inflicted at the Boston Tea Party. While these acts led to a tendency for merchants to side with the government more than they had earlier, the general effect of the coercive acts was to win converts to the radical position, to make the issues at stake in the conflict clearly political, and to increase hostility to the English government. Dr. Benjamin Franklin was one of many who, though antagonized by the earlier destruction of tea in Boston harbor, found the new acts even more offensive.[105] The closing of the port of Boston and transfer of the provincial capital from the city also aroused widespread indignation, opposition and resistance (not all nonviolent), instead of achieving the intended reimbursement for property losses and passive submission.[106] These acts against Boston were cited as a reason for the Continental Association program of noncooperation.[107] "The Coercive Acts made open rebellion inevitable."[108] Gipson also writes concerning the situation in September 1774: "Only the removal of the pressures brought to bear upon Massachusetts Bay to compel its obedience to the will of the government of Great Britain could now stem the revolutionary tide."[109]

During the nonviolent resistance to the Kapp *Putsch* there were several similar instances. When pro-Kapp *Freikorps* troops on March 14, 1920, occupied the offices of two newspapers supporting the legal Government, *Freiheit* and *Vorwärts,* the result was not the submission of all associated with newspaper publishing, but a strike of all the printers in Berlin.[110] One morning the Kapp group arrested all the ministers of the Prussian Government—which controlled a major section of Germany. Immediately, the railroad workers threatened to strike unless Minister Oesser —in charge of railroads—were released; he refused to leave unless the other ministers were also released, and they were all let go.[111] It is true that the *Putsch* was ill planned and inefficiently carried out. It would be a mistake, however, to attribute its collapse to faint-heartedness of Dr. Kapp in face of resistance, for he finally ordered that all strikers be shot (only to find that his own troops would not carry out the order).[112]

While French repression was sometimes effective during the *Ruhrkampf,* at other times it was not. In one case, for example, after an occupation ultimatum of twenty-four hours had expired, French troops evicted thousands of families of striking railworkers from their homes and left them in the streets. The German workers, however, did not return to their jobs. In fact German Transportation Minister Gröner instructed not only the workers, but also all higher functionaries and civil servants of the railroads in the occupied territory to refuse all cooperation with the French. Furthermore, Gröner promised them financial compensation for possible losses.[113]

Indians struggling nonviolently against British rule often found that severe repression, and especially brutalities (even when provoked), helped the independence movement by increasing the number of Indians opposed to the *Raj* and willing to resist it. The shootings at Jallianwala Bagh, Amritsar, in 1919 were unprovoked. They permanently alienated many Indians from British colonial rule. On an official goodwill visit for Britain sometime after the Amritsar shooting, the Duke of Connaught observed: "Since I landed I have felt around me bitterness and estrangement between those who have been my friends. The shadow of Amritsar has lengthened over the face of India." [114] Those shootings, which came to be called a massacre, helped to complete Gandhi's own disaffection from the British Empire for which he had once had warm and sympathetic feelings. Disillusioned with the manner in which Prime Minister David Lloyd George handled the killings and the question of reparations, Gandhi wrote in December 1920 that his "faith in the good intentions of the Government and the nation which is supporting it" had been "completely shattered." [115] In the coming years India and Britain were to experience the full effects of his alienation.

Severe unprovoked repression occurred during the 1930-31 campaign, but sometimes the Indians used nonviolent means that were deliberately provocative. A young Indian in Bombay attempted to stop a truck delivering foreign cloth by lying in front of it and was killed when the truck ran over him. Then the population throughout Bombay Presidency became indignant and the boycott of foreign cloth became highly successful. [116] After reporting a number of police brutalities against the nonviolent actionists, H. N. Brailsford commented:

> The importance of such affairs . . . was psychological. They helped to discredit the Government during the critical time when the masses were hesitating whether they should unreservedly support Congress. The privations . . . suffered by the main body . . . of the political prisoners in jail had the same effect. [117]

Specific provocative tactics were sometimes chosen to arouse extreme repression and discredit the regime. In Gandhi's view, nonviolent provocation was intended: 1) to reveal clearly the inherent violence upon which the British Empire rested; 2) to exert moral pressure on the British to change their attitudes; 3) to make clear to the world the nature of the empire in India and the determination of Indians to be free; and 4) very important, to expose the nature of the British system to the Indians themselves, thereby alienating them from it and increasing their resolution to destroy it.

The nonviolent raids on the salt works at Dharasana that year, described briefly in Chapter Eight, were deliberately planned by Gandhi with the knowledge that they would provoke extreme repression. He expected such repression to put the British *Raj* in a very bad light, strengthening the Indian position while weakening the British. Concerning this instance, J. C. Kumarappa has written:

> Dharasana raid was decided upon not to get salt, which was only the means. Our expectation was that the Government would open fire on unarmed crowds . . . . Our primary object was to show to the world at large the fangs and claws of the Government in all its ugliness and ferocity. In this we have succeeded beyond measure. [118]

Madeline Slade wrote: "India has now realized the true nature of the British *Raj,* and with that . . . the *Raj* is doomed." [119]

At the end of the 1930-31 struggle Britain still remained established in India, but from an Indian perspective Britain had not won. A psychological change had taken place which was comparable to that in Russia on Bloody Sunday 1905. Rabindranath Tagore described the change in these words:

> Those who live in England, far away from the East, have now got to realize that Europe has completely lost her former moral prestige in Asia, she is no longer regarded as the champion throughout the world of fair dealing and the exponent of high principle, but as the upholder of Western race supremacy and the exploiter of those outside her own borders.
>
> For Europe, this is, in actual fact, a great moral defeat that has happened. Even though Asia is still physically weak and unable to protect herself from aggression where her vital interests are menaced, nevertheless, she can now afford to look down on Europe where before she looked up.[120]

The effort by Soviet officials in East Germany to avoid provoking further resistance by overreaction to the initial demonstrations and strikes of the 1953 rising has already been noted.[121] While later intervention of the Soviet military forces defeated the demonstrators and strikers, on at least two occasions during those June days severe repression led to increased resistance. In the case of demonstrations in smaller towns near the zonal border on June 18, "it was largely the news of the brutal suppression of the strikes in the big industrial centers which drove the people into open resistance."[122] Similarly, when the news of the execution in Jena of a young motor mechanic reached Erfurt, "the employees of three large factories joined the strike."[123]

The Diem regime's repression of Buddhist resisters in 1963 greatly alienated other South Vietnamese from the regime and increased resistance instead of quelling it; conversely a reduction in repression seemed to reduce resistance. *The New York Times* on August 5 reported: "Some observers feel that the Buddhist movement has slowed down in the last two weeks because the Government had been shrewder and less repressive in handling the Buddhists."[124] One result of the severe pagoda raids the night of August 20–21 was a wave of revulsion against the government throughout the country.[125] Surveying the campaign and the effects of severe repression against nonviolently defiant Buddhists, David Halberstam concluded:

> Often the Government broke up their demonstrations with violence and bloodshed, and as Bull Connor and his police dogs in Birmingham were to etch indelibly the civil rights movement in the minds

of millions of Americans, so the Buddhists used the Government's repeated clumsiness to commit their people further to their cause and to strengthen the movement. "There is blood on the orange robes," a spokesman would say at a demonstration, and the emotional response was always astonishing.[126]

As Halberstam suggests, this general phenomenon has also occurred repeatedly in the United States in nonviolent struggles against racial discrimination and segregation. Both arrests and unofficial extremist violence failed to intimidate Negroes in Montgomery, Alabama, or to cause them to halt their famous bus boycott. Instead, the opposite results were achieved, as Dr. King reported: "Every attempt to end the protest by intimidation, by encouraging Negroes to inform, by force and violence, further cemented the Negro community . . ."[127] When mass arrests came, the results were anything but those desired by the white officials: "Instead of stopping the movement, the opposition's tactics had only served to give it greater momentum, and to draw us closer together."[128]

Various types of official and unofficial counteractions against the student sit-ins in 1960 were followed not by acquiescence but increased demonstrations. On successive days in late March, in Baton Rouge, Louisiana, seven and nine student sit-inners, respectively, were arrested. The results: 3,500 students marched through the center of town to the State Capital.[129] On April 19 in Nashville, Tennessee, the home of a well-known Negro attorney defending the sit-inners was bombed. The result: a few hours later 2,500 unintimidated demonstrators marched on City Hall.[130] The 1961 Freedom Rides began with thirteen people, with the organizers hoping there would still be that many at the end. Then one bus was burned in Anniston, Alabama, and the actionists on the other bus were cruelly beaten. The result: ". . . we were deluged with letters and telegrams from people all over the country, volunteering their bodies for the Freedom Rides," James Farmer reported. Hundreds of people inexperienced in nonviolent action arrived, and it became possible to begin filling the jails of Mississippi with opponents of segregation.[131]

Birmingham, Alabama, in the spring of 1963, also experienced this phenomenon of severe repression increasing resistance, especially when school children were arrested and police dogs were used against them. One of the effects was, writes Waskow, that, "it swiftly involved many more Negroes in active, vigorous support of the movement for integration—since that movement now meant not only an abstract demand for social change, but the concrete and immediate protection of their children."[132] In addition, the Birmingham struggle provoked new Negro demonstrations and demands throughout the South and also in Northern ghettos.[133]

After James Meredith was shot and wounded by a fanatical white supremacist in June 1966, the march through Mississippi—which he had only just begun with a tiny handful of supporters—became the biggest since the march from Selma to Montgomery, Alabama. *Newsweek* wrote that the three shotgun blasts "reverberated across the nation," echoing other cases of brutalities against Negroes and several civil rights martyrs, and once again leading to government action. "It was the same dark counterpoint of nonviolent protest and violent response that produced the Civil Rights Acts of 1964 and 1965." President Johnson called the shooting an "awful act of violence," and Congress began to move more quickly on civil rights legislation. Emanuel Celler, aged chairman of the House of Representatives Judiciary Committee, commented: "There are times when the civil-rights movement has no greater friend than its enemy. It is the enemy of civil rights who again and again produces the evidence . . . that we cannot afford to stand still." [134]

To avoid misunderstanding, let it be emphasized again that whether repression crushes or increases resistance to the opponent depends on a variety of conditions other than the repression itself. To a large degree these may be within the control of the nonviolent actionists and the general grievance group for which they are acting. Severe repression and brutalities against nonviolent people have lead to increased resistance by more people in too many cases in diverse circumstances for this result to be dismissed as an isolated and atypical occurrence. Instead, it is an important part of the general process by which nonviolent action combats repression and brutalities, using them to weaken the power position of the opponent and to strengthen that of the nonviolent actionists through the workings of political *jiu-jitsu*.

LESS SEVERE REPRESSION AND COUNTER-NONVIOLENCE?

Some opponents, or some members of the opponent group, sometimes realize that severe violence against nonviolent actionists is counterproductive. When the repression or brutalities have already been committed, this realization may lead to private recriminations and disagreements among officials within the opponent group. Where the realization preceeds the repression, there may be experiments in less severe counteractions or even counter-nonviolence.

Where the realization by some members of the opponent group that severe action is counterproductive follows the event, a reversal of steps already taken may not follow. In fact, there may be a great show of determination and haughty rejection of protests about the repression at the same time that the leadership of the opponent group realizes that the severity of the repression was a mistake. An example of this is official Nazi reaction to the mass arrests of Norwegian students at the University of Oslo November 30, 1943 under the orders of *Reichskommissar* Josef Terboven. The arrests followed a long conflict with the students, faculty and administration of the University on one side, and the Germans and their supporters in the Norwegian fascist party *Nasjonal Samling* on the other.[135] The immediate cause was a fire set November 28, in the *Aulaen,* a large hall in the main University building, located near the Palace. The Nazis charged that students had set the fire as part of their protest, and the Norwegians charged it was a Nazi provocation.[136] Action against students was decided upon. Warnings to students to escape were possible because of information leaked from German officers to the underground Homefront Leadership, and other warnings from high *Nasjonal Samling* sources. Nevertheless, between 1,100 and 1,200 male students were arrested, of whom about 700 were deported to Germany.[137] The University was closed.

Propaganda chief Goebbels, Interior Minister Himmler and Hitler himself all concluded that Terboven's action was excessive and more detrimental to Germany's position than milder action would have been. Goebbels wrote in his diary on December 5 and 6, 1943:

> The Fuehrer was somewhat put out—and rightly so—that this question was handled with a sledge hammer. The Fuehrer is also skeptical about the success to be expected. Undoubtedly it would have been possible to achieve an essentially greater effect with less effort, for there are only a couple of dozen rebels among Oslo students who could have been arrested without the public noticing it. Most decidedly it was a big mistake to arrest all students of Oslo. Terboven is especially to be blamed for not having informed the Fuehrer before acting. The whole affair would have run an entirely different course had he done so.
>
> . . . the whole Oslo affair stinks. The Fuehrer, too, is quite unhappy about the way it was handled. He received two representatives of Terboven and gave them an energetic scolding. Terboven has once more behaved like a bull in a china shop. Himmler is furious about the effects of Terboven's action. He was going to enlist about 40,000

to 60,000 volunteers in Norway during the coming months. Prospects for this seemed to be excellent. By Terboven's stupid action a good part of the plan has fallen in the water.[138]

There was no public apology or reversal of Terboven's action, however. Despite considerable turmoil in both Sweden and Finland about the arrests, Hitler ordered Foreign Minister Ribbentrop to reject the Swedish Government's official protest "in the sharpest language." Accordingly Ribbentrop gave the Swedish Chargé d'Affaires in Berlin "a very juicy and cutting reply." "Naturally we can't beat a retreat on this Oslo student question now," wrote Goebbels. "But it would have been better to think matters over before rather than after."[139]

In other cases there have been advance attempts to reduce the extent or intensity of the repression. In the United States in 1937 when confronted with unusual strike action in which workers occupied factories and unemployed coal miners simply appropriated coal, both industrialists and government officials sometimes found it best not to take severe repressive action.

> . . . General Motors evidently feels it would lose public support by evicting the strikers from the plants by force. Even though the sit-downers . . . are manifestly trespassers on others' property, the public is averse to violence and apt to blame the side which begins it, whatever the legal rights may be. For that reason, coal operators and public officials in Pennsylvania are shrugging their shoulders while unemployed miners dig and sell anthracite which does not belong to them.[140]

In South Africa also there were several instances in 1952 in which, despite advance notice from the volunteers, the police refused to arrest actionists committing civil disobedience, sometimes even when they paraded past the police in defiance of curfew regulations. In other isolated cases, the police cordoned off areas where civil disobedience might be committed in order to thwart the defiance of the laws without making arrests. In another case, at Mafeking, volunteers were convicted but not imprisoned.[141] Police in Britain sometimes refused to arrest large numbers of supporters of the Committee of 100 who were committing civil disobedience during their anti-nuclear campaigns.

Sometimes, in the midst of a struggle, the opponent has made a generous and challenging gesture or appeal intended to put the leadership of the nonviolent group in a situation in which they almost had to respond in a conciliatory way. In January 1931—in the midst of the nonviolent

Indian rebellion—the British Viceroy of India, Lord Irwin, in a speech to the Central Legislature, paid high tribute to Gandhi's spiritual force and invited his cooperation in constitutional revision and in the restoration of friendship between the British and Indian peoples. Later, he unconditionally released Gandhi and his chief colleagues and again made the Congress Working Committee a legal body. This clearly put the pressure for the next move on the Congress. [142]

In some instances another type of gesture has been offered. One cold winter day President Wilson invited the woman suffragists who were picketing him into the East Room of the White House to warm up. (They refused the invitation.) [143] In August 1966 United States Air Force police abandoned their guns in dealing with an attempted nonviolent invasion of a base by two hundred demonstrators, mostly children. The group was protesting a decision of the Armed Services Committee of the House of Representatives to block for five years use of the base for low and middle-income housing. The demonstrators were stopped at the entrance but, after a conference with the head of the group, Air Force officers invited them in for a free tour of the base in Air Force buses. The Associated Press dispatch called the counteraction "one of the coolest bits of public relations in military history." [144]

There is another type of response to nonviolent action which, though relatively undeveloped, may in future decades become as significant as violent repression, or more so. The British (both in India and in the American colonies) and the American segregationists have been pioneers in this response. It involves confronting nonviolent action with counter-nonviolent action. For example, on one day during the nonviolent raids on the Dharasana salt depot in 1930, the police stopped the nonviolent volunteers on the road before they could reach the salt mounds and, when the Gandhian raiders sat down in protest, the police did the same. For some hours the two groups sat facing each other, until the patience of the police expired and they again resorted to violent methods to remove the sit-downers. [145] Later in Bombay, police also sat down in front of thirty thousand people sitting in the street after their procession had been halted. After hours and much rain, during which the volunteers passed their food, water and blankets to the police, the police gave in and the procession ended in a triumphant march. [146]

After several bitter experiences of the effectiveness of the American colonists' nonviolent economic noncooperation, the British attempted to apply similar economic measures against the Americans, albeit *after* the colonists had largely shifted to reliance on violence following the skirmishes at Lexington and Concord on April 19, 1775. The measure was Lord North's Prohibitory Bill, introduced on November 20, 1775, and given the royal assent on December 22. It provided for the prohibition of all trade and intercourse with the colonies: it also provided for the appointment of commissioners with authority to exempt from that prohibition any person, group or colony which they determined to be at peace with His Majesty. Other important concessions to the colonists were also promised by Lord North. The trade ban, however, was not to be enforced nonviolently but by seizures by the navy of vessels and cargoes, and allowance for impressment of crews of seized ships. This Act was regarded by many as "a declaration of perpetual war" against the colonies. [147]

In the United States civil rights struggles, there has been a very large number of examples of forms of nonviolent action used by segregationists. Sometimes these have taken rather simple forms, such as closing down businesses or making gestures of conciliation. For example, the bus terminal facilities in Montgomery, Alabama, were closed in May 1961, just before the arrival of Freedom Riders intent on violating segregation practices there. [148] In Orangeburg, South Carolina, the management of a lunch-counter where students were holding a sit-in responded, first by a temporary closure, then by removing seats, and finally by closing completely for two weeks. [149] The Maryland State Guard in Cambridge, Maryland, in May 1964, asked demonstrators to sing a few songs, led the group in prayer, and then politely asked them to disperse. [150] Imitation by segregationists of the same forms of nonviolent action being used by the integrationists has also occurred. For example, the Ku Klux Klan members in Atlanta, in late 1960, imitated student picketers by appearing dressed in full K.K.K. regalia to hold a counter-demonstration wherever they learned the students were demonstrating. They also threatened to call a white boycott against any store that desegregated its eating facilities in response to the student pressures. [151] During the Freedom Rides to integrate busses, a group of American Nazis sent a "hate bus" from Washington, D.C. to New Orleans, where they were jailed for "unreasonably" alarming the public; in protest the Nazis went on a fast. [152] Economic pressures have been widely used against opponents of segregation in the South.

Such cases of counter-nonviolence may be the first feeble attempts to move toward a new type of conflict situation in which *both* sides to a conflict will rely on nonviolent action as their ultimate sanction. If that were to occur widely, it would have the deepest social and political implications and ramifications. Many people, of course, will object to their opponents' doing anything to defend or advance viewpoints or practices which they reject as undemocratic or unjust. However, agreement on issues within in a reasonable period of time is often impossible. In this situation the conflicting groups still hold contradictory views which each believes must not be compromised. Is it then preferable that the group whose views one detests continues to use murder and terror or instead adopts economic boycotts and other nonviolent methods? Although powerful, those nonviolent methods do not involve killing but allow a continuation of the conflict by nonviolent means—which may bring into play various human influences leading to its ultimate resolution. This special type of conflict situation requires thoughtful analysis.[153] One important question is: what factors would be most important in the dynamics of this technique and in determining success in that special conflict situation?[154] This speculative exploration lies outside the scope of the present study, however. For the more limited purposes of this book, these developments show on the one hand a variation in the usual pattern of nonviolent action being met with violent repression. They also indicate that the opponent sometimes perceives that even from his perspective a nonviolent response is preferable. This perception may be based on a recognition that repression, especially when brutal, does not always strengthen the side which uses it; it sometimes strengthens the apparently defenseless nonviolent actionists.

By choosing to fight with a technique which makes possible political *jiu-jitsu,* the nonviolent actionists unleash forces which though often less immediately visible and tangible may nevertheless be more difficult for the opponent to combat than violence.

ALTERING POWER RELATIONSHIPS

The power of each contender in a conflict in which nonviolent action is used by one side, or by both, is continually variable, as was pointed out at the beginning of Chapter Nine. Far more than in violent conflict, the nonviolent actionists are able to exert considerable control not only over their own group's power, but directly and indirectly over the power of the opponent group. This the nonviolent actionists do by the effects which their behavior has on the social sources of each group's power. As discussed in this chapter, the availability of these sources of power is regulated, among other ways, by the operation of political *jiu-jitsu,* which affects the roles of third parties, the opponent group itself and the grievance group. Each of these groups of people exercises influence and control over the distribution of power by making available their cooperation with one side or the other, or by restricting or withholding cooperation from one or the other.

Shifts in power relationships as a consequence of political *jiu-jitsu* will not always be immediately apparent; sometimes they may be obvious and dramatic only after they are completed, as when the army has mutinied. Nor are these shifts all-or-nothing changes. The steps may be partial ones, and may be expressed in a variety of ways. For example, persons and groups who once supported the opponent fully may simply become uncertain, take up neutral positions, and refrain from offering major help to either side. On the other hand, persons who were formerly indifferent or neutral may through this process move toward the nonviolent group, either offering it minor or major assistance or simply withdrawing cooperation with the opponent. There is a considerable variety of other ways in which changes in feelings, attitudes and opinions stimulated by the opponent's repression may shift the social sources of power; some of these shifts may be decisive.

Political *jiu-jitsu* is one of the important factors which break up and reverse the initial polarization, discussed in Chapter Ten, when at the very beginning of the campaign the opponent is likely to gain support. As the changes which have been described in this chapter occur, that initial polarization is revealed as highly unstable. As attitudes shift, and as actions are brought into line with the new attitudes, the relative power positions of the protagonists also shift. What Seifert called (as we already noted) the "progressive detachment of groups arranged in a spectrum of potential support" may develop. [155]

The power shifts produced by political *jiu-jitsu* do not operate in isolation. They are concurrent with the other ideational, psychological, social, economic and political influences and pressures induced by the operation of the methods of nonviolent protest and persuasion, noncooperation and nonviolent intervention—the methods described in detail in Chapters Three to Eight. A period in which the balance of forces may seem to be in the opponent's favor, or one in which the contending forces seem approximately equal, may therefore be followed by the build-up and extension of the forces supporting the nonviolent struggle, while those supporting the opponent's violent regime disintegrate.

The Kapp *Putsch* provides an example. After initial success (seizure of the capital and flight of the legal government), followed by uncertainty (as noncooperation was launched), support for the *Putsch* bit by bit collapsed as key groups (previously either pro-Kapp or discreetly undecided) shifted loyalty to the legal government. Three *Reichswehr* commanders, previously uncertain, announced support for the legal government. Britain announced it would never recognize the usurping regime. The Nationalist Party, which had given the rebels limited support, urged Kapp to withdraw. The powerful National Association of German Industries, after initial reservation about the general strike, formally denounced the Kapp regime. The hitherto neutral Security Police demanded Kapp's resignation. Kapp resigned and flew to Sweden, leaving General von Lüttwitz as his heir. But even Lüttwitz's troops and regimental officers did not help: the Potsdam garrison mutinied against the usurpers, and most of his officers favored calling off the *Putsch*. "The General was somewhat bewildered at the way in which the whole structure of the conspiracy had suddenly crumbled around him." [156]

Mass nonviolent struggle may become so overwhelming that it is impossible to crush. It may also undermine the very power of the opponent, so that even if he wants to continue fighting the movement, he is no longer effectively able to do so. Massive defiance of the people can make a government powerless. Whether this potential will be fully realized will depend on the circumstances. Influential will be the degree to which, by its nonviolent discipline, persistence, and choice of strategy and tactics, the nonviolent group promotes the operation of political *jiu-jitsu*.

This is one of the ways in which change may be achieved by nonviolent action, although, as we noted, nonviolent struggle can be successful even if the political *jiu-jitsu* is reduced or eliminated by an opponent's restraint in counter measures. We shall next consider in more detail the effects of the application of nonviolent action, and the nature and requirements of the three mechanisms by which change may be achieved with its effective use—conversion, accomodation and nonviolent coercion.

NOTES

1. In his 1935 study, **The Power of Nonviolence** (pp. 44-45), Richard Gregg described nonviolent action as "moral *jiu-jitsu*." He referred to the moral or psychological effects of nonviolent persistence on the people carrying out the repression themselves. For the purposes of this study of the social and political dynamics of the technique, "social *jiu-jitsu*" or "political *jiu-jitsu*" is a much more important process. It incorporates "moral *jiu-jitsu*" when it occurs as part of a much broader process. A violent opponent facing a determined and disciplined nonviolent struggle movement can never really come to grips with its kind of power, and the more he tries to do so by means of his violence and brutalities, the more he loses his political balance.

2. The use of repressive violence against persistent nonviolent actionists rebounds against the opponent's very sources of strength. "The might of the tyrant recoils upon himself when it meets with no response, even as an arm violently waved in the air suffers dislocation," Gandhi said. (Gandhi, **Nonviolent Resistance**, p. 57; Ind. ed.:**Satyagraha**, p. 57.) But the process is more complex than that. Nehru came closer in his description:
   Naked coercion . . . . is an expensive affair for the rulers. Even for them it is a painful and nerve-shaking ordeal, and they know well that ultimately it weakens their foundations. It exposes continually the real character of their rule, both to the people coerced and the world at large. They infinitely prefer to put on the velvet glove to hide the iron fist. Nothing is more irritating and, in the final analysis, harmful to a Government than to have to deal with people who will not bend to its will, whatever the consequences. (Jawaharlal Nehru, **An Autobiography**, p. 393.)

3. Ross, "Introduction," in Case, **Non-violent Coercion**, p. iv. See also Sharp, **Gandhi Wields the Weapon of Moral Power**, p. 186. Gregg, (**The Power of Nonviolence**, p. 86) and Hiller, (**The Strike**, p. 169) have also pointed to the tendency for the opponent's repression against nonviolent actionists to arouse public opinion and enlist it in sympathy for the nonviolent group.

4. Harcave, **First Blood**, p. 116.

5. *Ibid.,* p. 121.

6. Halperin, **Germany Tried Democracy**, p. 288.

7. Sharp, **Gandhi Wields . . . .** , pp. 123 and 151.

8. Kuper, **Passive Resistance in South Africa**, p. 132. The nonwhite campaigners had even organized special "U.N.O. batches" of volunteers to commit civil disobedience just before the U.N. General Assembly discussed apartheid.

9. **Ibid**, pp. 164-165.

10. **Ibid.**, p. 166.

11. Luthuli, **Let My People Go**, p. 222. For his comment on world attention on the Treason Trial, see p. 181.

12. Colin and Margaret Legum, **South Africa: Crisis for the West** (New York and London: Frederick A. Praeger, 1964), p. 75.

13. *The Pentagon Papers* as published by *The New York Times* (New York, Toronto, London: Bantam Books, 1971), p. 163.

14. *Ibid.*, p. 165.

15. *Ibid.*, p. 166: also *The New York Times* 24 August 1963, and *Daily Telegraph* (London), 24 August 1963, cited in Adam Roberts, "The Buddhist Revolt," MS p. 25.

16. *The Pentagon Papers*, p. 197.

17. *Observer* (London), 8 September 1963, cited in Roberts, "The Buddhist Revolt," MS p. 27.

18. *New York Times*, 26 and 27 August, cited in *ibid.*, MS p. 26.

19. *The Pentagon Papers*, p. 166.

20. *Ibid.*, pp. 194 and 168.

21. *Ibid.*, pp. 172-178.

22. *Ibid.*, pp. 168-232.

23. *The Times* (London), 8 July, 1963 and *The New York Times*, 6 October, 1963, cited by Roberts, "The Buddhist Revolt," MS p. 16.

24. *New York Times*, 23 August 1963, cited in *Ibid.*, MS p. 24.

25. *New York Times*, 5 and 6 October, 1963, cited in *Ibid.*, MS p. 36.

26. Roberts, "The Buddhists, the War, and the Vietcong," p. 215. Denis Warner's quotation is from his book **The Last Confucian** (London and Baltimore, Md.: Penguin Books, 1964), p. 221.

27. Gregg, **The Power of Nonviolence**, pp. 45-46.

28. See Peter Wallensteen, "Characteristics of Economic Sanctions," *Journal of Peace Research,* 1968, no. 3, p. 251.

29. Seifert, **Conquest by Suffering**, p. 58.

30. Sharp, **Gandhi Wields . . . ,** p. 124. When charged with causing feelings of contempt toward the government, J.C. Kumarappa claimed in court that it was not he but "the accredited agents of this Government that bring it into disrepute." *Ibid.,* p. 209.

31. Seifert, **Conquest by Suffering,** p. 56.

32. Gipson, **The Coming of the Revolution,** p. 108. Gipson cites Walpole's **Memoirs** as authority for that statement. During the period of the Continental Association program of colonial resistance, adopted by the First Continental Congress, in 1774-1775, wide public support for the colonists' grievances continued in England. See Gipson, **The British Empire Before the American Revolution**, vol. XII, **The Triumphant Empire, Britain Sails into the Storm, 1770-1776**, pp. 259-290.

33. Harcave, **First Blood**, pp. 94-95.

34. **Ibid.**, pp. 100-110.

35. Halperin, **Germany Tried Democracy**, p. 288.

36. Quoted in Sternstein, "The *Ruhrkampf* of 1923," p. 129.

37. Lewy, **The Catholic Church and Nazi Germany**, pp. 265-267.

38. Luthuli, **Let My People Go**, p. 176.

39. Miller, **Nonviolence**, pp. 280-281.

40. This white help was so widespread that the following are only scattered examples: there was significant white participation in the 1961 freedom rides (*ibid.,* pp. 313-317); the United Auto Workers and National Maritime Union provided bail money for jailed Birmingham Negroes in 1963 (*ibid.,* p. 337);

especially in 1963 there was significant endorsement of nonviolent action against segregation and discrimination from major religious denominational bodies and active participation in various demonstrations of major church leaders and a multitude of clergymen – who were sometimes arrested and imprisoned (*ibid.*, pp. 208-211 and 309).

41. Oppenheimer and Lakey, **A Manual for Direct Action**, pp. 23-24.
42. King, **Stride Toward Freedom**, pp. 166-167.
43. *Ibid.*, p. 10.
44. Seifert, **Conquest by Suffering**, p. 58; quoted from **The Freedom Ride**, p. 6, a "special report" issued by the Southern Regional Council, May, 1961.
45. King, **Why We Can't Wait**, pp. 100-101.
46. Miller, **Nonviolence**, p. 315.
47. *New York Herald Tribune*, 21 August 1963, quoted in Roberts, "The Buddhist Revolt," MS p. 23.
48. Roberts, "Buddhism and Politics in South Vietnam," pp. 246-247.
49. *New York Herald Tribune*, 5 June 1963, quoted by Roberts, "The Buddhist Revolt," MS p. 10.
50. *New York Times*, 26 August 1963, cited in *ibid.*
51. Wolfe, **Three Who Made a Revolution**, pp. 333-334.
52. Katkov, **Russia 1917**, p. 263.
53. *Ibid.*, pp. 263-264.
54. *Ibid.*, pp. 269.
55. *Ibid.*, pp. 270.
56. *Ibid.*, p. 272.
57. *Ibid.*, pp. 272-284.
58. Gopal, **The Viceroyalty of Lord Irwin**, pp. 68-69.
59. *Ibid.*, p. 69.
60. Associated Press dispatch, datelined Berlin, 22 June 1953, quoted in Miller, **Nonviolence**, p. 352.
61. Ebert, "Nonviolent Resistance Against Communist Regimes?" pp. 189 and 192, and Brant, **The East German Rising**, pp. 149-152.
62. See Dallin, **German Rule in Russia, 1941-1945.**
63. See Ebert, "Nonviolent Resistance Against Communist Regimes?" p. 183. He cites Martin Jänicke, **Der dritte Weg: Die Antistalinistische Opposition gegen Ulbricht seit 1953** (Cologne: Neuer Deutsche Verlag, 1964), p. 38.
64. Ebert, "Nonviolent Resistance Against Communist Regimes?" p. 186.
65. Eleanor Flexner, **Century of Struggle** (Cambridge, Mass.: Harvard University Press, 1959), pp. 250-251.
66. Sharp, **Gandhi Wields . . .**, p. 180.
67. Luthuli, **Let My People Go**, pp. 211-214.
68. Wheeler-Bennett, **The Nemesis of Power**, p. 79, and Goodspeed, **The Conspirators**, p. 134.
69. Venturi, **Roots of Revolution**, p. 433.
70. *Ibid.*, p. 348.
71. Lord Hardinge of Penschurst, **Old Diplomacy**, p. 114.
72. Schapiro, **The Communist Party of the Soviet Union**, p. 65.
73. Charques, **The Twilight of Imperial Russia** p. 113.

74. Harcave, **First Blood,** pp. 98 and 114. See also p. 110.
75. Keep, **The Rise of Social Democracy in Russia,** p. 154. See also p. 158.
76. Harcave, **First Blood,** p. 114.
77. *Ibid.,* pp. 124-125.
78. *Ibid.,* p. 104.
79. *Ibid..,* p. 171-172.
80. Seifert, **Conquest by Suffering,** p. 42.
81. Machiavelli, **The Discourses of Niccolo Machiavelli,** vol. I, p. 254.
82. Seifert, **Conquest by Suffering,** p. 43.
83. *Ibid.,* p. 42.
84. Sharp, **Gandhi Wields . . . ,** p. 186.
85. *Ibid.,* p. 176.
86. Seifert, **Conquest by Suffering,** p. 45.
87. *Ibid.*
88. Gregg, **The Power of Nonviolence,** p. 133.
89. Gandhi, **Non-violence in Peace and War,** vol. I, p. 130.
90. Sharp, **Gandhi Wields . . . ,** p. 196.
91. *Ibid.,* p. 106.
92. Brockway, **Non-co-operation in Other Lands,** pp. 62-65. Brockway's account is mostly based on F. A. Mackenzie's **Korea's Fight for Freedom.**
93. Shirer, **The Rise and Fall of the Third Reich,** p. 941. See also Dallin, **German Rule in Russia, 1941-1945,** *passim,* and Crankshaw, **The Gestapo,** pp. 230-231.
94. Crankshaw, **The Gestapo,** p. 214.
95. de J. Haestrup, "Exposé," in **European Resistance Movements 1939-1945,** p. 160.
96. Keep, **The Rise of Social Democracy in Russia,** p. 40. See also Schapiro, **The Communist Party . . . ,** p. 28.
97. *Ibid.,* p. 70. For other examples of the general phenomenon, see also pp. 72, 98 and 216, and Katkov, **Russia 1917,** p. 420.
98. Frederick Engles, **Anti-Dühring** (Moscow: Foreign Languages Publishing House, 1954), p. 440.
99. Schapiro, **The Communist Party . . . ,** p. 347.
100. Geyl, **The Revolt of the Netherlands 1555-1609,** p. 56. Later under Philip in 1565 there was another lesson that repression may produce the opposite to the intended results. See *ibid.,* pp. 78-79.
101. Gipson, **The British Empire Before the American Revolution,** vol. XI, **The Triumphant Empire: The Rumbling of the Coming Storm 1766-1770,** pp. 282-283.
102. *Ibid.,* p. 278; and Gipson, **The Coming of the Revolution 1763-1775,** pp. 201-202.
103. Gipson, **The British Empire. . . , vol. XI, p. 305.**
104. *Ibid.,* p. 190, and Schlesinger, **The Colonial Merchants and the American Revolution,** pp. 155, 181-186 and 194.
105. Schlesinger, **The Colonial Merchants . . . ,** pp. 305-311.
106. *Ibid.,* pp. 353, 360, 363, 366, 367, 373, 397, 425 and 430-431. It also produced, it is claimed, the first explicit call for an American union, from the town meeting of Providence, Rhode Island, a week after the news of the Boston

Port Act reached America. Gipson, **The British Empire** . . . , vol. XII, p. 157.

107. *Ibid.,* p. 608.

108. Gipson, **The Coming of the Revolution**, p. 227.

109. Gipson, **The Bristish Empire** ... vol. XII, p. 160. There were, of course, other instances when punishments, or threats, produced increased defiance. For example, in 1774 Brigadier Ruggles, a magistrate at Hardwicke, Massachusetts Bay threatened to jail any man who signed a Covenant not to purchase or use British goods, a hundred men defiantly signed it. (Schlesinger, **The Colonial Merchants** . . . , p. 323.) In the summer of 1774, Salem held a town meeting in defiance of the Governor's orders. (Gipson, **The British Empire** . . . , vol XII, p. 157.)

110. Goodspeed, **The Conspirators**, p. 132.

111. Eyck, **A History of the Weimar Republic,**, vol. I, p. 151.

112. Wheeler-Bennett, **The Nemesis of Power**, p. 79.

113. Ehrlich, "Ruhrkampen," in Lindberg, Jacobsen and Ehrlich, **Kamp Uden Vaaben,** p. 186.

114. Quoted in Case, **Non-Violent Coercion**, p. 381.

115. *Ibid.*, pp. 381-382.

116. Sharp, **Gandhi Wields** . . . , p. 167.

117. *Ibid.*, p. 193. See also pp. 165-166.

118. *Ibid.*, p. 151.

119. *Ibid.*, p. 151.

120. *Ibid.*, p. 157.

121. Ebert, "Nonviolent Resistance Against Communist Regimes?" pp. 186 and 190.

122. Brant, **The East German Rising**, p. 92.

123. *Ibid.*, p. 113.

124. Quoted in Roberts, "The Buddhist Revolt," MS p. 20.

125. Roberts, "Buddhism and Politics in South Vietnam," p. 246.

126. David Halberstam, **The Making of a Quagmire** (New York: Random House and London: The Bodley Head, 1965), p. 215.

127. Quoted in Peck, **Freedom Ride**, p. 57.

128. King, **Stride Toward Freedom**, p. 143.

129. Major Johns, "Baton Rouge: Higher Education — Southern Style," p. 89, in Peck, **Freedom Ride**.

130. Paul Laprad, "Nashville: A Community Struggle," in Peck, **Freedom Ride**, p. 87.

131. Farmer, **Freedom -- When?**, pp. 69-70.

132. Waskow, **From Race Riot to Sit-in**, p. 234.

133. *Newsweek*, 27 May 1963, cited in Ebert, "Theory and Practice of Nonviolent Resistance," MS p. 397.

134. *Newsweek*, 20 June 1966, pp. 27-31.

135. On the over-all struggle, see Sverre Steen, *"Universitetet i Ildlinjen,"* in Steen, gen. ed., **Norges Krig**, vol. III, pp. 127-194.

136. See *ibid.*, pp. 182-184.

137. *Ibid.*, pp. 186 and 190.

138. Lochner, ed., **The Goebbels Diaries**, pp. 542-544.

139. *Ibid.*

140. "Editoral Research Reports," *St. Louis Post-Dispatch* 20 January 1937; quoted in Bernard, **Social Control in its Sociological Aspects**, p. 389.

141. See Kuper, **Passive Resistance in South Africa**, pp. 82, and 125-126, and Luthuli, **Let My People Go**, p. 118.

142. Gopal, **The Viceroyalty of Lord Irwin**, pp. 98-100.

143. Seifert, **Conquest by Suffering**, p. 38.

144. *Baltimore Sun*, 2 August 1966.

145. Sharp, **Gandhi Wields . . .** , pp. 136-137.

146. *Ibid.*, pp. 166-167.

147. Gipson, **The British Empire . . .** , vol. XII, pp. 346-349.

148. Lomax, **The Negro Revolt**, p. 155.

149. Miller, **Nonviolence**, pp. 308-309.

150. Oppenheimer and Lakey, **A Manual for Direct Action**, p. 87.

151. C. Eric Lincoln, "The Strategy of a Sit-in,", in Sibley, ed., **The Quiet Battle,** pp. 295 and 298.

152. Lomax, **The Negro Revolt**, pp. 151-155.

153. For an interesting discussion on this, see Waskow, **From Race Riot to Sit-in**, pp. 276-303.

154. Gregg suggests that in such conflicts with both sides using nonviolent action, success would go to the side with the greatest understanding of nonviolent action, the best discipline, and preparations, the most self-purification and love, the best understanding of society, the greater inner unity and strength, and the more respect from the other side and from the public. Gregg, however, emphasizes the mechanism of conversion and gives very little consideration to the wider social, economic and political pressures, often coercive, which may be involved in nonviolent action. Hence, further analysis is required. See Gregg, **The Power of Nonviolence**, pp. 99-100.

155. Harvey J.D. Siefert, " The Use by American Quakers of Nonviolent Resistance as a Method of Social Change," MS p. 145.

156. Wheeler-Bennett, **The Nemesis of Power**, p. 80. For the specific cited changes in loyalty, see pp. 79-81.

PART THREE: DYNAMICS

13

Three Ways Success May Be Achieved

INTRODUCTION

Nonviolent struggle can only be successful when the necessary conditions exist or have been created. Despite the improvised character of most nonviolent action in the past, successes from which we can learn have occurred. Even failures can provide important insights. As understanding of the requirements for effectiveness grows, the proportion of successes is likely to increase. The question then increasingly becomes *how* success can be achieved.

The influences, causes and processes involved in producing success in nonviolent conflict are diverse, complicated and intermeshed. The determining combination of influences, pressures and forces will never be precisely the same, the possible combinations being infinite. It would be a distortion to impose on them an unnatural uniformity or an artificial simplicity.

It is, however, possible to distinguish three broad processes, or mechanisms, by which the complicated forces utilized and produced by nonviolent action influence the opponent and his capacity for action and thereby perhaps bring success to the cause of the grievance group. These are *conversion, accommodation* and *nonviolent coercion*,[1] which we introduced briefly in Chapter Two. Other consequences of nonviolent struggle, affecting the actionists themselves and the long-term distribution of power in the society, will be discussed in the next chapter.

In *conversion* the opponent has been inwardly changed so that he wants to make the changes desired by the nonviolent actionists. In *accommodation*, the opponent does not agree with the changes (he has not been converted), and he could continue the struggle (he has not been nonviolently coerced), but nevertheless he has concluded that it is best to grant some or all of the demands. He may see the issues as not so important after all, the actionists as not as bad as he had thought, or he may expect to lose more by continuing the struggle than by conceding gracefully. In *nonviolent coercion* the opponent has not changed his mind on the issues and wants to *continue* the struggle, but is *unable* to do so; the sources of his power and means of control have been taken away from him without the use of violence. This may have been done by the nonviolent group or by opposition and noncooperation among his own group (as, mutiny of his troops), or some combination of these.

Advocates and practitioners of nonviolent action have differed in their attitudes to these mechanisms. All too often their attitudes have been oversimplified, focusing primarily on the extremes of complete conversion or full nonviolent coercion. Thus, exponents of a nonviolence derived from religious conviction who emphasize conversion frequently see nonviolent coercion as closer to violence than to their own beliefs. Exponents of nonviolent coercion (say, use of the general strike to achieve social revolution) often deny even the possibility of conversion, and see that approach as alien to their own efforts. There are also middle positions. The choice of a preferred mechanism will influence the conduct of the struggle, including the strategy, tactics and methods used, the public statements made, the "tone" of the movement, and the responses to the opponent's repression. A choice or preference by actionists of one of these mechanisms is possible and even necessary, whether on ethical or strategic grounds. In practice, however, matters are rarely clear and simple between pure conversion and strict coercion, as exponents of these extreme mechanisms would have us believe. Not only may the mechanisms be variously combined and play different roles in the various stages of the struggle; different persons and subgroups within the opponent group may be diversely affected or even unaffected by the nonviolent action. We shall return to the ethical significance of these complexities later. First we must examine the three broad mechanisms of change themselves.

CONVERSION

"By conversion we mean that the opponent, as the result of the actions of the nonviolent person or group, comes around to a new point of view which embraces the ends of the nonviolent actor." [2] This change may be influenced by reason, argumentation and other intellectual efforts. [3] It is doubtful, however, that conversion will be produced solely by intellectual effort. Conversion is more likely to involve the opponent's emotions, beliefs, attitudes and moral system.

A. Seeking conversion

While Gandhi did not in certain circumstances rule out actions which produced change by accomodation or even nonviolent coercion, [4] he sought to achieve the change as far as possible by means which did not "humiliate" the opponent "but . . . uplift him." [5] Gandhi's statements provide good illustrations of this objective of conversion. He wrote to the Viceroy in 1930: "For my ambition is no less than to convert the British people through nonviolence, and thus make them see the wrong they have done to India." [6] On another occasion he wrote that a *satyagrahi* never seeks to influence the "wrong-doer" by inducing fear; instead the appeal must always be "to his heart. The Satyagrahi's object is to convert, not coerce, the wrong-doer." [7] The aim of nonviolent action with this motivation is thus not simply to free the subordinate group, but also to free the opponent, who is thought to be imprisoned by his own system and policies. [8]

In line with this attitude, while maintaining their internal solidarity and pursuing the struggle, the nonviolent actionists will emphasize that they intend no personal hostility toward the members of the opponent group. Instead, the actionists may regard the conflict as a temporary, but necessary, disruption which will make possible deeper unity and cooperation between the two groups in the future. [9] Gandhi said: "My non-cooperation is non-cooperation with evil, not with the evil-doer." He added that he wished by noncooperation to induce the opponent to cease inflicting the evil or harm so that cooperation would be possible on a different basis. [10] "My non-cooperation is with methods and systems, never with men." [11] This aim of conversion has in certain situations had significant effects on the opponent group. Replacement of hostile personal attitudes by positive attitudes will reduce the pressure on the opponent group to be defensively aggressive. "Thus the opponents may be influenced to engage in fewer acts of provocative hostility, and, in the long-run, some of their leaders and part of the membership may even become motivated to live up to the other group's view of them as potential allies." [12]

The extreme Gandhian emphasis on conversion is translated into action only rarely. However, efforts to convert sometimes occur in the absence of such a doctrine, and conversion sometimes occurs without conscious efforts. Also, conversion of *some* members of the opponent group (say, soldiers) may contribute to change by accommodation or nonviolent coercion.

Conversion efforts may sometimes take place side by side with the application of other nonviolent pressures, such as economic or political noncooperation. For example, even as Philadelphia merchants were in late 1765 cancelling orders already placed with British merchants and launching a campaign of economic noncooperation in an effort to obtain repeal of the Stamp Act, they sent a memorial to British merchants in which they urged those same merchants to help the Americans achieve repeal of the Act and the removal of certain commercial restrictions. [13] Almost exactly three years later under comparable conditions a similar memorial was sent from Philadelphia, seeking support for repeal of the Townshend duties. [14]

The opponent group of course consists of many members and a variety of subgroups, and the nonviolent group will be unable to apply equal influences for conversion to all of these. Furthermore, the nonviolent group may deliberately choose to concentrate its efforts to achieve conversion on certain persons or subgroups in the opponent camp. When the most direct personal contact in the course of the struggle occurs between the nonviolent actionists and the opponent's agents of repression—his police and troops—the actionists may attempt to convert these agents, instead of the general public or the policy makers. For example, during the resistance to the Kapp *Putsch,* striking workers carried on an open discussion with troops serving the usurpers who, it soon turned out, could no longer completely rely on their own soldiers. [15] Even in the East German Rising in 1953 demonstrators and strikers made significant, spontaneous and repeated appeals to police and troops, although there was no systematic effort to win them over. [16]

Variations will also occur in the type of influences utilized to induce conversion. One approach may be to change the social situation drastically, eliminating the opponent's power or profits, in order that he may see the ethical issues in his past policies in a new light. For example, when an oppressor's economic gains are eliminated he may find it easier to see that exploitation is morally wrong. Gandhi sometimes spoke of this path to attitude change.

More often, however, nonviolent groups which have sought to convert have emphasized direct appeals to their opponent's better nature, as Gandhi put it.[17] These appeals have not only been made with words, as in the Philadelphia examples, but have primarily utilized emotional pressures induced through the nonviolent actionists' own self-suffering, either at the opponent's hands (as in withstanding repression) or at their own hands (as in fasts). It is important to understand the rationale underlying this view.

B. The rationale of self-suffering

All nonviolent actionists who understand their technique accept the necessity of willingness to suffer and to persist in the face of repression. As has been discussed earlier, such willingness is the necessary price for maintaining resistance and possibly also a way to neutralize or immobilize the opponent's repression. Suffering in the context of the conversion mechanism is more than that, however. *Some* nonviolent actionists see an *additional* reason for acceptance of such nonretaliatory suffering: to them it is the main means by which the opponent may be converted to their views and aims. (Other nonviolent actionists, of course, reject that objective as undesirable, unnecessary or impossible, and instead stress change by accommodation or nonviolent coercion.)

Advocates of suffering to achieve conversion maintain that on some issues a strictly rational appeal to the opponent's mind will be inadequate, and insist that it is then necessary to appeal also to his emotions. Gandhi repeatedly argued along these lines:

I have found that mere appeal to reason does not answer where prejudices are age-long and based on supposed religious authority. Reason has to be strengthened by suffering and suffering opens the eyes of understanding.[18]

. . . if you want something really important to be done you must not merely satisfy reason, you must move the heart also. The appeal of reason is more to the head but the penetration of the heart comes from suffering. It opens up the inner understanding of man.[19]

He identified the appeal to the hearts of the opponent group as "evoking the best that is in them."[20] Bondurant explains it in these words: "Suffering operates in the satyagraha strategy as a tactic for cutting through the rational defenses which the opponent may have built in opposing the initial efforts of rational persuasion . . ." In other words, suffering "acts as a shock treatment . . ." [21]

It must be clear that just any kind of suffering is not likely to set in motion the processes which may lead to changes in the opponent's feelings, beliefs and attitudes. The suffering of nonviolent actionists has little or nothing to do with the suffering of those who passively accept their fate. For suffering to lead to conversion, Lakey points out, the opponent must experience feelings of identification with the nonviolent group. This identification in turn, he argues citing Freud, requires a new perception of a common quality between the two groups. Such perception depends not only on the actual suffering but on the way in which the nonviolent actionists behave prior to and during such suffering. Therefore, he continues, suffering by people who have demonstrated their bravery, openness and honesty, goodwill and nonviolent determination is far more likely to produce a significant sympathetic response in the opponent than is suffering by people who behave like cowards, and cringe, flee, lie and hate. [22]

The opponent's initial reactions to the suffering of nonviolent actionists may vary widely from situation to situation. Initial reactions are, however, often unstable and may be reversed. Self-suffering is likely to shatter normal indifference to the particular issue, producing instead (as it did in South Africa) extremes in reactions, "active emotions of hate or sympathy." [23] In face of challenge, as noted earlier, the opponent group may first unite, [24] but in face of the nonviolent actionists' suffering and other influences, that initial unity may be shattered as the actionists' demonstrated bravery and sincerity arouse sympathetic interest. [25]

The initial reaction of the general public may also be split, with the suffering evoking resentment among some, and pity among others. [26] This pity may lead members of the public to see the suffering actionists as men of integrity, determination and goodwill, [27] even while not agreeing with them. Suffering for a cause may also help move public opinion on the issues at stake, [28] as was discussed in the previous chapter. That shift may in turn influence the attitudes of members of the opponent group to the issues at stake. It is in the nature of conversion of this type that a considerable number of influences will operate simultaneously and often unconsciously, over a period of time.

It is unlikely to be easy to endure the suffering which can induce conversion. The actionists may be helped to continue their struggle and to maintain the necessary discipline by awareness that their courageous suffering without counter-violence may help both to frustrate and immobilize the opponent's repression and also to contribute to changes of attitudes and feelings. Hiller has pointed out correctly, however, that the sacrifice required of actionists must be "bearable," or depression will set in and their will will be broken.[29] It is not solely the opponent who determines what is bearable, however. The sufferings which one group may find trivial may be intolerable to another. It is also true and very important that the sufferings which one group will find intolerable may be quite acceptable to another as the price of change. The will power, determination, beliefs and emotional response of the nonviolent actionists will help to determine, sometimes decisively, how much suffering is tolerable as the price of change.

Gregg also has pointed out that when nonviolent actionists understand the role of suffering in the dynamics of their type of struggle, and regard suffering as not simply a necessary risk, as in war, but also as an effective weapon for strengthening their cause, casualties will not lower their morale.[30] Voluntarily accepted suffering for the sake of winning goals may instead enhance morale and unify the actionists and others in support of their objectives.[31] Summarizing the Gandhian view of suffering in this context, Kuper writes: "Hence, suffering being positively desired by the resisters becomes an armour against the tyrant rather than a weapon in his hands."[32]

In most types of nonviolent action suffering is not deliberately courted but neither is it avoided when it is a consequence of other appropriate stages of the campaign.[33] There are, however, certain forms of Gandhian *satyagraha* which at times do seek suffering by provocative acts of physical nonviolent intervention or by fasts, for example. Even in these, however, Gandhi insisted that the suffering not to be sought for its own sake and argued that previous personal and social preparation were important in order to achieve maximum beneficial effects. Even in such cases of nonviolent provocation there is little sign that actions are undertaken for masochistic purposes. In their study of student civil rights workers in 1963 (especially of some who took dangerous actions and were severely attacked), Drs. Solomon and Fishman, both psychiatrists, reported: "Only very rarely have we heard of a personally masochistic demonstrator—emphasis in the movement is always on group values and goals."[34]

C. The barrier of social distance

The "social distance" between the contending groups—the degree to which there is or is not "fellow feeling," mutual understanding and sympathy—is important in the operation of self-suffering as a tool for converting members of the opponent group. At one extreme, if members of the nonviolent group are not even regarded as fellow human beings, the chances of achieving conversion by nonviolent suffering are likely to be nil. This barrier needs to be examined.

The closeness or distance between the contending groups will help to determine the effect of the suffering of the nonviolent group on members of the opponent group. If the opponent group sees the grievance group as members of "a common moral order," this perception is likely to encourage better treatment and a more sympathetic response to their challenge. Conversely, if the subordinates are regarded as outside such a common moral order, or as traitors to it, or as inferiors or nonhumans, the opponent group is more likely to be both cruel and indifferent to their sufferings.

Citing Simmel's analysis, Kuper points out that the possibility of conversion through suffering in nonviolent action will be influenced by the structure of the social system.[35] Kuper argues that whether the members of *both* the dominant and subordinate groups in the system are recognized as full human beings, or are regarded simply as members of some category, will be important. Not only will the perception by the dominant group of the subordinates as a class of inferior creatures block sympathy and empathy for their suffering, but also, if the members of the opponent group see *themselves* not as individuals but as members of some overriding collectivity, they will be less responsive to the sufferings of nonviolent actionists. Seeing themselves simply as parts of a very important whole (party, race, etc.) members of the opponent group will be likely to surrender their own sense of responsibility, standards of behavior, and right of moral judgment to the group, and to hide behind the policy or decision of their government, party or other collectivity. Suffering then becomes institutionalized, and may take relatively impersonal forms. Brutalized elements of the population become the agents for inflicting severe repression or brutalities on the nonviolent group, and the average citizen may be protected from emotional involvement by an insulating barrier of institutional procedures. Arguments that the members of the grievance group are inherently inferior may be consciously used to keep the average citizen indifferent to their suffering.

The greater the social distance, the fewer the "reality checks" on each group's picture of the other,[36] and the more likely that the conflict can proceed with relative indifference to the human suffering involved. Censorship and other controls over the media of communication may increase the difficulties of using suffering to overcome the social distance between the two groups.[37] Conversely, the more sympathetic feelings the two groups have for each other, the more difficult it will be for the opponent to use violence against the nonviolent group.

Illustrations of how subordinate groups can be treated inhumanly because they are regarded as nonhuman or outside the common moral order can be found in the behavior toward the Negro by the Ku Klux Klan member, toward the Jew by the Nazi, and toward the "enemy" in many wars. Even within the institution of slavery, the degree of cruelty varied, with the same social distance, being generally less when the master knew the slave personally, and greatest when slave traders or overseers regarded the slave simply as a commodity or as a subhuman species.[38] When people were "debtor slaves," i.e., were bound into slavery in their own country because of debts, they were usually treated more considerately than were foreign slaves.[39]

Within the context of nonviolent action, a similar difference has occurred in repression and attitudes toward actionists who were members of the opponent's own people and toward actionists who were foreigners. For example, Harvey Seifert reports that during the New England Puritans' persecution of Quakers from 1656 to 1675 officials distinguished foreign Quakers from colonists who had become Quakers, penalties for colonist-Quakers being consistently more lenient than for Quakers who came from outside.[40]

The role of social distance as an insulator against influence by suffering helps to explain why governments sometimes use police and troops who have as little as possible in common with the people they are to repress. For example, the Soviet government used non-Russian speaking troops from Far Eastern sections of the U.S.S.R., who could therefore not talk with Russian-speaking Hungarians, to repress the Hungarian 1956 revolution, after there had been considerable unrest and defections among the Russian and Ukranian troops previously utilized.

Where a large social distance exists, the opponent may be insulated against empathy for the suffering nonviolent actionists by various interpretations of the suffering. Such misperceptions may be especially frequent in societies in which people already suffer a great deal *involuntarily* in the course of normal living.[41] When the actionists deliberately court suffering for a cause, the opponent may, initially at least, regard their act of defiance which leads to suffering and the actionists' taking the initiative themselves in inviting suffering, as a kind of impudence and status-usurpation.[42] By defying the opponent's expectations the challenge by self-suffering may therefore initially produce, not sympathy or pity, but hostility.[43] Alternatively, the nonviolent suffering may initially be interpreted as cowardice, the result of a "mental condition," or ridiculous. When the opponent group believes its dominance to be for the benefit of the subordinates, it may interpret the nonviolent suffering as an attempt to exploit its good nature by trying to arouse sympathy for a "bad" cause, or as the result of the subordinates being misled by subversive or foreign influences.[44] For example, the South African 1952 civil disobedience campaign was described by government supporters to be the result of Mau Mau influence, Russian Communism and Indian imperialism.[45]

After a time, certain misperceptions of the self-suffering of nonviolent actionists may be recognized by members of the opponent group as inaccurate. Other misperceptions may, however, not be so quickly corrected. Which each of these will be, and why, will vary with the particular case. When the social distance between the groups is considerable, all of the misperceptions of the grievance group and the actionists are likely to aggravate the difficulty of converting members of the opponent group by sacrificial suffering. That effort may still have some effect on some members of the opponent group, especially over a long period of time.[46] But for short-term or less costly changes it may at times be necessary to bring the other mechanisms of change into operation also.

Recognizing the importance of social distance, nonviolent actionists have taken a number of steps to overcome and remove it. When members of the grievance group have seen certain of their traits to be undesirable in themselves and also objectionable to others—such as lack of cleanliness, rudeness, etc.—they may make deliberate efforts at self-improvement, as Gandhi often urged. Participation in the struggle by persons with high prestige and status may also help to penetrate the barrier of social distance.[47] When the barrier involves language and lack of acquaintance with the people and issues at stake, the nonviolent action involving self-suffering may be used as a means of communication. Gregg pointed to this possibility: "Nonviolent resistance . . . uses facial expressions, bodily gestures and the tone of voice, just as in all personal communication . . . . conduct . . . itself may be a rapid, accurate, and efficient means of communication."[48] Even Gregg, who strongly favored conversion, recognized that this process may take place slowly or incompletely.

The opponent's fear of the challenge to the status quo, or his perception of the nonviolent group as a dangerous one with secret intentions and plans, work against the conversion. The nonviolent group which seeks a change in attitudes will need to relieve or counteract such fears. Nonviolent behavior is important here, but other means may also be helpful. For example, when the opponent is afraid of large numbers, a specific demonstration may be restricted to high quality action by a few actionists in order to minimize, or remove, that impediment to the influence of self-suffering.[49] Miller has succinctly pleaded for this approach:

> It is our task in any encounter with the opponent to strip away his fears and apprehensions and to deprive him of any rationalizations he may be using to distort the facts. It is distinctly to our advantage if we can summon sufficient empathy to see matters from his point of view so that we can help him to see the situation as it actually is.[50]

In some cases, the self-suffering of the nonviolent actionists may itself finally break down the social distance between the groups, as a result of repeated actions which finally explode the old stereotypes of the group and gradually arouse respect from the opponent group. Some of the initial negative reactions to the suffering may gradually be modified and reversed. The fact that the suffering is *voluntarily* accepted,[51] and that the actionists repeatedly demonstrate great bravery and heroism, may finally become decisive.

Just as an absence of respect for nonviolent actionists is a serious impediment to conversion by the self-suffering of the actionists, so a growth of respect can be an important step toward changed perceptions of the grievance group and the issues at stake. Respect does not automatically come with nonviolent behavior. Very courageous nonviolent actionists often gain respect from others, but in achieving that change it seems that while their nonviolence is important, their courage is primary. Indeed, their nonviolence may be perceived as a higher type of bravery. Their courage is more akin to the courage of brave violent fighters than to the behavior of people who use no violence but behave cowardly. Opponents are most unlikely to respect people who submit helplessly, or cringe or plead in fear of punishment. Respect for men with courage, and contempt for people who cringe, are especially likely responses from certain personality types which are most likely to be brutal in dealing with dissenters and resisters.

Bravery is so important in the context of nonviolent action that it has much in common with extreme courage demonstrated by violent resisters. The capacity of great bravery expressed in violence to arouse admiration from the most unlikely people is illustrated by the responses of two high Nazis to the Jews of the Warsaw ghetto rebellion of 1943. Even Adolph Eichmann, working hard at the extermination program, declared in total violation of Nazi racial theories that some of those Jews were "important biological material." That is, they had by their bravery demonstrated sufficient biological superiority to be important for "breeding" future generations, rather than being so biologically inferior and contaminating as to require extermination, as the Nazi ideology maintained. The Nazi police chief, S.S. Major-General Krueger, of the *General Government* (in the remnant of Poland), praised the endurance of the defiant Jews also.[52]

In a different situation, Hitler too seemed moved by the courage of a rebel, in this case a defiant Nazi, Hans Frank, *Reichskommisar* for Justice for Germany and Governor-General of occupied Poland. Frank had split with the S.S. and after a personal friend, who was a Nazi official in Poland, had been executed without trial, Frank went on a stormy speaking tour of German universities in July 1942, advocating a return to constitutional rule. This was an act of defiance for which Frank might well have been executed, but although he was removed as *Reichskommisar* for Justice, Frank was kept as Governor-General and even won his fight with the S.S. Reitlinger writes that "Hitler had an uncanny respect" for a man who could remain defiant in the face of death.[53]

These instances are very different from ideal nonviolent action; the Warsaw Jews were clearly violent and Frank was scarcely a model nonviolent actionist. But these instances do show that bravery and defiance can sometimes win respect even from the most unlikely persons. Some people have argued that by expressing heroism and courage nonviolently, nonviolent actionists may be braver than even courageous practitioners of violence, and thereby gain respect from the opponent through demonstrated courage, sincerity, nonretaliation and self-sacrifice.

Such bravery is likely to violate the opponent's stereotype of the nonviolent group. Some members of the opponent group may, Seifert suggests, feel more threatened by such an unexpected response, and hence react with more intense aggression, but others who are more open may begin to change to bring their perceptions closer to reality. The impact of such a dramatic demonstration and suffering, "combined with a comparative absence of personal threat, make this outcome more likely," Seifert writes. "Although perceptions always remain somewhat distorted, under these circumstances it is harder to maintain the bias of old steotypes in full force . . . Under the conditions created by nonviolent resistance, man's capacity for unreality is more likely to be limited."[54]

Farmer reports that newspaper and television accounts of the 1960 sit-ins in the United States presented images which reversed the common stereotypes of Negroes—stereotypes which extended beyond cowardice and passivity. The students taking part in the sit-ins were well-dressed, well-mannered, studious and quiet, while the crowds of white boys outside were disorderly and trying to start trouble.[55] Solomon and Fishman made similar observations: the movement was destroying both the *Southern* stereotype of the "contented Negro," and the *national* stereotype of the "violent Negro."[56]

When nonviolent actionists seek conversion through self-suffering, Miller argues, it is necessary to make "a maximum effort to establish rapport and to present the opponent with an image that commands respect and can lay a basis for empathy."[57] If a change of image and a growth of respect take place it may become possible for the opponent to "identify" with the suffering nonviolent actionist despite the former extreme social distance between the two groups. Such a breakdown of social distance has occurred both outside and within the context of nonviolent action.[58] The social distance between the orthodox Brahman Hindus and the untouchables in South India in the 1920s was about as great as can be imagined. Yet the 1924–25 Vykom temple-road *satyagraha* campaign ended sixteen months after it began with the Brahmans changing their attitude. This campaign, which was described in Chapter Two, persisted despite beatings, prison sentences, tropical sun and floods. The actionists sought not simply the right of the untouchables to use a road which passed the temple, but that the Brahmans should willingly agree to that change. In the end, the Brahmans said: "We cannot any longer resist the prayers that have been made to us, and we are willing to receive the untouchables."[59] This illustrates that under certain circumstances conversion is possible despite extreme social distance. For these cases, and the many more in which the barriers to conversion are not so high, it is important to examine *how* this conversion takes place.

D. Conversion through self-suffering

Because there has been so little research on conversion in nonviolent action it is impossible here to offer a full and accurate analysis of how conversion is achieved, when it is, or to give full consideration to all the important variations within this mechanism. It is, however, possible to summarize present insights into the process which raise hypotheses for further research and add to our understanding of the dynamics of the technique.

Conversion is, of course, not a single precise phenomenon. It includes various types of changes varying in their rational and emotional components, operating on different people, and differing with the length of time the change has been in operation.

Conversion includes various changes in the opponent's attitudes, beliefs, feelings and world views. There may be changes in opinions and reactions toward the grievance group, for example, or toward themselves, or toward the issues at stake in the conflict, toward the repression, their own social system, or, finally, toward their own belief system or that of the actionists. The conversion may be primarily focused on one of these or involve all of them to a significant degree, or a combination of several of them.

Conversion results from differing influences and also varies in the degree of rationality and nonrationality involved; it seems to range on a continuum from a relatively rational change of attitude on the specific issue at stake to a change almost exclusively in the person's emotions and deepest convictions. The latter type may involve a revulsion against past policies and behavior, contrition and repentence, and a change in an entire outlook on life, including the adoption of new beliefs. This type is apparently much the rarest type of conversion, although it is the type most often discussed in the writings of actionists who believe in principled nonviolence and who seek conversion. Most cases of conversion fall at various points between these extremes.

Nor will all members of the opponent group be equally converted simultaneously. Some may not change at all. Although members of the general public of the opponent group may change their views and feelings toward the conflict or the grievance group and even ordinary soldiers may do so, the persons occupying the top political positions may not be moved in the slightest. Nonviolent actionists, far more than their violent counterparts, view their opponent as a heterogeneous group. Although headed sometimes by strong leaders who may be hard to influence, the actionists see the opponent group as consisting of diverse subgroups and people who may be far less committed to the objectionable policies than are the leaders. These sub-parts of the opponent group may be much more susceptible to influence in favor of the nonviolent group, and their conversions may prove to be highly important.

Furthermore, conversion of any type takes place over a time span and the process goes through various stages. This means that if the process is interrupted or halted at a certain point, although the opinions and feelings of the person will differ from what they were previously, they will also differ from those which would have developed had the conversion process been completed.

Although believers in principled nonviolence derived from religious sources most often are the exponents of conversion, this mechanism occurs in the absence of such beliefs and even when conversion is not deliberately sought. For example, most of the attitudes thought to be needed to achieve conversion were apparently absent in the Irish peasants' boycott of the now famous Captain Boycott, mentioned briefly earlier. Although economically ruined by the peasants' action in 1879, he returned in 1883 from New York to Ireland, but this time as a *supporter* of the Irish cause.[60] This does not show that the peasants' boycott alone had changed his opinions, but that his personal experience was bound to have played a role in his thinking about conditions in Ireland.

Theory and opinions from Gandhi and others on how conversion operates may best be understood if an example of change by conversion is described first: the Quakers' struggle in Puritan Massachusetts Bay Colony, 1656–75.[61] When the Quakers attempted to proselitize in Puritan Massachusetts they became involved in a nonviolent action campaign for religious liberty. The Puritans regarded Quakerism as a "sink of blasphemies" and Quakers themselves as "ravening wolves." They were accused of defiance of the ministry and the courts, naked dancing, and a plot to burn Boston and kill the inhabitants. Perhaps most important, a grant of religious toleration would have ended the Puritan theocracy and political ideal. The Puritans believed they had a religious duty to persecute those who spread religious "error."

Two women Quakers were the first to arrive; they were sent back to England on the next boat. Two days later eight more Quakers arrived; despite harsh penalties the numbers constantly increased as they waged "a direct frontal attack." They met in private homes, tried to speak after sermons in churches, spoke during their own trials and from their jail cell windows, issued pamphlets and tracts, returned to the colony in defiance of the law, held illegal meetings, refused to pay fines, and when imprisoned refused to work at the cost of food being denied them. Despite expulsions, whippings through towns and executions, the Quakers repeatedly returned. One already banished on pain of death walked calmly into the court where another was on trial for his life.

Initially the general public and the theocratic leaders were united in favor of the persecution. Gradually, however, a split developed as the public began to see the Quakers in a new light. Sympathizers began to pay the jailers' fees and at night passed food to the Quakers through jail windows. The bearing of the Quakers as they were whipped and executed convinced people that they had "the support of the Lord" and were "the

Lord's people." The Governor expressed his determination to continue executions so long as the Quakers persisted.

Public unease increased. After a time that same governor even threatened to punish a jailer who had nearly killed an imprisoned Quaker by beating. The law on banishment under pain of death was modified to allow trial by jury. Later, opposition to enforcement of the law grew and after a woman Quaker was executed discontent increased. Finally, even the General Court (the legislature) began to weaken. The death penalty was virtually abolished. Although the laws became milder, it was difficult to obtain constables to enforce them. By 1675 in Boston the Quakers were holding regular Meetings undisturbed. The Quakers were now included in the category of human beings and a "common moral order," and religious liberty was then not far behind.

In a very different case, despite his rejection of nonviolence as a moral principle and his emphasis on economic and political forces, Nehru's experience forced him to conclude that something like conversion did at times take place in nonviolent struggle:

> That it has considerable effect on the opponent is undoubted. It exposes his moral defences, it unnerves him, it appeals to the best in him, it leaves the door open for conciliation. There can be no doubt that the approach of love and self-suffering has powerful psychic reactions on the adversary as well as on the onlookers.[62]

All writers on conversion by nonviolent action seem to see self-suffering by the actionists as the dominant factor which initiates conversion, but there are differences on whether the suffering directly initiates conversion or whether it does so indirectly. Sometimes such suffering is seen to operate *directly* on the consciences of members of the opponent group, and at other times the suffering is seen first to influence wider public opinion which then causes members of the opponent group to experience inner emotional conflict and to question their previous opinions and beliefs.

Gandhi sometimes spoke of this *indirect* type of conversion. In the case of the Vykom *satyagraha,* already described, he said: "The method of reaching the heart is to awaken public opinion."[63] The opponent's violence, then, first puts him in a bad light in the eyes of observers, and their disapproval contributes to the beginnings of inner uncertainty in the opponent himself. As Gregg put it:

> With the audience as a sort of mirror . . . the attacker with his violence perhaps begins to feel a little excessive and undignified—even a little ineffective—and by contrast with the victim, less generous and in

fact brutal. He realizes that the onlookers see that he has misjudged the nature of his adversary, and realizes that he has lost prestige. He somewhat loses his self-respect . . .[64]

The sufferings of the nonviolent actionists may also be a *direct* stimulus to inner change in the opponent, especially when the social distance between the groups is not great or can be overcome with time. Voluntary suffering for a belief or ideal, argues Gregg, is likely to induce in others feelings of "kinship with the sufferer"[65] and sympathy for him. If the severity of their suffering disturbs the opponent, awareness that granting the demands of the nonviolent actionists can quickly end the suffering may stimulate change. When the opponent starts to wonder if the demands of the nonviolent group are justified, he is on the way toward conversion.

The existence of a complex of strong emotions, which may swing between opposites, was regarded by Case as another factor facilitating conversion; this is said to make possible sudden rushes of sympathetic emotions such as admiration, remorse, compassion and shame. The changed views may focus on the violence of the repression or on the issues at stake.[66]

Among the possible effects of the self-suffering of nonviolent actionists on the members of the opponent group are three: the sincerity of the actionists may become clear; their courage and determination may bring reluctant respect; and the old image of the group may be replaced by a new, more favorable, one.

Willingness to endure sacrifices—such as poverty, injury, imprisonment and even death—in furtherance of their beliefs or cause is likely to demonstrate the sincerity of the nonviolent actionists. Sacrifices incurred in *violent* conflict also demonstrate sincerity, as already discussed, but, it is argued, sympathy for the actionists is more likely when they are not also inflicting suffering on the opponent.[67] "To be willing to suffer and die for a cause is an incontestable proof of sincere belief, and perhaps in most cases the only incontestable proof."[68] Willingness of leaders of social movements to make visible personal sacrifices for their cause has also been called a test of their sincerity.[69]

If the opponent recognizes the sincerity of the nonviolent group, this may be a very important step toward respect for them and toward a reconsideration of the issues. Gandhi saw respect of the opponent for the nonviolent actionists as an achievement which heralded approaching success. He argued that at the approach of this stage, the nonviolent actionists must conduct themselves with special care.

Every good movement passes through five stages, indifference, ridicule, abuse, repression, and respect. . . . Every movement that survives repression, mild or severe, invariably commands respect which is another name for success. This repression, if we are true, may be treated as a sure sign of the approaching victory. But, if we are true, we shall neither be cowed down nor angrily retaliate and be violent. *Violence is suicide* . . . power dies hard, and . . . it is but natural for the Government to make a final effort for life even . . . through repression. Complete self-restraint at the present critical moment is the speediest way to success. [70]

The self-suffering of the nonviolent actionists may also contribute to changes in the opponent group's perception of themselves. At times, instead of seeing themselves as the brave heroes courageously defending their loved ones, principles and society against vicious attacks, the events may break through their psychological defences and force them to recognize that it is *they* who have harshly attacked courageous men standing firmly for their cause without either threats or retaliation. On one occasion King expressed his confidence in the power of such self-suffering to bring inner disturbance to the perpetrators of such cruelties. [71]

In certain circumstances repression of the nonviolent group may lower the self-esteem of members of the opponent group. This change may affect their will to continue the repression and the struggle generally, especially if the opponent's objectives are difficult to justify.

Intermediary stages of the conversion mechanism may lead to reduced violent repression. While continued and increasingly severe violence is more likely against a violent action group—violence thrives on violence—violent repression tends to be reduced when confronted with nonviolent resistance. Another source of reduced repression is the growth of respect for the nonviolent actionists which may, according to Gregg, lead the opponent unconsciously to imitate them by reducing his own violence. [72] The absence of violence from the actionists may also lead individual members of the opponent group to reject a violent response; for example, during a lunch counter sit-in in Tallahassee, Florida, in February 1960, when tough-looking characters entered the store and looked as if they might attack the sit-inners, the waitress asked them to leave, and when some made derogatory remarks, she told them, "You can see they aren't here to start anything." [73]

In some instances the opponent's anger at the nonviolent group may prove to be physically and emotionally exhausting. Such exhaustion, combined with new inner uncertainties, may lead him to make mistakes in calculation and judgment, or may reduce his ability to make crucial decisions.[74]

When the influences which may bring about conversion are first set into operation the opponent is unlikely to be conscious of them. Gandhi described this conversion process as three-fourths invisible, its effect being in inverse ratio to its visibility. This led, he argued, to more effective and lasting change in the long run.[75] These inner influences may grow until the opponent realizes that he has doubts and has begun to question the rightness of his attitudes and behavior. When he becomes aware of these inner conflicts, the conversion process has already reached an advanced state. "If you want to conquer another man," wrote Gregg, "do it . . . by creating inside his own personality a strong new impulse that is incompatible with his previous tendency."[76] This inner conflict may be increased because the opponent finds that his usual outlook on life, his ways of behaving and responding to subordinates, opponents and crises—in which he has always had confidence—have failed to produce the expected results. In a very real sense this places him in a new world which requires that he reconsider many things.[77]

The willingness of nonviolent actionists to suffer rather than to submit may therefore lead the opponent to look once again at his dogma and policies, as Case suggests.[78] Initially, he may have intended to revel in their correctness, but now he may see them differently. Attitudes and feelings may then change, including some which seemed rigid. Some changes will appear as apparently sudden reversals of outlook.[79]

Such results will, of course, not take place easily, or even at all. There will be strong counterpressures, psychological, economic, political or other, to continue the old policy and activities, and the opponent may decide to do so no matter what the cost. He may also become brutalized and callous to the sufferings of others, and his mind may become closed to rational arguments.[80]

In order to avoid such brutalization, advocates of conversion in nonviolent action have often counseled restraint, and recommended that the opponent not be pushed too far at a single point. They have urged that he not be required to choose too often between being repeatedly brutal and acquiescing to demands. Whole campaigns, and even individual demonstrations, may therefore be planned to be implemented in phases which are intended to reduce hatred, to avoid extreme fury, and to provide time for one phase to work before the next begins. Such a phased campaign gives the opponent opportunity for reflection and thought, and is an effort to show him that not he personally but his policy is under attack. The choice of methods, the numbers participating at a given time and point, the tactics employed, attitudes conveyed, and even small personal gestures, may all be important in this attempt. These refinements may facilitate the operation of the conversion mechanism despite unfavorable circumstances by showing the opponent the sincerity of the actionists and by removing his misconceptions about them and their objectives.

As the opponent's first point of reference is himself,[81] he must keep a favorable self-image. His justification for the policy at issue and his dismissal of the grievance group as nonhuman or as outside the common moral order may have helped him to do this. If as a result of the nonviolent group's self-suffering, he begins to doubt his policy and also begins to see the members of the grievance group as fellow human beings, it will be difficult to keep that favorable self-image. In order to do so he must then change the policy and cease certain behavior.

The conflict may thus be resolved by a change of the opponent's will, aims and feelings. "He ceases to want in the same way the things he wanted before; he ceases to maintain his former attitude toward the resisters; he undergoes a sort of inner conversion."[82] The inner conflicts and uncertainty—which are certainly not easy to bear—may lead the opponent to become receptive to suggestions from the nonviolent group as to an honorable way out of the particular conflict,[83] as well as to new ideas which may lead to more fundamental conversion.[84] In such circumstances the opponent may be considerably more subject to influence and suggestion than the nonviolent group.[85] Gregg also argues that the emotional and moral perturbation taking place in the opponent during the struggle may bring to the surface "moral memories" which he had long since forgotten and which had ceased to influence his behavior; these, he suggests may also influence the opponent to make a more humane response to the conflict.[86] The conversion process may finally lead the opponent to come to see the situation "in a broader, more fundamental and far-sighted way . . ."[87] Gregg describes this change confidently in these words:

> Nonviolent resistance demoralizes the opponent only to re-establish in him a new morale that is finer because it is based on sounder values. Nonviolent resistance does not break the opponent's will but alters it; does not destroy his confidence, enthusiasm and hope but transfers them to a finer purpose.[88]

Gandhi's views on this mechanism may be illuminating. Although he fully recognized the importance of power in social and political conflicts and in certain circumstances justified action which would produce nonviolent coercion, Gandhi had full confidence in the power of voluntary suffering to convert the opponent. "Given a just cause, capacity for endless suffering and avoidance of violence, victory is certain." Another path was concentration over a long period on the reform of the nonviolent group itself; this would produce various influences and finally result in the opponent being "completely transformed." [89]

The results of voluntary suffering might not appear at once,[90] and especially difficult cases might require extreme suffering. This did not, however, alter his view: even "the hardest heart" must melt before "the heat of nonviolence," and there was no limit on the capacity of nonviolence to generate heat.[91] Gandhi credited the brave suffering of the Boer women of South Africa in concentration camps set up by Lord Kitchener with changing the English attitude toward the Boers and making changes possible in British government policy for that country.[92] Gandhi applied this same principle in India, incorporated in nonviolent action. He wrote in 1930: "If the people join me as I expect they will, the sufferings they will undergo, unless the British nation sooner retraces its steps will be enough to melt the stoniest heart." [93]

When results from voluntary suffering were not immediately forthcoming, Gandhi, perhaps using circular logic, explained that there had been not enough suffering, or not enough time, or the suffering had not been pure enough. Granted the quality of the suffering, however, Gandhi saw an almost mathematical relationship between the suffering and the results. "Success is the certain result of suffering of the extremest character, voluntarily undergone." [94] "Progress is to be measured by the amount of suffering undergone by the sufferer, the purer the suffering, the greater is the progress." [95] At times he even defined the technique of *satyagraha* as "a method of securing rights by personal suffering . . ." [96]

It is not necessary to share Gandhi's extreme view of the power of voluntary suffering to achieve conversion to recognize that under some circumstances this mechanism may be effective. However, an oversimplified view of conversion, whether held by exponents of that mechanism, or by sceptics, is bound to lead to misunderstanding and the unwarranted dismissal of conversion as a genuine mechanism of change in certain circumstances. It is important to recognize, as Ebert points out, that "if it occurs at all, it does so by way of intermediate stages." [97] Furthermore, there are distinguishable factors which may influence the operation of the conversion mechanism, and it is to these that our attention now turns.

E. Some factors influencing conversion

The factors influencing the operation of the conversion mechanism in nonviolent action may be roughly divided into external factors and internal factors—external factors being those inherent in the conflict situation and outside the direct control of the nonviolent group, and internal factors being those under the direct control of the nonviolent group and involving either its internal condition or the activities and gestures it may make in efforts to convert the opponent.

1. External factors   These factors will include the following:

(a) The degree of conflict of interest. If the issue at stake in the conflict is highly important to the opponent, the nonviolent actionists can reasonably expect that it will be more difficult to convert him to their point of view than if the issue at stake is of relatively little importance to the opponent. Janis and Katz describe this as "the degree of conflict of interest relative to the community of interest between the competing groups."[98] The gravity of the issues at stake, and the likely consequences if the demands of the nonviolent group are granted, may significantly influence the resistance of members of the opponent group to efforts to convert them.

(b) Social distance. In accordance with the earlier discussion, whether or not the subordinates are regarded by the opponent as members of a common moral order will be an important factor influencing the possibility of conversion.

(c) The personality structure of the opponents. Certain types of personalities may be particularly susceptible to conversion by nonviolent self-suffering, while others may be extremely resistant to such influences. (This does not imply that sadists, for example, would simply revel in the opportunity to inflict cruelties against nonviolent actionists, for other factors in the situation, especially the absence of masochistic fear, cringing, etc., among them, may make the relationship unsatisfactory for sadists.) Research, which takes into consideration both existing knowledge of personality structure and change, and also the nature of this technique of struggle, could contribute significantly to understanding the personality factor.

(d) Beliefs and norms—shared or diverse. If the opponent and the nonviolent actionists share common beliefs and norms of behavior, they will provide "a higher tribunal, standing above the parties" to which the nonviolent group can appeal with the expectation of understanding and perhaps sympathy.[99] Where such common ideals and standards are absent, however, and especially where the opponent group is committed to belief in the right or duty of domination, there will be "formidable barriers" to the conversion of the opponent. [100]

(e) The role of third parties. Whether or not the opponent group cares about praise or condemnation from third parties, and whether and how those groups respond to repression of the nonviolent actionists, will frequently be an important factor influencing conversion.

These five factors may at times be supplemented by others. Even when these five factors are unfavorable to conversion, a nonviolent group might be able to achieve conversion anyhow. However, the combination of a high degree of conflict of interest, great social distance, unfavorable personality types in the opponent group, absence of shared beliefs and moral standards, and unsympathetic third parties would make conversion exceedingly difficult.

2. Internal factors　　According to Gandhian thinking, there are at least eight factors influencing conversion which are under the control of the nonviolent group. [101]

(a) Refraining from violence and hostility. If the nonviolent group wants to convert the opponent, it generally emphasizes the importance of abstention from physical violence and also from expressions of hostility and antagonism toward the opponent. Deliberate rejection of violence in favor of nonviolent means is regarded as having an important psychological impact on the opponent which may influence his conversion, [102] removing or reducing his fear of the grievance group, and hence increasing his ability to consider its arguments and to respond sympathetically to its plight. Gandhi believed that when the Englishmen came to feel that their lives were protected, not by their weapons but by the Indians' refusal to harm them, "that moment will see a transformation in the English nature in its relation to India . . ." [103] When an opponent feels a campaign to be a personal attack on himself—psychological if not physical—he is more likely to resist changes in his outlook and policies, and to be more impervious to appeals from the actionists and third parties, than when the actionists are able to convince him they bear no personal hostility and are concerned only with policies. [104]

(b) Attempting to gain the opponent's trust. Trust of the nonviolent actionists may significantly increase the chances of conversion. This trust may be consciously cultivated, in at least four ways. 1) Truthfulness, in the sense of accuracy of one's word. Statements to the opponent and to the public should be as correct as possible. In describing the grievance, for example, the facts should not be exaggerated or falsified. All statements to the opponent should be accurate with no attempt at deception. 2)

Openness concerning intentions. Truthfulness is carried to the point of telling the opponent one's plans for action and broader intentions.[105] In addition to the factors discussed in Chapter Nine openness also has beneficial psychological influences on the opponent. 3) Chivalry. If the opponent experiences some unrelated difficulty, such as a natural disaster, the nonviolent action may be postponed, or he may even be offered assistance. This "don't hit a man when he's down" behavior may help gain his trust and promote conversion.[106] 4) Personal appearance and habits. Offensive appearance and behavior may, as Sir Herbert Read, the anarchist, observed, "create a barrier of suspicion and reserve which makes the communication of any truth impossible."[107] To gain trust, the actionists may try to make their appearance and behavior inoffensive without compromise on the issues at stake. If the opponent does gain more trust in the actionists, his own insecurity may be reduced, and hence his desire for dominance.[108]

(c) Refraining from humiliating the opponent. Humiliation is an unlikely step toward sympathy, voluntary change and conversion. Therefore, if the nonviolent group aims at conversion, it must refrain "from any action that will have the effect of humiliating the rival group."[109]

This implies various "do's" and "don'ts" for the nonviolent actionist. For example, *don't* rely on numbers to convert the opponent. Numbers as such may inspire fear, and hence work against conversion. Even an outward "victory," produced by massive numbers may produce only obstinacy or bitterness. *Do* rely on the power of a few determined, nonviolent, self-sacrificing volunteers, or even a single one. Gandhi believed one actionist might "induce a heart change even in the opponent who, freed from fear, will the more readily appreciate his simple faith and respect it."[110] Seeking conversion, actionists also sometimes may refrain from pressing home a "victory" within their reach while persisting in action, as at Vykom, until the opponent is ready to agree to the objective.

(d) Making visible sacrifices for one's own cause.[111] If the suffering is to have the greatest impact on the opponent, it should, argued Gandhi, be offered by people directly involved in the grievances. This is more likely to be perceived as sincerity, and therefore influence conversion, than if they are unwilling to do so, or if some other people are taking the risks. Even major sacrifices by other people who are, or are regarded as, "outsiders," may have comparatively little effect. Their participation may even arouse hostility as "outside intervention" and "trouble-making." The opponent may even see the whole campaign as originating with outsiders, not with the people directly affected by the grievance.[112]

Generally, in Gandhi's view, outside aid should be limited entirely to expressions of sympathy. When the aim is conversion of the opponent, sympathetic nonviolent action should be offered only in special circumstances. During the Vykom *satyagraha,* a Christian became leader of the nonviolent actionists at one point. Gandhi then urged that participants should be limited to Hindus (including untouchables).

> The silent loving suffering of one single pure Hindu as such will be enough to melt the hearts of millions of Hindus; but the sufferings of thousands of non-Hindus on behalf of the "untouchables" will leave the Hindus unmoved. Their blind eyes will not be opened by outside interference, however well-intentioned and generous it may be; for it will not bring home to them the sense of guilt. On the contrary, they would probably hug the sin all the more for such interference. All reform to be sincere and lasting must come from within. [113]

Self-sufficient nonviolent action by members of the grievance group was also necessary, Gandhi argued, to show the opponent his dependence on that group and that "without the cooperation, direct or indirect, of the wronged the wrong-doer cannot do the wrong intended by him." [114]

There are also some indications from the experience of nonviolent action movements in the Deep South that outsiders may arouse more antagonism than local people in initiating projects.

(e) Carrying on constructive work. Constructive program work and other efforts at self-improvement within the subordinate group may help to achieve conversion. Janis and Katz describe such work as "maintaining a consistent and persistent set of positive activities which are explicit (though partial) realizations of the group's objectives." [115] Such work may demonstrate sincerity and social concern. "Participation *(as individuals)* in wider community activities which are widely regarded as necessary in the common welfare" is listed by Robin Williams as one means by which a vulnerable minority group can reduce the majority's hostility towards it. [116]

It is relatively difficult to dismiss humanitarian and constructive work and to distort the motives behind it; when people who engage in such work are also practicing nonviolent action, the opponent may take their statements and behavior more seriously.

(f) Maintaining personal contact with the opponent. Nonviolent actionists seeking to convert the opponent repeatedly emphasize the importance of maintaining personal contact with him. Such contact may at times also be maintained by personal letters, or by discussions and conferences. Such contact may help keep personal relations friendly despite the conflict and achieve maximum accurate understanding of the other's views, motivations, aims and intentions.[117] Personal contact may at times contribute to conversion by both emotional and rational processes.

(g) Demonstrating trust of the opponent. The nonviolent group seeking to convert the opponent will, in Gandhian thinking, adopt "a consistent attitude of trust toward the rival group and [take] overt actions which demonstrate that one is, in fact, willing to act upon this attitude."[118] When the nonviolent group has high expectations of the opponent's intentions and future behavior, those expectations, it is believed, may encourage him to live up to them. Such high expectations of the opponent may also place the nonviolent group in a favorable light with third parties. The actionists do not, however, play down their indictment of the opponent's policies, or temporize about the justification for nonviolent action.[119] However, negotiations and other means of settling the conflict short of direct action will be fully explored, and the nonviolent group will deliberately appeal to the best in the opponent to facilitate a response in similar terms. All suggestions by him for negotiations will be seriously explored, even when they may be intended as diversions from the direct action campaign.[120] It is, of course, not necessary to suspend direct action for negotiations to take place, and if, after an agreement has been reached, the opponent does not fulfill his pledges, nonviolent action can always be resumed.

(h) Developing empathy, good will and patience toward the opponent. Conversion will be helped if the actionists can achieve an inner understanding of the opponent, ". . . a high degree of empathy with respect to the motives, affects, expectations, and attitudes of the members of the rival group."[121] With such empathy, the nonviolent actionists may be more able to anticipate the opponent's moves and reactions, and will also have a more sympathetic understanding of his outlook, feelings and problems—while disagreeing with him on policy.

The actionists can then refrain from action which would needlessly antagonize the opponent and, positively, in small ways—a glance, tone of voice, letter—or in large ways communicate the nonviolent actionists' lack of personal hostility and even their personal friendship in the midst of battle. This may aid the opponent's conversion. Demonstrated respect for the individual members of the opponent group, and understanding of their outlook and problems may in turn make them more sympathetic and less hostile to the nonviolent challengers.

The expression of personal goodwill for the opponents may express itself in such ways as continuation of personal friendships in the midst of the struggle or efforts not to inconvenience the opponent. Bondurant reports instances in India "of proper satyagrahis refusing to take action in the mid-day sun because of the hardship this would work on European opponents who were less accustomed to extreme heat, and again, of satyagrahis postponing an action to spare the Englishman for his Easter Sunday services and celebration." [122] When the police raided the *satyagrahis* camp at Dharasana in 1930, following two days of bloody repression which had turned the camp into a hospital, one of the *satyagrahis* wrote: "Some twenty policemen surrounded us. We were going on with our own work. As it was hot we gave our police brethren a drink of cold fresh water. On the mornings of the 21st and 22nd, we had given them our blood as patiently and quietly." [123] Nonviolent actionists intent upon converting the opponent must be willing to demonstrate considerable patience with him. This patience with him as an individual is combined with impatience with his policies.

F. Conversion may not be achieved

There are a variety of reasons why the self-suffering of nonviolent actionists may not convert the opponent. Sometimes only partial success may be achieved, while in other cases the struggle may end without outward indications that any degree of conversion has been achieved. Such factors as the conflict of interest, the social distance, absence of shared beliefs and norms, and the personality structure of members of the opponent group may have established a broad and deep chasm between the groups, so unfavorable to conversion that the suffering of the nonviolent group is insufficient to achieve conversion. Even Gregg—who stresses conversion —admits that "in the case of a very proud and obstinate opponent, there may have to be a complete outward defeat before the change of heart really takes place . . ." [124] Others acknowledge that certain groups may be especially difficult, or impossible, to convert. Miller singles out unofficial and anonymous attackers drawn from "the worst elements among the opponent's masses" who may bomb, shoot, beat and kill nonviolent actionists (he recommends appeals to "the more responsible elements in their community to quarantine them.") [125] Members of a terroristic secret police, such as the Gestapo, must also be expected to be nearly immune to conversion attempts, while ordinary conscript soldiers may be vulnerable. While it is easy on the one hand to dismiss the possibilities of conversion with excessive enthusiasm, it would also be naïve not to recognize that in some cases conversion will never take place.

Frequently all three mechanisms of change operate in the same situation. In many campaigns success cannot be attributed solely to conversion or nonviolent coercion, or even to the middle mechanism, accommodation. Instead, change may be produced by some combination of these mechanisms.

Sometimes, for example, although conversion is attempted, the conflict may produce other forces of change which contribute to accommodation or nonviolent coercion so rapidly that the aims of the actionists will be achieved before the conversion process has had time to work. In those cases in which the passive acquiescence of the grievance group has in the past been largely responsible for the grievance, their noncooperation and defiance may in itself be sufficient to abolish the objectionable policy or practice. The halt to their submissiveness may result from a "change of heart" within the members of the *grievance group,* rather than the different type of "change of heart" in the *opponent group,* which is more often discussed in the literature. The withdrawal of support by the grievance group may have a rapid impact on the operation of the system. "The unifying power of nonviolent resistance may often take effect more rapidly than does the breaking down of the morale of the opponents." [126]

Some advocates of conversion as the only ethical or moral mechanism in nonviolent struggle have a very simplistic view of the nature of change in nonviolent action, of possible courses of action, and of the ethical problems posed by the differing mechanisms. Some of these are revealed by the power of noncooperation even when conversion is sought. Extreme exponents of conversion reject all change which is not willingly agreed to by the opponent leadership. But where the victims of an objectionable policy have ended it by noncooperation and such moralists still insist on conversion, they must also advocate a resumption of cooperation and continuance of the "evil" to which they object until the leaders of the opposition group are converted. Should the grievance group, with its new sense of self-respect, courage and determination, then be counseled to continue to submit while the opponent's domination or objectionable social practices continue?

Related ethical problems concerning conversion are raised when some members of the opponent group are converted while others, such as the top officials or leaders, have not been changed. The effort to achieve conversion is not likely to win over *all* members of the opponent group simultaneously. The opponent's troops, administrators and general population may be converted before the top leaders. Soldiers, for example, carrying out repression against the nonviolent actionists may, despite their discipline and habits of obedience, come to question the use of such repression against nonviolent people. Such questions, combined perhaps with fraternization with the nonviolent group, may lead them to think for themselves, and then to lower their morale and finally to question orders, disobey and perhaps even mutiny.[127] A similar process may take place among the opponents' administrators, home civilian populations, and even officers. When such members of the opponent group begin to protest at the opponent's policies and finally refuse to obey orders, should they resume their roles as tools for maintaining the objectionable policies until their top officials have been converted?

Nonviolent actionists may, of course, not even attempt to convert the opponent. Or they may be willing to try to do so, while being ready after a certain point to use full nonviolent coercion. Nonviolent action can achieve social and political objectives by means other than conversion.

Difficulties in producing conversion have led many exponents and practitioners of nonviolent action, among them James Farmer, to reject the attempt to achieve it, and to concentrate on change by accommodation or nonviolent coercion: "In the arena of political and social events, what men feel and believe matters much less than what, under various kinds of external pressures, they can be made to *do.*"[128] Attention now turns to the mechanisms of change by *accommodation* and *nonviolent coercion*.

ACCOMMODATION

Accommodation as a mechanism of nonviolent action falls in an intermediary position between conversion and nonviolent coercion. In accommodation the opponent is neither converted nor nonviolently coerced; yet there are elements of both involved in his decision to grant concessions to the nonviolent actionists. This may be, as has been suggested, the most common mechanism of the three in successful nonviolent campaigns.[129] In the mechanism of accommodation the opponent resolves to grant the demands of the nonviolent actionists without having changed his mind fundamentally about the issues involved.[130] Some other factor has come to be considered more important than the issue at stake in the conflict, and the opponent is therefore willing to yield on the issue rather than to risk or to experience some other condition or result regarded as still more unsatisfactory. The main reason for this new willingness to yield is the changed social situation produced by the nonviolent action. Accommodation has this in common with nonviolent coercion. In both mechanisms, action is "directed toward . . . a change in those aspects of the situation

which are regarded as productive of existing attitudes and behavior." [131]
This means that the actionists

> . . . operate on the situation within which people must act, or upon their perception of the situation, without attempting directly to alter their attitudes, sentiments or values. The pressure for a given type of behavior then comes either from (a) revealing information which affects the way in which individuals visualize the situation, or from (b) actual or potential alteration of the situation itself. [132]

In nonviolent coercion the changes are made when the opponent no longer has an effective choice between conceding or refusing to accept the demands. In accommodation, however, although the change is made in response to the altered situation, it is made while the opponent still has an effective choice before him, and before significant nonviolent coercion takes place. The degree to which the opponent accepts this change as a result of influences which would potentially have led to his conversion, or as the result of influences which might have produced nonviolent coercion, will vary. Both may be present in the same case. Sometimes other factors not capable of leading to either extreme may contribute to achieving accommodation.

A. Violent repression seen as inappropriate

The opponent may become convinced that despite his view of the rights and wrongs of the issues at stake in the conflict, continued repression of the nonviolent group by various types of violence is inappropriate. The suffering of the nonviolent actionists may have moved him to the point where, although not converted, he sees them as fellow human beings against whom the continued infliction of violence is no longer tolerable. Or he may feel that his violence is losing him "face" among third parties whose opinions may be important to him, and that if he continues the repression, he will lose still more. As Seifert explained it,

> Humanitarians in government or in the general population may oppose the cause of the resisters, but also want to protect an image of themselves as decent, tolerant persons. In order to protect the second . . . they may yield on the first. For them the costs of terrorization and brutality have become greater than the costs of . . . whatever the resisters were contending for. Or opponents may . . . no longer consider the central issue to be as important as they once did . . . They would still like to have their own way on [it] . . . but . . . continuing the struggle is not worth the trouble. [133]

The change of opinion among Montgomery, Alabama, whites is an example of this type of accommodation. While still favoring segregation at the end of the bus boycott, many of them could no longer countenance extreme violence, such as bombings and shootings, to support it.[134] A similar reaction was noted by correspondent Negley Farson in India in 1930. His dispatch published on June 23 said:

> "Where is this going to end? What can we do with people like this?" These are some of the questions which at clubs, home, offices and on the streets Europeans in Bombay are now asking each other, many of them appalled by the brutal methods police employ against Mahatma Gandhi's nonviolent campaign.[135]

Four days later it was reported that the very Englishmen who had six weeks earlier been the "damn-well-got-to-rule" type had now come to say, "Well, if the Indians are so determined to have dominion status as all this, let them have it and get on with it."[136] A similar development occurred in the American woman suffrage movement. Seifert reports that many people

> . . . who objected to militant tactics or to woman suffrage, . . . objected even more to cruel handling of them . . . . The suffragists quoted an unnamed congressman as saying, "While I have always been opposed to suffrage I have been so aroused over the treatment of the women at Occoquan [a prison] that I have decided to vote for the Federal Amendment" . . . . When a choice had to be made between supporting the cause of the militants and cruelly suppressing them, many people preferred the former.[137]

The opponent may thus find that, although he is perfectly capable of continuing the repression and although he still has not agreed with the demands of the nonviolent actionists, "the campaigner is not really so bad after all and that, all things considered it 'costs too much' to suppress the campaigner."[138] He may thereby end the still unresolved inner conflict produced by the behavior of the nonviolent actionists.[139]

B. Getting rid of a nuisance

Sometimes opponents may grant the actionists' demands, or make major concessions, simply because they regard the group, or certain consequences of the conflict, as a nuisance which they wish to end. Lakey has argued that "when the campaigner succeeds in projecting an image of himself as a 'nuisance' and not as a 'threat,' he is close to a resolution of the conflict." [140] Seifert writes that some Americans may favor accommodation in face of nonviolent action because, for example, they are more devoted to orderly community life than to the issues, because they want quiet and an end to continued demonstrations; even segregationist parents may prefer open integrated schools to closed segregated ones. With these priorities, such persons "therefore detach their support from repressive policies." [141]

Sometimes when repression against nonviolent actionists is proving unsuccessful and frustrating, the government may itself conclude that the group is more of a nuisance than a threat, and that therefore partial or full concessions are in order.

The toleration of Christians in the Roman Empire seems to have resulted from this type of accommodation. The edict of toleration, issued by the Roman Emperor Galerius in April 311 A.D. frankly admitted that the attempt to get the Christians to return to the State religion, which had been reinforced by bloody repression, had not been successful. In granting toleration, the Emperor appears not to have been motivated by a sudden conversion to the principle of religious liberty, much less being coerced into making concessions. Rather, it appears, he wished to end the constant source of irritation posed by the Christians who would not bend to the Emperor. The reconsideration of the status of the Christians was made, the edict stated, in the context of various other arrangements "which we are making for the permanent advantage of the state." The edict spoke of the "willfulness" and "folly" of the Christians who "were making themselves laws for their own observance . . . and in diverse places were assembling various multitudes." Although in face of the repression many had given in and others had been "exposed to jeopardy," "very great numbers" had refused to yield. The edict stated that therefore, following the pattern of clemancy and pardon granted to others in the past, "Christians may exist again, and may establish their meeting houses, yet so that they do nothing contrary to good order." [142] There is other evidence that this edict was not, as the Christians then claimed, an act of repentance, but an act of State policy influenced by the lack of success of the policy of repression. [143]

C. Adjusting to opposition in his own group

As discussed repeatedly above, one likely consequence of nonviolent action is to create or deepen internal dissension and opposition over policies and repression within the opponent's group. These internal disagreements may become so serious that the leaders of the opponent group find it to their domestic political advantage to grant some or all of the demands of the nonviolent actionists. This is especially likely if such opposition is expected to grow, and it therefore seems best to cut the ground from under it. In some extreme cases failure to do so could result in the power-holders' being removed from their official positions. In such cases, Seifert points out, the officials "would prefer to continue the suppression, but they cannot do so and remain in office." Given that choice "they unwillingly give up the repression." [144] This does not imply that such internal opposition within the opponent's own group will always be successful, nor that a change in government will never be involved.

Although such opposition was a very important factor in achieving repeal of laws against which the American colonists were using economic and political noncooperation, Lord Chatham's plan of conciliation (which would have made the colonies autonomous, but subordinate, states within the Empire) failed to win approval of Parliament in early 1775, a crucial period before a major shift in the colonies to violent struggle. [145] As has already been shown, however, opposition in the opponent's own camp was highly important in achieving the withdrawal of French forces from the Ruhr, following electoral defeat for the French government produced in part by dissension over the occupation and repression. (German willingness to call off the noncooperation was obviously also important.) There are wide variations in the extent of internal opposition which is required to produce change and the forms in which it may be expressed.

D. Minimizing economic losses

The opponent may find it to his interest to accommodate to the demands of the nonviolent actionists, without either conversion or nonviolent coercion, if his economic position is important to him and the struggle is affecting his wallet more than would concessions. This is an extremely common motive in settlements of strikes and economic boycotts, when the objectives are improved wages and working conditions.(Various illustrations of this factor in accommodation may be found in Chapters Five and Six.)

Economic motives for settlement may also be important, however, in other cases where they are less obvious, and even when economic demands are not present or are secondary. Thus in American civil rights campaigns both economic boycotts of white-owned stores and peaceful demonstrations which discourage shoppers from buying in the area where they were held have sometimes helped Southern white businessmen to favor concessions to the Negro demands. [146] For example, during a sit-in campaign in Atlanta between November 25 and mid-December 1960,

Christmas buying was down sixteen percent, almost ten million dollars below normal.

Repeal of the Stamp Act, achieved partly because of support from British merchants, was certainly influenced by the effects of the American colonists' cutting off trade and refusing to pay commercial debts to those merchants. A Bristol merchant reported in August 1765, for example: "The present Situation of the Colonies alarms every Person who has any Connection with them . . . . The Avenues of Trade are all shut up . . . . We have no Remittances, and we are at our Witts End for Want of Money to fulfill our Engagement with our Tradesmen." [147] The merchants' petitions for modification or repeal of the relevant acts emphasized this economic motivation, [148] and the repeal statute itself stated that continuation of the Stamp Act would be accompanied by ". . . many Inconveniences, and may be productive of Consequences greatly detrimental to the Commercial Interests of these Kingdoms . . ." [149]

Economic motives for a settlement proved effective in achieving a victory for African bus boycotters in South Africa in 1957. Africans reported for work as usual during the boycott, but walking ten miles or more each way between their homes in Alexandra township and their jobs in the city of Johannesburg inevitably reduced their productivity. Despite the obstinacy of the Nationalist government, businessmen and industrialists became worried, and their intervention finally led to a settlement which gave victory to the Africans, as Luthuli reports:

> A stage was reached when an honorable conclusion became a possibility, as a result of a set of proposals made by the Chamber of Commerce—the fatigue of workers was not doing production any good. To put it briefly, the Chamber of Commerce appeared willing to do what the adamant Government refused to do, which was to subsidise the [bus] company indirectly rather than place a new burden on poor folk. [150]

E. Bowing gracefully to the inevitable

In other instances of accommodation, the opponent may concede because he sees inevitable defeat. He may, therefore, wish to bow to change gracefully, avoiding the humiliation of defeat and perhaps salvaging more from the situation than might be possible at a later stage. The degree of choice the opponent has in such a situation may vary. In some cases, the social and political situation may have so changed that while the opponent cannot be said to be nonviolently coerced it would nevertheless be most difficult for him to pursue an earlier intended course of action. This happened, for example, to the recommendations of the British government's Simon Commission concerning the future political development of India. The Commission had begun its work early in 1928, and, in face of widespread boycott and refusal of assistance by the Indians, concluded its work over a year later. By the time its report was published in June 1930, however, the three-month-old national civil disobedience movement had so changed the Indian political situation that it was impossible for the British even to attempt to follow the Commission's recommendations. "The report . . . was dead before it was born." [151]

In other cases, the opponent may decide to accommodate himself to the nonviolent actionists while he still has some freedom of action. If he expects the nonviolent movement to grow significantly in strength, he may be inclined to accede to the demands voluntarily. Strength may include numbers but, as discussed earlier, encompasses much more.

In some situations, the opponent may accede relatively easily to the demands of the nonviolent actionists if he anticipates that otherwise he will face a really powerful movement capable of causing considerable difficulties and perhaps of winning despite repression. The motivation for accommodation in this case may not be simply to bow to the inevitable, but to prevent the activists and the rest of the population from realizing by experience the power of which they are capable when united in nonviolent noncooperation and intervention.

This motivation is illustrated in Faulkner's novel, *A Fable,* which describes troops of both sides in World War I defying their generals, mutinying and bringing the war to a sudden halt. The threat implied in the troops' action was deeper than the mere stopping of the war, however. The more severe threat was the possibility that troops and people generally would learn that they were *able* to stop wars if they wanted to do so. The group commander in the novel saw this clearly:

> We can permit even our own rank and file to let us down on occasion; that's one of the prerequisites of their doom and fate as rank and file forever. They may even stop the wars, as they have done before and will again; ours merely to guard them from the knowledge that it was actually they who accomplished that act. Let the whole vast moil and seethe of man confederate in stopping wars if they wish, so long as we can prevent them learning that they have done so. [152]

After a struggle has reached an advanced stage, the opponent's fear of the awareness of people's knowledge of their own power may make him determined *not* to make concessions. For example, in January 1775

Lord Chatham's plan of conciliation with the American colonies was opposed in the House of Lords by the Earl of Suffolk for essentially this reason: victories for the colonists would give them confidence to demand independence. Suffolk condemned the First Continental Congress, which had adopted a noncooperation program:

> . . . the whole of their deliberations and proceedings breathed the spirit of unconstitutional independency and open rebellion . . . . Now, therefore, was the time to assert the authority of Great Britain, for . . . every concession on our side would produce a new demand on theirs; and in the end, bring about that state of traitorous independency, at which it was too plain they were now aiming. [153]

Fear that the people would learn their power also appears to have been one of the major obstacles to reaching a settlement of the Bardoli peasants' revenue-refusal campaign in 1928, waged against the government of Bombay Presidency. In this instance nearly the entire population of 87,000 had stood together and effectively blocked the government's will. More extreme repression might have caused the local campaign to spread to all India. There seemed little the government could do except to concede defeat. But that was difficult. Therefore, though the settlement finally agreed upon meant in practice that the government would grant the peasants' demands, it did not openly state that the demands were granted. The government was much concerned with "saving face" and with finding a formula which would grant the demands of the *satyagrahis* without directly admitting the government's defeat. This was done by establishing an Enquiry Committee whose eventual recommendations meant that there was virtually no increase in the revenue in Bardoli. [154] It is difficult to avoid the conclusion that it was not simply an empty gesture to support the prestige of the government, but a desire not to admit defeat in face of determined nonviolent action—an example which in the India of unrest and turmoil of 1928 might have had the most dangerous consequences for the British *Raj*.

The factors influencing accommodation may be summarized as the degree of conflict of interest, all factors influencing the conversion mechanism, actual and potential support for the nonviolent actionists and their cause in the opponent's group and among third parties, the degree of effectiveness of the opponent's repression and other countermeasures, economic losses produced by the conflict, the estimated present and future strength of the nonviolent actionists, and the estimated chances of victory and defeat and their consequences.

But not even accommodation may be achieved, for there are clearly some types of opponents who may be unwilling to grant any demands of the nonviolent group. Even if they know that they may be finally defeated, such opponents may prefer to remain firm to the end. For these cases, too, the question arises as to whether nonviolent action can win except by a change of will in the opponent? Is there such a thing as *nonviolent coercion?*

NONVIOLENT COERCION

In some cases of nonviolent action, the opponent is neither converted nor does he decide to accommodate to the actionists' demands. Instead he may be determined to win full victory against them. Under some circumstances he may do so, or he may at least achieve temporary success in crushing the actionists. Failure of both conversion and accommodation does not, however, always mean victory for the opponent. The demands of the nonviolent group may also be achieved *against* the will of the opponent, that is, he may be *nonviolently coerced.* This type of nonviolent change has often been neglected in favor of the other two mechanisms.

As James Farmer has pointed out, when change by conversion and accommodation is believed to be unrealistic, neglect of the mechanism of nonviolent coercion has left the field clear for advocates of violence:

Perhaps we at CORE have failed to show how effective and virile nonviolence can be . . . . We must show that nonviolence is something more than turning the other cheek, that it can be aggressive within the limits a civilized order will permit. Where we cannot influence the heart of the evil-doer, we can force an end to the evil practice. [155]

Roughly speaking, nonviolent coercion may take place in any of three ways: 1) the defiance may become too widespread and massive to be controlled by the opponent's repression; 2) the noncooperation and defiance may make it impossible for the social, economic and political system to operate unless the actionists' demands are achieved; 3) even the opponent's ability to apply repression may be undermined and may at times dissolve. In any of these cases, or any combination of them, despite his resolution not to give in, the opponent may discover that it is impossible for him to defend or impose his objectionable policies or system. In such an instance, the change will have been achieved by nonviolent coercion.

A. The concept of nonviolent coercion

The concept of coercion is not limited to the effects of threat or use of physical violence. Neither the *Oxford Dictionary* nor the *Webster Dictionary* suggests that its definition is restricted to the impact of that pressure or force which comes from physical violence. On the contrary, it is often made clear that coercion can be effected by nonphysical pressures including moral force.[156] Instead of violence, the key factors in coercion are: 1) whether the opponent's will is blocked despite his continued efforts to impose it, and 2) whether the opponent is *able* to act in an effort to implement his will. These two aspects are emphasized by Paullin and Lakey. "Coercion is the use of either physical or intangible force to compel action contrary to the will or reasoned judgement of the individual or group subjected to such force."[157] "Coercion . . . is taking away from the opponent either his ability to maintain the status quo or his ability to effect social change."[158] The concept of "coercion" is thus a very broad one, which clearly includes the imposition of certain conditions by means of nonviolent action without the opponent's agreement.

There is, however, a vast difference between nonviolent coercion and what might be called violent coercion. As Bondurant points out: "The difference between violent coercion in which deliberate injury is inflicted upon the opponent and nonviolent coercion in which injury indirectly results is a difference of such great degree that it is almost a difference of kind."[159] Involved in the former is the deliberate intention of *inflicting* physical injury or death; in the latter, the coercion largely arises from noncooperation, a refusal of the nonviolent group to submit despite repression, and at times removal of the opponent's ability to inflict violence: "nonviolent coercion forces the opponent to accept the [nonviolent actionists'] demands even though he disagrees with them, has an unfavorable image of [the nonviolent group], and would continue resisting if he could."[160] In such cases the nonviolent actionists have so grown in numbers and strength, or the opponent's sources of repressive sanctions have been so weakened, or both, that the opponent is unable to continue to impose his will on the subordinates.[161] The opponent can no longer wield power contrary to the wishes of the nonviolent group.

Nonviolent coercion is not simply a creation of theoretical speculation. Nor is it even a forecast of future potentialities of the technique based on extensions of previous experience. Despite the improvised nature of most past cases of nonviolent action, nonviolent coercion has sometimes occurred. In other cases it has nearly taken place. Noncooperation has sometimes been so effective that temporary paralysis of the opponent's power has been achieved, but total collapse of his regime did nevertheless not result. The regime may have regained ground because of the actionists' failure to capitalize strategically on the situation, the introduction of resistance violence or other disruptive influences, or some other factor. For example, as descibed earlier, effective British power in several of the American colonies was for a time paralyzed and it even collapsed in the face of noncooperation.

A similar situation existed at certain points in the Russian 1905 Revolution. *The Times* in London reported at the end of October: "The nation is still in passive revolt, and the Government is incapable of enforcing even the semblance of authority." [162] The Great October Strike, described above, was so effective and inclusive that the government was for a while unable to govern.

> For five days Nicholas II and his advisors found themselves virtually isolated at Peterhof, facing a country that appeared to be gripped by some strange paralysis. It was this situation that in the final instance induced the Tsar to issue the constitutional manifesto of 17 October—a turning-point in the 1905 revolution and a landmark in Russian history. [163]

The 1920 Kapp *Putsch* against the new Weimar Republic is a much clearer case of this mechanism. The general strike and political noncooperation made it impossible for the usurpers to govern, despite their successful occupation of Berlin. They were unable to win the assistance of those persons and groups whose help was essential. Without that assistance and the submission of the people, the Kappists remained an impotent group, pretending to govern a country whose loyalty and support were reserved for the legal government. The *Putsch* therefore simply collapsed.

Despite a limited amount of violence, the February 1917 Russian Revolution, to which reference has repeatedly been made above, provides another example of success through nonviolent coercion. There were massive strikes—on February 28 nearly a quarter of a million were on strike in Petrograd alone. There were massive peaceful street demonstrations in which the people talked with the soldiers trying to win them over, and even the Bolshevik leaders tried to prevent violence, which they saw would only provide an excuse for extreme repression. Revulsion at obeying orders to fire on such crowds contributed to unrest and to the mutiny of the Tsar's troops. When reinforcements were sent to replace ineffective or disobedient troops, they dissolved into the crowds. Soon organized government forces ceased to exist. The Commander of the Petrograd Military District, General S.S. Khabalov, was unable even to rely on the troops which had not disappeared. When he realized his powerlessness, he "probably did not even know to whom he could have surrendered." Meeting on the 27th, the Council of Ministers experienced "a sense of impotence and lassitude." Rodzyanko, Chairman of the Duma Committee, declared "the old regime has turned out to be impotent," while others asserted that it had fallen. On the night of March 2, Nicholas II quietly signed an act of abdication for himself and his son. The Tsarist government had been "dissolved and swept away." [164]

Economic shutdowns and other noncooperation produced two other cases of nonviolent coercion, the nonviolent paralysis in 1944 of the dictatorships of Martinez in El Salvador and of Ubico in Guatemala, described in Chapter Two. These cases involved far less violence than the February 1917 revolution, and their coercive character is unmistakable.

B. Withdrawing the sources of political power

The theoretical analysis of the sources of political power and their withdrawal by noncooperation, which was developed on Chapter One, now merges with our analysis of the dynamics of nonviolent struggle. In this section we shall recall the sources of political power which have already been discussed and examine how each of these may be restricted or severed by nonviolent action. Some of the examples which illustrate the restriction or severance of the particular source of power are from cases of nonviolent coercion, while others simply show the potential of nonviolent struggle to affect the particular power source. The discussion in this section will show the practical relevance of the earlier power analysis and will also help to explain how nonviolent coercion is possible. It is precisely the remarkable convergence of the necessary sources of political power with the ways in which nonviolent action strikes at the opponent's strength and position which gives this technique the potential for high effectiveness and greater political power than violence.

As the analysis in Chapter One showed, political power emerges from the interaction of all, or several, of the following sources of power, each of which derives from the cooperation, support and obedience of the subjects: *authority, human resources, skills and knowledge, intangible factors, material resources* and *sanctions.* As was noted, changes in the degree to which these sources are available to the ruler will determine the degree of the ruler's political power. Our earlier catalogue of the methods of nonviolent action and our analysis of the dynamics of this technique show that these sources are potentially highly vulnerable to a widespread, yet qualitative, application of nonviolent action.

It is the capacity of the nonviolent technique to cut off these sources of power which gives it the power of coercion. The precise ways in which these sources of power are restricted or severed, and the extent to which they are cut, will vary. This technique can both restrict and sever the availability of those sources of power to the opponent, and also reveal the the loss of those sources by other means. This technique becomes coercive when the people applying it withhold or withdraw to a decisive degree the necessary sources of the opponent's power. Nonviolent action makes possible "coercion through nonparticipation." [165] This potential is of the greatest political significance and requires detailed attention, even at the risk of repeating points made earlier, to show how each of these sources of power may be cut off.

1. Authority Nonviolent action affects the opponent's authority in three ways: 1) it may show how much authority the opponent has *already* lost, and a demonstrated major loss of authority will by itself weaken his power; 2) nonviolent action may help to undermine his authority *still further;* and 3) people who have repudiated his authority may transfer their loyalty to a rival claimant in the form of a parallel government, which may in turn weaken his authority yet more as well as create or aggravate other serious problems. Any of these consequences for the opponent's power may be serious.

Bloody Sunday—which produced a loss of authority—was followed by a warning to the Tsar from Minister of Finance Vladimir Kokovstev that something had to be done at once to regain public confidence, and also by the expressed fear of Count Witte, chairman of the Committee of Ministers, that the "aureole of the ruler would be destroyed" if Nicholas II did not publicly dissociate himself from the day's events. [166] Their warnings proved correct. Katkov points also to the Russian liberals' campaign over some years of denouncing and discrediting the autocracy, that is destroying its authority, as paving the way for the success of the February 1917 "popular rising and the mutiny of the Petrograd garrison [which] resulted in the bloodless collapse of the monarchy . . ." [167]

In his account of the East German Rising, Brant observes:

To the people of the Soviet Zone it [the declaration of the state of emergency by the Red Army, not the East German regime] was confirmation of what they already knew: after seven years in command the Red republicans were still dependent on power lent them by their protectors. But lasting domination depends less upon power than upon authority; power demands constant submission, and submission can quickly turn to mutiny. Authority requires and is granted respect, which in time of trouble and unrest is confirmed in willing obedience.[168]

In an extreme case, loss of authority in a system or regime may lead to recognition of the authority of a rival, nascent regime, and therefore the transfer of loyalty and obedience from the old to the new government. (At times loyalty may also be transfered, not to a rival regime, but to a more abstract authority, as a religious or moral system, or to a principle or ideology.)

A parallel government will emerge only in unusual instances of nonviolent action in clearly revolutionary situations. To be successful, the new government must possess widespread and deep support, and the old regime must have lost its authority among the vast majority of the populace. However, when a parallel government develops in a serious way, the opponent's *remaining* authority and power will also be severely threatened.

Such a parallel government obviously faces a number of difficult problems, and whether it succeeds or not will depend on how they are answered. Little analytical work has been done to date on the factors leading to success or failure of this particular method, or on the ways in which, when successful, the replacement may take place.

2. Human resources   Nonviolent action may also cut off the human resources necessary to the opponent's political power. Usually, in "normal times," rulers assume that they will receive general obedience and cooperation among the subjects who will obey and do all the things that need to be done to maintain them as rulers and to enable the system to operate. The widespread practice of nonviolent action, however, may shatter that assumption. The sheer numerical multiplication of noncooperating, disobedient and defiant members of the subordinate group and general population is likely not only to create severe enforcement problems but also to influence the ruler's power position. Nonviolent action is likely to lead not only to an increase in the refusal of consent among the subordinates directly affected by the grievance, but also to a related withdrawal of consent among the opponent's usual supporters (assuming there is a distinction between the two.)

This withdrawal of human resources will be most effective in 1) conflicts within the opponent's country in which the noncooperation of his own home population denies him the only available source of the human assistance he requires, and 2) in conflicts, as in a foreign occupation, in which the opponent is denied the assistance of *both* population groups, that is his usual supporters (the home population) and the grievance group (the people of the occupied country). However, even when two population groups are involved, and only *one* of these (as in an occupied country) withholds its human assistance, the noncooperation may nevertheless prove effective given the presence of certain other favorable conditions.

The increased withholding of human resources both in absolute and proportionate terms may lead to a disastrous situation for the opponent. These human resources, along with other sources of power, are likely to be reduced simultaneously with an increase in the demands upon that power which have been produced by the growth of noncooperation and defiance. The opponent then may lose control of the situation and the regime may become powerless. When this happens in politics nonviolent action has produced in the political arena results comparable to an effective strike in the industrial arena. Nonparticipation may paralyze the opponent's political system. This potentiality was clearly foreseen by Gandhi:

> I believe, and everybody must grant, that no Government can exist for a single moment without the cooperation of the people, willing or forced, and if people suddenly withdraw their cooperation in every detail, the Government will come to a stand-still. [169]

For major periods during the Russian 1905 Revolution the situation was completely out of the control of the government and the police were powerless to intervene, so massive was the popular defiance. [170]

In face of massive nonviolent defiance in Peshawar in April 1930 and the Garwali mutiny, already cited, the British temporarily gave up the attempt to control the city and withdrew their troops, abandoning the city for nearly ten days until reinforcements were available. [171]

The Devlin Commission's report to the British Government in 1959 revealed that the real reason for the 1958 Emergency in Nyasaland (now called Malawi) was fear that widespread African noncooperation and disobedience would lead to collapse of the government—not the "murder plot" which was so widely publicized at the time. By early March the situation reached the point where "the Government had either to act or to abdicate." [172] The Commission declared: "The decision to suppress Congress, we think, owed more to the belief that its continued activities were making government impossible than to the feeling that it was, or might be, a terrorist organization." [173]

3. Skills and knowledge   People do different jobs, have different skills and knowledge, and a particular regime or system needs some of these more than others. A withdrawal, therefore, by key personnel, technicians, officers, administrators, etc., of their assistance to the opponent (or their *reduced* assistance) may have an impact on the opponent's power quite disproportionate to the numbers actually noncooperating.

Refusal of assistance by key subjects may make it difficult for the opponent to develop and carry out policies appropriate to the situation he faces. This may lead to the acceptance of policies which prove to be political mistakes or to an inability to implement chosen policies, or difficulties in doing so.

For example, during the Inquisition imposed by Spain's Charles V on the Netherlands which Spain then ruled, the opposition of officials and magistrates, as well as of regular citizens, seems to have been decisive in blocking its implementation. In 1550 there was an attempt to impose the most severe measure yet, the "edict of blood," which imposed the death sentence for all trespasses. It proved, however, impossible to carry out the edict on a large scale. Pieter Geyl reports that both officials and magistrates opposed it and declined to give their cooperation. "In the opinion of those who designed the system, religious persecution in the Netherlands never worked anything but defectively." [174]

Gandhi maintained that if the Indians who held official posts under the British *Raj* were to resign them, the result would probably be the end of foreign rule without the need for the noncooperation of the masses. The alternative for Britain, he said, would be a pure despotic military dictatorship which, he argued, Britain did not dare contemplate. [175] Pleas were often made during the Indian struggle for officials to resign. [176] The key contribution made to the defeat of the Kapp *Putsch* by the noncooperation of civil servants and the refusal of experts to join the new cabinet has already been described above. The German government in 1923 recognized the special role of civil servants in the official passive resistance struggle against the French and Belgian occupation of the Ruhr, as it forbade all State, provincial and local authorities and civil servants from obeying the occupation officials' orders. [177]

Doubtless in some political and social situations the chances of the administrators and officials—the bureaucracy—shifting their loyalty are greater than in other situations, but if it happens, it may prove decisive. The opponent's political power may be weakened also by internal conflicts within his own regime, both at upper and lower levels. These conflicts may be independent of the nonviolent action, or may be accentuated by it, or perhaps even created by it—as on such questions as whether to make concessions and what repression should be applied. While the regime may give the impression to the outside world that it is firmly united, the actual situation may be quite different, with or without a major nonviolent action movement.

The theoretically omnipotent Russian Tsar, for example, in 1904 could neither impose his will on his advisors nor stop their intrigues and disputes. [178] The split inside the Soviet Communist Party and the regime in 1924-27 is another example. [179] Various splits also occurred within the Nazi regime over policy and administration of the occupied areas of the Soviet Union. [180] Khrushchev's admission of disputes within the Russian leadership on how to react to the Hungarian Revolution is confirmation that such conflicts may exist in response to a major challenge outside the regime. The mere existence of such internal conflicts under various conditions may accentuate the impact of nonviolent action.

The analysis of the dynamics of nonviolent action suggests that for a variety of reasons such internal conflicts may be *more* probable in face of major nonviolent action, although documentary proof is at present not available. Where they occur, such internal conflicts in the opponent's regime will affect detrimentally the degree to which the regime's full potential of skills, knowledge, insight, energy, etc., is available for dealing with the challenge.

4. Intangible factors   Such factors as habits of obedience, political beliefs and the like may be significantly threatened by widespread nonviolent action. Such a movement involves the destruction of the habit of *unquestioning* obedience and the development of conscious choice to obey or disobey. This development would tend to make the opponent's political power more dependent upon the active and deliberate support of the subjects.

Nonviolent action may also be associated with changes in outlook and political beliefs. Nonviolent action in some situations (not necessarily the majority) *reflects* the spread among the subjects of views which challenge officially blessed doctrines. In most situations, however, the actionists are likely to be concerned instead with either particular grievances or a single broad political principle or objective, or with both. Even such cases may contribute to *further* erosion of unquestioning belief in an official doctrine. In such a struggle, events may refute official dogmas. For example, effective nonviolent challenge to the dictatorship may refute the view that violence is omnipotent. Or, the doctrine that the dictatorship reflects the will of the "people," or is a "workers' State," may be questioned when the general population, or the workers, demonstrate in the streets against it, go on strike, or noncooperate politically. Or, a belief that the dictatorship is benevolent and humanitarian may be shattered by repression against nonviolent people whose demand seems reasonable. The degree to which members of the population as a whole, and particularly members of the dominant group (the government, the Party, etc.) will be able and willing to re-examine the official political ideology will vary. At times firm adherence to the official ideology may ensure that repression is swift and harsh, although this may be a temporary phase. In other conflicts the actionists may be seen as trying to implement the "real" principles underlying official doctrines, while the existing regime is viewed as violating and distorting them to support despicable policies.

This discussion is only illustrative of ways nonviolent action may alter the intangible factors which help to secure the subjects' obedience and to preserve the ruler's power.

5. Material resources   Nonviolent action also may regulate the degree to which material resources are available to the opponent. These resources include control of the economic system, transportation, means of communication, financial resources, raw materials, and the like. The capacity of nonviolent action to impose economic penalties on the opponent should already be clear, for of the 198 methods of this technique described in earlier chapters 61 are directly economic, boycotts, strikes or intervention. In addition certain other methods may also have indirect economic effects, as from political disruption or by increasing costs of enforcement, or by losing goodwill for the opponent, or public confidence, so that third parties withhold loans, investments, trade and the like. A view popular among economic determinists—that nonviolent action is inevitably ineffective and irrelevant because financial and material factors determine the course of politics—is therefore based upon a fundamental gap in their understanding of this technique.

The Townshend duties, against which the American colonists complained so harshly, had been imposed to reduce the burdens on the British taxpayer by raising revenue in North America. The colonists' campaign of noncooperation not only blocked achievement of that objective, but also imposed additional economic losses on the Mother Country. A correspondent (probably Benjamin Franklin) pointed out in the London *Public Advertiser* on January 17, 1769, that only a maximum revenue of £3,500 had been produced in the colonies, while the British business loss due to the American nonimportation and nonconsumption campaign was estimated at £7,250,000. He also pointed to the possibility of war if the policy were continued, which would take the British at least ten years to win, cost at least £100,000,000, and leave a loss of life and a legacy of hatred. In Britain by that time, says Gipson, ". . . most men in public life were persuaded that to attempt to collect such duties in face of colonial opposition was economically unsound and politically unwise." [181]

It would be possible to offer innumerable examples from the two centuries since 1769 in which nonviolent action has inflicted such material losses on opponents that their economic, and consequently their power position, were both placed in jeopardy. Many examples described in Chapters Five and Six are of this type, especially of generalized strikes, general strikes and economic shutdowns.

However, only one more example of how nonviolent action affects the economic resources of the opponent will be offered: the nonviolent Indian struggles against British rule. These economic losses are in the main attributed to three sources: direct revenue refusal, increased expenditure for administration and enforcement, and deliberate economic boycotts.

During the Indian 1930-31 struggle, as a result of tax refusal and boycott of goods providing government revenue, and with increased expenditure to deal with the civil disobedience movement, the British regime faced deficits in the provincial governments. At various times the government of the Punjab faced a deficit of Rs. 10,000,000, the Bombay government faced a deficit of Rs. 10,250,000, the Central provinces Rs. 5,000,000, Madras Rs. 8,700,000, Bengal Rs. 9,482,000 and Bihar Rs. 4,200,000. [182] Gandhi's *Young India* commented: "When we check the nourishment from passing from the victim to the parasite the latter naturally weakens and dies while the former revives." [183] It is clear that revenue refusal was an important aspect of that movement. [184]

Year	Total Exports of the United Kingdom to British India in Millions of Pounds
1924	90.6
1925	86.0
1926	81.8
1927	85.0
1928	83.9
1929	78.2
1930 (boycott year)	52.9 [185]

People who argue that Gandhi's nonviolence had nothing to do with the British leaving India, that the real reasons were instead economic, erroneously assume that there was no contact between the two. There was, however, a close relationship, which included an immediate reduction of trade and profits.

A survey of exports to India over several years is instructive.

For certain specific items the decrease in imports from Great Britain between 1929 and 1930 ranged from eighteen percent to forty-five percent. [186] The Secretary of State for India told the House of Commons at the end of 1930 that the general depression in world trade accounted for a drop of twenty-five percent in exports to India, while he credited a drop of a further eighteen percent to the Congress' boycott. [187] Even eighteen percent is a significant figure, but the boycott may have been even more effective. Imports of British cotton cloth to India dropped far more that year than imports of cotton cloth from all foreign countries combined. [188] Between October 1930 and April 1931, when the boycott was at its height, there was a decline of eighty-four percent in imports of British cloth. Lancashire millowners and workers petitioned the Secretary of State for India to "do something about India." [189]

These cases are simply illustrative, and quite mild at that. Large-scale strikes and economic shutdowns affect much more severely the economic resources available to the opponent and the degree of political power he can wield, as the Great October Strike of 1905 or the 1944 economic shutdowns in El Salvador and Guatemala illustrate. International consumers' boycotts and embargoes may also influence the outcome of the struggle.

6. Sanctions   Even the opponent's ability to apply sanctions may on occasion be influenced by nonviolent action. We saw in Chapter One that fear of the ruler's sanctions is one of the reasons for obedience. We also noted that the threat or use of sanctions does not necessarily produce obedience, and that they can be neutralized by massive defiance.

In addition, sanctions as a source of the ruler's power may be reduced or removed by nonviolent action by those who help to provide the sanctions. Usually, this means that police and troops carry out orders for repression inefficiently, or disobey them completely. Sometimes the actions of others may also cut off the supply of weapons and ammunition, as when foreign suppliers halt shipments, or when strikes occur in domestic arms factories and transport. These means of control may be very important in certain situations.

The opponent's ability to apply sanctions may also be influenced by the degree to which his agents of repression—police and troops—are willing to carry out orders. In some situations there may be too few such agents because they have not volunteered or because conscripts have refused duty. In other situations, the existing police or troops decline to carry out orders efficiently, or refuse them completely—i.e. mutiny. Mutinies have occurred in wartime, in face of violent revolution, and in cases of mixed violent and nonviolent struggle.

As we have already discussed, there is good reason to believe that mutiny is much more likely in face of nonviolent resistance. The troops or police then do not face injury or death from the "rebels" and they must decide whether to obey orders to inflict severe repression against *nonviolent* people. Laxity in obedience and finally open mutiny will only occur in special circumstances, however. Police and troops will vary in their sensitivity or callousness to the sufferings they inflict on the nonviolent group. The potential for reduced reliability of the agents of repression nevertheless exists; this may be descibed as a tendency in nonviolent conflicts. Gandhi was quite convinced that soldiers who wound and kill nonviolent actionists undergo a traumatic experience which in time will bring them to contrition: ". . . an army that dares to pass over the corpses of innocent men and women would not be able to repeat that experiment." [190]

Efforts to convert the opponent group may produce both laxity in obeying orders for repression and open mutiny among police and troops, which may lead to nonviolent coercion of the opponent leadership. In other cases, mutiny may occur without conscious efforts at conversion. In any case, disobedience by the agents of repression will reduce the opponent's power, in some cases decisively. Widespread mutinies of Russian troops during the revolutions of 1905 and February 1917 have already been described above. [191] In the latter case they played a major role in achieving the disintegration of the tsarist regime.

The Nazis recognized well that if they lost control of the Army their power would be drastically weakened; Goebbels reveals that in early February 1938 the Nazis feared most of all not a *coup d'etat* but the collective resignation of all high-ranking officers [192]—a form of noncooperation.

During the predominantly nonviolent East German Rising of June 1953 police sometimes withdrew completely or willingly gave up their arms. Among the East German armed forces there were some cases of mutiny and laying down of arms. There were even evidences of sympathy from Russian soldiers and of reluctance to fire on the civilians. The overwhelming number of Russians who obeyed orders apparently suffered reduced morale. [193] It is reported that some one thousand Soviet officers and other ranks refused to fire at demonstrators, and that fifty-two Party members and soldiers were shot for disobeying orders. [194]

Large-scale deliberate inefficiency among troops and police is likely to reduce the regime's power. When officials realize that obedience is uncertain, especially if small mutinies have already occurred, they may hesitate before ordering severe repressive actions which might provoke mutiny. That hesitation also limits sanctions as a source of power. A major mutiny is bound to alter power relationships radically, and the opponent is unlikely then to be able to withstand the demands of the nonviolent actionists. In fact, his regime may then disintegrate.

C. Some factors influencing nonviolent coercion

There is no single pattern for producing nonviolent coercion. The factors which produce it occur in different combinations and proportions; there appear to be at least eight such factors. The role and combination of these will not be the same when the nonviolent coercion has been largely produced by mutiny, for example, as when the coercion has been achieved by economic and political paralysis. The contribution of each factor will depend upon the degree to which it regulates one or more of the opponent's necessary sources of power.

Generally speaking, nonviolent coercion is more likely where the *numbers* of nonviolent actionists are very large, both in absolute numerical terms and in proportion to the general population. It is then possible for the defiance to be too massive for the opponent to control; paralysis by noncooperation is more likely. There, too, may be a greater chance of interfering with the sources of power which depend upon manpower, skilled or unskilled.

The *degree of the opponent's dependence* on the nonviolent actionists for the sources of his power is also important. The greater the dependence, the greater the chances of nonviolent coercion. It therefore becomes important to consider exactly *who* is refusing assistance to the opponent. "The extent of nonparticipation required to produce measurable political effects varies with the strategic position of the strikers," argued Hiller.[195] Under certain circumstances the opponent may be relatively indifferent to large numbers of noncooperating subjects and in other circumstances he may be nonviolently coerced by the action of a relatively few.

The *ability* of the nonviolent group *to apply the technique* of nonviolent action will be very important. The role of fighting skill here is comparable to its importance in any other type of combat. Skill here includes the capacity to choose strategy, tactics and methods, the times and places for action, etc., and ability to act in accordance with the dynamics and requirements of this nonviolent technique. Ability to apply nonviolent action skillfully will help to overcome the weaknesses of the nonviolent group, to capitalize on the opponent's weaknesses, and to struggle against the opponent's countermeasures.

Whether or not nonviolent coercion is achieved will also depend on *how long* the defiance and noncooperation can be maintained. A massive act of noncooperation which collapses after a few hours cannot nonviolently coerce anyone. Willingness and ability to maintain nonviolent action for a sufficient duration despite repression are necessary to reduce or sever sources of the opponent's power.

The sympathy and support of *third parties* for the nonviolent group may be important in producing nonviolent coercion if the opponent depends on them for such things as economic resources, transportation facilities, military supplies and the like. Such supplies may then be cut off and his power position thereby undermined.

The *means of control and repression* which the opponent can use, and for how long, in an attempt to force a resumption of cooperation and obedience are also important. Even more important is the actionists' response to them.

The final factor contributing to nonviolent coercion is *opposition within the opponent group* either to the policies at issue or to the repression, or to both. The number of dissidents, the intensity of their disagreement, the types of action they use, and their positions in the social, economic and political structure will all be important here. On occasion splits in the ruling group itself may occur. Should this happen, or should a general strike or major mutiny of troops or police take place in opposition to repression of the nonviolent actionists, it would be a major factor in producing nonviolent coercion.

A SUCCESSFUL CONCLUSION?

Contrary to a popular view, skillfully applied nonviolent action may offer greater chances of success than would political violence in the same situation. However, the simple choice of nonviolent action as the technique of struggle does not and cannot guarantee victory, especially on a short-term basis. Changes will take place when significant nonviolent struggle occurs, but there is no certainty that these changes will always be for the better, from the perspective of the actionists. Nor are the results of such conflicts always full defeat or full success, but *as in all conflicts* they are frequently mixtures of the two in differing proportions. The results of many cases of nonviolent struggle might be spread along a continuum with complete defeat and complete success at opposite poles, and a draw falling at the midpoint. This allows for various intermediary types of results, such as partial failures and partial successes, which is where most of the cases would fall. The terms "success" and "failure" will both require examination since, as we shall note, they are usually far less precise and lucid than they first appear. The risk of defeat and its possible consequences will be considered first.

A. The risk and nature of defeat

Defeat in immediate political terms is always possible in nonviolent action, just as it is in war or in other types of political violence. "Defeat" here indicates failure to achieve the objectives of the struggle. During the analysis in this Part, stress has repeatedly been laid on the need to develop various qualities and to fulfill a number of conditions if the actionists are to wield maximum power. If these requirements have not been met in sufficient degree, there is no reason to expect success. If the grievance group does not as yet possess sufficient internal strength, determination and ability to act to make this technique effective against their opponent, then the simple verbal acceptance of nonviolent action will not save them. There is no substitute for genuine strength in nonviolent action and if the subordinates do not possess sufficient to cope with the opponent, they cannot be expected to win until they develop that strength.

Comparative studies are urgently needed of cases of "failure" and "success" to see whether common features are present within each group and if so what they are. It might then be possible to seek ways to counter weaknesses and to overcome especially difficult external circumstances.

The possibility of defeat is not a characteristic limited to this technique, however. Comparative evaluations of nonviolent and violent means must take into consideration that political violence is often defeated also. By conventional standards, does not one side lose in each international war, civil war and violent revolution? Such defeats have usually been explained as resulting from certain weaknesses or inadequacies, such as lack of fighting spirit, insufficient or poor weapons, mistakes in strategy and tactics, or numerical inferiority. Comparable weaknesses may also lead to defeat in nonviolent action. The common practice of explaining defeats of political violence in terms of such *specific* shortcomings while blaming defeats of nonviolent action on the presumption of its *universal* impotence is both irrational and uninformed.

The precise consequences of defeat will vary from case to case depending on the particular conditions in each situation. In some cases there may be physical suffering and mental anguish. At times defeat will bring economic losses and worsened conditions, as for the defeated British miners in 1927. Defeat may also be followed by new legal restrictions and prohibitions designed to place the government in a more advantageous position to prevent or control future nonviolent action. The defeat of the British General Strike of 1926 was followed by the harsh Trade Disputes and Trade Union Act of 1927,[196] and the Defiance Campaign of 1952 in South Africa was followed by the Criminal Law Amendment Act, No. 8 of 1953 and the Public Safety Act, No. 3 of 1953.[197]

Where defeat leads to demoralization and loss of confidence in the effectiveness of nonviolent action, the chances of a later resort to this technique may be drastically reduced. This was the case, writes Symons, after the British 1926 General Strike: "One thing Governments, Conservative, Labour or National, could feel happily sure: the trade unionists would never again attempt to engage in a General Strike." [198] Previous successes or failures in the use of nonviolent action are likely to influence whether or not the technique is used again, and, if so, may also help to determine the outcome of those later campaigns.

It does not follow, however, that defeats are necessarily always total and permanent. There are two relevant perspectives here: first, it is sometimes better to have fought and lost than not to have fought at all, and second, even in the midst of defeat there may occur less obvious changes which contribute to a later success for the nonviolent group.

Nehru expressed the former view well, when it was becoming obvious that the current civil disobedience campaign (of 1932-34) was not going to win. He wrote in prison in 1933:

Outside, the struggle went on, and brave men and women continued to defy peacefully a powerful and entrenched government, though they knew that it was not for them to achieve in the present or the near future. And repression . . . demonstrated the basis of British rule in India. There was no camouflage about it now . . . It was better that we should be governed thus, we thought, than . . . sell our souls and submit to spiritual prostitution. . . . [T]he cause went on despite setbacks; there could be no failure if ideals remained undimmed and spirits undaunted. Real failure was a desertion of principle . . . and an ignoble submission to wrong. Self-made wounds always took longer to heal than those caused by an adversary.

THREE WAYS TO SUCCESS   *757*

There was often a weariness at our weakness . . . and yet . . . . it was good to feel oneself to be a member of a gallant band. [199]

Obviously defeat alone does not determine whether the actionists become demoralized and nonviolent action is abandoned permanently. Defeat can also be seen as a lost battle, leaving for the future the winning of the war. Other factors make the difference in perspective. One of these may be an awareness that the side effects of even defeated nonviolent action can be important. Sometimes in conventional war the cost of success is so great that the victor has won only a Pyrrhic victory, which contributes to the relative strengthening and final victory of the defeated side. A comparable situation sometimes also occurs in nonviolent action. The actionists appear to be defeated, but the opponent's power is in the process weakened, or the subordinates' determination and ability to resist are significantly strengthened.

L. de Jong has observed that the mass strikes in the occupied Netherlands against Nazi rule in February 1941, 1943 and again in September 1944 were met with "great ferocity." Although there were no changes for the better in German policy, the strikes were "a tremendous stimulant to solidarity" of the Dutch people and offered ". . . convincing proof of the will to resist animating the majority of the people . . ." [200]

Although not immediately successful, if the nonviolent actionists increase their spirit of resistance, expand their organizational strength, improve their skill in applying this technique, and gain sympathy and friends which may be useful in the future, then even defeat may become a prelude to success.

B. A draw or an interim settlement?

During difficult stages of the struggle various steps can be taken to maintain a high level of participation and high morale among actionists. These steps may include phasing the strategy and tactics, varying the specific methods used, shifting the degrees of involvement and of risk for various groups, and attempting to win certain smaller interim goals or partial successes. If spirits are sagging, or fear of repression is increasing, some form of fearless, dramatic and dangerous action may be undertaken by a few reliable people in an effort to restore morale and confidence and to rally continued participation.

If such steps are not taken, or are not successful, however, the actionists may have to face the reality that, despite their achievements, they do not as yet have sufficient strength to win. In any contest of strength there are likely to be periods of increased and reduced direct involvement, high and low morale, growing strength and loss of vitality. In reference to military war Clausewitz pointed to the need always to allow for a line of retreat in case of necessity.[201] He also spoke of the need to provide rest for certain population and reserve groups while others take up the most exhausting action and thus keep up constant pressure on the opponent.[202] In nonviolent struggle, the "troops" may also become afflicted with "war-weariness" and reach a limit to their capacity for tension and suffering. This was the situation by late January 1931 in India after ten months of the civil disobedience campaign, reports Gopal. "Repression," Gandhi had earlier argued, "does good only to those who are prepared for it."[203] Not all nonviolent actionists have an equal capacity for suffering, and the capacity of the same person may vary at different stages within a particular movement. "Suffering has its well-defined limits. Suffering can be both wise and unwise, and, when the limit is reached, to prolong it would be not unwise but the height of folly."[204] This must be considered by leaders who plan and launch a campaign and who can influence the time and circumstances of its termination.

If the participants are not capable of further voluntary suffering without demoralization then tactical or even strategic changes may be necessary. "A wise general does not wait till he is actually routed; he withdraws in time in an orderly manner from a position which he knows he would not be able to hold," wrote Gandhi.[205] It may be wise to halt the current phase of the movement while one is still strong enough to achieve a negotiated settlement, or an unwritten one, with certain gains.

In other situations, when the actionists would have to give up or compromise on *essentials,* there may be no formal or informal truce. Instead, the nonviolent group may simply make a major change in strategy and take steps to provide rest for the combatants while attempting to make the situation more propitious for major action at a future date. There is no standard rule for determining when to call a formal halt to the campaign under honorable conditions with partial gains, and when to continue the defiance by the many in spirit and by only a few in action. Careful assessment of the particular circumstances is required.[206] If a temporary halt is to be called, it should be done at the most favorable moment. One factor in the choice of that moment will be the opponent's readiness to negotiate and to offer significant concessions.

The opponent, too, may have good reasons for wishing to end the struggle. The course of the struggle may have placed him in an insecure position from which he may wish to extricate himself. While the non-violent actionists had been unable to win, the opponent may have been unable to crush the movement and may have found the losses due to the conflict unacceptable. The opponent may therefore seek, by means other than repression, a resumption of cooperation and obedience. He may be willing to make certain concessions, either explicit ones or in substance.

This may well involve formal negotiations with the nonviolent actionists. For example, Lord Irwin, the British Viceroy, at the end of the 1930–31 struggle made determined efforts to settle the conflict and to obtain the resumption of cooperation by the Congress with the British regime. It is clear that these efforts were in large degree politically motivated by the need for an end to the noncooperation.[207] Where such efforts take place they may be encouraged by the actions of less extreme groups which did not participate in the nonviolent action movement, but urged the opponent to grant concessions and offer a settlement as did the Indian Liberals in 1930–31.[208]

Following the negotiated settlement at the end of the 1930–31 struggle, Gandhi said in his Press statement:

> It would be folly to go on suffering when the opponent makes it easy for you to enter into a discussion with him upon your longings. If a real opening is made, it is one's duty to take advantage of it, and in my humble opinion, the settlement has made a real opening. Such a settlement has necessarily to be provisional, as this is. The peace arrived at is conditional upon many other things happening. The largest part of the written word is taken up with what may be called, "terms of truce." [209]

It should be stressed again that the nonviolent actionists may compromise on secondary, nonessential, matters, but will not on essentials or give up fundamental principles or demands. They may, however, state in a document that disagreements on such points continue, although direct action on them is being suspended for the time being. The policies of compromise and of this type of interim settlement are quite different.[210] Compromise requires willingness on each side to give up part of their aims and objectives, on essential as well as unessential issues. Nonviolent actionists see such compromise at times as morally and politically unacceptable. For example, how does one "split the difference" on such issues as freedom of religion or speech, equal treatment of minorities, international aggression, the existence of a dictatorship, and the like? Compromise on basic issues is thus rejected both as a substitute for nonviolent struggle and as a means of settling a nonviolent campaign. Nonviolent actionists are willing to negotiate, but not on essentials—even when they cannot be won.

Even the occurrence of negotiations may mark a recognition of changes which the nonviolent action has produced in the relationships between the opponent and the nonviolent group. If a government, or other powerful opponent, agrees to negotiate it is usually because the opponent recognizes that the other side is able to wield effective power. This capacity to wield power will also influence the course and outcome of the negotiations. For example, Gandhi argued that the struggle must continue unabated during the 1931 negotiations, since any slackening at that stage would lead to a prolongation of the struggle.[211]

In certain political circumstances, such negotiations may themselves be a major concession by the opponent and a recognition of the new status of the subordinates. In 1931, for example, "the Congress was negotiating with the Government on what was virtually an equal footing."[212] Gandhi came to the Viceroy as the representative of India to negotiate with the representative of the British Empire. Sir Winston Churchill condemned the "nauseating and humiliating spectacle of this one-time Inner Temple lawyer, now seditious fakir, striding half-naked up the steps of the Viceroy's palace, there to negotiate and to parley on equal terms with the representative of the King-Emperor."[213] While the British in that year had not been converted, nor yet forced to give full independence, they found it necessary to negotiate and thus give a kind of *de facto* recognition to India as a separate political unit. The terms of the truce and the specific concessions—either direct concessions or ones granted in substance without officially conceding the demands of the nonviolent actionists[214]—important though they were, were secondary to this more fundamental recognition in the change of the relationship between Britain and India. The settlement itself "was framed in the form of a treaty to end a state of war." Gandhi saw its most important feature to be the recognition of the Indian National Congress as the intermediary between the people and the government. Members of the government in London privately expressed disapproval of the acceptance of "the unique and semi-sovereign position of the Congress."[215]

Formal negotiations and agreements are not the only ways to produce a truce or interim settlement. Such negotiations or agreements do not create the changes in the relationships but reflect and result from them.

Such formal bargaining at the conference table may, of course, not occur at all. The opponent may refuse to negotiate or make significant concessions, or other political circumstances may be difficult. In such cases a tacit truce may develop and informal understandings may become the equivalent of a settlement. For example, the opponent may call a halt to arrests for certain types of nonviolent action, especially if he has not been able effectively to halt them anyhow and if the wider public has clearly expressed its belief that on these issues justice lies with the actionists. The nonviolent group, in turn, might refrain from launching new types of action, or might halt its most ambitious methods, such as nonviolent raids or civil disobedience of regulatory laws. Gains already achieved toward the long run wider objectives might then be tacitly accepted—such as advances in free speech, freedom of the press, desegregation and the like—without the opponent abandoning his intent to block full realization of wider objectives and without the nonviolent group disavowing its intent to implement the full goals.

For the nonviolent group, the period following such a truce or interim settlement will be difficult. They will need as a minimum to maintain their existing position and marginal gains; at best they need to utilize this as a period for regrouping and gaining new strength. If they can do that, then later under more favorable conditions the nonviolent actionists will be stronger and can press more effectively to their full goal.

Pressures to renew the attack along exactly the same line will have to be resisted.[216] So also must be pressures to jump to the offensive too soon and without good reason to believe that one's relative strength has in the interim been significantly increased. Clausewitz' insights on war are applicable here:

> The first movements [after a lost battle] should be as small as possible, and it is a maxim in general not to suffer ourselves to be dictated to by the enemy. This maxim cannot be followed without bloody fighting with the enemy at our heels, but the gain is worth the sacrifice; without it we get into an accelerated pace which soon turns into a headlong rush, and costs merely in stragglers more men than rear-guard combats, and besides that extinguishes the last remnants of the spirit of resistance.[217]

In nonviolent action where morale and psychological influences are so important, very careful consideration must be given to trying to understand and solve these problems. Periods of retreat, and even times of defeat, must be turned into opportunities for the recovery of strength, confidence and determination, and for preparations for more favorable action. As Nehru pointed out, one should not count on a chance "irrepressible upheaval of the masses," although it might occur, but instead anticipate "a long struggle with ups and downs and many a stalemate in between, and a progressive strengthening of the masses in discipline and united action and ideology." [218]

To some degree, increased understanding of the nature of the technique combined with advanced training, wise strategy and careful preparations will make major successes by campaigns of shorter duration more likely. These campaigns may involve larger numbers of participants, applying more extensive, disciplined and persistent noncooperation and defiance.[219] Even if increased knowledge of this technique brings shorter and more successful conflicts, there will still be cases in which the nonviolent actionists must regroup and strengthen themselves and the wider grievance group. If a given campaign is not successful, the actionists' attitude in such a case generally is that the people are externally defeated for the time being, but internally still determined and defiant. They may be, for example, a "subjected but unconquered people," [220] who in time will translate their inner spirit of independence and opposition into an overthrow of the external subjugation.

Strategy and tactics during the period of regrouping and regaining strength will be of particular importance. One should never remain completely passive, for the population must not sink again into submissiveness. In such periods nonviolent action may be continued by individuals or reliable small groups especially committed and prepared to act. Sometimes large numbers or even masses of people may be involved in limited actions of a symbolic nature which, although clearly showing the feelings and views of the participants and hence perhaps improving morale, involve a minimum of risk to the participants. Demonstrations, protest or resistance may be used briefly or occasionally. Various methods of nonviolent protest, or even protest strikes, may be used on such occasions. National days, religious holidays, anniversaries of events related to the struggle and the like, may provide occasions for these limited acts of mass participation. For example, although the South African Defiance Campaign was really over, on June 26, 1953, the first anniversary of its launching, Albert Luthuli in a message to Africans and their allies appealed to them to light bonfires or candles or lanterns outside their homes, "as a symbol of the spark of freedom which we are determined to keep alive in our hearts, and as a sign to freedom-lovers that we are keeping the vigil on that night." [221] Such limited acts of protest or resistance must be continued until the time for more severe struggle comes.

Organizational work and training in nonviolent action will also be highly important during such a period. Where appropriate local issues require remedies, and the necessary support, determination and resistance capacity are present, local campaigns may be highly important for correcting the particular grievance. They may also help to maintain the spirit of resistance, improve morale by producing victories, and train people by participation and example for wider future campaigns. Ebert calls these "continuity or revival struggles" or "local continuity actions." [222] The nonviolent group may also use the period for trying to undermine both the opponent's belief in the rightness of his policies and his confidence that he can win; they may also try to improve his attitudes toward the grievance group and the nonviolent actionists in particular. If such efforts are successful to a significant degree, then when struggle is resumed, .the opponent group may lack both the will power to refuse the demands and also the determination to impose severe repression.

In a different type of situation, when the nonviolent group wins its full objectives as the result of a series of struggles each of which achieves part of the full aim, the points actually won by each particular conflict are likely to correspond to more basic changes in attitudes, power positions and other relationships between the contending groups. If so, those limited successes are likely to be genuine and lasting, ones which cannot be easily taken from them by anyone, as they could if they had been given as an edict or a gift without struggle.

C. Success

Most of this chapter has been devoted to evaluations of the ways in which nonviolent action may make the changes which produce success by the three mechanisms of change. It is possible that the most successful cases of nonviolent action involve optimal combinations of the three mechanisms. A considerable number of the illustrative cases of nonviolent action which have been offered in the book as a whole were successful. It has also been shown that a few cases of nonviolent struggle—as in the Ruhr—which are commonly regarded as complete failures instead achieved a considerable degree of success. The time has come to offer some final observations on the nature of success with this technique, and the ways in which it may occur.

In internal political conflicts and in international wars the terms "success" and "failure" or "victory" and "defeat" are widely used in very diverse senses, some quite clear, others imprecise or misleading. In violent struggles attention is frequently paid only to that side which succeeds in crushing the combat forces of the other and to that side which surrenders. Is that a sufficient criterion for success? What is the situation when, despite military victory, the political objectives or war aims of the winning side are not achieved? Or are won only in part? What if the military struggle ends in a stalemate, but one side gets most or all of its political objectives? Many other similar questions could be asked. Examinations of violent struggles in which it is presumably clear who won and lost, to determine whether goals of each side were achieved or not, are revealing.

It is important to see the problem of defining "success" in nonviolent action in this wider context. Precise thought and careful criteria are needed in order to determine intelligently whether given cases of nonviolent action have, or have not, succeeded, and to what degree.

As is often the case with violent struggles, it is not always possible to conclude categorically that a particular nonviolent action movement has been a clear "success" or "failure." Elements of both success and failure may be present in the same situation. The particular struggle must often be seen in the wider context of a series of campaigns and of its contribution to the later struggles and relationships. Even though all the goals may not have been won at a particular stage, it is possible that the struggle may have paved the way for their later achievement. Much more work on the nature and conditions of success in nonviolent struggle is needed. Understanding of this technique could be considerably advanced by a comparative study of cases of nonviolent action in terms of the results which were produced. Such a study might take into consideration such factors as these: 1) were the goals of the nonviolent group achieved? fully? in part? as the result of nonviolent action? as the result of other means or factors? immediately, or some time after the struggle? 2) which mechanisms of change operated? 3) were the nonviolent group and the grievance group strengthened or weakened internally as a result of the campaign? 4) was the basis laid for later or wider achievement of their objectives, or both? 5) were there changes in attitudes and perceptions toward the issues and toward the various groups? 6) were there additional subtle and indirect effects, and if so of what types? 7) were there lasting effects on the social structure or social system generally, and if so of what kind? 8) what was the cost of the achievements, and how do they compare with the cost of other efforts to achieve similar results? Doubtless other relevant questions might also be added.

That type of study cannot, however, be attempted here. For our purposes "success" in nonviolent action will be measured by whether the avowed goals of the nonviolent group were achieved as a consequence of the struggle, either at its end or shortly thereafter. Where all (or almost all) of their goals or demands are achieved, then the movement is described as *a full success*. Where only some of those goals are achieved, the movement is described as *a partial success*. Both of these may be achieved by any one, or any combination, of the three mechanisms of change discussed above, conversion, accommodation and nonviolent coercion.

If the nonviolent actionists have persisted on their chosen course despite repression, and have achieved a significant number of the factors upon which change hinges, then they are in sight of a victorious conclusion of the struggle. This is a crucial period, and a dangerous one. The opponent, sensing his imminent defeat, may make special exertions and take unexpected measures to defeat the actionists. Members of the nonviolent group, sensing victory, may become victims of overconfidence, carelessness and reduced determination. Gandhi clearly warned that ". . . the danger is the greatest when victory seems the nearest. No victory worth the name has ever been won without a final effort, more serious than all the preceding ones." [223]

Where full success is achieved, or a partial success in which most of the goals are won, there is no single formula with which the campaign is ended. Indeed, some cases are successful even before direct action is launched, at the stage of negotiations. James Farmer reports significant cases of desegregation and of opening employment to Negroes during negotiations because the opponent was familiar with other cases of successful nonviolent action for similar objectives by the Congress of Racial Equality (C.O.R.E.) These "victory before struggle" cases included, for example, the desegregation of all sixty-nine Howard Johnson restaurants in Florida, the ending of employment discrimination at various Sears Roebuck stores, and at the First National Bank in Boston. [224]

Attention here, however, is on the more common cases in which success follows only after struggle. As might be expected, with a technique as broad and diverse as nonviolent action and with the multitude of possible variables, there is no uniform pattern for the successful conclusion. At times conflict situations, especially international ones, may be so complex that it is difficult to disentangle the relative roles of nonviolent action and other factors in producing the change, as for example the conclusion of the Hungarian struggle against Austrian rule. In other cases the proportionate role of the nonviolent action will be clearer.

The mechanism with which change has been effected—conversion, accommodation or nonviolent coercion—will influence the manner of conclusion. Negotiation with a formal settlement is possible in all three mechanisms.[225] Some negotiations will be real bargaining sessions, but others will simply formalize the changes already agreed or recognized as inevitable. Those nonviolent groups which seek conversion of the opponent, or at least accommodation, may be only satisfied by a settlement which involves real agreement with the opponent.[226]

In certain instances of conversion or accommodation, there may be no formal negotiations or settlement. The opponent may simply grant the full, or essential, demand. Where a full success is achieved by nonviolent coercion, negotiations may produce a formal surrender to the actionists' demands. In other cases, the nonviolent group may even refuse to negotiate with the opponent, on the ground that he deserves no recognition at all; this was the case in 1920 when the legitimate Ebert government in Germany refused negotiations with Lüttwitz, who headed the putschists after Kapp fled to Sweden.[227]

In some cases of nonviolent coercion there may be no agreement or negotiation at the end of the struggle because of the impact of a major mutiny of the opponent's troops and police, an economic shutdown, massive popular noncooperation and an effective parallel government. The opponent's power may have disintegrated and collapsed, and the people's loyalty shifted to the new regime or system.

D. Toward a genuine solution

Advocates of the use of nonviolent action in place of techniques of violence have sometimes argued that the results achieved by nonviolent action are likely to be more permanent and satisfactory than those achieved by violence. Gregg, for example, wrote that victory achieved by violence is likely to result in hatred and desire for revenge, which may in turn lead to a new war to achieve revenge or restitution. The results of a successful nonviolent struggle, Gregg maintains, are quite different; it is likely there will be "no aftermath of resentment, bitterness, or revenge, no necessity for further threats of force."[228] The solution has been reached on a deeper level, with better feelings on both sides and fewer ill effects. The readjustment of relationships, he says, is more likely to be permanent.[229] Gandhi was of the opinion that even the sufferings of nonviolent actionists inflicted by repression did not lead to bitterness which would cause lasting tension and hostility.[230] King also pointed to increased respect in the opponent group for the nonviolent actionists after their demands had been won, and a lack of bitterness toward them; he attributed the lack of bitterness to "our insistence on nonviolence" and the resulting absence of casualties among the opponent group.[231] Others, too, have maintained that changes won by nonviolent action are much more lasting both than those won by violence and also than those which have been bestowed without struggle.

Such claims merit investigation. Comparative studies of the results of cases of successful violent action and successful nonviolent action have yet to be undertaken. They could, however, help significantly an intelligent evaluation of the relative merits of the contrasting techniques. The analysis in the preceeding chapters, however, suggests that successful nonviolent action may well produce a number of long-term beneficial results.

For example, the likelihood of bitterness, hatred and desire for revenge may be indeed reduced, especially where the conversion and accommodation mechanisms have operated to any considerable degree. The incidence of political violence may be reduced in the future also. The defeated opponent may be less likely to use violence in new attempts to impose policies on people who do not want them, because he has learned that violence is not omnipotent. The grievance group, having won nonviolently, may be less inclined to use violent means in future conflicts if feasible nonviolent strategies can be developed. Under some conditions the nonviolent struggle may have had lasting repercussions on the opponent group, such as stimulating new ways to achieve their objectives, bringing new outlooks and goals, or modifying the system itself. To the degree that the nonviolent action has been able to remove the grievances which provoked the nonviolent action, these will not provide issues for future conflicts.

Where changes have been achieved in accommodation or nonviolent coercion because of power changes, a lasting alteration in the power relationships of the contending groups is likely. This, too, may contribute to more equitable and less contentious relationships in the future. Many of the most important changes are within the grievance group itself. It is to those changes, and the changes in power relationships, to which we now turn in the concluding chapter.

NOTES

1. This roughly follows Lakey's similar discussion of three mechanisms, except that I have offered a substitute title for the second and modified its description slightly. See Lakey, "The Sociological Mechanisms of Nonviolent Action" p. 23; *Peace Research Reviews*, vol. II, no. 6 (Dec. 1968), p. 14. Earlier writers have usually not included this intermediary mechanism, jumping directly from conversion by suffering to nonviolent coercion. See, for example, Kuper, **Passive Resistance in South Africa**, pp. 77-78, and Bondurant, **Conquest of Violence**, p. 11.

2. Lakey, "The Sociological Mechanisms . . ." p. 20; *Peace Research Reviews,* vol. II, no. 6 (Dec. 1968), p. 12.

3. See Case, **Non-violent Coercion**, pp. 397-398.

4. Gandhi did not like the term "nonviolent coercion" but sometimes spoke of "compelling change" and of "compulsion."

5. Gandhi, **Non-violence in Peace and War**, vol. I, p. 44.

6. Sharp, **Gandhi Wields the Weapon of Moral Power**, p. 65.

7. Gandhi, **Non-violent Resistance** p. 87; Ind. ed.: **Satyagraha**, p. 87. See also Gopal, **The Viceroyalty of Lord Irwin**, 1926-31, pp. 4-5.

8. See Kumarappa's statement in Sharp, **Gandhi Wields . . .** , pp. 190-191.

9. Gregg, **The Power of Nonviolence**, p. 85.

10. Quoted in Bose, **Studies in Gandhism**, p. 162.

11. *Ibid.*

12. Janis and Katz, "The Reducation of Intergroup Hostility," *Journal of Conflict Resolution*, vol. III, no. 1 (March 1959), p. 95.

13. Schlesinger, **The Colonial Merchants and the American Revolution**, p. 79.

14. *Ibid.*, p. 127.

15. Ehrlich, *"Den Ikke-voldelige Modstand, der Kvalte Kapp-Kupet,"* p. 201.

16. See Ebert, "Nonviolent Resistance Against Communist Regimes?" pp. 180, 188, and 191-193.

17. Gandhi, **Non-violence in Peace and War**, vol. I, p. 412.

18. Gandhi, **Non-violent Resistance**, p. 194; Ind. ed.: **Satyagraha**, p. 194.

19. Gandhi quoted in Bose, **Studies in Gandhism**, p. 162. See also Bose, **Selections from Gandhi**, p. 146.

20. Gandhi, **Non-violent Resistance**, p. 202; Ind. ed.: **Satyagraha**, p. 202.

21. Bondurant, **Conquest of Violence**, pp. 227-229. See also Seifert, **Conquest by Suffering**, pp. 69-70.

22. Lakey, "The Sociological Mechanisms . . . ," pp. 30-33; *Peace Research Reviews,* vol. II, no. 6 (Dec. 1968), pp. 19-20.

23. Kuper, **Passive Resistance in South Africa**, p. 22.

24. *Ibid.*, p. 178.

25. Hiller, **The Strike**, p. 159.

26. *Ibid.*, pp. 169-171.

27. Case, **Non-violent Coercion**, p. 400.

28. *Ibid.*, pp. 399-400.

29. Hiller, **The Strike**, p. 91.

30. Gregg, **The Power of Nonviolence**, p. 78.

31. *Ibid.*, p. 84.

32. Kuper, **Passive Resistance in South Africa**, p. 79.

33. Seifert, **Conquest by Suffering**, p. 18.

34. Frederick Solomon and Jacob R. Fishman, "The Psychosocial Meaning of Non-violence in Student Civil Rights Activities," *Psychiatry,* vol. XXVII (May 1964), p. 99.

35. Kuper, **Passive Resistance in South Africa**, pp. 87-91.

36. See Wolff, ed., **The Sociology of Georg Simmel**, pp. 224-249.

36. See Janis and Katz, "The Reduction of Intergroup Hostility," p. 88.

37. See Kuper, **Passive Resistance in South Africa**, p. 131.

38. E. Franklin Frazier, **Race and Culture Contacts in the Modern World** (Boston: Beacon Press, 1957), pp. 49-50.

39. Bernard J. Stern, "Slavery, Primitive," in **Encyclopedia of the Social Sciences**, (New York: The Macmillan Co., 1934), vol. 14, p. 73.

40. Harvey Seifert, "The Use by American Quakers of Nonviolent Resistance as a Method of Social Change," MS p. 41.

41. Kuper, **Passive Resistance in South Africa**, pp. 84-85.

42. *Ibid.*, p. 89.

43. Lakey, "The Sociological Mechanisms . . . ," pp. 83-84; *Peace Research Reviews,* vol. II, no. 6 (Dec. 1968), pp. 54-55.

44. Kuper, **Passive Resistance in South Africa**, pp. 85 and 89.

45. *Ibid.*, p. 91.

46. Hiller, **The Strike**, p. 170.

47. Kuper, **Passive Resistance in South Africa**, p. 85, and Gandhi, **Non-violent Resistance**, pp. 62-63; Ind. ed.: **Satyagratha**, pp. 62-63.

48. Gregg, **The Power of Nonviolence**, pp. 54-55.

49. Gandhi, **Non-violent Resistance**, p. 294; Ind. ed.: **Satyagraha**, p. 294.

50. Miller, **Nonviolence**, p. 146.

51. Kuper, **Passive Resistance in South Africa**, p. 85.

52. Reitlinger, **The Final Solution**, p. 277.

53. *Ibid.*, pp. 38-39 and 157-158.

54. Seifert, **Conquest by Suffering**, p. 68.

55. Farmer, **Freedom — When?**, pp. 67-68.

56. Solomon and Fishman, "The Psychosocial Meaning of Nonviolence in Student Civil Rights Activities," *Psychiatry*, vol. XXVII (May 1964), p. 97. See also Miller, **Nonviolence** pp. 312-313.

57. Miller, **Nonviolence**, p. 173.

58. McCleery has cited such a case in a Southern prison, where a Negro had defied officials: "In North Carolina, a Negro who had remained defiant through a reported 26 days in 'the hole' (solitary confinement) and repeated beatings was held in high respect by the predominantly Southern, white, members of his

group." Richard H. McCleery, "Authoritarianism and the Belief System of Incorrigibles," in Donald R. Cressey, ed., **The Prison: Studies in Institutional Organization and Change** (New York: Holt, Rinehart and Winston, 1961), p. 283. I am grateful to George Lakey for this reference.

59. Bondurant, **Conquest of Violence,** pp. 46-52.

60. Lindberg, *"Eksempler fra Irland,"* in Lindberg, Jacobsen and Ehrlich, **Kamp Uden Vaaben,** pp. 161-162.

61. Seifert, "The Use by American Quakers of Nonviolent Resistance as a Method of Social Change," pp. 22-54.

62. Jawaharlal Nehru: **An Autobiography,** p. 545.

63. Gandhi, **Non-violent Resistance,** p. 191; Ind. ed.: **Satyagraha,** p. 191.

64. Gregg, **The Power of Nonviolence,** p. 45.

65. *Ibid.*, p. 53. See also p. 78.

66. See Case, **Nonviolent Coercion,** p. 398. Gandhi describes how his wife's resistance and suffering in response to his efforts to dominate her "ultimately made me ashamed of myself, and cured me of my stupidity in thinking that I was born to rule over her, and in the end she became my teacher in non-violence. And what I did in South Africa was but an extension of the rule of satyagraha which she unwillingly practised in her own person." Gandhi, **Non-violence in Peace and War,** vol. I, p. 174.

67. Gregg, **The Power of Nonviolence,** p. 78.

68. *Ibid.*, p. 47. See also p. 133.

69. Bondurant, **Conquest of Violence,** p. 227, Janis and Katz, "The Reduction of Intergroup Hostility," p. 91, and Bose, **Studies in Gandhism,** p. 147, and Bertrand Russell, **Roads to Freedom: Socialism, Anarchism and Syndicalism** (London: Geo. Allen & Unwin, 1918), p. 14.

70. Quoted in Bose, **Selections from Gandhi,** p. 204.

71. King, **Stride Toward Freedom,** p. 177; Br. ed.: p. 207.

72. Gregg, **The Power of Nonviolence,** p. 54.

73. Peck, **Freedom Ride,** p. 75.

74. Gregg, **The Power of Nonviolence,** pp. 45-46.

75. Gandhi, **Non-violence in Peace and War,** vol. I, pp. 128-130.

76. Gregg, **The Power of Nonviolence,** p. 53.

77. *Ibid.*, pp. 44-45.

78. Case, **Non-violent Coercion,** p. 400.

79. Gregg, **The Power of Nonviolence,** pp. 55-56.

80. Lakey, "The Sociological Mechanisms . . ." (thesis), p. 33; *Peace Research Reviews,* vol. II, no. 6 (Dec. 1968), p. 21.

81. Lakey, "The Sociological Mechanisms . . . ," p. 87; *Peace Research Reviews,* vol. II, no. 6, p. 57.

82. Gregg, **The Power of Nonviolence,** p. 83.

83. *Ibid.*, pp. 46-47.

84. *Ibid.*, pp. 52-53.

85. *Ibid.*, p. 46.

86. *Ibid.*, pp. 56-57.

87. *Ibid.*, p. 97.

88. *Ibid.*, p. 73.

89. Gandhi, **Non-violence in Peace and War,** vol. II, p. 64.

90. *Ibid.*, vol. I, p. 178.

91. *Ibid.*, vol. I, p. 180.

92. Gandhi, **Satyagraha in South Africa,** pp. 16-17.

93. Quoted in Sharp, **Gandhi Wields . . . ,** p. 65.

94. Quoted in *ibid.,* p. 117.

95. Gandhi, **Non-violent Resistance,** p. 113; Ind. ed.: **Satyagraha,** p. 113. See also pp. 188-189.

96. *Ibid.,* p. 17.

97. Ebert, "Theory and Practice of Nonviolent Resistance," MS p. 297.

98. Janis and Katz, "The Reduction of Intergroup Conflict," p. 88.

99. Kuper, **Passive Resistance in South Africa,** p. 90. Kuper cites Wolff, ed., **The Sociology of Georg Simmel,** pp. 195-197.

100. Kuper, **Passive Resistance in South Africa,** p. 91.

101. The outline of these eight factors is based upon Janis and Katz, "The Reduction of Intergroup Conflict," p. 86, who based their listing upon Arne Naess' analysis of Gandhi's norms of action. See Naess, "A Systematization of Gandhian Ethics of Conflict Resolution," *Journal of Conflict Resolution*, vol. I (1957), pp. 140-155.

102. Gandhi, **Non-violence in Peace and War,** vol. II, p. 91.

103. Gandhi, **Non-violent Resistance,** p. 154; Ind. ed.: **Satyagraha,** p. 154.

104. Lakey, "The Sociological Mechanisms . . ." (thesis), p. 37; *Peace Research Reviews,* vol. II, no. 6 (Dec. 1968), p. 24.

105. Janis and Katz, "The Reduction of Intergroup Conflict" p. 86.

106. Bondurant, **Conquest of Violence,** pp. 119-120.

107. Miller, **Nonviolence,** p. 168.

108. Gregg, **The Power of Nonviolence,** p. 133.

109. Janis and Katz, "The Reduction of Intergroup Conflict," p. 86.

110. Gandhi, **Non-violent Resistance,** p. 295; Ind. ed.: **Satyagraha,** p. 295.

111. Janis and Katz, "The Reduction of Intergroup Conflict," p. 86.

112. Oppenheimer and Lakey, **A Manual for Direct Action,** pp. 21-22.

113. Gandhi, **Non-violent Resistance,** p. 181; Ind. ed.: **Satyagraha,** p. 181.

114. Quoted in Bose, **Studies in Gandhism,** p. 127.

115. Janis and Katz, "The Reduction of Intergroup Conflict" p. 86.

116. Williams, **The Reduction of Intergroup Tensions,** p. 77.

117. Janis and Katz, "The Reduction of Intergroup Conflict," p. 86.

118. *Ibid.*

119. See Gandhi's letter to Lord Irwin, in Sharp, **Gandhi Wields . . . ,** pp. 61-66.

120. Gregg, **The Power of Nonviolence,** pp. 78 and 55.

121. Janis and Katz, "The Reduction of Intergroup Conflict," p. 86.

122. Bondurant, **Conquest of Violence,** p. 120 n.

123. See Sharp, **Gandhi Wields . . . ,** p. 145.

124. Gregg, **The Power of Nonviolence,** p. 83.

125. Miller, **Nonviolence,** p. 164.

126. Gregg, **The Power of Non-violence,** p. 85.

127. *Ibid.,* pp. 73-76.

128. *Ibid.,* p. 17.

129. Lakey, "The Sociological Mechanisms . . ." (thesis), p. 21; *Peace Research Reviews,* vol. II, no. 6 (Dec. 1968), p. 12.

130. Lakey, "The Sociological Mechanisms . . . ," p. 22; *Peace Research Reviews,* vol. II, no. 6, p. 13. Lakey described this mechanism as "persuasion," interpreted as persuasion to discontinue resistance to the efforts of the nonviolent actionists, rather than persuasion over the demands and issues at stake. In my slightly different interpretation of this mechanism, emphasizing the importance of adjustment to a changed social situation, the term "accommodation" may be more descriptive. See Farmer, **Freedom — When?** p. 41.

131. Williams, **The Reduction of Intergroup Tensions,** p. 14.

132. *Ibid.,* p. 17.

133. Seifert, **Conquest by Suffering,** pp. 73-74.

134. King, **Stride Toward Freedom,** pp. 8 and 140-144; Br. ed.: pp. 10 and 164-168.

135. Sharp, **Gandhi Wields . . . ,** p. 165.

136. *Ibid.,* p. 166.

137. Seifert, "The Use by American Quakers of Nonviolent Resistance as a Method of Social Change," MS p. 94.

138. Lakey, "The Sociological Mechanisms . . ." (thesis), p. 23; *Peace Research Reviews,* vol. II, no. 6 (Dec. 1968), p. 14. For Gandhi's similar view, see Gandhi, **Non-violent Resistance,** p. 121; Ind. ed.: **Satyagraha,** p. 121.

139. Lakey, "The Sociological Mechanisms . . . ," p. 36; *Peace Research Reviews,* vol. II, no. 6, p. 23.

140. Lakey, "The Sociological Mechanisms . . . ," pp. 22-23; *Peace Research Reviews,* vol. II, no. 6, p. 13.

141. Seifert, **Conquest by Suffering,** p. 74.

142. "The Toleration Edict of Galerius, 30 April 311," in J. Stevenson, ed., **A New Eusebius: Documents Illustrative of the History of the Church to A.D. 337** (London: S.P.C.K., 1957), p. 296.

143. See Hans Lietzmann, **From Constantine to Julian** (London: Lutterworth Press, 1960), p. 72. I am grateful to J. D. Kemp for this and the above reference.

144. Seifert, **Conquest by Suffering,** p. 73.

145. Gipson, **The British Empire Before the American Revolution,** vol. XII, **The Triumphant Empire, Britain Sails into the Storm, 1770-1776,** pp. 277-307.

146. Seifert, **Conquest by Suffering,** p. 74.

147. Gipson, **The Coming of the Revolution, 1763-1775,** p. 106.

148. *Ibid.,* p. 107.

149. *Ibid.,* p. 115.

150. Luthuli, **Let My People Go,** p. 177.

151. Gopal, **The Viceroyalty of Lord Irwin, 1926-1931,** p. 91.

152. William Faulkner, **A Fable** (New York: Random House, 1954), p. 54.

153. Gipson, **The British Empire . . . ,** vol. XII, p. 279.

154. See Bondurant, **Conquest of Violence,** pp. 53-64, esp. pp. 60-61 and 64, and Mahadev Desai, **The Story of Bardoli,** esp. pp. 256-263.

155. Farmer, **Freedom — When?** p. 101.

156. In addition to those dictionaries, see Case, **Non-violent Coercion,** p. 403, and Horace M. Kallen, "Coercion," **Encyclopedia of the Social Sciences,** vol. III, pp. 617-619.

157. Theodor Paullin, **Introduction to Non-violence,** p. 6. Philadelphia: Pacifist

Research Bureau, 1944. Paullin defines "force" as "physical or intangible power or influence to effect change in the material or immaterial world." Elliott's definition of "force" is similar: ". . . force need not be limited to physical coercion. Any form of willed compulsion, whether it uses economic means or even moral pressure may become political force if it is used to accomplish political ends." W. Y. Elliott, "Political Force," **Encyclopedia of the Social Sciences** (New York: Macmillan, 1935), Vol. VI, p. 338.

158. Lakey, "The Sociological Mechanisms . . . (thesis), p. 18; *Peace Research Reviews,* vol. II, no. 6 (Dec. 1968), p. 10.

159. Bondurant, **Conquest of Violence,** p. 9.

160. Lakey, "The Sociological Mechanisms . . . ," p. 23; *Peace Research Reviews,* vol. II, no. 6, p. 13.

161. Some believers of nonviolence as a moral principle reject such "nonviolent coercion." Gandhi and some of his interpreters have often argued in these terms, although they have admitted that satyagraha contained a justifiable "compelling element." On Gandhi and "nonviolent coercion," see Bose, **Studies in Gandhism,** pp. 223-224; Dhawan, **The Political Philosophy of Mahatma Gandhi,** pp. 133-134, 254, and 261-266; Shridharani, **War Without Violence,** pp. 291-292, Br. ed.: pp. 249-250; Diwakar, **Satyagraha,** pp. 44 and 61; Bondurant, **Conquest of Violence,** pp. 9-11 and 173; and Johan Galtung and Arne Næss, **Gandhis Politiske Etikk** (Oslo: Tanum, 1955), pp. 223 and 258-259.
On the other hand, it has been argued, by Bondurant, Case and others, that it is precisely the combination of coercion and nonviolence which is so important, and which makes the ideals politically relevant, their achievement possible, and also makes the application of nonviolent means acceptable to people who would otherwise use violence. Case writes: "Perhaps it is only through a working partnership of seemingly incongruous forms of behavior as nonviolence and coercion that the problems of social collision can be permanently solved." (Case, **Non-violent Coercion,** p. 413. See also pp. 3, and 403-404.)

162. Crook, **The General Strike,** p. 165.

163. Keep, **The Rise of Social Democracy in Russia,** p. 222. See also Harcave, **First Blood,** pp. 191-197.

164. Katkov, **Russia 1917, pp. 249, 263-264, 269-276, 278-281, 284, 288, 296, 340-344 and 364.**

165. This is Hiller's phrase. See Hiller, **The Strike,** p. 125.

166. Harcave, **First Blood,** p. 121.

167. Katkov, **Russia 1917,** p. 423.

168. Brant, **The East German Rising,** p. 155.

169. Gandhi, **Non-violent Resistance,** p. 157; Ind. ed.: **Satyagraha,** p. 157. Sometimes specific tactics and methods of nonviolent action are used to make the optimal use of numbers in order to bring about the collapse of the government, as by massive nonviolent raids on government salt depots in India in 1930. "Such a widening of the salt campaign, by substituting collective action for individual breaches of the law, directly challenged the Government's ability to maintain the public peace." Gopal, **The Viceroyalty of Lord Irwin,** p. 70.

170. Schapiro, **The Communist Party of the Soviet Union,** p. 66, and Charques, **The Twilight of Imperial Russia,** pp. 119, 125 and 132. See also, Katkov, **Russia 1917,** p. 262.

171. Gopal, **The Viceroyalty of Lord Irwin,** p. 69.

172. Report of the Nyasaland Commission of Inquiry, p. 74.
173. *Ibid.,* p. 88.
174. Geyl, **The Revolt of the Netherlands (1555-1609),** pp. 55-56.
175. Gandhi, **Non-violent Resistance,** p. 121; Ind. ed.: **Satyagraha,** p. 121. See also Bose, **Selections from Gandhi,** p. 199.
176. Gopal, **The Viceroyalty . . . ,** p. 80.
177. Sternstein, "The *Ruhrkampf* of 1923," p. 114. See also pp. 111, 115, 117, 123, and 132-133.
178. Seton-Watson, **The Decline of Imperial Russia,** p. 214.
179. Schapiro, **The Community Party of the Soviet Union,** pp. 286-308.
180. Dallin, **German Rule in Russia, 1941-1945,** *passim.*
181. Gipson, **The Coming of the Revolution, 1763-1775,** p. 193.
182. Sharp, **Gandhi Wields . . . ,** pp. 190, 179, 200, 210, 189, and 204, respectively.
183. *Ibid.,* p. 179.
184. *Ibid.,* pp. 106, 126-128, 134, 160, 175, 182-183, 190, 192-193, 196, 205, and 211, and Gopal **The Viceroyalty . . . ,** pp. 79-80 and 86-87.
185. Shridharani, **War Without Violence,** p. 24; Br. ed.: p. 43.
186. Gopal, **The Viceroyalty . . . ,** p. 97, based on telegrams of the Viceroy to the Secretary of State.
187. Cited by Kumarappa in "*Young India*", and quoted in Sharp, **Gandhi Wields . . . ,** p. 186.
188. Shridharani, **War Without Violence,** p. 25; Br. ed.: p. 44; Shridharani reports that these figures are based upon the **Statistical Abstract for the United Kingdom** 74th number, and **Trade and Navigation, The United Kingdom.**
189. Shridharani, **War Without Violence,** p. 25, Br. ed.: p. 44.
190. Gandhi, **Non-violent Resistance,** p. 361; Ind. ed.: **Satyagraha,** p. 361.
191. See also Katkov, **Russia 1917,** pp. 262, 274, 276-282, and 340-341.
192. Görlitz, **The German General Staff,** p. 319. See also p. 341.
193. Stefan Brant, **The East German Rising,** pp. 86, 106, 149-153. On the behavior of the East German police and troops, and the Russian troops during the rising, see also Ebert, "Nonviolent Resistance Against Communist Regimes?" pp. 187-190.
194. *Das Parlament* (Bonn), 15 June 1955. Cited in Ebert, "Theory and Practice of Nonviolent Resistance," MS p. 254.
195. Hiller, **The Strike,** p. 233.
196. Symons, **The General Strike,** pp. 224-227.
197. Kuper, **Passive Resistance in South Africa,** pp. 62-63.
198. Symons, **The General Strike,** p. 228.
199. Nehru, **An Autobiography,** p. 360.
200. L. de Jong, "Anti-Nazi Resistance in the Netherlands," in **European Resistance Movements, 1939-1945,** p. 142.
201. Clausewitz, **On War,** vol. I, pp. 249-250.
202. *Ibid.,* pp. 231-234.
203. Gopal, **The Viceroyalty . . . ,** p. 100.
204. Sharp, **Gandhi Wields . . . ,** p. 220.
205. Bose, **Selections From Gandhi,** p. 154. See also p. 153.
206. Opposite views were, for example, offered by Nehru in differing conditions.

THREE WAYS TO SUCCESS

Nehru, **An Autobiography**, pp. 405-406, and Ebert, "Theory and Practice of Nonviolent Resistance," MS pp. 427-430 and 437-439.

207. Gopal, **The Viceroyalty** ..., pp. 97-100 and Sharp, **Gandhi Wields** ..., p. 203.

208. Sharp, **Gandhi Wields** ..., pp. 124, 202 and 207, and Gopal, **The Viceroyalty** ..., pp. 92-94.

209. Sharp, **Gandhi Wields** ..., pp. 220-221.

210. Bondurant, **Conquest of Violence**, pp. 196-197.

211. Sharp, **Gandhi Wields** ..., p. 207.

212. Gopal, **The Viceroyalty** ..., p. 101.

213. Sharp, **Gandhi Wields** ..., p. 206.

214. See *ibid.*, pp. 213-219, or Gopal, **The Viceroyalty** ..., pp. 140-144.

215. Gopal. **The Viceroyalty** ..., pp. 112-113.

216. Liddell Hart, **Strategy: The Indirect Approach**, p. 348.

217. Clausewitz, **On War**, vol. I, pp. 306-307.

218. Nehru, **An Autobiography**, p. 339.

219. See Ebert's discussion of a nonviolent *Blitzkrieg* strategy for use in national defense through prepared nonviolent resistance (civilian defense), in his chapters "Preparations for Civilian Defense" p. 155 and "Initiating Popular Resistance to Totalitarian Invasion," in Mahadevan, Roberts and Sharp, eds., **Civilian Defence: An Introduction**, pp. 159-161.

220. O'Hegarty, **A History of Ireland Under the Union**, p. 487. This discussion draws upon Ebert, "Theory and Practice of Nonviolent Resistance," MS pp. 431-438.

221. Kuper, **Passive Resistance in South Africa**, p. 145.

222. Ebert, "Theory and Practice of Nonviolent Resistence" MS p. 435.

223. Bose, **Selections from Gandhi**, p. 203.

224. Farmer, **Freedom — When?**, pp. 38-39.

225. For some general observations on the role of negotiations in civil rights struggles, see Oppenheimer and Lakey, **A Manual for Direct Action**, pp. 24-25.

226. See Gandhi's view, Bose, **Selections from Gandhi**, p. 187.

227. Halperin, **Germany Tried Democracy**, pp. 181-182.

228. Gregg, **The Power of Nonviolence**, p. 98.

229. *Ibid.*, pp. 61-62, 98, 100-101 and 120. Aldous Huxley argued that the results of nonviolent action were preferable to those of violence because "... the means employed inevitably determine the nature of the result achieved ..." Aldous Huxley, **Ends and Means: An Enquiry into the Nature of Ideals and into the Methods Employed for Their Realization** (New York: Harper Bros., 1937 and London: Chatto and Windhus, 1948), p. 55.

230. Gandhi, **Non-violent Resistance**, p. 31; Ind. ed.: **Satyagraha**, p. 31.

231. King, **Stride Toward Freedom**, p. 148; Br. ed.: p. 174.

14

The Redistribution
of Power

INTRODUCTION

The nonviolent technique of action inevitably has important effects on the nonviolent group itself and on the distribution of power among the contenders in the conflict and within the wider system. These consequences of the technique require consideration. As is the case with all other areas which this study has been exploring, very little research has been carried out on these subjects. This discussion must, therefore, be limited to those effects which are now fairly clear. Further investigation may correct possible errors in our present understanding, reveal other important effects, and explore the complexities of these consequences of nonviolent action.

EFFECTS ON THE NONVIOLENT GROUP

Reference has already repeatedly been made to the fact that the strength of the nonviolent actionists may grow as the struggle proceeds, both in comparison to their earlier strength and to the capacity of their opponent. Although some of this strengthening of the nonviolent group may be temporary, other aspects of this increased internal strength are likely to last. There are also other important effects of the use of this technique. For example, to start with, the people end their submissiveness and learn a technique of action which shows them they are no longer powerless. They are also likely to experience a growth of internal group solidarity. Certain psychological changes will occur which spring from their new sense of power and their increased self-respect. Finally, members of the group which uses nonviolent action seem during and after the struggle to cooperate more on common tasks. We shall now explore these, and related, consequences in more detail.

A. Ending submissiveness

Participation in nonviolent action both requires and produces certain changes in the previous pattern of submissiveness within the grievance group. A change of the opponent's outlook and beliefs may or may not be an objective of the campaign, but some kind of "change of heart" must take place in the nonviolent group and in the wider grievance group. Without it there can be no nonviolent action. Without a change from passive acceptance of the opponent's will, from lack of confidence and helplessness and a sense of inferiority and fear, there can be no significant nonviolent action and no basic transformation of relationships.

Erik Erikson has pointed out the close association between hierarchical systems and the subordinate's view of himself:

> Therapeutic efforts as well as attempts at social reform verify the sad truth that in any system based on suppression, exclusion, and exploitation, the suppressed, excluded, and exploited unconsciously believe in the evil image which they are made to represent by those who are dominant.[1]

As long as members of the subordinate group regard themselves as inferiors, are submissive, and behave in a deferential and humiliating manner to members of the dominant group, repeating the customary habits of acknowledging inferiority (the lowered eyes, and "Yes, sir," for example), they confirm the dominant group's view of them as inferiors and as creatures or persons outside the "common moral order."[2] Submissive behavior by the subordinates helps to support the views which serve to "justify" the established system. Also, such a pattern of submission makes possible the system's continuation, for that behavior helps the system to operate smoothly.

Gregg related this self-image to an inability of subordinates to act to change their condition. He argued that an inferiority complex created in childhood and regularly reinforced in later years is "the most potent of all methods of restraining independent creative action among individuals and masses of people. It makes them feel utterly helpless and in times of crisis it creates a fatal hesitation and lack of confidence."[3] Use of nonviolent action requires at least a partial end to the former pattern of self-deprecation and submission. Gregg has argued that people using nonviolent action also cease to experience such social weaknesses as lack of self-respect, dislike of responsibility, the desire to be dominated, and political and economic ignorance.[4]

B. Learning a technique which reveals one's power

One of the most important problems faced by people who feel that they are oppressed, or that they must oppose dominant "evil" policies and systems, is: *how can they act?* Nonviolent action provides a multitude of ways in which people, whether majorities or minorities, can utilize whatever potential leverage they may possess to become active agents in controlling their own lives. People learn a "new" way of acting which immediately frees them from feelings of helplessness. As the movement develops and they become a formidable force, they become freed from the sense of impotence and they gain confidence in their own power. The specific ways this operates differ with the situation and the leverages utilized—labor, buying power, public sympathy, self-sacrifice, political behavior and the like. But to gain a sense of power, it is often necessary to learn how to use the leverage effectively. As they learned how to strike, industrial workers realized they could act together effectively, instead of being individually helpless. They learned to wield power by withdrawing their labor in order to gain certain objectives from their employers. During the rise of industrialism, workers did not always have this knowledge and ability. They were often unfamiliar with earlier cases of strikes. We frequently forget that this type of nonviolent action also had to be learned, experimented with, and tested in struggle.

As strikes became more widespread the participating workers gained confidence in their ability to improve their lot by their own efforts, and this example stimulated other workers to form unions and similarly to withdraw their labor in case their demands were not met. The workers had to achieve group solidarity, learn how to act, and be willing to undergo temporary suffering during the struggle as the price of winning improvements in their condition and status. These are qualities common to most instances of nonviolent action.

This process among industrial workers took place in a variety of situations and countries. In Russia, for example, industrial workers began to learn the weapon of the strike about 1870.[5] In the following three decades the process which we have described in general terms above occurred. "The modest ameliorations [produced by the strikes] were often in practice nullified by evasion and corruption, but," writes Schapiro, "they taught the workers the important lesson that they could improve their lot by striking."[6] The strikes in the late 1890s not only gave the workers confidence that they could achieve immediate concessions but also made them aware that they possessed the power, given time, to make much more fundamental changes in the system. "By making concessions only when faced with organized force [in the form of strikes], it [the autocracy] nurtured the hope that the fortress could one day be stormed."[7] Strikes became commonplace at the beginning of the 1905 revolution. Although usually spontaneous and unorganized, each strike "helped to impress the 'strike habit' more firmly on Russian workers" and strikes spread.[8] The workers were soon convinced that this was an appropriate form of action for more fundamental changes. The process continued to develop, and in a few months the Great October Strike dramatically demonstrated the increased use of the weapons of noncooperation against the government. Both supporters of strikes and of the autocracy had to take notice of the change which had been introduced.[9]

The success of the noncooperation against the 1920 Kapp *Putsch* gave even the calmest and most responsible labor leaders an unexpected sense of great power (sometimes they forgot the roles in that struggle played by others: civil servants, the Berlin population, etc.). The labor leaders then sought to use this power in bargaining to achieve their own political demands. Despite only partial success in that effort "many workers and their leaders . . . nourished long memories of how effective their weapon had been."[10]

The Indian experiments under Gandhi produced a similar sense of power among nonviolent actionists as they learned a "new" way to act. Gandhi often described a nonviolent action campaign as a means by which the people would generate the strength to enable them to advance toward achieving their political goals.[11] It was through noncooperation, Gandhi said, that people come to realize "their true power."[12] Referring to the experience of the Bardoli revenue-refusal campaign of 1928, he pointed to the importance of the participants learning the lessons "that so long as they remain united in nonviolence they have nothing to fear" and that they could wield "the unseen power of nonviolence." [13] At the beginning of the 1930–31 struggle, Gandhi wrote: "The mission of the Satyagrahis ends when they have shown the way to the nation to become conscious of the power lying latent in it." [14] Gandhi insisted that nonviolent action enables people to feel their own power, and added that "possession of such power *is* independence." [15]

The phenomenon is not new. It occurred also as a result of the American colonists' successful noncooperation campaign against the Townshend Acts (September 1767 to April 1770). Schlesinger writes: "The workingmen had emerged from the struggle against the Townshend duties conscious for the first time of their power in the community." [16] The South African civil disobedience campaign by the Indian minority in 1908 (against registration certificates, similar to the present passes) gave the Indians "some consciousness of their strength." [17] The mutiny of the 2nd Division of the Colonial Infantry (Tenth French Army) in May 1917 gave the defiant soldiers a similar awareness. So many mutinied that they were not generally punished, but were instead talked into returning to the trenches—with the important difference that they were not required to make the almost suicidal attack on German trenches.

> And the soldiers sensed with an ominous thrill that they could defy their officers, could shrug off the faceless inevitability of discipline with near-impunity, could refuse to attack. In short, it was up to the troops themselves whether they would live or die. And, marveling at this simple but heretofore unsuspected truth, they marched forward to share it with the Army. [18]

Reluctant support for this view of the effect of nonviolent struggle came from Lenin who was firmly committed to violence for revolutionary aims. Writing of the impact of the mass strike on the exploited class during the 1905 revolution, Lenin observed that ". . . only the struggle discloses to it the magnitude of its own power . . ." [19]

The capacity of nonviolent action to give the people who use it increased power has been described by Seifert as a general characteristic of the technique. Nonviolent resistance movements, he writes, "have demonstrated that the powerless can wield power and that social means can be democratized." People who have been politically subjugated and economically dispossessed "have accomplished on country roads and city streets" the power changes usually associated "only with paneled board rooms and marble legislative halls." A chief result of resistance campaigns, Seifert continues, has been to "give to disprivileged groups the conviction that there is something they can do about their plight. Nonviolent strategies have given a powerful voice to those otherwise inarticulate." [20]

Individual nonviolent campaigns may be primarily intended to strengthen the subordinate group through the learning and use of nonviolent struggle, even though their avowed objectives are to win concessions from the opponent. The strengthening of the subordinates will be the most fundamental of these changes and have lasting consequences.

C. Increasing fearlessness

That the grievance group needs to cast off fear in order to use nonviolent action effectively has already been discussed. The other side of the story is that experience in the use of nonviolent action tends to increase the degree of fearlessness among the actionists. It may be that initially both fear and anger among nonviolent actionists must be consciously controlled.[21] Discipline and training may assist in this, as they do in military conflict. The nonviolent actionists learn, through explanation, training, example and experience, that they can remain firm in face of the opponent's repression, that he is not omnipotent, even that his violence betrays his weakness.[22] The actionists learn that if they act together and refuse to be terrorized, they are powerful. Imprisonment and other suffering can be withstood. In common with heroes of violent combat, they also risk death as a chance not too high to take on behalf of fundamental principles and goals. Casualties are interpreted as assertions of the dignity and importance of individuals[23] who refuse to bend in face of wrong and who struggle with others to achieve their objectives. Hence, casualties may simply prod the others to make still stronger efforts.

Beyond this conscious discipline there appears, however, to be a stage in which the nonviolent actionists do not have to control their fear because they cease to be fearful. Gandhi has pointed out that in actual cases people who had previously been "fear-stricken" of the government had "ceased to fear" its officials.[24] Interpreting the 1930–31 Indian campaign, Gregg wrote that its activities had been intended to end the fear of the government among the masses and "to stimulate courage, self-reliance, self-respect and political unity." He concluded that these aims had been largely achieved.[25] It might be possible to dismiss the testimony of both Gandhi and Gregg on the ground that, as believers in an ethic of nonviolence, they were not objective observers. However, Nehru, who was never such a believer and only reluctantly came to accept the practicality of nonviolent struggle, pointed to the same effect. He wrote that "the dominant impulse" in British-ruled India was "fear, pervasive, oppressing, strangling fear." Sources of this fear were the army, the police, the widespread secret service, the official class, laws, prisons, the landlord's agents, moneylenders, unemployment and starvation. "It was against this all-pervading fear that Gandhi's quiet and determined voice was raised: Be not afraid." It was not quite so simple, Nehru admitted, but in substance this was accurate. Although "fear builds its phantoms . . . more fearsome than reality itself," the real dangers, when calmly faced and accepted, lose much of their terror. Nonviolent struggle resulted in the lifting to a large degree of that fear from the people's shoulders.[26]

Noncooperation gave the masses "a tremendous feeling of release . . . , a throwing-off of a great burden, a new sense of freedom. The fear that had crushed them retired into the background, and they straightened their backs and raised their heads."[27]

There is evidence that not only masses of people but even individual actionists lose fear in the midst of nonviolent struggle. After being personally beaten by a mounted policeman using a *lathi,* Nehru wrote that he forgot the physical pain in the "exhilaration that I was physically strong enough to face and bear *lathi* blows."[28] Other participants in nonviolent defiance, too, he reported, experienced a growth of inner "freedom and a pride in that freedom. The old feeling of oppression and frustration was completely gone."[29]

Experience in the American nonviolent civil rights movement was similar. As a result of participation in the Montgomery, Alabama, bus boycott, wrote King, "a once fear-ridden people had been transformed."[30] The 1960 sit-ins created, wrote Lomax, a new type of Negro: "They were no longer afraid; their boldness, at times, was nothing short of alarming."[31] Student sit-inners and freedom riders frequently experienced a "strange calm" immediately before especially dangerous actions. Physical injury was feared more than death, and when lives were indeed in danger, the actionists tended to think: "One of us is going to die, I bet, but it's not going to be me; it's going to be him, the next guy." When these student nonviolent actionists did face the prospect of their own deaths, they felt it might arouse sympathy for their cause and they were sometimes inspired by heroes who had died in *violent* campaigns against oppression.[32]

The development of fearlessness is seen both as having important consequences for the personal growth of the individual actionists, as they develop such qualities as self-sacrifice, heroism and sympathy,[33] and also as having far-reaching social and political implications. Absence of fear may not only threaten the particular hierarchical system being opposed. It will greatly enhance the ability of those people to remain free and to determine their own future.

D. Increased self-esteem

If hierarchical systems exist in part because the subordinates submit as a result of seeing themselves as inferiors, the problem of how to change and end the hierarchical system becomes twofold: first, to get the members of the subordinate group to see themselves as full human beings, not inferiors to anyone, and, second, to get them to behave in ways consistent with that enhanced view of themselves, i.e., to resist and defy the patterns of inferiority and subordination.

People who are not, and do not regard themselves as, inferior must not behave as though they were: they must act to refute those conceptions and to challenge the social practices based on those views.[34] Some change of self-perception among at least certain members of the subordinate group must precede action, and further changes or extensions of those changes among more members of the subordinate group are likely to occur as a result of participation in nonviolent struggle.

An improved self-image often must precede action against the stratified system, and indeed an enhanced view often requires such action. When people who have accepted domination come to see their previous submission as unworthy of their new estimate of themselves, they must bring their behavior in line with their enhanced self-image. They must cease cooperation with that system, noncooperate with and disobey its behavior patterns, and the established "rules" which symbolize and perpetuate the inferior status. Self-image and resistance are thus seen to be closely linked. Lakey points out that "there is a tendency for the initiators of campaigns of exploited groups to be persons closest to the exploiting group in status in terms of self-image."[35] This changed behavior by the subordinates may then be important in changing the views of them held by members of the dominant group, who are confronted by behavior which refutes their stereotyped and distorted picture of the subordinate group.

The focus here, however, is primarily on the changes in self-perception which participation in nonviolent struggle has on the nonviolent

PART THREE: DYNAMICS

actionists and other members of the subordinate group. Behavior which itself defies and refutes the former self-image of the subordinates becomes a major factor in spreading and deepening their new enhanced view of themselves. Even the very initiation of action and tackling the underlying conflict may improve the self-image of members of the subordinate group. To many of them it may come as a revelation that they are capable of standing up to the opponent, and that by acting together they become formidable challengers of whom notice must be taken. They then gain a new sense of importance.[36] By their action they throw off and refute the opponent's image of themselves as inferior and stand up to him as equals. They demonstrate courage and determination. Even injuries and deaths incurred in struggle are not viewed as cruelties inflicted on helpless victims but as the price of change paid by determined resisters struggling to alter their present condition and to create their own future. These people who have been subordinates are no longer a passive mass of malleable humanity, but men and women acting powerfully against conditions they oppose. They have learned to rely on themselves, and to shape their own lives.

Willingness to undergo punishment without retaliation does not destroy this new image. There is a crucial difference in the self-esteem of the person who suffers because he is punished for defying a law which he regards as violating his dignity, and he who suffers out of passive acquiescence to the same law which he regards in the same way, as Luthuli said: "Nationalist laws seek to degrade us. We do not consent. They degrade the men who frame them. They injure us—that is something different." [37] Because of the importance of this element, although Indian civil disobedience prisoners in 1930 had been instructed by Gandhi to obey most prison rules, they were not to submit to orders which were "contrary to self-respect," nor would they submit "out of fear." During that campaign the Indians outside of prison refused to cooperate with the British census because, they reasoned, as long as they remained a subject people such a census was in their eyes like a "stocktaking" of "slaves." [38]

Standing up against the opponent and fighting back by *some* means, even if violent ones, may contribute to greater self-respect. For example, Negroes of Washington, D. C. who fought back violently when attacked during the 1919 riots gained increased self-respect.[39] However, there are indications that when the struggle is conducted by nonviolent means the group will gain additional self-respect not only because they are struggling instead of submitting but also because they are acting with means which are seen to be ethically superior.[40] Nehru records, for example, that in the Indian nonviolent struggles the Indians saw their goal and their nonviolent type of struggle as better than the goal and methods of their British rulers, and this gave the Indians "an agreeable sense of moral superiority over our opponents."[41]

An enhanced view of themselves and a new sense of their own importance has been noted among strikers and other nonviolent actionists.[42] Hiller points out that increased self-esteem may result from success.[43] But success is not the only factor, for Hiller also indicates, as does Lakey,[44] that even when the nonviolent group is not successful, increased self-confidence and less inner tension tend to develop.[45]

The capacity of nonviolent action to change the participants themselves was, writes James Farmer, one of the reasons why the early Congress of Racial Equality (C.O.R.E.) concentrated on nonviolent direct action projects instead of working for new laws and court decisions:

> CORE . . . wanted to involve the people . . . personally in the struggle for their own freedom . . . [I]n the very act of working for the impersonal cause of racial freedom, a man experiences . . . a large measure of private freedom . . . which, if not the same thing as freedom, is its radical source.

Having described a courageous initial attempt at nonviolent defiance by Negroes of Plaquemine, Louisiana, Farmer pointed to a change within them:

> Gradually, during . . . those two violent days, they made the decision to act instead of being acted upon . . . [They] refused to be victimized any longer by the troopers, [and] had been transformed into a community of men, capable, despite the severest limitations, of free and even heroic acts. Their subsequent activity at the polls and in initiating a school boycott suggests that this kind of freedom, though essentially personal, will inevitably lead to social action, and that freedom once won is not readily surrendered.[46]

Nehru described the change wrought by Gandhi on the Indian millions as one "from a demoralized, timid and hopeless mass, bullied and crushed by every dominant interest, and incapable of resistance, into a people with self-respect and self-reliance, resisting tyranny, and capable of united action and sacrifice for a larger cause.[47] Describing a similar change among the fifty thousand Negroes of Montgomery, Alabama, during the year-long bus boycott, King wrote that they "acquired a new estimate of their own human worth."[48] Seen in this context certain instances of Gandhi's moralizing have strong political implications. He insisted on dignity, discipline and restraint which would bring the Indians self-respect. Their self-respect would bring them the respect of others, and this would bring them freedom. "To command respect is the first step to *Swaraj* [self-rule]."[49]

The growth of self-esteem, with its impact on the opponent, the subordinate group, and the ability and determination of that group to defy the behavior patterns of inferiority, may have highly significant long term consequences.

E. Bringing satisfaction, enthusiasm and hope

Despite the dangers and hardships encountered in the struggle, non-violent actionists may find the overall experience a satisfying one. The precise source of the satisfaction has varied, but it has occurred in diverse cases, including the pro-Jewish strikers of Amsterdam in February 1941:

> To those who had participated, the strike provided a sense of relief, since it represented an active repudiation of the German regime. . . . In the strike the working population of Amsterdam had discovered its own identity in defiance of the occupying power.[50]

Tens of thousands of British citizens found the 1926 General Strike to be "the most enjoyable time of their lives."[51] A high society lady from Washington, D.C., who supported woman suffrage by doing picket duty, maintained that "no public service she had ever done gave her such an exalted feeling."[52] In England, woman suffragist public demonstrations had a similar effect on the actionists; Mary Winsor wrote that "to make women feel at ease in the streets of the city helped to break the sex dominance that man had set up."[53] Nehru wrote: "In the midst of strife, and while we ourselves encouraged that strife, we had a sense of inner peace."[54]

Of similar experiences in the United States, Farmer has observed that tens of thousands of young Negroes who participated in marches, sit-ins, or went to jail experienced "the joys of action and the liberating effect" of working to determine their own future. Consequently, "they began to regard themselves differently." ". . . men must achieve freedom for themselves. Do it for them and you extinguish the spark which makes freedom possible and glorious . . ." The many Negroes who participated in the nonviolent civil rights movement, Farmer continued, achieved "a measure of spiritual emancipation" which no legal document could give them: "The segregation barriers . . . . have ceased to be an extension of their minds . . . They do not feel inferior . . . We feel dignified . . ." People who had formerly felt little and insignificant changed as a result of taking part in nonviolent struggle, he reports, so that afterwards they "in their own eyes, stand ten feet tall." Farmer quotes a student in Atlanta: "I, myself, desegregated that lunch counter on Peachtree Street. Nobody else. I did it by sitting-in, by walking the picket line, by marching. I didn't have to wait for any big shots to do it for me. I did it myself." Farmer adds: "Never again will that youth and the many like him see themselves as unimportant." [55]

Participants in nonviolent action may also experience increased enthusiasm, dedication and hope.[56] Luthuli concluded that the 1952 Defiance Campaign in South Africa "had succeeded in *creating* among a very large number of Africans the spirit of militant defiance. The Campaign itself came to an untimely end, but it left a new climate, and it embraced people far beyond our range of vision. Since then there have been a number of unexpected demonstrations, especially among women." Luthuli goes on to cite several instances in which Africans after that campaign was over applied nonviolent action and "the refusal to comply" because they had caught the "mood" of the campaign "and sometimes its technique." [57]

The 1962 civil rights campaign among Mississippi Negroes (which consisted largely of the "freedom registration" and "freedom ballot") "energized Negroes who had never before dreamed of participating in their state's political process . . ."[58] The 1961 Freedom Riders "went back to their homes with a deep and abiding commitment to the movement of the sort that only direct participation can inspire." The gains that were won through nonviolent action also produced a "sense of possibility . . . in the ghetto."[59] Hope was restored, or perhaps born.

Lenin was no friend of nonviolent action, but in his "Lecture on the 1905 Revolution" he acknowledged the role which some methods of this technique played in radically altering the attitudes of the masses. Before January 9, 1905 the revolutionary party in Russia, he writes, "consisted of a small handful of people . . ." Within a few months "slumbering Russia became transformed into a Russia of a revolutionary proletariat and a revolutionary people." How had this transformation come about? What were its methods and ways? Lenin had no doubt, although the answer was contrary to his elitist conception of revolution. "The principal means by which this transformation was brought about was the *mass strike."* The social content of that 1905 revolution, he wrote, was a *"bourgeois-democratic* revolution" but "in its methods of struggle it was a *proletarian* revolution." It was this type of action which had made the change: ". . . the specifically proletarian means of struggle—namely, the strike—was the principal instrument employed for rousing the masses . . ." This struggle had imbued the masses with "a new spirit." "Only the struggle educates the exploited class." Only struggle reveals to that class the extent of its own power, while it also "widens its horizon, enhances its abilities, clarifies its mind, forges its will . . ." Even reactionaries had to admit, concluded Lenin, that the year 1905 had "definitely buried patriarchal Russia." [60]

F. Effects on aggression, masculinity, crime and violence

Participation in nonviolent action has at times reversed or demonstrated a reversal of the usual assumed relationships between nonviolent behavior and human aggressiveness, masculinity, crime and future violence.

The use of nonviolent struggle by multitudes of ordinary people should make it clear beyond dispute both that human beings are not by nature too aggressive to use such means, and that human aggressiveness can be expressed nonviolently. It is fairly obvious that aggressiveness and feelings of hostility may be expressed in economic boycotts which inflict financial losses on the opponent, and that demonstrators who sit down in the street may realize that by this nonviolent act they are being more difficult to deal with than if they had used violence. There are also indications that the show of friendliness toward opponents may be associated with contempt for them, and that even extreme gestures of humanity in nonviolent action may at times derive from feelings of aggressiveness. Solomon and Fishman point to this association in their studies of American student civil rights actionists: "The friendliness of demonstrators toward their foes . . . sometimes is displayed at moments when the students *feel* the most hostile and contemptuous." They cite an instance in which a member of the American Nazi Party, carrying and shouting extremely offensive racial expressions, taunted a civil rights picket line near Washington, D.C. One student demonstrator wanted for the first half hour to hit the Nazi, but for the sake of the movement he didn't. Then, the student started smiling at the Nazi every time he saw him. In a quarter of an hour, the Nazi started smiling back, but then felt ridiculous for not hating the student enough, got mad, and left. That student had found in other cases also that friendly behavior to hecklers made them "quite exasperated at themselves." He adopted a Mississippi journalist's motto: "I always love my enemies because it makes them mad as hell." [61]

Nonviolent action has also been used by groups which have been famous for their very aggressive behavior and violence. Bondurant points to the case of the Pathans, in the North-West Frontier Province of British India. She quotes William Crooke's observation of their nature, published in 1896: "The true Pathan . . . is cruel, bloodthirsty and vindictive in the highest degree . . . . He leads a wild, free, active life in the rugged fastnesses of his mountains; and there is an air of masculine independence about him . . ." Bondurant quotes others who have said that war has traditionally been the "normal business of the land" among the Pathans, who had "no hesitation to kill when the provocation causes sufficient wrath." It should also be noted that the Pathans were Muslims, adherents of a religion widely regarded as approving of war for a good cause. Yet among these Pathans, Khan Abdul Ghaffar Khan, "the Frontier Gandhi," organized a powerful movement of the Khudai Khidmatgar, or Servants of God, which was pledged to complete nonviolence and whose members became some of the bravest and most daring and reliable nonviolent resisters of India's struggle for independence. Bondurant writes: "The achievement of the Khudai Khidmatgar was nothing less than the reversal in attitude and habit of a people steeped in the tradition of factious violence . . . . The instrument for this achievement was a Pathan version of satyagraha." [62] It seems clear from this extremely important case that there was no basic change in the "human nature" of the Pathans, but that the aggressiveness, bravery and daring of those people found new nonviolent expressions through the nonviolent technique.

Jerome D. Frank, Professor of Psychiatry at Johns Hopkins University, writes that nonviolent action struggles have also broken "the psychological link between masculinity and violence, thus circumventing one of the major psychological supports for war." He points to Kenneth Boulding's "First Law": "What exists, is possible." Frank continues: "Nonviolent action exists and has succeeded under some circumstances, and this alone destroys the contention that nonviolent methods of conflict are hopelessly at variance with human nature." The Indian campaigns under Gandhi and the American nonviolent civil rights struggles, in very different societies with quite unlike traditions,

> . . . have reversed the relationship between masculinity and violence, and shown that this may be based more on cultural expectations than on the usually assumed biology of maleness. They suc-

ceeded in establishing group standards in which willingness to die rather than resort to violence was the highest expression of manly courage.

Frank cites as supporting evidence the findings of two studies of participants in the American sit-in movements and Freedom Rides, which ". . . have revealed that by refusing to resort to violence, the participants gain a heightened feeling of manliness and a sense of moral superiority over their opponents, who in effect, act out their own aggressive impulses for them." [63]

Nonviolent action may also help reduce crime and other anti-social behavior among the general grievance group. At the end of the Montgomery, Alabama, Negro bus boycott, King observed a decline in heavy drinking, crime and divorce among the Negroes, and in the number of fights on Saturday nights. [64] Others reported the same trend from other cities. Hentoff wrote:

> Significantly, again and again in recent years, when a large section of a Negro community has been caught up in a movement against discrimination, the crime rate in that community has gone down and remained down so long as mass action continues. [65]

Mrs. Gloria Richardson, Chairman of the Cambridge, Maryland, Non-Violent Action Committee, said in 1963:

> It's funny, but during the whole time we were demonstrating actively, there were almost no fights in this ward and almost no crime. . . . Now they've gone back to fighting each other again. They've been thrown back to carrying a chip on their shoulder. [66]

Farmer cited both the above cases also, pointing in addition to Jackson, Mississippi, which before the 1961 Freedom Rides had "a shocking incidence of petty and violent crime of Negro against Negro. When the Freedom Buses came, the city united in support and the crime rate dropped precipitately." He added: "Whenever people are given hope and the technique to get the heel off their necks, crime will decline." [67] Solomon and Fishman also cited reports of sharp decline in crime and delinquency during public protest campaigns, noting generally: "The movement provides a release of pent-up resentment and anger in a socially and politically advantageous and morally superior manner. . ." [68] There has also been a psychiatric study on this result of nonviolent action. [69]

Participation in nonviolent action, under some circumstances at least, may contribute to an extension of the areas of life in which the person may feel able to act nonviolently, instead of violently, and to an increased sympathy for nonviolence as an overall moral principle. Lakey reports changes among participants in the sit-in movement in the Deep South: some began taking part while being rather hostile and aggressive persons, but later came gradually to "accept the Gandhian values of nonviolent action as a part of their everyday behavior."[70] This is in line with Gregg's view that "in actual life action often precedes and clarifies thought and even creates it."[71] Similar developments in some individual participants of the British Committee of 100 civil disobedience demonstrations were reported.

Of course, such changes may not take place at all, or if they do, they may occur only among a small percentage of the actionists; this will depend on various factors. Given sufficient time and favorable experiences (not necessarily pleasant ones), such changes are likely, however, among *some* of the participants. A process of "emotional relearning" may take place in which, by testing out a new way of behaving, the actionist learns that his earlier fears about the consequences of nonviolent behavior may not in fact materialize.[72] Janis and Katz have suggested that the prospect of taking part in a future act of violence in a conflict situation may produce at least a small degree of anticipatory guilt feelings, and hence emotional tension; they add that this inner tension may be reduced by a group decision to abstain from violence and to use "an effective form of nonviolent action instead." They argued that even when the group's approval of nonviolent behavior is only lip service, that approval may increase the individual's self-esteem concerning his own adherence to nonviolence. The combination of this reduced inner tension and this increase in self-esteem for his own nonviolence, may make the individual increasingly sympathetic to nonviolent behavior more generally.

If each act of abstention [from violence] is rewarded in this way, a new attitude will gradually tend to develop such that the person becomes increasingly more predisposed to decide or vote in favor of nonviolent means. Perhaps under these conditions, good moral "practice makes perfect."

Even where success is ambiguous, they argued, this type of process is likely to take place among those members of the group "who have a relatively low need for aggression," and people who, without thinking, formerly accepted violent methods may instead accept nonviolent methods for dealing with opponents.

Other factors and processes are of course involved in such a change. Just as the person may have inner hesitations about using violence, he may also be apprehensive about using nonviolent means only, Janis and Katz continued. Such a pressure against nonviolence may arise, for example, from the widely accepted view that violence is the only suitable response in severe conflicts, or from such a question as "Am I a sissy?" The person using nonviolent action may therefore have to justify to himself his participation in a campaign which rejects violence or withdraw from the struggle. Janis and Katz have argued that the process set in motion by this is likely to "contribute to two types of attitude change: 1) reduced hostility toward the rival group, and 2) more favorable evaluations of the desirability of using positive [i.e., nonviolent] means in general." [73] Gregg argued that nonviolent action is also less exhausting and requires less emotional energy than violence:[74] if so, this factor too may make the nonviolent actionist sympathetic to use of non-violent methods in other areas of his life.

There may also be certain social-psychological effects of adherence to nonviolent methods on the group as a whole. Janis and Katz have suggested that reliance on nonviolent action may strengthen the group's commitment to its avowed goal, whereas reliance on violence may lead to the original goals being abandoned and to other "corrupting" effects.[75]

On a more conscious and rational level, participation in nonviolent action may convince people that such behavior may be practical and effective in conflicts in which they have presumed only violence to "work." Moral imperatives to refrain from violence—contained in various philosophical and religious systems to which lip-service is widely paid—are often violated because people believe that nonviolent behavior is not practical in serious social, political and international conflicts.[76] If people become convinced by participation, observation and new knowledge that nonviolent action is practical, it may be used in more serious conflict situations, and the tension between a desire to adhere to a nonviolent ethic and a wish to be effective in real conflicts may be reduced or removed. This process will not, of course, operate unless concrete and practical nonviolent courses of action are worked out to deal with each conflict situation.

G. Increased group unity

The effectiveness of nonviolent action is increased when the actionists and the general grievance group possess a high degree of internal unity. In addition, the use of nonviolent action in itself contributes significantly to the growth of such internal solidarity. This growth has often been seen in the labor movement. Conflict, said Hiller, "solidifies the group." "Under attack, strikers perceive the identity of their interests." Comradeship is generated in the group during the conflict and a feeling of elation is produced by acting with the whole group. "Mutual stimulation increases the readiness to act." [77]

There is evidence that the nonviolent actionists are likely to find it easier to achieve and maintain group unity than is the opponent group; and also easier than if they use violent means. Violence is likely to exclude certain persons from full participation, both because of age, sex, physical condition and the like, and because of beliefs, or simple distaste and revulsion against the use of violence in the conflict.

For example, there was much greater unity among the American colonists during the predominantly nonviolent campaigns against English laws and policies than there was later, after the struggle had shifted to a military confrontation. The Morgans point out that the colonies had never been able to unite for any purpose, even against the French and Indians in war, prior to the Stamp Act struggle. Not only did the Stamp Act Congress show this unity: the solidarity of merchants in several cities in supporting nonimportation agreements, despite temptations to profit by violating them, was also new. A proposal for an intercolonial union was making rapid progress when the Stamp Act was repealed. Joseph Warren in March 1766 wrote that Grenville's legislation had produced ". . . what the most zealous Colonist never could have expected. The Colonies until now were ever at variance and foolishly jealous of each other, they are now . . . united . . . nor will they soon forget the weight which this close union gives them." [78] Further noncooperation followed, and greater unity among the colonies. This unity grew, so that during the deliberations of the First Continental Congress in 1774 (which drafted the most ambitious noncooperation campaign yet), Patrick Henry of Virginia was able to declare: "The Distinctions between Virginians, Pennsylvanians, New Yorkers, and New Englanders, are no more. I am not a Virginian, but an American." [79]

The initial period of the 1905 Revolution in Russia, which was significantly more nonviolent than the concluding period, produced a "strong feeling of camaraderie and unity," wrote Harcave. It was possible to achieve a common front uniting everyone from revolutionaries to conservatives against the regime, under the limited but common conviction that it was impossible to continue without change.[80] It was under the program urged by Gandhi and the application of nonviolent action to achieve independence that the Indian National Congress was transformed from a very small group of intellectuals who met for discussions and consideration of resolutions once a year into a mass membership political party engaged in active struggle with the British Empire. During this same period, despite diverse linguistic, cultural and religious groups, very considerable if inadequate steps were taken in developing Indian unity. The 1952 South African Defiance Campaign also saw increased solidarity and a sense of power among the nonwhites. The various nonwhite Congresses were strengthened, and in particular the number of paid members of the African National Congress jumped from seven thousand at the beginning of the campaign to one hundred thousand at the end.[81] The South African 1957 bus boycott by Alexandra township Africans also produced similar effects. African National Congress leader Walter Sisulu said later that "the bus boycott has raised the political consciousness of the people and has brought about a great solidarity and unity among them."[82] Repeatedly, the use of nonviolent action against racial discrimination and segregation in the United States led to a significant increase in Negro unity. The June 1963 Boston Negro boycott of the public schools, in protest against *de facto* racial segregation, produced this result, as Noel Day, one of its leaders, pointed out: "The boycott was a success in terms of getting the Negro community organized for action. It was never as united before the boycott as it has been since."[83] Feelings of group unity are closely associated with increased cooperation, self-help and organization within the grievance group.

H. Increased internal cooperation

The withdrawal of cooperation from the opponent and his system by nonviolent actionists does not lead simply to chaos and disorganization. On the contrary, such noncooperation and defiance are balanced by increased cooperation within the grievance group in general and among the nonviolent actionists in particular. The effective conduct of a nonviolent action movement requires considerable organization, cooperation and self-help.

At the same time, increased cooperation within the grievance group is required in order to provide alternative ways of meeting those social needs formerly met by the institutions with which cooperation has been now refused. The reverse side of noncooperation is cooperation, and that of defiance is mutual aid. These make it possible both to preserve social order and to meet social needs during and following a nonviolent action movement. Without such positive efforts, even though the nonviolent action were effective and successful—which is doubtful—the result would be social chaos and collapse which would lead the way toward quite different results than those intended by the nonviolent group, unless there were a prompt resumption of cooperation under the old system. The alternative arrangements for preserving social order and meeting human needs depend upon the willingness of the grievance group to give them their cooperation and to make them a success.

The close relationship between noncooperation and cooperation was repeatedly emphasized by Gandhi:

> The movement of non-cooperation is one of automatic adjustment. If the Government schools are emptied, I would certainly expect national schools to come into being. If the lawyers as a whole suspended practice, they would devise arbitration courts . . . [84]

Bondurant makes the same point: ". . . the non-cooperation of satyagraha has the necessary concomitant of cooperation among the resisters themselves . . . for establishing a parallel social structure, [and] also in . . . conversion of the system against which the group is resisting." [85]

This building up of cooperation to fulfill the social needs formerly met by the opponent's institutions is illustrated by the Montgomery bus boycott. With the decision of the Negroes to refuse to ride on the segregated buses, fifty thousand people were left without a public transportation system. This was one of the first problems to be tackled by the planning committee. Through a series of efforts, they established a highly efficient alternative transportation system. The importance of this rival institution was clearly recognized by the city officials who made repeated efforts to crush it. [86]

There is considerable variation in the degree to which this balancing of noncooperation with cooperation is consciously developed or just "happens" without advance consideration. There are even some cases in which a broad program of social change and development based on this developing cooperation has been thought out and deliberately promoted to take place both between and during nonviolent action struggles. A whole series of alternative national Hungarian cultural, educational, economic and political institutions were built up during Hungarian opposition to Austrian rule in the mid-nineteenth century, especially during the passive resistance phase from about 1850 to 1867. It is clear that these alternative institutions were important in the continuation of Hungary as a nation and in its ability to resist domination from Vienna.[87]

In India, Gandhi also developed his "constructive program"[88] on the need for parallel substitute institutions to replace those of the opponent. With this theory and program, new institutions and social patterns need not wait for the capture of State machinery: far better, they could be initiated immediately, Gandhi maintained. Social "evils" were to be attacked directly by nonviolent action when necessary. Along with such struggle, however, had to go the broader educational and institutional work, a balancing cooperation to meet social needs. To the extent that there is support for this constructive program and that it succeeds, the new efforts will gradually weaken and replace the former system. Also in Gandhi's view, as it showed results that constructive program would increase support for the resistance movement by showing that change was both desirable and possible. Gandhi constantly pressed for constructive work, both between and during direct action struggles. He believed it helped to train volunteers, to educate the masses, and was a necessary accompaniment to all nonviolent action struggles except in cases of a local specific common grievance.[89]

Both Gandhi and the Hungarians in the mid-nineteenth century apparently had an explicit theory about the need for alternative social institutions. However, even in the absence of such theories, nonviolent action struggles tend to be accompanied by increased cooperation within the grievance group expressed in organizational, institutional and often economic forms. Some type of compensating process seems to be involved: noncooperation with certain institutions tends to produce increased alternative cooperation with other institutions, even if these have to be created especially for the purpose.

Economic noncooperation campaigns by American colonists against England, for example, led to strong efforts to build up American self-sufficiency in both agriculture and manufactures.[90] Strikes and political noncooperation in the Russian Empire in 1905 were balanced by a growth of organizational strength among the revolutionaries, especially among trade unions and the creation of *soviets* (councils) as institutions of direct popular government.[91] A logical consequence of this development of internal cooperation and of alternative institutions for meeting social needs and maintaining social order in a revolutionary situation is dual sovereignty and parallel government.

I. Contagion

When nonviolent action is used with at least moderate effectiveness, the technique will tend to spread. The same people may use it again under other circumstances, and the example set may be followed by other people in quite different circumstances. This effect of contagion is not unique to nonviolent action—political violence too seems to be contagious—but the spread of nonviolent action is important, especially because that technique enhances the power of the nonviolent actionists. Those consequences, as we shall see, are different from those of political violence.

The royal governors of American colonies claimed that it was the contagious example of Boston's initial defiance of the Stamp Act (not strictly nonviolently) which had set off resistance in their colonies, too, and produced the situation in which no one was willing and able to put the Act into operation on November 1, 1765, when it was to come into force. Reports which exaggerated the radical nature of resistance in Virginia led to resistance in other colonies more extreme than had actually occurred in Virginia.[92]

Success in achieving repeal of the Stamp Act paved the way for the colonists to use comparable methods when facing new grievances, such as the Townshend taxes. The very influential "Letters from a Farmer in Pennsylvania" (authored anonymously by John Dickinson) reminded the American colonists of the previous effectiveness of their legislative petitions and nonimportation agreements, and urged that those means of protest be revived against the new Townshend Acts. Arthur Schlesinger wrote: "These articles were read everywhere and helped to prepare the public mind for the mercantile opposition of the next few years."[93]

This additional colonial experience with noncooperation made possible in turn the development of a more comprehensive program of such resistance embodied in the Continental Association, adopted by the First Continental Congress. It was, wrote Schlesinger, in part "the standardization and nationalization of the systems of commercial opposition which had hitherto been employed on a local scale." There was, however, a significant difference, for initiative and control had been seized by the radicals, who were now using the weapons which the merchant class had earlier developed and used for their own purposes; the radicals "had now reversed the weapons on them in an effort to secure ends desired solely by the radicals."[94]

There were repeated instances during the 1905 Revolution in which strikes and other forms of struggle spread by imitation. Small successes from strikes earlier in the year led to expansion of trade union organizations and more use of strikes. Similarly, limited political successes have sometimes prodded resisters and revolutionaries to press on to larger objectives. The Tsar's October Manifesto which granted civil liberties and a limited *Duma,* wrested from the Tsar by the Great October Strike which had paralyzed the country and the government, convinced the revolutionaries that they had the power to press on. The majority considered, Harcave reported, that they had won "a preliminary victory" which should be followed "by a final assault on autocracy." [95]

To my knowledge, studies have not been made specifically on the contagion effect of the nonviolent technique. However this contagion seems to operate even across national borders and around the world as descriptions of nonviolent struggles are relayed by radio, television and newspapers. Printed accounts in books or pamphlets may also serve a similar purpose at times. When nonviolent struggles are failures, contagion is not likely to occur; but when successes follow each other nonviolent action may spread and the use of the technique may multiply almost geometrically.

J. Conclusion

The bulk of the earlier analysis in this Part was focused on the dynamics of nonviolent struggle in terms of its effects on the opponent. That is obviously an extremely important aspect of the technique. However, as the discussion in this section has shown, the effects of this technique on its practitioners are far-reaching and in light of the analysis of power on which this technique rests, may in the long run be the most important. For if people are strong and know how to resist effectively, it becomes difficult or impossible for anyone to oppress them in the first place. Future analysis of the dynamics of nonviolent action may, therefore, give more attention to the changes the technique produces among the nonviolent actionists than to the immediate effects on the opponent. The strengthening of the grievance group is bound to alter power relationships in lasting ways.

DIFFUSED POWER AND THE NONVIOLENT TECHNIQUE

Tocqueville pointed out that a society needs strong social groups and institutions capable of independent action and able to wield power in their own right; when necessary, these may act to control the power of the established government or any possible domestic or foreign usurper. If such groups (*loci* -or places-of power) are not present to a significant degree, it may prove extraordinarily difficult or impossible for that society to exercise control over its present ruler, to preserve its constitutional system, and to defend its independence.[96] People are better able to act together against the ruler or usurper when they can act through groups, organizations and other institutions than when each person is isolated from all others, and no group of them has collective control over any of the sources of the power of the State.

According to this view, lasting capacity for popular control of political power, especially in crises, requires the strengthening of such nongovernmental groups and institutions in the normal functioning of the society in order that in crises they will be able to control the sources of political power, and therefore control rulers who do not wish to be controlled. In this establishment of effective control over the political power of rulers, questions of social organization and of political technique converge.

There may be a causal connection between the relative concentration or diffusion of power in the society and the technique of struggle, or final sanction, relied upon by that society to maintain the social system or to change it. Political violence and nonviolent action may produce quite different effects on the future concentration of power in the society. Therefore, the choice between the various political techniques will become that society's ultimate sanction and technique of struggle and may help to determine the future capacity of that society to exercise popular control over any ruler or would-be ruler.

This brief discussion necessarily deals in broad generalizations and tendencies, which may not give full appreciation to the complexities of a given case. It may be remembered not only that many other factors may be operating in a given situation, but that under particular conditions the tendencies discussed here might not be realized.

A. Violence and centralization of power

It has been widely recognized that violent revolutions and wars have been accompanied and followed by an increase both in the absolute power of the State and in the relative centralization of power in its hands. This recognition has by no means been limited to opponents of political violence and centralization. Following successful violent revolutions, the new ruler may in some cases behave in a more humanitarian and self-restrained way than the former regime, but this is not always so, and there is nothing in the new structure which requires it. Furthermore, the increased power of the new government frequently puts the general populace in a more unfavorable position to exert control over it in the future than the populace was under the old regime. The weakening of other social groups and institutions and the concentration of increased power in the hands of the State—whoever might hold the position of ruler—thus generally has not brought to the subjects increased ability to control political power. This process, Jouvenel has argued, laid the foundation for the monolithic State.[97]

The centralizing effect of conventional war has similarly been widely recognized. This has been especially obvious in the twentieth century, but the tendency was apparent earlier.[98] Technological changes and the breakdown of the distinction between civilians and the armed forces have accentuated this tendency. Effective mobilization of manpower and other resources into an efficient war machine, the necessity of centralized planning and direction, the disruptive effect of dissension, the need for effective control over the war effort, and the increase in the military might which is available to the government, all contribute to the strong tendency of modern war to concentrate more and more effective power in the hands of the ruler—whoever occupies that position. There seems to be a causal connection between the use of political violence and the increased centralization of power in the government. Political violence, therefore, even when used against a particular tyrant, may contribute to increased difficulties in controlling the power of future rulers of that society and in preventing or combatting future tyranny.

There are various factors in the dynamics of political violence which appear to influence this connection; all of these seem to be aggravated by modern developments in technology and political organization. For example, centralized control of the preparations for and the waging of violence is generally necessary if the violence is to be applied efficiently. In order to provide control over the preparations and waging of violence, centralized control of the weapons (and other material resources), the active combatants, and the groups and institutions on which these depend, is also required.

The combination of all these types of control means increased power before and during the struggle for those exercising that control. The controllers will also be able to use violence against the population to maintain that control. After a successful violent struggle, the group which controlled the conduct of the struggle, and which now controls the State, is likely to retain at least most of the power which they accumulated during the conflict. Or, if a *coup d'etat* takes place, others will obtain control of that increased power. In addition, when violent revolutionaries take over the old State, now strengthened by the additional centralized power accumulated by them during the violent conflict, the overall effective power of the new ruler will be increased, compared to that of the old one.

Furthermore, the power of the State is likely also to be increased relatively as a result of the destruction or weakening during the struggle of the effective *loci* of power—the independent institutions and social groups. The combination of an increase in the power of the State and a weakening of the *loci* of power among the people will leave the subjects under the new regime relatively weakened *vis à vis* the ruler, compared with their condition before the change. In addition, the new regime which was born out of violence will require continued reliance on violence, and therefore centralization, to defend itself from internal and external enemies. In a society where subjects and ruler alike regard violence as the only kind of power and the only effective means of struggle, the subjects may feel helpless in face of a ruler which possesses such vast capacity to wield political violence. Technological developments in modern weaponry, communications, police methods, transportation, computers and the like all contribute to the further concentration of control of effective political violence and to a diminution of what can be called freedom or democracy. All these various factors and related ones may thus help to reduce the capacity of subjects to control political power in a society which has relied upon violence as its supreme sanction and technique of struggle.

B. Nonviolent action and decentralization of power

Nonviolent action appears to have quite different long term effects on the distribution of power in the society. Not only does this technique lack the centralizing effects of political violence, but nonviolent action appears by its very nature to contribute to the diffusion of effective power throughout the society. This diffusion, in turn, is likely to make it easier in the long run for the subjects to control their ruler's exercise of power in the future. This increased potential for popular control means more freedom and more democracy.

There are several reasons why widespread use of nonviolent action in place of political violence tends to diffuse power among the subjects.

These reasons have to do with the greater self-reliance of the people using the technique, as related to leadership, weapons, the more limited power of the post-struggle government, and the reservoir capacity for nonviolent struggle which has been built up against future dangers.

Leadership in nonviolent struggle, although important, is an unstable and often temporary phenomenon, while the dynamics of the technique promote and even require greater self-reliance among the participants. The chances of continuing domination by a leadership group are thereby drastically reduced. Although strong leadership may play an important role in initiating the movement and setting its strategy, as the struggle develops the populace takes up its dominant role in carrying out the noncooperation or defiance, and the original leadership is often imprisoned or otherwise removed by the opponent. A continuing central leadership group then ceases to be so necessary or even possible in many situations. The movement thus tends to become self-reliant, and in extreme situations effectively leaderless. Under severe repression, efficiency in nonviolent action requires that the participants be able to act without reliance on a central leadership group.

A nonviolent struggle movement cannot be centrally controlled by regulation of the supply and distribution of weapons to the combatants and populace, because in nonviolent action there are no material weapons. There are, it is true, a multitude of nonviolent "weapons"—the many specific methods examined in Chapters Three to Eight—but their availability cannot be centrally controlled. The nonviolent actionists depend not on weapons which can be restricted or confiscated or ammunition which may not be freely available, but on such qualities as their bravery, ability to maintain nonviolent discipline, skill in applying the technique and the like. These qualities and skills are likely to develop with use, so that during and at the end of a nonviolent struggle the populace is likely to be more self-reliant and powerful than in a violent struggle when the fighting forces are dependent on the supply of equipment and ammunition. This is important for the distribution of power in the post-struggle society, for people who have, or believe they have, no independent capacity for struggle are likely to be treated by elites as a passive populace to be controlled and acted upon, not as people capable of wielding effective power for their own objectives.

Irving L. Janis and Daniel Katz have suggested that the choice of violent action or nonviolent action may also have significant effects on the *type* of leadership likely to arise in the movement, to be perpetuated in it, and to carry over into the post-struggle society. Violence, they suggest, tends to result in a more brutal, less democratic leadership than does nonviolent action, and also in the long run reduces adherence to the movement's original humanitarian goals as motivating principles for both leaders and participants. "That individuals and groups can be involved in anti-social practices in the interests of desirable social goals and still maintain these goals in relatively pure fashion is a doctrine for which there is little psychological support." They add that ". . . repeated behavior of an anti-social character, though originally in the interests of altruistic social goals, will probably lead to the abandonment of those goals as directing forces for the . . . leaders as well as the followers within any group or organization." Social approval for violence, they continue, is likely to increase the amount of violence in the society by weakening super-ego controls and by releasing latent violence. Where the violence becomes institutionalized, Janis and Katz conclude, even assuming the political "success" of the movement, it tends to lead to rigidity and to the filling of political and social positions involving violence with individuals whose basic personality patterns (deriving satisfaction from such work) are reinforced by rewards of status, salary and social approval.[99]

Nonviolent leaders do not use violent sanctions to maintain their positions and hence are more subject to popular control than leaders of violent movements which may apply violent sanctions against internal opposition. During nonviolent campaigns, their leaders depend for their positions upon voluntarily accepted moral authority, acceptance of their political and strategic judgment, and popular support—not upon any capacity to threaten or use violence against the participants themselves. After the struggle, the leaders who do not accept official positions in the State will have no means of violence for use against the populace to maintain their leadership positions or to impose a nondemocratic regime. In such cases as national independence struggles or social revolutions in which some of the leaders after the conclusion of the conflict accept official positions in the State, that capacity of the State for violence against the populace, as we have seen, will be more limited than it would have been had the struggle been violent. After the nonviolent struggle, then, the State power remains unenlarged while the popular capacity for resistance has increased; greater chances for future popular control and a greater degree of diffused power therefore exist.

Whereas violent struggles tend to erode or destroy the independence of the society's *loci* of power, with nonviolent struggle those groups and institutions are likely to have been strengthened. That increased capacity will in turn contribute to greater institutional vitality, capacity for opposing autocratic tendencies, and to the general diffusion of power in the post-struggle society.

It cannot be expected that a nonviolent campaign for specific objectives will be followed immediately by that society's full rejection of violence in all situations. However, effective use of nonviolent struggle may be a step in the direction of increased substitution of nonviolent for violent sanctions in that society. Increased confidence and understanding of the potential and requirements of the nonviolent technique will need to be accompanied by efforts to work out specific strategies to deal with specific issues, since lasting substitution hinges on the nonviolent alternative being, and being seen to be, effective for each specific conflict. That is, replacement of violence with nonviolent action is likely to be a continuing series of particular substitutions instead of a single sweeping adoption of nonviolent means, regardless of the reason it might be chosen. In addition, changes won by nonviolent means are unlikely to be seen to "require" violence to maintain them, in contrast to changes won by violence. When, to cite a third possibility, the changes have been "given" by the opponent without struggle by the grievance group, those changes may be taken away, either by the donor or some other group, as easily as they were received. However, changes won in struggle by nonviolent action are accompanied by the capacity developed in struggle to defend those changes nonviolently against future threats. Such changes achieved by nonviolent action are therefore likely to be relatively lasting, and not to require political violence to maintain them.[100]

Members of grievance groups which have, respectively, used violent struggle and nonviolent struggle successfully, are likely—following the conflicts—to have different perceptions of their own power in the new situation. With confidence in violence as the real type of power, after a nominally successful violent struggle which has, for example, changed the elite which controls the State, the populace viewing the concentrated capacity for violence held by the new government is likely to see it in comparison as relatively helpless in any possible serious struggle against it. A quite different situation is, however, likely to follow a successful nonviolent struggle. Training in nonviolent "battle" contributes to increased future capacity to apply the technique in crises and to the ability of that populace to control whatever ruler may seek to impose his will on the people. Nirmal Kumar Bose has written that experience using nonviolent action puts people "on their own legs." In contrast to violence which, when all accept it as the "real" power, gives the upper hand to the group which uses it most effectively, nonviolent struggle distributes power among all. Given determination and bravery, every person can apply the nonviolent technique which brings power to each actionist. Consequently, Bose continued, in a nonviolent revolution power "spreads evenly among the masses . . ." [101] This is, of course, a tendency and not a nothing-or-all process. The degree to which power is diffused among the populace, and whether in the course of time this continues and grows or is diminished and largely lost, is dependent on the course of that nonviolent struggle and later events. However, experience in the effective use of nonviolent action "arms" the populace with knowledge of how to wield nonviolent weapons; this technique thereby tends toward the diffusion of power throughout the society and contributes decidedly toward the capacity of the populace to control the ruler should he on future occasions alienate the support of the majority of the subjects. All these indications are suggestive that nonviolent action and political violence may contribute to quite different types of societies.

Gregg argued in the 1930s that the adoption of nonviolent action in place of violence might break the constant circle of the violence of one group leading to violence by the other, and also break the frequent escalation in the extent and severity of violence.[102] If valid, the social consequences of breaking the spiral of violence are obviously important for reducing the amount and intensity of violence, especially political violence. Since violence may be particularly compatible with hierarchical and especially dictatorial systems, the ramifications of such breaks in the spiral of violence may be wide and profound.

CONCLUSION

This book has been an exploration of the nature of nonviolent struggle. We began with an examination of political power, which has been often assumed to derive from violence and to be ultimately controlable only by still greater violence. We discovered that political power derives instead from sources in the society which may be regulated or severed by the withholding or withdrawal of cooperation by the populace. The political power of governments may in fact be very fragile and even the power of dictators may be destroyed by withdrawal of the human assistance which has made their regime possible. At least that was the theory.

The technique of nonviolent action is rooted in that theory of power.

We surveyed its basic characteristics and sketched part of the history of its development. Then we turned to an examination in detail of the multitude of specific methods which fall within that technique, under the general classes of nonviolent protest and persuasion, noncooperation and nonviolent intervention. These methods make possible the application of diverse leverages against the opponent in the effort to achieve the objectives of the actionists: psychological, ideational, economic, social, political, physical and other leverages. Attention then shifted to the complex ways in which this technique may operate in conflict with a violent opponent. The groundwork which may precede the launching of nonviolent action was examined, and some of the basic requirements for the effective use of the technique. Then we focused on the initial impact which the launching of nonviolent action may have on the social situation and the opponent, to the probability of repression and the need for a determined, yet nonviolent, continuation of resistance. The opponent's repression, we saw, may rebound to weaken his power position through the process of political *jiu-jitsu*.

Instead of nonviolent action achieving change in one simple way, we discovered that there were three main processes, or mechanisms, by which change was produced, ranging from conversion of the opponent, so that he now agrees with the nonviolent group—probably the rarest type of change—to nonviolent coercion on the other extreme in which changes are forced, albeit nonviolently, on the opponent, with accommodation falling at midpoint and being the most usual mechanism. Nonviolent struggle also brings changes of various types to the nonviolent group itself, as we examined in this concluding chapter. These changes are especially associated with a new sense of self-respect, self-confidence, and a realization of the power people can wield in controling their own lives through learning to use the nonviolent technique. These changes within the nonviolent group gain greater significance in light of the analysis of power in the first chapter which showed it to derive ultimately from the people who are ruled or otherwise subordinated. The changes in the nonviolent group, the relative strengthening of the non-State institutions of the society in which nonviolent action is used, and the development of a nonviolent struggle capacity by which the opponent's violence may be made impotent, combine to redistribute power in that society.

This book has thus been limited to an attempt to understand the nature of the technique of nonviolent action. Despite its widespread application on many issues against diverse opponents, nonviolent struggle has remained an underdeveloped political technique, largely neglected not only by the officials of governments and leaders of the society's dominant institutions but also by social reformers, avowed revolutionaries, even pacifists, and very importantly also by academics. We are only becoming aware of the past history of this type of conflict and of the vast armory of nonviolent weapons it utilizes. The ways it operates in major struggle to produce change are still new to us and its long term possibilities and significance are still primarily matters of speculation rather than careful analysis based on adequate understanding. One thing is, however, abundantly clear: this is a significant technique of great past importance and of considerable future potential.

As the brief historical survey of the development of this technique showed, nonviolent struggle has in the past century undergone major innovations, development and expansion as compared at least to what we know of its previous history. Certain other characteristics of this same century stand in sharp contrast: the extension and growth of control by centralized States, the development and expansion of depersonalized industrial production, the emergence of total war with World War I and then with World War II the invention of nuclear and other weapons of mass destruction, the development in the 1920s and 1930s of modern totalitarian systems, the deliberate extermination of whole population groups, and the mass killings of still more millions in pursuit of domestic political objectives or in the course of war. Even many of the rebels against the old order have adopted its belief in the omnipotence of political violence, now in the forms of guerrilla warfare, domestic repression, or even nuclear weapons. There have been other similar developments in political violence. Yet it was in this same century that nonviolent action became more significant and powerful than in any previous era.

Nonviolent struggle may now be entering a new phase of its development. One of the most important factors in this phase is the conscious effort to increase our knowledge and understanding of the nature of the technique, to improve its effectiveness, and to extend the areas in which it may be substituted for violence, even as a replacement for military defense. This new phase has begun, but only just, and it remains to be seen how and to what extent it will develop. Once again, it is remarkable that this development in nonviolent alternatives should begin at the same time that important trends in politics, technology, social control, social organization and violence are moving in the opposite direction: toward capacity for super destruction, toward vast State controls over institutions and people, toward computer and other technological aids to regimentation, toward psychological and chemical control of people's behavior, toward an increased police capacity for political surveilance, toward centralized control of the economy by small elites, and even toward genetic control of future mankind. For those of us who still believe that human dignity, creativity, justice and freedom are important, the nonviolent technique of struggle may provide one of our last hopes for effective reversal of the current directions toward dehumanization, regimentation, manipulation, and the dominance of political structures of violence and tyranny.

Such a hope may or may not be achieved, for between our present condition and the current underdeveloped status of the nonviolent technique on the one hand, and a reversal of present trends, on the other, lies a great gap. All the requirements for filling that gap are not yet clear, but it is possible to indicate at least a few of them which are directly associated with nonviolent action.

One step is clearly research and analysis on the nature of this technique. The insights, theories and hypotheses of this study require continual testing, evaluation and modification in light of other cases of nonviolent action, future experience and further research. This book has been intended to stimulate further explorations of the politics of nonviolent action. These explorations include opening this field to a greater degree than hitherto to academic investigation. This is only the beginning.

A related step involves efforts to explore and develop various extensions in the practical application of this technique in place of violence in a variety of specific tasks for meeting pressing problems. These vary widely and may include its potential for securing rights for suppressed minorities, for obtaining, maintaining or extending civil liberties, for expanding social justice, for restructuring social, economic or political institutions, for disintegrating and replacing political dictatorships, for achieving social revolution with freedom, for preventing internal usurpations by *coup d'état* and other political violence, and even as a substitute for military defense in deterring and defeating foreign invasions and foreign-aided *coups*. These and various other areas for basic research and investigation of policy alternatives are outlined elsewhere as parts of a comprehensive program which needs to be launched.[103] Needless to say, this research, analysis and policy exploration must include attention to weaknesses, limitations and possible undesirable ramifications of the nonviolent technique, as well as its more positive potentialities.

Another step is public education using various media to share widely the information we now have or soon gain about the nature of non-violent action, its requirements and know-how, as well as new proposals for its application to problems for which people now rely upon violence. One of these areas of possible future application would be "civilian defense"—the use of prepared nonviolent resistance to defeat domestic usurpations and foreign invasions. Others might focus on current or anticipated problems of a country or area, such as conflicts of color, poverty, freedoms, institutional restructuring, prevention and disintegration of tyranny and many others. Courses in nonviolent alternatives in schools and universities at all levels would be an important part of such public education and would help develop qualified future researchers on these phenomena.

Then too, there is the field of action. Many people would place this first. While in some ways it is primary, it is given a slightly lower priority here since nonviolent action which is ill-conceived, based on ignorance of the requirements of the technique or of the conditions and issues of the conflict, on poor strategy and tactics and similar inadequacies is likely to be counterproductive in advancing the adoption of nonviolent alternatives. On the other hand, until and unless people have themselves gained experience in the use of this technique for limited objectives, and have observed others applying it also effectively, they will be unlikely or may even be unable to use it in the more difficult and crucial conflicts.

Attention is also needed to the ways in which nonviolent action may be related to milder peaceful ways of action and to regular institutional procedures, either private or governmental ones, for nonviolent action is not a substitute for, but an aid to, other peaceful ways of dealing with problems and carrying out common tasks where they are responsive to popular control.

There are other important things to be done. Each person who is familiar with the needs of his neighborhood, people, country and world will be able to propose and tackle additional problems.

For all its many pages and hundreds of thousands of words, this book is not the last word on nonviolent action. It is hoped that instead it may turn out to be one of the first in this new stage of the development of nonviolent alternatives. If we are to gain new knowledge and increased understanding, and if deliberate efforts are to be made to apply nonviolent action in place of violence in the crucial conflicts of today and tomorrow, then the responsibility must fall on all of us who see these as tasks which need to be accomplished. This means the responsibility is ours. It falls on each of us, on me and on you.

NOTES

1. Erik Erikson, **Identity and the Life Cycle,** in *Psychological Issues* (New York: International Universities Press, 1959), vol. I, monograph 1, p. 31.

2. Lakey, "The Sociological Mechanisms of Nonviolent Action" (thesis), p. 43; *Peace Research Reviews,* vol. II, no. 6 (Dec. 1968), p. 26.

3. Gregg, **The Power of Nonviolence,** pp. 85-86.

4. *Ibid.,* p. 133.

5. Venturi, **Roots of Revolution,** p. 445.

6. Schapiro, **The Communist Party of the Soviet Union,** p. 20.

7. *Ibid.,* p. 28.

8. Harcave, **First Blood,** p. 133.

9. *Ibid.,* p. 189.

10. Eyck, **A History of the Weimar Republic,** vol. I, p. 154.

11. See Gandhi, **Non-violent Resistance,** p. 356; Ind. ed.: **Satyagraha,** p. 356, and Sharp, **Gandhi Wields the Weapon of Moral Power,** pp. 72 and 100.

12. Gandhi, **Non-violent Resistance,** p. 154; Ind. ed.: **Satyagraha,** p. 154.

13. *Ibid.,* p. 218.

14. Sharp, **Gandhi Wields . . . ,** p. 71.

15. Bose, **Selections from Gandhi,** p. 205.

16. Schlesinger, **The Colonial Merchants and the American Revolution,** p. 280.

17. M. K. Gandhi, **Satyagraha in South Africa,** p. 203.

18. Watt, **Dare Call it Treason,** p. 183.

19. Lenin, "Lecture on the 1905 Revolution," in Lenin, **Selected Works in Three Volumes,** vol. I, p. 792.

20. Seifert, **Conquest by Suffering,** p. 174.

21. Gregg, **The Power of Nonviolence,** p. 55. Gregg also argues that fear, anger, and hatred are closely related emotionally, and that therefore the capacity to control or replace one of them is associated with the capacity similarly to deal with the others. See pp. 66-67.

22. Lakey, "The Sociological Mechanisms . . ." (thesis), p. 63; *Peace Research Reviews,* vol. II, no. 6 (Dec. 1968), p. 43.

23. See Bondurant, **Conquest of Violence,** p. 29.

24. Gandhi, **Non-violent Resistance,** p. 8; Ind. ed.: **Satyagraha,** p. 8.

25. Gregg, **The Power of Nonviolence,** p. 64.

26. Jawaharlal Nehru, **The Discovery of India** (New York: John Day, 1946), p. 361.

27. **Nehru, An Autobiography,** p. 69.

28. *Ibid.,* p. 178.

29. Nehru, **Toward Freedom,** p. 129.

30. King, **Stride Toward Freedom,** p. 119; Br. ed.: p. 140. See also Peck, **Freedom Ride,** pp. 51-54.

31. Lomax, **The Negro Revolt,** p. 137.

32. Frederic Solomon and Jacob R. Fishman, "The Psychosocial Meaning of Nonviolence in Student Civil Rights Activities,"*Psychiatry,* vol. XXVII (1964), p. 96.

33. See Hiller, **The Strike,** p. 19.

34. See Gandhi, **Satyagraha in South Africa,** p. 199.

35. Lakey, "The Sociological Mechanisms of Nonviolent Action," p. 45; *Peace Research Reviews,* vol. II, no. 6, p. 28.

36. Hiller, **The Strike,** pp. 22 and 168-169.

37. Luthuli, **Let My People Go.** p. 10.

38. Sharp, **Gandhi Wields . . . ,** pp. 67-68 and 188.

39. Waskow, **From Race Riot to Sit-in,** p. 37.

40. Gregg, **The Power of Nonviolence,** p. 85.

41. Nehru, **An Autobiography,** p. 70.

42. Lakey, "The Sociological Mechanisms . . ." (thesis), pp. 44-45; *Peace Research Reviews,* vol. II, no. 6 (Dec. 1968), pp. 27-28.

43. Hiller, **The Strike,** p. 19.

44. Lakey, "The Sociological Mechanisms . . . ," p. 74; *Peace Research Reviews,* vol. II, no. 6, pp. 51-52.

45. Hiller, **The Strike,** p. 88.

46. Farmer, **Freedom – When?** pp. 17-18.

47. Nehru, **India and the World,** p. 173.

48. King, **Stride Toward Freedom,** p. 7; Br. ed.: p. 9.

49. Sharp, **Gandhi Wields . . . ,** pp. 44-45.

50. Warmbrunn, **The Dutch Under German Occupation, 1940-1945,** p. 111.

51. Symons, **The General Strike,** p. 53.

52. Inez Haynes Irwin, **The Story of the Woman's Party** (New York: Harcourt, Brace and Co., 1921), p. 219. I am grateful to George Lakey for this and the next reference.

53. Mary Windsor, "The Title is Probably This Long," *The Annals of the American Academy of Political and Social Science,"* (Season, 1914).

54. Nehru, **An Autobiography,** p. 70.

55. Farmer, **Freedom – When?** pp. 67 and 80-81.

56. Ebert, "Theory and Practice of Nonviolent Resistance," MS p. 249.

57. Luthuli, **Let My People Go,** p. 136.

58. Waskow, **From Race Riot to Sit-in,** p. 264.

59. Farmer, **Freedom – When?** pp. 72 and 76.

60. Lenin, "Lecture on the 1905 Revolution," in Lenin, **Selected Works in Three Volumes,** vol. I, pp. 789-792.

61. Solomon and Fishman, "The Psychosocial Meaning of Nonviolence in Student Civil Rights Activities," *Psychiatry,* vol. XXVII (1964), p. 97.

62. Bondurant, **Conquest of Violence,** pp. 131-145. Quotations are respectively from pp. 132 and 144.

63. Frank, **Sanity and Survival,** pp. 270-271. He cites C. M. Pierce and L. J. West,

"Six Years of Sit-ins: Psychodynamic Causes and Effects," in *International Journal of Social Psychiatry*, vol. XII (1966), pp. 29-34, and Solomon and Fishman, "The Psychosocial Meaning of Nonviolence in Student Civil Rights Activities."

64. King, **Stride Toward Freedom**, pp. 177-178.

65. Hentoff, **The New Equality**, p. 55.

66. *Ibid.*

67. Farmer, **Freedom — When?** pp. 35-36.

68. Solomon and Fishman, "The Psychosocial Meaning of Nonviolence in Student Civil Rights Activities," p. 99.

69. F. Solomon, W. L. Walker, G. O'Connor, and J. R. Fishman, "Civil Rights Activity and Reduction in Crime Among Negroes," *Archives of General Psychiatry*, vol. XII (March 1965), pp. 227-236.

70. Lakey, "The Sociological Mechanisms . . . (thesis), pp. 74-75; *Peace Research Reviews*, vol. II, no. 6, p. 52.

71. Gregg, **The Power of Nonviolence**, p. 63.

72. See Janis and Katz, "The Reduction of Intergroup Hostility" p. 93.

73. *Ibid.*, pp. 93-95.

74. Gregg, **The Power of Nonviolence**, pp. 45, 47, and 60-61.

75. Janis and Katz, "The Reduction of Intergroup Hostility" pp. 88 and 90-93.

76. See Sharp, "The Need of a Functional Substitute for War" *International Relations* (London), vol. III, no. 3 (April 1967), pp. 187-207.

77. Hiller, **The Strike**, pp. 30, 90, 19 and 17.

78. Morgan and Morgan, **The Stamp Act Crisis**, pp. 368-369.

79. Gipson, **The British Empire Before the American Revolution**, vol. XII, **The Triumphant Empire: Britain Sails into the Storm, 1770-1776**, p. 244. On other general indications of this tendency, see Schlesinger, **The Colonial Merchants . . .** , pp. 371ff. and *passim.*

80. Harcave, **First Blood**, pp. 116-117.

81. Kuper, **Passive Resistance in South Africa**, p. 215 and 146. See also Luthuli, **Let My People Go**, pp. 125 and 192.

82. Miller, **Nonviolence**, p. 275. See also Luthuli, **Let My People Go**, p. 180.

83. Hentoff, **The New Equality**, p. 205. For mention of a similar effect in Chicago, see p. 206.

84. Gandhi, **Non-violent Resistance**, p. 152; Ind. ed.: **Satyagraha**, p. 152.

85. Bondurant, **Conquest of Violence**, p. 186. See also Hiller, **The Strike**, p. 31.

86. King, **Stride Toward Freedom**, pp. 46, 65, and 69-74, 120-122 and 152-154.

87. Griffith, **The Resurrection of Hungary**, p. 170.

88. On the theory and content of the constructive program, see M. K. Gandhi, **Constructive Programme: Its Meaning and Place** (pamphlet; Ahmedabad: Navajivan Publishing House, 1941 and later), and Sharp, "The Constructive Programme," *Mankind* (Hyderabad), vol. I, no. 12 (July 1957), pp. 1102-1112, and Dhawan, **The Political Philosophy of Mahatma Gandhi**, pp. 190-208.

89. Gandhi, **Constructive Programme**, pp. 5 and 30 (1957 edition), and Dhawan, **The Political Philosophy of Mahatma Gandhi**, pp. 191-193.

90. See Gipson, **The Coming of the Revolution, 1763-1775**, pp. 181 and 187, and Schlesinger, **The Colonial Merchants . . .** , pp. 97, 106-107, 109-110, 112, 117, 121-123, 128, 130-131, 140, 143, 147, 151-152, 243, 369-370, 482, 492,

500-502, 517-518, 524, 528 and 610.

91. See Harcave, **First Blood,** pp. 110-111, 134, 143-144, 154, 171, 176-177 and 215.

92. Morgan and Morgan, **The Stamp Act Crisis,** pp. 203 and 243.

93. Schlesinger, **The Colonial Merchants . . . ,** p. 114.

94. Schlesinger, **The Colonial Merchants . . . ,** pp. 423-424 and 432.

95. Harcave, **First Blood,** pp. 77, 79-81, 179, 181, 183-184, 225 and 174. The quotation is from p. 200.

96. Tocqueville, **Democracy in America,** vol. I, pp. 9, 92-93, 333-334, and vol. II, pp. 93, 258, 271-272, and 296. See also Jouvenel, **Power,** pp. 244-246 and Gaetano Mosca, **The Ruling Class** (New York and London: McGraw-Hill, 1939), p. 134.

97. Jouvenel, **Power,** pp. 18-22 and 244-246.

98. Quincy Wright, **A Study of War** (Chicago: University of Chicago Press, 1942), vol. I, pp. 232-242, 302 and esp. 311; Bronislaw Malinowski, "An Anthropological Analysis of War," *American Journal of Sociology,* vol. XLVI, no. 4, esp. p. 545; and Malinowski, **Freedom and Civilization** (New York: Roy Publishers, 1944), esp. pp. 265 and 305.

99. Irving L. Janis and Daniel Katz, "The Reduction of Intergroup Hostility," in *Journal of Conflict Resolution,* vol. III, no. 1 (March 1959), pp. 90-91.

100. See Sharp, **Gandhi Wields . . . ,** p. 125, and Gandhi, **Non-violence in Peace and War,** vol. I, pp. 87 and 235, and vol. II, p. 340. Gregg writes: "Reforms will come to stay only if the masses acquire and retain the ability to make a firm veto by mass nonviolent resistance. . . . Hence reformers would be wise to lay less stress upon advocacy of their special changes and concentrate on the teaching of nonviolent resistance. Once that tool is mastered, we can make all sorts of permanent reforms." Gregg, **The Power of Nonviolence,** p. 146.

101. Bose, **Studies in Gandhism,** p. 148.

102. See Gregg, **The Power of Nonviolence,** p. 134.

103. See Sharp, **Exploring Nonviolent Alternatives** (Boston: Porter Sargent, 1970), pp. 73-113.

Appendix:
Summary of Factors Determining the Outcome of Nonviolent Struggles

The factors which determine the outcome of nonviolent struggles may be grouped in four classes: the factors associated with the social system, the opponent group, third parties and the nonviolent group. Those associated with the social situation are the most stable ones, within the limitations of which nonviolent action must usually operate. Long-run changes in these are possible, but within the time span of a nonviolent action struggle they cannot be relied upon, except in certain circumstances (item A.4, below). The remaining factors in the other three groups are mostly highly variable during the course of the struggle. The very nature of the dynamics of nonviolent action not only depends upon such changes but produces them, probably to a much greater degree than in comparable violent struggles. Almost all of these will constantly vary during the struggle; the only question is whether the changes will strengthen relatively the nonviolent actionists or their opponent.

A. *Factors in the social situation.*
    1. The degree of conflict of interest between the two groups.
    2. The social distance between the groups.

3. The degree to which beliefs and norms are shared by the two groups.
4. The degree to which the grievance group (and in some cases the opponent group) consists of atomized individuals with most social and political power concentrated in a center, or of social groups and institutions (*loci* of power) capable of wielding and withholding power.

B. *Factors associated with the opponent group.*
1. The degree to which the opponent is dependent for his sources of power upon those withdrawing their cooperation and obedience.
2. The degree of noncompliance which the opponent can tolerate without his position being seriously endangered; the less nonconformity and dissent normally allowed, the greater challenge it will be when it does occur.
3. The degree to which the opponent and the opponent's usual supporters are convinced of the rightness of their views and policies and/or their necessity in the situation.
4. The degree of conviction among the opponent and his usual supporters in the rightness of and justification for the means of repression used against the nonviolent actionists.
5. The means of control, including repression, which the opponent may use in an effort to defeat the nonviolent challenge.
6. How long the opponent can continue to maintain his position and power in face of the nonviolent action.
7. The degree to which the opponent's agents of repression, administrators and other aides serve him efficiently or refrain from doing so, whether by deliberate inefficiency or by mutiny.
8. The degree and type of support or opposition within the opponent group for the opponent's policy and repression of the nonviolent group; this refers to the general population as distinguished from special agents, aides, etc.
9. The opponent's estimate of the future course of the movement, the chances of victory or defeat, and the consequences of either.

C. *Factors associated with third parties.*
1. The degree to which third parties become sympathetic to either the opponent or the nonviolent group.
2. The degree to which the opinions and good will of third parties are important to the opponent and to the nonviolent group respectively.
3. The degree to which third parties move from a noninvolved position to active support for, or to noncooperation with, or obstruction of, either of the contending groups.
4. The degree to which either of the contending groups will be assisted by such support or hindered by such noncooperation or obstruction.

D. *Factors associated with the nonviolent group.*
1. The opportunity and ability to organize nonviolent action *or* to act spontaneously on a group level in accordance with the requirements of nonviolent action.
2. The degree to which the nonviolent actionists and the general grievance group are convinced of the rightness of their cause.
3. The degree of confidence in nonviolent action among the nonviolent

actionists and the general grievance group.

4. The choice of the methods of nonviolent action, especially whether these are symbolic or involve noncooperation and intervention, and whether they are within the capacity of the nonviolent actionists.

5. The degree of soundness of the strategy and tactics chosen or accepted for the struggle.

6. Whether the demands of the nonviolent group are within their capacity to achieve them.

7. The relative ability of the nonviolent actionists to practise the technique as influenced, for example, by their past experience or their understanding of it.

8. The degree of voluntarily accepted discipline within the nonviolent group, so that the plans are carried out effectively, with a maximum of clarity and unity of action.

9. The numbers of nonviolent actionists, seen within the context of the quality of the movement and the mechanism by which change is sought.

10. The degree to which the nonviolent actionists are aided or hindered by the general grievance group, on whose behalf they may be acting.

11. The balance between the degree of terror the opponent is able and willing to use and the degree of determination to act (regardless of sanctions), due to fearlessness, courage or willingness to accept suffering as the price of change.

12. The length of time that the nonviolent actionists are able and willing to continue their course of action.

13. The ability of the nonviolent actionists to keep the struggle nonviolent.

14. The capacity of the nonviolent actionists to maintain openness and nonsecretiveness in their actions in normal circumstances.

15. The presence and quality of some type of effective leadership, formal or informal, or the ability of the actionists to act with unity, and discipline, and wisely chosen strategy, tactics and methods without a significant distinguishable leadership group.

16. The degree to which the nonviolent actionists can demonstrate the attitudes and actions which may help convert the opponent.

17. The degree to which the nonviolent actionists and the general grievance group control their own sources of power or to which these are subject to control by the opponent.

Most of these factors, especially in the last three groups, it is emphasized once again, are potentially subject to considerable and constant variation during the course of the nonviolent action struggle. The outcome is then determined by the direction and extent of these changes. The degree to which these factors, directly or indirectly, are subject to the control of the members of the grievance group is disproportionately high in nonviolent action as compared with the factors influencing the outcome of struggles using violent techniques.

Bibliography

Abramowitz, Isidore, **The Great Prisoners: The First Anthology of Literature Written in Prison**. New York: E.P. Dutton and Co., 1946.

Aczell, Tamas and Tibor Meray, **The Revolt of the Mind: A Case History of Intellectual Resistance Behind the Iron Curtain**. New York: Frederick A. Praeger, 1959. London: Thames & Hudson, 1960.

Adams, Henry, **History of the United States During the Second Administration of Thomas Jefferson**, vol. II. New York: Charles Scribner's Sons, 1890.

Agar, Herbert, ed., **The Formative Years**, vols. I and II. Edited from the writings of Henry Adams. Boston: Houghton Mifflin, 1947. London Collins, 1948.

Alinsky, Saul, a conversation with Marion K. Sanders, "The Professional Radical, 1970," *Harpers Magazine*, vol. 240, no. 1436 (January 1970), pp. 35-42.

American Archives, Fourth Series, vol. I, no. 18. Washington, D.C.: M. St. Clarke and Peter Force, 1937.

American Foreign Policy, 1950-1955: Basic Documents, vol. II. Washington, D.C.: Department of State, 1957.

American Foreign Policy: Current Documents, 1956. Washington, D.C.: Department of State, 1959.

American Foreign Policy: Current Documents, 1960. Washington, D.C.: Department of State, 1964.

Amundsen, Sverre S., general editor, **Kirkenes Ferda, 1942.** Oslo: J.W. Cappelens Forlag, 1946.

Aptheker, Herbert, **American Negro Slave Revolts.** New York: International Publishers, 1964.

"A Rhode Islander." See "Rhode Islander."

Austin, John, **Lectures on Jurisprudence of the Philosophy of Positive Law.** Two vols. Fifth edition. London: John Murray, 1911 (orig. 1861).

Baer, G. W., **The Coming of the Italian-Ethiopian War.** Cambridge, Mass.: Harvard University Press, 1957.

Bagby, Jeanne, "Witness Against Germ Warfare," *Christian Century*, vol. 76, 23 September 1959.

Bailey, Thomas A., **A Diplomatic History of the American People.** Sixth edition. New York: Appleton-Century-Crofts, 1958.

Bakke, E. Wight and Charles Kerr, **Unions, Management and the Public.** New York: Harcourt, Brace & Co., 1948.

Barbash, Jack, **Labor Unions in Action: A Study of the Mainsprings of Unionism.** New York: Harper and Bros., 1948.

Barker, J. Ellis, **Modern Germany: Its Rise, Growth, Downfall and Future.** New York: E. P. Dutton & Co., 1919.

Barnard, Chester I., **The Functions of the Executive.** Cambridge, Mass.: Harvard University Press, 1948.

Barraclough, Solon L., "Agricultural Policy and Land Reform." Duplicated MS. 106 pp. Conference on Key Problems of Economic Policy in Latin America, University of Chicago, 6-9 November 1966.

——, "Farmers' Organizations in Planning and Implementing Rural Programs." Duplicated MS. 22 and iv pp. Prepared for a study being edited by Professor Raanan Weitz.

Barton, Paul, "The Strike Mechanism in Soviet Concentration Camps," in *Monthly Information Bulletin of the International Commission Against Concentration Camp Practices* (now titled *Saturn*), (Brussels), no. 4 (August-November 1955).

Bauer, Raymond A. and Alice H., "Day to Day Resistance to Slavery," *Journal of Negro History,* vol. XXVII, no. 4 (Oct. 1942), pp. 388-419.

Belfrage, Sally, **Freedom Summer.** New York: Viking Press, 1965.

Bennett, Jeremy, "The Resistance Against the German Occupation of Denmark 1940-5," in Adam Roberts, ed., **Civilian Resistance as a National Defence,** pp. 154-172.

Bentham, Jeremy, **A Fragment on Government.** London: Oxford University Press, Humphrey Milford, 1931 (orig. 1891).

Berger, Carl, **The Korea Knot: A Military-Political History.** Philadelphia: University of Pennsylvania Press, 1950.

Berger, Suzanne, **Peasants Against Politics: Rural Organization in Brittany 1911-1967.** Cambridge, Mass.: Harvard University Press, 1972.

"The Berkeley Free Speech Controversy," prepared by "A Fact-Finding Committee of Graduate Political Scientists." Duplicated. Berkeley, Calif: The Authors, 1964.

Bernard, L.L., **Social Control in Its Sociological Aspects.** New York: Macmillan, 1939.

Blaustein, Albert P. and Clarence Clyde Ferguson, Jr., **Desegregation and the Law: The Meaning and Effect of the School Segregation Cases**. New Brunswick, New Jersey: Rutgers University Press, 1957.

Bloom, Murray Teigh, "The World's Greatest Counterfeiters," *Harpers Magazine*, vol. 215, no. 1286 (July 1957), pp. 47-53.

Blum, Robert, **The United States and China in World Affairs**. Ed. by A. Doak Barnett. New York: McGraw-Hill (for the Council on Foreign Relations), 1966.

de La Boétie, Etienne, *"Discours de la Servitude Volontaire,"* in **Oeuvres Completes d'Etienne de la Boétie**, pp. 1-57. Paris: J. Rouam & Coe., 1892.

——, **Anti-Dictator: The "Discours sur la servitude volontaire" of Etienne de la Boétie**, New York: Columbia University Press, 1942.

Bondurant, Joan V., **Conquest of Violence: The Gandhian Philosophy of Conflict**. Princeton, New Jersey: Princeton University Press. London: Oxford University Press, 1958.

Bontemps, Arna, **100 Years of Negro Freedom**. New York: Dodd, Mead & Co., 1962.

Borton, Hugh, **Peasant Uprisings in Japan of the Tokugawa Period**. Second Edition. New York: Paragon Book Reprint Corp., 1968. First published in *The Transactions of the Asiatic Society of Japan* (Second Series), vol. XVI, 1938.

Bose, Nirmal Kumar, **Selections from Gandhi**. Ahmedabad: Navajivan, 1948.

——, Studies in Gandhism. Calcutta: Indian Associated Publishing Co., 1947.

Brailsford, H.N., **Rebel India**. New York: New Republic, Inc., 1931. London: Leonard Stein (with Victor Gollancz), 1931.

Brant, Stefan, **The East German Rising**. New York: Frederick A. Praeger, 1957. London: Thames and Hudson, 1955.

Brinton, Crane, **The Anatomy of Revolution**. New York: Vintage Books, 1962.

Brockway, A. Fenner, **Non-co-operation in other Lands**. Madras: Tagore & Co., 1921.

Browne, Edward G., **The Persian Revolution of 1905-1909**. Cambridge: University Press, 1910.

Buckler, W. H., "Labour Disputes in the Province of Asia Minor," in W.H. Buckler and W.M. Culder, eds., **Anatolian Studies Presented to Sir William Mitchell Ramsay**. Manchester: University Press, 1923.

Bullock, Alan, **Hitler: A Study in Tyranny**. Revised edition. New York: Harper and Row, 1962. London: Odhams, 1964.

Busk, Sir Douglas, **The Craft of Diplomacy: How to Run a Diplomatic Service**. New York: Frederick A. Praeger, 1967.

Carter, April, **Direct Action** (pamphlet). London: Peace News, 1962.

Case, Clarence Marsh, **Nonviolent Coercion: A Study in Methods of Social Pressure**. New York: The Century Co., 1923.

Catt, Carrie Chapman and Nettie Rogers Shuller, **Woman Suffrage and Politics: The Inner Study of the Suffrage Movement**. New York: Charles Scribner's Sons, 1923.

Chakravarty, Amiya, **A Saint at Work. A View of Gandhi's Work and Message** (pamphlet). William Penn Lecture 1950. Philadelphia: Young Friends Movement of the Philadelphia Yearly Meetings, 1950.

Chang, Chung-li, **The Chinese Gentry: Studies in their Role in Nineteenth-**

Century Chinese Society. Seattle: University of Washington Press, 1955.

Charques, Richard, **The Twilight of Imperial Russia**. Fair Lawn, N.J.: Essential Books, 1959. London: Phoenix House, 1958.

Chaudury, P.C. Ray, **Gandhiji's First Struggle in India**. Ahmedabad: Navajivan, 1955.

Clark, Evans, ed., **Boycotts and Peace**. New York and London: Harper & Bros., 1932.

von Clausewitz, General Carl, **On War**. Three volumes. Trans. by Col. J.J. Graham. Edited by Col. F.N. Maude. New York: Barnes and Noble, 1956. London: Routledge and Kegan Paul, 1956.

Coleman, McAlister, **Men and Coal**. New York: Farrar and Reinhart, 1943.

Coleman, Peter J., **The Transformation of Rhode Island 1790-1860**. Providence, R.I.: American History Research Center, Brown University Press, 1963.

Commager, Henry Steele, ed., **Documents of American History**. New York and London: Appleton-Century-Crofts, 1948.

Comte, Auguste, **The Positive Philosophy of Auguste Comte**. Two volumes. London: George Bell & Sons, 1896.

Contempt (no author). Chicago: Swallow Press, 1970.

Coser, Lewis, **The Functions of Social Conflict**. Glencoe, Ill.: The Free Press, 1956.

Cottam, Richard W., **Nationalism in Iran**. Pittsburg: University of Pittsburg Press, 1964.

Cowell, F.R., **The Revolutions of Ancient Rome**. New York: Frederick A. Praeger, 1962. London: Thames and Hudson, 1962.

Craig, Gordon A., "Totalitarian Diplomacy," in Lawrence W. Martin, ed., **Diplomacy in Modern European History**, pp. 74-92. New York: Macmillan, 1966. London: Collier-Macmillan, 1966.

Crankshaw, Edward, **Gestapo: Instrument of Tyranny**. New York: Viking Press, 1956. London: Putnam, 1956.

Cremeans, Charles D., **The Arabs and the World: Nasser's Arab Nationalist Policy**. New York and London: Frederick A. Praeger (for the Council on Foreign Relations), 1963.

de Crespigny, Anthony, "The Nature and Methods of Non-violent Coercion," *Political Studies,* (London), vol. XII, no. 2 (June 1964), pp. 256-265.

Cressey, Donald R., ed., **The Prison: Studies in Institutional Organization and Change**. New York: Holt, Rinehart and Winston, 1961.

Crook, Wilfred H., **Communism and the General Strike**. Hamden, Connecticut: The Shoestring Press, 1960.

———, "General Strike," **Encyclopedia of the Social Sciences**, vol. VI, pp. 607-612.

———. **The General Strike: A Study of Labor's Tragic Weapon in Theory and Practice**. Chapel Hill: University of North Carolina Press, 1931.

Dallin, Alexander, **German Rule in Russia, 1941-1945: A Study of Occupation Policies**. New York: St. Martin's Press, 1957. London: Macmillan, 1957.

Daniels, Dan, "Non-violent Actions in Canada," in *Our Generation Against Nuclear War* (Montreal), vol. III. no. 1 (June 1964).

Davidson, Philip, **Propaganda and the American Revolution**. Chapel Hill: University of North Carolina Press, 1941.

Davis, John P., **The American Negro Reference Book**. Englewood Cliffs, N.J.: Prentice-Hall, 1966.

Davison, W. Phillips, **The Berlin Blockade**. Princeton, N.J.: Princeton University Press, 1958.

Deanesly, Margaret, **A History of the Medieval Church, 590-1500**. London: Methuen & Co., 1965.

Delarue, Jacques, **The Gestapo: A History of Horror**. New York: William Morrow, 1964.

DeMarco, Margaret, "The Use of Non-violent Direct Action, Tactics and Strategy by American Indians." Unpublished student research paper. Upland School of Social Change, Chester, Pa., July 1968.

"Demonstrators—" (leaflet). London: Committee for Direct Action Against Nuclear War, 1958.

Department of State, United States Government. See also **American Foreign Policy**. Department of State *Bulletin*, vol. XLVI.

Desai, Mahadev, **The Epic of Travancore**. Ahmedabad: Navajivan, 1937.

——, **The Story of Bardoli**. Ahmedabad: Navajivan Publishing House, 1929.

Deutsch, Karl W., "Cracks in the Monolith: Possibilities and Patterns of Disintegration in Totalitarian Systems," in Carl J. Friedrich, ed., **Totalitarianism**, pp. 308-333. Cambridge, Mass.: Harvard University Press, 1954.

Deutscher, Isaac, **The Prophet Armed: Trotsky: 1879-1921**. New York and London: Oxford University Press, 1963.

——, **Stalin: A Political Biography**. New York and London: Oxford University Press, 1961.

Dhawan, Gopinath, **The Political Philosophy of Mahatma Gandhi**. Third revised edition. Ahmedabad: Navajivan, 1962.

"Discipline for Public Witness Demonstrators" (leaflet). New York: various peace organizations, 1962.

Diwakar, Ranganath R., **Satyagraha: Its Technique and History**. Bombay: Hind Kitabs, 1946.

Drake, St. Clair, and Horace R. Cayton, **Black Metropolis: A Study of Negro Life in a Northern City**. New York: Harcourt Brace, 1945.

Dulles, Forster Rhea, **Labor in America: A History**. New York: Thomas Y. Crowell, Co., 1949.

Dunne, John Gregory, **Delano: The Story of the California Grape Strike**. New York: Ferrar, Straus & Giroux, 1967.

Ebert, Theodor, "Effects of Repression by the Invader," *Peace News* (London), 19 March, 1965.

——, "Nonviolent Resistance Against Communist Regimes?," pp. 175-194, in Roberts, ed.: *Civilian Resistance as a National Defence*, pp. 175-194.

——, "Organization in Civilian Defence," in Roberts, ed., *ibid.*, pp. 266-273.

——, "Theory and Practice of Nonviolent Resistance: A Model of a Campaign". MS. Unpublished English translation (by Hilda Morris) of a doctoral thesis in political science presented at the University of Erlangen, Germany, 1965. A revision of this thesis has now been published entitled: **Gewaltfrier Aufstand: Alternative zum Bürgerkrieg**. Freiburg: Verlag Rombach, 1968. Paperback abridgement: **Gewaltfrier Aufstand: Alternative zum Bürgerkrieg**. Frankfurt am Main and Hamburg: Fischerbücherei GmbH, 1970.

Ehrlich, Karl, (pseud. for Karl Raloff), *"Den Ikke-Voldelige Modstand, Der*

Kvalte Kapp-Kupet," in Ehrlich, Lindberg and Jacobsen, **Kamp Uden Vaaben**, pp. 194-202.

———, "*Ruhrkampen*," in Ehrlich, Lindberg and Jacobsen, **Kamp Uden Vaaben**, pp. 181-193.

Ehrlich, Karl, Niels Lindberg and Gammelgaard Jacobsen, **Kamp Uden Vaaben: Ikke-Vold som Kampmiddel mod Krig og Undertrykkelse**. Copenhagen: Levin & Munksgaard, Ejnar Munksgaard, 1937.

Elliott, W. Y., "Force, Political," **Encyclopedia of the Social Sciences**, vol. VI, p. 338. New York: Macmillan, 1935.

Engels, Frederick, **Anti-Dühring**. Moscow: Foreign Languages Publishing House, 1954.

Erikson, Erik, **Gandhi's Truth: On the Origins of Militant Nonviolence**. New York: W. W. Norton & Co., 1969.

———, **Identity and the Life Cycle**, in *Psychological Issues*, vol. I, monograph 1. New York: International Universities Press, 1959.

European Resistance Movements, 1939-1945. First International Conference on the History of the Resistance Movements held at Liège-Bruxelles-Breendonk, 14-17 September 1958. (No editor listed.) Oxford: Pergamon Press, 1960.

Eyck, Erich, **A History of the Weimar Republic**, vol. I, **From the Collapse of the Empire to Hindenburg's Election**. Cambridge, Mass.: Harvard University Press, 1962.

Fairbank, John King, **The United States and China**. Cambridge, Mass.: Harvard University Press, 1958.

Farmer, James. **Freedom—When?** New York: Random House, 1965.

Faulkner, William. **A Fable**. New York: Random House, 1954.

Fehrenback, T. R. **This Kind of War**. New York: Macmillan, 1963.

The Fifty States Report. Submitted to the Commission on Civil Rights by the State Advisory Committees, 1961. Washington, D. C.: U.S. Government Printing Office, 1961.

Fischer, Louis. **The Life of Lenin**. New York: Harper and Row, 1965. London: Weidenfeld and Nicolson, 1965.

———, **The Life of Mahatma Gandhi**. New York: Harpers, 1950.

Fitch, John A., "Strikes and Lockouts," **Encyclopedia of the Social Sciences**, vol. XIV, p. 422. New York: Macmillan, 1935.

Fleischer, Wilfred, **Sweden: The Welfare State**. New York: John Day, 1956.

Flexner, Eleanor, **Century of Struggle**. Cambridge, Mass.: Harvard University Press, 1959.

Fogg, Richard W., "Jazz Under the Nazis," in **Music 66**, "*Down Beat*'s Annual," 1966, pp. 97-99.

Foley, Hamilton, **Woodrow Wilson's Case for the League of Nations**. Princeton, N.J.: Princeton University Press, 1933. London: Humphrey Milford, Oxford University Press, 1933.

Follett, Mary, **Creative Experience**. New York and London: Longmans, Green & Co., 1924.

Fontaine, André, **History of the Cold War: From the October Revolution to the Korean War 1917-1950**. New York: Pantheon Books, 1968.

Ford, Paul Leicester, ed., **The Works of Thomas Jefferson**. New York and London: G. P. Putnam's Sons, 1904.

Forster, H. O. Arnold, *The Truth About the Land League, Leaders and its Teaching* (pamphlet). London: National Press Agency, Ltd. (published for the Property Defence Association), 1883.

Foster, William Z., **The Great Steel Strike and Its Lessons**. New York: B. W. Huebsch, 1920.

Fox, George. See Nickalls, J.L., ed.

Frank, Jerome D., **Sanity and Survival: Psychological Aspects of War and Peace**. New York: Random House, and Vintage Books, 1968.

Frazier, E. Franklin, **Race and Culture Contacts in the Modern World**. Boston: Beacon Press, 1957.

Friedman, Philip, "Jewish Resistance to Nazism: Its Various Forms and Aspects," in **European Resistance Movements, 1939-1945**, pp. 195-214.

Friedrich, Carl J., ed., **Totalitarianism**. Cambridge, Mass.: Harvard University Press, 1954.

Fromm, Erich, **Escape from Freedom**. New York: Holt Rinehart and Winston, 1961. British ed.: **The Fear of Freedom**. London: Routledge and Kegan Paul, 1961.

Galenson, Walter, **Labor in Norway**, Cambridge, Mass.: Harvard University Press, 1949.

Galtung, Johan, "On the Effects of International Economic Sanctions, with Examples from the Case of Rhodesia," *World Politics*, vol. XIX, no. 3 (April 1967), pp. 378-416.

Galtung, Johan and Arne Naess, **Gandhis Politiske Etikk**. Oslo: Tanum, 1955.

Gandhi, M.K., **An Autobiography or the Story of My Experiments with Truth**. Ahmedabad: Navajivan Publishing House, 1956.

——, **The Constructive Programme** (pamphlet). Ahmedabad: Navajivan, 1941.

——, **Economics of Khadi**. Ahmedabad: Navajivan, 1941.

——, **Hind Swaraj or Indian Home Rule**. Ahmedabad: Navajivan, 1958.

——, **Non-violence in Peace and War**. Two volumes. Ahmedabad: Navajivan, 1948 and 1949.

——, **Non-violent Resistance**. New York: Schocken Books, 1967. Indian ed.: **Satyagraha**. Ahmedabad: Navajivan, 1951.

——, **Satyagraha in South Africa**, Trans. from the Gujarati by Valji Govindji Desai. Revised second edition. Ahmedabad: Navajivan, 1950.

——, **Young India**, vol. I. Triplicane, Madras: S. Ganesan, 1922.

Gerassi, John, **Great Fear in Latin America**. New York: Collier, 1965.

Gerland, Brigitte, "How the Great Vorkuta Strike was Prepared," and "The Great Labor Camp Strike at Vorkuta," in *The Militant* (New York), 28 February and 7 March 1955.

Gerth, Hans and C. Wright Mills, **Character and Social Structure**. New York: Harcourt, Brace & Co., 1953. London: Routledge and Kegan Paul, 1954.

Gerth, Hans, and C. Wright Mills, editors, From **Max Weber: Essays in Sociology**. New York: Oxford University Press, Galaxy Books, 1958 (orig. 1946). London: Kegan Paul, Trench, Trabner and Co., 1948.

Geyl, Pieter, **The Revolt of the Netherlands 1555-1609**. New York: Barnes and Noble, 1958. London: Ernest Benn, 1962.

Gipson, Lawrence Henry, **The British Empire Before the American Revolution**, vol. X, **The Triumphant Empire: Thunder-clouds Gather in the West, 1763-1766**, vol. XI, **The Triumphant Empire: The Rumbling of the Coming Storm, 1766-1770**, and vol. XII, **The Triumphant Empire: Britain Sails into the Storm, 1770-1776**. New York: Alfred A. Knopf, 1961-1965.

————, **The Coming of the Revolution, 1763-1775.** New York and Evanston: Harper Torchbooks, 1962.

Gleditsch, Nils Petter, ed., **Kamp Uten Våpen: En Antologi.** Oslo: Pax Forlag, 1965.

Godwin, William, **Enquiry Concerning Political Justice and its Influence on Morals and Happiness.** Two volumes. London: G. G. and J. Robinson, 1796.

Goldberg, Art., "Negro Self-Help," *New Republic*, vol. 156, no. 23 (10 June 1967), p. 6.

Goldhamer, Herbert and Edward A. Shils, "Power and Status," *American Journal of Sociology*, vol. XLV, no. 2 (September, 1939), pp. 171-180.

Goldman, Emma, **The Individual Society and the State** (pamphlet). Chicago: Free Society Forum, n.d.

Goodspeed, D.J., **The Conspirators: A Study of the Coup d'Etat.** New York: Viking Press, 1962. Toronto: Macmillan Co. of Canada, 1962.

Goodrich, Leland M., Edvard Hambro and Anne Patricia Simons, **Charter of the United Nations: Commentary and Documents.** Third and revised edition. New York and London: Columbia University Press, 1969.

Gopal, S., **The Viceroyalty of Lord Irwin, 1926-1931.** London: Oxford University Press, 1957.

Gordon, King, **U. N. in the Congo: A Quest for Peace.** New York: Carnegie Endowment for International Peace: 1962.

Görlitz, Walter, **History of the German General Staff, 1657-1945.** Trans. by Brian Battershaw. New York: Praeger, 1962.

————, ed., **The Memoirs of Field-Marshal Keitel.** Trans. by David Irving. New York: Stein and Day, 1966.

Government of India, **India in 1930-31, A Statement prepared for Presentation to Parliament in accordance with the requirements of the 26th section of the Government of India Act (5 & 6 Geo. V, Chapter 61).** Calcutta: Government of India, Central Publication Branch, 1932.

Grant, Joan, ed., **Black Protest: History, Documents, and Analyses 1619 to the Present.** Greenwich, Conn.: Fawcett, 1968.

de Grazia, Sebastian, **The Political Community: A Study of Anomie.** Chicago: University of Chicago Press, 1948.

Green, Thomas Hill, **Lectures on the Principles of Political Obligation.** London: Longmans, Green & Co., 1948 (orig. 1882).

Gregg, Richard, **The Power of Nonviolence.** Second revised edition. New York: Schoken, 1966. London: James Clarke & Co., 1960.

Griffith, Arthur, **The Resurrection of Hungary: A Parallel for Ireland.** Third edition. Dublin: Wheland & Son, 1918.

de Haestrup, J., "Expose," in **European Resistance Movements 1939-1945,** pp. 150-162.

Halberstam, David, **The Making of a Quagmire.** New York: Random House, 1965. London: The Bodley Head, 1965.

Hall, Fred S., **Sympathetic Strikes and Sympathetic Lockouts,** New York, published Ph.D. dissertation in Political Science. New York: Columbia University, 1898.

Halperin, S. William, **Germany Tried Democracy: A Political History of the Reich from 1918 to 1933.** Hamden, Conn. and London: Archon Books, 1963 (orig. 1946).

Hanh, Thich Nhát, "Love in Action: The Nonviolent Struggle for Peace in Vietnam" (duplicated pamphlet) Paris (?): Overseas Vietnamese Buddhists Association, 1967.

Harcave, Sidney, **First Blood: The Russian Revolution of 1905**. New York: Macmillan, 1964. London: Collier-Macmillan, 1964. Paperback edition entitled: **The Russian Revolution of 1905**. New York: Collier-Macmillan, 1970.

Hardinge of Penschurst, Lord, **Old Diplomacy: The Reminiscences of Lord Hardinge of Penschurst**. London: John Murray, 1947.

Hare, A. Paul, and Herbert H. Blumberg, eds., **Nonviolent Direct Action: American Cases: Social-Psychological Analyses**. Washington, D.C. and Cleveland: Corpus Books, 1968.

Harris, Errol E., "Political Power," *Ethics*, vol. XLVIII, no. 1 (October 1957), pp. 1-10.

Harris, Herbert, **American Labor**. New Haven: Yale University Press, 1938.

Heath, Dwight B., Charles J. Erasmus and Hans C. Buechler, **Land Reform and Social Revolution in Bolivia**. New York: Frederick A. Praeger, 1969.

Helset, Major General Olaf, "*Idrettsfronten*," in Steen, gen. ed., **Norges Krig**, vol. III, pp. 7-34.

Hentoff, Nat, **The New Equality**. New edition. New York: Viking Press, 1965.

Higgins, Trumbull, **Korea and the Fall of MacArthur: A Precis in Limited War**. New York: Oxford University Press, 1960.

Hilberg, Raul, **The Destruction of the European Jews**. London: W. H. Allen, 1961.

Hildebrandt, Rainer, **2 x 2 = 8: The Story of a Group of Young Men in the Soviet Zone of Germany** (pamphlet). Bonn and Berlin: Federal Ministry for All-German Affairs, 1961.

Hillenbrand, Martin J., **Power and Morals**. New York: Columbia University Press, 1949.

Hiller, E. T., **The Strike: A Study in Collective Action**. Chicago: University of Chicago Press, 1928.

Hirst, Margaret E., **The Quakers in Peace and War**. New York: George H. Doran Co., 1923. London: Swarthmore Press, 1923.

Hitler, Adolph, **Mein Kampf**. New York: Reynal and Hitchcock, 1941.

Hobbes, Thomas, **Leviathan**. New York: Everymans E. P. Dutton, 1950. Oxford: Clarendon Press, 1958.

Hoffman, Frederik, "The Functions of Economic Sanctions: A Comparative Analysis," *Journal of Peace Research*, 1967, no. 2, pp. 140-160.

Holmsen, Andreas, **Norges Historie Fra de Eldste Tider til 1960**, (Third Edition). Oslo and Bergen: Universitetsforlaget, 1964.

Holt, Edgar, **Protest in Arms**. London: Putnam & Co., Ltd., 1960.

Holter, Harriet, "Disputes and Tensions in Industry," reprint from *Scandinavian Democracy* (Copenhagen), 1958.

Hoskyns, Catherine, **The Congo Since Independence: January 1960-December 1961**. London: Oxford University Press, 1965.

Houser, George, **Erasing the Color Line** (pamphlet). Revised edition. New York: Congress of Racial Equality, 1948.

Howe, Irving and B. J. Widick, **The U.A.W. and Walter Reuther**. New York: Random House, 1949.

Høye, Bjarne and Trygve M. Ager, **The Fight of the Norwegian Church Against Nazism**. New York: Macmillan, 1943.

Hsiao, Kung-ch,üan, **Rural China: Imperial Control in the Nineteenth Century**. Seattle: University of Washington Press, 1960.

Huntington, Samuel P., **Political Order in Changing Societies**. New Haven and London: Yale University Press, 1968.

Hurum, Hans Jørgen, **Musikken Under Okkupasjonen, 1940-1945**. Oslo: H. Aschehoug, 1946.

Hutchinson, Royal D., **The Radio and the Resistance: A Case Study from Czechoslovakia**. Hellerup, Denmark: Institute for Peace and Conflict Research, 1970.

Hutchinson, Thomas, editor, **The Complete Poetical Works of Percy Bysshe Shelley**. Oxford: Clarendon Press, 1904.

Hutchinson, Thomas, **The History of the Colony and Province of Massachusetts-Bay**. Edited by Laurence Shaw Mayo. Cambridge, Mass.: Harvard University Press, 1936. See also C.B. Mayo, ed.

Huxley, Aldous, **Ends and Means: An Enquiry into the Nature of Ideals and into the Methods Employed for their Realization**. New York: Harper Bros., 1937, and London: Chatto and Windus, 1948.

India in 1930-31. See Government of India.

Irwin, Inez Haynes, **The Story of the Woman's Party**. New York: Harcourt, Brace and Co., 1921.

Jacob, Philip E., See Sibley and Jacob.

Jameson, A.K., **A New Way in Norway** (pamphlet). London: Peace News, 1946 or 1947.

Janis, Irving L. and Daniel Katz, "The Reduction of Intergroup Hostility: Research Problems and Hypotheses," in *Journal of Conflict Resolution*, vol. III, no. 1 (March 1959), pp. 85-100.

Jensen, Magnus, "*Kampen om Skolen*," in Sverre Steen, gen. ed., **Norges Krig**, vol. III, pp. 73-110.

————, **Norges Historie: Norge Under Eneveldet, 1660-1814**. Oslo and Bergen: Universitetsforlaget, 1963.

de Jong, L., "Anti-Nazi Resistance in the Netherlands," in **European Resistance Movements 1939-1945**, pp. 137-149.

de Jouvenal, Bertrand, **On Power: Its Nature and The History of its Growth**. Trans. by J.F. Huntington. Boston: Beacon Paperback, 1962. British edition: **Power: The Natural History of its Growth**. London: The Batchworth Press, 1952 (1945).

————, **Sovereignty: An Enquiry Into the Political Good**. Chicago: University of Chicago Press, 1959. London: The Batchworth Press, 1952.

Joyce, Patrick, **A Social History of Ancient Ireland**, vol. I. London: Longmans, Green, 1903.

Jungk, Robert, **Brighter than a Thousand Suns: The Story of the Men Who Made the Bomb**. New York: Grove Press Black Cat Edition, n.d.

Jutikkala, Eino, **A History of Finland**, with Kauko Pirinen. Trans. by Paul Sjöblom. New York: Frederick A. Praeger, 1962. London: Thames and Hudson, 1962.

Kallen, Horace M. "Coercion." **Encyclopedia of the Social Sciences**, vol. III, pp. 617-619. New York: Macmillan, 1935.

Karski, Jan, **Story of a Secret State**. Boston: Houghton Mifflin, 1944.

Katkov, George, **Russia 1917: The February Revolution**. New York: Harper

& Row, 1967.

Keep, J.H.L., **The Rise of Social Democracy in Russia**. Oxford: Clarendon Press, 1963.

Kendall, Carlton W., **The Truth About Korea**. San Francisco: Korea National Association, 1919.

King, Dan, **The Life and Times of Thomas Wilson Dorr with Outlines of the Political History of Rhode Island**. Boston: The Author, 1859.

King, Martin Luther, Jr., **Stride Toward Freedom: The Montgomery Story**. New York: Ballantine Books, 1958. London: Victor Gollancz, 1959.

——, **Why We Can't Wait**. New York: Signet Books of The New American Library, 1964.

King-Hall, Sir Stephen, **Defence in the Nuclear Age**. Nyack, N.Y.: Fellowship, 1959. London: Victor Gollancz, 1958.

Kirchhoff, Hans, Henrik S. Nissen, and Henning Pulsen, **Besaettelsestidens Historie**. Copenhagen: Forlaget Fremad, Danmarks Radios Grundbøger, 1964.

Knapp, Wilfrid F., **A History of War and Peace 1939-1965**. London, New York and Toronto: Oxford University Press, 1967.

Knowles, K.G.J.C., **Strikes—A Study in Industrial Conflict with Special Reference to British Experience Between 1911 and 1945**. New York: Philosophical Library, 1952. Oxford: Basil Blackwell, 1954.

Koestler, Arthur, **Reflections on Hanging**. New York: Macmillan, 1967.

Korbel, Josef, **The Communist Subversion of Czechoslovakia 1938-1948: The Failure of Coexistence**. Princeton, New Jersey: Princeton University Press, 1959.

Kornhauser, Arthur, Robert Dubins, and Arthur M. Ross, eds., **Industrial Conflict**. New York: McGraw-Hill.

Krehbiel, Edward B., **The Interdict: Its History and its Operation**. Washington, D.C.: American Historical Association, 1909.

Kripalani, Krishna, ed., **All Men Are Brothers: Life and Thoughts of Mahatma Gandhi as told in his Own Words**. Ahmedabad: Navajivan, 1960. (Also, Paris: Unesco, 1958.)

Kropotkine, P. (sic), **In Russian and French Prisons**. London: Ward and Downey, 1887.

Kuper, Leo, **Passive Resistance in South Africa**. New Haven, Conn.: Yale University Press, 1957. London: Jonathan Cape, 1956.

Laidler, Harry, "Boycott," **Encyclopedia of the Social Sciences**, vol. II, pp. 662-666. New York: Macmillan, 1935.

——, **Boycotts and the Labor Struggle, Economic and Legal Aspects**. New York: John Lane Co., 1913.

——, See also James Myers and Harry Laidler.

Lakey, George, "Cultural Aspects of the American Movement for Woman Suffrage, Militant Phase." Duplicated MS. Philadelphia, 1968.

——, "The Sociological Mechanisms of Nonviolent Action." Duplicated M.A. thesis in Sociology, University of Pennsylvania, 1962. Published in *Peace Research Reviews* (Oakville, Ontario: Canadian Peace Research Institute), vol. II, no. 6, whole number, (Dec., 1968).

Lasswell, Harold D., **Power and Personality**. New York: Norton, 1948.

Lees, Hannah, "The Not-Buying Power of Philadelphia Negroes," *The Reporter*, vol. 24, no. 10 (11 May 1961), pp. 33-35.

Lefebre, George, **The French Revolution from its Origins to 1793**. New York: Columbia University Press, 1962. London: Routledge & Kegan Paul, 1962.

Legum, Colin & Margaret, **South Africa: Crisis for the West**. New York and London: Frederick A. Praeger, 1964.

Leiss, Amelia, C., ed., **Apartheid and United Nations Collective Measures**. New York: Carnegie Endowment for International Peace, 1965.

Lenin, Nikolai (sic), **The Essentials of Lenin in Two Volumes**. London: Lawrence and Wishart, 1947. (N.B.: Lenin is now usually called V.I. Lenin.)

Lenin, V.I., **Collected Works**. Moscow: Foreign Languages Publishing House, 1962.

——, **Selected Works**. Moscow and Leningrad: Co-operative Publishing Society of Foreign Workers in the U.S.S.R., 1934(?).

——, **Selected Works in Three Volumes**. New York: International Publishers, and Moscow: Progress Publishers, 1967.

——, **Selected Works in Two Volumes**. Moscow: Foreign Languages Publishing House, 1950.

Lewis, Anthony and *The New York Times*, **Portrait of a Decade: The Second American Revolution**. New York: Random House, 1964.

Lewis, Flora, **A Case History of Hope: The Story of Poland's Peaceful Revolutions**. New York: Doubleday & Co., 1958. British edition: **The Polish Volcano: A Case History of Hope**. London: Secker & Warburg, 1959.

Lewy, Guenter, **The Catholic Church and Nazi Germany**. New York and Toronto: McGraw-Hill Co., 1964. London: Weidenfeld and Nicolson, 1964.

Liddell Hart, Sir Basil, **Defence of The West: Some Riddles of War and Peace**. New York: William Morrow Co., 1950. London: Cassell, 1950.

——, "Lessons from Resistance Movements—Guerilla and Nonviolent," in Roberts, ed., **Civilian Resistance as a National Defence**, pp. 195-211.

——, **Strategy: The Indirect Approach**. New York: Frederick A. Praeger, 1954. London: Faber and Faber, 1954.

Lipscome, Andrew A., editor-in-chief, **The Writings of Thomas Jefferson**. Washington, D.C.: Thomas Jefferson Memorial Association of the United States, 1903.

Littell, Robert, ed., **The Czech Black Book: Prepared by the Institute of History of the Czechoslovak Academy of Sciences**. New York, Washington and London: Frederick A. Praeger, 1969.

Lloyd, Clifford, **Ireland Under the Land League: A Narrative of Personal Experiences**. Edinburgh and London: William Blackwood & Sons, 1892.

Lochner, Louis P., ed., **The Goebbels Diaries, 1942-1943**. Garden City, N.Y.: Doubleday & Co., 1948.

Locker-Lampson, G., **A Consideration of the State of Ireland in the Nineteenth Century**. New York: E.P. Dutton & Co., 1907. London: Archibald Constable, 1907.

Loh, Robert (as told to Humphrey Evans), **Escape From Red China**. New York: Coward-McCann, 1962.

Lomax, Louis E., **The Negro Revolt**. New York: Signet Book, New American Library, 1963.

Luihn, Hans, **De Illegale Avisene: Den Frie, Hemmlige Pressen i Norge Under Okkupasjonen**. Oslo and Bergen: Universitetsforlaget, 1960.

Luthuli, Albert, **Let My People Go: An Autobiography**. New York McGraw-

Hill Book Co., Inc., 1962. London: Collins, 1962.

Lynd, Staughton, ed., **Nonviolence in America: A Documentary History**. Indianapolis: Bobbs-Merrill Co., 1966.

Lyttle, Bradford, **Essays on Non-violent Action** (duplicated booklet). Chicago: The Author, 1959.

——, "Haymarket; Violence Destroys a Movement" (duplicated). New York: Committee for Nonviolent Action, 1965.

——, "The Importance of Discipline in Demonstrations for Peace" (duplicated). New York: Committee for Nonviolent Action, 1962.

Mabee, Carleton, **Black Freedom: The Nonviolent Abolitionists from 1830 Through the Civil War**. New York: Macmillan, 1970. Toronto: Macmillan, 1970. London: Collier-Macmillan, 1970.

Machiavelli, Niccolo, **The Discourses of Niccolo Machiavelli**. London: Routledge and Kegan Paul, 1950.

——, **The Prince**. New York: E.P. Dutton Everyman's Library, 1948. London: J.M. Dent & Sons, Everyman's Library, 1948.

MacIver, R.M., **The Modern State**. Oxford: Clarendon Press, 1926. New York and London: Oxford University Press, 1964.

——, **The Web of Government**. New York: Macmillan, 1947.

Macmullen, Ramsay, "A Note on Roman Strikes," *Classical Journal*, vol. LVIII (1962-1963), pp. 269-271.

Mahadevan, T.K., Adam Roberts and Gene Sharp, eds., **Civilian Defence: An Introduction**. New Delhi: Gandhi Peace Foundation and Bombay: Bharatiya Vidya Bhavan, 1967.

Malinowski, Bronislaw, "An Anthropological Analysis of War," *American Journal of Sociology*, vol. XLVI, no. 4, pp. 521-549.

——, **Freedom and Civilization**. New York: Roy Publishers, 1944.

Maritain, Jacques, **Man and the State**. Chicago, Illinois: University of Chicago Press, 1954. London: Hollis & Carter, 1954.

Matthiessen, Peter, **Sal Si Puedes: Cesar Chavez and the New American Revolution**. New York: Random House, 1969.

Mayer, J.P., ed. and trans., **The Recollections of Alexis de Tocqueville**. New York: Meridian Books, 1959.

Mayo, Catherine Barton, ed., **Additions to Thomas Hutchinson's "History of Massachusetts Bay."** Worcester, Mass.: American Antiquarian Society, 1949.

McWilliams, Carey, **Factories in the Field: The Story of Migratory Farm Labor in California**. Boston: Little, Brown, & Co., 1939.

Menashe, Louis and Radosh, Ronald, eds., **Teach-ins: U.S.A.: Reports, Opinions, Documents**. New York: Frederick A. Praeger, 1967.

Michels, Robert, "Authority," **Encyclopedia of the Social Sciences**, vol. I, p. 319. New York: Macmillan, 1935.

Mikes, George, **The Hungarian Revolution**. London: Andre Deutsch, 1957.

Miles, Michael, "Black Cooperatives," *New Republic*, vol. 159, no. 12 (21 September 1968), pp. 21-23.

Miller, William Robert, **Nonviolence: A Christian Interpretation**. New York: Association Press, 1964.

Mills, C. Wright. See Hans Gerth and C. Wright Mills.

de Montesquieu, Baron. **The Spirit of the Laws**. Trans. by Thomas Nugent. Intro. by Franz Neumann. New York: Hafner Publishing Co., 1959.

Monthly Information Bulletin of the International Commission Against Concentration Camp Practices, no. 4, Aug.-Nov. 1955. Now titled *Saturn*.

Morgan, Edmund S. & Helen M., **The Stamp Act Crisis: Prologue to Revolution**. New revised edition. New York: Collier Books, 1963.

Morley, John, **The Life of William Ewart Gladstone**, vol. III. New York and London: MacMillan & Co., 1903.

Morris, John, "Early Christian Civil Disobedience," *Peace News* (London), 5 January 1962.

Mosca, Gaetano, **The Ruling Class**. New York and London: McGraw-Hill, 1939.

Mowat, Charles Loch, **Britain Between the Wars 1918-1940**. London: Methuen & Co., 1955.

Mowry, Arthur May, **The Dorr War or the Constitutional Struggle in Rhode Island**. Providence, R.I.: Preston & Rounds, 1901.

Muse, Benjamin, **The American Negro Revolution: From Nonviolence to Black Power, 1963-1967**. Bloomington and London: Indiana University Press, 1968.

——, **Virginia's Massive Resistance**. Bloomington: Indiana University Press, 1961.

Myers, James and Harry W. Laidler, **What Do You Know About Labor?** New York: John Day, 1956.

Naess, Arne, "A Systematization of Gandhian Ethics of Conflict Resolution," *Journal of Conflict Resolution*, vol. I (1957), pp. 140-155. See also Johan Galtung and Arne Naess.

Napoleon, **The Officer's Manual** or **Napoleon's Maxim of War**. New York: James G. Gregory, 1861.

Nayar, Pyarelal. See Pyarelal.

Nehru, Jawaharlal, **An Autobiography**. New edition. London: The Bodley Head, 1953.

——, **The Discovery of India**. New York: John Day, 1946.

——, **India and the World: Essays by Jawaharlal Nehru**. London: Geo. Allen & Unwin, Ltd., 1936.

——, **Toward Freedom: The Autobiography of Jawaharlal Nehru**. Revised edition. New York: John Day Co., 1942.

Neumann, Franz, **Behemoth: The Structure and Practice of National Socialism 1933-1944**. New York: Octagon Books, 1963.

——, **The Democratic and the Authoritarian State: Essays in Political and Legal Theory**. Glencoe, Ill.: The Free Press and Falcon's Wing Press, 1957.

Neustadt, Richard E., **Presidential Power: The Politics of Leadership**. New York and London: John Wiley and Sons, 1960.

Nevins, Allan and Henry Steele Commager, **America: The Story of a Free People**. Boston: Little, Brown and Co., 1943.

Nevinson, Henry W., **The Dawn in Russia or Scenes in the Russian Revolution**. New York and London: Harper & Bros., 1906.

Nicholson, Harold, **Diplomacy**. Second edition. London, New York and Toronto: Oxford University Press, 1960 (orig. 1950).

Nickalls, John L., ed., **The Journal of George Fox**. Cambridge: University Press, 1952.

Niebuhr, Reinhold, **Moral Man and Immoral Society**. New York: Charles Scribner's Sons, 1960 (orig. 1932). London: S.C.M. Press, 1963.

Nirumand, Bahman, **Iran: The New Imperialism in Action**. New York and London: Modern Reader Paperback, 1969.

O'Hegarty, Patrick Sarsfield, **A History of Ireland Under The Union, 1880-1922**. With an Epilogue carrying the story down to the acceptance in 1927 by De Valera of the Anglo-Irish Treaty of 1921. London: Methuen Press, 1952.

Olmsted, Frederick Law, **A Journey in the Seaboard Slave States, with Remarks on Their Economy**. New York: Dix and Edwards, 1956. London: Sampson Low, Son & Co., 1956.

Oppenheimer, Martin and George Lakey, **A Manual for Direct Action**. Chicago: Quadrangle Books, 1965.

Oxford English Dictionary. See **Shorter Oxford English Dictionary on Historical Principles**.

Pattabhi Sitaramayya, Bhagaraju, **The History of the Indian National Congress, 1885-1935**, vol I. Madras: Working Committee of the Congress, 1935.

Paullin, Theodor, **Introduction to Nonviolence** (pamphlet). Philadelphia: Pacifist Research Bureau, 1944.

Peck, Graham, **Two Kinds of Time**. Boston: Houghton-Mifflin, 1950.

Peck, James, **Freedom Ride**. New York: Simon and Schuster, 1962.

The Pentagon Papers as published by "The New York Times." New York, Toronto and London: Bantam Books, 1971.

Perkins, Dwight H., **Market Control and Planning in Communist China**. Cambridge, Mass.: Harvard University Press, 1966.

Perlman, Selig, **A History of Trade Unionism in the United States**. New York: Macmillan Co., 1923.

Peters, William, **The Southern Temper**. Garden City, New Jersey: Doubleday & Co., 1959.

Peterson, Florence, **American Labor Unions: What They Are and How They Work**. New York: Harper and Bros., 1945.

——, **Survey of the Labor Economics**. Revised edition. New York: Harper and Bros., 1951.

Phillips, Ulrich Bonnell, **American Negro Slavery: A Survey of the Supply, Employment and Control of Negro Labor as Determined by the Plantation Regime**. New York: Peter Smith, 1952 (orig. 1918).

Phillips, Norman, **The Tragedy of Apartheid**. New York: David McKay, 1960.

Pigors, Paul, **Leadership or Domination**. Boston: Houghton Mifflin Co., 1935. London: George G. Harrap, 1935.

Plamenatz, John, **The Revolutionary Movement in France 1815-1871**. London: Longmans, Green and Co., 1952.

Post, R. H., "Mourning Becomes Patriotic," in *Win* (New York), vol. 3, no. 13 (July 1967), p. 23.

Postgate, R. W., ed., **Revolution from 1789 to 1906**. New York: Harper Torchbooks, 1962.

Prasad, Rajendra, **Satyagraha in Champaran**. Ahmedabad: Navajivan, 1949.

Prawdin, Michael, **The Unmentionable Nechaev: A Key to Bolshevism**. London: Allen and Unwin, 1961.

Proudfoot, Merrill, **Diary of a Sit-in**. Chapel Hill, North Carolina: University of North Carolina Press, 1962.

Pyarelal, "Gandhiji Discusses Another 1942 Issue: Nonviolent Technique and

Parallel Government," reprinted from *Harijan* in *The Independent* (Bombay), 25 March 1946.

——, **Mahatma Gandhi: The Last Phase**, vol. I. Ahmedabad: Navajivan Publishing House, 1956.

Radosh, Ronald. See Lewis Menashe and Ronald Radosh.

Roloff, Karl. See Karl Ehrlich.

Ramachandran, G. and T. K. Mahadevan, eds., **Gandhi: His Relevance for Our Times**. Revised and enlarged second edition. Berkeley, Calif.: World Without War Council, 1971 and Bombay: Bharatiya Vidya Bhavan and New Delhi: Gandhi Peace Foundation, 1967.

Rao, G. S., **Gora—An Atheist**. Vijayawada, India: Atheistic Centre, 1970.

Ratcliffe, S. K., "Hunger Strike," **Encyclopedia of the Social Sciences**, vol. VII, pp. 532-533. New York: Macmillan, 1935.

Rayback, Joseph G., **A History of American Labor**. New York: Macmillan, 1964.

Reitlinger, Gerald, **The Final Solution: The Attempt to Exterminate the Jews of Europe 1939-1945**. New York: A. S. Barnes, 1961.

Remington, Robin Alison, ed., **Winter in Prague: Documents on Czechoslovak Communism in Crisis**. Cambridge, Mass. and London: M.I.T. Press, 1969.

Report of the Advisory Commission on the Review of the Constitution of Rhodesia and Nyasaland, Cmnd. 1148. London: H. M. Stationery Office, 1960.

Report of the Nyasaland Commission of Inquiry, Cmnd. 814. London: H. M. Stationery Office, 1959.

Report of the Special Committee on the Problem of Hungary, General Assembly, Official Records: Eleventh Session, Supplement No. 18 (A/3592). New York: United Nations, 1957.

Reynolds, Lloyd G., **Labor Economics and Labor Relations**. Englewood Cliffs, New Jersey: Prentice-Hall, 1959.

"A Rhode Islander," **Might and Right**. Providence: A. H. Stillwell, 1844.

Richman, Irving Berdine, **Rhode Island: A Study in Separatism**. Boston and New York: Houghton Mifflin Co., 1905.

Roberts, Adam, "Buddhism and Politics in South Vietnam," in *The World Today* (London), vol. 21, no. 6. (June 1965), pp. 240-250.

——, "The Buddhist Revolt: The Anti-Diem Campaign in South Vietnam in 1963." London: The Author, duplicated MS, 1964.

——, "The Buddhists, the War, and the Vietcong," in *The World Today*, vol. 22, no. 5 (May 1966), pp. 214-222.

——, co-ed., **Civilian Defence: An Introduction**. See Mahadevan, T. K.

——, "Four Strategies in Resisting Invasion," unpublished MS.

——, ed., **Civilian Resistance as a National Defence: Non-violent Action Against Aggression**. Harrisburg, Pa.: Stackpole Books, 1968. British ed.: **The Strategy of Civilian Defence: Non-violent Resistance to Aggression**. London: Faber & Faber, 1967. Paperback ed.: **Civilian Resistance as a National Defence**. Baltimore, Maryland, Harmondsworth, Middlesex, England and Ringwood, Victoria, Australia: Penguin Books, 1969.

——, See also Philip Windsor and Adam Roberts.

Robertson, J. R., "On-the-Job Activity," in E. Wight Bakke and Charles Kerr, **Unions, Management and the Public**.

Rosenthal, Mario, **Guatemala: The Story of an Emergent Latin-American**

Democracy. New York: Twayne Publishers, 1962.

Rostovtzeff, M., **The Social and Economic History of the Roman Empire**, vol. I. Second edition revised by P. M. Fraser. Oxford: Clarendon Press, 1956.

Rousseau, Jean Jacques, "The Social Contract" in **The Social Contract and Discourses**. New York: E. P. Dutton & Co., Everyman's Library, 1920. London: J. M. Dent & Sons, Ltd., Everyman's Library, 1920.

The Royal Institute of International Affairs, **International Sanctions**. London: Oxford University Press, 1938.

——, **Sanctions**. Second edition. London: Royal Institute of International Affairs, 1935.

Rubin, Jerry, **Do It!** New York: Simon and Schuster, 1970.

Rudé, George, **The Crowd in The French Revolution**. Oxford: Clarendon Press, 1959.

Rudlin, W. A., "Obedience, Political" in **Encyclopedia of the Social Science**, vol. XI, p. 415. New York: Macmillan, 1935.

Russell, Bertrand, **Authority and the Individual: The Reith Lectures for 1948-1949**. New York: Simon and Schuster, 1949. London: George Allen and Unwin, 1949.

——, **Power: A New Social Analysis**. New York: W. W. Norton & Co., 1938. London: George Allen and Unwin, 1938.

——, **Roads to Freedom: Socialism, Anarchism and Syndicalism**. London: George Allen and Unwin, 1918.

Salvemini, Gaetano, **The French Revolution, 1788-1792**, Trans. I. M. Rawson. New York: Henry Holt and Co., 1954. London: Jonathan Cape, 1963.

Schapiro, Leonard, **The Communist Party of the Soviet Union**. New York: Random House, 1960. London: Eyre & Spottiswoode, 1960.

——, **The Origin of the Communist Autocracy, Political Opposition in the Soviet State, First Phase 1917-1922**. Cambridge, Mass.: Harvard University Press, 1955. London: G. Bell & Sons, The London School of Economics and Political Science, 1956.

Schelling, Thomas C., **International Economics**. Boston: Allyn and Bacon, 1958.

Schlesinger, Arthur M., **The Colonial Merchants and the American Revolution 1763-1776**. New York: Frederick Ungar, 1966.

Schneider, Ronald M., **Communism in Guatemala 1944-1954**. New York: Frederick A. Praeger, 1958.

Scholl, Inge, **Six Against Tyranny**, Trans. by Cyrus Brooks. London: John Murray, 1955.

Scholmer, Joseph, **Vortuka**. New York: Holt, 1955.

Schwarz, Solomon M., **The Russian Revolution of 1905: The Workers' Movement and the Formation of Bolshevism and Menshevism**, Trans. by Gertrude Vakar. Preface by Leopold H. Haimson. Chicago and London: University of Chicago Press, 1967.

Schweitzer, Arthur, **Big Business in the Third Reich**. Bloomington, Indiana: Indiana University Press, 1964. London: Eyre and Spottiswoode, 1964.

Segal, Ronald, ed., **Sanctions Against South Africa**. London and Baltimore, Md.: Penguin Books, 1964.

Seifert, Harvey, **Conquest by Suffering: The Process and Prospects of Nonviolent Resistance**. Philadelphia: Westminster Press, 1965.

————, "The Use by American Quakers of Nonviolent Resistance as a Method of Social Change." Unpublished Ph.D. dissertation, Boston University, 1940.

Seton-Watson, Christopher, **Italy From Liberalism to Fascism, 1870-1925.** New York: Barnes and Noble, 1967. London: Methuen, 1967.

Seton-Watson, Hugh, **The Decline of Imperial Russia.** New York: Frederick A. Praeger, 1952. London: Methuen & Co., 1952.

Sharp, Gene, **An Abecedary of Nonviolent Action and Civilian Defense.** Cambridge, Mass.: Schenkman, 1972.

————, "Can Non-violence work in South Africa?" "Problems of Violent and Non-violent Struggle," "Strategic Problems of the South African Resistance," and "How Do You Get Rid of Oppression?" in *Peace News* (London) 21 and 28 June, 5 July, and 25 October, 1963.

————, co-ed., **Civilian Defence: An Introduction.** See T.K. Mahadevan, Adam Roberts and Gene Sharp.

————, "The Constructive Programme," *Mankind* (Hyderabad), vol. I, no. 12 (July 1957), pp. 1102-1112.

————, "Creative Conflict in Politics," *The New Era*, January, 1962. Pamphlet reprint edition: London: Housmans, 1962.

————, "Dilemmas of Morality in Politics," *Reconciliation Quarterly* (London), First Quarter 1965, no. 128, pp. 528-535.

————, "Ethics and Responsibility in Politics: A critique of the present adequacy of Max Weber's classification of ethical systems," *Inquiry* (Oslo), vol. VII, no. 3 (Autumn 1964), pp. 304-317.

————, **Exploring Nonviolent Alternatives.** Boston: Porter Sargent, 1970.

————, **Gandhi Wields the Weapon of Moral Power: Three Case Histories.** Introduction by Albert Einstein. Ahmedabad: Navajivan, 1960.

————, "Gandhi's Defence Policy," in T. K. Mahadevan, Adam Roberts and Gene Sharp, eds., **Civilian Defence: An Introduction,** pp. 15-52.

————, "Gandhi's Political Significance Today," in G. Ramachandran and T.K. Mahadevan, eds., **Gandhi,** pp. 44-66.

————, "The Meanings of Nonviolence: A Typology (revised)," *Journal of Conflict Resolution*, vol. III, no. 1 (March 1959), pp. 41-66. See latest revision "Types of Principled Nonviolence."

————, "The Methods of Nonviolent Resistance and Direct Action" Duplicated MS. Oslo: Institute for Social Research, 1960.

————, "The Need of a Functional Substitute for War," *International Relations* (London), vol. III, no. 3 (April 1967), pp. 187-207.

————, "Non-violence: Moral Principle or Political Technique?" *Indian Political Science Review* (Delhi), vol. IV, no. 1 (Oct. 1969-Mar. 1970), pp. 17-36.

————, "The Political Equivalent of War—Civilian Defence," *International Conciliation*, Whole Number, no. 555. New York: Carnegie Endowment for International Peace, November 1965.

————, "A South African Contribution to the Study of Nonviolent Action: A Review," in *Journal of Conflict Resolution*, vol. II, no. 4 (Dec. 1961), pp. 395-402.

————, "The Technique of Nonviolent Action," in Adam Roberts, ed., **Civilian Resistance as a National Defense,** pp. 87-105.

————, "Types of Principled Nonviolence," in A. Paul Hare and Herbert H.

Blumberg, eds., **Nonviolent Direct Action**, pp. 273-313.

———, **Tyranny Could Not Quell Them** (pamphlet). London: Peace News, 1958 and later editions.

Sheehy-Skeffington, F., **Michael Davitt: Revolutionary, Agitator and Labour Leader**. London and Leipsic: T. Fisher Unwin, 1908.

Shimbori, Michiya, "Zengakuren: A Japanese Case Study of a Student Political Movement," in *Sociology of Education*, vol. 37, no. 3 (Spring 1964), pp. 229-253.

Shirer, William L., **Berlin Diary, The Journal of a Foreign Correspondent, 1934-1941**. New York: Alfred A. Knopf, 1941.

———, **The Rise and Fall of the Third Reich**. New York: Simon and Schuster, 1960. London: Secker and Warburg, 1962.

The Shorter Oxford English Dictionary on Historical Principles, vol. II. Third edition revised. Oxford: Clarendon Press, 1959.

Shridharani, Krishnalal, **War Without Violence: A Study of Gandhi's Method and Its Accomplishments**. New York: Harcourt, Brace, and Co., 1939. London: Victor Gollancz, 1939. Reprinted with an Introduction by Gene Sharp, New York: Garland, 1972. Revised and enlarged paperback edition: Chowpatty and Bombay: Bharatiya Vidya Bhavan, 1962.

Shuller, Nettie Rogers. See Carrie Chapman Catt and Nettie Rogers Shuller.

Sibley, Mulford Q. and Asa Wardlaw, "Conscientious Objectors in Prison," in Lynd, ed., **Nonviolence in America**.

Sibley, Mulford Q. and Philip E. Jacob, **Conscription of Conscience: The American State and the Conscientious Objector, 1940-1947**. Ithaca, N.Y.: Cornell University Press, 1952.

Sibley, Mulford Q., ed., **The Quiet Battle: Writings on the Theory and Practice of Nonviolent Resistance**. Garden City, N.Y.: Anchor Books, Doubleday, 1963.

Sitaramayya. See B. Pattabhi Sitaramayya.

Skodvin, Magne, "Det Store Fremstøt," in Steen, gen. ed., **Norges Krig**, vol. II, pp. 573-734.

———, "Norwegian Nonviolent Resistance During the German Occupation," in Roberts, ed., **Civilian Resistance as a National Defense**, pp. 136-153.

Smith, T. Lynn, ed., **Agrarian Reform in Latin America**. New York: Alfred A. Knopf, 1965.

Solomon, Frederic and Jacob R. Fishman, "The Psychosocial Meaning of Nonviolence in Student Civil Rights Activities," *Psychiatry*, vol. XXVII, no. 2 (May 1964), pp. 91-99.

Solomon, F., W. L. Walker, G. O'Connor and J. R. Fishman, "Civil Rights Activity and Reduction in Crime Among Negroes," *Archives of General Psychiatry*, vol. XII (March 1965), pp. 227-236.

Spitz, David, **Democracy and the Challenge of Power**. New York: Columbia University Press, 1958.

Stalberg, Benjamin, **Tailor's Progress: The Story of A Famous Union and the Men Who Made It**. New York: Doubleday, Doran and Co., 1944.

Steen, Sverre, gen. ed., **Norges Krig 1940-1945**. Three volumes. Oslo: Gyldendal Norsk Forlag, 1947-50.

Steinberg, I.N., **In the Workshop of the Revolution**. New York: Rinehart & Co., 1953.

Steiner, Stan, **The New Indians**. New York: Harper & Row, 1968.

Stern, Bernard J., "Slavery, Primitive," Encyclopedia of the Social Sciences, vol. 14, pp. 73-74. New York: Macmillan, 1935.

Sternstein, Wolfgang, "The *Ruhrkampf* of 1923: Economic Problems of Civilian Defence," in Roberts, ed., Civilian Resistance as a National Defense, pp. 106-135.

Steuben, John, Strike Strategy. New York: Gaer Associates, 1950.

Stevens, Doris, Jailed for Freedom. New York: Boni and Liverwright, 1920.

Stevenson, J., ed., A New Eusebius: Documents Illustrative of the History of the Church to A.D. 337. London: S.P.C.K., 1957.

Stokes, Whitley, ed., Tripartite Life of St. Patrick. London: Her Majesty's Stationery Office, by Eyre and Spottiswoode, 1887.

Suhl, Yuri, ed., They Fought Back: The Story of the Jewish Resistance in Nazi Europe. New York: Crown Publishers, 1967.

Sykes, Brigadier-General Sir Percy, A History of Persia. Two volumes. London: Macmillan & Co., 1963.

Symons, Julian, The General Strike: A Historical Portrait. London: The Cresset Press, 1957.

Taber, Robert, M-26: Biography of a Revolution. New York: Lyle Stuart, 1961.

Taft, Philip, The A. F. of L. in the Time of Gompers. New York: Harper and Bros., 1957.

Taubenfeld, Rita Falk and Howard J. Taubenfeld, "The 'Economic Weapon': The League and the United Nations," *Proceedings of the American Society of International Law*, 1964, pp. 183-205.

Taylor, George R., The Struggle for North China. New York: Institute of Pacific Relations, 1940.

Taylor, Mary, ed., "Community Development in Western Sicily." Duplicated. Partinico: Centro studi e iniziative per la piena occupazione, 1963.

Tendulkar, D. G., Mahatma: Life of Mohandas Karamchand Gandhi. Eight volumes. Delhi: Publications Division, Ministry of Information and Broadcasting, Government of India, 1962.

Thayer, Charles W., Diplomat. New York: Harper & Bros., 1959.

Thompson, Daniel, The Negro Leadership Class. Englewood Cliffs, New Jersey: Prentice-Hall, 1963.

Thoreau, Henry David, "On the Duty of Civil Disobedience" (pamphlet). Intro. by Gene Sharp. London: Peace News, 1963. Or, in Walden and Other Writings of Henry David Thoreau. New York: Random House, 1937.

Tobias, Fritz, The Reichstag Fire. New York: G. P. Putnam's Sons, 1964.

de Tocqueville, Alexis, Democracy in America. Translated by George Lawrence. Edited by J. P. Mayer. Garden City, N. Y.: Anchor Books, Doubleday & Co., 1969.

Tolstoy, Leo, The Kingdom of God is Within You. New York: Thomas Y. Crowell, 1899. London: William Heinemann, 1894.

———, The Law of Violence and the Law of Love. Translated by Mary Koutouzow Tolstoy. New York: Rudolph Field, 1948. Also published in a different translation in *The Fortnightly Review*. London: Chapman & Hall, 1909.

———, "A Letter to a Hindu: The Subjection of India—Its Cause and Cure," with an Introduction by M. K. Gandhi, in Leo Tolstoy, The Works of

Tolstoy, vol. XXI, **Recollections and Essays**, pp. 413-432. Translated by Mr. and Mrs. Aylmer Maude. London: Oxford University Press, Humphrey Milford, 1937. Also in Kalidas Nag, **Tolstoy and Gandhi**. Patna, India: Pustak Bhandar, 1950.

Trevelyan, Sir George Otto, **The American Revolution**, vol. I. New edition. New York, London and Bombay: Longmans, Green & Co., 1908.

Trotsky, Leon, **My Life**. New York: Universal Library, Grossett & Dunlap, 1960.

Ulan, Adam B., **The Bolsheviks: The Intellectual and Political History of the Triumph of Communism in Russia**. New York: Macmillan, 1965. London: Collier-Macmillan, 1965.

Ullstein, Heinz, **Spielplatz Meines Lebens: Erinnerungen**. Munich: Kindler Verlag, 1961.

United Nations. See **Report of the Special Committee on the Problem of Hungary**.

Urutia, Miguel, **The Development of the Colombian Labor Movement**. New Haven and London: Yale University Press, 1969.

Vali, Ferenc A., **Rift and Revolt in Hungary: Nationalism versus Communism**. Cambridge, Mass.: Harvard University Press. London: Oxford University Press, 1961.

Vassilyev, A.T., **The Ochrana: The Russian Secret Police**. Edited and with an Introduction by Rene Fülöp-Miller. Philadelphia and London: J.B. Lippincott Co., 1930.

Venturi, Franco, **Roots of Revolution: A History of the Populist and Socialist Movements in Nineteenth Century Russia**. New York: Alfred A. Knopf, 1960. London: Weidenfeld and Nicolson, 1960.

Walker, Charles C., **Organizing for Nonviolent Direct Action** (pamphlet). Cheney, Pennsylvania: The Author, 1961.

Wallensteen, Peter, "Characteristics of Economic Sanctions," *Journal of Peace Research* (Oslo), 1968, no. 3, pp. 248-267.

Walter, E. V., "Power and Violence," *American Political Science Review*, vol. LVIII, no. 2 (June 1964), pp. 350-360.

Walters, F. P., **A History of the League of Nations**. London: Oxford University Press, 1960.

Warmbrunn, Werner, **The Dutch Under German Occupation 1940-1945**. Palo Alto, California: Stanford University Press. London: Oxford University Press, 1963.

Warner, Denis, **The Last Confucian**. London and Baltimore, Md.: Penquin Books, 1964.

Warriner, Doreen, **Land Reform in Principle and Practice**. Oxford: Clarendon Press, 1969.

Washington, H. A., ed., **The Writings of Thomas Jefferson**. Washington, D.C.: Taylor and Maury, 1853.

Waskow, Arthur I., **From Race Riot to Sit-in: 1919 and the 1960s**. Garden City, N.Y.: Doubleday, 1966.

Watkins, Frederick, ed., **Hume: Theory of Politics**. Edinburgh: Thomas Nelson & Sons, Ltd., 1951.

Watt, Richard M., **Dare Call It Treason**. New York: Simon and Schuster, 1963.

Webb, Sidney and Beatrice, **The History of Trade Unionism**. Revised edition to 1920. New York: Longmans, Green & Co., 1920.

Weber, Max, "Politics as a Vocation," in H. H. Gerth and C. Wright Mills, eds. and trans., **From Max Weber: Essays in Sociology**, pp. 77-128. London: Kegan Paul, Trench, Trabner & Co., 1948.

Wechsberg, Joseph, **The Voices**. Garden City, N. Y.: Doubleday, 1969.

Westin, Alan F., ed., **Freedom Now: The Civil-Rights Struggle in America**. New York: Basic Books, 1964.

Wheeler-Bennett, John W., **The Nemesis of Power: The German Army in Politics, 1918-1945**. New York: St. Martin's Press, 1953. London: Macmillan, 1953.

Williams, George Huntston, "The Ministry and the Draft in Historical Perspective" in Donald Cutler, ed., **The Religious Situation—1969**. Boston: Beacon Press, 1969.

Williams, Robin M., **The Reduction of Intergroup Tensions**. New York: Social Science Research Council, 1947.

Willigan, J. Dennis, S.J., "Sanctuary," *Union Seminary Quarterly*, vol. XXV, no. 4 (Summer 1970).

Wilson, James Q., "The Negro in Politics," *Daedalus*, vol. 94, no. 4 (Fall 1965).

Windsor, Philip and Adam Roberts: **Czechoslovakia 1968: Reform, Repression and Resistance**. New York: Columbia University Press, 1969. London: Chatto & Windus, 1969.

Wolfe, Bertram D., **Three Who Made a Revolution**. New York: Dial Press, 1948. London: Thames and Hudson, 1956.

Wolff, Kurt H., ed. and trans., **The Sociology of Georg Simmel**. Glencoe, Ill.: Free Press, 1950.

Wolman, Leo, **The Boycott in American Trade Unions**, Johns Hopkins University Studies in Historical and Political Science, series XXXIV, no. 1, 1916. Baltimore, Md.: Johns Hopkins Press, 1916.

Woodward, E. L., **French Revolutions**. London: Oxford University Press, Humphrey Milford, 1939.

Wright, Quincy, **A Study of War**. Two volumes. Chicago: University of Chicago Press, 1942.

Wyller, Thomas Chr., **Nyordning og Motstand: Organisasjones Politiske Rolle Under Okkupasjonen**. Oslo: Universitetsforlaget, 1958.

Yarmolinsky, Avrahm, **Road to Revolution: A Century of Russian Radicalism**. New York: Macmillan and Co., 1959. London: Cassell, 1957.

Yellen, Samuel, **American Labor Struggles**. New York: Harcourt, Brace & Co., 1936.

Yoder, Dale, **Labor Economics and Labor Problems**. New York and London: McGraw-Hill Co., 1939.

Yunus, Muhammed, **Frontier Speaks**. Bombay: Hind Kitabs, 1947.

Zinn, Howard, **Albany**. Atlanta: Southern Regional Council, 1962.

Ziskind, David, **One Thousand Strikes of Government Employees**. New York: Columbia University Press, 1940.

Index

African slaves, 124.

Afro-Americans, 5, 70, 73, 95-97, 98, 134, 138, 166, 198, 199, 203, 223-224, 235, 239-240, 243, 335-337, 371-372, 373-377, 378, 379-380, 383-384, 386, 388, 391-392, 395, 398-399, 402, 411, 414-415, 472, 534, 548, 559-560, 569 n. 102, 591, 616-617, 640, 670, 671, 689-690, 700 n. 40; 713, 716-717, 737, 766, 771 n. 58, 785, 786-788, 791, 795, 796. See also Negroes.

Afro-American Society of Tufts University, 378-379.

Aga Bey, Lydia (Asia Minor), 124.

Agents provocateurs, 112, 592-594, 601, 627.

Ager, Trygve M., 122.

Agrarian Reform Decree, Bolivia, 407.

Agrarian Reform Law, Colombia, 441 n. 192.

Agrarian Reform Law, Venezuela, 408.

Agricultural strikes, 261-264.

Agricultural union, 398.

Ahimsa (nonviolence), 212, 456.

Ahmedabad, India, 466, 583, 591.

Ahmedabad, India, Municipal Board of, 339.

Ahmedabad strike, 367, 583.

Akron, Ohio, 277, 403.

Akwesasne Notes, 439 n. 131.

Alabama, 95, 151, 159, 201, 233, 414-415.

Albany, Georgia, 138, 471-472.

Albany County, New York, 226.

Albrecht, Emil, 325.

Alcatraz Island, 389, 439 n. 131.

Aldermaston Atomic Weapons Research Establishment, 148.

Aldermaston march, 171, 631.

Alexander II, Tsar, 645 n. 79, 679.

Alexander, King of Serbia, 344.

Alexandra, South Africa, 223, 464, 536, 669, 738, 795.

Alfieri, Dino, 589.

Algeria, 363, 385, 544-545, 552.

Algerian nationalists, 73, 544.

Algerian War, 310, 544, 552. See also France.

Algerine Law, of Rhode Island, 427, 428.

Algiers, Algeria, 165, 385.

Alien and Sedition Acts, U.S., 338.

Alinsky, Saul, 139.

Allied Commission of Control, 381.

Allied "terror fliers," 324.

Allies, 87, 90, 267, 312, 324, 409, 586, 626.

All-Russian Peasant Union, 237.

All Souls College, Oxford, Preface.

Almon, John, 317.

Alternative communication system, 400-401.

"Alternative Days" strike. See Strike, limited.

Alternative economic institutions, 415-416.

Alternative institutions, 433, 797.

Alternative markets, 413-414.

Alternative political institutions, 423.

Alternative social institutions, 398-400, 797.

Alternative transportation system, 414-415, 796.

Alternatives to violence, Preface.

Altgeld, Governor John, 598.

Ambrose, Bishop, 388.

America, 70, 76, 90, 132, 171, 212, 229, 233, 245, 250 n. 49, 265, 382, 397, 404, 425, 671, 689, 736, 794. See also United States of America, South America, Latin America and individual countries.

American Antislavery Almanac, 376.

American Antislavery Society, 391.

American Cigar Makers Union, 269.

American colonists, 4, 70, 73, 74, 76, 124, 140-141, 157, 160, 165, 185-186, 224, 225, 229, 231, 234, 238-239, 241-242, 246-247, 266, 274, 287, 299, 308, 337, 361-362, 352 n. 169, 412, 424, 481, 495, 507, 511, 519 n. 132, 519 n. 142, 531, 534-535, 536, 540, 551, 553, 569 n. 115, 578-579, 580-582, 595, 600, 602-603, 605, 646 n. 99, 648 n. 147, 611-615, 622-623, 631-632, 633, 636, 667, 685, 693, 708, 713, 737, 738, 740, 743, 750, 781, 794, 797-798.

American Congress of Deputies for All the Colonies, 362.

American Federation of Labor, 404.

American Federation of Labor and Congress of Industrial Organizations, 297.
———. Union Label Department, 413.

American and Foreign Antislavery Society, 384.

American Nazis, 694, 789.

American Railway Union, 233.

American War of Independence, 221, 264, 337, 425, 611.

Americus, Georgia, 243.

Ami du Peuple, 35.

Amnesty International, 172.

Bloom, Murray Teich, 409-410.
"Blowing In the Wind" (song), 129.
Bobrikov, General Nikolai I., 593.
Bock, Field-Marshal Fedor von, 322.
Boddie, Jan, Preface.
de la Boétie, Etienne, 17, 24, 34, 35, 36, 54 n. 52, 60 n. 158.
Boghari, Algeria, 385.
Bohemia, 234; Catholic newspapers in, 234; National Socialists in, 234.
Bolivia, 246, 406-407; *coup d' état* in, 407; Ministry of Rural Affairs, 262.
Bolsheviks, 4, 79, 160, 328, 430, 606-607, 646 n. 99, 649 n. 159, 673, 743. See also Communist Party, Soviet Union.
Bombay, India, 155, 311, 385, 432-433, 687, 693, 735, 740, 751.
Bombay Congress Committee, 432.
Bombay Presidency, British India, 687.
Bombing (as sabotage), 3, 12, 77, 96-97, 139, 539, 548, 598, 610, 670, 689, 735.
Bombings, U.S. of Vietnam, 342.
Bondurant, Joan V., 146, 211, 299, 477, 519 n. 182, 503, 552-553, 709-710, 731, 742, 774 n. 161, 790, 796.
Books, publication and distribution of, 127.
Bordeaux, France, 326.
Border Government, North China, 232, 424.
Bormann, Martin, 324, 669.
Borisov, U.S.S.R., German Army Group Center at, 320.
Borton, Hugh, 212-213.
Bose, Nirmal Kumar, 500, 503, 509, 557, 563, 638, 805-806.
Bose, Subhas Chandra, 86.
Boston, Massachusetts, 137, 141, 157, 165, 274, 361, 381, 720; and occupation of Boston by British, 338, 553, 578; Boston School Committee, 373; Boston City Hospital, 393; Boston Massacre, 557, 685.
Boston Edison Company, 131.
Boston Globe, 297, 394.
Boston Port Act and Bill, 361-362, 702 n. 106.
Boston Tea Party, 507, 602, 612, 632, 685.
Boston University, 205.
Boston Vigilance Committee, 369-370.
Boulding, Kenneth, 790.
Bowditch, Dr. Henry, 391.
Boycott: general, 12, 71, 76, 77, 126, 719. See Social boycott, Economic

boycott and Political boycott. See also Noncooperation; Social noncooperation; Economic noncooperation; Political noncooperation; all specific methods under those classes; also Primary and Secondary boycotts.
Boycott, Captain, 220, 719.
Boycott of elections, 291-292.
Boycott of government departments, agencies and other bodies, 295-297.
Boycott of government employment and positions, 292-295.
Boycott of government-supported organizations, 199, 298, 302.
Boycott of legislative bodies, 289-291.
Boycott of social affairs, 196.
Boycott, political. See Political boycott and Political noncooperation.
Boycott, social. See Social boycott, Boycott of social relations, and Selective social boycott.i,
Brady, Dennis, Preface.
Braemer, General Friedrich, 326.
Brailsford, H.N., 432-433, 687.
Brahmins, 83, 393, 717.
Brandeis University, Preface, 198.
Brando, Marlon, 319.
Brandt, Heinz, 172, 529.
Brant, Stefan, 170, 172, 303, 386-387, 519 n. 132, 542, 550, 566 n. 21, 567 n. 47, 629, 688, 745-746.
Bratislava, Slovakia, 234, 313.
Brauchitsch, Commander-in-Chief Walter Von, 295, 322.
Bräutigam, Dr. Otto, 683.
Brazil, 262, 406, 408; coup d'etat in, 262.
Brest, Katherine, Preface.
Breton peasants, 189.
Brewers' Association, U.S., 231.
Brewers' Employers' Association, Germany, 222.
Brezhnev, Leonid I., General Secretary, Communist Party of the Soviet Union, 126.
Brinton, Crane, 337, 423-424.
Bristol, James, 243.
Bristol, Rhode Island, 185.
Britain (also British, England and English): American colonists' struggles against, 4, 76-77, 124, 137, 141, 158-159, 160, 165, 172, 185, 221, 224-226, 229, 231, 238-239, 246-247, 274, 287, 299, 361-363, 412-413, 424-425, 464, 507, 531, 534-535, 540-541, 553, 578, 699 n. 32, 702 n. 109, 708, 738, 740, 750-751, 794. See also American colo-

nies, Stamp Act, Townshend Acts, Continental Association, First Continental Congress, etc.; Subjection of India, 30, 57 n. 100, 59 n. 144, 78, 84, 210, 512-513, 687, 783. See also British *Raj*; Indian struggles against, 4-5, 82, 83, 84-85, 86-87, 135, 212, 229-230, 295, 413, 420, 421, 432-433, 490, 494, 513-514, 529, 546, 552, 556, 593, 605, 659, 665, 676, 677, 681, 687-688, 693, 701, 727, 747, 748, 751-752, 785, 795, 797. See also India, Gandhi, satyagraha; Egyptian struggle against, 125; Irish struggles against, 161, 188, 189, 366. See also Ireland; nuclear disarmament movement in, 148, 167, 171, 289, 419-420, 482, 631, 632, 634-635, 692. See also Committee of 100, Campaign for Nuclear Disarmament, Committee for Direct Action Against Nuclear War, and Direct Action Committee Against Nuclear War; conflict with U.S. over impressment and U.S. economic sanctions against, 245-246, 247. See also T. Jefferson and J. Madison; and Federation of Rhodesia and Nyasaland, 126-127; Disputes and Trade Union Act of 1927, 133; refusal to recognize Kapp regime, 344; broadcasts from, 305. See also British Broadcasting Corporation; capital punishment in, 329; restrictions on picketing, 133; perceptions of threat of nonviolent action, 41-42, 528, 531-532; repression of Mau Mau in Kenya, 666; Quakers returned to, 719; *Chargé d'Affaires* in Tehran, Persia, 208; and anti-slavery plan, 411; and Berlin airlift, 408-409; travellers in China, 350 n. 88; sabotage in Norway organized in, 609; specific nonviolent methods applied in: teach-ins, 169; rent-withholding, 226; handler's boycott, 233; lock-out, 235; tax refusal, 242; international trade embargo, 246-247, 248; lightning strike, 261; sympathetic strike, 268; detailed strike, 268; ca'canny, 269; general strikes in, 134, 276, 277, 464, 485, 531, 542, 578, 593, 757, 787; judicial noncooperation, 329-330; fasts, 366. See also Fasts; nonviolent interjection, 385; counterfeit money, 410; seizure of assets, 410-411; civil disobedience of "neutral" laws, 420; parallel govern-ment, 424; social boycotts, 580; general demonstrations, 659; railway strikes, 71, 273; constitutional system, 532; General Election of 1959, 292; Parliament of, 76, 132, 238, 292, 315, 316-317, 361, 362, 425, 481, 536, 636, 665, 685, 737. See also Ireland, Scotland, Wales, individual towns and cities, organizations, woman suffrag-ists, Trades Union Congress, Devlin Commission, names of officials, and Occupations, British of.

British Broadcasting Corporation, Welsh Service, 242.

British Columbia, Canada, 140.

British Empire, 513, 534, 737, 761.

British General Strike of 1926. See General Strike, Britain 1926.

British Government, 42, 84, 127, 133, 187, 433, 495, 512, 574, 584, 591, 614, 639, 725.

British Honduras, 155.

British Isles, 541.

British Legation, Tehevan, Persia, 208-209.

British North America, 238.

British Quartering Act, 337.

British Railway Wage Dispute 1949, 271.

British *raj* (rule) in India, 41, 84, 383, 526, 529, 562, 681, 686, 687, 740, 748, 757. See also Britain, subjection of India.

British Treasury, 338.

British West Indies, 541.

Brochures, 128.

Bronx, New York City, 228.

Brooklyn, New York City, 228, 388.

Brown, William Wells, 392.

Browne, Edward G., 207, 209.

Bruenn, Czechoslovakia, 590.

Brussels, Belgium, 684.

Brutalities, 555-565.

Buchenwald concentration camp, 161.

Büchs, Major Herbert, 324.

Buckler, W.H., 231, 266, 568 n. 72.

Buck's Stove and Range Co., 222.

Budapest, Hungary, 93, 163, 171, 200, 344.

Buddhist struggle against Diem regime, 1963, South Vietnam, 158, 279, 288, 293-294, 363, 461, 534, 542, 628, 660, 671, 688.

Buddhists, 136, 137, 138, 151, 158, 279, 288, 292, 296, 363, 385, 534, 537, 542, 628, 660-661, 671, 688.

Buffum, James N., 376.
Bugunda, Uganda, 291.
Bulawayo, Southern Rhodesia, 191.
Bulgaria, 120, 121, 153, 325, 326, 340, 384.
Bulgarian Executive Council of Doctors, 121.
Bullock, Alan, Preface, 369.
Bulwer, British Ambassador to Spain, 341.
Bumper strike, 269.
Bundestag, West German, 290.
Bunyoro, Uganda, 291.
Bureaucracy, 10, 36, 39, 63, 80, 323-325, 748.
Bureaucratic obstruction, 36-41.
Bureau of Indian Affairs, U.S., 372.
Bureau of Zemstvo Congresses, Russian Empire, 431.
Burke, Edmund, Member of Parliament, 535.
Burmeister and Wain shipyard, 274.
de Bus, Gervaise, 152.
Busk, Sir Douglas, 340, 344.
Busoga, Uganda, 291.
Bus segregation laws, 415.

Ca'canny. See Slowdown strike.
Caja Agraria (agricultural credit bank), 406.
Calcutta, India, 306.
Calcutta University, 383.
Calhoun, Senator John C., 339.
California, 130, 262, 267, 413, 418.
California Attorney General, 418.
Campaign for nuclear disarmament: Britain, 631; Christian group of, 138.
Camouflaged meetings of protest, 167-168.
Cambay. See Gulf of Cambay.
Campesinos of Bolivia, 262.
Canada, 140-141, 205, 288, 314, 384, 392.
Canaris, Admiral Wilhelm, 321.
Canners Association of Northern California, 267.
Cannery and Agricultural Workers' Industrial Union, 263.
Cannery Workers Union (A.F.L. Teamsters), 267.
Canton, China, 220.
Cao Van Luan, Father, 138, 293.
Caper, Dr. Philip, 393.
Capetown, South Africa, 167, 419, 585, 629, 670.
Capetown University, South Africa, 155.
Capital punishment, 329.

Capitulation, reducing grounds for, 578-579.
Carbonell, Guatemalan opposition spokesman, 92.
Cardiff, Wales, 578.
Caricatures, 125-126.
Carl von Ossietsky Peace Medal, 172.
Carpenter, General, 427.
Carter, April, Preface, 544.
Cary, Massachusetts merchant, 381.
Case, Clarence Marsh, 212, 220, 698 n. 3, 723, 774 n. 161.
Cass Lake Region, Minnesota, 372.
Castellammare del Golfo, Sicily, 363.
Castle William, Boston, 685.
"Cat and Mouse Act," 366.
Catholic Church. See Roman Catholic Church.
"Cause-Consciousness," 470, 473-475.
Celler, Emanuel, 690.
Censorship, 4, 79, 86, 88, 120, 127-128, 305-306, 489, 538, 585, 712.
Center for International Affairs, Harvard University, Preface.
Central African Federation. See Federation of Rhodesia and Nyasaland.
Central Africa, 295. See also individual countries.
Central America, 5, 90. See also specific countries.
Central Asian Railroad, 549.
Central Bureau of the Union of Railroad Workers, Russia, 549.
Central Labor Union Council, Czechoslovakia, 173 n. 19.
Central Committee of the Trade Union Organizations, Czechoslovakia, 173 n. 19.
Central Legislature, India, 693.
Central Prison, Lodz, Poland, 313.
Central Provinces, India, 642.
Central Sierra, Peru, 407.
Central Trade Union Council, Czechoslovakia, 173 n. 19.
Centre de Tri de Vincennes, France, 310.
Cernik, Prime Minister Oldrich, 99, 100.
Ceylon, 135.
Chacao War, 1933-36, 246.
Chakravarty, Amiya, 473.
Chamber of Commerce, South Africa, 223, 738.
Chambers of Industry, Nazi Germany, 296.
Chambly, Canada, 264.
Champaran, Bihar, India, 497.

Champs Elysées, Paris, 310.
Chaney, James, 198.
Chang Chung-Li, 155, 242.
Changes in diplomatic and other represen-
    tation, 340-341.
Channing, William Ellery, 392.
Chapman, Colin, 100.
Charles I, King of England, 424.
Charles II, King of England, 426.
Charles V, King of the Netherlands, 684,
    748.
Charleston, South Carolina, 141, 221.
Charlestown, Massachusetts, 613.
Charles University, Czechoslovakia, 127,
    162.
Charques, Richard, 261, 287, 430-431,
    679.
Chase Manhattan Bank, 237.
Chase, William, 205.
Chatham, Lord (William Pitt, First Earl of
    Chatham), 737, 740.
Chauri-Chaura, India, 593.
Chavez, Cesar, 263.
Chelm Telegraph Station, Poland, 304.
Chemin des Dames, France, 166.
Chernigov, Russia, 261.
Chernyshevsky, N. G., 128, 163.
Cherokee Indians, 2372.
Cheyenne, Wyoming, 385.
Chicago, Illinois, 139, 198, 233, 236,
    371-372, 402, 437 n. 55, 598, 624,
    813 n. 83; City Hall of, 139.
Ch'ien Yung, 359.
Chikuni, Northern Rhodesia, 197.
Childs Security Corp., 233.
China, 73, 76, 131, 155, 196-197, 210,
    212, 220, 229, 233, 234-235, 242,
    246, 272, 277, 303-304, 307-308, 350
    n. 88; Nationalist China, 343, 345-346;
    People's Republic of China, 145, 167,
    272-273, 306, 323, 343, 346; Labor
    Insurance Regulations, 272; Health
    Committee of Trade Unions, 273.
China, North, 211, 307-308, 424. See also
    Occupations, Japanese of China.
Chipembere, H.B., 419.
Chippewa Indians, 288, 372.
Chipping Norton, England, 235.
Chita, Russian Empire, 333.
Chōcen, Czechoslovakia, 327.
Chōsan. See Desertions.
Christian Action, 138.
Christian II, King of Denmark, 241.
Christians, 368, 736.
Christiansand, Norway, 305.
Christison, Wenlock, 549.
Cherokee Indians, 372.

Chrysler Corporation, 404.
Chungking, China, 308.
Churches, 121, 191, 199, 204-205, 294,
    469. See also names of individual
    churches, religions and denominations.
Church of Dolores, Cuba, 153.
Church of San Francisco, Guatemala City,
    Guatemala, 92.
Churchill Boulevard, Warsaw, 144.
Churchill, Winston, 87, 432, 531, 761.
Chu Van An High School, Saigon, 136.
Cierna, Czechoslovakia, 327.
Cinema Strike, 196.
Circulation of hostile rumors and jokes,
    445 n. 301.
Citizens' alternatives to obedience,
    303-319.
Citizen Army, Ireland, 161.
Citizens' catechism, 186.
City College of New York, 205, 373.
Civil disobedience, 4, 41, 67, 73, 84,
    85-86, 118, 122, 129, 153, 162, 167,
    304, 308, 310, 312, 315, 372, 382,
    418, 420, 459, 466, 470, 483, 487,
    497, 504, 512-513, 523, 533, 535,
    541, 544, 546, 552, 558, 576, 584,
    599-600, 622, 638-639, 640-641, 642,
    652 n. 213, 667, 681, 682, 692, 698 n.
    8, 762, 785, 792; defensive, 316; in In-
    dia, 42, 497-498, 502, 739, 751, 757,
    759; against "illegitimate" laws, 315-
    319; against "neutral" laws, 420-421;
    purificatory, 316; reformatory, 316;
    revolutionary, 316.
Civil liberties, 455, 483.
Civil Rights Act, 1964, U.S., 384, 690.
Civil rights campaigns, U.S., 74, 95-97,
    134, 159, 198, 233, 371, 380, 383,
    475, 483, 488, 498, 517 n. 94, 534,
    587, 596, 603, 625, 626, 628, 632,
    670, 671, 682, 688, 690, 694, 711,
    722, 737-738, 766 n. 225, 783,
    787-788, 789, 790.
Civil servants, 40, 81, 82, 297, 293, 323,
    328, 459, 460, 498, 748.
Civil war: general, 3, 34, 551, 637, 756;
    Austria, 589; England, 970; Holy Ro-
    man Empire, 192; U.S., 203, 376, 392,
    399, 411.
Civilian defense, 421, 496, 517 n. 93,
    519 n. 128, 776 n. 219, 810.
Civilian insurrection, 90.
Civilian Public Service, 200.
Civilian resistance, 90, 100, 155, 505, 513,
    530.
Civilian Resistance, Directorate of Poland,
    188.

ČKD, Czechoslovak factory, originally Ceskomolavska-Kolben-Danék, 402, 440 n. 171.

Clarke, Moira, Preface.

Clausewitz, General Carl von, 495, 496, 506, 759, 762.

Clay, Senator Henry, 384.

Cleveland, Ohio, 386, 392, 403.

Clogging the channels of justice, 445 n. 301.

"Closely Watched Trains," (film), 301.

Clyde, Scotland, 235.

Codex juris cannonici, 204.

Coercion, 12, 26, 27-28, 30, 42, 58 n. 122, 67-68, 83, 245-246, 367, 431, 433, 536, 548, 703 n. 154, 742, 807.

Coercion by direct physical violation, 12, 27, 30. See also Nonviolent coercion.

Coercion Act, Ireland, 603.

Coercive acts, colonial America, 685.

Coffin, Rev. William Sloane, 204.

Cohoes, New York, 236.

Coimbra, Portugal, 195.

Colijan government, Netherlands, 422.

Collaborators, 188-189, 410.

Collective disappearance, 210-211.

Collective indiscipline. See Mutinies.

Collier, John, Commissioner of Indian Affairs, 372.

Collins, John A., 375.

Colombia, 406.

Colombo, Ceylon, 267.

Colonialism: in Africa, 43, 293, 297, 483; Nazi, 43, 483.

Colored American, 374, 392.

Cominform, 347.

Commando order, Nazi, 353 n. 182.

Commissar Decree, Nazi, 322.

Committee of Correspondence, 165.

Committee for Direct Action Against Nuclear War, 635.

Committee for Nonviolent Action, 653 n. 254.

Committee of 100, Britain, 145, 167, 419-420, 482, 631, 632, 652 n. 213, 653 n. 253, 692, 792.

Committee on Appeal for Human Rights, Atlanta, Georgia, 464.

Committee of Observation and Prevention, American colonies, 274.

Committee of Safety, Massachusetts Bay Colony, 612.

Commodus, Emperor of Rome, 123, 201.

Communication, means of, 11, 15, 78, 100, 125, 369, 400, 474, 627, 640, 712, 714, 750, 802.

Communism, 5, 39-40, 93, 125, 172, 260

297, 343, 532, 619, 714; Belgian Communists, 683; Hungarian Communists, 125; South African Communists, 619. See also Communist Parties and individual countries.

Communist Party, Czechoslovakia, 98-100; Extraordinary Fourteenth Congress of, 99-100, 121, 129, 170, 173 n. 19, 234, 260, 288; All-Unit Committee of, 173 n. 19, 288, 301; University Committee of, 174 n. 19; Presidium, 131, 310, 327, 390; Presidium of the Central Committee, 131, 174 n. 19; Presidium of the Prague City Committee of the National Front, 173 n. 19; Party Presidium, 99; Presidium of the Prague City Committee of the Communist Party, 131.

Communist Party, East Germany. See Socialist Unity Party, East Germany.

Communist Party, Poland, 316.

Communist Party, Hungary, 125.

Communist Party, Soviet Union, 39, 40, 170, 171, 684, 749, 753. See also Bolsheviks.

Communist Party, United States, 263.

Communist Party, Yugoslavia, Central Committee of, 340.

Company of Commerce, Hungary, 398.

Compliants, Finland, 186.

Compliance (pattern of), 15, 25, 26, 57 n. 110.

Comply-in, 417.

Compromise, 3, 65, 81, 100, 534, 547, 695, 760.

Comte, Auguste, 11, 49 n. 5; 49 n. 8; 49 n. 9.

Concentration camps, 88, 485, 585, 725.

Concessions, 45, 86, 94, 202, 207, 213, 258, 268, 283 n. 89; 470, 532-534, 567 n. 47; 694, 737, 739, 748, 759-761, 780, 782.

Conciliation, 65, 534.

Concord, New Hampshire, 199, 396.

Concord, Massachusetts, 246, 287, 536, 600, 603, 605, 611-614, 694.

Confiscation, 86, 538.

Conflict: acute, 3, 537, 793; scale of, 793; responses to, 65; in democratic system and dictatorships, 71; facing conflicts, 74; armed, 53; military, 111, 782; violence in, 133, 695, 792, 794, 801-802; international, 793; noncooperation in, 183; nonviolent action and assumptions about, 109, noncooperation in, 183, differences in development of strategy, 523; sharpened by

nonviolent action, 524; within opponent camp, 675-676; Gandhi's use of nonviolent action in 82-83; conclusion of conflict and concentration of power, 799-806; underlying, 785, 810; violent, 133, 551, 695, 782, 802.
Confronting the opponent's power, 451-454.
Confucius, 359.
Congo, 237.
Congregational Church, Concord, New Hampshire, 396.
Congregational Church, Plymouth, New Hampshire, 199.
Congress of Democrats, South Africa, 526.
Congress of Industrial Organizations (CIO), 404.
Congress of the People at Kliptown, Johannesburg, South Africa, 123.
Congress of Racial Equality (CORE), 134, 139-140, 373-374, 377, 383, 395, 402, 419, 617, 632, 741, 766, 786.
Congress of the United States of America, 126, 245-247, 338, 379, 428, 690. See also House of Representatives, Senate, and United States of America.
Congressional Union, 126.
Connaught, Duke of, 686.
Connecticut, 429, 581, 633. See also individual towns and cities.
Connor, Bull, 138.
Conscientious objector(s), U.S., 200, 265, 366.
Conscription, 260, 312, 539; resistance to, 125, 149, 204-205, 261, 312, 314, 507, 752.
Consent, 25, 27, 28, 29, 30-31, 58 n. 123; 59 n. 128; 44.
Consent, withdrawal of, 3, 13, 30, 47, 476, 524. See also Obedience.
Conser, Walter, Preface.
Conservation Department, State of Washington, 318.
Conservatives, England, 532.
Consolidated Edison Co., 223.
Conspiracy, 80, 81, 322.
Constantine, 385.
Consumer boycott, 221-224, 231-232, 234, 358, 395, 412, 504, 538.
Constitution, Atlanta, Georgia, 671.
Constitutionalists, Finland, 186.
Constitutional Movement, Persia, 206.
Continental Association, 5, 186, 224, 225, 229, 234, 424-425, 481, 511, 578, 581, 600, 603, 612-615, 633, 648 n. 124; 685, 699 n. 32; 798. See also Continental Congress.

Continental Congress, First, 5, 224-225, 229, 239, 274, 317, 424, 481, 507, 511, 581, 595, 600, 612, 699 n. 32; 740, 794, 798. See also Continental Association and Continental Congress, Second.
Continental Congress, Second, 123, 614-615. See also Continental Congress, First.
Control of communication and information, 538.
Control of political power: general, 3, 7, 13, 33, 34, 35, 52 n. 23; 54 n. 47; traditional means, 32-33.
Conversion, 69, 83, 85, 358, 363, 367, 455, 458, 477, 501, 502, 528, 601, 634, 666, 697, 703 n. 154; 706-733, 734, 737, 741, 753, 766, 767, 768, 769 n. 1.
Cooperation: power dependent upon, 8, 12, 13, 16, 18, 22, 23, 24, 27, 28, 29, 30, 42, 44, 47, 59 n. 144; 59 n. 145; 64, 423, 490, 695, 744, 746, 747; sanctions dependent on, 14, 15, 112, 755, 760; refusal of, 31, 34, 40, 41, 69, 80-81, 82, 183, 681, 686, 785. See also need for in Gandhi's view, 43, 78; among nonviolent actionists, 423, 778, 795-797. See also Noncooperation.
Copenhagen, Denmark, 274, 275, 277, 305.
Corporative state, Norway, 5, 70, 88, 89, 298, 585.
Corvées, India, 264; Russia, 270.
Cossacks, Russia, 163, 207, 333.
Cottam, Richard, 210.
Council of Art and Culture, Poland, 316.
Council of Limoges, 193.
Council of Massachusetts Bay, 685.
Council of Union of Liberation, Russia, 168.
Council of Workingmen's Delegates or Deputies of St. Petersburg, Imperial Russia, 430-431.
Coup d'etat: general and resistance to, 9, 25, 34, 294, 328, 421, 433, 464, 480, 500, 753, 802, 809; in Guatemala, 93; in Czechoslovakia, 98-99, 234; in Brazil, 262, 408; in Russia, 328; in Bolivia, 407; in South Vietnam, 672; in Sachsen, Germany, 619; in Germany, see Kapp *Putsch.*
"Coventry, Send to," 508.
Craft strike, 265.
Craft, William and Ellen, 418.
Craig, Gordon A., 342.
Cranswick, Yorkshire, England, 395.

Crawfordville, Florida, enterprises, 416.

Crespigny, Anthony de, 290, 291, 340.

Criminal Law Amendment Act, No. 8 of 1953, South Africa, 541, 757.

Criminal Syndicalism Act, U.S., 263.

Cripps, Sir Stafford, 270.

Criterion, 378-379.

Croatans, American Indians, 372.

Crook, Wilfred Harris, 80, 275-276, 283 n. 111, 432.

Cuba, 153-154, 171, 248, 653 n. 254.

Curfews, 274, 538.

Cuzco, Peru, 407.

Czechoslovakia: war with Germany expected in 1938, 170, 295, 589; government-in-exile during World War II, 222; resistance during Nazi occupation, 163, 222; Communist-controlled trade union activities under parliamentary government, 233-234; resistance to 1968 Warsaw Pact invasion and occupation, outline of events, 98-101; resistance, etc.: general, 4, 5, 5-6, 74, 97, 98; resistance, etc., description of specific forms of, 121, 122-123, 128, 131, 136, 142-143, 144, 151, 162, 188, 260-261, 288, 289, 310, 327-328, 389-390, 402; radio and television in resistance, 128, 129-130, 300, 327, 328, 401; activities of organizations and institutions: National Assembly, 121, 122, 390; ČTK (government news agency), 99; Academy of Sciences, 121; Union of Czechoslovak Journalists, 371 n. 19; Central Trade Union Council, Presidium of, 174 n. 19; Czechoslovak Writers' Union, 174 n. 19; Czechoslovak Association of Anti-Fascist Fighters, 174 n. 19; Czechoslovak Union of Journalists, 188; State Security, 174 n. 19; Public Police, 100; State Police, 100. See also Occupation, German of Czechoslovakia; Occupation, Russian of Czechoslovakia; Communist Party of Czechoslovakia; trade unions of Czechoslovakia, individual cities, names of persons, etc., Central Labor Union Council, Central Committee of Trade Union Organizations, and Central Trade Union Council.

Czechs. See Czechoslovakia.

Dagmarhus, Copenhagen, Denmark, 274.

Daily Chronicle, London, 648 n. 154.

Daily Mail, London, 587.

Daily Telegraph, London, 587.

Daley, Mayor Richard, 139.

Dallin, Alexander, 42-43, 353 n. 182.

Danbury, Connecticut, 265.

Dandi, India, 153, 497.

Danubia, Hungary, 388.

Dartmouth, Second Earl of, William Legge, 425, 613.

Dartmouth, Massachusetts, 632.

Daulatram, Jairamdas, 639.

Davidson, Philip, 172.

Davidson, W. Philips, 409.

Davis Cup, 383.

Davitt, Michael, 185, 603.

Day, Noel, 795.

Deák, Francis, 77, 594-595.

Deanesly, Margaret, 192.

Debrecen, Hungary, 309.

Debs, Eugene V., 233.

de Bus. See Bus, de.

Decentralization of power, 802-806.

Declaration, 536, 664.

Declaration of Independence, American, 123, 127.

Declarations by organizations and institutions, 121.

Declarations of indictment and intention, 123.

Declaration of women's rights, 127.

Defeat, 71, 72, 755-758. See also Success, and Outcome of the Conflict.

Defense Ministry, Germany, 41.

Defense Research Corporation, 455 n. 301.

Defiance campaign, South Africa, 1952, 123, 137, 142, 167, 318, 483, 525-526, 512, 514, 541, 547, 576, 579, 587, 591, 599, 601, 628, 652 n. 216; 659, 714, 757, 763, 788, 795.

Defiance of blockades, 401, 408-409.

Degoutte, General, 541.

de Jong. See Jong.

de Jouvenal. See Jouvenel.

de la Boétie. See Boétie.

Delaney, Martin R., 411.

DeLano, California, 263-264.

DeLarue, Jacques, 532.

Delaware River, 412.

Delay and cancellation of diplomatic events, 341-342.

Delft, Netherlands, 197.

Delhi, India, 367. See also New Delhi.

Deliberate inefficiency and selective non-cooperation by enforcement agents, 330-332.

Delivering symbolic objects, 139-140.

DeMarco, Margaret, 288.

Democratic Party, Slovakia, 234.

Democratic Party, U.S. 134, 373.

Democracy, 33, 46, 49 n. 6; 71, 75, 90,

92, 93, 96, 133, 316, 487, 543, 662, 781, 802, 804.

Demonstrations: advance notice of, 491; time gaps between, 509, 723; of unity, 536; repression of, see Repression; nonviolent demonstrations defusing violence, 623-625, 629; promoting nonviolent discipline in, 630, see also Nonviolent discipline: by third parties, 664; in periods of regrouping, 763; for particular demonstrations, see group of demonstrators, or place of demonstration. For particular types of demonstrations and examples of them, see all specific methods of the class nonviolent protest and persuasion, and all other methods of nonviolent action which operate primarily by calling attention to the grievance, viewpoint, etc., especially methods of social noncooperation, and the sub-classes of symbolic strikes, rejection of authority and often many of the methods of nonviolent intervention.

Demonstration, strike. See Protest strike.

Demonstrative funerals, 159-162.

Demoralization, 100.

Denmark, 87, 129, 136, 150, 194, 196, 231, 251 n. 64; 274, 275, 586, 683. See also Occupation, German of Denmark.

Department Deutschland, Nazi Germany, 325.

Department of Defense, U.S., Preface.

Deportation, 305, 312-313, 314, 321, 325, 326, 332, 484.

Deputations, 130-131.

Deravyanko, General, 533.

Desegregation, 97, 335, 388, 475, 788.

Despotism, 128, 339, 456. See also Dictators, Tyrants, Tyranny, Totalitarianism.

Desertions, 212-213. See also protest emmigration.

Destruction. See Material destruction.

Destruction, of own property, 140-142, 359.

Detailed strike, 268-269.

Detention camps, 86, 312.

Detroit, Michigan, 205.

Deutsch, Karl W., 15, 23, 52-53 n. 31.

Devlin Commission, 747.

De Waarheid 401.

Dharasana Salt Depot, 380, 564, 687, 731.

Dharasana salt raids, 311, 330, 687, 693.

Dhawan, Gopinath, 565, 813 n. 88.

Dhurna (or "Sitting Dhurna"), 364, 367.

Dickenson, John, 798.

Dictators (also dictatorship), 5, 29, 38, 71, 75, 90, 91, 92, 97, 298, 423, 482, 483-484, 493, 495, 744, 748, 749, 760, 806, 809. See also Tyranny, Totalitarianism, Oppression.

Diefenbaker, Prime Minister John, 140.

Diels, Rudolf, 330.

Diem, Ngo Dinh, 151, 660-661.

Diem Regime, 136, 137, 138, 279, 534, 537, 542, 587, 660-661, 671, 688.

Diet, Finland, 131.

Dillon, John, 603, 632.

Dimitroff, Georgi, 369.

Direct action, 537, 543, 544, 551, 797.

Direct Action Committee Against Nuclear War, 128, 148, 289, 631, 632, 653 n. 253.

Directives of 1937, Netherlands, 422.

Directorate of Civilian Resistance, Poland, 188.

Direct physical violence, 539-540.

Disarmament conference, 1933, 345.

Discipline: general, 54 n. 51; 333, 763, 782, 787; necessity of in nonviolent action, 615-620. See also Nonviolent discipline and Self-discipline.

Disclosing identities of secret agents, 418.

Discountenancing, 185.

Discrimination, 95, 358, 373, 375, 378, 419, 791, 795.

Disguised disobedience, 306-308.

Disobedience, 46, 285, 576; withdrawal of obedience, 12, 20, 21; and sanctions and repression, 27, 28, 32, 35, 58 n. 122, 58 n. 123, 204, 681; relationship to obedience and enforcement, 15, 35; and self-confidence, 23; always exists, 25; and self-interest, 27; potential and limits of, 32, 35, 45, 82, 84; perceived threat of, 45, 61-62 n. 201; ethical justification of, 45; resistance by, 47, 84; disintegrates political power, 63, 434, 753; by ruler's agents, 77, 667, 675, 753. See also specific methods subclassed as "Action by Government Personnel," and fraternization, 146. See also Fraternization, to military system, 204-205; judicial, 329. See also Judicial noncooperation; and leadership, 426. See also all the following particular methods: Social disobedience, Nonobedience, in absence of direct supervision, Popular nonobedience, Disguised disobedience, Refusal of an assemblage or meeting to disperse, Sitdown, Noncooperation with conscription and deportation, Hiding escape and false identities, Selective refusal of assistance by government aides, Blocking lines of command and information, Stalling and obstruction, General administrative noncooperation, Judicial noncooperation, Deliberate inefficiency and selective noncooperation by enforcement agents, Mutiny, Quasilegal evasions and delays, Noncooperation by constituent governmental units, Disclosing identities of secret agents, Seeking imprisonment, Civil disobedience of "neutral" laws, Work-on without collaboration, Dual sovereignty and parallel government.

Display of flags and symbolic colors, 135-136, 522.

Displayed communications, 126.

Displays of portraits, 143.

Disputes and Trade Union Act of 1927 Britain, 133.

Diwakar, Ranganath R., 85.

Doane, Don, 675.

Dobrolubov, N.A., 163.

Dolci, Danilo, 363, 402.

Domestic embargo, 244.

Dominican Republic, 248.

Donbas, U.S.S.R., 150.

Don Cossack region, Russian empire, 261.

Dorr's rebellion, Rhode Island, 426-430.

Dorr, Governor Thomas Wilson, 427-430.

Douglass, Frederick, 375-376, 379, 391-392, 523.

Doukhobors, 140, 141.

Dracy, France, 327.

Draft card burning, 142.

Draga, Queen of Serbia, 344.

Drake, St. Clair, 411.

Dresden, Germany, 80.

Drill Hall, Johannesburg, 150.

Dual sovereignty and parallel government, 4, 69, 79, 93, 232, 416, 423-433, 502, 633, 745, 746, 767.

Dubček, Alexander, First Secretary, Communist Party of Czechoslovakia, 98-99, 100, 111, 121, 122, 143.

Dubček, regime, 98, 100, 122, 173 n. 19, 402.

Dubček shift, 402.

Dubček's Sunday, 402.

Dublin, Ireland, 161, 227, 300.

Duc, Venerable Thich Quang, 138.

Dühring, Eugen, 684.

Duisburg, Germany, 610.

Dulany, Daniel, 76, 412.

Dulles, John Foster, 248, 343.

Duluth, Michigan, 372.

Duma of Imperial Russia, 152, 160, 191, 238, 242, 290, 291, 519 n. 132, 533, 799.

Dumbarton Oaks conversations, 346.

Dumping, 411.

Dunmore, Governor John Murray, 137, 425, 613-614.

Dunn, North Carolina, 372.

Dunn High School, North Carolina, 372.

Duplex Printing Co., 221.

Durban, South Africa, 200, 167.

Dutch. See Netherlands.

Dutchess County, province of New York, 226.

Dutch Reformed Church, 122.

Duy Tan Clinic, 363.

Dylan, Bob, 129.

Earthwriting, 130.

Eastern Railroad, Massachusetts, 376.

Eastern Transvaal, South Africa, 223.

East Europeans, 42-43. See also individual countries.

East German Peace Council, 172.

East German rising, 1953, 5, 93, 125, 143, 172, 277, 298, 405, 463, 474, 484, 515 n. 30, 519 n. 132, 533-534, 550, 597, 566 n. 21, 615, 629, 647 n. 99, 675, 676, 688, 708, 745-746, 753.

East Germany, 97, 121, 125, 136, 148, 153, 170, 172, 213, 242, 303, 529, 545, 566 n. 21, 675-677, 688, 745.

East India Company, 224-225, 361, 507, 685.

East Indies, 221.

East Prussia, 213.

Eberhard, Prof. Wolfram, 350 n. 88, 359.

Ebert government, Germany, Weimar Republic, 4, 40, 80, 81, 339, 767.

Ebert, President Friedrich, 80, 170, 678.

Ebert, Theodor, Preface, 421-422, 470, 472, 473, 480, 491, 509, 515 n. 30, 517 n. 93, 523, 529, 550, 566 n. 21, 567 n. 47, 567 n. 50, 574-575, 647 n. 99, 764, 775 n. 193, 776 n. 219.

Eccleston Square, London, 574.

Economic boycotts: general characteristics, 219-221; methods of, defined with examples, 221-248; general, 4, 70, 77, 86, 95, 118, 185, 186, 196, 258, 338, 461, 503, 538, 580, 667, 695, 737, 750, 789; relation to selective patronage, 412-413; laws and other countermeasures against, 540-541, 685; and smuggling, 612; American colonial, 580-582, 667, 750; See also American colonies, Britain—American

public opinion, 530, 584; dissatisfaction with concessions, 533; opponents' reaction to civil disobedience, 535; maintaining rapport, 576, 583; limits to effectiveness of opponents' violence, 544, 545, 698 n. 2; inhibiting repression, 584, 753; persistence, 547, 548; opponent prefers violence, 591; avoiding hatred, 634; resisting provocations to violence, 594; violence weakens movement, 597, 599; provocative nonviolent action, 563, 564, 687; nonviolence weakens opponent, 565; sabotage, 609, 651 n. 168; need for financial self-reliance, 663; escalation of disobedience, 641; reaction to Amristar shooting, 686; counter-nonviolence, 693; seeking conversion, 707, 709, 720, 723, 724-725, 727, 728; rationale of self-suffering, 709, 711; overcoming social distance, 714; sense of nonviolent power, 780, 781; increasing self-respect of Indians, 786; reversal of perceptions of masculinity and violence by, 790; effect on Indian National Congress, 795; increasing internal cooperation, 796; constructive program, 797, 813 n. 88; effect of nonviolence on British trade, 751-752; negotiated settlement, 760, 761; struggle during negotiations, 761; dangers of overconfidence, 766; aftermath of repression, 767-768; nonviolent coercion, 769 n. 4, 774 n. 161; effect of wife on, 771 n. 66; respect of opponent for actionists, 721; need for self-sufficient nonviolent action, 728, 729; *Young India*, 751.

Gandhian(s), 73, 131, 393, 563, 564, 693, 792.

Gandhian struggles, India, 74, 79, 83, 403, 413, 510, 512, 528, 665, 677.

Ganu, Babu, 385.

Gapon, Father Georgii, 155-156, 483, 640.

Garhwali Mutiny in India, 675, 747.

Garhwali Regiment, 335, 432.

Garnet, Henry Highland, 411.

Garrison, William Lloyd, 369, 371, 376, 384, 412.

Garrisonian nonviolent actionists, 371, 375, 396.

Gaspée, 299.

Gates, Seth, 379.

Gauche Dynastique, 168.

Gauldal, Trøndelag, Norway, 253 n. 119.

Gaul 124.

Gayle, Mayor, 415.

Gazette, official newspaper of Persia, 207.

Gazetteer, Britain, 317.

General administrative noncooperation, 328.

General Assembly, Rhode Island, 426, 428-430.

General Committee, South Carolina, 614.

General Council's Strike Organization Committee, Britain, 464.

General Court, Massachusetts Bay Colony, 720.

General Governement, in Nazi-occupied Poland, 127.

General Motors, 269, 403, 403-404, 692.

General Agrarian Strike, Russia, 507.

General strike: general, 45, 80, 133-134, 165, 259, 265, 271, 275-277, 278, 289, 422, 431, 441 n. 191, 477, 498, 507, 751, 815-817; "localized," 275; and nonviolent coercion, 502, 706, 755; and economic shutdown, 279; economic, 276; political, 276; revolutionary, 276; in support of hunger strike, 366; in support of mutiny, 503; feared as powerful weapon, 532; measures against, 542, 593; and parallel government, 432; against Kapp *Putsch*, Germany 1920, 40, 41, 80, 619, 743. See also Kapp *Putsch*. Turned into armed rising, 79; Czechoslovakia 1968, 260; Britain 1926, 271, 432, 463, 464, 485, 519 n. 128, 531, 532, 542, 574, 578, 593, 757, 787; Belgian general strikes, 276; Russian general strikes, 604, 606, 607-608, 649 n. 154; Great October Strike, Russia 1905, 139, 152, 166, 276, 533, 743, 752, 780, 799; Guatemala 1944, 93; during Hungarian Revolution 1956, 93; Haiti 1956, 266; Ghana (then called Gold Coast) 1949, 788; Italy 1904, 432; Netherlands, 536.

Genessee County, New York, 379.

Geneva, Switzerland, 131, 297.

Geneva Committee of Parents, London, 131.

George III, King of England, 317, 363.

Georgia, Russian Empire, 242, 296, 431.

Georgia, United States, 200, 202, 221, 582, 615.

Gerbrandy, Prime Minister P. S., 422.

Gerland, Brigitte, 533.

Germany: general, 342, 545, 554, 562, 584, 659, 676, 682, 781, 787; submarine campaign 1917, 344; military attaché von Papen, 341; official backing for nonviolent action, 5; Weimar Republic. See Kapp *Putsch* and *Ruhrkampf*; abolition of Weimar Republic and Reichstag fire, 588-589; plantations in Guatemala, 90; assets frozen in U.S. 1941, 341; Nazi system: deportations of Jews, 153, 313, 314. See also Jews. Euthanasia program, 469; jazz banned, 306-307; and Portuguese cinemas, 233; pro-Jewish resistance in, 89-90, 136, 304, 305, 325-326. See also Jews. And right of resistance, 45; provocation by violence desired by, 588-589; Minister of War, 296; Ministry of Justice, 320-323; Minister of Economics, 244; East Ministry, 323; Order Police, 321; War Office, 320-322; Army High Command (O.K.H.), 295, 321-322; High Command of the Armed Forces (O.K.W.), 321; Foreign Office, 325, 327; Army band, 307; German Democratic Republic, Politbureau of, 533-534, 676. See also East Germany and Socialist Unity Party. West German farmers and Berlin blockade, 409; methods: public speeches, 119-120; pastoral letters, 122; slogans and symbols, 125-126; posters, 126; leaflets etc., 128; wearing of symbols, 136; silence, 170; social boycott, 189; consumers boycott, 222, 223; slowdown strike, 270-271; selective strike, 275; general strike, 276-277; refusal of industrial assistance in, 236; revenue refusal, 242; domestic embargo, 244; boycott of government employment etc., 293, 295; boycott of government agencies, 296; disguised disobedience, 306-307; "escape," 314; selective refusal of assistance by government aides, 320, 321; blocking lines of command and information, 321-322; stalling and obstruction, 323-324; noncooperation by constituent government units, 337; withdrawal from international organizations, 345; reverse trial, 368; nonviolent air raid, 381; political counterfeiting, 410. See also Berlin Airlift, Kapp *Putsch*, *Ruhrkampf*, East German Rising, Invasions, Occupations, Nazis, Hitler, Colonization, names of specific organizations and persons, or of occupied countries and cities.

Gerth, Hans, 18, 54 n. 51.
Gestapo, 88, 89, 90, 164, 306, 327, 331, 585, 549, 731.
Geyl, Pieter, 287, 684, 701 n. 100, 748.
Ghana (Gold Coast), People's Party Convention, 788.
Ginty, J. P., 273.
Gipson, Lawrence Henry, 124, 186, 239, 299, 317, 362, 425, 519 n. 132, 534, 602, 568 n. 67, 569 n. 115, 667, 685, 699 n. 32, 750-751.
Gladstone, William, 603.
Glasgow, Scotland, 197, 233, 270, 385.
Glazunov, Ilya, 311.
Glocester, Rhode Island, 430.
Goa, 382.
"Go-Home-Early" strikes. See Strikes, limited.
"Go-Slow" strike. See Strike, slowdown.
Godwin, William, 22, 29, 31, 32, 35, 50 n. 15, 55 n. 65.
Goebbels, Joseph, 120, 122, 164, 233, 270, 320, 323-324, 484, 644 n. 66, 669, 691-692, 753.
Goering, Hermann, 236, 324, 369. See also Hermann-Goering Works (steel plant).
Goerlitz, East Germany, 597, 629, 675.
Goffman, Erving, 477.
Going-limp, 200, 205, 300.
Goldhamer, Herbert, 52 n. 23.
Goldman, Emma, 55 n. 65.
Goodman, Andrew, 198.
Goodspeed, Lt. Col. D. J., 41, 81, 381.
Goodyear rubber workers, 267.
Gopal, S., 546, 585, 587, 638-639, 642, 675, 739, 759, 761.
Gora, 393.
Gordon, King, 237.
Gorky, Maxim, 551.
Görlitz, Walter, 170, 321, 322, 324, 353 n. 182.
Gothenburg, Sweden, 275.
Goulart, President of Brazil, 408.
Gounaris, M., 344.
Government: general, 78; and nonviolent action, 67, 98; depends on cooperation and consent, 64, 84; prevention of collaborationist, 99-100; resistance to, 85, 86, 88, 91-92; refusal to pay debts of, 237-238; revenue refusal and, 240-241, 242; blacklisting of traders by, 244-245; international sellers' embargo by, 245; reverse trial against, 368.
Governments-in-exile, 5, 87. See also individual countries.

Hannecken, General Hermann von, 321.

Harassment. See Nonviolent harassment and Psychological harassment.

Harbin, U.S.S.R., 333.

Harcave, Sidney, 139, 156, 160, 168, 266, 276, 287, 333, 353 n. 226, 483, 519 n. 132, 536, 567 n. 44, 567 n. 50, 606, 607, 626, 659, 679, 780, 794, 799.

Hardinge, Lord of Penschurst, 561, 679.

Hardwicke, Massachusetts Bay, 702 n. 109.

Harlan, John Marshall, 377.

Harlem, New York City, 223, 228, 395, 617, 625.

Harold, Hardråde, 251 n. 64.

Harrington, England, 289, 382.

Harris, Errol E., 29-30, 47, 48 n. 4, 49 n. 5, 51 n. 17, 52 n. 27.

Harris, Herbert, 267.

Hartal, 199, 277-278, 504, 576, 639.

Hartford County, Connecticut, 633.

Harteneck, General, 43.

Hartnett County School Board, North Carolina, 372.

Harvard University, Preface, 297, 427.

Harvard Divinity School, 205.

"Haunting" officials, 145-146, 369.

Haverhill, Massachusetts, 273.

Havlin, James, Preface.

Haymarket Square, Chicago, Bombing in, 598.

Hawaii, 205.

Hawaii, University of, 205.

Hawaii, University Resistance Group of, 205.

Heal-in, 393-394.

Hearn, John, Preface.

Heath, William, 341.

Heidelberg, Germany, 376.

Helset, Olaf, 194-195.

Henderson, Arthur, M.P., 539.

Henry IV, Emperor of the Holy Roman Empire, 192.

Henry, Patrick, 361, 794.

Hentoff, Nat, 791, 813 n. 83.

Hermann- Göring Works, 236.

Hernandes Martinez. See Martinez.

Heroes' Square, Budapest, 163.

Herrnstadt, Rudolf, 676.

Herst, Pawel, 316.

Herzen, Alexander, 163, 456.

Het Parool, 400.

Heydrich, Reinhardt, 325, 590.

Hiding, escape and false indentities, 313-314.

Hijrat, 211-212, 642.

Hijrat-i-Kubrá ("The Great Exodus"), 208.

Hilberg, Raul, 173 n. 7, 306, 322, 323.

Hildebrandt, Rainer, 148-149, 405.

Hillenbrand, Martin J., 7, 33, 34, 48 n. 1.

Hiller, E. T., 267, 269, 431, 449, 525, 557, 575-576, 584, 597, 698 n. 3, 711, 745, 754, 786, 794.

Himalayas, 264.

Himmler, Heinrich, 553, 691.

Hind Swaraj or Indian Home Rule by M. K. Gandhi., 84.

Hindu-Muslim unity, Gandhi's campaign for, 367.

Hindus, Orthodox, 83, 148, 156, 368, 393, 729.

Hingst, *Stadtkommissar*, 325.

Hipp, Jutta, 307.

Hird, 88, 196, 332.

Hiroshima Day, 117.

Hitler, Adolf: general, 90, 119, 126, 170, 484; government depends on consent, 29, 43; limits on imposition from above, 46; and Quisling's Corporate State, 89; public hostility to, 170; opposition to, 293, 295, 320-322, 324, 327; and Commando Order, 353 n. 182; reverse trial, 368; withdrawal from international organizations, 345; use of provocation, 588-590; less severe repression by, 669, 691; admiration of courage by, 716.

Hoarding, 445 n. 301.

Hobbes, Thomas, 18, 19, 45, 46, 58 n. 123, 61-62 n. 201.

Hobson, Charles, 370.

Hoepner, Colonel General Erich, 322.

Holland. See Netherlands.

Holland, Ambassador Jerome, 341.

Holmsen, Andreas, 251 n. 64, 253 n. 119.

Holt, Edgar, 161, 260, 366.

Homage at burial places, 162-163.

Homefront leadership, Norway, 691.

Home rule, Hungary, 135.

Home rule, Ireland, 260, 603.

Honan, China, 146.

Hong Kong, 220.

Honington, England, 145.

Honoring the dead, 157.

Hooper, Isaac, 392.

Hoorn, Count of, 294.

Hooton, Elizabeth, 549.

Hoover- Stimson Doctrine, 343.

Hopei-Chahar Political Council, 307.

Hostages, 313, 328.

Hoth, 320.

Hottentots, 556.
House of Burgesses, Virginia. See Virginia.
House of Commons, Britain, 124, 132, 316-317, 366, 752.
House of Lords, Britain, 316, 740.
House of Ministries, East Berlin, 629.
House(s) of Parliament, London, 141, 531.
House of Parliament, Persia, 210.
House of Representatives, Massachusetts Bay, 362-363.
House of Representatives, United States, 135, 427, 693; Judiciary Committee of, 690; See also Congress.
Houser, George, 377, 437.
Howard Johnson Restaurant, 766.
Høye, Bjarne, 122.
Hradec, Czechoslovakia, 328.
Hsiao, Kung-Chuan, 217 n. 107, 242, 301-302, 307, 536.
Hudson River, New York, 392.
Hué, Vietnam, 138, 158, 279, 628, 660.
Hué, University of, 138, 293.
Huerta, Victoriano, 342.
Human resources as source of power, 11, 453, 744, 746-747.
Hume, David, 19, 20-21, 22, 44-45, 46, 50 n. 15, 54 n. 51, 55 n. 70, 56 n. 85.
Humorous skits and pranks, 148.
"Hundred Flowers Blossoming," China, 167.
Hundred Years' War, 151.
Hungary: general, 74, 135, 659, 713; alternative national institutions, 398, 796-797; army officers, 388; assemblies of protest or support in, 164; Calvinists, 309; economic boycott against, 230; boycott of legislative bodies in, 290; home rule in, 135; homage at burial places in, 163; fraternization in, 146; nonviolent resistance in, 76-77; boycott of government employment and positions in, 293; revenue refusal in, 242; noncooperation with conscription and deportation in, 312; nonviolent obstruction in, 388; countering economic nonviolent resistance of, 541; nonviolence urged for, 594; silence used in, 170; Parliament of, 164; Protestants' resistance to Austria in, 157, 309; Revolution of 1956-57, 93, 97, 99, 146, 170, 200, 212, 288, 343, 713, 749; struggle against Austrian rule, 594-595, 767, 796.
Hunger strike, 360, 363-364, 365-367, 404, 642. See also Fasts.

Hunter Committee, 504.
Huntington, Samuel, 407, 441 n. 192.
Hurum, Hans Jørgen, 149.
Hus, Jan, Statue of, 162-163.
Husak, Gustav, 99.
Hutcheson, Federal Judge Sterling, 240.
Hutchinson, Governor Thomas, 172, 308, 581-582, 636, 646 n. 99.
Huxley, Aldous, 776 n. 229.
Ickes, Harold, 372.
Imâm-Jum'a, 206.
Imâm Rizâ, Shrine of, 206.
Imes, Rev. William Lloyd, 223.
Imperial Parliament, Vienna, 290.
Imprisonment, 12, 86, 466, 540, 541, 548, 555, 580, 620, 636, 638, 689, 721, 782, 785, 803.
Imprisonment of leadership. See Leadership, jailing of.
Inaction, 64, 65-66.
Independence, 3, 87, 781. See also Home rule and individual countries.
Independence Day, January 26, 1930, India, 84, 135.
India: general, 74, 468, 545; British, 642 (United Provinces Government), 529 (Indian Army), 290 (National Legislative Council), 290 (Provincial Legislative Councils), 85 (Penal Code), 41 (Legislative Assembly), see also Britain; castes, 393; South India, 82, 148, 210; national flag, 576; uprising of 1857, 552, 584; British problem of repression, 546, 559, 681, 682, 686-8; casualties, 552; camps for volunteers, 576; pledges of nonviolent discipline, 631; decentralization of later resistance organization, 639; Gandhi on noncooperation for independence, 84-85, 748; Gandhi on fearlessness for independence, 457; Tolstoy on voluntary subjection of, 30, 78; need for cooperation of subjects, 41-42; subjection and English education, 57 n. 100; historical context for Indian struggles, 79; force needed for freedom, 85, 512-513; terrorism, 85-86, 624; violent revolution, 86; nonviolent action adopted as weapon, 87; panchayats, 133; untouchability violated, 198; negotiations by leaders, 470; negotiations with Britain, 761; secret resistance network, 487; strategies of campaigns, 504; Britain's economic ties, 512-513; people transformed into resisters, 524, 529, 780-781, 783, 786; resisters' sense

200, 223, 464, 536, 669, 738.
John, King of England, 193.
Johnson, President Lyndon B., 341, 690.
Joint Boycott Committee, South Africa, 223.
Jong, L. de, 270, 282 n. 62, 284 n. 125, 313, 758.
Journeymen Stone Cutters Association, 231.
Jouvenel, Bertrand de, 16, 18, 19, 20, 24, 27, 34, 35, 36, 51 n. 17, 51 n. 19, 54 n. 50, 55 n. 63, 56 n. 74, 57 n. 105, 60 n. 158, 801.
Joyce, Patrick, 364.
Judenrat (Jewish Council) of Athens, 313.
Judicial Noncooperation, 328-330.
Jungk, Robert, 324.
Junin, Peru, 407.
Jutikkala, Eino, 186, 312, 646 n. 99.
Kádár regime, Hungary, 343.
Kagal, 149-150, 186.
Kaluga, Russia, 168.
Kanara, India, 210.
Kao-Yu District, China, 155.
Kapp, Dr. Wolfgang, 40-41, 80, 81, 277, 339, 529, 626, 686, 696-697. See also Kapp *Putsch*.
Kapp *Putsch*, 4, 36, 40-41, 70, 79-81, 170, 276, 277, 328, 339, 344, 381, 529, 619, 626, 677-678, 686, 696-697, 708, 743, 748, 767, 780.
Karakozov, D. V., 645 n. 79, 679.
Karski, Jan, 126, 137, 144, 157-158, 196, 232.
Kashmir, 135.
Kathrada, Ahmed, 514.
Katkov, George, 191, 333, 519, 532, 602, 673-674, 744, 745.
Katyn graves, 344.
Katz, Daniel, 491-492, 561, 708, 726, 728, 729-730, 772 n. 101, 792-793, 803-804.
Kaunda, President Kenneth, 293.
Kazan, Russia, 261.
Kazansky Square, Petrograd, 673.
Keep, J.H.L., 273, 333, 607, 649 n. 163, 679, 684, 743.
Keitel, Field-Marshal Wilhelm, 170, 322, 324, 683.
Kellogg-Briand Pact, 343.
Kennedy, President John F., 139.
Kentucky, United States, 377, 399.
Kentucky Resolutions, 338-339.
Kenya, 294, 666.
Kerensky, Alexander, 328.
Kerry Volunteers, Ireland, 366.

K.G.B. – Committee for State Security, Soviet Union, 99.
Kgosana, Philip, 419, 629.
Khabalov, General S. S., 334, 673, 743.
Khan Abdul Ghaffar Khan, 790.
Kharkov, Russian Empire, 261.
Kharkov Prison, 365.
Kherson, Russian Empire, 360, 365.
Khrushchev, Premier Nikita, 342, 749.
Khudai Khidmatgar, 432, 790.
Kiangsu, China, 155, 236.
King, Rev. Martin Luther, Jr.: general, 111, 569 n. 102; bus boycott in Montgomery, Alabama (1955-56), 95-96, 249 n. 18, 414; on casting off fear, 457, 458; sharpening the focus for attack, 472; on 'tokenism,' 534; on generating incentives, 577; pleas for nonviolent behavior, 628; nonviolence and love urged by, 635; segregationist defections reported by, 670-671; effects of repression against, 689; and self-suffering, 722; and effects of nonviolence on opponent, 678; and effects of nonviolence on Negroes, 786-787, 791.
Kitchener, Lord H. H., 725.
Kiev, Ukraine, 168, 261, 268, 318, 640.
Kihss, Peter, 388.
Kilmallock, Ireland, 189.
Kimberly, South Africa, 601.
King, Governor Samuel, 427-428.
Kirchhoff, Hans, 279.
Kirkenes, Norway, 88.
Klarov, Czechoslovakia, 390.
Klunder, Rev. Bruce William, 386.
Knapp, Wilfrid, Preface, 342, 345.
Kneel-in, 380.
Knights of Labor, 222, 231, 236.
Knowless, K.G.J.C., 233, 261, 271.
Knoxville, Tennessee, 437 n. 566.
Koch, *Reichskommissar* Erich, 323.
Koestler, Arthur, 329.
Kokovtsev, Russian Minister of Finance, 659, 745.
Kolin, Czechoslovakia, 328.
Koller, General Karl, 324.
Kooperativa Förbundet, 415.
Korbel, Josef, 163, 222, 234, 271.
Korea, 152, 172, 682.
Korean War, 345.
Kossuth, Louis, 77.
Kostroma, Russian Empire, 168.
Kota-Kota District, Nyasaland, 310.
Kotgiri, India, 264.
Krasnoyarsk, Russia, 333.

compared with nonviolent action, 569 n. 116; not mentioned in "Continental Association," 613, French in Ruhr alienates support, 668; crushed in Hungary as general strike continues, 93; both sides use knowledge of to defeat other, 111; may be defeated, 71; conceptual tool for exists, 73; economic intervention used in, 402; nonviolent air raids used in, 381.

Military means and forces, 3, 63, 75, 76, 453; in *coups d'etat*, 80-82, 671-672, 743, see also *coups d'etat*; in occupations, 31, 42-44, 84, 98-101, 121, 141, 146-147, 149, 162-164, 178 n. 152, 189-190, 261, 274, 300, 337-338, 388, 550, 557, 590, 600, 606, 668-669, 686; as internal police, 31, 92, 94, 146, 156, 206, 208, 304, 385, 387, 429, 532, 561, 593, 629-630, 660, 668, 671-675, 684, 688, 713, 775 n. 193; in revolutionary role, 428, 600, 612-613, 649 n. 160, 650 n. 161; similarity to nonviolent action, 616. See also repression, mutiny, deliberate inefficiency and selective noncooperation by enforcement agents.

Miller, William Robert, 128, 151, 309, 352 n. 169, 463, 471, 550, 591, 595, 632, 653 n. 239, 715, 717, 731.

Miller, Webb, 330.

Mill-in, 378-379.

Mills, C. Wright, 18, 54 n. 51.

Milner, Lord, 295.

Milorg, 332.

Miner, Myrtilla, 399.

Ming Dynasty, 350 n. 88.

"Minute Men," 612, 614.

Miramar Naval Air Station, San Diego, California, 130.

Mirza, Crown Prince Mohamed Ali, 206.

Mirza, Nasru'lláh Khán, 209.

Mississippi, 134-135, 198, 373, 388, 419, 596, 689-690, 788-789.

Missouri Pacific Railroad, 268.

Mobilization committee to end the war in Vietnam, 417.

Mock awards, 131.

Mock election, 134-135.

Mock funeral, 157-159, 630.

Mogilev, Russia, 191.

Mohammed, 211.

Mohawk Indians, 389.

Molineux, William, 381.

Molotsi, Peter, 508, 519 n. 175.

Mommsen, Theodor, 76.

Monashki, 94.

Monckton Commission, 126, 188, 197, 296.

Montague, F.C., 57 n. 105.

Montesquieu, Charles Louis, de Secondat Baron de, 12, 53 ns. 33 and 63.

Montgomery Advertiser, 670.

Montgomery, Alabama, 73, 95, 96, 159, 233, 249 n. 18, 670, 690, 694; bus boycott, 5, 95, 222, 414-415, 457, 535, 548, 575, 577, 626, 640, 670, 689, 735, 783, 786, 791, 796.

Montgomery, Field Marshal Sir Bernard Law, 282 n. 62.

Moral *jiu-jitsu*, 657 n. 1.

Morale, 88, 99, 467, 479, 481, 490, 508, 511, 529, 573, 596, 625, 626, 664, 711, 724, 733, 758, 762-764; maintenance of, 575-583.

Moral obligation to obey, 20-22, 24, 27, 55 n. 65.

Moravany, Czechoslovakia, 327.

Moravian Church, 556.

Moravian Indians, 556.

Morgan, Edmund S. & Helen M., 159, 306, 315, 337, 352 n. 169, 519 n. 132, 630, 794.

Morioka, Japan, 213.

Morley, John, 603-604.

Morocco, 374.

Mosca, Gaetano, 47, 56 n. 82.

Moscow, Russia, 39, 78, 79, 94, 98, 100, 121, 131, 148, 153, 160, 166, 168, 171, 260, 261, 276, 289, 310, 320, 366, 368, 374, 507, 533, 604, 646 n. 79, 650 n. 159, 651 n. 167.

Moser, Nazi Gauleiter for Warsaw, 158.

Moses, Robert, 596.

Moslems. See Muslims.

Mossadegh's government, Iran, 234, 411.

Motorcade, 156.

Mott, Lucretia, 391.

Mountjoy Gaol, Ireland, 366.

Mowat, Charles Lock, 188.

Mowry, A.M., 428.

Mpopoma, Southern Rhodesia, 191.

Mujtahids, 208.

Mullaney, Father Anthony, 205.

Mullás, 206-210.

Multi-industry strikes, 275-277.

Munich, Germany, 126, 128.

Munro, Sir Thomas, 210.

Münster, Germany, 669.

Muravev, M.N., 645 n. 79.

Murcia, Spain, 289.

Murphy, Governor Frank, 404.

Mushiru 'd-Dawla, 209.

Music, American, 129. See also performances of plays and music, and singing.

Muslims, 155, 156, 368, 432, 433, 790.

Mussolini, Benito, 88, 326, 404.

Mutiny: general, 112, 113, 118, 146, 332-333, 453, 498, 502, 503, 595, 596, 671-672, 696, 706, 708, 733, 739, 753, 754, 755, 767; sanctions against, 24; Kapp *Putsch* 1920, 708; India 1930, 335, 432, 675, 747; Russia 1905, 79, 333-334, 354 n. 226, 606-608; Russia 1917, 596, 672-675, 743-744, 753; France 1917, 144, 166, 334, 464, 511, 529, 781; East Germany 1953, 675, 745.

Muzaffaru'd-Din, Shah of Persia, 206-210.

M.V.D., Ministry of Internal Affairs, U.S.S.R., 94.

Myers, J., 318, 413.

Myshkin, Ippolit Nikitch, 368.

Naess, Arne, Preface, 722 n. 101.

Nage, Premier Imre, 200.

Naidu, Sarojini, 311.

Nairobi, Kenya, 385.

"Naming," 581-582.

Nantucket, Massachusetts, 375.

Napoleon I, Emperor of France, 93, 452, 499.

Nashville, Tennesse, 223-224, 632, 689.

Nasjonal Samling, 193-195, 331-332, 691.

National Academy of Sciences, Hungary, 398.

National Agrarian Institute, Venezuela, 408.

National American Woman Suffrage Association, 154.

National Antislavery Standard, 387.

National Assembly, Czechoslovakia, 99, 173 n. 19, 188, 390.

National Assembly, France, 241.

National Association for the Advancement of Colored People, 378, 383.

National Association of German Industries, 697.

National Buddhist Institute, Vien Hoa Doa, 385.

National Consultative Assembly, Persia, 210.

National consumers' boycott, 228-230.

National Farm Workers Association, U.S., 263.

National Labor Relations Board, U.S., 404.

National Land League, Ireland, 227.

National Liberation Front, Vietnam, 296, 342, 381.

National Maritime Union, U.S., 700.

National Museum, Czechoslovakia, 143, 260.

National Museum, Hungary, 398.

National Palace, Guatemala City, 91.

National Protective Union, Hungary, 398.

National Theatre, Hungary, 398.

National University, Guatemala, 197, 268.

National Wages Agreement of 1924, Britain, 233.

"National Week," Indian, 498.

"National Work Effort," Norway, 332.

Nationalist Party, Germany, 697.

Nationalist Party, South Africa, 525.

Nationalistic Revolutionary Movement, Bolivia, 407.

Nationalists, Irish, 160, 366. See also Ireland.

Nationalists, African, 785. See also individual countries.

Nationalists, Indian, 135, 187, 295. See also India.

Nationalists, Puerto Rican, 291.

Native Labour (Settlement of Disputes) Act, South Africa, 542.

Natural Resources, 11.

Nazis: general, 172, 397, 545, 562; nonviolent resistance in countries occupied by, 5; and cooperation of populations, 42-43; Hitler's regime, 45; Norwegian occupation by, 5, 47, 74, 88, 126, 149, 626; Polish occupation by, 127, 188, 399; Danish occupation by, 150; Czechoslovakian occupation by, 163; occupation of Soviet Union by, 322; struggles against, 87-90; methods used against: public speeches, 119-120; protest against propanganda campaigns of, 127-128; illegal newspapers, 129; performances of plays and music, 149; singing, 150; political mourning, 158; homage at burial places, 163; social boycott, 188; producers boycott, 232; revenue refusal to pro-Nazi leaders, 242; limited strike, 274; resignation, 293, 295; boycott of government departments and agencies, 296; disguised disobedience, 306-307; noncooperation with conscription and deportation, 312; escape, 314; selective refusal of assistance by government aides, 320-321; blocking of lines of command and communication, 321-323; stalling and obstruction, 323-327; deliberate inefficiency and selective noncooperation by enforcement agents, 330-332; reverse trial, 369; nonviolent interjection, 386; alternative social institutions, 399; alternative communication system, 400-401; politically motivated counterfeiting, 410; general strike, 532, 536; openness and secrecy in resistance against, 484, 485; provocation by, 588-590; persistence against, 549; repression by, 553; morale in struggle against, 626; susceptible to public opinion, 662; defections from, 669; internal disputes of, 675, 676, 749; resistance spurred by repression by, 682-683; less severe repression urged by, 691; influence of Gandhi on resistance against, 98; swastika of, 126; domestic embargo used by, 244; interest payments refused by, 239; anti-Jewish measures of, 325-326; attitude toward Jews, 713; Labor Front of, 296; investigation of, 469. See also Germany, Hitler, Colonization and Invasions.

Nechaev, Sergei, 365.

Necker, Jacques, Minister of Louis XVI of France, 54 n. 51.

Negotiations, 65, 67, 77, 86, 90, 95, 100, 273, 277, 331, 341, 510, 514, 531, 639, 730, 759, 761, 766, 767, 776 n. 225; as preparation for nonviolent struggle, 470, 474, 510.

Negroes. See Afro-Americans.

Nehru, Jawaharlal: general, 42, 555, 776 n. 206; on power of noncooperation, 41; on length of struggles, 763; advocate of violence, 86; on nonviolent method of Gandhi, 87; on openness and lack of secrecy, 487, 490-491; halting submission, 522, 524; on timing of tactics, 497; on initiative in nonviolent action, 500; on repression, 537; on British perception of nonviolence, 528, 529; ineffectiveness of repression, 545-546, 585, 698 n. 2; beaten by police, 559, 783; on *agents provocateurs*, 593; effect of nonviolence on terrorism, 624; *hartal* used to protest imprisonment of, 638; reducing fear through nonviolence, 783; on nonviolence and self-respect, 786; nonviolent struggle brings satisfaction, 787; on nonviolent conversion, 720; on effect of defeat on later success, 757-758; photograph displayed, by supporters, 143.

Nehru, Motilal, 554-555.

Nekrasov, Nikolai A., 645 n. 79.

Neo-Gandhian struggles, 510.

Nepszabadsag, 289.

Netherlands: general, 129, 586; and nonviolent resistance, 87; resistance to Spanish rule 1565-1576, 4, 76, 287, 294; resistance to Inquisition, 684, 748; Nazi repression of strike in, 553; methods used in: strikes, 87, 758; letters of opposition and support, 120, 122; wearing of symbols, 136; vigils, 147; student strike, 197; industry strikes, 267; general strike, 277; producers' boycott, 232; seizure of assets by, 410; work-on without collaboration, 422; hiding, escape and false identities, 313-314; alternative communication system, 422; parallel government, 423; Commander of the *Wehrmacht* in, 683; repression brings solidarity in, 758; government-in-exile, 267, 422. See also Occupation, German of Netherlands.

Neues Deutschland, 597, 676.

Neumann, Franz, 18, 270-271, 283 n. 89.

Neurath, Foreign Minister, 295.

Neustadt, Richard, 36-39.

Nevinson, Henry W., 648-649 n. 154, 649 n. 167.

Newark, New Jersey, 379.

New Bedford, Massachusetts, 375.

New Bedford Railroad, 375-376.

Newbern, North Carolina, 318.

Newbury Church, Massachusetts Bay Colony, 140.

New Delhi, India, 290, 294, 367.

New England, 376, 379, 574, 794. See also individual colonies and states.

New Forward, 306.

New Hampshire, 186, 199, 225, 275, 430.

New Haven County, Connecticut, 633.

New Jersey, 157, 225, 374.

New Jersey Civil Rights Bill of 1949, 374.

New Orleans, Louisiana, 166, 377, 694.

Newport, Rhode Island, 158, 221, 380, 426, 428, 623, 630.

New Republic, 416.

New signs and names, 143-144.

Newsletter, National Strike Information Center, 198.

Newspapers, 128-129, 188, 306, 369, 377, 400, 542, 799. See also names of individual newspapers.

Newsweek, 690.

Newton, Isaac, 73.

New York City, 142, 198, 205, 226, 228, 375, 376, 379, 384, 391, 392, 616-617, 619, 654 n. 254, 719; colonial, 124, 141, 165, 186, 239, 265, 274, 413, 464, 574, 623, 647 n. 99, 794.

New York Herald Tribune, 671.

New York, Province of, 225, 226; General Assembly of, 337.

New York State, 230, 236, 379, 386, 429.

New York Times, 142-143, 388, 417, 660, 688.

New Zealand, 312.

Ngo Dinh Diem, President. See Diem, Ngo Dinh. (Most Vietnamese names are, however, here listed in the standard way by the first name of the series.)

Ngo Dinh Nhu, 660.

Nguyen Thanh Le, 342.

Nguyen Van Binh, Archbishop of Saigon, 671.

Nicolson, Harold, 344.

Nicholas, Robert Carter, 362.

Nicolas II, Tsar of Russia, 4, 79, 131, 156, 186, 191, 238, 312, 334, 530, 532, 533, 534, 542, 659, 668, 672-674, 678-680, 743-745, 749, 799.

Niedzialkowski Avenue, Warsaw, 144.

Nikolaev, Russia, 268.

Nivelle, General Robert, 335.

Nixon administration, 341.

Nixon, E. D., 458.

Nizhny Province, Russian Empire, 261.

N.K.V.D. (People's Commissariat of Internal Affairs), U.S.S.R., 365.

Noakhali, Bengal, India, 156.

Nolting, Ambassador Frederick E., 661.

Nonconformity, 524, 816.

Nonconsumption of boycotted goods, 186, 224-225, 229, 425, 613-614, 750.

Noncooperation: general, 4, 71, 114, 117, 429, 434, 455, 460, 522, 544, 763, 807; defined, 69, 183; and nonviolent action, 64, 67, 595; compared with nonviolent protest and persuasion, 118, 119, 169; compared with nonviolent intervention, 357; covert, 5; social, 169, 184, 188, 192, 211, 390, Chapter 4; political, 143, 184, 188, 212, 347, 504, 797, Chapter 7; economic, 184, 797, Chapter 5, 6; personal, 200, 201; by citizens with government, 289-303; works despite sanctions, 17; and habitual obedience, 25; and withdrawal of consent, 32; withdrawal of cooperation, 45, 46, 69, 84, 114, 183, 257, 285, 476, 501, 531, 696, 747,

806; withdrawal of support, 34, 85, 657, 666; popular, 41, 45, 767; and control of political power, 32, 44, 47; clues on political impact of, 36; as weapon of choice, 502; as intangible factor, 749; methods of: excommunication and interdict, 191; student strike, 196, 197; stay-at-home, 199; *hijrat*, 211, 212; social boycott used to encourage, 185, 187; producers' boycott, 231; withdrawal of bank deposits, 236; domestic embargo, 244; blocking lines of command and communication, 322; by constituent governmental units, 337-340; and removal of signs, 143; and fraternization, 146; with social events, 184; and alternative social institutions, 398, 796-797; and seeking imprisonment, 419; and civil disobedience of neutral laws, 420; reasons for nonrecognition of, 72; singing used against, 149; assemblies in support of, 164; persuasion by, 383; avoiding violence through, 454; aimed at conversion of opponent, 513, 706, 707, 732; as problem for opponent, 528, 532, 546-547, 747, 753; laws against, 540, 542; as defensive moral action, 501; when most effective, 494; action against refusal to engage in, 580-582; as substitute for war, 647; government-sponsored, 337, 604; effectiveness depends on organization, 480, and nonviolent coercion, 742-743, 744, 754, 755; and withdrawal of human resources, 746; altering power relationships through, 696; and withdrawal of skills and knowledge, 748; sensing power of, 739, 780, 781; and firmness, 548; discipline needed for success of, 631; increasing the use of, 638, 642, 780; increasing fearlessness through, 783; and self-image, 784; relation to cooperation, 795-796, 797; in absence of leadership, 803; and third parties, 818; and settlement, 760; Gandhi on, 84-85, 454, 480, 707, 748, 796; Gandhi's use of, 82, 84; Shelley on, 35; Nehru on, 41; by American colonies, 352 n. 169, 553, 580, 582, 600, 602, 611, 633, 636, 647, 685, 740, 743, 750, 781, 794, 797, 798; during American Revolution, 77, 337; in Northern Rhodesia and Nyasaland, 188, 747; in Guatemala 1944, 97; in Germany, 604; and

German generals' plot 1939, 322; against Kapp regime, Germany 40-41, 80, 696, 748; during the *Ruhrkampf* 1923, 82; in Egypt 1919, 97; in 1930-31 Indian campaign of Gandhi, 504, 682, 760; Noncooperation Committee in India 1920, 631; in Ephesus, Second Century A.D., 540; in Russia 1905, 797. See Economic boycotts, Strikes, Social noncooperation, and specific methods within those categories.

Noncooperation Committee, India, 631.

Noncooperation, general administrative. See General administrative noncooperation.

Noncooperation, judicial, 328-330.

Noncooperation with conscription and deportation, 311-313.

Noncooperation with social events, customs and institutions, 193.

Nonexportation, 186, 229, 239, 425, 507, 511, 600, 612, 615.

Nonimportation, 140-141, 186, 225, 229, 239, 425, 511, 540-541, 553, 574, 580-582, 612-614, 622, 636, 750-751, 794, 798.

Non-Importation Act, U.S., 246.

Non-Intercourse Act, U.S., 246.

Nonobedience, 350 n. 88. See also Popular nonobedience.

Nonobedience without direct supervision, 304.

Nonparticipation, economic, 431.

Nonrecognition, 72-74.

Nonresistance Society, 199, 375.

Nonsecrecy, in nonviolent struggle, 481-492.

Nonviolence: general, 47, 70, 83, 94, 111, 141, 387, 615, 794, 790; and political behavior, 65; and nonviolent action, 68, 71; and nonviolent coercion, 774 n. 161; and violence, 72, 77, 187, 528, 543, 552, 553, 565, 622; sometimes premeditated, 5; association with effective action, 82; and power of actionists, 110, 526, 781; and splits in opponent's group, 676; opponent's response to, 531, 557; repression of brings outrage, 657; and third parties, 660; produces unity, 794; and conversion, 719, 720; and element of surprise, 530; and increased self-esteem, 792; and Gandhi, 751-752, 771 n. 66; Gandhi on, 187, 229, 522, 565, 622, 725, 781; Nehru and ethic of, 87, 720; and Indian Campaign, 1930-31, 85; and anti-*Apartheid* movement, 123; and anti-slavery protests, 370; and anti-segregation protests, 375-376.

Nonviolent action, technique of. See Table of Contents.

Nonviolent air raids, 381-382.

Nonviolent *Blitzkrieg*, 776 n. 219.

Nonviolent coercion: general, 193, 455, 501, 709, 725, 737, 738, 769 n. 1; defined, 69, 706, 742-744; mechanism of change, 69, 71, 502, 697, 706, 732, 733, 734, 766, 767, 769 n. 1, 807; factors influencing, 754-755; economic boycott as form of, 220; linked to nonviolent intervention, 358; linked to conversion, 708, 732, 733; and numbers, 498; violence undermines, 601; and refusal to hate, 634; and negotiations, 767; alters power relationships, 768; and Gandhi, 769 n. 4.

Nonviolent discipline: general, 93, 101, 130, 264, 466, 573-642, 703 n. 154; necessary part of nonviolent technique, 455, 648 n. 99; need to maintain, 485, 537, 545, 549, 583, 638, 639; related to planning action, 462, 466; role of organization, 479, 480; and secrecy, 488; codes and pledges of, 481, 619, 631-632, 654 n. 254; and numbers 476, 478, 498, 501; and leadership, 638, 639, 817; possible without training, 620, 653 n. 216; and repression, 113, 537, 583, 585, 587, 591, 594, 657, 711; and nonviolent intervention, 501, 502, 508; prerequisite for shifts in power, 70, 545, 657; as test for future action, 504, 640; tested by tactical changes, 508; undermines opponent's support, 605, 666; promoting, 620-633; impact of, 565, 620, 710-711; and political *jiu-jitsu*, 697; as self-reliant weapon, 803; voluntarily accepted, 817; in Czechoslovakia 1968, 130; urged by Cesar Chavez, 264. See also Discipline, Codes of.

Nonviolent harassment, 369-371, 418.

Nonviolent interjection, 310, 382-387, 580, 582.

Nonviolent intervention: general, 64, 67, 321, 347, 494, 504, 528, 817; defined, 69; as class of methods, 114, 357-445; 455, 807; compared with other classes of methods, 117, 118, 119, 310, 358, 501-502; physical, 358, 371-390; political, 416-433, 461; psychological,

and Sports, 194; peasants of, 231, 241, 253 n. 119; teachers' protests, 1942, 70, 88, 237, 419, 422, 457, 585; Quisling regime, 70, 120, 122, 196, 298, 457, 626; Quisling's Education Department, 88. See also Occupation, German of Norway.

Norway-Denmark, 305, 414, 691-692.

Noske, Minister of Defense Gustav, 80.

Notre Dame Cathedral, Paris, 136.

Nottingham, England, 395.

Nova Scotia, 275.

Novgorod, Russia, 261.

Nuclear disarmament symbol, 130, 360.

Nuclear testing, 131, 310.

Nuclear weapons, 3, 9, 259, 311, 324, 808.

Numbers and strength, in nonviolent struggle, 498-499.

Nyanga, South Africa, 585-586.

Nyasaland, 126, 188, 296, 747. See also Malawi.

Nyasaland African Congress, 242, 419.

Nyasaland Commission of Inquiry, 310.

Obedience: general, 20; sources of power depend on, 12-16, 18, 28, 744, 746, 817; as habit, 19, 25, 51 n. 17, 749; essentially voluntary, 26-30; not equally given, 30; and sanctions, 12, 14, 15, 19-20, 26, 28, 752; not inevitable, 18, 25, 57 n. 110; not uniform, 26; withdrawal of, 31, 32, 34, 45, 63, 817; different from coercion, 27; ruler's use of, 24; role of self-interest, 22, 27; varies with strength of reasons given, 31; interdependent with enforcement, 15; springs from fear, 18; and psychological identification with ruler, 23; and intangible factors, 749, 750; and zone of indifference, 23; and absence of subjects' self-confidence, 23-24; and common good, 20-21, 56 n. 74; and ruler's legitimacy, 21; and suprahuman factors, 21; and authority, 746; and conformity of commands to accepted norms, 21; duty of, 45; of many to the few, 54 n. 51; and repression, 112; and moral obligation, 20-22, 55 n. 65. See also individual authors.

The Observer, 171.

Occupations: general, 39, 40, 42, 44, 64, 71, 74, 82, 101, 118, 122, 126, 127, 136, 137, 143, 144, 147, 190, 211, 296, 298, 300, 302, 323, 325, 328, 414, 421, 423, 498, 686, 746. See also Nonviolent occupations; military, 129,

189, 422; British of Boston, 337, 603; British of India, 82, 330, 339, 585. See also India. British and French of Port Said, 190; French and Belgian of Germany, 126, 149, 287, 296, 541, 578, 604, 610, 659, 668, 737, 748. See also *Ruhrkampf*; German of Austria, 589; German of Czechoslovakia, 163, 177, 222, 271, 301; German of Denmark, 136, 189, 196, 277, 683; German of Europe, 87, 232, 270, 418, 586, 683; German of France, 305, 314, 326, 410; German of Netherlands, 231, 270, 274, 282 n. 62, 305, 313, 422, 536, 758; German of Norway, 47, 74, 88, 126, 129, 149, 170, 193, 294, 330, 314, 545, 577, 609, 626; German of Poland, 126, 127, 137, 143, 188, 222, 399, 716; German of Russia, 42-43, 322, 682-683, 749; Italian of France, 326; Japanese of China, 211, 231, 232; Russian of Czechoslovakia, 100, 144, 147, 300, 327-328, 402; Russian of Germany, 542, 550. See also Military forces, Occupations.

Ochakov, 287.

Ochrana, 330, 333, 593.

"October Manifesto" of Tsar Nicholas II, 79, 152, 291, 533, 567 n. 50, 799.

Odense, Denmark, 275.

Odessa, Russia, 168, 268, 276, 604.

O'Donovan, Patrick, 437 n. 56.

Oesser, Rudolf, 686.

Office of Strategic Services, U.S., 410.

O'Hegarty, P. S., 603, 632, 763.

Ohio, 200, 556.

Ohio State University, Preface.

Oklahoma, 335.

Olbricht, Friedrich, 322.

Olmstead, F. L., 203.

Olomouc, Czechoslovakia, 327.

Omaha, Nebraska, 382.

Omission, Acts of, 68.

Ons Volk, 401.

Open letter, 120.

Openness and secrecy in nonviolent struggle, 481-492.

Opera Dei Congressi, 416.

Oppenheimer, Martin, 300, 474, 488, 517 n. 94, 525, 547, 587, 630, 776 n. 225.

Opponent: general, 65, 67, 78, 92, 496, 500, 503, 508, 521, 564, 778, 786, 792, 795, 800, 816,; effect of nonviolent action on, 68, 69, 508, 754, 795, 799; violence of, 71, 547, 554, 698 n. 1, 807; repression by, 500, 536, 542,

708; Tolstoy on, 44; in various countries: Cuba, 153; India, 42, 83, 187, 311, 318, 330, 432, 529, 552, 559, 591, 682, 687, 693, 731, 735, 783; Germany, 80, 90, 288, 302, 354 n. 216, 542; East Germany, 161, 197, 405, 529, 629, 675, 677, 708, 753, 775 n. 193; Guatemala, 90, 91, 92; Russia, 94, 197, 333, 365, 483, 485, 553, 561, 593, 640, 646 n. 79, 684; Ireland, 161, 188-189; South Africa, 138, 223, 419, 541, 550, 587, 591, 629, 670, 692; Nyasaland, 310, 419; United States, 138, 166, 319, 374, 378, 386, 397, 404, 587, 677, 692; Spain, 171; Finland, 278; France, 310, 326, 327; Belgium, 312; Italy, 326, 363, 403; Brazil, 408; Norway, 330-332; Netherlands, 330; Hungary, 388; Japan, 682; South Vietnam, 661. See also specific methods, individual countries and particular struggles.

Policy of austerity, 225-226.

"Polite procrastination," 323. See Stalling and obstruction.

Political boycott, 285. See also Political noncooperation.

Political *jiu-jitsu*, 110, 112, 113, 453, 496, 557, 563, 596, 600, 642, 657-697, 698 n. 1; 807.

Political mourning, 157-158.

Political noncooperation: general, 69, 184, 394, 504, 737: defined, 285-286; methods of, 285-347; related to methods of social noncooperation, 193, 195, 199, 212, 213; related to methods of economic noncooperation, 240, 279; compared with methods of nonviolent intervention, 394, 421; effect of, 536, 613, 614, 743; and sanctions, 12; practiced under repression, 640; and nonviolent protest, 118, 129, 133, 143; conversion by, 70; Continental Association, program of, 186. See also Noncooperation and specific struggles.

Political violence, Preface; defined, 543; compared with nonviolent action, 459, 485, 523, 679, 755, 756, 802, 805, 806; effect of nonviolent action on, 809; effect on nonviolent action, 513; linked to kind of social system, 543, 800, 806, 808; relation to centralization of power, 800-801, 802; and repression, 545, 547, 552; and suffering, 551, 552; contagion of, 798; exposure of leadership, 637; in Latin America,

90. See also Violence, Repression and individual countries.

Politically-motivated counterfeiting, 409-410.

Politika, 327, 389-390.

Poltava, Province, Russian Empire, 261.

Ponce, General, 92.

Poor People's Corporation, Jackson, Mississippi, 416.

Popular nonobedience, 304-306, 308, 312.

Populists, Russia, 128, 163.

Port-au-Prince, Haiti, 279.

Port Elizabeth, South Africa, 138, 167, 200, 601.

Portsmouth, New Hampshire, 159, 653 n. 252.

Portsmouth, Virginia, 559.

Portugal, 195, 233, 237, 243, 291, 297, 347, 382, 410; Minister of Education, 311; opposition, 291; recognition of Republic, 344.

Postal service, 86.

Posters, 126, 127, 132, 152, 154, 156, 171, 188, 369, 370.

Posters and other displayed protest, 117.

Potsdam Garrison, 697.

Powell, Rev. Adam Clayton, 223.

Power: general, 4, 5, 6, 13, 40, 72, 79, 81, 85, 124, 431, 532, 659, 706; social power defined, 7; political power defined, 7-8; nature of, 8, 48 n. 4, 49 n. 5, 523; social roots of, 10-16; sources of, 11-12, 16, 28, 69, 453; monolith theory of, 9-10, 44; pluralistic-dependency theory of, 9, 39; relation to authority, 13; depends on consent, 3, 13, 16, 25, 29, 49 n. 8, 51 n. 17, 53 n. 33, 54 n. 51, 55 n. 61, 61 n. 201, 63, 490, 524, 745; depends on interaction, 11, 16, 17-18, 25, 26, 49-50 n. 9, 52 n. 23, 54 n. 47, 744; and nonviolent action, 3, 7-8, 64, 65-67, 69, 70, 76, 97, 110, 112, 113, 321, 451, 453-454, 470, 471, 485, 489, 490, 579, 657, 658, 698 n. 1, 743, 756, 816; and nonviolent coercion, 744-745; control of, 10, 18, 29, 32, 36, 39, 41, 47, 50 n. 13, 817; theory of nonviolent control of, 32-34; technique of control of, 43-48, 461, varies with control of social forces, 15-16; social sources of power changes, 458-461; altering relationships of, 695-697; power problem, 36-38, 39; Gandhi's theory of, 83-86, 724-725; withdrawing sources of, 47, 64, 85, 112, 453-454, 706, 744-754,

816; and sanctions, 14, 19; and repression, 35, 496, 588, 594; shifts in, 434, 524, 527, 537, 657, 658, 662, 690, 758, 767; redistribution of, Chapter 14; indirect approach to, 495-496; and political *jiu-jitsu,* 496, 690, 768; and concessions by opponent, 532, 543, 588, 594, 739; and conversion of opponent, 725; role in negotiations, 470; compared with authority, 745; and violence, 683; as factor in social situation, 618; awareness of, 739, 740; and Jouvenal, 54 n. 50; Weberian 'types', 56 n. 86.

Prace, 301.

Prague, Czechoslovakia, 73, 127, 129, 131, 136, 142, 151, 162, 163, 188, 189, 234, 260, 300, 310, 327, 328, 590; Lord Mayor of, 288; City Committee of the Communist Party, 131; Praha-Vrsovice railroad depot, 127.

Prasad, Rajendra, 591.

Prawdin, Michael, 457, 607.

Prayer and worship, 137-139, 480.

Pray-in, 379-380.

Preclusive purchasing, 410.

Prelouc, Czechoslovakia, 328.

Preparations for nonviolent struggle, 467-481.

Presbyterians, 376, 386, 670.

Press Ordinance, India, 641.

Preston, Katherine, 439 n. 131.

Pretoria, South Africa, 164, 167, 223.

Primary boycott, 220-221.

Prince Edward County, Virginia, 239.

Princeton, New Jersey, 140.

Princeton University, 144.

Principled nonviolence, Preface.

Prison, 77, 125, 138, 200, 452, 486, 491, 537, 576, 771 n. 58.

Prison camps, 93.

Prisoner-of-war camps, 485.

Prisoners and political prisons, 90, 93, 94, 265, 328, 470, 642.

Prisoners' strike, 265.

Producers boycott, 231-232.

Professional strike, 265-266, 334.

Prohibitory Act, Britain, 247, 694.

Propaganda, 20, 89, 120, 127, 146, 148, 332, 529, 683.

Property, 11.

Protest. See Nonviolent protest and persuasion.

Protest disrobing(s), 140, 177 n. 121, 359.

Protest emigration, 202, 204, 211-213. See also *hijirat.*

Protest meetings, 117, 165-167, 445 n. 301. See also Assemblies of protest or support, Camouflaged meetings of protest and Teach-ins.

Protest strike, 259-261, 763.

Protestants, 669.

Protopopov, Minister of the Interior, 190.

Proudfoot, Merrill, 437 n. 56.

Providence, Rhode Island, 141, 185, 205, 299, 426, 428-430, 517 n. 66, 702 n. 106.

Prussia, 213, 604, 686.

Psychological changes in nonviolent actionists, 777-793.

Psychological harassment, 369.

Psychological identification with ruler, 23, 24, 27.

Public opinion, 92, 110, 113, 119, 316, 321, 337, 340, 530, 584-585, 589, 626, 657, 659, 662, 710, 698 n. 3, 720.

Public Safety Act, No. 3 of 1953, South Africa, 541, 757.

Public statements, 122, 461, 511.

Publication of names, 186.

Puerto Rico, 388.

Puget Sound, State of Washington, 319.

Pullman Palace Car Co., 233.

Punjab, India, 751.

Puritans, 362, 540, 548, 681, 713, 719, 720.

Putrament, Jerzy, 316.

Quakers. See Society of Friends.

Quang Nang Province, South Vietnam, 296.

Quantity and quality in nonviolent action, 475-479.

Quantri, South Vietnam, 138.

Quasi-legal evasions and delays, 335-337.

Quebec, Canada, 264.

Quickie walkout, 261.

Quillayute River, State of Washington, 319.

Quisling, Vidkun, 5, 88, 89, 331, 410, 419, 585. See also Norway, Quisling regime.

Qum, Persia, 207, 208, 209, 210.

Radhakrishnan, President S., 290.

Radio, 129, 190, 799.

Radio Prague, 162.

Rainbow Beach, Lake Michigan, 378.

Rajasthan, India, 290.

Raleigh, North Carolina, 464.

Rally, 445 n. 301.

Rampur, Gujarat, India, 677.

Randolph, A. Philip, 223.

Randolph, Edmund, 362.
Randolph, Massachusetts, 379.
Rapport, maintainance of, 575-577.
Rath, Ernst von, 590.
Rauter, Lieutenant General Hans, 330.
Rawza-Khwáns, 208.
Ray, Charles R., 392.
Rayback, Joseph G., 403, 404.
Read, Sir Herbert, 728.
Reading, Lord, Viceroy of India, 529.
Reading, Pennsylvania, 383.
Recinos, María Chincilla, 92.
Reconciliation, 359.
Reconstruction period, post U.S. Civil War, 335.
Records, 129.
Records, radio and television, 129.
Red Army, U.S.S.R., 629, 745.
"Redcoats," 612.
Red Square, Moscow, 148.
Rees, J. C., Preface.
Refusal of an assemblage or meeting to disperse, 308-310.
Refusal of assistance to enforcement agents, 298-300.
Refusal of government's money, 244.
Refusal of industrial assistance, 236.
Refusal of membership in international bodies, 346.
Refusal of public support, 288-289.
Refusal to accept appointed officials, 301-302.
Refusal to admit a government to membership in an international organization, 445 n. 301.
Refusal to dissolve existing institutions, 302-303.
Refusal to hate, 633-635.
Refusal to let or sell property, 235.
Refusal to pay debts or interest, 237-239, 667.
Refusal to pay fees, dues and assessments, 237.
Refusal to pay taxes, 389, 405, 504, 507, 536, 568 n. 72, 583, 641, 751.
Refusal to rent, 228.
Reggan, North Africa, 382.
Regicide, 3, 9, 294.
Regner, C. F., 670.
Reich Chancellery, Berlin, 41.
Reichsbank, Germany, 40.
Reichstag, 589.
Reichstag, fire, 369, 532, 588.
Reichswehr, German Army, 81, 696.
Reitherman, Robert, Preface, 440 n. 168.
Reitlinger, Gerald, 312, 325-327, 484, 549, 590, 716.

Rejection of government's paper money, 536.
Religious procession, 155-156.
Reluctant and slow compliance, 303-304.
Remembrance Sunday, 138.
Removal of own signs and placemarks, 300-301.
Renouncing honors, 171-172.
Rent-refusal campaign, Ireland, 582.
Rent with-holding, 189, 226-228, 521.
Reporting "sick" ("sick-in"), 271-273.
Repression: general, 44, 48, 82, 94, 110, 207, 262, 294, 313, 330, 341, 455, 457, 476, 489, 675, 709, 731, 739, 748, 757, 760, 766, 768, 807, 808; violent, 541-546, 559, 657, 658, 665, 666, 674, 698 n. 2; seen as inappropriate, 734-735; police brutality, 671; forcing submission through, 35, depends on approval of population, 460; opponent likely to use, 71; submission to contrary to nonviolent action, 548, 680; nonviolent action designed to operate against, 71, 807; effect of killings, 660, 673-674; effect on world opinion and third parties, 113, 660, 657, 698 n. 3, 727; relation to nonviolent action, 109, 110, 127; effectiveness of nonviolent action against, 111, 112-113, 330, 452, 453; relation to nonviolent methods chosen, 115, 367, 501; need for nonviolent discipline in face of, 70, 100, 499, 594, 615, 755, 782; persistence against, 110-111, 112, 113, 211-212, 476, 709; less "justified" and effective than vs. violence, 93, 545, 546, 583, 657, 665, 681-682, 698 n. 15; fear strengthens, 486; challenge brings, Chapter 10; strengthens cause of actionists, 473, organization against, 479; methods used against strikers, 263; need for initiative despite, 500; actionists must expect, 537; appeals to limit, 550; limiting by avoiding mass confrontations, 509, 550; by control of communication and information, 538; unofficial attacks, 206, 300, 377; by psychological pressures, 538; by confiscation, 538; by economic sanctions, 538; by bans and prohibitions, 538; by arrests and imprisonments, 539; by exceptional restrictions, 539; by direct physical violence, 539; nonviolent behavior limits, 583, 596, 634, 657-658, 732, 753, 764;

against revolutionaries, 646 n. 79; violence of actionists provides excuse for, 597, 603, 604, 605, 743; *agents provocateurs* used to justify, 593, 599; sabotage increases, 610, 611; undisciplined action facilitates effective, 618; opponent's means of and cause questionable, 665-667; problems in opponent's exercise of, 596, 665, 676-677, 752, 753, 755, 816; actionists provoke, 677, 687; increases resistance, 678, 682, 690, 740; strength needed to withstand, 680, 758-759; may legitimize resistance, 681; reduction of, 477, 565, 722; less severe forms and counter-nonviolence, 502, 690-695; and psychological effects, 698 n. 1, 722; and institutionalized indifference, 712; and differential treatment, 713; and mechanisms of success, 706, 708, 740, 722; neutralization through self-suffering, 709, 710-711; need for self-reliance against, 803; and nonviolent coercion, 741, 753, 755; inefficacy of, 636-642; solidarity and discipline needed to fight, 573-642; limitations on against nonviolent actions, 583-586; may become new point of resistance, 640-642; political *jiu-jitsu* a means to counter, 657, see also Political *jiu-jitsu*. See also Violence, Violent action and struggle, Sanctions and Political *jiu-jitsu*.

Republican Party, U.S., 134, 245, 246.

Resistance: general, 23, 35, 36, 76, 80, 81-82, 89, 98, 99, 113, 146, 185, 187, 196, 302, 312, 313, 321, 332, 418, 423, 452, 453, 480, 484, 485, 488, 498, 508, 586, 639, 640-642, 658, 763-764, 786; conditions when impossible, 56 n. 82, 524; and repression, 35; continuing under repression, 680-688, 709, 785; people adverse to, 21; right of, 45-46; by noncooperation, 47; corporate, 48; violent, 87; contagious, 798-799; advocacy of, 289; symbolic, 136, 360; economic, 76, 481, 534, 540, 578; and constructive program, 795-797; capacity for expanded, 804. See also Passive resistance and listings in Table of Contents.

Restraints or sanctions for solidarity of actionists, 580-583.

Restricted strike, 268-275.

Reverse strike, 114, 401, 402-403.

Revolutionary strike, 432.

Revolutionary struggle. See Struggle, revolutionary.

Reuter, Ernst, 550.

Revenue refusal, 84, 86, 240-243.

Reverse trial, 368-369.

Révész, Imre, 309.

Revolution: general, 33, 34, 78, 80, 97, 296, 332, 423, 424, 457, 460, 488, 551, 554, 753, 756; nonviolent, 78, 79, 806; social, 97, 477, 706, 809; right of, 45; and parallel government, 424; and centralization of power, 800, 802; and general strike, 532; and terrorism, 624; and leadership, 637; nonviolent, 86; Lenin on, 650-651 n. 160, 651 n. 161; support for violent, 86; Russian, 128, 456, 602; socialist, 291.

Reynolds, Lloyd G., 132-133.

Rhineland, German, 81, 259, 553.

Rhode Island, 225, 299, 337, 362, 375, 413, 426, 427, 428-429, 430, 582; Supreme Court, 427, 430; parallel government (Dorr's Rebellion), 426-430. See also individual towns, cities and persons.

Rhode Island Antislavery Society, 369, 387.

Rhodesia. See Southern Rhodesia and Northern Rhodesia.

Ribbentrop, Foreign Minister Joachim, 325, 326, 692.

Richardson, Gloria, 791.

Ride-in, 371, 375.

Riga massacres, 325.

Rinde, Erik, Preface.

Rioting, 3, 34, 77, 587, 591, 599, 600, 601, 603, 604, 616, 623-625.

Risør, Norway, 305.

Roberts, Adam, Preface, 173 n. 1.

Robin Moor, 341.

Rock Hill, South Carolina, 380.

Röchling concern, 236.

Rodman, Edward, 559.

Rodzyanko, M. V., 190, 744.

Rogers, abolitionist editor, 199.

Roman Campagna, Italy, 405.

Roman Catholic Church, 122, 234, 366, 399, 406, 416, 669. See also individual churches, clergy, popes, etc.

Roman Catholic Law, 204.

Roman Catholic minority, South Vietnam, 671.

Roman consuls, 75.

Rome: general, 192; ancient, 4, 57 n. 105, 75-76, 124, 266; Roman Empire, 123-124, 312, 388; toleration of Chris-

ers Association, 668; Merchants Club, 668; Kushka Station, 549; Academy of Sciences, 668; Bureau of the Central Committee of the Party, 673. See also Union of Soviet Socialist Republics, Occupation, German of Soviet Union, Russian of... specific methods of nonviolent action and Russian Revolutions of 1905, 1917.

Russian peasants, 228.

Russian Revolution of 1905, 4, 5, 78, 79, 139, 152, 166, 168, 197, 209, 236, 237, 242, 260, 261, 276, 296, 305, 306, 312, 333, 430, 431, 483, 507, 519 n. 132, 532, 533, 604, 606-608, 626, 640, 647 n. 99, 650 n. 160, 651 ns. 161 and 167, 672, 743, 747, 573, 780, 781, 788-789, 794, 798.

Russian Revolution of February-March 1917, 4, 5, 79, 333, 430, 519 n. 132, 542, 569, 596, 672, 743, 744, 745, 753.

Russian Socialist Federated Soviet Republic (R.S.F.S.R.), 39, 40.

Russian Soldiers' Councils, 464.

Russification, 279.

Russo-Japanese War, 78, 312.

Rustin, Bayard, 377.

Sabotage, 82, 274, 323, 403, 590, 597, 600, 604, 651 n. 168, 651 n. 173, 683; and nonviolent action, 608-611.

Sachsen, Germany, 619.

Sacramento, California, 264.

Sacred Mount, Rome, 75-76.

Saigon, Vietnam, 136, 661.

St. Donats Holiday Estates, Nash, Wales, 227.

St. Hedwig's Cathedral, Berlin, Germany, 120.

St. Lamberti Church, Münster, Germany, 669.

St. Lawrence Seaway, 389.

St. Louis, Missouri, 197.

St. Patrick, 361.

St. Petersburg, Russian Empire, 73, 78, 122, 155, 160, 162, 166, 168, 190, 197, 260, 266, 273, 333, 339, 368, 530, 645 n. 79, 659; Soviet of, 237, 242, 430, 606. See also Petrograd and Leningrad.

Salem, Massachusetts, 141, 317, 376, 549, 702 n. 109.

Salt Acts, British India, 86, 380, 483, 497, 513, 533, 641, 682.

Salt March of 1930, India, 4, 86, 153, 497, 504, 584, 775 n. 169. See also India, Gandhi, Indian National Congress and Britain.

Salvador. See El Salvador.

Salvemini, Gaetano, 137, 309.

Samara Province, Russian Empire, 261.

Sanctuary, 204; Christian examples, 204-205; Islamic examples (Persia 1906), 205-210.

Sanctions: defined, 12; social, 183-213; religious, 191-193; international, 12, 346, 663; diplomatic, 340-347, 664; economic (general), 141, 219-284; 401-416, 613, 652 n. 192, 664; (against nonviolent actionists) 538, (international), 132, 244-248, 251 n. 55, 409-411; nonviolent, 12, 537, 805, (to support nonviolent discipline), 466, 615-616; nonviolent action as, 165, 694; fear of as source of a ruler's power, 12, 14, 19, 22, 25, 27, 30, 55 n. 61, 453, 456, 744; nonviolent fearlessness makes impotent, 546, 752. See also Fearlessness. Fear of produces obedience, 19-20, 24, 27-28, 30, 456; and pattern of submission, 14, 15, 16-17, 23, 25-26, 35; must operate on will of subject, 26-29, 111, 545; willingness to undergo in resistance, 30-31, 32, 458, 476, 504, 551, 817; unwillingness to undergo in resistance, 547; derive from obedience and cooperation, 14-15, 21; nonviolent action may restrict opponent's, 752-754; against nonviolent action, 536-546; police and troops subject to, 558; and negotiations, 67. See also Repression, Obedience, Disobedience, Suffering, Self suffering, and Violent sanctions.

San Diego, California, 130, 395.

San Francisco Bay, 389.

San Francisco to Moscow Peace March, 153.

Sans-Culotte, 136.

Santiago, Cuba, 153, 154.

Saratov Province, Russian Empire, 168, 261.

Sargent, Porter, Preface.

Satyagraha: theory of power, 83, 85, 548, 711, 774 n. 161, 781; dynamics of, 211, 367, 707, 709-710, 725, 771 n. 66; and Dharsana raid, 311; and preparations, 467, 503, 505; reveals implicit violence, 544; casualties in, 553; widespread leadership in, 633; by Pathans, 790; at Vykom, 82; parallel social structures, 796; need for few

Southern Regional Council, 373.

Southern Rhodesia, 191, 420.

South Vietnam. See Vietnam, South.

South West Africa, 664.

Southwest Alabama Farmers Cooperative Association, 416.

Southwestern System Railroad, 231.

Soviet Union. See Union of Soviet Socialist Republics.

Sovremennik, 128.

Spain, 4, 76, 97, 171, 267, 276, 294, 341, 410, 423, 659.

Spitalfields, England, 152.

Spitz, David, 33.

Splits in the opponent regime, 675-677.

Sports strike, 195.

Spy flights, 342.

S.S. (*Schutzstaffel*), Nazi, 89, 90, 330, 716.

St. Catherine's College, Oxford, Preface.

Stabekk School, Stabekk, Norway, 419.

Stack, Austin, 366.

Staffordshire, England, 235.

Stalin, Josef, 49 n. 6, 94, 141, 148, 340, 342, 347, 562, 604.

Stall-in, 394-395.

Stalling and obstruction, 323-328, 335, 394.

Stamm, Eugen, 463.

Stamp Act Congress, 794.

Stamp Act, 70, 157, 158, 185, 221, 225, 229, 231, 238-239, 241, 266, 306, 337, 412, 602, 611, 623, 630, 667, 708, 738, 794, 798.

Stand-in, 374-375.

Stang, Axel, 194.

Stanley, Governor Thomas, 240.

The State: general, 9, 10, 17, 22, 25, 57 n. 105, 67, 81, 199, 328, 451, 532; and "force," 15, 26, 49 n. 5; violence and origin of, 20; violence and centralization in, 800-802; obedience to, 26; control of, 34; Hitler on restructuring of, 46; dependence on authority, 50 n. 14; 51 n. 19, 52 n. 24; 53 n. 33; sanctions to induce obedience, 123 n. 61, 536-537. See also Sanctions. Dissolution of, 62 n. 201; and civil resistance, 530.

State Department, U.S., 661.

States General, France, 137.

"Statement of the 342," by Russian academics, 122.

Stauffenberg, Count Claus von, 322.

Stavanger, Norway, 196.

Stay-at-home, 170, 199-200, 259.

Stay-at-home strikes, 507, 508.

Stay-down strike, 403.

Stay-in strike, 401, 403-405, 550.

Steblova, Czechoslovakia, 328.

Steel strike, U.S., 535.

Steiner, Stan, 191, 319.

Sternstein, Wolfgang, 149, 287-288, 578, 648 n. 144.

Steuben, John, 265.

Stevenage, Hertfordshire, England, 259.

Stevens, Edmund, 145.

Stock Exchange, New York City, 397.

Stralsund shipyard, East Germany, 143.

Strategy, 48, 67, 101, 455, 462, 518 n. 24, 519 n. 22, 523, (definition) 493; importance of, 493-495, 628, 756, 763; elements of, 495-500, (geographical) 496-497, (psychological) 490, (timing) 497-498; choice of weapons, 501-510; Gandhi's attention to, 82, 84, 85-86, 87, 492-493; grand strategy, 87, (definition) 493; and concentration of strength, 499-500; and influence of actionist behaviour, 527.

Strikes: general references and diverse cases, 4, 5, 67, 71, 73, 77, 87, 91, 97, 113, 118, 124, 125, 172, 219, 257-279, 282 n. 62, 421, 453, 459, 474, 479, 522, 529, 534, 544, 550, 553, 629, 686, 747, 749, 750, 752; defined, 257-258, 280 n. 5; as sanction, 12; learning how to use, 779-780; "flight" as precursor of, 201-204; violence in, 597-598; illegal, 45; injunction against ignored, 318; countermeasures and repression against, 535, 536, 540, 568 n. 72, 584, 585-586, 640, 686, 688, 692, 758, see also Repression; reduced violence against, 476; perceptions of power of, 532-533; morale and solidarity in, 575-583, 794; strategy in, 495, 519 ns. 127 and 128; settlements of, 737; control organizations in, 431-432, 797; as repudiation of authority, 531; and self-respect, 524, 786; increased self-confidence from, 798-799; Lenin on impact of, 781, 788-789; Lenin on limits of, 650-651 n. 161; and picketing, 132-133, 134, 503; and social boycott, 184; and stay-at-home, 199; and appeals to mutiny, 677-678; and lockout, 235; and nonviolent interjection, 383; and fast, 466; combined with economic boycott, 232-233, 258, 227-279; in

1905 Revolution, 78-79, 139, 431, 483, 530, 532, 549, 567 n. 44, 647 n. 99, 650 n. 161, 668, 780, 788-789; see Russian Revolution of 1905. In resistance to Kapp *Putsch*, 80-81, 743; see Kapp *Putsch*; at Vorkuta, 93-95, 533, 548; see also Vorkuta. See also specific methods of the strike, invidual countries, places etc. for other specific cases.

Strike breakers, 263, 476, 576.

Strike by resignation, 273.

Strike committees, 94, 95, 464, 578; at Vorkuta, 548.

Strik-Strikfeldt, Captain Wilfried, 43.

Student strike, 93, 196-198.

Struggle, general, 85, 101, 109, 110, 526, 531, 533, 547, 547 n. 50, 564; characteristic of nonviolent action, 65-67, 71-72, 87, 548; and anarchism, 67; forms of imitated, 798; violent, 802, 803, 805, 815; military, 71; and nonviolent action, 97-98; withdrawal from, 535, 793; testing nonviolent action in, 779; means of, 546.

Stuttgart, Germany, 80, 381.

Submission of subjects: sanctions to induce, 14; psychological means to induce, 16; indirect economic rewards induce, 22; moral obligation induces, 20; lack of self-confidence induces, 24; alien education induces, 57 n. 100; basic to nondemocratic rule, 78, 84, 490, 745; needed to preserve government *per se*, 45; pattern of, 14, 543; to oppression destructive of society, 46; suffering of submissive people, 554; psychological and attitudinal changes halt, 31-32; rejection basic to nonviolent action, 64-65, 67, 70, 87, 522, 523, 549, 785; pattern of submissiveness ended, 778-779; withdrawal of, 31, 34-36, 84, 521-524, 528, 778; repression to force resumption of, 32, 545, 681, 683, 684; to violence spells defeat, 680; repression may fail to induce, 111-112, 546-547, 683-687. See also Sanctions, Obedience, Passivity, Repression, Disobedience, Noncooperation.

Subordination, 58 n. 122, 779.

Subversion, 36.

Success-failure, factors influencing. See Outcome of the conflict, factors influencing.

Suffering: penalty for disobedience, 29; impact of, 634; acceptance as price of defiance, 636; capacity to endure, 680, 759; in nonviolent action (general), 638, 550, 769 n. 1; necessity of, 551-555; Gandhi on purity in, 655 n. 264; inflicted by general strike, 532. See also Self-suffering and Conversion.

Suffolk County, Massachusetts Bay, 595.

Suffolk, Henry Howard, Twelfth Earl of, 740.

Suffolk Resolves, 595.

Suhl, Yuri, 314.

Sumter County Civil Rights Movement, 243.

Sunakawa, Japan, 388.

"Sundays Only" strikes. See Strike, limited.

Sunday Times (London), 145, 162.

Sung Cheh-yuan, General, 307.

Suppliers and handlers boycott, 232-234.

Suppression, 541, 683, 688, 778. See also Repression.

Suppression of Communism Bill, South Africa, 199-200, 542.

Surrender, 534.

Suspension of social and sports activities, 193-196.

Svoboda, 127.

Svoboda, President Ludvik, 99, 100, 143.

Svyatopolk-Mirsky, Peter, 640.

Swadeshi, 413.

Swaffham, England, 385.

Swaraj, 41, 490, 576, 787.

Sweden, 81, 231, 241, 276, 341, 415, 659, 692, 697, 767.

Switzerland, 303.

Sykes, General Percy, 208, 209.

Symbolic Acts, 114, 117, 135-145, 287, 475, 576-577.

Symbolic lights, 142-143.

Symbolic public acts, 135-136.

Symbolic reclamations, 145.

Symbolic sounds, 144.

Symbolic strikes, 259-261.

Symbolic withdrawal, 172.

Symbols, 125, 126, 130, 136.

Symons, Julian, 134, 518 n. 105, 519 n. 128, 531, 574, 757.

Sympathetic, strike, 233, 267-268.

Syndicalists, 276.

Taber, Robert, 153-154.

Tabriz, Persia, 206.

Tagore, Rabindranath, 176, 688.

Tallahassee, Florida, 722.

Tambov Province, Russian Empire, 261.

Tamils, 135.

United Farm Workers, 413.
United Farm Workers Organizing Committee, AFL-CIO, 263.
United Mine Workers, 267.
United Nations, 237, 288, 345-346, 507, 660; Charter of, 345, 346; General Assembly of, 346, 659, 698 n. 8, (president of), 345; Security Council of, 345-346; Secretary-General of, 345; "U.N.O. batches" of South African resisters, 698 n. 8.
United Party, South Africa, 525.
United States of America: political system of, 33; limits on president's power, 36-39; Cabinet, 38; Department of Justice, 201, 319; See Congress of the U.S.; Supreme Court, 96, 335, 336, 373, 377, 404, 415; House of Representatives Committee on Internal Security, 343; Constitution, procedures for determining violations of, 338-339; Ambassadorship to Sweden, 341; Embassy in Guatemala, 91; Civil War, 203, 376, 392, 399, 411; State Department statement on Communist regime in China, 343; Germany closes consulates of, 341; consulate in Göteborg, Sweden, closed, 341; orders German and Italian consulates closed, 341; security pact with Japan, 155, 161; atomic bombing of Hiroshima, 117-118; student protest at invasion of Cambodia, 196; intervention called for in Rhode Island, 428; and Puerto Rico, 291; support of Diem regime withdrawn, 660-661, 661-662; treaties with Indians, 318; "U-2" plane incident, 342; planned air base at Sunakawa, Japan, 388; evasions of Constitution and court orders, 335-336, 399; role in Berlin airlift, 408-409; nonviolent air raid by, 381; embargo by, 245-246, 248; noncooperation by constituent government units, 337-339; presses to refuse Chinese government U.N. seat, 346; role in politically-motivated counterfeiting, 410; preclusive purchasing by, 410; anti-boycott laws in, 412; general references and instances of nonviolent action in, 4, 5, 77, 95, 98, 113, 140, 169, 191, 192, 197, 198, 202, 204, 220, 226, 231, 235, 236, 239, 245, 261, 262, 288, 313, 337, 372-373, 387, 397, 403, 411, 413, 417, 559, 562, 585, 587, 626, 659, 670, 682, 689, 692, 694, 716, 729, 787, 795. See also diverse other cases indexed by reference to cities, states, organizations, persons, etc.

Universities' *Apartheid* Bill, South Africa, 155.
University College, Swansea, Wales, Preface.
University of California at Berkeley, 169, 171, 373.
University of Madrid, 196.
University of Massachusetts at Boston, Preface.
University of Minnesota, 169.
University of Mississippi, 388.
University of Moscow, 168, 293.
University of Munich, 128.
University of Oslo, Preface.
University of Oslo, 331, 691; Institute for Philosophy and the History of Ideas, Preface.
University of Oxford, Preface.
University of Washington, 319.
University of St. Petersburg, 163, 164, 166, 684.
Untouchables, India, 83, 185, 198, 393, 717, 721.
Urrutia, Miguel, 406-407, 441 n. 191.
Uruguay, 659.
Utrecht, Netherlands, 422.
Vacaville, California, 263.
Vladimir, Grand Duke, 561.
Váli, Ferenc, 344.
Valle, Colombia, 406.
Vallat, Xavier, 326.
Vassiltchikoff, Prince, 561.
Vassilyev, A. T., 330, 333, 593.
Vatican, 661. See also Catholic Church and individual popes.
Venezuela, 248, 406.
Venice, 410.
Venturi, Franco, 128, 164, 202, 223, 228, 261, 270, 456, 515 n. 14, 518 n. 104, 646 n. 79, 679.
Versailles Peace Conference, 125. See also Treaty of Versailles.
Viborg Manifesto, 237-238, 242.
Viceroy of India, 42, 85, 86. See also Irwin, Lord India, and Britain.
Vichy, France. See France, Vichy.
Victoria Monument, London, 167.
Vienna, Austria, 148, 278, 797.
Vietnam: war, 171, 341, 397; anti-war demonstrations in U.S., 130, 132, 138, 139, 142, 397; North Vietnam (bomb-

ing of), 139; (peace delegation of), 342; peace talks, 342; South Vietnam (peace delegation), 342; (Special Forces), 660; Viet Cong (National Liberation Front), 136; Buddhist struggles in South Vietnam, 136-137, 151, 288, 363, 385, 461, 534, 537, 542, 628, 659, 660-662, 671, 688-689; Buddhist noncooperation with N.L.F., 296; U.S. alienated from Diem by repression of Buddhists, 660-661.

Vigilantes, 263.

Vigils, 69, 117, 147-148, 580.

Vilna, Lithuania, 287, 326.

Violence: defined, 608; defined by some as that disliked, 64; unusual definition, 441 n. 191; physical struggle, 523; shown within spectrum of social and political action, 66 Chart Two; not part of nonviolent action, 64, 84, 634; sabotage tied to, 609; dichotomy of violent and nonviolent social behavior untenable, 64-65; relation to material destruction, 65, 66 Chart Two; refraining from aids conversion, 727; and hostility, 727; Lenin committed to, 781; view that power comes from, 109, 683, 749, 793, 805, 806; power potential of, claimed exceeded by nonviolent action, 744; public adverse to, 692, 794; against violence reinforcing, 112, 722; nonviolent action against breaks circle of, 806; and "human nature," 72; diverse attitudes toward revealed by anthropologists, 72; Western civilization biased toward, 72-73; nonrational belief in, 73; none in civil disobedience, 316; of opponent's domination, 513; of system revealed by nonviolent action, 543-544, 557, 678-680; abstention from no guarantee of safety, 556-557; abstention from rewarded, 792; opponent prefers by resisters, 586-594; users of vulnerable, 110; need to prevent in nonviolent action, 465, 526, 595-608, 620, 647-648 n. 99, 722, 725, 727. See also Nonviolent discipline. By resisters reduces support in opponent's camp, 461; by resisters reinforces troop's loyalty, 606; warned against in Czechoslovakia, 130; factors likely to produce in nonviolent action, 608-615, 620; (spontaneity), 486; (improvization), 627; in nonviolent action loses support, 670; choice of methods to reduce chances

of, 403; means to prevent in nonviolent action, 618-633, 653 ns. 220 and 224, 654 ns. 252, 253, and 254; preventing in February 1917 Russian Revolution, 673, 743; expected by British in India, 528; attributed to nonviolent actionists, 573, 583; provocation of opponent to with nonviolent action, 476, 573, 583, 590-594; by resisters causes even radicals to desert American colonial cause, 602; nonviolent struggles tinged with, 97, 319, 404, 644 n. 40, 743; nonviolent struggles mixed with, 87, 94, 101, 146, 223, 235, 354 n. 226, 405, 424, 466, 519 n. 128, 580, 610. See also Violent action and struggle, Violent sanctions, Military struggle, Power, Conflict, War, Political violence, Struggle.

Violent action and struggle: and monolith view of power, 8-9, 678; forms of in conducting conflicts, 3, 34; has received disproportionate attention, 74; qualities and means appropriate to differ from those in nonviolent struggle, 485; defiance by may bring self-respect, 785; heroes of may inspire nonviolent actionists, 783; replacement in a series of particular nonviolent substitutions, 805, 808, 809, 810; meaning of success and failure in, 765; risks in compared to nonviolent struggle, 110; motives for substituting nonviolent action for, 67-68; conditions under which nonviolent action substituted for, 480; incapacity for leads to nonviolent means, 209; rejected for nonviolent means, 77, 98, 101, 318, 475; courageous but hopeless cases (compared to nonviolence), 554; (bridge social distance), 715-716; threat of may induce concessions, 258; opposition terrorism strengthens regime, 645-646 n. 79; unsuccessful cases idealized, 77; nonviolent action commonly unfairly compared with, 74; practical limitations of recognized, 97; time to achieve results, 70; usual means of repression designed to defeat, 111; enforcement problems against differ from those against nonviolent action, 111; group unity in less than in nonviolent action, 794; and centralization of power, 800-802; population less self-reliant than in nonviolent action, 803; may reduce population's perception of own power, 805; less control over opponent's power sources than with nonviolent action, 817; percentage of combatants lower than in nonviolent struggle, 460, 682; more soldiers required in than in nonviolent struggle (Gandhi), 478; change in relative strengths of protagonists slower than in nonviolent action, 527; used to control rulers, 34, 46, 47; not needed to collapse rulers, 34; weakens *loci* of power, 804; and centralization of power, 800-802; maintenance of contrast from in nonviolent action essential, 113, 489; results claimed less permanent and satisfactory than with nonviolent action, 767-768, 776 n. 229, 806; efficiency increased by conscious efforts, 3; nonviolent coercion occurs without, 706, 742; advocates of aided by neglect of nonviolent coercion, 741; worst aspects avoided by nonviolent coercion, 774 n. 161; seen closer to nonviolent coercion than latter to religious nonviolence, 706, 774 n. 161; suffering during, 551; limited social distance reduces, 713; movements may murder police agents, 488; may be defeated, 71; influences type of leadership, 803-804; comparison of casualties with nonviolent struggle, 552-553; shift to from nonviolent means (American colonials), 536, 614-615; (Algeria), 545; bravery in less powerful than in nonviolent action, 458; advocates of in India gain, 513; in extermination camp, 304; not unconditionally excluded by American colonists, 595; not way for India's freedom, 84; and parallel government, 424; to defend land seizures, 406; in Polish resistance, 223; to back embargoes, 408; to back blockade defiance, 408; ineffective for Czechoslovakia 1968, 100-101; less effective against Nazi occupation than nonviolent resistance, 586; comparison of possible costs of in Ruhr with nonviolent *Ruhrkampf*, 553-554; not needed to destroy tsarist system, 672; in 1905 Revolution, 5, 61, 78-79, 519 n. 128, 648 n. 106, 649-650 n. 154, 650 n. 160, 650-651 n. 161. See also Russian Revolution of 1905. See also Violence, Violent Sanctions, Military struggle, Power, Conflict, War, Political violence, Struggle.

Violent sanctions: general, 12, 19, 109, 466, 537, 543, 804, 805; not needed against passive submission, 543; threat of as sanction, 543; capacity to wield removed, 742, 752-754; for disobedience in violent conflicts, 580; to produce obedience, 55 n. 61; capacity for provided by cooperation, 44; may increasingly be replaced by nonviolent sanction, 805. See also Sanctions.

Viramgam, India, 591.

Virginia: general, 370, 384, 399, 481, 507, 613, 647 n. 99; House of Burgesses, 137, 239, 361; Virginia Resolutions, 338; colonists' parallel government, 424-425.

Vi Vill Oss et Land, 47.

Volhynia Province, Russia, 261.

Volkseigener Betrieb Industrie-bau, 547.

Voluntary exile, 211.

Volynsky Regiment, Russia, 333, 674.

Vorkuta prison camp, U.S.S.R., 93, 94, 265, 365, 533, 548, 553, 640.

Vorwärts, 686.

Voter Registration campaign, Mississippi, 198.

"Voters' Veto" campaign, Britain, 292.

Vrij Nederland, 400.

Vu Van Mau, 137.

Vykom Satyagraha Campaign, India, 82, 148, 472, 717, 720, 728, 729.

Wabash Railroad Company, 231.

Wade-in, 378.

Wagner Act, United States, 404.

Wagner, Mayor Robert, 228.

Wait-in, 139.

Wales, 242, 404. See also individual towns or cities.

Wall Street, New York City, 623.

Walk-alongs, 391.

Walk-outs, 169-170.

Wallace, Governor George, 233.

Wallensteen, Peter, 248.

Walker, Charles C., 621, 625, 632.

Walpole, Horace, 238, 699 n. 32.

Walter, E. V., 54 n. 47.

War: general, 35, 42, 97, 553, 750, 790, 794, 808; and monolith theory of power, 9-10; substitute for, 29, 245, 247, 470, 647 n. 99; as sanction, 12, 36; as control, 32, 34; similarity to nonviolent action, 67, 452, 471, 494, 496, 504-505, 509, 527, 551, 554, 620, 637-638, 678, 711, 756, 758, 762; study of, 73, 75, 492; support for by populace, 460; adoption of by

American colonists, 614-615. See also Violence, shift to. As seedbed for future wars, 767; centralizing effect of, 801; not simply uncontrolled outburst of violence, 494. See also Violence, Violent action and struggle, and Military struggle.

"Walter Ulbricht," The (ship), 143.

Watton, Jacob, 632.

Wardel, Lydia, 140.

Warmbrunn, Werner, 267, 282 n. 62, 283 n. 85, 314, 401. 422. 536, 787.

Warner, Denis, 587, 662.

Warpath, The, 493 n. 131.

Warren, Joseph, 794.

Warriner, Doreen, 407-408.

Warsaw, Poland, 126, 143, 157, 314, 399, 553, 585.

Warsaw Treaty Organization, troops of, 98, 121, 122, 127, 128.

Washington, D.C., U.S.A., 38, 132, 141, 154, 169, 341, 374, 377, 397, 399, 413, 428, 631, 661, 694, 785, 787, 789; police of, 397.

Washington, George, 238, 341, 473, 615.

Washington State, Supreme Court of, 319.

Waskow, Arthur, 133, 134, 224, 374, 503, 689, 788.

Watkins, Frances, 376.

Watt, Richard M., 144, 166, 334, 532, 781.

Weapons: relation to cooperation, 15, 59, n. 144; "weapons systems," 110, 112, 113, 452-453, 601; choice of, 501-504. See also Strategy.

Wearing of symbols, 136.

Weber, Max, 53 n. 33, 56 n. 86.

Webster, Secretary of State Daniel, 384.

Webster Dictionary, 742.

Wechsberg. Joseph, 629.

Wedderburn, Solicitor General, 535.

Weimar Republic. See Germany, Weimar Republic.

Weisse Rose, 126, 128.

Weizäcker, Baron Ernst von, 325.

Welhaven, Kristian, 331.

Wenceslas Square, Prague, 136, 142-143, 151, 260.

Wenceslas, Statue of, 136, 143.

Wentzcke, Paul, 611.

Westchester County, New York, 226.

West, L.J., 813 n. 63.

Westminster, London, 152.

Westmoreland County, Virginia, 239.

Westphalia, Germany, 669.

Wharton, Edward, 549.

Wheble, John, 317.

Wheeler-Bennett, John, 321-322, 344.

Whipple, Charles K., 369.

White House, 133, 540, 693.

White Terror, 646 n. 79.

"Wildcat" strike, 258, 261.

Wilhelm II, Emperor, 80, 302.

Wilhelm Tell, 149.

Wilkes, John, 317.

William, Frederick, 213.

Williams, Robin, 729, 734.

Wilmington, North Carolina, 159.

Wilson, Edmund, 386.

Wilson, President Woodrow, 126, 133, 141, 247, 342, 344, 540, 693.

Winnipeg, Canada, 275, 432.

Winsor, Mary, 787.

Winter Palace, St. Petersburg, 78, 155, 190, 483, 530, 640.

Withdrawal from government educational institutions, 297.

Withdrawal from international organizations, 345.

Withdrawal from social institutions, 199.

Withdrawal from social system, 184, 199-200.

Withdrawal of authority, 424.

Withdrawal of bank deposits, 236.

Withdrawal of cooperation. See Noncooperation.

Withdrawal of economic cooperation. See Economic noncooperation.

Withdrawal of labor. See Strikes.

Withdrawal of obedience. See Disobedience and Civil disobedience.

Withholding of allegiance, 286-288.

Withholding of cooperation, 36, 295. See also Noncooperation.

Withholding of diplomatic recognition, 342-344.

Witte, Prime Minister, Count S.Y., 431.

Wolfe, Bertram D., 430-431.

Wolff, Kurt H., Preface.

Wolman, Leo, 220, 222, 230.

Woman suffrage: in United States, 126, 133, 141, 154, 540, 682, 693, 735, 787; in Netherlands, 147; in England, 366, 677.

Wood, Amos, 199.

Woodlawn Organization, 139.

Woodward, E. L., 291.

Woolworth's, 373.

Workmen's boycott, 230-231.

Work-on without collaboration, 416, 421-422.

"Working-to-rule" strike, 271, 417.

World War I, 74, 125, 314, 341, 739.

World War II: general, 42, 90, 129, 245, 259, 261, 304, 584; nonviolent resistance against Germans, 5, 9, 121, 122, 136, 274, 305-307, 313-314, 410, 418, 586; nonviolent resistance by American prisoners, 200, 265.

Worms, Germany, 192.

Women's Party, U.S., 141.

Wright, General Agent, 199.

Wright, Governor Sir James, 425, 551.

Writers Union, Czechoslovakia, 174.

Wyller, Thomas Christian, 195.

Xa Loi Pagoda, Hué, Vietnam, 587.

Yakimas, 319.

Yang-chou, Kiangsu, China, 235.

Yang-ku, Shantung, China, 264.

Yarmolinsky, Avrahm, 318, 648 n. 127.

Yaryan, Rev. John J., 319.

Yellen, Samuel, 598.

Yoder, Dale, 413.

Yoruba rulers, 411.

Young India, 368, 483, 504, 576, 639, 641, 751.

Young Trudi, 417.

Yugoslavia, 340, 342, 347.

Yulzari, Matei, 121, 153, 384.

Zaandam, Netherlands, 553.

Zaisser, Minister for State Security, Wilhelm, 676

Zeiss factory, Jena, East Germany, 125, 170.

Zemstvo Congress, Third, 160.

Zengakuren, 155, 161.

Zion, Rabbi Daniel, 153.

Zinn, Howard, 471.

Znamensky Square, Petrograd, 333, 673-674.

Zomba Government House, Nyasaland, 419.

"Zone of Indifference" as reason for obedience, 23, 27.

Acknowledgments

Appreciation is gratefully acknowledged to the authors and publishers whose works are quoted in this volume. Complete publication details are provided in the footnotes and bibliography.

Aptheker, Herbert, *American Negro Slave Revolts*. Copyright © 1963 by International Publishers, Inc. New York: International Publishers, 1964. Permission courtesy of International Publishers, Inc.

Bailey, Thomas A., *A Diplomatic History of the American People*. Sixth edition. Copyrighted. New York: Appleton-Century-Crofts, 1958. Permission courtesy of Appleton-Century-Crofts.

Bauer, Raymond A. and Alice H. Bauer, "Day to Day Resistance to Slavery," *Journal of Negro History*, vol. XXVII, no. 4 (Oct. 1942), pp. 388-419. Copyright © 1942 by the Association for the Study of African-American Life and History, Inc. Permission courtesy The Association for the Study of African-American Life and History, Inc., and Raymond A. and Alice H. Bauer.

Blum, Robert, *The United States and China in World Affairs*. ed. by A. Doak Barnett. Copyright © 1966 by the Council on Foreign Relations. New York: McGraw-Hill (for the Council on Foreign Relations), 1966. Permission courtesy McGraw-Hill Book Co.

Bondurant, Joan V., *Conquest of Violence: The Gandhian Philosophy of*

Conflict. Copyright © 1958 by Princeton University Press. Princeton, New Jersey: Princeton University Press. London: Oxford University Press, 1958. Passages reprinted by permission of Princeton University Press.

Borton, Hugh, *Peasant Uprisings in Japan of the Tokugawa Period*. Second Edition. New York: Paragon Book Reprint Corp., 1968. First published in *The Transactions of the Asiatic Society of Japan* (Second Series), vol. XVI, 1939. Passage reprinted courtesy of Paragon Book Reprint Corp.

Brant, Stefan, *The East German Rising*. Translated and adapted by Charles Wheeler. Copyright © 1955 by Stefan Brant. New York: Frederick A. Praeger, 1957. London: Thames and Hudson, 1955. Permission courtesy of Praeger Publishers, Inc.

Brinton, Crane, *The Anatomy of Revolution*. Copyright © Prentice-Hall Inc. Englewood Cliffs, N.J. New York: Vintage Books, 1962. Passages reprinted with permission of Prentice-Hall, Inc.

Case, Clarence Marsh, *Nonviolent Coercion: A Study in Methods of Social Pressure*. Copyright 1923. New York: The Century Co., 1923. Permission courtesy of Appleton-Century-Crofts, Inc.

Charques, Richard, *Twilight of Imperial Russia*. Copyright © 1958 by Richard Charques. Fair Lawn, N. J.: Essential Books, 1959. London: Phoenix House, 1958. Permission courtesy of Dorothy Charques.

Clark, Evans, ed., *Boycotts and Peace*. New York and London: Harper & Bros., 1932. Permission courtesy Harper & Row Publishers, Inc.

Crankshaw, Edward, *Gestapo: Instrument of Tyranny*. Copyright 1956. New York: Viking Press, 1956. London: Putnam, 1956. Permission courtesy of Edward Crankshaw.

Crook, Wilfrid H., *The General Strike: A Study of Labor's Tragic Weapon in Theory and Practice*. Chapel Hill: University of North Carolina Press, 1931. Passages reprinted by permission of the Shoe String Press, Inc., present copyright owner.

Dallin, Alexander, *German Rule in Russia, 1941-1945: A Study of Occupation Policies*. Copyright 1957. New York: St. Martin's Press, 1957. London: Macmillan, 1957. Permission courtesy of St. Martin's Press and Macmillan, London and Basingstoke.

Daniels, Jonathan, *Frontiers on the Potomac*. New York: Macmillan, 1946. Permission courtesy of Brandt & Brandt.

Davison, W. Phillips, *The Berlin Blockade: A Study in Cold War Politics*. Copyright © 1958 by the Rand Corporation. Princeton, N. J.: Princeton University Press, 1958. Passage reprinted by permission of Princeton University Press.

Deanesly, Margaret, *A History of the Medieval Church, 590-1500*. London: Methuen & Co., 1965. Permission courtesy of Associated Book Publishers Ltd.

Delarue, Jacques, *The Gestapo: A History of Horror*. New York: William Morrow, 1964. Passages reprinted courtesy of Macdonald & Co. (Publishers) Ltd.

Ebert, Theodor, "Theory and Practice of Nonviolent Resistance," unpublished English translation of a doctoral thesis presented at the University of Erlangen, Germany, 1965. Permission courtesy of Theodor Ebert.

Eyck, Erich, *A History of the Weimar Republic*, Vol. I. *From the Collapse of the Empire to Hindenburg's Election*. Copyright © 1962 by the President and Fellows of Harvard College. Cambridge, Mass.: Harvard University Press, 1962. Permission courtesy of Harvard University Press.

Farmer, James, *Freedom—When?* Copyright © 1965 by the Congress of Racial Equality, Inc. New York: Random House, 1965. Permission courtesy of James Farmer and Random House.

Faulkner, William, *A Fable*. Copyright © 1950, 1954 by William Faulkner. New York: Random House, 1954. Permission courtesy of Random House, Inc.

Fogg, Richard W., "Jazz Under the Nazis," in *Music 66, "down beat*'s Annual," 1966, pp. 97-99. Copyright © 1966 by *down beat*, 1966. Permission courtesy of *down beat*.

Frank, Jerome D., *Sanity and Survival: Psychological Aspects of War and Peace*. Copyright © 1967 by Jerome D. Frank. New York: Random House and Vintage Books, 1968. Permission courtesy of Jerome D. Frank.

Friedrich, Carl J., ed., *Totalitarianism*. Copyright © 1954 by President and Fellows of Harvard College. Cambridge, Mass.: Harvard University Press, 1954. Permission courtesy of Harvard University Press.

Gandhi, M. K., *An Autobiography, The Constructive Programme, Economics of Khadi, Hind Swaraj, Non-violence in Peace and War*, Two vols., *Satyagraha, Satyagraha in South Africa, Young India*, Vol. I; publication details as cited in the bibliography; Gandhi's works are copyrighted by Navajivan Trust, Ahmedabad, India, and the passages reproduced in this volume are reprinted with the permission and courtesy of Navajivan Trust.

Gipson, Lawrence Henry, *The British Empire Before the American Revolution,* vols. X, XI and XII (see Bibliography). Copyright © by Alfred A. Knopf, 1961, 1965 and 1965 respectively. New York: Alfred A. Knopf, 1961-1965. Permission courtesy of Alfred A. Knopf, Inc.

——, *The Coming of the Revolution, 1763-1775*. Copyright © 1954 by Harper and Brothers. New York and Evanston: Harper Torchbooks, 1962. Permission courtesy of Harper & Row, Publishers, Inc.

Goodspeed, D. J., *The Conspirators: A Study of the Coup d'Etat*. Copyright © 1962 by D. J. Goodspeed, 1962. New York: Viking Press, 1962. Toronto: Macmillan Co. of Canada, 1962. Permission courtesy of Viking Press and of Macmillan (London and Basingstoke).

Gopal, S., *The Viceroyalty of Lord Irwin, 1926-1931*. Copyright 1957. London: Oxford University Press, 1957. Permission courtesy of Oxford University Press.

Görlitz, Walter, ed., *The Memoirs of Field-Marshal Keitel*. Trans. by David Irving. Copyright © 1965 by William Kimber and Co., Ltd. Passages reprinted with permission of William Kimber and Co., Ltd., and Stein and Day Publishers.

Gregg, Richard B., *The Power of Nonviolence*. Second revised edition. Copyright © 1935, 1959, 1966 by Richard B. Gregg. New York: Schocken, 1966. London: James Clarke & Co., 1960. Permission courtesy Schocken Books Inc. for Richard B. Gregg.

Halberstam, David, *The Making of a Quagmire*. Copyright © 1964, 1965 by David Halberstam. New York: Random House, 1965. London: The Bodley Head, 1965. Permission courtesy of Random House.

Halperin, S. William, *Germany Tried Democracy: A Political History of the*

Reich from 1918 to 1933. Copyright © 1946 by Thomas Y. Crowell Co. Hamden, Conn. and London: Archon Books, 1963 [1946]. Used with permission of Thomas Y. Crowell Co.

Harcave, Sidney, *First Blood: The Russian Revolution of 1905.* Copyright © 1964 by The Macmillan Co. New York: Macmillan, 1964. London: Collier-Macmillan, 1964. Permission courtesy of The Macmillan Co.

Harris, Errol E., "Political Power," *Ethics,* vol.XLVIII, no. 1 (Oct. 1957), pp. 1-10. Copyright © 1957 by the University of Chicago Press. Permission courtesy of University of Chicago Press.

Hentoff, Nat, *The New Equality.* New Edition. Copyright © 1964 by Nat Hentoff. New York: Viking Press, 1965. Permission courtesy of Nat Hentoff.

Hiller, E. T., *The Strike: A Study in Collective Action.* Copyright © 1928 by University of Chicago Press. Chicago: University of Chicago Press, 1928. Permission courtesy of University of Chicago Press.

Hsiao, Kung-ch,üan, *Rural China: Imperial Control in the Nineteenth Century.* Copyright © 1960 by University of Washington Press. Seattle: University of Washington Press, 1960. Permission courtesy of University of Washington Press.

Janis, Irving L. and Daniel Katz, "The Reduction of Intergroup Hostility: Research Problems and Hypotheses," in *Journal of Conflict Resolution,* vol. III, no. 1 (March 1959), pp. 85-100. Excerpts are reprinted by permission of the present publisher, Sage Publications Co., Inc. and the authors.

Karski, Jan, *Story of a Secret State.* Boston: Houghton Mifflin, 1944. Permission courtesy Houghton Mifflin Co.

Katkov, George, *Russia 1917: The February Revolution.* Copyright © 1967 by George Katkov. New York: Harper & Row, 1967. Permission courtesy of George Katkov.

Keep, J. H. L., *The Rise of Social Democracy in Russia.* Copyright © 1963 Oxford University Press. Oxford: Clarendon Press, 1963. Permission courtesy of the Clarendon Press.

King, Martin Luther, Jr., *Stride Toward Freedom: The Montgomery Story.* Copyright © 1958 by Martin Luther King, Jr. New York: Harper & Row and Ballentine Books, 1958. London: Victor Gollancz, 1959. Permission courtesy of Harper & Row, Publishers.

———, *Why We Can't Wait.* Copyright © 1963, 1964 by Martin Luther King, Jr. New York: Signet Books of The New American Library, 1964. Permission courtesy of Harper & Row, Publishers, publishers of the hardcover edition.

Knapp, Wilfrid F., *A History of War and Peace: 1939-1965.* Copyright © 1967 by Royal Institute of International Affairs. London, New York and Toronto: Oxford University Press (issued under the auspices of the Royal Institute of International Affairs), 1967. Permission courtesy of Wilfrid F. Knapp.

Koestler, Arthur, *Reflections on Hanging.* Copyright © 1957 by The Macmillan Co. New York: Macmillan, 1967. Permission courtesy of The Macmillan Co.

Korbel, Josef, *The Communist Subversion of Czechoslovakia, 1938-1948: The Failure of Coexistence.* Copyright © 1959 by Princeton University Press, 1959. Excerpts reprinted by permission of Princeton University

Press and Oxford University Press.

Kuper, Leo, *Passive Resistance in South Africa*. New Haven, Conn.: Yale University Press, 1957. London: Jonathan Cape, 1956. Permission courtesy of Yale University Press and Leo Kuper.

Lasswell, Harold D., *Power and Personality*. Copyright © 1948 by W. W. Norton & Co., Inc. New York: W. W. Norton & Co., 1948. Permission courtesy W. W. Norton & Co., Inc.

Lenin, V. I., *Selected Works in Three Volumes*. English language translations copyrighted. New York: International Publishers, and Moscow: Progress Publishers, 1967. Passages reprinted with permission of International Publishers, Inc.

Liddell Hart, Sir Basil, *Strategy: The Indirect Approach*. Coprighted. New York: Frederick A. Praeger, 1954. London: Faber & Faber, 1954. Permission courtesy of Lady Kathleen Liddell Hart.

Littell, Robert, ed., *The Czech Black Book: Prepared by the Institute of History of the Czechoslovak Academy of Sciences*. Copyright © 1969 by Praeger Publishers, Inc., New York. New York, Washington and London: Frederick A. Praeger, 1969.

Lochner, Louis P., ed., *The Goebbels Diaries, 1942-1943*. Copyright © 1948 by the Fireside Press, Inc. Garden City, New York: Doubleday & Co., 1948. Permission courtesy of Doubleday & Co., Inc.

Loh, Robert (as told to Humphrey Evans), *Escape from Red China*. Copyright © 1962 by Robert Loh and Humphrey Evans. New York: Coward-McCann, 1962. Passages reprinted by permission of Coward, McCann and Geoghegan, Inc.

Luthuli, Albert, *Let My People Go: An Autobiography*. Copyright © 1962 by Albert Luthuli. New York: McGraw-Hill Book Co., Inc., 1962. London: Collins, 1962. Used with permission of McGraw-Hill Book Co., Inc.

Mabee, Carleton, *Black Freedom: The Nonviolent Abolitionists from 1830 Through the Civil War*. Copyright © 1970 by Carleton Mabee. New York: Macmillan, 1970. Toronto: Macmillan, 1970. London: Collier-Macmillan, 1970. Permission courtesy of The Macmillan Co.

MacIver, R. M., *The Web of Government*. Copyright © 1947, 1965 by Robert MacIver. New York: Macmillan, 1947.

Miller, William Robert, *Nonviolence: A Christian Interpretation*. Copyright © 1964 by National Board of Young Men's Christian Association. New York: Association Press, 1964. Permission courtesy of Association Press.

Morgan, Edmund S. and Helen M., *The Stamp Act Crisis: Prologue to Revolution*. New, revised edition. Copyright © 1953 by the University of North Carolina Press; Copyright © 1962 by Edmund S. Morgan. New York: Collier Books, 1963. Permission courtesy of Edmund S. Morgan, the University of North Carolina Press and the Institute of Early American History and Culture, Williamsburg.

Mosca, Gaetano, *The Ruling Class*. Introduction by Arthur Livingstone. Copyright © 1939 by McGraw-Hill. New York and London: McGraw-Hill, 1939. Permission courtesy McGraw-Hill Book Co.

Jawaharlal Nehru, *An Autobiography* (sometimes cited as *Jawaharlal Nehru. An Autobiography*). New edition. London: The Bodley Head, 1953. Excerpts quoted with permission of The Bodley Head and the John Day Company. U.S. copyright: Copyright © 1941, The John Day Company.

Renewed 1968 by Indira Gandhi.

———, *Toward Freedom: The Autobiography of Jawaharlal Nehru*. Revised edition. Copyright 1941, The John Day Company, New York: John Day Co., 1942. Permission courtesy of The John Day Co., Ind., publishers.

Neumann, Franz, *Behemoth: The Structure and Practice of National Socialism, 1933-1944*. Copyright © 1942, 1944 by Oxford University Press, New York. New York: Octagon Books, 1963. Passages reprinted courtesy of Farrar, Straus & Giroux, Inc.

Neustadt, Richard E., *Presidential Power: The Politics of Leadership*. Copyright © 1960, 1964 by John Wiley & Sons, Inc. New York and London: John Wiley and Sons, 1960. Permission courtesy John Wiley & Sons, Inc.

Nicholson, Harold, *Diplomacy*. Second edition. Copyrighted 1950, 1960. London, New York and Toronto: Oxford University Press, 1960 [1950]. Permission courtesy of Oxford University Press.

Nickalls, John L., ed., *The Journals of George Fox*. Cambridge: University Press, 1952. Quotations reprinted by permission of Cambridge University Press.

Oppenheimer, Martin and George Lakey, *A Manual for Direct Action*. Copyright © 1964, 1965 by Martin Oppenheimer, George Lakey, and the Friends Peace Committee. Chicago: Quadrangle Books, 1965. Permission courtesy of Quadrangle Books.

Peace News (London), passage from issue of July 2, 1965. Permission courtesy of Peace News Ltd.

Peck, Graham, *Two Kinds of Time*. Copyright © 1950 by Graham Peck. Houghton Mifflin, 1950. Permission courtesy of Houghton Mifflin Co.

•Peck, James, *Freedom Ride*. Copyright © 1962 by James Peck. New York: Simon & Schuster, 1962. Permission courtesy Simon & Schuster.

The Pentagon Papers as published by "The New York Times", Copyright © 1971 by The New York Times Company. New York, Toronto and London: Bantam Books, 1971. Permission courtesy of *The New York Times*.

Prawdin, Michael, **The Unmentionable Nechaev: A Key to Bolshevism**. Copyright 1961. London: Allen and Unwin, 1961. Permission courtesy of Reneé C. Prawdin.

Rayback, Joseph G., *A History of American Labor*. Copyright © 1959, 1965 by Joseph G. Rayback. New York, Macmillan, 1964. Permission courtesy of The Macmillan Co.

Révész, Imre, *History of the Hungarian Reformed Church*. Washington, D.C.: Hungarian Reformed Federation of America, 1956. Passage reprinted from p. 128. Courtesy of the Hungarian Reformed Federation of America.

Reynolds, Lloyd G., *Labor Economics and Labor Relations*. Copyright © 1949 by Prentice-Hall, Inc. Englewood Cliffs, New Jersey: Prentice-Hall, 1959. Permission courtesy of Prentice-Hall, Inc.

Roberts, Adam, "Buddhism and Politics in South Vietnam," in *The World Today* (London), vol. 21, no. 6 (June 1965), pp. 240-250. Permission courtesy of Adam Roberts.

———, *Civilian Resistance as a National Defence*. Harrisburg, Pa., Stackpole Books, 1968. Original British edition: *The Strategy of Civilian Defence*. Copyright © 1967 by Adam Roberts, 1967. London: Faber & Faber, 1967. Permission courtesy of Adam Roberts.

Rosenthal, Mario, *Guatemala: The Story of an Emergent Latin American Democracy*. Copyrighted, New York: Twayne Publishers, 1962. Permission courtesy of Twayne Publishers, Inc.

Rostovtzeff, M., *The Social and Economic History of the Roman Empire*, Vol. I. Second edition revised by P. M. Frazer. Copyright © 1957 by Oxford Universtiy Press. Oxford: Clarendon Press, 1956. Permission courtesy of Clarendon Press.

Rubin, Jerry, *Do It!* New York: Simon and Schuster, 1970. Permission courtesy of Jerry Rubin.

Schapiro, Leonard, *The Communist Party of the Soviet Union*. Copyright © 1960, 1971 by Leonard Schapiro. New York: Random House, 1960. London: Eyre & Spottiswoode, 1960. Permission courtesy of Leonard B. Schapiro.

Schelling, Thomas C., *International Economics*. Copyright © 1958 by Allyn and Bacon, Inc. Boston: Allyn and Bacon, 1958.

Seifert, Harvey, *Conquest by Suffering: The Process and Prospects of Nonviolent Resistance*. Copyright © 1965 by W. L. Jenkins. Philadelphia: Westminster Press, 1965. Permission courtesy of the Westminster Press.

Seton-Watson, Christopher, *Italy From Liberalism to Fascism, 1870-1925*. Copyright © 1967 by Christopher Seton-Watson. New York: Barnes and Noble, 1967. London: Methuen, 1967. Permission courtesy of Christopher Seton-Watson.

Shirer, William L., *The Rise and Fall of the Third Reich*. Copyright © 1959, 1960 by William L. Shirer. New York: Simon and Schuster, 1960. London: Secker and Warburg, 1962. Permission courtesy of Simon and Schuster.

Shridharani, Krishnalal, *War Without Violence: A Study of Gandhi's Method and Its Accomplishments*. New York: Harcourt Brace and Co., 1939. London: Victor Gollancz, 1939. Permission courtesy of S. K. Shridharani.

Soloman, Frederic and Jacob R. Fishman, "The Psychosocial Meaning of Nonviolence in Student Civil Rights Activities", *Psychiatry*, vol. XXVII, No. 2 (May 1964), pp. 91-99. Permission courtesy of *Psychiatry: A Publication*.

Steiner, Stan, *The New Indians*. Copyright © 1968 by Stan Steiner, 1968. New York: Harper & Row, 1968. Permission courtesy of Stan Steiner and Harper & Row.

Suhl, Yuri, *They Fought Back: The Story of Jewish Resistance in Nazi Europe*. New York: Crown Publishers, 1967. London: MacGibbon and Kee, 1968. Permission courtesy of Yuri Suhl.

Sunday Times (London), a passage from the issue of March 19, 1967. Permission courtesy of the *Sunday Times*.

Symons, Julian, *The General Strike: A Historical Portrait*. Copyright © 1957 by Julian Symons. London: The Cresset Press. 1957. Permission courtesy of the Cresset Press, and Julian Symons.

Tabor, Robert, *M-26: Biography of a Revolution*. Copyrighted 1961. New York: Lyle Stuart, 1961. Permission courtesy of Lyle Stuart, Inc.

Taylor, George R., *The Struggle for North China*. Copyright © 1940 by the Secretariat, Institute of Pacific Relations. New York: Institute of Pacific Relations, 1940. Permission courtesy of William L. Holland, Editor, *Pacific Affairs*.

Ullstein, Heinz, *Spielplatz meines Lebens: Erinnerungen*. Copyright © 1961 by Kindler Verlag München. Munich: Kindler Verlag, 1961. Permission courtesy of Kindler Verlag. English translation in text by Hilda von

Klenze Morris.

Vassilyev, A. T., *The Ochrana: The Russian Secret Police.* Edited and with an Introduction by Rene Fülöp-Miller. Copyright © 1930 by J. B. Lippincott Co. Philadelphia and London: J. B. Lippincott Co., 1930. Passage reprinted by permission of J. B. Lippincott Company.

Warmbrunn, Werner, *The Dutch under German Occupation 1940-1945.* Copyright © 1963 by Board of Trustees of the Leland Standford Junior University. Stanford, California: Stanford University Press, 1963. London: Oxford University Press, 1963. Passages reprinted with permission of Stanford University Press.

Warriner, Doreen, *Land Reform in Principle and Practice.* Copyright © 1969 by Oxford University Press. Oxford: Clarendon Press, 1969. Permission courtesy of Clarendon Press.

Waskow, Arthur I., *From Race Riot to Sit-in: 1919 and the 1960s.* Copyright © 1966 by Doubleday and Co., Inc. Garden City, N. Y.: Doubleday, 1966. Permission courtesy of Doubleday & Co.

Wheeler-Bennett, Sir John W., *The Nemesis of Power: The Germany Army in Politics, 1918-1945.* New York: St. Martin's Press, 1953. London: Macmillan, 1953. Permission courtesy of Sir John Wheeler-Bennett.

Williams, Robin M., *The Reduction of Intergroup Tensions.* New York: Social Science Research Council, 1947. Permission courtesy of Robin M. Williams.

Wolfe, Bertram D., *Three who Made a Revolution.* Copyrighted. New York: Dial Press, 1948. London: Thames and Hudson, 1956. Permission courtesy of Bertram D. Wolfe.

Zinn, Howard, *Albany.* Atlanta: Southern Regional Council, 1962. Permission courtesy of Howard Zinn.